A Guide to Forensic Testimony

The publisher offers discounts on this book when ordered in quantity for bulk purchases and special sales. For more information, please contact:

U.S. Corporate and Government Sales
(800) 382-3419
corpsales@pearsontechgroup.com

For sales outside of the United States, please contact:

International Sales
(317) 581-3793
international@pearsontechgroup.com

Visit Addison-Wesley on the Web: www.awprofessional.com

Library of Congress Cataloging-in-Publication Data

Smith, Fred Chris.
  A guide to forensic testimony : the art and practice of presenting testimony as an expert
technical witness / Fred Chris Smith, Rebecca Gurley Bace.
    p. cm.
  Includes bibliographical references and index.
  ISBN 0-201-75279-4
  1. Evidence, Expert—United States. 2. Evidence, Expert. I. Bace, Rebecca Gurley. II Title.

KF8961 .S63 2003
347.73'47—dc21

2002074702

ISBN 0-201-75279-4
Text printed on recycled paper
1 2 3 4 5 6 7 8 9 10—CRS—0605040302
First printing, September 2002

This book was conceived at the time that Georgiana Faggioli learned she was passing on. She encouraged me to write about things we cannot do without, but risk losing by taking them too much for granted. This book is dedicated to her memory and to her daughter and her daughter's children.

FCS

In loving memory of two of my first mentors, Bertha Nel and Robert, and of my youngest mentor, Joey. To all those who mentor me and to those who allow me to carry on that fine tradition. May the circle be unbroken.

RGB

Legal Disclaimer

Nothing in this book represents the opinions of the United States Department of Justice. The Department neither endorsed nor accepts responsibility for any of the contents of this book. These contents are based solely on the opinions of the coauthors and are neither intended to nor can represent those of the United States Government or any of its branches.

Although the types of relationships between the lawyer and the expert are central to much of the material in this book, the discussion of these relationships and of the kinds of decisions that must be made concerning them—sometimes by the lawyer and sometimes by the expert—should always be guided in the real world by the advice of competent legal counsel whenever legal advice is required. This book is not to be taken as legal advice in any shape or form.

The coauthors and their publishers wish to make clear that no one should rely in any way on the discussions and materials in this book for legal guidance in any matter. Nor is there any intention to interfere in any way with the kind of relationships that lawyers and experts may decide, after due consideration, to form and maintain over time or to decline to enter into or depart from. The purpose of this book is simply and solely to stimulate thought and discussion about some of the many problems that occur in the presentation of technical expert witness testimony.

Contents

Taking Testimony Seriously 31

Creating Stories about Complex Technical Issues 55

Enhancing Objectivity in a World of Bias   195

The Role of Visual Exhibits in Expert Testimony   301

Demeanor and Credibility   335

Nonverbal Communications   355

Appendix A: Major Cases   401

Appendix B: Federal Rules   481

Index   495

Foreword

The explosion of networked information systems and microcircuits since the 1970s has made surprisingly modest changes in everyday life. After 45 years, a 1957 Chevrolet still looks modern in a way that a 1912 Model T Ford did not look in 1957. The Boeing 747, introduced in 1969, is still the mainstay of intercontinental air transport. The cubicle of the *Dilbert* strip has replaced the bullpen of desks in *The Apartment*. Electronic commerce has extended, but not drastically altered, catalogue shopping and telephonic reservations. Amazon.com's promotions use arguments little changed since Montgomery Ward, Sears, and others developed direct mail in the 1890s. The latest laptop computers and even personal digital assistants (PDAs) use a keyboard layout and spacing developed over 125 years ago. And despite all movements to equip schools with computers, the size and weight of paper textbooks is beginning to alarm some physicians.

Why has life remained, on its surface, so surprisingly conservative? For the same reason that our houses do not look like the sets of Fritz Lang's *Metropolis*. Ours has been a concealed and silent technological revolution, permeating almost everything yet often transparent to users who don't have to know what is being done with the data from their purchases at the supermarket, drugstore, or discounter—and, as in their knowledge of restaurant kitchens, may not want to know.

The revolution has also profited from the benevolent indifference that many new technologies encounter from the law in their early years, a moratorium as the authors call it, and a time of the blissful suspension of normal principles of accountability comparable to the creative accounting of the dot-com era.

As an innovation becomes less of an experiment and more of a foundation, the freewheeling spirit seems out of place. The illusion of technological transparency ends when something goes wrong: when hackers break into records and steal customers' credit card numbers, when holders of broad software patents claim infringement, when software failure threatens the survival of organizations. If our still-familiar world is actually a front end for products with so many million lines of code that their own vendors may not understand them fully, if the electronic components of some contemporary automobiles cost more than some whole cars of a decade ago, if even the simplest goods will soon have microprocessors, then just about all law becomes technology law. And technology law decisions often rest on the performance of expert witnesses.

Litigation surrounding engineering is hardly a novelty. And as the civil engineer and historian Henry Petroski has shown in *To Engineer Is Human* and *Engineers of Dreams*, fatal errors have long been part of the history of his profession, even essential to its progress. But most of the older branches of engineering have been developing for at least 150 years if not for centuries. If a pyramid under construction for a resort collapsed because of a too-steep angle, the knowledge that could have prevented the failure would have a history of millennia. Yet even in construction engineering, a mix of innovative techniques and unforeseen hazards—most apparent in the fate of the World Trade Center—is calling established standards into question. Our ability to develop new materials and processes grows geometrically, our skills in simulating their long-term behavior only arithmetically. Yet the expert is called on to give a prognosis.

Software design has been replacing other kinds of engineering. And some great software writers, especially in highly mathematical fields like cryptology, have also been distinguished academics. But others may have little theoretical background. They may be people with ordinary formal educations who happen to think efficiently and rapidly in certain ways. Their work is highly collaborative. And because software and hardware systems can interact under so many different real-world conditions, their products can never be fully debugged; the correction of one problem often creates others. The successful management of development teams has turned out to be a skill separate from invention itself. Thomas Edison, who introduced the first great research laboratory, had hundreds of patents in his name; in 2000, Bill Gates shared a single one, for a word-processing feature.

In such a regime, what are best practices? What credentials and experience are relevant? Who is an expert? When and how can concepts of software architecture and management be conveyed to nontechnical judges and jurors? These questions concern us all, because almost no professional is immune from involvement in a case involving information technology (IT). Physicians, attorneys, managers, teachers, clerics, writers, performers—nearly all of us can cite some technology case that is striking close to home. And we all have a stake in the outcome of the federal and state antitrust suits against Microsoft, which is about not only our experiences in the present but also the predictions of consequences of various resolutions by each side's academic witnesses.

For IT professionals this book is not just a painless but also a witty and absorbing introduction to an exotic logic and language. For lawyers it is a window on the concealed clockwork of the twenty-first century—and on the moral hazards of partisanship. For the certifiable laity it is a panorama, in lucid and readable English, of the heroic meeting of the twin specters of technological failure and litigation. And for everyone it is the model of a category-defying book. Most of us claim some kind of expertise. Few of us will ever have to defend it in court. But all of us can benefit from some reflection.

Advanced societies work through webs of knowledge so complex that nobody understands their ramifications. Even the most distinguished scientists, as the authors and their sources observe, rely on and trust the skills and integrity of their colleagues, building them into their work. Tug too hard at any thread and the fabric of social and technological certainty would begin to unravel; yet the miracle is that it coheres and that disasters occur as rarely as they do. Paradoxically, it may be the rise of expertise that leads to litigation. As Mark Grady has suggested, it was the new scientific power of medicine in the late nineteenth century, the improvement rather than the deterioration of care, that produced the expansion of malpractice litigation.

What will be the unintended consequences of the courts' new rigor in evaluating expertise? And how might judicial decisions feed back into the design of products and services in surprising ways? I won't begin to speculate. But I can't think of a better starting point than this book, *A Guide to Forensic Testimony*, for contemplating our legal-technological future.

—Edward Tenner

Preface

Mark Twain is reported to have said, "An expert is just some guy from out of town." As usual, Twain is on the mark in suggesting that there should be something suspicious about a stranger who shows up and offers to help us with his expertise and then quickly hits the road. For our purposes this apothegm could be slightly altered to make an expert out to be someone from out of town who has an opinion. The revised adage may say as much about communities of interest and the part they play today in deciding whom to trust as an expert as it says about experts and how they worked in Twain's era.

This book is all about expert witnesses, with particular attention paid to those who specialize in information technologies—the hardware, software, and data that make up computers and other digital systems used for data processing and communications. The level of technical knowledge needed to deal with these systems often makes the question of assessing the expertise of a particular person daunting to all but other experts in the technical domain in question.

This is not by any means meant to be a legal textbook. Indeed, we explicitly disclaim any intention to offer or suggest legal advice to any reader. Such legal advice must come from legal counsel engaged to offer it, and the materials in this book should not be relied on as legal advice or passed onto others as such. Nor is this book meant to be treated as yet another technical manual, to be consulted only when the reader is in the midst of a crisis and in search of specific answers to specific technical problems. The book is perhaps best considered as analogous to a general travel guide to an exotic destination that the reader anticipates visiting in the near future.

We appreciate the paucity of time available for technical experts to devote to reading a book such as this. Accordingly, although the book attempts to convey neither legal advice nor specific technical information, the chapters should still prove useful to the techie and his or her managers. The chapters can guide the consideration of "what if" scenarios that may well come to pass in the lives of many who read this book. Furthermore, like a travel book, this primer may at least provide some of the right questions (asked in the appropriate local dialects) that an expert can use to ask for directions as he or she navigates to the interesting places and events often found in the world of litigation.

One of many ways you might use this book to prepare for visiting the land of litigation as an expert is to begin with the first chapter to get a quick and entertaining overview of the process of becoming a recognized expert and testifying in court. Chapter 1 introduces technical expert witnesses who testify in criminal and civil trials and focuses on the communities of interest that society ultimately relies upon to certify the genuine expertise of their representatives and members in good standing. When you begin to think about what makes a particular individual an expert in the eyes of the law, and hence entitled to testify about his or her opinions in the course of litigation, you are led back to the specialized knowledge, training, and experience that an organized and socially recognized community of interest creates and maintains. The most peculiar thing about the technical domains that comprise what is generally described as information technology (IT) is how little they resemble the traditional, professional, licensed communities of interest that exist in other areas, such as structural engineering and medicine. These communities become important to the law as it tests the reliability of the expert and his or her methods. Most judges and jurors first hear about such communities when a community member is proffered as an expert witness in the course of litigation. For IT expert witnesses, the lack of an organized, licensed community of interest with the traditional trappings of a socially recognized expert community creates a number of issues that the courts are just beginning to confront.

We introduce established experts from a number of communities of interest that lie outside the realm of IT. These experts within ancient areas of expertise as well as new disciplines have coped with the special demands of the legal system. Their stories may provide some organizing analogies for IT professionals who become interested in forensic practices and also enable IT experts to build the lattice of disciplines, processes, and professional networks necessary to assure lawyers and courts that they are competent IT practitioners. The experiences of Raemarie Schmidt and her students bring us back to how some of the pioneers in IT forensics can contribute to recognized expert communities by developing standards and training that have become generally recognized by the courts.

A discussion of the film *My Cousin Vinny* offers a lighthearted account of the problems that a technical expert encounters while testifying in court. In the film, the community of expertise represented by the character Mona Lisa Vito (played to perfection by Marisa Tomei) is that of the automobile mechanic. This particular community reminds us that certain roles associated with IT are rapidly becoming as commonly accepted as those of the car mechanic or washing machine repairperson. That these areas of expertise are generally recognized and often encountered illustrates another aspect of the community of interest. In this scenario, too many members claim an expertise with too little self-regulation, peer review, and evaluation by a recognized community of professionals. This erodes the ability to separate the charlatans from the qualified and recognized practitioners of the IT trades.

The choice of a second chapter is not critical to making the best use of this guide. In fact, the techie reader may wish to go directly to Chapter 13, which includes the experiences and lessons learned by several accomplished IT experts. These technical experts, who are all widely recognized as such in their communities of interest, have varying degrees of experience as expert witnesses in criminal and civil litigation. Their observations can serve as either reviews or introductions to the chapters found between the first and the last.

Chapter 2 provides a real-world tale of just how serious this kind of communication performance can be to individual and corporate parties. This chapter also explores the kind of expectations that legal and IT social critiques bring to bear on performances by important IT witnesses in landmark cases. Passages from the deposition of Bill Gates in the Microsoft antitrust case introduce a number of the recurring themes and issues associated with expert testimony developed further in the rest of the book. The most important of these is the perception of the demeanor and overall credibility of the witness and his or her performance on the stand. This perception by the fact finder overrides, as it should, all the other components of the process of communicating complex concepts in formal testimony.

The return of Bill Gates to the witness stand two years later (and the dramatic change in the reporting of his second coming by the same IT and legal reporters) is an example of the point of this book. Judicial fact finders and the public have lofty expectations of experts, especially when the expert's testimony is key to understanding the merits of the case. Meeting those expectations requires certain things from the expert: experience, preparation, and a commitment to communicating not only the obvious expertise of the witness but also the credibility and willingness to provide useful information throughout the testimony. This set of requirements might appear excessive, but in certain cases, such as Gates', the members of the public with interest in the expert's testimony number in the millions.

Chapter 3 reprises the well-known story of how IT security experts Tsutomu Shimomura and Andrew Gross developed forensic tools to track down the hacker who broke into Shimomura's computer at the San Diego Supercomputer Center. The text recounts the investigation in the form of a hypothetical direct examination of Andrew Gross as the government's expert witness and illustrates the case with graphics designed to introduce and narrate the complex technical steps taken in the investigation. The sample testimony also explains the expert analysis of the computer network evidence used to establish that Kevin Mitnick was the original intruder and to account for how he came to possess the stolen computer data taken from Shimomura's computer.

Chapter 4 provides some historical background, outlining the evolution of the legal process and also exploring the growing importance of expert witness testimony that accompanies the evolution of society's dependence on technology. The different roles of the expert witness as consultant, strategist, and testifying witness are introduced along with some of the problems that can arise when the expert and his or her attorney do not keep these often conflicting roles clear and distinct throughout the course of litigation.

Chapter 5 gives the beginning expert several examples by analogy of the kinds of problems that may persist due to the pace of advances in IT. Some of the problems are considered to be a direct consequence of the inherent immaturity of the IT field. In particular, issues arise in areas where no rigorous community of interest has been established or where no formal education or training is available. In these cases, the expert cannot point to generally accepted standards or a formal peer review process for determining the reliability of the concepts and techniques that he or she uses to decide what happened in a given case. Discussions of astrologers, phrenologists, handwriting analysts, and fingerprint comparison experts and their communities of interest illustrate the kinds of problems that IT domain experts may encounter when their expertise is challenged in court.

Chapter 6 provides examples, many of them extreme, of what can go wrong when commonsense rules of professionalism and ethics are misapplied. It also outlines how the traditions of the legal system regarding the preparation and introduction of expert testimony place certain restrictions on the behavior of IT and other experts who perform expert witness tasks in the course of litigation. Expert witnesses must understand that while in civil litigation they ultimately work for a private party, through their legal counsel, the advocacy decisions made by the party and the attorney about the course of litigation must be segregated from the objective judgments that legal and professional ethical rules require expert witnesses to make about the application of their expertise and the communication of their opinions in court.

Chapter 7 shows how some experienced IT experts have handled the challenging task of solidly constructing and maintaining the professional relationship between the expert, the attorney, and the client or party. One of many metaphors for enabling both the lawyer and the expert to reach useful conclusions about issues within the expertise of the witness is an aviation checklist. In this analogy, the expert must learn a lot about his or her role before he or she can reliably check out all the things that need to be in working order and notice all the indicators of problems before taking off. Another approach that has worked for both beginning and experienced IT expert witness practices is to find an agent or agency that specializes in matching appropriate experts with legal teams requiring particular expertise.

Chapter 8 presents what is in some ways the most difficult information in the book—involved legal material that explores the kinds of criteria courts have estab-

> **A Note on Legal Documents**
>
> In some of the opinions, rules, and other legal documents cited throughout the book, we took the liberty of editing inline references from the quoted material. We performed this editing for the sole purpose of making the material easier to read and comprehend for readers unaccustomed to reading legal documents. We provide full case references (and for some cases, the complete opinions) in Appendix A in case you want to go to the source.

lished for expert witnesses in general. The legal approach to screening expert witnesses has undergone significant change over the past decade through a series of Supreme Court decisions. The result of this series of decisions, starting with the landmark case *Daubert v. Merrell Dow Pharmaceuticals*, is that an expert must now pass additional tests in order to testify as an expert. The major differentiation between the old and new qualification processes for expert witnesses involves the addition of a "gatekeeper" function, assigned to trial judges. Although it may be difficult for techies to master the cases and the analysis of the legal issues concerning the gatekeeping duties of trial judges, it is crucial for the beginning expert to understand how the decision to allow a proffered expert to testify at a hearing or trial is made in different courts across the country.

The gatekeeping function that most courts have now accepted in one form or another is a distinct departure from the traditional role of the courts with regard to the use of experts. Under the old system, the courts passively allowed attorneys to proffer their chosen experts, allowing the jury to decide what weight to give to the respective witnesses' opinions. In the post-*Daubert* world, the judge acts as a gatekeeper, charged with weeding out unqualified experts as well as qualified experts who deliver unreliable opinions irrelevant to the particular case at hand. A process enabling adversaries to challenge the qualifications or relevance of a particular expert often triggers this function. The challenges are conducted in addition to and in advance of the more traditional impeachment of witnesses through cross-examination.

This expert qualification and challenge process requires additional work on the part of expert witnesses. First, the expert needs to consider whether he or she is adequately qualified by education, training, and experience to investigate and testify about particular matters before the court. While acting as an expert witness, the expert must also keep abreast of legal developments and make additional efforts to determine all that will be involved in a particular assignment. The expert may also need to determine how a soliciting attorney has dealt with past cases in which judges have entertained gatekeeping challenges against other judges. The expert must accept additional responsibility for anticipating and dealing with serious challenges to his or her qualifications and expertise. Finally, the expert must understand this rapidly changing body of case law on the fly since it has only recently been used to challenge IT experts.

The good news is that experts don't have to take this on all by themselves. All competent trial lawyers can be expected to keep up with the most recent changes in the way this challenge round is evolving in their jurisdictions and should be able to explain it clearly to the beginning expert. The information in Chapter 8 is presented in hopes that it will enable IT experts to pose relevant and concise questions about this new area of the law and at the same time prepare them to better understand the significance of the legal advice they receive from trial counsel concerning these new developments and their impact on the performance of the witness.

Chapter 9 provides detailed examples of how judges look at qualifications and the different approaches taken by the witnesses when deciding between competing theories and methods of opposing experts, as in the landmark case of *Gates v. Bando*, which established one of the practice standards for computer forensics. The testimony of Robert Wedig, the expert witness for the defendant who prevailed in that case, illustrates the factors affecting the judge's decision to favor Dr. Wedig's opinion over that of the opposing expert. The historical example of Houdini illustrates the different roles of the expert—both as a performer, demonstrating a known expertise, and as a skeptic uncovering the abuse of known techniques used by an opposing expert to obfuscate the facts or deceive the fact finder.

One of the most important tools that any IT expert can employ in court is a visual display. Chapter 10 explores the subject of graphic images in detail and provides a visual metaphor to allow the beginning expert to think about the entire process of approaching a technical problem involved in litigation through the eyes of graphics designers. The litigation graphics consultants who work with lawyers and their technical experts enable them to focus on the most important concepts and to organize their presentations with visual aids. The resulting visual displays vastly enhance the expert's ability to communicate the analysis and conclusions to judges and juries. We have selected several examples of the work and the methodology that Chris Ritter, a former litigator who now works for The Focal Point, LLC, has developed to assist both lawyers and expert witnesses in preparing for court.

Although experts are often tempted to focus on the content of their testimony, in court the *context* of testimony is also very important. This means that even the most brilliant and accurate technical analysis may not be accepted if the demeanor and nonverbal communications skills of the expert witness are lacking. Chapters 11 and 12 contain various analogies and techniques for improving the ways that expert witnesses integrate their demeanor and nonverbal communication with their testimony.

With all the provisions and restrictions of the legal process outlined, Chapter 13 provides a wealth of wisdom from the front lines. The chapter presents the advice of three noted IT experts with different degrees of experience. Professor Rebecca Mercuri, a world-renowned specialist in the area of voting technology, offers insights gleaned during a decade of testimony in a wide variety of cases, ranging from a murder trial to the appeal of the 2000 U.S. presidential election results in Florida. Don Allison, whose expertise in the discovery and analysis of digital evidence has placed him on the stand in a number of cases, offers his feedback loop methodology that not only carries him through the trial process but also allows him to refine his expert witness skills. Finally, Professor Gene Spafford, noted for his accomplishments in the software engineering and network security area, offers insights gained testifying in cases involving allegations of intellectual property theft and patent infringement.

For many technical experts, manuals and guides serve as references of last resort. These technical gurus enjoy and excel at learning by doing and may welcome the first opportunity to testify as an expert witness as similar to learning a new programming language or system troubleshooting technique. Unfortunately, they often fail to gauge the complexity of the preliminary processes required to get to the moment of truth, when the expert actually explains a technical process to a judge or jury. Furthermore, testifying in a serious legal controversy may be one of the few situations a technical expert will encounter where he or she must prepare for battle. At a minimum, the expert needs to read some rules and some literature before being cross-examined by a lawyer who has spent months preparing to call into question the testimony the expert plans to give.

Even with that preparation, the best-planned testimony has a way of making some dramatic detours and complete changes in direction when subjected to cross-examination by an experienced trial lawyer. The expert must assume that the lawyer has had the benefit of reading all the available literature and of being prepared by an equally qualified expert of his or her own. As Bill Spernow (a widely recognized expert in many IT domains) likes to say, "This is not something you can afford to learn by doing, at least if you plan to testify more than once in your life."

Spernow proposes that the topic addressed by this book is actually a prime example of the age-old question: "How do you get techies to read the manual before they jump in with both feet and try to make something work?" This is an especially important question for those in IT, where the archetypical personality thrives on improvising solutions in the trenches and getting code and systems to work by tinkering with them, not by formally planning ahead. Spernow also asks whether or not this kind of perspective would ever fly within the legal community, where ritualistic procedures and time are such serious and constant constraints.

Spernow is certainly right to raise these issues about the kind of fit that can be expected between techies and attorneys, and he is correct in his suspicion that it was more likely the legal system and not Benjamin Franklin who first coined the phrase "Time is money." Besides their time, lawyers keep track of the performances of expert witnesses. Even if experts have not yet started to monitor their peers and to evaluate their performances in the courtroom or in recorded depositions, lawyers have created their own networks for efficiently sharing this accumulated wisdom as to whom to trust as an expert in an IT-related case. Make no mistake, the record made of an expert's performance will be consulted to determine whether lawyers can rely on the expert in any future litigation for which they are being considered.

The legal profession may not easily understand or embrace the ways of the techie who prefers to tackle problems on the fly. Lawyers may not care about the techie's demonstrated success in using these methods to solve a purely technical problem. It is much more likely that, should the techie decide to play this expert witness game, he or she will need to understand the perspectives of lawyers and judges and consider making certain accommodations to the ritualistic and traditional procedures that the legal process brings with it. Furthermore, the techie must understand and accommodate the accompanying constraints on his or her freedom and time.

Consider the function of this book to be twofold. First, a number of the chapters of this book are primarily concerned with acquainting the technical expert with this very different world by using various analogies, cases, and stories of the involvement of other techies in the litigation game to accomplish this goal. Secondly, there are recommendations and tactics for dealing with specific challenges that the legal system presents to the technical expert. It is our hope that this combination of features will eliminate many of the potential headaches you might face as a techie headed for your day in court.

James Boyd White, a law professor and respected author, wrote:

> [T]he law can be seen as a particular instance of a human activity that is far more widespread than law itself, and of which we have splendid exemplars from which to learn: the activity of making meaning in language in relation to others. To see law this way opens a whole set of issues for analysis in the law (and in other instances of meaning-making too): the quality of the language that a particular person inherits and uses; the nature of her transformation of that language in her use of it; and the kind of relation she establishes with the people she speaks to or about.[1]

In several thousand times as many words, this book attempts to explain the significance of Mark Twain's single, cynical quote and to do it with the optimism and hope of Professor White.

At the outset, we want to make clear that, unlike Samuel Clemens, we are not professional writers, humorists, or entertainers extraordinaire. If we could have figured

---

1. White, James Boyd. "Dialogue: A Conversation Between Milner Ball and James Boyd White." *Yale Journal of Law and Humanity* 8(1996), p. 466.

out how to make a living being professional philosophers, we would have done so already. Instead, we chose to pursue careers in the fields of information technology and law.

Nor, in retrospect, are we as clear as we would like to be about the points we set out to make in all these pages. The problem that brought us together to write this book emerged from doubts about the ability to communicate the idealistic goals tempered by the cynical observations that color the world of the expert witness. We concluded that simply sending something as wonderful as the Twain quip and as thoughtful as the White quote to all the potential technical experts who had asked us for advice would be viewed as inadequate—they would still need a path to follow.

So, the main impetus for writing this book is to define some paths that can allow technical experts to more easily gain an understanding of why it is critical for those qualified and capable to join the fray. In doing so, they contribute to White's "making meaning in language in relation to others" involved in the litigation of IT issues.

Our subject, then, is the art of presenting effective IT expert witness testimony. This testimony, in the best case, enables a judge or juror to make meaning in relation to complex technical concepts involved with information technologies. This art in turn enables the fact finders in litigation to relate that meaning to an important controversy in order to make sound judgments about it.

And yet Twain must keep bringing us back with his words to the way we suspect things really are in the world of litigation. And we realize that we must deal with that as well. No one wants to be perceived as a circus clown in a setting where everyone else is pretending to be serious about another game. Our suspicion that we are being foolish or that we will be made the fool by following White in his optimism about the law and our legal rituals makes it all the more difficult to sustain this essential optimism for honest experts to give command performances. Yet the sustained effort to communicate carefully and objectively the professional experiences and special knowledge true experts and great trial lawyers wish to share with others is not difficult to justify. It is both the essence of the scientific method and the most rewarding kind of trial advocacy.

We have chosen to undertake the job of overcoming the cynical force of Twain's apothegm with analogies, metaphors, stories, disciplines, opinions, and anecdotes. It is our hope that the humor of some of these stories and the insights and analysis of other experts will go some way in overcoming that convenient cynicism. There will always be those who would rather remain uninvolved, while technical experts and their lawyers increasingly command the center stage of a growing number of legal performances. Our hope is that the number of those temporarily on the sideline will be reduced by some who are encouraged and challenged by the materials collected in this primer.

Acknowledgments

It is popular these days to assert that it takes a village to raise a child. Based on our experiences during the past year, we gratefully acknowledge that it took a community to produce this book. Our respective communities of support have given us access to resources and wisdom that proved critical to our success in this undertaking.

First, of course, we have received a great deal of support from our families and friends. Their encouragement smoothed the often rocky path we traveled. Becky's partner, Terri Gilbert, and friends—Bob Correa, B. Lissah, Michelle Baker, Kwai Tom Lam, Mike Johnson, and Dan Buckler—provided invaluable assistance to us in handling the numerous permissions required for the various images and quotes used throughout the book.

We are amazed and gratified by the amount of support we received from the community of experts in information technology, law, and other domains as we conducted our research and documented our findings. We have benefited from the generosity of many world-class experts, many of them pioneers in their respective domains of expertise, who shared with us their time, energy, and insights gained over the courses of their illustrious careers. Gene Spafford, Rebecca Mercuri, David Liddle, David Bailey, Don Allison, David Rhoades, Raemarie Schmidt, Bernard Ewell, Chris Stippich, Ross Mayfield, Kevin Manson, Ed Skoudis, Jonathan Dowell, Vic Hogsett, and Andrew Gross have all been generous to a fault.

At the beginning of our project, a chance meeting with Robert Wedig and Jack Grimes grew into connections that set the tone for the entire work. Christopher Ritter, Shana van Ort, and the rest of the gifted team at The Focal Point, LLC, have contributed in countless ways to what you see here in printed form. Brooke Gamble, an accomplished actress and attorney whose lovely image graces our latter chapters, and Daniel Pearlman, a professional jazz musician and trial lawyer who photographed her and also added greatly to the aikido section of Chapter 11, not only understood what we were trying to accomplish in our chapters on demeanor and nonverbal communications but also took on the task with enthusiasm and a wonderful sense of humor.

An array of skilled attorneys contributed their experiences and helped make whatever in this book proves useful to experts and their lawyers a great deal better than it otherwise would have been. They include Michael Pezzulli, James Skinner, Filmore Rose, James Rowles, Richard Klein, Kip Byrne, Robert Kimball, Chuck Barth, John Gallagher, Michael Hemmenway, Bruce Kohl, Mitch Dembin, Jack Burton, Tim Butler, Beth Davenport, Robert Vizas, Jack Hiatt, and Erin Kenneally, who did triple duty as consulting IT expert, attorney reviewer, and major contributor to Chapter 3.

Our reviewers, Ruth Nelson, Bill Tafoya, Marvin Schaefer, Jay Heiser, Bill Spernow, and Christopher Wee, all offered thoughtful, concise feedback on our draft manuscripts during the production phases. We are grateful to them, and we acknowledge the influence they exerted on the final product.

Finally, our editorial and production teams—Karen Gettman, Emily Frey, Patrick Cash-Peterson, Diane Freed, Gillian Hall, and Chrysta Meadowbrooke—have weathered the events of the past year with considerable patience, providing guidance as the events of September 11, 2001, disrupted the best of plans and schedules.

Fred Chris Smith
Santa Fe, New Mexico

Rebecca Gurley Bace
Scotts Valley, California

July 2002

Introduction

W. C. Fields (to Charlie): Quiet, you flophouse for termites, or I'll sic a beaver on you.
Edgar Bergen: Now, Bill. . . .
Charlie McCarthy: Mr. Fields, is that a flame thrower I see or is it your nose?
W. C. Fields: Why, you little blockhead, I'll whittle you down to a coat hanger.[1]

Every Dummy Wants to Be the Ventriloquist

As David Goldblatt says, ventriloquism is a bizarre practice.[2] From its origins as the purported voice of God and in the abuses of spiritualist seances, ventriloquism emerged into popular culture on stage, first as part of magic shows and vaudeville. Later, as pure entertainment, ventriloquism became an art form of nearly universal appeal. Ventriloquists were admired and renowned to the degree that they perfected the illusion of having a conversation with an inanimate object.

If ventriloquism (which we understand very well) is best described as "deviant conversation," why do trial attorneys like to talk about an effective presentation of expert testimony as a serious conversation between two good friends? It is clear to everyone that this conversation is carefully scripted and quite often rehearsed before its presentation at trial. And in most hotly contested trials, by the time the expert testifies and is subjected to deposition and cross-examination before the jury, it is unlikely that the best characterization of the relationship between at least opposing counsel and the expert would be that of friends. If not as deviant a conversation as the art of

---

1. From the *Charlie McCarthy Radio Show*. Quoted by David Goldblatt in
"Ventriloquism," in *Aesthetics: A Reader in Philosophy of the Arts* (David Goldblatt
and Lee B. Brown, eds.). Upper Saddle River, NJ: Prentice Hall, 1997, p. 470.

2. Goldblatt, David. "Making Things Talk: Ventriloquism." *Art Issues* March–April,
1994, pp. 20–26.

ventriloquism, is the practice of allowing experts to tell a judge or a jury what to believe, based on the expert's "opinions" while all other witnesses are restricted to testifying about facts, any less bizarre?

As expert witnesses were allowed to testify in more and more types of cases, advocates increasingly used and abused the illusion of the objective, unbiased expert witness as a powerful technique to pursuade fact finders of what they should believe about things they did not really understand. The pattern of abuse that was initially tolerated by the courts ultimately came to be seen as out of control, and eventually courts began to manage and then to control who could be qualified to testify as experts. Through the precedent of case law, the definition of experts and of what techniques and methods they could use to justify their opinions evolved into guidelines. From an open acceptance of the majority of proferred experts, the courts began to seriously apply new rules in an attempt to disqualify quacks and charlatans and to provide fact finders with more "reliable" expert witness testimony.

Why We Wrote This Book

We wrote this book for experts who are genuinely interested in maintaining their objectivity and independence from the significant pressures toward affinity with the party who calls on and pays for the witness. In an advocacy system of justice, these pressures to bias expert testimony will always be present. We assume that no self-respecting expert wants to become the blockhead for a ventriloquist advocate any more than a lawyer wants to be made to play the puppet to a manipulative expert before the client, judge, or jury. The image of either the expert witness or the examining advocate as a dummy whose strings are visibly pulled is also a very poor picture to present when attempting to persuade the fact finders in a trial. One of us has acted as an expert and the other as an attorney, and we have both had first-hand experiences with assuming the role of the dummy. While this role may have worked well for Bergen and McCarthy on the radio, it fails miserably in court. In this book we describe several approaches that can prevent such a picture from developing during the course of the professional relationships created between attorneys and technical experts engaged in litigation.

This book provides technical experts in the IT field with a primer on the art of presenting testimony as an expert witness. We selected particular examples of the kinds of cases and problems apt to be encountered in digital forensic assignments to give the uninitiated expert some idea of what may be involved.

In this age of accelerating social dependence on IT, many technical experts will be forced to testify in litigation whether they want to or not. We propose to provide information to these experts that will allow them not only to survive an initial expert witness experience but also to be able to see it as a significant social and professional responsibility of any dedicated IT expert. Ironically, some of the most experienced experts, who would prefer not to be called to the stand under any circumstances, may be best equipped to remain disinterested in the outcome of the case at hand because they remain reluctant witnesses. And it is precisely those reluctant experts—the ones who are equipped with the deep, objective understanding of information technologies and an appreciation of the difficulties of communicating that knowledge and understanding in a forensic ritual—that the legal system needs the most.

Voices of Experience

In this book, a lawyer and a technical expert collect and present a number of different ways to think about IT expert witness testimony. All of these suggested ways to think about the art of testifying are based on our collective experiences and on those of other lawyers and experts who have shared their own stories. Some of the stories come from experienced technical expert witnesses such as Robert Wedig, who testified in a landmark case that established standards for the collection and analysis of computer evidence, standards that are still followed to this day. Wedig and other accomplished technical experts like Jack Grimes have shared their experiences in preparing for and giving lengthy depositions in major intellectual property cases. Pioneers like David Liddle, Raemarie Schmidt, Rebecca Mercuri, and Gene Spafford have more recently found their way into court as consultants and experts in major cases. In their journeys, they have found approaches that help manage the potentially chaotic experience of attempting to apply the scientific method in an advocacy system of justice. Other stories are told by first-time experts like Ross Mayfield, Andrew Gross, and Don Allison, who have found their initial experiences as experts in civil and criminal cases to be both challenging and rewarding.

Still more stories come from attorneys who spend much of their time working with IT expert witnesses. We gleaned several of these stories from the opinions of judges who had to choose between contending experts who testified at deposition or trial. We have also included stories from other experts who specialize in various aspects of the competitive storytelling of advocates and experts. These are the litigation teachers, jury consultants, public-speaking coaches, and graphics exhibit creators who provide tools and techniques that allow the expert and attorney to succeed in communicating complex technical matters to the judge and jury.

Finally, we selected both funny and tragic stories from the history of expert witnessing and from the entertainment industry. These stories can tell us what can go wrong when experts go astray. They can suggest what good can result when stories about expert witnesses not only entertain us but also make sense to the witness's audience—even when these stories are created by screenwriters for Hollywood rather than by lawyers and experts for judges and juries.

When the idea for this book first began to take shape, there appeared to be one very good reason for collecting these various points of view and parables in one place: an ever-growing number of cases that require courts and counsel to seek the advice of a wide array of technical experts. We proceeded to locate and interview IT experts about their experiences. From this body of knowledge, we derived some philosophical and practical approaches for IT practitioners who need to understand the role of an expert witness and how testimony works. A year after we began researching this book, the rationale for sharing these insights is all the more apparent as the demand for IT experts in the courts is not just growing but skyrocketing.

Experts Called as Witnesses Aren't Always Expert Witnesses

One of the highest-profile IT experts of recent times is Bill Gates, founder and former CEO of Microsoft Corporation. The book includes an analysis of Gates's testimony during his appearance in a deposition in September 1998 for the case of *U.S. v. Microsoft Corporation*, the federal antitrust action against Microsoft. Although the primary focus of analysis is the testimony delivered in the federal case, Gates's performance as a witness in a subsequent appearance in the continuing antitrust case demonstrates a larger point.

In testimony, as in other areas of life, sometimes the most valuable lessons are learned by analyzing the most abject failures. When Bill Gates was deposed by the government during the course of the antitrust litigation against Microsoft, his testimony was heavily criticized by both legal and IT industry press commentators. Our intent is not to add to the criticism of that earlier testimony but to illustrate some important points. First, the increase of the risk of litigation by or against individuals and organizations directly results in an increase in the individual's risk of being called as a witness, whether as an expert or as a witness to fact. That is, if you are in a position of responsibility, chances are that sometime you'll have to serve as a witness in a legal process. Second, although you may not be called as an expert witness, the fact that you possess expertise in IT may require you to act as if you were an expert witness. Finally, and Gates is an example of this point, not even the weathiest and most powerful individuals can consider themselves sheltered from this aspect of the judicial process.

Bill Gates was not called to testify as an expert witness by either party to the government's original antitrust suit, but he was certainly the most important and arguably the most expert of any witness who testified. And it is no accident that part of the reason his testimony was so important is that he is also an acknowledged technical expert in all the areas involved in the litigation. His well-known expertise contributed to the importance of his testimony in many ways. Furthermore, his performance—and the widespread reaction to that performance—placed in the public domain many of the issues concerning how to be an effective witness.

As this manuscript went to press, Gates was recalled to the stand to testify in yet another hearing in a challenge brought by several states to a proposed settlement between the federal government and Microsoft. By all accounts Gates testified extremely well and was animated and engaged throughout several days of intense testimony. In short, he testified like the world-class expert that he is. This sounds an encouraging note for the reluctant IT expert who sees an expert witness stint in his future. The dramatic improvement in the performance of Bill Gates, as evidenced by his persuasive performance in April 2002, suggests that our working hypothesis is valid—practice, preparation, and experience can indeed improve the performance of IT experts, either as witnesses of fact or as expert witnesses.

The Gates deposition plays but a tiny part in the ongoing debate about what to do about allegations of anticompetitive behavior in the twenty-first century. The important realization to be drawn is that the wider social revolution wrought by IT (like all other massively embraced new technologies) inevitably contributes to existing legal issues or creates entirely new legal disputes that end up in court. Accordingly, the courts will be called upon to fashion new legal remedies as well as reshape old familiar ones. Furthermore, the courts will rely on testimony from IT experts to enable them and their juries to find and understand the relevant facts involving the use and alleged abuse of these information technologies.

Finding Magical Ways to Think about Honest Expert Testimony

There is no real magic to be found in the excerpts from the Gates deposition that appear here. Neither the attorneys, who are considered highly skilled, nor the witness, who may or may not have been performing at his best, were able to attain the status of master conjurers. Again, Gates was not called as an expert witness, although he certainly could have been. But for many judges and most potential jurors there is real magic in the new technologies that IT professionals are called upon to explain to judges and juries in their testimony when they act as expert witnesses. Ordinary people tend to think of IT as a kind of magic, and they may tend to think about IT experts in the same way they came to admire the ability of the great stage magician, Harry Houdini, to set up a situation that only he understood how to manipulate successfully. Throughout the book, we attempt to explain how judges and jurors come to rely on the expert's special knowledge and demonstrated abilities to use IT tools and techniques to explain what has happened in a computer or in a complex network.

Later in the book, when we more fully turn our attention to the historical Houdini, the challenge for honest experts may become clearer. As a society we pride ourselves on having created a wonderful alternative to the resolution of serious conflicts by violence. We also credit ourselves with having created a legal system whose hallmark is the pursuit of truth. Given the growing dependence on expert witnesses of all kinds and the likely increase in the need for IT experts, it becomes ever more important for these potential experts to understand some fundamental truths. First, it is not enough just to pretend to be objective and unbiased when testifying for a party to litigation. To perform the role of expert witness, the expert must remain objective. Second, the trick that faces the expert witness is that he or she must balance the art of successfully communicating his or her own competence and objective knowledge while exposing the magic of an opposing expert who may have become an advocate first and an expert second.

Houdini, the world's most expert stage magician, in mid-career became committed to an advocacy of sorts. Although he continued to practice his fine art of illusion as a magician, he eventually used his expertise to expose the spiritualists for the frauds they were. In distinguishing the skeptical pursuit of fraudulent practices, Houdini always sought to preserve magic as an art. He made no secret that he was performing a trick, and although he never explained the most complex tricks, his audience knew they were watching an exhibition.

By analogy, it is important that jurors be made aware of whether they are watching a biased or an objective technical expert and whether they are seeing an application of scientific methods that reveal relevant information or magic tricks that keep too many things concealed. Expert witnesses need to understand that in most highly complex technical litigation, the fact finders must ultimately rely on the expert's own avoidance of advocacy. The application of this ethic allows the fact finders to accept the expert witness's findings and conclusions without ever being able to become experts themselves. The most effective experts throughout history have applied their skepticism not only to the theories and conclusions of those who oppose them but also and especially to their own conclusions.

The Complete Expert Package: Showing as Well as Telling

Our favorite example of the ideal expert witness is an early epidemiologist, Dr. John Snow. As a classic example of illustrative evidence, we include in Chapter 8 his famous map depicting the cause of the great cholera outbreak in London in 1854. Snow's equally classic approach to the use of the scientific method, his effective use of graphic images, and his exhaustive collection and analysis of data that ultimately persuaded the world that he had found the truth about how cholera spread can still inspire lawyers and experts alike.

One of the revolutions wrought by modern technologies has been in the area of graphic arts. In order to understand the potential of modern graphics we also sought and received the expert advice of the professional litigation graphics artists at The Focal Point, LLC, to pass on new methods of applying these skills.

Why Do Technologists Need Expert Witness Skills?

You may be wondering: If you need only be qualified, honest, objective, and skeptical about the opinions of others and of your own methods and conclusions, why do you also need a number of other skills to be an effective expert witness? We believe that several factors suggest that the demand for expert technical witnesses will significantly increase during the next decade. If this proves to be the case, there will be greatly increased demands and financial rewards for these experts. These factors combine to guarantee a predictably large increase in the number of technical experts who will make themselves available for service in these cases. Not all of these candidates for service will be qualified, and not all of those who qualify will be objective. Some will be "magician advocates," and opposing lawyers will require honest and objective experts to adequately expose those "magic tricks" in deposition and at trial while presenting objective expertise to prove their cases.

In other words, no matter how obvious the conclusions are to a qualified expert, there will more than likely be other experts with adequate or slightly stretched credentials who may be allowed to testify. Experts may be found to counter the most straightforward conclusions or at least to create significant doubts in the minds of the fact finders as to the qualifications or credibility of the most objective expert. Yet, for all the moralizing about the need for honest expert testimony, to be truly effective, scientific or technical skills form a necessary but not sufficient set of practices for an effective expert witness. In addition to understanding the information technologies that may be at issue in a given case, an effective expert must master and practice the arts of communication and must understand the contexts that the legal system creates for those communications to occur. To succeed, the expert must have some essential performance skills, just like any other public speaker, teacher, or storyteller.

Let's examine generally some of the factors that have convinced us of the new demand for IT expert witness testimony—and for IT expert witness skills.

Making Sense of the March of Technical Progress

Debora Spar, a professor at the Harvard Business School, has examined a number of new technologies, beginning with the European development of navigation in the fifteenth and sixteenth centuries and continuing through the computer revolution in the twentieth and twenty-first centuries, including the opinion of the Federal Court of Appeals that upheld the trial court decision that Microsoft had violated the nation's antitrust laws. Just as privateering and piracy on the high seas were eventually brought under control through governments' coordinated enforcement of new laws, so too have IT companies found their way to the courtrooms at the end of the millennium to address the modern analogies to the evolution of maritime commerce. In her book,

Ruling the Waves, Spar argues that four essential stages mark the maturation process of a new technology.[3]

1. During the incubation and hatching of the new technology, developing the new technology is the main goal, and making profit is of little concern or likelihood.
2. The initial stage is followed by a gold rush to capture the profits in a newly discovered space, such as the open sea or new lands that suddenly become available for plunder, exploitation, and colonization by private or state-backed armies or companies intent on conquest and driven by profit.
3. These newly available resources, riches, and sources of value and assets are in turn subject to pirates who operate in a kind of symbiosis with the original plunderers. Spar calls this stage "creative anarchy."
4. Ultimately, private enterprises and governments alike see that it is in their interest to preserve or expand existing markets through state-backed legislative and judicial enforcement of the law.

Where Technology Marches, Law Follows

Until very recently almost all IT expert witness experiences have been in the area of litigation over the rights to intellectual property. Until the 1990s it was often an open question as to which of the parties in a dispute should be considered the lawful plunderer, which the unlawful pirate. In some cases perhaps both parties could be given the benefit of the doubt, for whatever moral high ground that distinction deserved at the time of the lawsuit.

Focusing on the Microsoft antitrust case, as Spar points out, from Microsoft's point of view, the legitimate entrepreneur had played by the rules of engagement in this new economic space and time. Microsoft had managed to succeed and to establish workable standards in an especially chaotic market for IT products and services. This success served as the rising tide that lifted the vast majority of all boats and helped shape a very successful market. Microsoft argued at trial that it was unfair for the government to criticize this successful business just for having sunk a few ships like Netscape in the process. On the other side of the argument was a long list of both former friends and long-time enemies who believed Microsoft represented the archetypical pirate band and needed to be stopped. In fact, many believed that if Microsoft were not dismembered, its monopolistic practices would destroy the economic poten-

---

3. Spar, Debora L. *Ruling the Waves: Cycles of Discovery, Chaos, and Wealth from the Compass to the Internet.* New York: Harcourt Brace, 2001.

tial of the World Wide Web for everyone else attempting to make a profit in that market space. Since there was apparently no middle ground on which the warring factions could settle and agree to move forward without government intervention, the matter ended in litigation.

In other words, this was an ideal conflict for settling through litigation and for determining what the rules would be henceforth in similar situations. Spar reminds us that this has been a predominant pattern of evolution when new technologies are introduced to society. We should not be surprised when contending companies and regulatory agencies of state and federal governments make increased use of the courts in the coming years to settle the rules for competition. In fact, we probably should expect exactly this turn to the authority of government and the courts for rule making and enforcement to deal with the fast-moving targets of an IT-driven economy. This will necessarily require a large number of competent experts to testify about these new technologies and their uses. It will also require experts to give testimony as witnesses of fact merely because of their position with the government or the companies involved in litigation. While this trend is predictable, it is only one of the driving forces that will contribute to an enormous increase in the demand for IT expertise in the courtroom.

Risky Business

Just as governments and private businesses jockey for control over the rules for how powerful new technologies can be put to use in gaining economic advantage, eventually individuals and organizations will refuse to continue to accept the risk of maturing and newly developed technologies when they fail and cause economic or physical damage. For at least two hundred years civil and criminal laws have focused on the deterrence of irresponsible behavior by companies and individuals trying to take economic advantage of the use of new technologies that lead to injury or death.

Some would suggest that the majority of criminal law enforcement and a good deal of insurance litigation is focused on the deterrence of the reckless driving of automobiles and the recompense for injuries caused by negligent use of these vehicles or incurred as a result of their defective design and manufacture. This is beginning to happen in the IT industry as well. IT is breeding new forms of very large civil claims for everything from damages for the failures of large, enterprise-wide system installations to the downstream liability claims of innocent third parties who were harmed by the failure of companies to adequately secure network system resources to prevent their use as platforms for attacks. The IT industry is also giving birth to new claims for the abuse of individual privacy rights brought by employees against their employers or others who use IT to conduct surveillance or investigations. Again, our society needs IT experts to assist in the assessment and litigation of these claims.

Is It Real or Is It Spoofed?

Another example of the rising IT-related litigation tide is the growing number of cases that question the authenticity of digital evidence created, manipulated, and stored on individual and corporate computer systems. A recent assertion that over 90 percent of all information is now created and stored in computers implies an arguably infinite demand for digital forensic expertise. Experts in this new technology domain will be called into play in routine criminal investigations and prosecutions wherever evidence is suspected or found to exist in a computer or where system behavior is relevant to establishing identity or causation. In the civil arena, where the discovery of evidence is designed to be managed by the attorneys for the opposing parties, questions of whether the evidence disclosed has been altered or whether additional evidence has been deleted or destroyed by one of the parties are routinely argued at great length. In some cases, such disputes have spawned litigation over evidence authenticity that has dwarfed the underlying cause of action itself.

Defense against Bad Legal Precedents

We believe that society is entering an era in which legal precedents regarding information and communications technology will be delivered by a legal system itself struggling to understand the technological landscape. We furthermore believe that expert witnesses who are capable of guiding the courts through clear, accurate explanations of technical issues and evidence are the best insurance against bad decisions. The historical legal landscape is strewn with the wreckage of badly engineered and constructed legal decisions and dogma, created to deal with poorly or even wrongly understood social consequences of widely adopted new technologies. To the extent that the best and brightest IT experts can enlighten judges and juries who must sit in judgment of conflicts hinging on the application of information technologies, misdirected decisions and counterproductive legal doctrines may be avoided.

The Missing Links in Technical Education

Technologists are often ill prepared to step into the roles that the legal system defines for them as expert witnesses. Many technical education curricula do not expose fledgling technologists to details of the interaction between the legal system and technology. Although some technologists may be inclined to believe that they can learn anything (including legal principles) on their own by reading documentation and manuals, this self-study process rarely provides adequate preparation for the vagaries and subtleties of legal precedent, strategy, and procedure.

Furthermore, technologists may need some help communicating with those who have little or no expertise in technology. Legal process is built on a 2,000-year tradition of storytelling, in which the stories enable the court to decide the facts of a case. If technologists do not understand how to convey their understanding of technology in a fashion compatible with this storytelling tradition, the quality of legal decisions will suffer, to the detriment of all of society.

The effective communication of complex technical information about rapidly changing technologies and their use and abuse, if not bordering on stage magic, can often be a very complicated business. IT experts working with lawyers to present testimony in criminal and civil cases need to bear in mind that opposing technical experts, attorneys, judges, and jurors all have their individual histories. Both judicial fact finders and legal professionals are often constrained in their decision making by their own broad and deep traditions and by narrow local influences of which the naive expert has no inkling. At the same time, in our experience, effective communication of the histories of particular technologies can, and most often does, make the difference in whether the fact finder correctly gets the big picture, rather than some other competing picture that is not supported by the most competent scientific and technical information and opinion. In other words, regardless of the relative sophistication of the judge or jurors, results can vary, but far more often than not they come down to the story the expert chooses to tell and how well he or she tells it. To be able to effectively communicate information about these new technologies requires the expert and the lawyer to understand the communication technologies and techniques that have been developed and applied in the western tradition of dispute resolution through advocacy.

The need for IT professionals to prepare for giving testimony in a courtroom, in arbitration, during the course of a governmental investigation, or at a regulatory or administrative hearing should be clear. Although it may not always be the case that attorneys will subpoena experts to testify as experts per se, it is almost certainly the case that, due to the experts' experience and training, they will be among the most valuable and effective witnesses to testify about what has occurred in the use or alleged abuse or failure of some type of IT. Technologists should consider whether this new demand for IT expert testimony and the likelihood that they will be called upon to testify are real, and if so whether these new realities require them to add the art of forensic testimony to their professional expertise.

What This Book Provides

Although we wrote this book primarily for the technologist who is a neophyte expert witness, we recognize that other audiences may derive value from the contents. Following are the primary audiences for this book and the specific information they stand to gain.

- **Beginning IT experts** who accept expert witness assignments can gain much by reading this book:

— An understanding of certain aspects of the legal system, ranging from processes to specific rules

— An understanding of the different types of experts who may testify or consult about litigation, with specific focus on expert witnesses and the different roles they play within the legal process

— Courtroom communications skills applicable to a broad audience (both inside and outside the legal system)

— Skills for enduring cross-examination by an experienced and skilled adversary

— Skills for preparing for legal testimony, including specific physical and mental conditioning exercises

— An understanding of how expert witnesses are selected for specific types of cases

— An understanding of how legal needs and constraints affect expert witnesses

— An understanding of what judges may look for to qualify an IT expert when the opposing party challenges the expert

— Specific recommendations on how to effectively manage expert witness assignments, from the initial meeting with the attorney in the case to the final question from the cross-examining attorney at trial

- **Legal professionals** who work with IT experts can also benefit. Lawyers who hire experts can gain new insights into the concerns that technical experts have about becoming involved in litigation for the first time. Judges who must decide on the qualifications and methods of IT experts can consider how experienced experts think about these challenge rounds and how such challenges affect the willingness of the best and the brightest experts to enter the fray.

- **Clients** whose interests are affected by the performance of IT experts can benefit. Clients who want to win at all costs can gain an understanding of why expert objectivity and credibility are often indistinguishable and why, when those qualities are combined with competence and experience, they most often lead to the best results.

- **Risk managers** can learn how the process of the trial team's brainstorming with the help of an accomplished expert and trial consultants can lead to an early, cost-effective, and equitable settlement with the other side or a more effective framing and presentation of the technical issues and evidence at trial.

What This Book Does Not Provide

Although many technologists voiced a desire that we provide a concise "rule book" for the U.S. legal system, we do not satisfy that desire in this book for two simple reasons: (1) the legal system cannot be described in any acceptable detail in a book of this size, and (2) the rules and decisions are in a constant state of flux.

In declining to tackle the problem of explaining the legal system in all its constantly evolving detail or to state what the rules are at any given time, we advise beginning IT experts to focus instead on one of the main forensic facts of life. The expert witness is meant to serve the court as an objective witness, in order to assist the fact finder, be that judge or jury. The expert is best served by working closely and openly with the attorney or, in some cases, with the court who hires the expert to provide analysis, reports, and testimony, to come to a clear understanding of the different tasks each will take on in the course of the proceedings. As we discuss throughout this book, it is the attorney who is charged with advocacy for his or her client, and the best efforts of the expert are applied by the attorney toward this client-centric goal.

Caveats and Disclaimers

From time to time we may feel compelled to remind you of the important disclaimers made earlier in the beginning pages of this book. Discussions of the types of relationships between lawyers and experts and of the kinds of decisions that must be made concerning them should always be guided in the real world by the advice of competent legal counsel. We wish to make clear that we are not offering legal advice—no one should rely in any way on the discussions and materials in this book for legal guidance in any matter. Nor do we intend to interfere in any way with the kinds of relationships that lawyers and experts may decide, after due consideration, to form and maintain over time. Our purpose is simply and solely to stimulate thought and discussion about some of the many problems that occur in the presentation of technical expert witness testimony.

Should you disagree with any or all of these materials, so much the better for the candid and open discussion of these important issues. Whether you agree or disagree with any part of this discussion, if you think you need independent legal advice, you should always seek out and follow your own lawyer's advice. No advice of a legal nature is contemplated or offered to readers of this book or to people relying on the legal or other advice of any of its readers.

Examples of Expert Witnesses and Their Communities of Interest

Our world is awash with technology. The operation of the most common technical devices remains a mystery to mere mortals. In this chapter, expert witnesses from several different specialty areas describe the nature of their work. Of particular interest here is how each of these experts contributes to and draws on the expertise of other experts within their own professional community of interest. Included among these examples is a look at an Academy Award–winning portrayal of an expert witness who shares several common attributes with effective expert witnesses who testify in real courtrooms. The expert in *My Cousin Vinny* is extremely well qualified, competent, and credible. She is also able to correct in a clear and convincing way the serious technical mistakes made by the opposing expert in rendering his opinion. The movie version of competing expert witnesses shows how easily the expert with all the facts and the competence and experience to comprehend their meaning wins. The movie and the real-life examples presented in this chapter underscore the importance of the traditional expert community of interest that establishes clear standards of practice and the reputations of experts who apply them. These standards and qualifications are central to the process of the qualification of experts, the evaluation of the credibility of expert testimony, and the ultimate resolution of disagreements between legitimate, qualified experts.

1

Who Decides Whether an Expert Is Really an Expert?

There is an ongoing debate about whether or not it makes any sense to allow judges and juries to decide that an expert is sufficiently qualified to testify when neither judges nor juries can hope to understand the issues in question as well as the expert does. At the most basic level, this debate is resolved by accepting the consensus of an existing professional community of interest that endorses the proffered expert as a properly qualified member in good standing.

Professor C. A. J. Coady has considered this problem at length in *Testimony*.

We have certifying bodies and institutions and their various certificates and, typically, the courts require that the witness be shown to have some relevant certification from such bodies. Doubt can arise, of course, about the credentials of supposedly expert institutions (as admissions officers in universities and similar institutions are well aware) but usually the courts do not doubt such credentials. Were they to require for every such certifying body some proof of its credentials, it is hard to see what could be forthcoming, other than more of the same. In fact their attitude is one of trust in most such bodies and, given that the general reliability of testimony is not in doubt, this attitude can be given an indirect justification. Unless we take a thoroughgoing sceptical stance we can assume that it is, for instance, in the nature of scientific expertise to be communal. There are leaders and initiators in the various sciences but their work is recognized, criticized, expanded, carried forward, by a group who understand[s] what the initiators have done and are doing. Such a group will have an interest in protecting the standards of inquiry in the area of science they practise, in exposing pretenders to the expertise that gives a focus to their lives, and, especially if their expertise has direct practical value for the outside community, in providing certification or warranties of expertise.

. . . [T]he lay person can reason to the conclusion that there will inevitably be expert bodies with the sort of features discussed above and he can then observe the existence of what appear to be just such bodies. Various people tell him that they are members of the expert bodies and that the bodies really are expert, others tell him that their sons and daughters are being trained by such bodies in some expertise or other, and so on in a complicated web of testimony.[1]

Unfortunately, in the world of IT, the types of expert groups that have formed a recognized professional community of interest are often quite different in form and function than the scientific and professional communities of interest the courts have traditionally relied on to begin to consider the appropriateness of a proffered expert.

This is not just an academic or a philosophical problem. It can also impact the fact finder when one of the competing experts is not qualified and is essentially making up "facts" or inventing nonexistent standards on the stand. This issue also affects the will-

---

1. Coady, C.A.J. *Testimony: A Philosophical Study*. New York: Oxford University Press, 1992, pp. 282–283.

ingness of qualified experts to step forward and offer reliable expert testimony. In fact, a number of IT experts interviewed for this book who have experience in both litigation and arbitration described their abhorrence of testifying in a case when the opposing expert lacks adequate qualifications or experience to render an opinion about a complex issue. The problem becomes both uncomfortable and ultimately unmanageable for the witness because the genuine expert's sense of ethics prohibits him or her from going after the opposing expert during their testimony. Often for strategic reasons, the attorney has chosen not to do so during cross-examination. This creates a situation in which the judge or the jury hears diametrically opposed opinions from two people who have been presented, at least for purposes of testifying, as being approximately equal in knowledge, training, and expertise in the area in question.

This concern is echoed by Harry Hollien, a respected expert and author on forensic issues who has written lucidly about the ethics of expert testimony. Hollien points out that when courts adopt a cavalier approach to attributing the requisite expertise to a potential expert witness, it creates a major ethical and practical problem for a genuine, recognized expert to deal with on the stand. It is extremely difficult for the true expert to appear objective as a witness should he or she be required by the attorney to attack the qualifications, experience, and acceptance (by the common community of interest) of the opposing expert.

> [M]ost experts dread those trials in which they have to explain their findings and conclusions to a court that is not aware that the witnesses for the other side are only superficially competent and actually lack the scientific or professional expertise necessary to comment on the relevant issues. Small wonder then that many scientists and practitioners simply refuse to testify or even to offer their talents on a consulting basis.[2]

A Potpourri of Expert Witnesses from Other Disciplines

The legal system settles disputes that occur in everyday life. These disputes can involve individuals, governments, and organizations, both commercial and nonprofit, in every conceivable combination. The nature of the disputes can run the gamut of topics, with many resolutions hinging on highly technical evidence. In addition to the automobile mechanic expert witness scene from *My Cousin Vinny*, we present real-world examples of expert witnesses drawn from technical areas other than IT. All of these experts have achieved success as educators or consultants within their recognized areas of expertise and as forensic witnesses in the courtroom. The issues they discuss include many that are relevant to IT experts. We include details about how they contribute to and rely on

2. Hollien, H. "Expert Witness: Ethics and Responsibilities." *Journal of Forensic Sciences* 35(6), 1990, p. 1418.

active professional communities of interest, in hopes that their insights, drawn from a wide variety of such expert bodies, might serve as road maps to IT experts and their potential communities of interest.

Mona Lisa Vito: Reluctant Expert Witness in *My Cousin Vinny*

The popular movie *My Cousin Vinny* offers the fledgling technical expert an entertaining introduction to the performing arts of the expert witness in a criminal trial. Joe Pesci plays the lead role as the attorney from out of town, Vinny Gambini. Vinny is defending his cousin and a friend who are mistakenly charged with murder. Marisa Tomei steals the show in an Oscar-winning performance as Vinny's fiancée, Mona Lisa Vito, the reluctant expert witness whose testimony sets the wrongfully accused boys free. This film is a classic comedy of errors, but the play within the play that is most remarkable for our purposes is the battle of technical experts over the question of the identification of the getaway car. The courtroom testimony of the contending witnesses offers an extremely helpful introduction to the art of presenting expert witnesses at trial for both beginning experts and litigators.

As the trial unfolds, the viewer learns that Vinny has never tried a case before and is not even licensed to practice law. He has, however, learned a thing or two about human nature, and his street smarts and his ability to communicate with witnesses and score with jurors has succeeded in making mincemeat of the eyewitnesses for the prosecution. Although his case is badly damaged, the prosecutor has kept an ace up his sleeve and plays it in the form of his last witness—an FBI forensic expert on tire track identification. The prosecution expert is well qualified and testifies convincingly that he conducted reasonable experiments to determine that the rubber from the tires on the defendants' car is identical in chemical composition to the rubber left on the road by the vehicle in which the killers fled from the scene of the crime. He also correctly determines through his research that the type of tires that made the tracks left at the scene are identical to the kind of tires on the defendants' car.

The fairy-tale staging alerts us to two of the basic rules that would have precluded this scene from taking place in the real world of trials (or at least would have guaranteed that Vinny would win an appeal if his clients had been convicted). After a long history of trial by ambush, modern federal and state rules of procedure and evidence governing the disclosure of expert witnesses and their opinions were amended. The current rules would have required the prosecutor to advise Vinny well in advance of the trial that he intended to call an expert witness and, furthermore, to disclose the substance of that witness's testimony and opinions. But here, for dramatic purposes, the scriptwriters have the judge, played by Fred Gwynne, deny Vinny's proper protests about the surprise expert witness and his reasonable request for a continuance to find his own witness to render an opinion for the defense. With these erroneous rulings by the judge, the stage is set for Vinny to call his temporarily estranged fiancée to the stand to testify as an expert witness for the defense.

Vinny sets up Mona Lisa's testimony by deciding to conduct a constructive cross-examination of the defense expert. David M. Malone and Paul J. Zwier, in their book, *Effective Expert Testimony*, describe this technique in the following way:

> Constructive cross-examination enlists the support of the opposing expert, seeking his agreement that certain fundamental facts, principles, or limitations are correct. The appropriateness of a particular methodology that is generally accepted in the field, the unavailability of Bureau of Labor Statistics data for certain time periods, the inability to determine a nuclear particle's mass and velocity at the same time, or his own decision not to conduct certain additional tests—these are the kinds of areas in which a reasonable expert (or an unreasonable one who nevertheless recognizes the danger of denying the truth of matters which can be proved) is likely to agree, thereby saving energy for more important battles. Constructive examination depends upon the credibility of the opposing expert; the trial lawyer wants the jury to believe [the expert witness] when he says he is right on something, or his expert is right on something. Such agreement makes the "something" equivalent to a universal truth—no one disagrees, so the jury can accept it.[3]

Rather than attempting to confront the damning conclusions of the prosecution's expert, Vinny gets him to agree with what appear to be minor and uncontestable points. In this way, Vinny actually gains the support of the prosecution expert for a fact that will be essential to Vinny's own argument. In doing so, he establishes the fact that the kind of tires on the defendants' car, which match the tire tracks found at the scene of the crime, are indeed the most popular tires used on cars manufactured in the same year as the defendants' car. Without attacking the prosecution expert, Vinny elicits this admission on cross-examination that expands the number of possible vehicles that could have left those tracks. This weakens the FBI expert's implication that the car that left the tracks belonged to the defendants. After the constructive cross-examination, the jury understands that the class of cars that could have left those tracks includes hundreds of thousands of other vehicles. Vinny politely thanks the witness for his testimony.

Although in the movie the FBI expert gets off lightly as an honest government employee with limited resources, there is a darker side to this performance that can serve to highlight the problem with results-oriented expert testimony in general. Here the prosecution did not ask the expert to rule out all the other plausible theories that might account for the challenged identification of the defendants' car as the murderer's vehicle but simply to collect enough facts and to make enough comparisons to give the prosecution's theory of the case some credibility after Vinny had demolished the

---

3. Malone, David M., and Paul J. Zwier. *Effective Expert Testimony*. Notre Dame, IN: National Institute for Trial Advocacy (NITA), 2000, p. 179.

so-called eyewitnesses. The expert has become the prosecutor's best argument to the jury as to why they should still convict the defendants, because all the eyewitnesses have been impeached.

But note that this is not an objective expert's attempt to consider all the possible explanations for the apparent similarities between the tracks the murderer's vehicle left at the scene and the tires on the defendants' car. As we will see, Vinny's witness will take into account all the relevant facts and be able to conclusively demonstrate that the FBI's tire expert was simply wrong to suggest that the defendant's car was capable of leaving the tracks at the murder scene.

After cross-examining the FBI expert, Vinny attempts to convince his fiancée to take the stand as his expert witness. There is no one else to turn to, especially since the judge has given him five minutes to put up or shut up. Mona Lisa adamantly refuses to take the stand, and by the time she is brought kicking and screaming into the courtroom and forced to take the oath by the judge, it is clear to the audience that Vinnie has figured out a way to get two things he needs. For not only does he get the evidence he needs but also, and equally important, he gets beyond the problem of the appearance of bias due to the amorous relationship between the witness and the attorney. As the scene is presented, the judge, jury, and prosecutor can clearly see that, at the moment, Mona Lisa hates Vinny's guts and wants no part of testifying on behalf of the defense.

This cartoon caricature of how to handle the inherent problems of witness bias helps us understand its fundamental nature in all cases involving experts. Incidentally, this situation is one that can and will be examined by opposing counsel whenever an expert has been hired by one party to give an opinion that is helpful to the hiring party or harmful to the interests of the opposing party. The slapstick staging provides an amusing illustration of how an extreme form of this constant problem can be overcome. Here in its most ridiculous pose—that of a beleaguered lawyer resorting to calling his fiancée and paralegal to take the stand as an expert witness in order to give her opinion on what may be the ultimate issue in the case—we can more easily see how less severe problems of bias can and do arise in nearly every case, if only because the witness is usually being paid by the proponent for his or her time. Steven Lubet, in his excellent book, *Expert Testimony*, puts the problem of "relationship bias" in its more typically encountered forms this way:

> *An expert's relationship with a party or counsel may also be used to imply a lack of impartiality. Some witnesses seem to work repeatedly with certain law firms (or litigants), testifying to similar conclusions in case after case. While such an ongoing relationship is not proof of actual bias, cross-examiners can be counted on to insinuate that the association must have been sustained for a reason.*[4]

---

4. Lubet, Steven. *Expert Testimony: A Guide for Expert Witnesses and the Lawyers Who Examine Them.* Notre Dame, IN: National Institute for Trial Advocacy (NITA), 1998, p. 106.

Alternatively, Lubet suggests that "positional bias," where it can be demonstrated to exist in an expert by the opponent, is also likely to be challenged in cross-examination and should be kept in mind by an expert who may have become identified with a particular stance or position on an area of expertise.

Another typical kind of impeachment on bias involves the fees paid to an expert. Jack Matson offers the expert the following advice on this perennial problem when an aggressive attorney attempts to impeach on cross-examination for large payments for contested opinions.

> . . . [T]he examiner is trying to show how mercenary you were, and how much you charged for such minimal and flawed work. You are another living example of a high priced hired gun willing to say anything for a price. About all you want to do in these circumstances is maintain your composure and be dignified. Don't be defensive![5]

Once you begin to think about expert testimony like a trial lawyer, you begin to see why an attack on the various kinds of bias that may exist is considered to be one of the most fertile fields for cross-examining an expert. So, ironically, the fact that Mona Lisa Vito is not being paid at all for her testimony is also a promising area for cross-examination on the issue of bias. The reader may initially think that because Mona Lisa is not being paid for her testimony, this would count in her favor as indicating a lack of bias. However, the combination of a longstanding relationship with the defense attorney coupled with the total lack of compensation could be turned nicely by the cross-examiner into a ladder of bias questions. The point here is simply that compensation will always be an issue—either at the deposition or at trial—so experts should be prepared to explain how they came to the conclusion that some fee (or no fee) was appropriate for the work at hand.

Stanley L. Brodsky, who has 30 years of experience training health professionals in giving expert testimony, points to an even subtler form of the bias issue. This may totally escape the questioning of the cross-examining attorney, but it needs to register in the mind of every expert as he or she undertakes each assignment to testify. Brodsky calls it the "pull to affiliate."

> Bought experts may or may not exist, depending on one's perspective. Those who believe experts can be bought describe individuals who conform their opinions to the side that employs them. Although a few rare birds may indeed be bought, my perspective is that a subtle social-psychological process influences many witnesses toward "our" side. The courtroom drama does have an "us-versus-them" dichotomy. Just as the attorneys accept the viewpoint of their side, some expert witnesses may do the same. The affiliation process is rarely deliberate or conscious. Instead the pull, and sometimes the reality, is to shape one's opinions in small ways to conform to

---

5. Matson, Jack. *Effective Expert Witnessing*, 3rd ed. New York: CRC Press, 1999, p. 102.

what is seen as the "right side." Almost all expert witnesses would deny that their opinions are so influenced. However, the affiliation process begins early. From the time the attorney first speaks with a potential expert, the attorney probes, suggests, assures, and woos.

As often as I withdraw, I stay with cases—and so do most experts. As the cases progress, a litmus test for continued involvement occurs at the findings stage. The expert reports, usually by telephone, and the attorney decides about using the expert in court. If this decision is positive, then a series of additional stimulus demands to affiliate with this side take place. Meetings occur with the attorney. There is talk about the best way to present the expert's findings and opinions. Discussions may take place about the likely strategy of the opposing attorneys. A meeting prior to deposition may have the attorney helping the expert prepare. It is not unusual to observe an exchange of cooperative actions and warm feelings. Under these conditions, the impartiality of the expert may be compromised. . . . These events constitute a far greater hazard to impartiality than the mythical bought witness. Their impact is gradual and beyond the immediate awareness of the expert. These influences are sufficiently powerful that they may be the single greatest threat to expert integrity. Becoming aware of these events is a first way of preventing them.[6]

Regardless of all the potential pitfalls involved in attempting to place Mona Lisa on the stand, Vinny has no other options. As a car buff, he has noticed something about the photographs of the tire marks that shows that the tracks could not have been left by a car with the equipment on his cousin's car. Since he can't testify himself, and he can't rely on the depth of knowledge or the honesty of the government's witness to produce the right answer on a complete cross-examination, he has to get his fiancée on the stand and qualify her as an expert witness. He knows that Mona Lisa is an accomplished mechanic and a highly qualified expert who is able, based on her knowledge, training, and experience with cars, to point out to the court what Vinny has seen in the pictures and furthermore to explain why the tire marks exonerate the defendants.

It turns out that Vinny's method of getting his fiancée on the stand has effectively disarmed the prosecutor as to the bias issues, and his tender of Mona Lisa as an expert invites the overconfident prosecutor to make a fundamental mistake. The prosecutor acts on his obvious belief that his knowledge about cars will suffice to put this nice little lady in her proper place and make her appear in the eyes of the jury much less of an expert about cars than he is. He asks for and is granted the right to conduct what is called in the trade a voir dire examination of the tendered expert. Cocky as can be, the prosecutor decides to ask his questions designed to test Mona Lisa's qualifications as an expert witness in front of the jury. This is a strategic decision in which the attorney attempts to display the lack of expertise of an untested expert before the jury

---

6. Brodsky, Stanley L. *Testifying in Court: Guidelines and Maxims for the Expert Witness.* Washington, DC: American Psychological Association, 1991, pp. 8–9.

in an effort to discredit the witness even before testimony occurs. Technically, the voir dire is only supposed to test the legal sufficiency of the expert's qualifications to give an opinion and is often conducted outside of the presence of the jury when either attorney requests it. But Vinny knows his expert's qualifications and experience, and he is not about to deprive the jury of the chance to find out just how good an expert she is. Neither does he want to save the overconfident prosecutor from the just desserts of his male chauvinist appetite.

Steven Lubet explains the function of voir dire as follows:

> In esssence, the voir dire is a mini-cross, aimed exclusively at the legal sufficiency of the expert's qualifications. In legal terms, the only question is whether the witness is "qualified as an expert by knowledge, skill, experience, training, or education." No matter what the voir dire uncovers, the witness will usually be allowed to proceed with her testimony so long as she meets this minimum requirement.[7]

Without objection the judge allows the prosecutor to question Mona Lisa with the jury present. The prosecutor immediately attempts to challenge her qualifications and experience by asking her profession, which she happily admits is that of an out-of-work hairdresser. He then asks her what qualifies her as an expert in the field of automobiles. She effortlessly recounts her family's tradition of expertise in repairing and maintaining autos for most of the century. Her father, like his father before him, was a mechanic, as were her maternal grandfather, her four uncles, and her three brothers.

Before Mona Lisa can continue, the prosecutor concedes that her family is obviously qualified, but he then wants to know what makes her think that she is also an expert mechanic. Mona Lisa begins what quickly becomes an apparently unending inventory of the kinds of repair jobs she has personally performed as an automobile mechanic. The prosecutor immediately cuts her off again by asking why, even with all that experience maintaining and repairing all kinds of cars, she feels qualified as an expert in the specific area of tire mark identification.

For our purposes in this chapter, this is probably Vinny's key strategic move. Vinny has carefully carved out the general area of automobile technology as Mona Lisa's expertise but has not offered her as a specialized expert on tires. He needs to establish her as a general expert about all automobiles, not as a specialized tire expert, in order to explain to the judge and the jury the meaning of the photographs of the tire marks in the context of her expert analysis of what sort of automobile could have made those particular types of tracks. She is not being offered as a tire expert but as a more general kind of expert. This more general expertise will allow her to render an opinion about more relevant evidence in the case that will also make clear that the

---

7. Lubet, *Expert Testimony*, pp. 96–97.

opinion of the more specialized tire expert was erroneous due to ineptitude or ignorance. And if necessary this will also allow Vinny to argue that the prosecutor has attempted to mislead the jury by bringing an expert who lacked the necessary expertise to adequately address the real problem. But for Mona Lisa to be able to give her opinion, the judge and the jury must believe two things that are crucial for every technical expert to appear competent and credible to the fact finder.

The genius of this tactical move of presenting the witness as a general expert is that it gets over the two largest hurdles encountered when qualifying any technical expert witness.

1. Is this expert qualified by knowledge, experience, and training?
2. Is the expertise that this expert claims one that is generally recognized to exist by society and a socially recognized community of experts?

The staging of the voir dire by the prosecutor leaves no doubt in his mind or the minds of the audience that Mona Lisa is a genuinely qualified and experienced expert in the area of how cars are built and repaired. Remember that this fiction takes place in a rural Southern town where people's cars are an important part of their lives. The judge and the jury all know who the good mechanics are and which families turn out the best mechanics; that's the way someone becomes a good mechanic and gets recognized as an expert. The judge and the jury, like the prosecutor, also believe they know a little bit about cars themselves, or they have a sibling or an uncle who knows a great deal about cars and knows how to explain how they work and what to do to fix them. To claim a family tradition of expertise in auto mechanics is even more natural to this set of fact finders than the academic and professional qualifications of the FBI expert witness when he is called to the stand and qualified as a tire expert.

It is crucial to bear in mind that Vinny has called Mona Lisa as a general expert and that he has already somewhat defused the specific tire-related expert testimony of the FBI witness with his constructive cross-examination about the popularity of the tires in question. With automobile technology, it is a simple matter to find the statistics about which tires are used on which vehicles and which treads appear on which tires. These standards and statistics are widely available and accessible to everyone with an interest. There are also reasonable assurances that manufacturing standards have been scrupulously followed by the major automobile and auto parts manufacturers. This also holds true for the performance criteria of the different technologies and vehicles that have those technologies installed in particular models. And all of this objective information is available to any expert (or for that matter, to any judge or juror) to confirm. What Vinny still needs to prove to the judge and the jury for his witness to be allowed to give her opinion is that she has become expert as a result of her inheritance of the family tradition of expertise and through her own experience and training. There are many ways to demonstrate this economically in technical areas where licensing and certification are not required to become a recognized expert. Once again the sexist prosecutor comes to Vinny's aid.

Having nowhere to go with his challenge to her qualifications, since she has testified to her family tradition and her experience as a mechanic practicing with these other experts, the prosecutor next frames a question that appears to be highly technical. However, he poses it as if it were a fair test of Mona Lisa's experience and ability to provide a technical solution to a hypothetical mechanical problem. The witness instantly recognizes that the prosecutor has asked her a trick question, and she refuses to answer it. Furthermore, she explains to the judge and the jury why it is a trick question without an answer and goes on to add sufficient facts to the question to give it some sense. She then supplies and explains her answer to the clarified question, to the humiliation of the prosecuting attorney. The lawyer sits down, and the judge and jury are obviously impressed with Mona Lisa's control of the situation.

By her ability to listen carefully to the trick question and to refuse to play a blatantly bogus game with the lawyer, Mona Lisa has succeeded in shifting the balance of control in her favor. By taking the time to understand the question and the situation and by carefully explaining the correct question and answer to the judge and the jury, she has eliminated any doubt that she is an expert in the area about which she was called to testify. She has also set the stage for Vinny to ask her expert opinion on the ultimate question that will win the case.

After this masterful defense of her qualifications as an expert, we finally see Mona Lisa, on direct examination, handle exhibits and questions that she has never seen before. The movie audience knows full well that this would never take place in the real world, but the staging of this portion of the screenplay makes her testimony even more credible in the context of the story. It is obvious to one and all on the jury that this is in no way rehearsed or coached testimony. (This is something that jurors can worry about, and it needs to be explained by the lawyer and the expert during the course of the testimony so that the necessary preparation of expert testimony is seen as a normal process.) The staging of this piece of testimony in the movie removes that line of questions from the cross-examiner's normal arsenal. Mona Lisa goes on to destroy the opinion of the government's expert by pointing out that he had failed to consider all the information in the photos in light of the known capabilities of the defendants' car and other similar-looking cars on the market.

She is able to demonstrate, by using the photographic evidence in combination with her extensive knowledge and experience with cars, that there is only one reasonable explanation for the kind of tracks that the killer's vehicle left at the scene. In her expert opinion, the vehicle must have had both positraction and independent rear suspension in order to have left such tracks over both the pavement and curb. She then narrows the field of vehicle models that have both these features. This process of elimination leaves only two possible models. One is the Corvette, which could not possibly have been mistaken for Vinny's cousin's car. The other is the 1963 Pontiac Tempest, which just happens to have the same wheel base and body shape as the defendants' vehicle. This model was also available in the same color as the defendants' vehicle. In other words, the defendants' car could not have made the tire marks at the scene, but another kind of car, which looks a lot like theirs, could have.

Vinny then recalls the FBI expert, who turns out to be an honest man despite being an inept expert. Having been as impressed with the defense expert's testimony as everyone else in the courtroom, the FBI expert promptly corroborates Mona Lisa's conclusions and admits that he was mistaken in his testimony. Meanwhile, the sheriff has a change of heart and discovers that a stolen 1963 Tempest has just been recovered upstate and that the murder weapon has been recovered in that stolen vehicle. Faced with these new developments, the district attorney dismisses the charges against the boys, and Vinny and his beaming expert beat it out of town before the judge can discover Vinny's masquerade as an attorney.

Fairy-tale staging aside, *My Cousin Vinny* is a classic demonstration of how two honest and highly qualified experts can give persuasive testimony about relevant issues in a case, and yet only through the advocacy system can it become clear to the fact finder that only one of the experts possesses the ability to adequately resolve the technical questions in the case. It is not unusual for an attorney and his or her expert to simply fail to consider all of the facts that have a bearing on the issues in the case. In fact, sometimes an attorney requests only a selective review of all the available facts. Experts who do not insist on accessing all the relevant and material facts risk being placed in the position of the FBI forensic expert *in My Cousin Vinny*. And experts, unaided by screenwriters' scenarios, need ample time and resources to properly prepare for their testimony.

Unfortunately, the trial-by-ambush techniques first used by the prosecutor and later by Vinny may reinforce for the beginning expert other dramatic but unrealistic TV and movie portrayals of the justice system. Many people still believe that entertaining fictional accounts of courtroom events are also an accurate account of the way things are done in the courts. This fear, based on the fiction that we all consume in our daily dole of entertainment, can make potential experts reluctant to become involved in the legal system. They view the system as a ritual of conflict resolution designed to allow and abet attorneys to hide the ball or to humiliate the expert witness. In fact, as we will see in great detail in subsequent chapters of this book, the rules of procedure for both civil and criminal trials together with the reasonable exercise of judicial discretion by the courts attentuate the most objectionable of these behaviors. In particular, they require the parties to disclose nearly everything in the process of discovery and pretrial litigation.

Many things about the legal system's tradition and philosophy allow the opposing parties to test each other's theories and proof, including their respective expert's qualifications, methods, and opinions. However, the rules that are consistently followed by both court and counsel in all state and federal jurisdictions do not allow for the kind of dramatic surprise and comic relief in the staged litigation that makes *My Cousin Vinny* and other courtroom dramas so entertaining.

Bernard Ewell: Fine Art Appraiser and Salvador Dali Expert

Bernard Ewell specializes in the appraisal and authentication of questioned works attributed to the surrealist artist Salvador Dali (Figure 1-1). To testify in court, an art expert needs to conduct a comprehensive, independent investigation of a questioned piece. There are striking similarities between the techniques that the forensic art expert uses to carry out this sort of investigation and the work of an IT forensic expert. Regardless of the training, experience, and knowledge of the art expert, due to the complexity of the problem of authenticating and appraising centuries-old art, there is always the possibility that the expert will reach the wrong conclusion. This well-

Figure 1-1. Slave Market with the Disappearing Bust of Voltaire *(1940).*
Oil on canvas, 18 ¼ × 25 ⅜ inches. Collection of The Salvador Dali Museum,
St. Petersburg, Florida. Copyright © 2002, Salvador Dali Museum, Inc.

known risk in the art world is readily admitted by honest experts in nearly every forensic field that must rely more on art than science.

Consider the following observation by Mark Jones, introducing the exhibit he produced and the the book he edited by the same title, *Fake? The Art of Deception*:

> *Fakes can teach us many things, most obviously perhaps the fallibility of experts. Not a single object has been included here merely because it deceived an untutored layman. Most have been validated thrice over, on initial purchase by an experienced collector, on publication by a leading scholar and on acquisition by a great museum. What is being asserted is not that the less well informed may sometimes make mistakes, though that is evidently true, but that even the most academically and intuitively gifted of individuals, even the most rigorously organised of institutions, can and will occasionally be wrong. And this is not, or not simply, because knowledge and experience can never be complete, but because perception itself is determined by the structure of expectations that underpins it.*[8]

For IT experts, such authentication and appraisal work may involve the forensic reconstruction of data in a computer, network behavior in an intrusion case, penetration testing and reconstruction of system security in connection with an allegation of inadequate security or application failures, and the identification and authentication of digital evidence and its authors or users in civil discovery disputes, spoliation litigation, or criminal prosecutions.

As with most issues that engage the IT expert, Bernard Ewell's forensic detective work requires him to examine one or more artifacts and to render an opinion on the authenticity of the questioned piece. This process often requires almost as much work attempting to ascertain the authenticity of the standards previously used for comparison with other questioned works and the provenance, or absence of provenance, for or against authenticity of the questioned work itself. The methods he uses to support this opinion include testing the objects themselves and comparing the results of those tests with the accumulated knowledge compiled by collectors, curators, museums, and the literature relating to the physical and stylistic attributes of the artist, his known works, and known or suspected fakes of those works.

Ewell's forensic expertise and his experience as a testifying expert is uncommon and therefore of great value to stakeholders in the work or other works by the artist and to the ultimate fact finders who must resolve legal disputes involving works that Dali may or may not have created. The difference in value between a fake and an authenticated and accepted original can be several million dollars. (The complex job of appraising a piece involves market and legal analysis techniques that go beyond the scope of our comparison of forensic work in the art and IT worlds.) A determination

---

8. Jones, Mark, ed. *Fake? The Art of Deception*. Berkeley, CA: University of California Press, 1990, p. 11.

that a particular work is a fake can also destroy the reputations of collectors and dealers in the art market.

Ewell has testified as an expert witness for over 20 years. Perhaps the most important jury trial in which he took part was the famous case brought by the United States against Center Art Gallery, located in Hawaii, and its two principals, William Mett and Marvin Wiseman. In *The Great Dali Art Fraud and Other Deceptions*,[9] Lee Caterall tells the story of Ewell's involvement as an expert in that case, one of the largest art scams ever uncovered. Ewell also testified in another major civil proceeding involving the Federal Trade Commission and thousands of allegedly fake Dalis.

To understand how a successful businessman like Bernard Ewell came to enjoy being attacked by highly paid and highly motivated criminal defense attorneys in high-profile criminal trials, and by the best and the brightest from the boutique civil litigation firms of Manhattan, it helps to understand a little bit of his philosophy.

In addition to doing art detective work and fine art appraisals, Ewell also teaches other art appraisers how to testify effectively as experts in this highly subjective field. Since 1985, he has conducted training for the American Society of Appraisers as an Accredited Senior Appraiser. The lessons he has drawn from his experiences on the witness stand and in preparing for and giving lengthy depositions in cases destined to settle have made his lesson plans for passing on his skills as an expert witness easy to understand and to apply by those students who catch the testifying bug.

First, Ewell teaches that becoming an expert witness, whether as a public service or for profit, is the best way to test yourself periodically and to find out if you are as good as you need to be to provide day-to-day expert services to your clientele. As in any other teaching role, the best way to learn new things and to develop better ways of explaining the things you already know is to accept the responsibility of communicating that knowledge to others. You must also determine how you did by critiquing your own performance. In educational settings you make this determination of your performance by testing the students. In the case of forensic work, the effectiveness of your performance is indicated by a verdict and feedback from attorneys, judges, and jurors.

The bonus that comes from earning a reputation as an accomplished expert witness is that it may also give you the opportunity to do research that you need or want to do to hone your expert skills and to be paid for that research. You can explore new things and develop broader expertise or a deeper understanding of ever more specialized areas within your general area of expertise while earning a living.

If you decide to add forensic expertise to your resume, serving as a consulting or testifying expert also enables you to further bolster your standing as an expert outside of the courtroom. In the course of doing directed research for a particular case, you

---

9. Caterall, Lee. *The Great Dali Art Fraud and Other Deceptions*. Fort Lee, NJ: Barricade Books, 1992.

may be paid to develop new material for an article, a speech, or even a book about the substance of your research. The ability to document your methods and to give examples of acceptance of your methods by recognized peers in professional and other publications is invaluable in building your general reputation. Such publication of your work is worth even more as documentation that you have become a recognized and peer-reviewed expert in your field. Obviously, should you begin to spend increasing amounts of time as an IT forensic expert, your experiences with the attorneys and the judicial process can lead to new opportunities for publication, speaking, and general employment as well as to new and more challenging assignments in the forensic world.

Over time, with additional assignments, your résumé and reputation for demonstrated expertise will grow, provided you exercise strict quality control with regard to your selection of assignments and your performance as an expert. As we discuss in more detail in Chapter 6, it is important that you ensure that the assignments you accept are consistent with the highest principles of your professional peers, associations, and communities of interest. This consideration also comes into play should there be challenges to your qualifications, theories, or methods, as discussed in Chapter 8.

All these benefits require that you do your homework as an expert. For instance, you must be aware of the professional and ethical principles of your professional community of interest and also of the responsibilities that the law places on an expert for practices that attain or exceed the relevant standards of practice in the general field of experts. You must learn to be brutally honest with regard to your level of expertise. Furthermore, you must subject yourself to periodic reexaminations to assure that you are current in your field of practice and that you are taking appropriate measures to maintain your technical skills. Malpractice is an appropriate claim to make against people who hold themselves out to be something they are not or fail to measure up to the generally accepted standards of practice for their area of expertise. This applies whether the expertise involves determining the authenticity of fine art or the authenticity of logs in a computer network intrusion detection system.

That said, Ewell asserts that a well-trained and professional expert witness can expect to receive the benefits that he personally has garnered in his forensic practice. In addition, such an expert has the luxury of leaving the courtroom or the deposition chamber at the end of his or her testimony without the risks of liability that the parties to litigation bear, while having helped the judge or the jury understand complex facts and thereby resolve important matters in a serious legal controversy.

J. W. Lindemann: Forensic Geologist and Clandestine Grave Expert

J. W. Lindemann is a forensic geologist who has developed a fascinating practice working as part of a group that searches for clandestine graves. Like most IT professionals whom we interviewed for this book, Lindemann has found that his peers were not prepared for the number of different and demanding contexts in which the forensic services of geologists were required. In particular, an increasingly regulated and litigious society demands that forensic geologists be able to support litigation. Lindemann's experience in applying his skills and knowledge to the solution of serious forensic problems is mostly in law enforcement contexts. Like Ewell, Lindmann finds that, despite occasional frustrations, his involvement with law enforcement as a forensic expert has been very rewarding both personally and professionally. Unlike Ewell, Lindmann joined a group of professional volunteers to advance his forensic interests. About ten years ago they incorporated a not-for-profit interdisciplinary group called NecroSearch International to assist with forensic investigations of alleged homicides.[10]

While this group arrangement is certainly not for everyone with an interest in forensic testimony, it may be an idea whose time has come for IT forensic experts and associated professionals who depend on a diverse network of skills, share many mutual interests, and want to solve what may at first blush seem to be very different kinds of problems. NecroSearch International has worked on over 200 forensic cases, involving the coordinated search for clandestine burials in 20 states and 6 foreign countries. In addition to the in-house associates, the organization often calls upon individuals, groups, and other resources in related fields of expertise, increasing its inventory of available experts in order to take on new and challenging cases or research projects. In addition to creating the flexible network of accomplished experts in an ever-growing number of different disciplines, Lindemann has learned how to communicate his science to people who have little or no training in his field. This experience of learning how to talk about his scientific knowledge to other scientists and law enforcement officers with no scientific training has made it much easier to communicate as a forensic expert witness.

Like other professionals, the forensic geologist faces many changing codes of practice and ethics, both written and unwritten. In fact, experts like geologists are often called in to determine whether one or more of their peers has failed to live up to those standards, resulting in an alleged crime, serious property or financial damage, or the loss of life or limb. Lindemann suggests that one of the rewards that comes from testifying in cases involving charges of negligence or criminal culpability of professional peers is the chance to set the record straight and in the process repair the potential damage to one's chosen profession by assisting in the determination of responsibility

10. Lindemann, J. W. "Forensic Geology: The Example of Professional Contribution to NecroSearch International." *The Professional Geologist* 37(9), 2000, pp. 4–7. See also *No Stone Unturned: The True Story of NecroSearch Interniational, the World's Premier Forensic Investigators*, by Steve Jackson. New York: Kensington Publishing, 2002.

for intentional or unintentional lapses in professional judgment.

After years of appearing as an expert witness in criminal cases, Lindemann now believes it is almost a given that the average practicing professional will be called to the witness stand to give testimony in some form of compliance or regulatory proceeding, civil or criminal litigation, or a preliminary or ongoing investigation by any number of legally authorized authorities.

> *It therefore behooves the professional geologist to conduct his activities in strict adherence to professional standards, to thoroughly document his work, and to make sure his results and conclusions are based on data, information, and knowledge that fall within his field of expertise. Further, the geologist must strive to maintain both his academic and professional credentials to the very best of his ability and resources. It must be remembered that the side presenting the expert witness will present him as a knowledgeable professional, an expert in his field, and as an experienced, competent scientist/engineer. In contrast, the opposition will attempt to compromise the competence, the integrity and the professionalism of the expert witness, often focusing on mundane and irrelevant points of that witness'[s] professional credentials, performance, or testimony. It has been said that any courtroom trial is not about guilt or innocence, right or wrong, but about theater—the best performance wins the Oscar. The geologist as expert witness must then be prepared professionally, technically, and personally to give the "performance" of his career.*[11]

Lindemann reminds interested parties that the work of the forensic scientist often is based on information that comes from highly questionable sources that may prove to be completely erroneous. In other words, without the facts there are no guarantees that proper theories, methods, and adequate skills will succeed in solving a forensic problem.

> *At the end of the day, a particular clandestine grave may in fact not exist. But then what guarantees that the minerals exploration geologist or the petroleum geologist finds the ore body or the reservoir at the end of a given project? However, if the grave, the ore body, or the reservoir is present, the chances of its discovery are enhanced by thorough planning, meaningful field activity, intelligent evaluation of resultant data, persistence, and a positive outlook relative to the problem at hand. The uncertainty of result, the "risk of failure" is an aspect of professional evolvement that the geologist learns to handle whatever his specific field of interest.*[12]

Some valuable lessons from the forensic application of field sciences like geology can remind IT practitioners that investigations into the human use of complex or simple computer systems and networks are still based in space and time. Just as in the real world of forests and mountains, IT forensic experts need to be familiar with a mind-

---

11. Lindemann, "Forensic Geology," p. 5.

12. Lindemann, "Forensic Geology," p. 6.

numbing number of field settings in order to solve field problems when, for example, attempting to reconstruct a pattern of application and network behavior. If you can bear these things in mind, much like forensic geology field work, you can undertake IT forensics with a remarkably easy transition.

We dedicate much of this book to assisting technical experts in communicating their knowledge, experience, and opinions to lawyers, judges, and jurors. Lindemann, in focusing on the investigations that experts need to conduct in order to reach their conclusions and to formulate valuable opinions relevant to case issues, eloquently reminds his audience of the need to apply these same skills with other experts and nonexperts alike, who may become involved in the research and investigation of a given problem in the field.

> *As with all aspects of professional endeavor, communication is paramount. As a professional geologist working with other professionals without an earth science background, the idea is not to simplify your science but to clarify your science. Most professionals can understand what you say and why you say it if your explanation is clearly presented in understandable terms. You are not on site to amaze and confound your non-geologist colleagues, you are on site to get the job done! Work with your non-geologist colleagues and communicate with them.*[13]

Whether we are considering grave site identification or network intrusion detection, the rewards of solving forensic problems go beyond the expert's involvement in a particular investigation or litigated case. Because of the peculiar nature of judicial record keeping, regardless of whether or not the individual expert has a professional group with a corporate memory, the undertaking of a forensic assignment may pleasantly surprise the investigator by providing a better understanding of the problems encountered and the solutions attempted for future reference. Through the process of experts applying their forensic expertise to solving important problems, the record over time will reflect why some experts may have failed while others succeeded in solving the problems presented in the investigation or litigation. IT experts should keep in mind the problems that other professions have invited by their reluctance to record and subject to open criticism the errors they make. The medical profession has only recently begun to keep track of errors as a way to determine how effective its methods and its ability to predict outcomes of treatment or nontreatment really are. Unfortunately, many aspects of IT are simply written off as successful or unsuccessful hacks or fixes, without being subjected to a peer review leading to the establishment of reliable standards. Over time, IT standards will be established, and these lessons learned will feed back into the next case to the benefit of those IT professionals, their organizations, the judicial process, and society in general.

---

13. Lindemann, "Forensic Geology," p. 7.

Madison Lee Goff: Forensic Entomologist and Bug Doctor

Entomology, the scientific study of insects, is a major subdiscipline of biology and zoology. In recent times, homicide crime scene investigators have come to value the contributions of entomologists in solving some of the grisliest and most challenging cases. The specialized science of forensic entomology, where insect-related evidence is collected and analyzed, has rapidly evolved into a standard operating procedure for determining time of death and in some cases the location of the body when the murder took place (i.e., when the body may have been moved before it was discovered). Of course, in the world of IT, the identification of "bugs" and their systematic study have a very different—but no less important—place.

> *From at least the time of Thomas Edison, U.S. engineers have used the word "bug" to refer to flaws in the systems they developed. This short word conveniently covered a multitude of possible problems. It also suggested that difficulties were small and could be easily corrected. IBM engineers who installed the ASSC Mark I at Harvard University in 1944 taught the phrase to the staff there. Grace Murray Hopper used the word with particular enthusiasm in documents relating to her work. In 1947, when technicians building the Mark II computer at Harvard discovered a moth in one of the relays, they saved it as the first actual case of a bug being found [Figure 1-2]. In the early 1950s, the terms "bug" and "debug," as applied to computers and computer programs, began to appear not only in computer documentation but even in the popular press.[14]*

Unlike the engineers of the early days of computing, Dr. Madison Lee Goff is interested in bugs of a different sort. For almost 20 years he has engaged in forensic entomology as it relates to the cause, time, and circumstances of death. When he first became involved in forensics, medical investigators did not regard insects as a significant source of information and seldom used such evidence in cases in which proof of the time, place, or other conditions relating to the cause of death was important.

Figure 1-2. *The first computer bug. (Photo #NH 96566-KN. Washington, DC: U.S. Naval Historical Center, 1945.)*

14. Kidwell, P. A. "Stalking the Elusive Computer Bug." *IEEE Annals of the History of Computing* 20(4), 1998, pp. 5–9.

In the world of IT, it is practically a given that information is available. In fact, too much evidence is often the main problem for computer and network forensic detectives. Nevertheless, in IT forensic analysis, as with the beginnings of forensic entomology and any other new forensic frontiers of a science or technology, there is always the need to educate the public as well as the legal and forensic communities about the potential of IT forensic evidence.

Goff is an entomology professor in Hawaii, where he is also a consultant to the chief medical examiner. He has been a major contributor to the process of educating the public about forensic entomology. He led an aggressive public information campaign, using workshops, lectures, and memberships in various societies to deliver his message. Today, Goff admits that he and his colleagues may have been too successful in convincing the public that the entomologist has valuable forensic evidence to contribute in death investigations. In his own words:

> *In 1983, entomological evidence was viewed with skepticism. By the early 1990s the situation had changed and people involved in death investigations were willing to believe almost anything we told them. Entomologists who had never consulted on a single homicide case were conducting training sessions for law enforcement agencies as well as other entomologists. With a number of people having a minimal exposure to forensic entomology entering the field, it was only a matter of time before major problems cropped up.*[15]

Goff has found that his involvement as a forensic expert in criminal cases follows a familiar pattern. After agreeing to work on a case, he collects (or arranges to have collected) specimens from the corpse to be analyzed. An IT expert might consider this analogous to making an exact copy of the data image from the computer system or the storage device for further analysis and testing. Once Goff has done the necessary experiments and made his observations, he files away his report and the evidence in his possession and waits to be contacted about future involvement. Because these cases tend to become routine and because criminal cases, like civil cases, routinely settle before trial with a plea bargain or dismissal, he may never be asked to deliver his results to anyone but the case agent or prosecutor for the government.

Goff has always been involved in training both his peers and law enforcement and medical investigators in how to conduct forensic examinations of the insect evidence. He is committed to constantly improving his skills and to developing new cutting-edge techniques for recognizing and presenting admissible evidence related to the cause or time of death. The inevitable delays in being called to the stand are not a serious problem for two reasons. First, he has only a few cases at any given time. Second, he is constantly rethinking those cases that he does have in order to improve his tech-

---

15. Goff, M. Lee. *A Fly for the Prosecution: How Insect Evidence Helps Solve Crimes.* Cambridge, MA: Harvard University Press, 2000, p. 173.

nique and to develop new tools to assist him in his investigations and presentations of the evidence.

Goff's experience may not be typical among forensics experts. Forensics experts who are not in business for themselves but are employed at state crime labs or other public organizations where the sheer volume of cases often require them to testify in court frequently may find greater challenges. For instance, many experts report some difficulty recalling the particulars of one case compared with another due to the large number of these cases assigned to each forensic examiner. Therefore, each case requires a very clear set of policies, practices, and procedures, including the preparation of routine reports, in order to allow the public expert to clearly recall the work done on a particular case up to 12 months or more before testifying in court. Consequently, the better government crime labs require their forensics experts to devote a great amount of time to training and practice. This preparation enables the experts to perform competently in those few but important cases that do end up in court and that may contribute to the establishment of new standards of practice and proof in the form of legal precedent.

Goff describes his feelings of estrangement in court as follows:

> The goal of every forensic entomologist is to produce a set of carefully analyzed data that can be used in a court of law. A courtroom is about as foreign and hostile an environment for a scientist as can be imagined. I have now appeared in court many times as an expert witness, both for the defense and for the prosecution, and every time I enter the courtroom, I still feel much as if I am leaving the planet. The fact that a homicide or some other crime has occurred seems almost irrelevant to what takes place in the courtroom, crowded with the judge, the jury, the bailiffs, the sheriffs, the attorneys, and the court reporter, who frequently has to ask me how to spell the Latin names of insects.[16]

Goff has helped form societies, regulatory bodies, and certification procedures for forensic entomologists. Contrary to what might be characterized as a paradise for practitioners who were essentially unregulated, his own experience and observation revealed that the lack of regulation presented a nightmare for lawyers and judges who had no way to evaluate a particular entomologist's qualifications or abilities. This remained the case until 1996, when the American Board of Forensic Entomology was formed. Goff is a Diplomate of the Board.

Goff also has advice for aspiring forensic expert witnesses that applies to more than his peers in entomology. He warns that because most potential experts have an academic background, they tend to conform to behavior usually associated more with a golden retriever than a distinguished scientific or technical expert when approached by a person of some authority, such as a prosecutor or a law enforcement agent bran-

---

16. Goff, *A Fly for the Prosecution*, p. 174.

dishing a gun and a badge. This wildly enthusiastic eagerness to please must be carefully managed by the expert if he or she wants to have effective and objective involvement as a forensic expert.

Experts who come from a scientific background, regardless of whether they remain in academia or not, can be surprised by a couple of phenomena that take place if and when the investigation gets to the litigation stage. Academics and scientists are often very uncomfortable with the rules of engagement in the adversarial legal system, in contrast to the principle of collegiality that is at least in theory associated with academia and the world of science. Furthermore, even Goff admits to being constantly amazed by the ease with which lawyers seem to move in and out of their respective roles as learned legal opponents and aggressive advocates in a particular case.

> *I am often considered the opposition while I am giving testimony or during cross examination, but the situation changes as soon as a recess is called or the day is over. In the absence of the judge and jury, conversation turns to the game the night before, sports in general, and occasionally politics, movies, and other current events—people even tell lawyer jokes. These conversations often include both the defense and the prosecution's attorneys, the suspect, and the bailiff. But when the jury returns, each reassumes correct courtroom demeanor and the trial continues. This has happened so often that I am no longer surprised when it does, but I'm still amazed.*[17]

IT experts, like other forensic expert witnesses, should learn to appreciate not only the many lawyer jokes that are often told at times like these but also the stories that lawyers and judges love to tell about experts, complete with examples of preposterous or incomprensible testimony. Both experts and attorneys today play important roles in resolving some of the most controversial and important problems in our society. Thus, it is necessary to the preservation of their respective sanity to be able to step outside the formal roles of witness and advocate and to reassert the humanity of the formal but social process of judicial dispute resolution whenever possible and appropriate.

Approaches to Building Professional Communities of Interest

You may be wondering just what these examples have to do with IT expertise. For heaven's sake, IT is a far cry from automobile mechanics, art fraud, the geology of clandestine graves, and entomology! Or, you might be thinking, "There just doesn't seem to be much need for IT experts at this time, or I would have already found myself involved." Besides, doesn't it really all boil down to whether or not you can stand to work with a bunch of lawyers and are willing to exhibit yourself before a judge or jury?

17. Goff, *A Fly for the Prosecution*, p. 174.

On the other hand, you might finish reading what has been covered so far in this chapter and come away with the idea that you would simply like to give IT forensics a try and that there is little left to be said on the subject of technical expert witnesses. What could be simpler for a qualified expert than to be shown some pictures, traipse around the countryside or collect some bugs, and, based on his or her knowledge, education, and training, to give a reasoned opinion about an issue in a lawsuit? Furthermore, the expert's conclusions based on his or her careful analysis of the relevant facts should be obvious not only to the expert witness, the judge, and jurors but also to any other honest expert who looks at the same facts.

The technical expertise featured in *My Cousin Vinny* is simple enough to understand. We have grown accustomed to the technology of the motor car. But that technology, like the steam engine and the railroad before it, began as an invention and then slowly moved into mass production and widespread assimilation by mainstream society over a number of decades. There is nothing really surprising about learning that an aspiring hairdresser just happened to grow up with expert auto mechanics and mastered the subject to the point that she can provide useful testimony as an expert witness. Similar expertise is applied in hundreds of cases almost every day involving legal disputes over automotive products liability, accident reconstruction, or the alleged criminal use or abuse of motor vehicles. Indeed, we have all become experts to a degree about how automobiles function and fail to function.

The point of considering the lessons to be learned from Mona Lisa Vito, as well as the real experts cited in this chapter, is to try to determine whether their stories can instruct us about how to build fledgling IT expert witness communities or to evolve existing ones into something useful for those who do find themselves on the witness stand. Consider the following analogies drawn between cited examples from other areas and similar community structures in the IT area.

Professional Problem-Solving Associations

Lindemann found that he needed to become associated with a group of professionals who could address the diverse set of requisite skills required to perform complex investigations. Lindemann's organization, NecroSearch International, specializes in the search for clandestine grave sites, and its member scientists and investigators work on a volunteer basis at the request of law enforcement agencies.

An example of an analogous international organization for IT professionals who feel they may have a forensic bent might be the Forum for Incident Response and Security Teams (FIRST). FIRST was chartered in 1990 as an umbrella organization under which incident response teams worldwide could exchange information and coordinate investigations. Among the charter member teams is the Computer Emergency Reponse Team, which was formed in response to the 1988 Morris Internet worm incident and charged with the reponsibility for handling security incidents on the Internet. FIRST has grown steadily over the past decade to its current level of more than 100 member teams. It is structured as a coalition of incident response teams drawn from academic institutions, commercial organizations, and governmental agencies. FIRST is an international organization, with members in all the major global regions. The members comprise a network of resources for incident information sharing and prevention for both the members themselves and society at large.

As most network intrusion cases occur over the Internet, the ability to analyze the artifacts of such attacks requires cooperation across the entire global network infrastructure. Furthermore, as the time during which such attacks take place is compressed, it is also very important to have a competent set of incident-handling peers, all sharing information on current attack methods and observed activity trends. Add to this the need to conduct analyses in consultation with cross-discplinary technical experts and the appeal of consortium-structured professional organizations such as FIRST and NecroSearch International is understandable.

Note that the information sharing and discussion venues provided by FIRST to its members conform to the advice given by both Ewell and Goff regarding experts' needs to stay current and competent in their areas of expertise. It behooves those fortunate enough to find that they enjoy and do well in forensic assignments to contribute to communities of interest and to the establishment of standards and certification for the forensic application of their expertise by others. Almost every forensic discipline sooner or later must find an efficient and equitable way to report, criticize, and correct any poor or unethical practices of expert witnesses. Few professional communities have come up with effective solutions for handling this problem.

What would the charter of an international computer forensics organization look like? The founders of FIRST have defined their mission as follows.[18]

- Provide members with technical information, tools, methods, assistance, and guidance.
- Coordinate proactive liaison activities and analytical support.
- Encourage the development of quality products and services.
- Improve national and international information security.
- Enhance the image, recognition, and status of the incident response and security community.

The strategic plans and goals for this voluntary (membership by invitation only) organization include those listed on the following page.[19]

---

18. FIRST.ORG, Inc. "FIRST Statement of Mission and Strategic Goals." Accessed in July 2002 at *http://www.first.org/about/mission.html*.

19. FIRST.ORG, "FIRST Statement of Mission and Strategic Goals."

- Encourage trust and cooperation.
- Implement effective, secure communications.
- Streamline operational coordination.
- Improve internal FIRST operations and organization to meet the needs of the changing environment.
- Promote the FIRST concept and approach to incident response.
- Create cooperative research and development.
- Facilitate sharing of tools, techniques, and information.
- Provide technical education and support.
- Exhibit organization and leadership.
- Investigate funding, support, and collaboration.

IT experts should constantly scan the Web and the available literature for information about new and evolving organizations, offering collaboration and training in their professional areas of interest and also in other relevant areas of interest. The fact is that both judges and jurors look to the existence and the social significance of these organizations and communities to decide how much credibility to give to the qualifications and experience of anyone claiming to be a technical expert. FIRST is just one example of these communities that are beginning to spring up and establish standards, thereby providing judicial confidence in the expertise of individuals who wish to enter the forensic fray.

Government Training Programs for Forensic Experts

Goff, the forensic entomologist, has offered advice regarding skills required by forensics experts who were subject to frequent court appearances. You may remember that such experts reported that due to their heavy caseloads, they have problems recalling the details of each individual case. Goff's advice was to compensate for these caseload issues by providing clear sets of policies, practices, and procedures. To accomplish this, nonprofit groups of volunteer experts can collaborate on cases and train each other or provide training for others, or statewide or national professional communities of interest can establish standards, certification, and training programs. Either way, the nature of forensic presentations in every recognized discipline sooner or later requires some consensus about what state-of-the-art forensic performance entails at the state or national level.

Whether the expert handles only one case or becomes a seasoned veteran of forensic assignments with his or her own specialized and staffed systems for maintaining numerous cases, the fact remains that accepting a forensic assignment usually means the expert will face an opposing attorney, who has some level of experience in expert witness examination, and in all likelihood an opposing expert, who will quarrel with the methods or opinions of the witness. Training in what to expect when testifying in an advocacy proceeding will prove not only helpful to the beginner but essential to anyone who wants to continue to provide an adequate performance as an expert witness in case after case as the beginner becomes habituated and his or her habits become known to opposing attorneys.

This is certainly not news for IT experts whose job descriptions include forensic duties. Raemarie Schmidt developed a training program for forensic experts of all kinds over ten years ago when she ran the Milwaukee drug identification section for the Wisconsin state crime lab. Like more traditional experts, her computer forensic evidence examiners were required to complete a lengthy training program, with actual moot court experience and periodic practice sessions, to become qualified by the lab as competent witnesses. This qualification was required before any of the computer forensic examiners were allowed to sign off as the examining expert and to give testimony in a hearing or trial. Many of the graduates of this training program have moved on to successful careers as computer evidence forensic experts in both the public and private sectors.

Schmidt continues to train computer forensic experts in law enforcement and to learn about new tools and techniques for conducting computer forensic examinations and for testifying in court about the results of those examinations. She is presently affiliated with the cybercrime section of the National White Collar Crime Center, a nonprofit organization headquartered in Richmond, Virginia, that provides support to state and local law enforcement organizations as they deal with economic and high-tech crime. Schmidt and other experienced experts provide basic and advanced training in digital forensic tools and techniques and help prepare law enforcement investigators and prosecutors for courtroom presentations of digital forensic evidence.

This program annually trains approximately 500 state and local law enforcement agents to conduct basic computer forensic examinations, but as yet it does not have a dedicated program similar to the one Schmidt put in place ten years ago in Wisconsin. Such programs as Schmidt's current training programs offered at the National White Collar Crime Center provide a beginning for law enforcement organizations interested in the problems that accompany the ever-increasing docket of IT-related crimes. Schmidt is eager to find the time and resources needed to add more forensic training programs for law enforcement investigators and prosecutors. Such programs focus on the skills state and local government experts require in order to testify competently and convincingly about technical and scientific findings.[20]

---

20. Personal communication from Raemarie Schmidt, February 2002.

Beginning forensic examiners can quickly come to understand and apply the basic tools, practices, and procedures of computer forensics for purposes of examining data in a computer or digital forensics for application to digital media. They then need to recognize there is a very big difference between finding all the relevant evidence without contaminating or altering it and communicating those findings as well as opinions about the significance of those findings to a judge and a jury. When the resources and the mandate to prepare staff experts to perform well in the field, the lab, and the courtroom exist, the success of the parties and their legal counsel who must rely on those experts is dramatically improved. Conversely, when an expert who lacks this extensive forensic training and experience is asked to perform a forensic assignment for the first time, it may behoove that expert to consider what sort of training and experience in testifying the opposing expert may have had, in addition to his respective expertise in the relevant technical or scientific fields. Proficiency in the field and in the lab will not necessarily suffice for effectively communicating the significance of the evidence on the witness stand.

Chris Stippich was one of Schmidt's best forensic examiners in Milwaukee. He graduated from the expert witness training program there and has gone on to train law enforcement and private corporate security professionals as experts in conducting computer forensic evidence examinations. Currently he helps to lead a private company, which provides computer evidence forensic equipment and training to corporations and government agencies. Stippich and his company, Digital Intelligence,[21] have taken the packaging of computer forensic investigation equipment to the level of forensic network construction. Their products allow multiple forensic clients to access case and image files simultaneously without duplicating information on several forensic workstations. Stippich now designs, implements, and maintains forensic laboratory networks around the world.

Reminiscing recently at a cybercrime conference, Stippich had both good and bad news to report about the training he received in Schmidt's program back in Milwaukee. He recalled his first appearance many years ago as a forensic expert in a jury trial, after he completed his rigorous training. With Schmidt sitting in the audience to evaluate Stippich's first appearance as a forensic expert, he strode confidently to the witness stand. As he stepped up to take his seat, unbeknownst to him, his right suit pant pocket caught on an exposed piece of wood moulding. As Stippich moved to the seat to take the oath, he felt and heard his pant leg ripping from the edge of his pocket to his cuff. The quite audible sound announced to the expectant jurors the sudden appearance of his fully exposed right leg clad in unfashionably short socks. There was nothing for Stippich to do but to cross his still-clothed left leg over his right one.

---

21. See *http://www.digitalintel.com*.

So the bad news is that even the best forensic training program in the world will not prepare you for everything that can happen in the courtroom![22]

Jury consultants and others who study the dynamics of nonverbal communication like to point out that the head and hands are the only naked parts of the body that the judge and the jurors can see during the taking of testimony from the witness stand. For that matter, this is the case in most other verbal communication situations where people are speaking at close range and that don't take place on the beach or in the sauna. So it is a very dramatic turn of events when the previously clothed leg of a male technical expert is suddenly exposed in this way. This is also why most judges become concerned and tend to frown on female experts, even those with the most attractive, athletic legs, who alight the witness stand wearing a microminiskirt.

Nevertheless, these things happen, and that's the point of sharing with you the embarrassment of a torn garment. In this case, the judge immediately asked Stippich if he would like a recess. Stippich shook off the shock and allowed himself to laugh with the judge and the jurors at the unexpected and quite humorous turn of events, then persevered and gave his testimony in an organized and effective way. Thus he won the emotional as well as the rational support of the judge and jurors. Instead of a problem, the torn pants created instant sympathy and effectively disarmed the opposing counsel from even thinking about trying to take advantage of Stippich on cross-examination due to his predicament.

Once again, the good news is that diligent preparation for what is expected, coupled with solid testing through staged moot court appearances in a dedicated training program like the one pioneered by Schmidt, yield a witness who is better able to deal with the unexpected as well as the mundane. When the unanticipated happens, this preparation can make all the difference when you actually take (or attempt to take) the stand. What may seem to be a completely negative, disturbing, or destructive event can be turned into an advantage for the well-prepared and composed expert witness.

In Forensics, No Expert Is an Island

The advice from experienced expert witnesses in other forensic scientific specialties as well as the entertaining example of Mona Lisa Vito in *My Cousin Vinny* offer a wide array of views that point to some of the elements the IT community must build in order to support the testimony of IT experts testifying in litigation. One of the most important areas for exploration and involvement by individual experts is the appropriate professional communities of interest for their areas of expertise. Experts may well find that such involvement is required before they can count on being qualified and approved as an expert witness.

---

22. Personal communication from Christopher J. Stippich, February 2002.

You may believe that the existing communities of interest for your technical area of expertise are less than adequate. Or, you may bemoan the necessity of such formal structures in order to vouch for the technical credentials of those involved. However, it appears inevitable that such formal communities will be required in order to allow the rest of society to make sense of an increasingly complex technological landscape when it needs to be traversed in the course of a highly technical lawsuit.

The story of Robinson Crusoe is one of the most potent myths about the ability of individuals to go it alone and to create entire worlds of meaning and practical application. Unfortunately, that myth of rugged or extreme individualism, so much a part of the general American psyche, has little utility for the practicing technical expert witness. In fact, when he or she sets sail from some isolated island of successful technical enterprise into the shark-infested waters of litigation, isolation from the support of a community spells doom. For some of the reasons already given, and for many more reasons that are yet to come in the following pages of this book, it is clear that without establishing membership in a recognized professional or technical community of interest, it will be very difficult for a technical expert to convince a judge and jury that his or her particular expertise and proffered testimony should be taken seriously.

Taking Testimony Seriously

Why Do So Many People Cringe at the Thought of Testifying?

For some IT professionals, participation in any of the formal, regimented rituals of life is mind-numbing, something to be avoided at all costs. For other IT experts, legal and business tasks and functions are unappealing because they violate two of the most important conditions for happiness in the technical world: first, the need for a great deal of control over the environment and conduct of one's life and work, and second, the need for a constant stream of intellectual stimulation. Were members of the IT community asked to name two things universally reviled by IT experts, they'd likely select micromanagement and boredom.

For those IT wizards who possess these aversions, the first question that might arise in the discussion of expert witness skills is "Why would I ever want to do something like that?" Why should any self-respecting IT expert ever want to get involved in the legal process? After all, the worst attorneys (who seem to be the only ones we ever see featured on the nightly news, depicted in TV shows or movies, or described in novels) are usually characterized as ranging from obnoxious to sleazy, terminally bureaucratic to heavy-handed, archaic to simply slow-paced. This implies that any involvement with the legal community is likely to produce either intense discomfort or boredom for the IT professional who is unfortunate or foolish enough to be caught in its clutches.

31

In this chapter, we begin the process of arguing the case for why you, as a technical expert, should look forward to your day in court. Our message is simply that it is far better for you to prepare to be a witness (expert or otherwise) as a basic part of your professional duties and skills than to continue to deny that your day is coming and then become bitter about the results when you are finally called to the stand. As you will see evidenced in a major case, *U.S. v. Microsoft*, regardless of your status and personal views of the desirability of becoming involved as a witness, you might not be able to opt out of it. The witness stand is a powerful symbol within our legal system. Potential witnesses (even when they are as important an individual and as highly acknowledged an expert as Bill Gates) do not always have the final say about whether they end up there. The power of testimony is a two-edged sword, one that can devastate those associated with the witness as easily as help to defend them in a criminal case or advance their just cause in civil litigation. Once compelled to serve as a witness, it is too late to begin rationalizing about why you don't want to be there and the fact that you don't know how to prepare for the experience. Unless you have taken the time to carefully prepare both yourself and your testimony, there are no guarantees that you will survive the experience with reputation, finances, and sanity all intact.

However, the reality of the litigious world in which we live does not need to terrify the potential expert witness. Much like learning to dance gracefully, to competently play a competitive sport, or to persuasively speak in public, we believe that you can develop some basic skills that will enable you to survive the experience of serving as an expert witness. With guidance from the attorneys who are involved with the witness, a beginner can also learn to master the practice to the extent that it becomes an enjoyable and profitable experience. In this book, we provide information and techniques for motivated technologists that will prepare them for this journey.

Why Should a Technical Expert Want to Work in the Legal System?

There are three very good reasons to acquire the skills necessary to become a good expert witness: (1) simple self-preservation, (2) the duty of any professional to help shape his or her community of interest, and (3) the very practical need of any expert to improve communication skills. Beyond these personal and professional responsibilities, experts must also attempt to affect the controls that society will inevitably impose on their own IT industry. When the industry does not develop its own acceptable standards and professional self-regulatory safeguards, outside of those imposed through the judicial process on a case-by-case basis, experts must be prepared to contribute to that process, in lieu of any other effective alternatives.

Given that our legal system is based on precedent, it's important to encourage courts to resolve conflicts involving technology using adequate and accurate explanations of the technology. Bad legal judgments based on poor or incomplete understanding of technical systems or devices are especially problematic since they are likely to affect the development of industry standards. Bad decisions can also create confusion in understanding where the definition of best practices stands for a given forensic discipline at any given time. These ad hoc standards tend to subject the profession to legal control by default rather than to gradual improvement resulting from constant peer review and constructive criticism, followed by general acceptance of improved standards by recognized experts within the discipline. This can stall needed technological advances—even those that remedy acknowledged flaws in existing systems and technology. For similar reasons, it's also important for information technologists to be heard in regulatory and legislative processes. These can lead to carefully crafted laws or regulations contributing to appropriate solutions to recognized problems.

Technological advances can drive broadscale, even revolutionary changes in everyday life. This often intimidates the general populace, many of whom neither work with nor understand the technologies. Although technological change in the United States has been going on constantly for nearly two hundred years, IT has sped up the velocity of that change and arguably also the pace of social changes in adopting and then adapting to these new technologies. Similar to the adoption of motor vehicles, IT has had unanticipated and profound effects on modern life, changing common perceptions of ownership, control, time, and space. As IT enables access to information that many people believe should remain private, it provokes considerable debate about privacy rights and personal information control. Its automation tends to eliminate human intervention from many mainstream processes (and the employment that human intervention represents), thereby threatening the personal security of some members of society. This introduces subsequent complications, making it difficult for society to fully understand how best to assign responsibility when IT failures result in financial or physical injuries—without killing the technological goose that lays the golden eggs.

It is predictable, even understandable, that those people most threatened by technology should seek to alter its perceived ill effects by lobbying their government representatives for additional regulation. At times, government can consider restrictions so Draconian that they can serve as roadblocks to technological progress. Similarly, many seeking to control perceived threats and the inevitable damages that accrue from new technology may attempt to deal with such problems by using the court system in both appropriate and inappropriate ways. Some file lawsuits, while others allege criminal violations by those who use the technology in a less orthodox fashion. Determining whether a lawsuit is appropriate or inappropriate often requires the early assistance of competent experts who can help the attorneys and the courts separate the dross from the gold in claims and counterclaims. Experts help provide a layperson lawyer and his or her client with a correct and comprehensible understanding of what the technology was designed to do and what it actually did in a particular situation.

All of this is quite in keeping with the American tradition of the law playing catch-up with an evolving technology that large portions of society are embracing. The problem is that we have never had to deal with a new technology quite as pervasive as IT adopted in so short a time. Not only does IT radically change the ways we communicate and process all kinds of information; it also has a dramatic effect on the very nature of a particular kind of information that the legal system calls evidence. Given the precedent-driven nature of common law, technology-related legal actions carried forth in the absence of objective and thoughtful technical experts can create problems. They represent a very shaky foundation on which to erect a set of standards and precedents to guide future attorneys and judges in the essential discovery, production, and sharing of evidence required for the efficient and equitable litigation of cases. As problematic as it is to have too few decisions to guide us (as is the case now with regard to IT problems and solutions), once even a few bad decisions are made it can be very difficult to correct or reverse them through the legal system.

Even if you do not believe that either your own self-interest or your duty to contribute to the creation of appropriate standards requires you to get involved with giving testimony in court, a prudent IT professional should still acquire expert witness skills. There has been a steady growth over the past few years in the number of lawsuits involving IT-related services and issues raised in civil cases regarding the discovery and authenticity of electronic evidence. Though you may read this book and never anticipate volunteering to be qualified as an IT expert or even as a non-expert witness in court, you will almost certainly be called on to serve in such a capacity if you continue to work in this area. You may be asked by an employer or a party to a lawsuit to play the additional role of a witness or a consultant to in-house counsel or to another expert witness. Furthermore, the different roles IT professionals are asked to play may depend on their existing roles in managing or consulting on a technical issue that becomes involved somehow in litigation. In other words, it is very likely that during the course of your IT career you will sooner or later be called upon to serve as a witness, at least to the facts relevant to some issue in a case in controversy. Your expertise will be at issue one way or another. This may be due to a discovery that occurs on your professional turf or a disaster that occurs on your watch. Everyone needs certain core skills to be the most effective witness he or she can be. While these threshold skills will not necessarily be sufficient to qualify you as a top-flight expert witness, they will serve as the foundation on which to build solid expert witness skills that you can apply to provide effective testimony.

Everyone Is Subject to Subpoena

In Western culture, when push comes to shove and we really need to figure out what happened, our legal system has decreed that we're all potential witnesses. On reflection, this should not seem all that unusual. We are, after all, members of an open society that has endorsed neither royalty nor a privileged aristocracy as immune from giving testimony in our courts. Most of the belief systems underlying the everyday conduct of the culture rely on testimony to convey key information to us on a daily basis. As in other life skills, your skills as a witness can vary based on personality, experience, training, and attitude. The ability to communicate, both verbally and nonverbally, and the ability to relate to those outside your inner circle of friends and associates are clearly skills that you can hone over time. What may not be as clear to those who are celebrated for their mastery of technology is the impact of neglecting the development of such skills.

An example of this point should be familiar to most readers since it was splashed in lurid detail across most of our television and computer screens in 1999 during *U.S. v. Microsoft Corporation*, the antitrust case against the Microsoft Corporation. In late April 1999, the U.S. government released the full transcripts of the deposition of Bill Gates, President and CEO of Microsoft. At the same time, the government released the video recordings of that deposition.

The negative reaction to the public display of the three-day deposition (which surfaced for the first time during the trial that took place several months after the deposition) was immediate and intense. Gates has been criticized as not having been at his best during the deposition, with a demeanor that has been characterized as swinging from agitated, bored, or just plain irritated to impatient and uncooperative. The legal experts retained by the media to comment on the trial were flabbergasted by Gates's performance in the deposition; they mused about and openly questioned the quality of the Microsoft legal strategy in not better preparing Gates for his testimony.

Consider this exchange between Gates and David Boies, lead counsel for the government. Some commentators have suggested that this deposition is a textbook example of how *not* to conduct oneself during testimony. The questions explore Gates's communications concerning the intentions of Microsoft to give away its browser.

Q (David Boies): Were you in 1996 trying to get financial analysts to develop a more negative and more pessimistic view about Netscape's business prospects?

A (Bill Gates): Except through the indirect effect of them seeing how customers received our products and our product strategies, that was not a goal.

Q: If that was not a goal, sir, why did you say in substance that the Internet browser would be forever free?

A: That was a statement made so that customers could understand what our intent was in terms of that set of technologies and how it would be a part of Windows and not an extra cost item, and so people would have that information in making their decisions about working with us on Windows.

Q: Now, is it your testimony that when Microsoft told the world that its browser would be forever free, that the desire to affect financial analysts' view of Netscape played no role in that decision?

A: I can be very clear with you. The reason we told people that it would be forever free was because that was the truth. That's why we told them that, because it was the truth.

Q: Now, Mr. Gates, my question to you—

A: That's the sole reason we told them.

Q: And my question to you is whether or not the truth was, in part, due to your desire to adversely affect financial analysts' view of Netscape. Did that play any role, sir?

A: You've been asking me a question several times about why did we say something. We said it because we thought our customers would want to know and because it was the truth. And that explains our saying it completely.

Q: And what I'm asking you, sir—and it may be that the answer to my question is, "no, it played no role." But if that's your answer, I want to get it on the record. And my question—

A: Are you talking about saying it?

Q: Yes.

A: Or how we came up with our decision about how to price our products?

Q: Let's take it each step at a time, one step at a time, so that your counsel doesn't say I'm asking you a compound question, okay? And first let's talk about saying it. I know you're telling me it was the truth. In addition to it being the truth, did the fact that this would, in your view, adversely affect the view of financial analysts of Netscape play any role at all in your decision to announce that your browser would be forever free?

A: I actually think that came up in response to some questions that people asked in an event we had on December 7, 1995. So it wasn't so much a question of our saying, okay, we're going to go make this a headline, but rather, that there were questions that came up during that, including our future pricing plans.

Q: This was a meeting on December 7 of what year?

A: 1995.

Q: And was it attended by people outside Microsoft?

A: It was a press event.

Q: And prior to attending that press event, had you made a decision that it would be forever free?

A: Well, if you really want to probe into that, you'll have to get into the different ways that we made Internet technology available. In terms of what we were doing with Windows 95 and its successors, yes. In terms of some of the other ways that we offered the Internet technologies, there was some—there hadn't been a clear decision about that.

Q: When you refer to other ways that you offer Internet technologies, would you explain for the record what you mean?

A: Oh, we created an offering that ran on the Macintosh OS that offered some but not all of the capabilities that we put into Windows and used a common branding for that. And we came up with a package that ran on a previous version of Windows, Windows 3.1, and made an offering of that. Subsequently I mean, not on that day, but subsequently.

Q: And those were charged for; is that what you're saying?

A: I'm saying that before the December 7th event, it was clear to everyone that in the Windows 95 and its successors, that the browser technology would be free for those users. But it was unclear to people what we were going to do with the other ways that we packaged up the technologies.

Q: Would you read the question back, please?

(The following question was read: "**Q:** And those were charged for; is that what you're saying?")

The Witness: Well, they weren't available. So if we're talking about December 7, 1995, it's not a meaningful question. Subsequently those products were made available to the customers without charge. But I'm saying that there was some lack of clarity inside Microsoft even up to the event itself about what we were going to do with those other ways we were providing Internet Explorer technology.

Q (Mr. Boies): Uncertainty as to whether you would charge for them; is that what you're saying?

A: That's right.

Q: Okay. Prior to the December 7, 1995 meeting, had a decision been made to advise the world that not only would the browser be free, but it would be forever free?

A: Well, it's always been the case that when we put a feature into Windows, that it remains part of Windows and doesn't become an extra cost item. So it would have been kind of a silly thing for anyone to ask, including about that particular feature. And by this time, of course, browsing is shipping with Windows 95.

Q: Exactly sort of the point I wanted to come to, Mr. Gates. When you put things into the operating system generally, you don't announce that they're going to be forever free, do you?

A: Yes, we do. If anybody—

Q: You do?

A: If anybody asks, that's obviously the answer we give.

Q: Have you finished your answer?

A: Yes.

Q: Okay. Could you identify for me the products other than browsers that Microsoft has announced that they would be forever free, expressly said, "These are going to be forever free"?

A: As I said to you, I think that actually came up only in response to some questions. So it's not proper to ask me and suggest that we announced it like it was some, you know, press release announcement or something of that nature.

Q: Well, let me come back to that aspect of it and just ask you for the present. What products has Microsoft said publicly, whether in response to a question or otherwise, that these would explicitly be forever free?

A: I've said that about the broad feature set that's in Windows.

Q: When did you say that, sir?

A: I remember an analyst talking to me about that once at an analyst meeting.

Q: When was that?

A: It would have been one of our annual analysts meetings.

Q: When?

A: Not this year. Either last year or the year before.

Q: Is there a transcript of that analyst meeting?

A: Not with the conversation with that analyst, no.

Q: There are transcripts of analysts meetings, aren't there, Mr. Gates?

A: Only of the formal Q and A, not of the—most of the Q and A, which is where people are mixing around with the press and analysts who come to the event.

Q: And this question that you say happened happened after the transcript stopped being taken; is that what you're saying?

A: That's my recollection, yes.[1]

So What Happened in This Deposition?

We do not intend to second-guess the strategy of Gates and his legal team. Many analyses performed by experts in the business and legal communities alike criticize either the behavior of the witness or the legal team's performance. A typical critique comes from David Bank, staff reporter at *The Wall Street Journal*, in his book *Breaking Windows*:

> *As a legal tactic, Gates's approach backfired. Microsoft's attorneys claim they believed the videotaped deposition would never be played in court. That's plausible, if only because they could hardly have staged the deposition more poorly. In the harshly lit Microsoft conference room, Gates projected a visual image of an evasive smart aleck. It was a win for the government. The video effectively countered Gates's popular persona as Chief Digital Seer.[2]*

Regardless of the Microsoft legal team's strategy and its relative effectiveness in the final analysis, the transcripts of Gates's testimony emphasize the importance of a witness considering what the fact finder sees when testimony is given. What becomes evident to a spectator who is also a technologist is the mismatch between the naïve expectations of the technical witness and those of the ultimate fact finder in the formal context of a trial. Technologists may initially think this is reasonable and appropriate conduct for an antagonistic exchange between two technically savvy people. But this may not be as apparent to a fact finder who is reviewing these deposition tapes at a later date to determine what actually happened and to decide an important legal case. So, what could conceivably be considered acceptable, though rather cantankerous, technical discussions by an acknowledged technical expert with an attorney, about things they both presumably know a great deal about, can still place the witness in a bad light with a judge or jury. The sort of demeanor that is necessary to present and preserve personal and professional credibility in formal legal proceedings turns out to be oceans apart from just getting the best of another techie or dodging a difficult ques-

---

1. All quotations of Gates's deposition testimony in this chapter are taken from the U.S. Department of Justice Antitrust Division Web site, accessed in July 2002 at *http://www.usdoj.gov/atr/cases/ms_gates2.htm.*

2. Bank, David. *Breaking Windows: How Bill Gates Fumbled the Future of Microsoft.* New York: The Free Press, 2001, p. 149.

tion posed by an astute attorney. In this particular case, such decorum was even more important, given that Gates's opponent had a stacked deck comprised of hundreds of prejudicial e-mails to and from the witness, already thoroughly analyzed by a team of lawyers and now in the mind and hands of a highly skilled cross-examiner.

It was no secret that the government and Boies had powerful statements in the form of e-mails before the deposition began. The record of the decisions by the witness as to how to react to such locked and loaded questions, obviously based on Gates's and others' multiple prior statements, allows future witnesses the luxury of benefiting from Gates's discomfort. These transcripts can provide hours of free training in considering how you would have handled these kinds of questions in a deposition or trial. The point of this chapter is not to criticize Gates or his lawyers for what happened in the Microsoft trial but to learn from the record of that performance. Fortunately, these videos of one of the most important depositions in the world of IT litigation are all available for viewing, through the interlibrary loan services of state depository libraries for public government documents.

Every Transcript Tells a Story

During the widely covered courtroom proceedings associated with *U.S. v. Microsoft*, most trial observers realized that Bill Gates was testifying as a witness to facts—*and as something like an interested party witness.* While Gates was clearly not the corporate party to the lawsuit, he was at least the personification of Microsoft in the popular mind, and his testimony was probably the most important testimony in the entire case. Gates's special status as a witness, whether regarded as a fact, expert, or symbolic party witness, was especially apparent given his testimony regarding e-mail communications and meetings with Microsoft officials during which competitive strategies were discussed. However, few commentators acknowledged that, at times, Gates also could have been perceived by the fact finder, who in this case was a federal judge rather than a jury, as testifying (or at least as having been characterized by the government examiners from time to time) as an expert. After all, Gates was acknowledged for his technical acumen and was certainly able to address and explain technical details of Microsoft's software products to the court.

When perusing all the examples of testimony contained in this book (and in the online and videotape versions available for sale or library loan), keep in mind that when someone is called to the stand, that witness may be qualified as an expert but used only to testify about what he or she saw, heard, or did. In this role, the witness's expertise may be largely irrelevant to his or her role as a witness in a particular hearing or trial. In the example cited here, Gates is a special kind of witness, offering testimony that can be considered by the fact finder as going well beyond his knowledge of the facts and touching on his presumed expertise. He is also testifying in a context that places him in a very similar position to a party witness in the case, which heightens the importance of his performance to the fact finder. Gates is, in the eyes of the fact finder, at least the most influential person in deciding on and recalling in his testimony the acts of Microsoft, the corporate party, which were alleged to have given rise to the claims made by the United States. For such witnesses, certain expectations and presumptions by the fact finder naturally come into play as to how to view and consider the testimony that the witness chooses to give.

This is high-risk testimony for anyone placed in such a role, especially with the well-known expertise and depth of involvement that this witness is assumed to have had in the technologies his company produced. Nevertheless, any witness, whether a routine fact witness or the most important representative of a party involved in high-profile, high-stakes litigation, arrives at the witness stand in possession of his or her skills and experiences. This accompanying baggage of expertise or the lack thereof can be injected into the case by either or both parties. More importantly, perhaps, in the case in point is the assumption the fact finder is likely to make about the knowledge and expertise that such a witness has that can help the fact finder determine all the facts in the case. It therefore behooves the attorneys and the witness to consider carefully how this potential expertise may be used or abused and what the fact finder can be anticipated to make of it. In the Microsoft case, the reasonable expectations of the fact finder as to how such a witness should behave in the course of testimony apparently came into play, to the dismay of the defendant company. The judge's determination of the credibility of this key witness, as well as other witnesses for the company, and the judge's decision in deciding the outcome of the case tried before him may have been affected by Gates's behavior during the three days of deposition testimony.

Quibbling with Counsel Can Be Counterproductive

On further review of the transcript, several commentators suggested that Gates was less helpful than he might have been to the questioners in his deposition, weaving and dodging what appear to be the simplest questions asked him by the government's counsel.

Q (Mr. Boies): Let me show you a document that has been marked as Exhibit 386. The second item here purports to be a message from you to a number of people dated April 6, 1995. Do you see that?

A (Gates): Yes.

(The document referred to was marked by the court reporter as Government Exhibit 386 for identification. . . .)

Commentary: Note that this is one of many instances during the deposition when the government's attorneys confronted the witness with a copy of an e-mail and introduced it into the record so that it would be clear to the fact finder what was being discussed. This forces the witness to admit or deny that this e-mail is indeed his prior statement, regardless of what interpretation he attempts to give its text. This is also an example of the power of e-mail and other recorded statements to shape and control the examination of a witness and to limit or change the inclinations of witnesses to explain away suggestions of counsel in the absence of such prior statements.

Attorneys also recognize that this power can serve as an impediment to an expert in communicating with attorneys appropriately, effectively, and efficiently during the assignment. As they further recognize that e-mail exchanges have replaced telephone conversations and that the rules of procedure dictate what attorney-expert communications must be disclosed, they often enter agreements not to subpoena e-mail communications between attorneys and their experts during the expert's assignments.

Let's return to Gates's deposition.

Q (Mr. Boies): Did you send this message on or about April 6, 1995?

A: I don't remember sending it, but I don't have any reason to doubt that I did.

Q: Now, attached to this message, as it was produced to us, I believe, by Microsoft, is a two-page document headed "Netscape as Netware." Do you see that?

A: I see a three-page document, yes.

Q: Yes, three pages. Pages 3558 through 3560. Have you seen this before?

A: I don't remember seeing it before.

Q: Now, the title of this three-page attachment is "Netscape as Netware" and there is a footnote that says, "The analogy here is that the major sin that Microsoft made with Netware was to let Novell offer a better (actually smaller and faster with simpler protocol) client for networking. They got to critical mass and can now evolve both client and server together." Do you see that?

A: Uh-huh. Yes.

Q: In or about April of 1995, was Microsoft concerned with Netscape getting to what is referred to here as critical mass?

A: I don't know what Paul meant in using that word.

Q: Do you have any understanding at all about what Mr. Maritz meant when he referred to a competitor getting "to critical mass"?

A: He seems to be using that phrase with respect to Netware or Novell, but I'm not sure what he means by it.

Q: He is also using it with respect to Netscape in the analogy, is that not so?

A: It's not clear that the term "critical mass" is part of the analogy, is it? It's not to me.

Q: Okay. This document is about Netscape, it's not about Novell; correct, sir?

A: I didn't write the document. The document appears to refer to "Netscape as Netware" as its title, so Novell is talked about in this document and a lot of things seem to be talked about here. Do you want me to read it?

Q: If you have to, to answer any of my questions. Netware is something from Novell; correct, sir?

A: Fact.

Q: What?

A: Fact.

Q: Does that mean yes?

A: Yes.

Q: And what Mr. Maritz here is doing is analogizing Netscape to Netware; correct?

A: It's kind of confusing because Netscape is the name of a company and Netware is the name of a product and so I'm not sure what he is doing. Usually you think of analogizing two products to each other or two companies to each other, but he appears to be analogizing a company to a product, which is a very strange thing.

Q: Well, sir, in April of 1995, insofar as Microsoft was concerned, was Netscape primarily a browser company?

A: No.

Q: It was not?

A: No.

Q: All right, sir. In this document do you understand what Mr. Maritz is saying is that Microsoft should not make the same mistake with Netscape's browser as it did with Novell's Netware?

A: I'd have to read the document. Do you want me to?

Boies continues the questioning.

Q: And the question is, do you understand that what this document is saying is that Microsoft should not make the same mistake with Netscape's browser as it did with Novell's Netware? And you can read any portion that you want, but I am particularly interested the heading which says "Netscape as Netware" and the footnote right off that heading, "The analogy here is that the major sin that Microsoft made with Netware was to let Novell offer a better (actually smaller and faster, with simpler protocol) client for networking. They got to critical mass and can now evolve both client and server together."

A: Are you asking me a question about the whole document?

Q: No, I didn't think I was. I thought it was possible for you to answer the question by looking at the title and first footnote.

A: I thought you were asking me what the document is about.

Q: I think it's possible to answer the question by looking at the heading and that footnote. My question is whether, as you understand it, what Mr. Maritz is saying here is that Microsoft should not make the same mistake with Netscape's browser as it did with Novell's Netware?

A: Does it say "mistake" somewhere?

Q: All I'm asking you is whether you interpret this that way.

A: Does it say "mistake" somewhere?

Q: Mr. Gates, we have had a conversation about how I ask the questions and you give the answers. I think—

A: I don't see where it says "mistake."

Q: It doesn't say "mistake." It says "major sin." If you think major sin is something different than mistake, you can answer the question no, that's not what you think Mr. Maritz means. My question is clear. You can answer it yes, no, or you can't tell.

A: What is the question?

Q: My question is whether—as you understand what Mr. Maritz is saying here, is he saying that Microsoft should not make the same mistake with Netscape's browser as it did with Novell's Netware?

A: No, I think he is saying something else.

Q: Okay. Do you think that when Mr. Maritz uses the term "major sin" that Microsoft made, he is referring to what he thinks is a mistake?

A: Probably.

One might argue that Gates was, in these depositions, fulfilling his responsibility to answer the questions posed by the opposing counsel and furthermore to answer them in as truthful a fashion as required without volunteering any information. One might further posit that he answers these questions while complying with the most minimal requirements of testifying. Unfortunately, he may have neglected one of the most important considerations for an effective witness—appearing credible in the eyes of the court. It is typical for attorneys to advise almost any witness, whether an expert or not, to just answer the questions and in doing so to avoid volunteering information beyond that necessary for an adequate answer to what is being asked. Before depositions were routinely videotaped, this served as standard operating procedure. Everyone knew that if the case did not settle, as most cases do, the witness would testify at trial anyway. Furthermore, and perhaps more importantly, concise answers were advisable because reading lengthy depositions was boring for the jury. Videotaping depositions changes this. When a deposition is videotaped and can be introduced as substantive evidence at the trial in lieu of calling the witness to the stand, the witness must balance the original desire for terse answers with the desire to enhance his or her credibility.

Fact finders (in this case the judge) take many factors into account when considering the testimony of witnesses. The most crucial of these is credibility. A necessary part of establishing and maintaining credibility is acting with a demeanor proper to a witness who has a great deal of relevant information to bring to bear on the issues in a given case. For whatever reasons (strategic or otherwise), Gates is generally considered by his critics to have missed getting the highest marks in demeanor, which may have undermined the credibility of his deposition.

When Bad Strategy Happens to Competent Technologists

As the deposition continued, Gates's testimony descended into increasing murkiness.

Q (Mr. Boies): The November 27, 1996, Nehru e-mail that you sent around is headed "Netscape Revenues"; correct, sir? And it is a discussion of an analysis of Netscape's revenues?

A (Gates): I didn't send it around. Amar sent it around. I enclosed it.

Q: I thought we established that you then sent it around.

A: I enclosed it, yes.

Q: When you say you enclosed it, that means it's enclosed with what you have written so that it goes around to everybody that your e-mail is directed to; correct?

A: Well, Amar had already sent it to quite a large superset of the people I copied on my e-mail, so he sent it to them.

Q: He sent it to them and then you sent it to everybody that is on the addressee or copy list of your e-mail; correct?

A: I enclosed it to those people who had already all gotten it from Amar.

Q: And by enclosing it means you sent it around?

A: That's not the word I would use, but it was enclosed in the e-mail I sent to those people who had already received it directly from Amar.

Q: So when people got your e-mail—all I'm trying to do is—I don't think this is obscure. All I'm trying to do is establish that when you sent your e-mail to the five people that you sent it to, with your e-mail they got Mr. Nehru's e-mail?

A: Which they had already gotten.

Q: And they got it again?

A: As an enclosure, yes.

Q: As an enclosure to your e-mail?

A: Right.

Q: And that e-mail from Mr. Nehru that you enclosed with your e-mail is a discussion of Netscape's revenues; correct, sir?

A: That's the subject line of his e-mail.

Q: Not only is it the subject line, that's what the substance of the e-mail is?

A: Do you want me to look at it?

Q: If you need to to answer the question.

A: It appears to be a discussion of Netscape's revenue, or what he was able to find out about it at a 70 percent confidence.

Q: And the first line of your memo that you sent to the five people indicated here, including Mr. Maritz and Mr. Ballmer, is, "What kind of data do we have on how much software companies pay Netscape?" correct, sir?

A: Yes.

Q: And did they furnish you with that information?

A: I don't think so.

Q: You say in the next line, "In particular, I am curious about their deals with Corel, Lotus and Intuit." Do you see that?

A: Uh-huh.

Q: You've got to say yes or no for the—

A: Yes.

Q: Did you ever receive information about what revenues Netscape was getting from any of those companies?

A: I'm quite sure I didn't.

Q: Netscape was getting revenues from Intuit. You knew that in December of '96; correct, sir?

A: I still don't know that.

Q: You still don't know that? You tried to find that out in December of 1996; correct?

A: I did not myself try and find that out.

Q: You tried to find it out by raising it with people who worked for Microsoft, didn't you? That's what this message is?

A: It says I'm curious about it.

Q: Well, the first line says, "What kind of data do we have about how much software companies pay Netscape? In particular I am curious about their deals with Corel, Lotus and Intuit." That's what you wrote to Mr. Nehru, Mr. Silverberg, Mr. Chase, Mr. Ballmer and Mr. Maritz; correct, sir?

A: Right, because Amar's mail didn't seem to have any data about that.

Q: And is it your testimony that you never got any data about that?

A: That's right. I don't remember getting any data. I'm quite sure that I didn't.

Q: Did you follow up to try to get an answer to those questions?

A: No.

Q: After December of 1996, Microsoft entered into an agreement with Intuit that would limit how much money Intuit paid Netscape; correct, sir?

A: I'm not aware of that.

Q: Are you aware of an agreement that Intuit entered into with Microsoft?

A: I know there was some kind of an agreement. I wasn't part of negotiating it, nor do I know what was in it.

When reading this portion of the transcript of the deposition and when viewing the videotapes, one can almost sense the frustrations building in the witness, who at various points appears not to want to be testifying. The novice might assume that Boies is also frustrated by Gates's vague and evasive answers. However, experienced experts and legal strategists can recognize when the playing field of a deposition is under their control. The extraordinary number of prior e-mail statements that Boies could use to control the ability of Gates to answer and explain his answers represented a formidable advantage. Regardless, it is clear at this point in the deposition that any witness would be in for a rough time. Almost any strategy that attempts to get around the massive amount of impeachment material is likely to make it look like the witness is attempting to frustrate the legitimate efforts of the examining attorney to establish the facts that are most relevant to the lawsuit.

Furthermore, Boies is widely acknowledged in legal circles as an expert linguist and a consummate examiner of witnesses. We get the idea that he was delighted with what he was eliciting from the witness over the three days of the deposition. Therefore, he was content to appear in the video and written transcript to be fairly but futilely attempting to get from the witness a straight answer that contained all the information that was available as to a particular issue. From the government's perspective, Boies was in a win-win situation. After all, he had already obtained most of the essential evidence in the form of admissible prior statements of the witness or others discussing these issues. Gates's only real hope was to come across as a knowledgeable and helpful witness while explaining these e-mail messages, in order to score any points at all with the fact finder.

On the other hand, in fairness to the witness, the last exchange is also an example of testimony that, in the absence of the cumulative effect of dozens of other exchanges that put Gates at a distinct disadvantage, might almost as easily be scored by the fact finder in favor of the witness. Such an isolated exchange as the one quoted immediately above could reasonably be interpreted as nitpicking questioning by the lawyer, rather than as a failure by the witness to be responsive or cooperative and therefore completely credible. It is important for technical experts to pick their fights carefully and not to assume that if they consistently react defensively to all lines of questions, the fact finder will continue to empathize with the witness. After enough of these defensive answers, the most open-minded fact finder may conclude that the witness is simply refusing to explain what he or she knows, whether the questions are reasonable or not.

Some legal observers have wondered why the Microsoft counsel did not call more time-outs. From time to time the Microsoft counsel objected and in other ways attempted to smooth over a situation that was, in retrospect, not helping to make the witness appear credible. This loss of control over the impressions made during the deposition had an impact on the future trial strategy. Some commentators have suggested that after viewing the videos, the existence of the taped deposition may have convinced the legal team members of their inability to effectively rehabilitate the witness once the deposition was introduced into evidence at the trial. This may have persuaded the Microsoft counsel not to present Gates as either a factual witness or as an objective and wise expert—his bias and interest in the outcome of the case notwithstanding.

Although it may appear to the reader that Boies is being unnecessarily picky in his repeated questioning of Gates on details of the e-mail messages, he is expertly and dramatically drawing the attention of the court to the witness's antagonistic and picky behavior, which could be construed as that of someone failing to adequately respond to a legitimate line of questioning.

David Bank has a less generous interpretation of Gates's intent:

Gates tried to stall Boies. While he otherwise had crisp recall of the pros and cons of every strategy debate since Microsoft's inception, he, in his deposition, claimed not to remember whether he did or did not write or receive any of the dozens of e-mails put before him. . . .

In what turned out to be his only chance to influence the trial, Gates had opted for obfuscation rather than clarity. His evasiveness and forgetfulness in the deposition had disqualified him as a witness in the courtroom. The forceful defense he might have later chosen to make would be fatally undermined by his lack of credibility. So Gates effectively gave up his chance to defend Microsoft's strategy as simply the best adapted to the new form of competition in high-technology markets. . . .[3]

A Learning Experience for Both Litigators and Witnesses

Lawyers have not missed the opportunity to use Gates's performance to make a number of points about the art of giving and taking depositions for the education of trial attorneys. Such depositions are especially well suited for instructional purposes when they are videotaped, as this one was, and then dramatically introduced in relevant portions during the presentation of the case and the examination of other witnesses at the trial. Former Federal Judge Herbert J. Stern and George Washington University Law School Professor Stephen A. Saltzburg have devoted an entire chapter to the analysis of portions of the Gates deposition in the fourth volume of their series for attorneys, *Trying Cases to Win.*[4]

Along with Bank, Stern and Saltzburg also have pointed out that, regardless of the reasons that prompted Gates to testify as he did, the resulting performance made it extremely difficult for him to take the stand after the deposition had been introduced by the plaintiff in the trial before the judge. They also discuss why it makes good sense to treat the videotaped deposition as if it were itself the trial. According to Stern and Saltzburg, the strategy of having as knowledgeable and important a witness as Bill Gates (the personification of the defendant in the lawsuit) appears to deny the plain meaning and significance of one evidentiary document after another ultimately harms the case for the defendant. It erodes the credibility of one of the main witnesses and may also enhance the importance of the documents to the fact finder, in this case, the judge. These are heavy potential losses to incur during the discovery phase of litigation. Such losses can turn out to be powerful and persuasive admissible trial testimony from which the legal team cannot recover during the actual trial.

---

3. Bank, *Breaking Windows*, pp. 149–150.

4. Stern, Herbert J., and Stephen A. Saltzburg. *Evidence: Weapons for Winning, Trying Cases to Win.* Vol. 4 in the *Trying Cases to Win* series. New York: Aspen Publishing, 2001.

What Fact Finders Say about the Importance of Testimony

You may wonder what impact Gates's demonstrated difficulties in deposition had on the outcome of the case. In other words, what real damage could testimony, perceived as Gates's performance was generally perceived, actually incur? This is an unusual case because shortly after the trial the judge supplied a journalist with significant evidence that supports the conclusion that the fact finder did score points against the defendant and for the plaintiff, based on his analysis of the witness's performance. Ken Auletta, a reporter for *The New Yorker*, interviewed Judge Robert Penfield Jackson (who presided over the Microsoft case) many times during the trial. Ultimately, Jackson's comments on the trial were published in an article that appeared in *The New Yorker* in January 2001.[5] Jackson's remarks quoted in the article led to a remanding of his judgment against Microsoft on appeal and to further proceedings. Furthermore, the Court of Appeals returned the case to the lower court and assigned a new judge to reconsider it.

In his article (and in his subsequent book on the Microsoft case[6]), Auletta quoted Jackson as saying that Jackson became irritated with what he called Microsoft's "obstinacy" displayed, for example, by Gates during his videotaped deposition. Jackson was also disturbed by the apparent contradictions between the text of some Microsoft e-mails presented as evidence and the testimony of its witnesses.

Another exchange, this time between Gates and Stephen Houck, illustrates a key problem.

Q (Stephen Houck): Do you understand that in this e-mail here Mr. Siegelman is opposing a proposal to give MCI a position on the Windows 95 desktop as an Internet service provider?

A (Gates): I don't remember anything about MCI. This talks about how we'll have a Mosaic client in Windows 95. I don't see anything in here about the desktop.

Q: It references in this e-mail the Windows box. What do you understand the Windows box to mean?

A: Well, the Windows box is certainly not the Windows desktop. The Windows box is a piece of cardboard.

---

5. Auletta, Ken. "Final Offer-What Kept Microsoft from Settling Its Case (Annals of Communications)." *The New Yorker*, January 15, 2001, p 26.

6. Auletta, Ken. *World War 3.0–Microsoft and Its Enemies.* New York: Random House, 2001.

Jackson later asserted in remarks to Auletta that Gates's deposition was a critical mistake because it essentially supported the prosecution's contention that Microsoft was arrogant and unfair. The judge asserted that after observing Gates's testimony, he had no choice but to rule for the prosecution, returning a judgment that ordered a split of Microsoft into two separate companies.

Gates himself later came close to admitting his mistake in the approach he took as a witness in the case. After Jackson's findings and his order to break up the company, Gates offhandedly acknowledged that perhaps he should have chosen to testify in Microsoft's defense. "If we look back, I think it's clear that the whole story of personal computing—how the great things that have been done there and how we created an industry structure that's far more competitive than the computer industry before we came along—that story didn't get out," Gates said on Good Morning America. "And I do wonder if I'd taken the time to go back personally and testify, if we might have done a better job in getting that across."[7]

When Auletta was asked to identify the most critical flaw in Microsoft's legal team's strategy, he responded, "[The Microsoft legal defense team] ignored things like credibility, intent. They handled [the trial] like an engineer would. And they are paying for it."[8]

Testifying Effectively Is Not the Same as Solving Engineering Problems

Auletta's analysis of the flaws in Microsoft's legal strategy is of special interest to those who might serve as expert witnesses. Technologists often want to believe that the law is logical and that they can therefore understand the tenets of the law and how it applies to most situations. This view might lead them to believe that they can afford to ignore the illogical details of the legal ritual that has evolved over centuries. This is a disaster in the making.

We live in an age when the massive effect of technology on everyday life has accorded those who demonstrate mastery of technology the status of court magicians. Understanding technology involves a great deal of academic effort and certain analytical talents, attributes that do not come easily to everyone. Technologists are understandably proud of their skills and their accomplishments won by using those skills. It's only natural to believe that the systematic analytic process learned in the course of a technical education can be generalized to dealing with all the challenges of life.

---

7. As quoted in Bank, *Breaking Windows*, p. 150.

8. As quoted in Garfield, Matt. "*New Yorker* Author Analyzes Microsoft 'Trial of the Century.'" *Davidson News & Events* (Davidson College newspaper, Davidson, NC), January 22, 2001, p. 1.

However, this technical approach does not satisfy some of the key requirements of the adversarial legal system, which relies in the end on the understanding by judges and jurors of the facts that are crucial to reaching a decision. In every case the facts are developed either in whole or in part by the testimony of lay and expert witnesses. It is often the credibility of those witnesses that makes all the difference.

Testimony—Take Two

In April 2002, as this book went to press, Bill Gates returned to the witness stand in *U.S. v. Microsoft*, this time concerning the claims of nine states and the District of Columbia. This set of claims asserted that the settlement reached between the Department of Justice and Microsoft was insufficient to serve the best interests of the consumers in their respective jurisdictions.

The media and press celebrated a "different Bill Gates," one who was well prepared and appropriately deferential to the judge and the plaintiff counsel. According to press accounts, Gates was initially nervous but soon regained his composure, delivering a clear message to the judge that the punitive measures proposed by the plaintiffs would inflict significant damage on both Microsoft and the U.S. economy as a whole.

Consider and contrast this description of Gates's assuming the mantle of the prepared and composed expert with his previous performance in the original deposition:

> *On Monday, Gates began his testimony with an elaborate PowerPoint presentation and painstaking definition of technical terms. He said that arbitrarily "removing code" from Windows would have disastrous consequences because software would lose application program interfaces—he called it "published ways of calling on functions"—and cease to work.*[9]

In another turnabout from his previous witness persona, Gates was clear and candid when asked by the states' attorney about a previous claim of improper activity:

> *"Cloning is a strategy that Microsoft has employed, isn't it?" asked [states' attorney Steven] Kuney.*
> *"We have done it," Gates responded, adding that he believes cloning is appropriate if a company does it without improperly obtaining another firm's source code.*[10]

Consider the contrast between this succinct exchange and Gates's endless parrying with Boies during the deposition (and consider the difference made to the court). Clearly Gates learned from his first experience as a witness in the deposition. In

---

9. McCullagh, Declan, and Robert Zarate. "Gates: Leave My Windows Alone." *Wired News*, April 23, 2002. Accessed July 10, 2002, at *http://www.wired.com/news/print/0,1294,52027,00.html.*

10. Krim, Jonathan. "Gates Tries Softer Voice in Loud Court Battle." *Washington Post*, April 22, 2002, p. E01.

reflecting those lessons learned in his return visit to the court, he demonstrated that with experience and preparation, an expert can indeed learn new tricks about the art of testifying!

If Credibility Is Always the Answer, What Are the Questions?

The legal system has slowly evolved, reflecting the influences and experiences of Western culture through many generations and regenerations of theories and practices of conflict resolution. One point that may be difficult for technologists to accept, given that so much of the IT revolution is driven by the need for speed, is that the law is "designed" to function slowly. This is to accommodate the "one step forward, two steps back" nature of technological and societal progress without making social policy that either cripples further advance or creates too many unacceptable risks for society in the adoption of new technologies. Furthermore, the law ultimately attempts to deal with the most difficult scenarios that arise when scientific crispness meets human messiness—the addition of humans to even the most elegant analytical constructs can result in wildly unpredictable results. Because it deals with human frailties, the law tends to focus its attention in the process of litigation on human attributes of trust and believability, and not solely or even primarily on the absolute properties of correctness.

Thus some of the things that matter most when participating in the legal rituals of litigation and dispute resolution are determined by legal and philosophical concepts that have been around at least since the time of Cicero.

- Is the testimony relevant?
- Is the witness believable?
- Do other similarly qualified and credible witnesses agree with these conclusions?
- Is the witness's testimony comprehensible?
- Is there admissible evidence to show that the testimony is factual?

Contrast that set of criteria to the questions asked when testing a scientific or technical argument.

- Is the argument logical?
- Is it based on a provable hypothesis?
- Has it been rigorously tested?
- Does it follow from established scientific fact?
- Has it been subjected to published peer review and critique?

Although one might argue that the goal of the legal process is to derive the truth—presumably the same goal as an unbiased scientific or technical inquiry into causation or proof—there are differences in the techniques applied for the process of considering the issues and for reaching the final judgment about the results of the inquiry. In particular, the treatment of context is quite different. In technical inquiry, in order to use mathematical models of process, researchers and design engineers often try to eliminate or else dampen the effect of context. In legal process, given the importance of bias, motive, and interest to the credibility of witness testimony, establishing the full context is critical to establishing all the relevant facts of a matter in litigation. This context is established through an objective assessment of all the evidence as subjected to rhetorical interpretations by the advocates. In the end, the fact finder applies his or her common sense to those arguments and the evidence and seeks to reach a fair and final verdict.

Creating Stories about Complex Technical Issues

U.S. v. Mitnick: A Case That Defined the Internet Threat

Perhaps the best-known computer crime story that resulted in a successful criminal prosecution is the widely publicized 1995 apprehension and prosecution of Kevin Mitnick. The network investigation was chronicled by John Markoff in a spectacular series of articles in the *New York Times* and later by the same reporter in the book *Takedown*, coauthored by the hero of the story, Tsutomu Shimomura.[1] Shimomura, one of the better known of Mitnick's many hacking victims over the years, took on the challenging investigation into the use of a theoretically understood—but hitherto unproven—intrusion method to obtain access to his personal computer. Shimomura considered the intrusion an invitation to a duel and proceeded to become Mitnick's dogged pursuer. With the assistance of Andrew Gross (then his fellow researcher at the San Diego Supercomputer Center), a great deal of help from the government (which had been unsuccessfully searching for Mitnick as a fugitive for years), and the critical

---

1. Shimomura, Tsutomu, with John Markoff. *Takedown*. New York: Hyperion Press, 1996.

cooperation of Internet service providers, Shimomura tracked the defendant to his hideout in North Carolina a few weeks after the initial intrusion.

A criminal trial that considered Mitnick's manipulation of the telecommunications and computer networks of the world, including his successful intrusion into the computer of one of the best computer security experts, would in all likelihood have taught law enforcement and the public a great deal about just how exposed users of the Internet are. It would also have served to clarify some unresolved issues concerning the degree to which the roles of private-sector monitors and law enforcement can interact within the confines of the Electronic Communications Privacy Act (ECPA).

Due to a plea agreement reached in March 1999, no trial of any of the many charges lodged against Mitnick occurred. In August 1999, Mitnick pled guilty to four counts of wire fraud, two counts of computer fraud, and one count of illegal interception of wire communications. He was sentenced to serve 46 months in federal prison and ordered to pay restitution to his victims.[2]

It is not our intention to argue the merits of the Mitnick case, but rather to use it as a worked example of a type of case that will, in all probability, be more common in the future. Regardless of the type of case, prosecutions usually culminate in plea bargains or dismissals before trial. This creates a real problem in that only by trying some of these cases can the legal system give practical guidance to those investigators and prosecutors who are actually out in the trenches digging up cases based on digital evidence of network crimes and bringing them to court.

The terrorist attacks of September 11, 2001, and the general increase in vigilance concerning critical infrastructures have resulted in a change in the public's perception of threat. In particular, the threat posed by computer criminals and their crimes largely escaped many executive and legislative decision makers prior to the terrorist attacks. Law enforcement is now finding evidence that suggests that the number of crimes investigated by experts but never prosecuted may be astronomical. Attempts to quantify the problem have been only minimally effective, although nearly every business surveyed reports large losses due to computer crimes.

Andrew Gross investigated this case as an employee of the San Diego Supercomputer Center. Erin Kenneally is an attorney with a master's degree in forensic sciences who works at the San Diego Supercomputer Center. Gross and Kenneally collaborated with us in preparing the following narrative and simulated testimony outlining Gross's explanation of the investigation. We created this simulation in order

---

2. "Kevin Mitnick Sentenced to Nearly Four Years in Prison; Computer Hacker Ordered to Pay Restitution to Victim Companies Whose Systems Were Compromised." Press release, U.S. Department of Justice, U.S. Attorney's Office, Central District of California, Los Angeles, California. August 9, 1999. Accessed July 21, 2002 at *http://www.usdoj.gov/criminal/cybercrime/mitnick.htm*.

to give you a sense of how Gross, through his expert testimony, might have explained in court the analysis of the intrusion. Without the original expert investigation by Gross, the following story could never have been told. Without the persistent efforts by Kenneally to elicit Gross's story and to structure it as testimony, this simulation could never have been produced.

Hiding and Seeking Digital Evidence

Setting aside the philosophical debate over what is or is not a computer crime, let us assume that whatever Mitnick did that caused him to be prosecuted by the authorities in North Carolina and by the federal government clearly qualifies. Let us also simply assume that whether Mitnick was properly referred to as a committed cyberterrorist, a career criminal, or a cantankerous cracker, he probably deserved to be prosecuted for what he did. But a prosecution does not guarantee a conviction, and a criminal conviction requires that a story be created and presented to a judge or a jury that convinces them beyond a reasonable doubt of the defendant's guilt. In this section we present a fictional account of what the trial testimony of the government's expert witness might have been had Mitnick's case gone to trial. The testimony concerning the tracing of evidence in this complex case will also give you an idea of the kinds of problems that private security professionals, investigating law enforcement officers, and prosecuting attorneys are beginning to face as they deal with computer intrusions and other criminal attacks.

Though Gross originally discovered the Christmas 1994 break-in of Shimomura's computer system, the rest of the world first heard about the incident a few weeks later at a Computer Misuse and Anomaly Detection (CMAD) workshop in Sonoma, California. CMAD was an annual workshop for researchers working on computer security and intrusion detection and was sponsored by the National Security Agency and the Air Force Information Warfare Center. The decision by Shimomura to publicize the story of the compromise of his system and to begin describing it to both the media and law enforcement at the CMAD workshop led directly to the clues that allowed Shimomura and federal agents to pick up the digital trail of evidence.

Shimomura presented a description of the intrusion incident to the CMAD conference attendees, believing that this audience might have some insights as to whether the artifacts left by the intruder supported the initial diagnosis by Shimomura and Gross of the intrusion techniques. At the time of the CMAD presentation, Mitnick had not yet been identified as the culprit.

Accepting that security is a relative concept and computer intrusions are inevitable, there is much to be said for capitalizing on the potency of digital evidence that can be collected. Technology will constantly raise the sophistication of attacks and countermeasures, but digital evidence will persist. As London School of Economics security expert Peter Sommer has suggested, the more corroborating streams of digital evidence that can be captured, the more persuasive the case will be for the prosecution.[3] Recognizing that digital evidence embodies a way of turning technology, which is the intruder's strength, against him or her, common sense dictates that more concern must be paid to its proper use in the exercise of discretion.

What follows is a simplified, fictional presentation of the evidence that Gross might have given had Mitnick gone to trial. This tale helps to illustrate how the sharing of information among the victims, their technical experts, and law enforcement officers in the course of efforts to trace back and identify the intruder can lead to success in even the most difficult cases. The testimony is designed to tell the story of the investigation and eventual "red-handed" apprehension of Mitnick. The expert's narrative is approached from the perspective of Mitnick's trackers and focuses on the evidentiary trail that led to his arrest. The story contains the forensic approach to all network intrusion analysis work that is essential to fostering trace-back capabilities leading to the eventual identification of computer criminals and the collection and preservation of admissible digital evidence. Furthermore, the credibility of a criminal prosecution and the efficacy of a civil action hinge on the proper handling of this digital evidence used to identify the miscreant and accurately assess the damage done by the intrusion.

Although the Mitnick case illustrates only a handful of the myriad techniques whereby a system can be compromised, this simulated testimony, based on a real investigation of an intrusion and trace-back, underscores the existence of generally applicable responses that forge the necessary link between the intruder, a user account, an IP address, a physical node, and/or the data transmitted. By extrapolating common forensic capabilities amid an array of intrusion scenarios, you can make these incidents become both manageable and useful. This study illustrates grounded and practical methods for recognizing and recovering digital evidence of intrusions. It also places in perspective some areas of potential forensic contention.

We have inserted commentary in italics at key points throughout the fictional testimony, outlining additional questions that experts for the opposing counsel and court-appointed experts might suggest in an attempt to identify discrepancies or other flaws in the prosecution's case or the expertise of the witness. This commentary is meant to remind you that expert input isn't limited to a prepared script for the case, and that the purpose of the trial is to provide the fact finder with all the information he or she needs in order to make a just decision.

---

3. Sommer, Peter. "Intrusion Detection Systems as Evidence." First International Workshop on the Recent Advances in Intrusion Detection, Louvain-la-Neuve, Belgium, September 1998.

The Simulated Testimony of Andrew Gross

In any computer network intrusion case there are likely to be two key expert witnesses for the prosecution: namely, the company expert who discovered and initially investigated the crime, and the hired expert who prepares a report and provides an expert opinion to the prosecutor in the process of investigating and prosecuting the case. Here, Andrew Gross played both roles.

Q (Prosecutor): Please state your name and occupation.

A (Gross): Andrew Gross. I'm the Principal Investigator for PICS—the Pacific Institute for Computer Security at the San Diego Supercomputer Center.

Q: Briefly describe your background, skills, and experience in the field of computer security.

A: I have a Ph.D. in Electrical and Computer Engineering and an M.S. in Electrical Engineering from the University of California at San Diego. I also have a B.S. in Electrical Engineering from Duke University. Without getting too technical, my main areas of research are network monitoring, auditing, and analysis. This has led to the development of new tools for intrusion analysis and tracing and eventual system recovery. I have also provided consulting for federal law enforcement agencies, private industry, and public collaborations.

Q: How did you become involved in the tracking of Kevin Mitnick?

A: Part of my responsibilities while I was completing my dissertation at SDSC was looking after Tsutomu Shimomura's machines at SDSC. In doing so, I discovered in the early morning hours of Christmas Day, December 25, 1994, that his system had been compromised.

Q: At what point did you begin to make substantial headway and realize that you were onto the trail of the intruder or intruders?

A: We received a call from an account owner at The Well, which is an ISP in Sausalito, California. His account was apparently being hacked, and there were some interesting things about it that connected back to Tsutomu.

Commentary: On cross-examination, Gross may be asked how much time elapsed between the detection of the Christmas Day intrusion and the call from the account holder at The Well. Also, Gross may be asked how he knew that the intrusion actually took place on Christmas Day—that is, how does he know that someone hadn't intruded at an earlier time and simply changed the system clock to make it appear that the intrusion happened on December 25? Finally, the witness may be asked whether a warning banner was displayed to anyone accessing the system, informing legitimate users and hackers alike that they were being monitored. If these things are not addressed during the direct examination (in order to keep the story line tight and the testimony as brief as possible), the expert should be thoroughly prepared to deal with them as issues that opposing counsel is likely to raise on cross-examination.

Q: How was this determined, and how was the connection made to contact you?

A: The Well had informed the account owner that his "cfp" account had surpassed its quota of allowable space. It was something like 600MB, which is a relatively large file size, especially in light of the fact that he rarely used that account. When he accessed the account he noticed files owned by Tsutomu.

Q: How did he determine that they were Tsutomu's files?

A: He saw Tsutomu's name in various places in the text and made the connection to news he had read about the Christmas break-in, which had been publicized by Tsutomu in an effort to spread the word about the use of this technique to break into systems by pretending to be another trusted system.

Q: What did you do next?

A: We talked to the head systems administrator and also to legal counsel at The Well and discussed how we would respond to the situation. They decided to hire us to assist them in getting to the bottom of their problem. They agreed to give us access to the log files so that we could examine the compromised accounts. They pointed us to areas they knew to be problematic, such as the names of the compromised accounts. We also looked at other account activity to find any further tracks of the intruder.

Commentary: *On cross-examination, Gross may be asked whether he and Shimomura were also conferring with law enforcement, especially the FBI, at this time. These kinds of questions lead to efforts to impeach the witness on previously decided legal issues and may or may not be allowed by the court, as discussed below. Nevertheless, in preparation for testifying, the witness must cover approaches for dealing with these questions. In particular, the witness needs to reach a comfort level with these kinds of questions in case they do come up and the court allows the defense attorney to pursue them. This pursuit may occur either in front of the jury or outside the jury's presence but always on the record.*

Q: Were the log files the only source of information made available that would confirm that the account was indeed being hacked?

A: Essentially . . . aside from examining the logs we looked around The Well for other entry points or interesting files to make sure we were monitoring everything in question.

Q: What did you find upon analyzing this information?

A: We were able to understand the magnitude and intent of the intruder. There were several files of an unusual nature, such as one that had copies of large numbers of credit card numbers from another Internet service provider. Other files contained tools for breaking into computers and hiding files; still other files contained electronic mail from well-known computer security professionals. We also found and confirmed that there were copies of the files taken from Tsutomu's machine. Also, there was evidence of log tampering.

Q: Would there be any legitimate reason for these "log tampering" events to have occurred? For example, could these artifacts have simply recorded a system administrator who may have been moving around or restructuring directories or something innocent such as that?

A: No. If that were the case we would have found missing chunks of data, whereas here, the only thing missing was data from a compromised account. One log contained information that it should not have had under any normal circumstances, while another was found in a totally different place than it should have been in the file structure. For instance, the log showed a session where the intruder created a new file to give himself privileges not associated with the compromised account and then deleted the log records of the original privileges. After doing those things, the intruder then renamed the file containing new privileges to be the same as the deleted file; finally, he reviewed the log file to make sure any reference to the original files had been eradicated.

Commentary: After the testimony above, Gross can be cross-examined on how the log files and file system records he and Shimomura were using were protected from alteration and tampering. He might also be asked how they knew that someone else hadn't touched them and, furthermore, what assurance they had that Mitnick was responsible for the events recorded in the logs. The decision as to whether to include these explanations in the direct examination is a strategic one. If they are left out for tactical reasons, the witness must be prepared to handle them and explain them fully when they come up on cross-examination.

Q: How did you know the same person or persons had done all of this?

A: At that point we weren't certain. We did know that there were no overlapping sessions, which would be expected if there were multiple intruders. This would have indicated some sort of collaborative effort. However, there were actually a bunch of different IP addresses associated with the tampering activities. The IP address is like a telephone number for a computer. The numbers correspond to a particular network and host. In this way, the IP address identifies the last source of the person connected into the network. So, we used a domain-name reference that is available through a service known as the

InterNIC to determine that all four IP addresses had come from the same network. In this case, they were all coming from Netcom, which is another large Internet service provider, located in San Jose, California. Next, we configured "sniffers" to catch all incoming logins from those IP addresses at Netcom. These are monitoring tools that were set on the connection port between The Well and the Internet. They were configured to trap packets of information that had any of the above-mentioned IP addresses in their headers.

Commentary: *Depending on his or her level of expertise in network security, the opposing counsel's expert may make the following point. Although the case relies on demonstrating that the sessions were coming from Netcom, the IP addresses could easily be spoofed (that is, faked so that traffic appeared to come from places it didn't).*

The level of expertise in areas such as network security is really uneven across the landscape of experts (and the attorneys they advise). Some experts might understand that although the IP addresses used to trace back the sessions to Netcom appear to be correct, it's relatively easy for an attacker to make the computer give out a false IP address. The attorney needs to make a critical strategic decision about whether to raise this issue (and any other points that fall in the realm that only leading-edge experts are likely to know) during the expert's initial testimony or whether to wait and see if the other side raises it during cross-examination. If neither side raises the technical point, it goes into the category of a can of worms that remains blessedly unopened. Both the expert and the lawyer need to be prepared to handle this point regardless of whether they plan to bring it up themselves. To do otherwise leaves them vulnerable to the possibility of a surprise attack by the other side.

Q: How did the people at The Well know what to look for when initially obtaining the four logins?

A: Basically we pieced out the information from the most recent login sessions that had suspicious activity associated with them.

Q: But since the log files were tampered with, couldn't they have been manipulated to make it look like someone else, identified by another IP address, had done the tampering?

A: Yes, but only one log file was tampered with, and the only thing done was to erase information that had to do with the intruder's activity. The sniffing gave us crucial additional data that couldn't be modified by the intruder and in turn would also show us whether modification was going on. After about a week of monitoring we attempted to trace back the intruder by pattern matching. This involves taking the incoming log records from The Well and comparing them to the outgoing log records at Netcom.

Q: How was this comparison conducted? Do you have any physical evidence of this matching?

A: Each login record contains the start time, duration, user name, and IP address from which the account user came. We took the four login entries having a Netcom IP address source and extracted the time, date, and duration between each one and the next consecutive login from Netcom. Then we simply looked at the Netcom logs of outgoing messages and found matching times and dates, lengths, and elapsed times.

Q: With the vast number of people accessing the Internet these days, couldn't this merely be coincidental? How could you rule out that possibility, or the possibility that the login name was forged?

A: It's certainly possible, even though all the logins used the same user name. What is significant about the information we were getting by setting up the sniffer is that we were actually looking at the session as it was taking place and observing what the intruder was doing in real time. We were accessing the packet data that was being passed as the user was in a session, which couldn't have been manipulated by anyone else. The big question at that point was whether we could tie this observed activity to a single account at Netcom in order to trace the activity to a specific account and ultimately to a specific machine and user.

Commentary: (The following colloquy would in all likelihood have occurred in pretrial hearings, but we include it here simply to illustrate how legal issues sometimes arise in testimony.) The law that relates to this issue is too complicated to cover here in detail. However, in a nutshell, the point is a crucial one that could determine whether or not the government can proceed with part or all of the evidence collected by the expert after the issue is resolved in a pretrial hearing. Even if it were resolved pretrial, defense counsel may still wish to go into the issue in a slightly different way on cross-examination for the effect it could have on the jury relating to other issues such as the fairness of the prosecution or the credibility of the witness.

Some jurors may be concerned about law enforcement tactics that can be made to appear to come too close or to cross over the line of what is commonly thought of as fair or legal policing or surveillance techniques. This determination of legality is made by the judge in light of the constraints that the ECPA and other statutes place on the ability of law enforcement to gather information from networks. Jurors may be bothered by what was done, regardless of how the judge rules on the admissibility of the questioned evidence.

It is also important to remember that the laws that address these issues are constantly changing. For example, new legislation, including portions of the Patriot Act, passed after the terrorist attacks of September 11, 2001, have significantly altered the rules that applied at the time of the Mitnick investigation. Regardless of how the pretrial hearings are decided, these issues may be dealt with in the course of direct examination or left unmentioned until cross-examination. The attorney and the witness who deal with these issues need to make sure the expert has adequate common-sense explanations for his or her actions, about which legal decisions have been made by the court. Without going to law school, it helps to have a good understanding of the current laws and court decisions that relate to these areas that are crucial to the expert's work, in case the judge allows this line of questioning to proceed on cross-examination or voir dire before the jury (as in My Cousin Vinny*).*

Defense Attorney: Objection, Your Honor. We move to quash this evidence since it was obviously obtained without a court-ordered wiretap. It violated the ECPA and cannot be used against my client.

Prosecutor: Dr. Gross was acting at the behest of and in the employ of The Well, which is a private enterprise. Dr. Gross was not acting as a public law enforcement official. Under the Electronic Communications Privacy Act (ECPA), a provider may protect itself with reasonable precautions, such as hiring computer security experts to investigate whether or not the company and its network are under attack. The ECPA was not violated by any of the actions of Dr. Gross, who acted as a private security consultant for The Well.

Defense Attorney: But Dr. Gross must be construed as an "agent" of the government since he was communicating and consulting with law enforcement, that is, the FBI, throughout the entire course of his tracking. This so-called employment is simply a ruse to avoid the requirement that government agents obtain a warrant before they intercept electronic communications over the Internet.

Prosecutor: Your Honor, counsel for the defense simply has not read the clear exceptions to the ECPA. This entire investigation and certainly the sniffing and tracing activity of Dr. Gross, as a consultant to The Well, would fall well within the "service provider" exception to ECPA. Merely because Dr. Gross's actions appear to be similar to the actions that law enforcement agents might take after applying for and receiving a warrant to intercept Internet communications pursuant to the ECPA, those actions are done routinely by systems administrators in order to deal with the anomalies they constantly encounter when maintaining their service to their customers and in guarding against unlawful attempts to hack into their system or deny service to their legitimate and authorized users. As the Court is well aware, that Act specifically allows an employee of an electronic communications service provider to intercept or disclose communications in the normal course of employment while engaged in any activity incident to rendering service or protecting the service provider.

Defense Attorney: This activity went beyond the bounds necessary to render service or protect The Well, and therefore those investigative actions by Mr. Gross were well outside of the exceptions to the Act. Any electronic or other evidence seized by Gross or Shimomura was therefore seized as part of a law enforcement operation without the benefit of the required warrant for a real-time interception of protected communications. Such activities are not allowed by the Act without prior court authorization, and the evidence obtained must be suppressed, together with the fruits of this poisonous tree that grew from this sham employment.

Prosecutor: The statute does not make "necessity" a requisite element, and furthermore, the ECPA allows any activity incident to protection—it is justified to avoid downstream liability for damage done to third-party systems via access through that ISP.

Commentary: For our purposes, we will assume that the court overruled this objection and instructed Gross to proceed with his testimony.

Q (Prosecutor): Did you contact someone at Netcom immediately?

A (Gross): Actually, we had been in contact with Netcom several days before because we had also found some of its files in one of the compromised accounts. The management at Netcom called us back to offer the company's cooperation.

Q: What did you do at Netcom, which appeared to be the next link in your tracking activities?

A: With the assistance of the system administrator, we ran a shell script to catch all logins from user name "joeblow." This was the account that was being used to access the Netcom service. When that user logged on, the system administrator was automatically notified by pager. These are logins that link the intruder to accounts at Netcom and The Well. Netcom had approximately 20 hosts through which its users could gain access. Trackers accessed the log files at each machine and ran a command, LAST gkremen, to glean the intruder's logins per machine. Each one of these lists was then placed in a file and chronologically ordered. This allowed pattern matching with other login and phone records in order to trace the intruder's path.

Commentary: On cross-examination, Gross may be asked what file is used by the LAST command and how well it is protected. The LAST command uses a system log file that is not particularly well protected. (Many hacker scripts wipe entries from the file in order to cover their tracks. It would be trivial for someone to alter this system log file and make it appear that the purported intruder was present.)

This is another area that the trial attorney must consider as he or she decides which items to bring up in direct examination, rather than simply preparing the witness to be able to respond to this line of questions if it comes up on cross-examination. The dilemma that the lawyer and the expert face here, as elsewhere, is that not all of these problems or complications will be understood sufficiently by the opposition to be troublesome on cross-examination. They may never come up. While they can be handled on direct, to handle every such issue may make the direct examination less dramatic and much more difficult to follow than is either necessary or desirable. This is a recurrent problem.

Q: If you had the user name and corresponding IP address, why didn't you just use that information to trace back to the previous location?

A: We had to link up the "joeblow" logins and the accesses by that user name at Netcom to the compromised "dono" accounts, which had been identified as having been stored at The Well. So we needed to monitor the sessions that were occurring at Netcom. We did this by fine-tuning the sniffer at Netcom to catch network traffic from that IP address associated with the "joeblow" user logins. The sniffer gave us a whole session of "joeblow" access, and we were able to observe the intruder going into The Well and logging in as "dono." This confirmed that we were on the right track. We were able to reach this conclusion because, had we been tracking the wrong account, we would have observed activity not associated with the deviant activity we had already found at The Well. Rather than seeing what we did and making the connection at The Well with the hijacked account activity, maybe we would have just seen someone reading his mail or something else equally innocuous.

Q: Once it was confirmed that you were in fact dealing with the same person, did you then use the IP address to track that person to the next location?

A: Yes, we would get an IP address when the user logged in. The system administrator at Netcom then logged into the terminal server associated with the IP address and got the port number being used. This was necessary because there were 23 ports per machine, and we needed a specific one in order get a trap and trace on the number.

Commentary: Gross may be asked how he knew that the port number corresponding to the IP was correct. (The terminal server file that maintains the mappings of ports to IP addresses is often badly protected and thereby subject to unauthorized alteration.) Again, the attorney and witness need to think about such questions before the testimony begins and reach a decision about how much diversion of attention to the narrative or unnecessary confusion these types of issues will create if they are handled during direct examination or simply deferred until they arise, if they do, during cross-examination.

Q: Were you dealing with just one IP address?

A: No, there were multiple sessions from "joeblow" from three locations most frequently called Atlanta, Denver, and Raleigh. So we got trap-and-trace orders to obtain incoming call information from all three dial-ins. This was done with the help of an Assistant United States Attorney in San Francisco.

Q: How long was this carried out, and what did you obtain from the trap and trace?

A: About 4 to 5 days. The only trap and trace that was completed was the Raleigh one. We learned that the Raleigh phone switch had been having problems, which explained why the intruder had gone through Denver and Atlanta to log sessions.

Q: How do you know that you didn't just miss some logins from the other sites?

A: Netcom's system was configured to log all accesses.

Commentary: On cross-examination, Gross may fairly be asked how he knows that Netcom's system was (1) administered correctly—that is, did the systems administrator test on configuration to determine that the logging of accesses worked as expected?—and (2) adequately secured—that is, how does he know that someone didn't access the log files and selectively erase entries?

Q: So, what was the link that led you from Netcom to Raleigh, as opposed to the other two sites?

A: We were trying to get data from all three sources. We had no preconceived notions of where the intruder would be, but it just worked out that the only good trap resulted from Raleigh. If anything, we thought the intruder might have been in Denver based on rumors floating around. It was fortuitous because as it turned out, all the calls coming into the Raleigh switch were local. We were thus more inclined to believe the intruder was physically there.

Commentary: On cross-examination, Gross may need to be prepared to explain himself here. Had he and Shimomura decided that Mitnick was the intruder? How else could they have heard "rumors floating around" about him perhaps being in Denver? Isn't this a case of throwing a dart and then drawing a bull's-eye around it? Seriously, there appears to be nothing in the logins or evidence collected up to this point in the testimony to suggest that the intruder might be Mitnick. The problem is that the narrative thread that has been presented about the investigation and capture of the hacker can be twisted during a clever cross-examination by suggesting that both the experts and the law enforcement agents knew who they were after all the time—Kevin Mitnick. The suggestion would be that they sought Mitnick, not the perpetrator of the original intrusions targeting Shimomura's system. This could conceivably create some confusion in the minds of some jurors. The expert witness needs to carefully explain the causal steps here or risk unwittingly creating the suggestion of too much coincidence in selecting the right taps and so forth. Coincidence that leads to the solution does happen, as it apparently did here, but it needs to be care-

fully explained in the context of the overall logic and discipline of the expert investi-
gation. Some jurors will naturally try to read more significance into a coincidence
than they will into the methods used to take advantage of the opportunity that pre-
sented itself in the form of coincidence. The expert needs to be prepared to show that
coincidence is merely that and should not be confused with causation in the analysis
of the evidence.

Q: What did you do at the Raleigh site?

A: The FBI contacted the local carrier that controlled the Raleigh phone switch
and got a trap and trace on that site.

Q: What happened at that point?

A: We obtained access to the log records at the Southern Bell/Raleigh POP and
engaged in pattern matching, just as we had done at The Well. We took
Netcom's log of accesses coming from the Raleigh phone switch, which were
connected to the accesses we were looking at using the "joeblow" user name
as the source, and extracted the time, date, and duration data. Then we compared this to the outgoing log records for Raleigh and found matching times,
dates and durations . . . all associated with the same user name, "joeblow."

Q: Once again, couldn't that have been a coincidence, or someone forging or
spoofing the user name and trying to make it look like the activity was coming from one source?

A: Just like we did at Netcom, we had packet data from "joeblow" that showed
the user to be using files at The Well, logging into compromised sites, and
engaging in similar activity that helped us tie this account from Netcom to
The Well.

Q: At this point, I understand that you were certain from the monitoring you
had done that you were dealing with "joeblow." Then, did you have to repeat
the process of running a trap and trace at the Raleigh switch to get the location where the intruder was dialing from?

A: Yes, but we also had realized by then that the Raleigh switch had been hacked.

Q: Explain what you mean by hacking the phone switch in Raleigh and how you
were able to come to this conclusion.

A: When I say a "hacked" telephone switch, I mean a switch, which is a kind of
computer, whose configuration files have been modified to create an indirect
route to the intended number by rolling over a series of unrelated numbers.
Thus, the real telephone number the intruder is dialing from is not evident. We
knew this when we dialed the number produced by the trap and trace and could
hear subtle clicking noises on the other end. You learn to detect this from listening to lots of phone traffic over the years. In other words, the trap and trace

was working alright, but because of the hack done on the telephone switch, it revealed a wrong number. The actual telephone entity on the other end when we checked it out turned out to be some fax number for a doctor's office.

Commentary: *Gross needs to resolve a conflict here. He and his colleagues were trusting access logs from this telephone switch, even as they knew that the switch had been hacked. Did this switch being hacked also compromise the veracity of the trap-and-trace results? An independent expert might have a hard time attesting to the level of trust one should place in a system one knows has been hacked. So, in a real trial, the attorney and expert might decide to address this issue beyond the brief treatment our simulation gives to this important issue.*

In preparing for testimony, the more the expert can help the attorney recognize potential cross-examination weaknesses, the easier it will be for the attorney to organize the direct examination to anticipate and deal with these potential problems in advance. Notice how the prosecutor in the simulation is asking leading questions in the following exchange. Leading questions will usually be allowed by the court if they establish basic, foundational facts for additional testimony, or simply repeat a previous answer in order to make the questioning flow more quickly in the long run. However, if the attorney persists in leading the witness, opposing counsel will almost surely raise an objection . Worse yet, the judge may raise the issue from the bench and then chide the attorney for leading the witness. Such an interchange can damage the credibility of the attorney and the witness in the eyes of the jury.

Q: So, if I am following your testimony, at that point in your trace, your only lead was a bogus number. Were you concerned at that point that the intruder had effectively steered you off the trail?

A: No. . . . Since we knew that the phone switch recorded all incoming and outgoing calls, we pattern-matched the date, time, and duration information of outgoing call logs to the logs for incoming calls to determine the location of those calls.

Q: Didn't the hacked phone switch cast doubt on the authenticity of the location you traced?

A: It did in terms of the actual number that we got back, but we were able to look at data more closely. By that I mean that we could go to the phone switch itself and get the location of the number that was being used.

Q: Could you have traced back to the previous phone switch by some other method, like tracking each rolled-over number until you got to the source in each instance?

A: Yes, but that would require other tools, techniques, and resources to go after each number along the chain. This would have taken a lot longer. Also, we could have waited until the actual call was being made and had a technician trace it back. But, yes, we had other options to get behind the efforts of the intruder to disguise his path and his identity. In this case, the intruder's behavior was repetitive, as determined from several weeks' worth of monitoring at The Well and several days of monitoring at Netcom. In that sense, we were forewarned of his probable behavior patterns and prepared for further sessions to occur.

Q: From your pattern matching at the phone switch, what were you able to determine?

A: The calls were all coming from the same location. We determined that the calls were coming from another phone switch in the local area, which turned out to be a cellular phone switch.

Q: How did you determine that it was a cellular switch as opposed to the hacked land-line switch, and how did it affect your next steps?

A: The number configuration told us it was a cell switch. The numbers led us to a switch within a mobile telephone switching office, which is a central location that coordinates all the cells in a cellular phone system. Essentially, we just compared the incoming and outgoing calls from the call detail records with Netcom's login records and found matching dates, times, and durations, as well as ESNs, cell sites, and sectors.

Q: Is the ESN, cell site, and sector information analogous to getting the originating phone number in a traditional phone system?

A: Not exactly. But that information allows tracking of the ESN to establish a pretty narrow search area. The ESN is the electronic serial number that is programmed into each phone unit. It is used with the MIN, or mobile identification number, which is assigned by the carrier, to identify and track the phone. In order for a call to be made, the switching office has to verify that the ESN and MIN correspond. Also, the cell sites that make up a cellular system cover defined areas that can range from 3 to 5 miles across. So, we could determine roughly from this information where the calls were being made from. Since the cell and sector numbers were constant, we inferred that the calls were coming from a fixed source.

Q: Since the calls were ultimately connected, does that mean that switching office validated the ESN and MIN against a subscriber database? Could you use the subscriber information records to obtain the address of the intruder?

A: That would be the most obvious course of action, but we were pretty confident that the phone's registered user would not be the actual intruder. Based on the intruder's past evasive actions and attempts to conceal his identity, we had good reason to believe that we were dealing with a cloned phone. This means that the intruder's phone was probably reprogrammed to duplicate the MIN and ESN of a legitimate subscriber. In order to get subscriber information, we would have needed to get a subpoena. However, we didn't necessarily need the specific subscriber data in order to confirm or deny whether this was a viable lead to follow. For example, the phone switch technician can be used as a sort of "oracle" to provide generic information, like whether or not the registered owner lived in the vicinity. In this way we were able to conclude that we didn't need to pursue the subscriber data and get a subpoena.

Q: Does the fact that you suspected you were dealing with a cloned phone have any bearing on tracing the location of the call?

A: Not really. Since the call data records provided us with the cell site, sector location, and ESN, we could electronically track the intruder to a pretty narrow search area. However, the intruder had switched cellular carriers within a day or so of our determining his location.

Commentary: At times, the value of including certain testimony must be balanced against the possibility or risk that opposing counsel will explore so many possibilities for a set of events that the fact finder will lose sight of why an expert did what he or she did.

By introducing the factors associated with cloned phones, Gross opens the door to a plethora of alternative explanations of the events. For example, the defense attorney could say on cross, "It is common for folks who clone cell phones to clone multiple phones and then switch phones periodically. Is it possible that the person you observed hacking The Well accounts could have switched off to another cloned phone and escaped?"

Again, the possibility of this sort of digression on cross-examination needs to be factored in as part of the witness's preparation, even when it is not included on direct examination.

Q: How did you determine that the intruder had switched cellular carriers, and did that effectively curtail your trace-back activities?

A: We were able to determine this because we were continuing to observe his logins as "joeblow" at Netcom, but there was no activity at the cellular phone switch. Since there are two cellular providers per market area, we knew to check the records at Carrier B. Consequently, we compared time, date, and duration information from Netcom's logs to the Call Detail Record (CDR) at Carrier B. These matched, so we knew we hadn't lost him.

Q: But since the Mobile Identification Number (MIN), Electronic Send Number (ESN), and cell information gave only a 3 to 5 mile range within which he was located, how did you pinpoint the location?

A: We used a technique called "triangulation." We waited until the intruder was online, and then we drove around the area. Since we knew what frequency the call was on, we could lock on with radio direction-finding equipment to measure signal strength and get a specific location.

Q: If the intruder was calling from the same origin, regardless of what cell carrier he used, if you had the location information from Carrier A, why did you need to even trace the Carrier B call?

A: We wanted to catch the intruder when he was online, and since the activity had ceased through Carrier A, we needed the information from Carrier B for tracking purposes.

Q: So, after you had this information, what did you do?

A: We continued monitoring sessions as they occurred and passed on this information to FBI officers so they could draft a warrant. When the warrant was served on the location, we pretty much caught the intruder red-handed: the cell phone used to make the calls had his fingerprints, the cell phone was cloned with the Number Assignment Module (NAM) [the cell phone hardware programmed with the phone's identification numbers and codes] that was last used to dial into the systems, and the laptop contained data from the various sites he had compromised, for example.

Q: Would you mind just briefly sketching the chronological progression of your tracking activities?

A: I'll do my best, but please realize that this is merely an illustration, not a demonstration, of laboratory tests conducted to show that computer crime investigations run more quickly when their Internet-tracing capability is turned on.

Q: Could you identify the evidentiary exhibits of some of the logs and transaction records that have been marked for identification?

Commentary: At this point, Gross would continue his testimony, aided by charts, tables, and other graphic displays devised to help jurors understand the technical issues involved.

Visualizing Gross's Technical Testimony

We selected the Mitnick case for inclusion in this book because the story is well known. A great deal of information has been recorded about the incident and the technologies that were used both to commit the crime and to track down the perpetrator. However, it's important to understand that when you're offering expert testimony, especially when the fact finders are not themselves technology experts, the story is only the beginning. Showing is as important as telling, and you should be prepared to illustrate his testimony with some basic graphics.

As mentioned before, we worked with Gross and Kenneally to develop the training example of the direct examination of the government's expert. Kenneally also developed some basic exhibits intended to show the key events in the trace-back performed by the investigators together with an abbreviated time line to orient the fact finder to the different techniques used and how they were related over time.

Demonstrative and Substantive Graphic Evidence

Two exhibits were developed, each serving different functions, within the context of this simulated technical litigation. The common goal for these graphic exhibits is to tie the digital act (be it electronic communication or transaction) to an individual wrongdoer by way of an evidentiary trail linking his digital identity (user account) to an IP address bound to a physical node.

In the physical world, when a crime is committed, there is often a transfer of evidence linking the perpetrator to the crime scene. For example, a murderer will almost always leave trace evidence (blood, fibers, or fingerprints) at the scene of a bludgeoning because the event has taken place on a physical level. This trace evidence can then be compared to known exemplars from the suspect (DNA or threads from a shirt in the suspect's closet, for example) to identify the culprit or rule out suspects.

However, crimes committed over electronic networks create a new forensic playing field, where contact transfer does not occur in the same way that traditional forensic sciences have come to expect. Hence traditional forensic scientists have developed techniques that are not likely to suffice when collecting, preserving, and analyzing electronic evidence. Indeed, evidence linking the suspect to the crime may exist, but proving that Jane Doe was typing the commands that caused the buffer overflow that shut down Yippee.com at a given point in time involves reconstructing a chain of digital contacts, which may or may not still be available to detect and collect. Any weakness in that chain may invite reasonable doubt in a criminal case.

The following graphics designed to support Gross's simulated testimony help create a conceptual linkage between the physical evidence that can still be found (or captured in real time) and the digital actions (or the electronic traces of those actions) and consequences.

1. *Chart.* The purpose of Table 3-1 is to help organize and verbally illustrate the theory underlying the Mitnick investigation. It is a case analysis methodology that can be used by both the attorney and expert in "telling the story" of how and why this expert was able to conclude that Mitnick was the person who intruded into the victim's computer and committed various other offenses. Although particular methodologies used in IT investigations may certainly

Table 3-1. Chart Graphic for Outlining Events in the Mitnick Investigation[a]

	The Well	Netcom	Raleigh	Cell Switch
TARGET/ASSET VALUE	• **Data warehouse/ archive:** Compromised accounts used to – Store credit card numbers – Store hacker tools – Store stolen e-mail – Store Tsutomu's files • **Self-preservation:** Allowed concealing of identity when attack launched elsewhere	• Conduit point to access The Well (loged in to Netcom as legitimate user and used Telnet to The Well) • Platform from which to launch other attacks	• Conduit point to access Netcom, etc. • Evasion platform (hackable phone switch) • Free local and long distance calls	• Conduit point to access Netcom, etc. • Evasion platform • Free calls
PATTERN	• **Historical tampering activities:** – Missing data – Altered logs (for data and locations) – Extraction of tools to use for attacking other sites – Addition of data to repositories in files – Cleansing of log files after each session	• Logged in as normal user and used Telnet to other victims/ compromised sites	• Call patterns repetitive • Social engineering attempts to get passwords and phone numbers to phone switches • Used hacked phone switch	• Call patterns repetitive • Used alternate cellular switch

(continues)

Table 3-1. Chart Graphic for Outlining Events in the Mitnick Investigation[a] *(continued)*

	The Well	Netcom	Raleigh	Cell Switch
EVALUATION	**Who:** Reasonable assumption that one person/small group made the attacks. (No overlapping sessions; observed definite interest in certain person's e-mail, news and info. about Kevin Mitnick.) **Where from:** Netcom (most recent and frequent calls traced there) **When:** Definite patterns of activity (consistent active times) **Where to:** Surmised that intruder was actively attacking other sites, but The Well was not used to direct attacks	**Who:** Same person who compromised The Well. ("joeblow" and "dono" log activities match.) **Where from:** Three POPs (most recently and most frequently used to dial in) **When:** Definite periods of activity **Where to:** – The Well – Other compromised machines	**Who:** More certain just one intruder. (No overlapping sessions; "joeblow" activity matched call data records for one particular cell phone.) **Where from:** Cell switch with serial number **When:** Definite periods of activity **Where to:** – Netcom – Other ISPs – Other hotline numbers	**Who:** Same person in local calling area **Where from:** Transmitter location within several miles **When:** Definite periods of activity **Where to:** – Raleigh POP – Other dial-ins
FORENSICS		• Trap-and-trace records (got Raleigh IP address; obtained via warrant and probable cause) • Data packets (sniffed "joeblow" sessions) • Sys logs showing last logins at Netcom • Contact info. from PortMaster informing what ports were used	• Trap-and-trace records (got cell switch number) • Call data records (used to pattern-match time/date/duration with Netcom's login logs)	• Cloned phone records • Call data records at Cell 1 (used to pattern-match with Netcom's logins) • Call data records at Cell 2 • Data packets travelling to Netcom

a. Table adapted with permission of Erin Kenneally.

vary, this particular case lends itself to the development of graphics that work to break down the potentially confusing and disparate events in a complex investigation by focusing on the targets of the hacking, the pattern of activity at each target, the forensic evaluation carried out at each target, and the potential evidence gleaned during each step of the process. Although the more detailed, wordy chart would lend itself to pretrial preparation for both the attorney and expert, a stripped-down version of the chart highlighting key points may be applicable in the trial phase during the expert's testimony or when cross-examining an opposing witness. The strength of this type of graphic is that it brings order to a series of events and allows you to align the fact finders to your theory more easily. By framing facts, evidence, and testimony in this way, you paint a cohesive and logical picture in the minds of the fact finders.

2. *Basic flow drawing*. A rudimentary line drawing can also be used with charts like Table 3-1 to help the fact finder conceptualize the linking process that is so vital to your case. It may lend itself to the expert testimony in the form of a real-time illustration on a drawing board. In addition to contextualizing the expert's testimony, the flow drawing also offers a respite from what can be dry, lifeless testimony. Jurors may be more inclined to follow the story if the expert is allowed to sketch the trail as he or she presents the basis for testimony. Further, this may reinforce the impression that the expert was organized and methodical in his or her approach, rather than haphazardly following any number of digital trails.

The static simulation diagram shown in Figure 3-1 (pages 77–78) attempts to paint a physical recreation of the link between the defendant, a physical node, an IP address, an account and user name, the various conduits through which the criminal activity took place, and the initial and related computer crimes. This graphic would also work well during closing arguments, when the attorney wants to leave an indelible reminder of his or her theory of the case in the minds of the fact finder. The diagram wraps up the case in a tight package and links the digital and physical acts and consequences. Further, it places the theory of the case in the realm of the knowable and reasonable, which may empower the fact finders to connect with the expert and may forestall defense attempts to have the jurors believe that any number of possible pictures can be painted. It is designed to be used in conjunction with the bulleted outline that follows.

The exhibits presented in this chapter were prepared to be used for demonstrative purposes. If the Mitnick case had gone to trial, something like them would have been used in conjunction with the foregoing testimony to give the judge and jurors a road map of the expert testimony. At the conclusion of his testimony, Gross would have initialed the chart and action flow diagram and offered them as evidence—a summary of the complex set of records and documents that formed the foundation of his testimony and his various opinions. Both the flow diagram and the charts would have been used during the testimony and hopefully taken with the jury to deliberations to enable them to conclude as did the experts that there is proof beyond a reasonable doubt as to the criminal acts and as to the identity of the perpetrator.

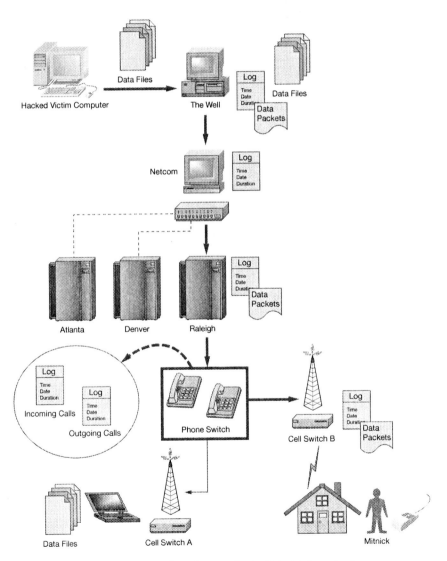

Figure 3-1. *Action flow diagram for the Mitnick investigation.*
(Reprinted with permission of Erin Kenneally.) (continues on page 78)

The Well
- This was a key site where Tsutomu's files from the December break-in were found in the hacked "dono" account.
- Examined log files, compromised accounts.
- Configured sniffers to catch incoming logins from IP addresses at Netcom; monitored these packets.
- Pattern-matched incoming Netcom logs from The Well to login logs.

Netcom
- Attempted to tie criminal activity at The Well to a specific account at Netcom.
- Determined that the account being used to access the Netcom system was "joeblow."
- Because of the large size of this network, ran a shell script to catch all logins from "joeblow," which alerted us when the user of that account logged on.
- Needed to monitor sessions to try and link "joeblow" to "dono" at The Well, so configured sniffers to catch packets from the IP addresses associated with "joeblow."

Trap and Trace
- System administrator at Netcom logged into terminal server of the "joeblow" IP address and got port number being used.
- This was necessary because there were 23 ports per machine; we needed a specific one in order to get packet data and trap and trace the dial-in number.
- Since there were multiple sessions from "joeblow" from multiple locations (ATL, DEN, RAL), got trap-and-trace orders to obtain incoming call information from all three dial-ins.

Raleigh POP
- Fortuitous that the only complete trap was RAL.
- FBI contacted local carrier which controlled the RAL phone switch and got trap-and-trace order for that line.
- Pattern-matched Raleigh POP dial-in logs to Netcom's incoming logs and got matching time, date, duration information for user name "joeblow."
- Packet data from "joeblow" showed user accessing files at The Well and engaging in same activities that tied the account from Netcom to The Well.

Hacked RAL Phone Switch
- Real telephone number from which intruder was dialing was concealed via hacked phone switch (trap-and-trace number was not the number from which intruder called).
- Pattern-matched date, time, and duration of outgoing and incoming call logs to get location of call.

Cell Phone Switch
- Compared call data records with Netcom logs and found matching dates, times, durations, ESNs, cell sites, and sectors.
- Intruder switched cellular systems.
- Checked call data records at Cell Switch 2 and compared outgoing log information to the incoming log information at the land-line switch.
- Continued to monitor sessions and observed same types of sessions (access to Netcom, The Well, compromised accounts).

The Roundup
- Passed information to FBI. Drafted warrant. Triangulated call.
- Caught intruder red-handed: cell phone with fingerprints, cloned phone, laptop with previous session displayed, and so on.

Figure 3-1. *Action flow diagram for the Mitnick investigation.*
(Reprinted with permission of Erin Kenneally.) (continued from page 77)

Seeking Professional Graphics Assistance

To better illustrate how the visualization of this sort of complex case can change the way experts and attorneys think about organizing the testimony and integrating more visual information in the presentation, we asked Christopher Ritter of the courtroom graphics firm The Focal Point, LLP, in Oakland, California, to sit down with us, as if for an initial brainstorming session for a real case, and to apply the skills of his organization to the illustration of Gross's scripted testimony. Ritter is an experienced litigator, and he will have much more to say about using graphic images to enhance technical expert testimony in Chapter 10.

When we first presented Ritter with Gross's testimony, he had no other information about the case. His initial approach was to determine how extensively we wanted The Focal Point to delve into the structure of the story that had been scripted and whether we simply wanted to consider how to improve on the graphics that Kenneally had already prepared or to create a new series of visual exhibits that would tackle one or two possible problems in comprehending the complexity of the investigation and the technical tools and techniques applied by Gross and Shimomura.

Choosing the Focus for Visual Aids

We first discussed the possibility of taking the existing exhibits to additional levels of exposition and recreating these or a number of other images to show more detail about where the investigation started and what information the investigators had then. Tracing back the clues uncovered over time, we considered individual images and link diagrams, as well as what might go into a final image that would show the investigators' final evidence and conclusions. Additional images could be created to illustrate why the investigators took the steps they did.

Professional groups that specialize in consulting on the presentation of complex trials are prepared to do a full-scale review for the entire trial. Here, we were interested only in improving the testimony of the key expert witness, so we asked Ritter to limit his analysis to what would clarify for a lay judge or jurors the points being made in the scripted direct examination.

Considering Which Elements to Emphasize

The next step was to discuss what things needed to be stressed and to sketch out the kinds of exhibits that might be helpful in focusing on these perceived needs for visual support.

Ritter first raised the possibility that the primary reason for this expert's testimony was to demonstrate as both a fact witness and as an expert why the defendant must have been responsible for the intrusion. Now this will certainly not always be the job of the expert witness. As recent challenges to the reliability of traditional fingerprint identification methods and theories make clear, experts who stick their necks out beyond the comfort of the demonstrable uses of the scientific method are likely to have the credibility and significance of their opinions cut back by the court. The fact that "scientific method" has been redefined in a line of recent Supreme Court cases (that will be discussed in some detail later in the book) represents an additional challenge to even the best-qualified expert witness, who may find the court's definition to be conservative.

It just so happens that in this case the investigation did lead inexorably to the defendant, who at least had the stolen data that came from the original intrusion into Shimomura's computer network. But to explain how that was possible and why the results are so conclusive requires visual aids because of the complexity of some of the techniques that led to the discovery of the essential links in the investigation. So, the issue for visualization becomes the following: How can the witness show the jury that, out of the entire universe of millions of Internet users, this particular defendant is involved in the illegal intrusion of a computer system and the possession and distribution of stolen data?

Going Back to the Basics in a Network-Based Plotline

Considering the scripted testimony without any outlines or other graphic aids, you can see how even the clearest narrative of an expert's investigation of an intrusion could create obstacles to understanding for computer-phobic jurors or those who begin with only a vague picture of how computer systems and the Internet work. It could conceivably be an even bigger conceptual problem for jurors who have some knowledge about how computers and computer networks work if some of their ideas or preconceptions are mistaken. So the first issues are these:

- How can we illustrate what the Internet is really like?
- How it is possible to identify who did what on a particular date?

The task for the expert and the graphic designer is to come up with a big picture or a series of images (or both) that make it easy for jurors who have little or no computer knowledge to follow the steps of this complex investigation and to see the logic of moving from the computer break-in back through those many digressions and progressions until arriving at the keyboard of the defendant at the end of the chase.

Let's now consider the other possibility—that at least some of the jurors will have considerable faith in computers and the abilities of software engineers and computer programmers to solve computer and real-world problems by creating computer programs. Considering such jurors, we are likely to think of completely different kinds of images to help them understand the testimony. Assuming that some jurors will be sophisticated and receptive to detailed explanations, then perhaps some visuals should be created that take advantage of this. In particular, such visuals would use the jurors' belief that computers and computer experts do understand how to make systems work, how to discover what went wrong when they don't work, and how to detect when someone disrupts their normal operation. Ritter reported in our discussion that he finds many jurors accept other technologies at face value, and some exhibits need to appeal to that sort of juror. Meanwhile, without offending or boring those jurors, you must also go the extra mile to explain these same technologies to the Luddites and technophobic members of the panel.

Combining these different sets of needs associated with different fact finders, your overall goal must be to create enough information for both audiences. If you are successful in this goal, the jurors can walk away concluding that, while they do not fully understand the details of everything the expert witness testified to, they can see that what he or she did was based on experience and expertise and that he or she used a logical approach to solve the problems. In order to accomplish this goal, the expert needs to identify a target audience for his or her presentation, a "middle ground" defined as the juror who is neither ignorant of nor in awe of the technologies.

Using Familiar Analogies to Describe What Computer Experts Do

In general, when these middle-ground jurors are presented with a new problem, they can and do apply their common sense to understand it. Furthermore, they understand from their own life experiences that for most problems, some basic techniques will produce the desired solutions. Following this line of reasoning, more complex problems may require more sophisticated tools and techniques. If you know how to contact the people who have those specialized tools and techniques and the person you call uses them correctly in order to solve your problem (such as a plumbing or electrical problem), you are inclined to trust that person the next time you need help. We all need plumbers and electricians from time to time, and we tend to return to the service providers who have helped us in the past. In recent years, we have also come to recognize that we need computer experts and reliable network service providers when we have a problem at home or at work. Some of the visual aids used to support expert witness testimony may need to indicate the expert's experience with the tools and techniques about which he or she is testifying.

In the example of the fictional Mitnick trial, you want the jury to believe that Gross has the experience and qualifications to perform the operations he did during the investigation. Once that fact is established, it is also important to assure the fact finders that the methods used were used fairly and properly and did not cut any unnecessary ethical or scientific corners. Neglecting to address those points might allow the opposing counsel to cast doubt on the credibility of the witness or the techniques used in the investigation. Creating visuals that bolster this sort of assurance requires a great deal of sophistication. However, you must provide this assurance, realizing that some jurors will worry about such issues, especially when they are having trouble understanding the fundamental steps and the overall logic of the technical process about which the expert is testifying.

Remembering the Real Goal of Expert Testimony

When the trial team and the expert are brainstorming about visual aids and how to best integrate them into the expert's testimony, it is best to assume that the technicalities of what actually took place are simply too complex to describe in detail. This is true for even the brightest of judges and jurors. This is the real reason that expert witnesses are allowed to testify and are, in fact, absolutely essential: so that judges and jurors can follow the logic of the case and place their trust in a trustworthy expert (in lieu of becoming experts themselves) before deciding the case one way or the other. In other words, the goal of the expert's testimony is not to turn the fact finders into sorcerer's apprentices but to lead them to rely on the expertise of the witness and his or her explanations of the events and evidence.

In the Mitnick case, visual aids can highlight some very positive aspects of Gross's testimony to keep the jurors' attention long enough to establish him as a very credible expert and to get the jurors to accept the facts and implications of everything he did in the trace-back.

Ritter read Gross's scripted testimony as a classic case of cat and mouse. Jurors can relate to this story line and in the process become fascinated by the kinds of tools that had to be invented along the way and how the two investigators improvised with their tools and techniques to keep the search going. Technical jargon is always a problem that the attorney and expert alike must address. This can be dealt with through a combination of careful use of language by the attorney and the expert and interesting visuals to depict what key terms used in the testimony mean and how they are being used. At the same time, words and phrases like "configured sniffers" and "trap and trace" are intriguing; the attorney and the expert can use them to keep the jurors' interest in the search by stopping to discuss each term as it comes up and illustrating how it fits into the story line. Sometimes these new terms need to be considered an opportunity for visualization, rather than handicaps of unnecessary jargon.

Here is an example from another kind of search or surveillance case that The Focal Point worked on that makes the following point: what may be routine to the technical expert can be fascinating to a lay juror who is trying to follow the story. Ritter was involved in a case in which the FBI conducted a lengthy surveillance of a suspect. Many law enforcement agents will gladly tell you that 99 percent of this work is excruciatingly boring. They will also tell you that they do it a lot. However, to the jurors, who have never done it, even the boring act of surveillance becomes interesting as an integral part of the story they are hearing. In the case in question, the jurors indicated that they wanted to know how the agents could sit there for hours on end and still remain awake and alert enough to make the observations they did. In a way this is also a credibility check on the witnesses, who needs to satisfy the fact finders that they were awake and alert so as to see what was going on when the action took place. In particular, the jurors needed to know and wanted to know how the agents relieved themselves during the surveillance.

The trick became using these instances when the jurors were listening to something they could identify with to introduce some of the basic technicalities associated with the surveillance and to reassure the jurors that the agents followed standard operating procedures at all times in both the mundane details of their surveillance and the highly technical things they also had to do. By analogy, in many of the processes that Gross described in his testimony, the work was in fact boring, but it had to be meticulously carried out and recorded in order to get to the next step in the trace. So one of the opportunities in this testimony is to focus on how Gross kept track of all the mind-numbing routines that he needed to conduct in order to find the data that led him to the next step in the trace-back chain. With the right visual aids, this otherwise boring activity can become an opportunity to spark interest in the fact finders and to insert some additional information about the technology while the fact finders are becoming more interested in and conversant with how the witness could continue to concentrate on all of these routines and activities over time.

Selecting the Visual Components of the Story Line

Once the story line is developed, there needs to be some analogy to show the jurors that the process that the story describes really works. Given the complexity of the search, the simpler the analogy, the better. While selecting the pictures for the depiction of the steps in the story, you should keep in mind that specific characteristics of an investigation make it reliable to almost all qualified experts. Building these indices of reliability into the methods used by the expert will only enhance the credibility of the witness and his or her testimony and encourage the jurors to have confidence in the logic of the presentation.

For example, for the Mitnick investigation, if it can be said that it was essential to obtain the data while the hacker was online, then the logic of going to the trouble of setting up alarms so that the intruder can be observed in action while he is actually online not only makes sense but also leads logically to the next step in the trace. This allows Gross to explain a little bit more about the technologies and the techniques applied to this case and should also serve to bridge over to the details of how all these applications work to allow the expert to monitor the behavior he is looking for. While describing the criteria for reliability of the results of the search, the expert can show that he did comply with each and every one of these criteria and is therefore highly confident of the trustworthiness of his results.

Finally, in our initial brainstorming session with Ritter, we attempted to anticipate how the defense would challenge Gross or his evidence and the case as a whole and to prepare explanations and graphics that show the jurors why this challenge is ineffective or misleading. For example, we could have created a visual aid that addressed the defense's challenge that the investigating team had violated the ECPA due to allegedly excessive government involvement with the private investigators when they were acting as agents of the Internet service providers in order to monitor the activities of the hacker in the systems. If this or some other area is going to be of concern at trial or at pretrial motions, exhibits showing the exact nature of the challenged activities should be prepared to assist the expert.

For the purposes of this demonstration, we imagined the flowchart created by Kenneally presented on a large exhibit board to enable the expert and in turn the jurors to easily trace the path of the search and to connect with other visual aids in order to annotate each step visually. Ideally, with the court's consent, this board would be left up during the entire testimony. Magnetic arrows or other indicators could tie the master chart to the other visual aides for purposes of annotation, and Gross could use them during the course of his testimony. Basically, the expert could move to and from the chart and handle individual visuals at the stand. The markers would enable the jury to keep in mind "where they were" at any particular time during the testimony. Depending on the budget and the preferences of the expert and the trial team, the flowchart could be coordinated with more detailed graphics that break down each step in the investigation. These additional visuals could be displayed electronically on computer screens in front of the jury in courtrooms that are equipped for such presentations.

Showing and Telling Is Better Than Just Telling

Hopefully the transcript of simulated testimony for a criminal trial (and the comments for the opposing counsel) have given you a sense of the interactions between the attorney and the technical expert witness. The explanation of the steps that Shimomura and Gross went through in their trace-back of an intruder may still be a bit of a challenge for the most technophobic of jurors and judges to assimilate. However, as evidenced by the popularity of press and literary accounts of the tale of Mitnick's pursuit and apprehension, the process that the investigators went through in order to isolate the source of the attacks is of interest to many. Our approach, in addition to careful preparation for direct examination and the anticipation of all the imagined problems in preparing for cross-examination, is to construct simple and honest graphics to allow the expert and the attorney and then the jurors to put it all together as the elements are presented through the testimony of the witness.

Understanding the Rules of the Game

After reading through the deposition testimony of Bill Gates and the hypothetical direct examination of Andrew Gross, a techie might initially assume that the demands of forensic duties are relatively trivial when compared to the rigors of actually applying the scientific method in the research, development, and integration of new technologies. After all, an expert witness is only required to show up in court, wear nice clothes, take an oath, politely answer a few questions about technology from a non-technologist, and leave, right? Well, it's actually a bit more complicated than that. In considering the complexities of this activity, especially if one has never thought about it before, it helps to consider some analogies.

Serving as an expert witness can be reasonably compared to other creative business and social relationships:

- Learning to speak a new language in preparation for traveling abroad
- Trying out for an athletic team as a specialty player
- Applying for a new job that involves a number of challenging new technical functions and responsibilities
- Learning to play in an orchestra or a jazz ensemble
- Becoming friends with someone you respect as an accomplished individual but whose professional background is totally different from your own

As you make your way through this book, you will find other analogies to the art of testifying as an expert. For all of these analogical activities and roles there are plenty of guidebooks outlining how to acquire basic skills and how to develop practice routines and more advanced skill sets. Still other manuals suggest strategies for success in auditions and how to practice and play with partners and teams. Some of these guides may prove just as helpful as this book, especially when you have developed an avocation or activity with a passionate commitment to excelling.

Unfortunately, few such guides tell the beginning technical expert witness how to prepare for giving testimony about IT issues. On the other hand, many books attempt to prepare trial lawyers to hire and work effectively with expert witnesses. There are also a growing number of books for the general expert witness that consider what lawyers are being told (and what they are telling each other) about initiating and managing professional relationships with expert witnesses. The technical expert can also learn a great deal from reviewing the expanding volume of literature in the area of general expert witness advice and instruction for some special areas of expertise, such as health care professionals, accountants, and structural engineers. Finally, a growing number of journals such as the *Journal of Forensic Science* often feature articles on testifying as an expert about IT and other technical issues.

As a first step, let's revisit the roots of our current legal system. The purpose of catching a glimpse of the origins of the advocacy system of justice in a lighthearted, if not slightly insane, dash through the history of evidence in western civilization is to clarify otherwise apparently nonsensical practices you may encounter in your service. Who better to be our guide than Monty Python?

Knights Errant as Experts

Monty Python and the Holy Grail (1975) is a hoot. The witch trial that takes place near the beginning of the film makes most experienced technical experts laugh. Initially, it may make some potential expert witnesses who have their doubts about the wisdom of getting involved as a witness wonder just how far we have come in making rules and procedures more logical and more fair to the parties that come to court today. But by the end of this book, when you have seen how far we have traveled, we think it may help to make you cringe a little less at the irrational origins of the practices of the modern jury trial.

Many experts believe that the battle of advocates staged in front of a jury has little to do with serious considerations of the finer points of science. The Monty Python production gives us a metaphor to help us to laugh at ourselves when we're tempted to stretch the scientific method and logical arguments based on sound technical chains of reasoning. Today, experts are necessary to assist parties whose fate is placed in the hands of juries instead of mobs, and experts' qualifications are considered by judges instead of foolish barons. Modern juries expect to hear from witnesses with real scientific and technical training and experience, instead of listening to an errant knight who says whatever comes into his helmeted head while he and his lackey run around the kingdom clapping coconuts together to make it sound like the knight is riding a horse. So much for his credentials as a knight let alone as an expert.

The witch trial opens with a scene of priests and penitents slamming their heads with boards as they march through their medieval town. Suddenly a mob surges in, screaming that the "witch" with them must be burned. The members of the mob are on a mission in search of authority to bless their madness, and it's clear they have determined that they need to burn this witch as quickly as possible before another townsperson is bewitched. But apparently the custom in this shire is to first obtain the approval of the local lord. We get the feeling that the lord is a bit (just a bit) off, and clearly in need of a technical expert, when we see him testing the flight capabilities of a pigeon to which he has attached a large rock. The experiment doesn't work, unless it was designed to kill the bird.

What happens next is one of the great send-ups of how scientific experts report they often feel when called on to present complicated scientific or technical evidence to a jury. At the same time, the viewer gets the idea that the degree of ignorance of the mob members and their ability to think logically is sometimes difficult to distinguish from the ignorance of those in authority over the proceedings. John Cleese, in the front row of the mob, swears loudly that the witch has turned him into a newt. When the lord raises the visor on his helmet to take a closer look, Cleese quickly has to admit that he has improved.

Other evidence that the crowd offers to the lord includes the size and shape of the witch's nose. Here the accused patiently explains to the lord that the crowd put a fake nose on her. Sure enough, the lord examines the nose and sees that it is in fact a carrot that has been strapped to her face. Forced to abandon the arguments about being turned into a newt and believing in the witch's nose, the crowd next urges the lord to declare her a witch because of the way she is dressed. The accused claims that the mob dressed her up and the crowd finally admits this is the case. Within a very short time the lord has realized that the crowd is unable to come up with any real evidence that would support the charges. But the lord does not wish to disappoint merely on the grounds of a technicality. At this point the lord takes over the production of admissible evidence and asks the crowd a series of questions to get to the bottom of things.

First, he quizzes the assembled townspeople on what they know about the general nature of witches, for example, what they are made of. This is not easy for them to think about, but they finally figure out that since witches burn, they must be made of wood. The lord commends them on their reasoning power and then asks them to think of what they could do to determine whether this particular accused might be made of wood. This is even harder for the crowd members to follow, and their answers indicate to the lord that they could use some expert advice if they are ever going to figure this out. Finally, after a few false starts in their reasoning, such as the suggestion to build a bridge out of the woman, they figure out that the thing to do is to throw her into the bog and see if she floats. Of course, this was in fact one of the ways that mobs of that period decided who was and was not guilty of a given offense.

But this enlightened lord is interested in being thoroughly scientific about the proof that the accused is or is not a witch. He calms the mob and asks what else floats besides wood and witches. This appears to have stumped the entire crowd, until Sir Arthur, presumably with the requisite expertise, confidently announces what the lord immediately accepts as the correct answer—namely, a duck. Having just completed his own unsuccessful experiments with birds tied to large rocks, this is just the kind of answer the lord wanted and one that he is confident he can test on the scales of justice. And fortunately for the lord and the mob, there is a duck at hand. Someone from the mob quickly places the accused on one side of the largest scale in the town and then puts a duck in the other weighing pan. Lo and behold, they weigh the same. Meanwhile, as the mob begins to light the fire, we hear the lord asking Sir Arthur how he became such an expert scientist. And we know the answer. He is from out of town.

Monty Python created this masterpiece of comedy long before the U.S. Supreme Court decided it was time to do something about the foolishness taking place in front of American juries in the form of equally bizarre expert testimony sometimes based on precious little more than blatant surmise. This testimony was allowed by judges who thought it was their role to simply allow each side to bring in a recognized expert and let the attorneys have at the experts in cross-examination and then argue about the merit and meaning of their respective opinions.

Many litigators will frankly tell you that, at least before the gatekeeping revolution that now requires trial judges to screen expert evidence, the real purpose of hiring experts who could corroborate the scientific and technical issues in their cases was to reduce those factors in the case to a vote by the jury on which expert they believed. Not all cases required experts, but the practical use of technical experts to attempt to eliminate the consideration of certain issues in almost every case became one of the standard operating procedures of many trial attorneys, forcing opposing counsel to come up with their own expert. This is not to say that there was anything wrong with this practice, assuming that both sides went along with the ritual of producing legitimate experts to testify about important issues that had just never been raised through expert testimony before. The problem was that after a while, these practices acquired an undue importance and then almost a life of their own, tempting experts to take on the role of advocates rather than objective witnesses whose job it is to explain things that the jury could not otherwise easily understand.

The witch trial shows us how the lord of the manor, acting as both a prosecutor and a judge, is quite willing to use Sir Arthur's expertise to invade the province of the jury and essentially tell the mob what to think and decide. All that is missing here is to have another expert attempt to explain to the incensed mob members that their reasoning is defective. (That expert would probably end up on the pyre too.) In *Monty Python and the Holy Grail*, the fact that the judge endorses the expert's opinion is enough for the jury. After the demonstration that the accused weighs the same as a duck, they are off to burn the witch.

For those who wish to see the jury come to the right conclusion for the right scientific or technical reasons, a few things bear remembering as we discuss some of the basic rules of the game. These are developed in more detail in later chapters (we include an entire chapter on the use of visual aids and another on the use of nonverbal communication strategies), but briefly considering some of those things here is worthwhile.

There are a few simple keys to thinking about communicating effectively with a modern jury, which is after all a group of people with their own lives and interests. Foremost among these strategies is to remember that at any given time, one or more members of the jury may not be paying all that much attention to what is going on in the courtroom. This can be hard for accomplished experts to accept, but in a lengthy trial this is certain to be the case at one time or another for all the jurors. This is not to say that the jurors aren't extremely interested in the case and in doing a good job as jurors but simply to point out the obvious—our minds often wander, and we simply get tired from time to time during an eight-hour day, no matter what jobs we are doing. That said, it is a wise expert who develops different tools and techniques to interest different types of jurors in following the testimony. We also recognize that minds can wander while reading, and for some an occasional image is helpful to maintain overall focus on the material being presented through the text—which brings us to a cartoon.

Why Does Everyone Love to Hate Lawyers?

The law has always provided artists and social critics with ample material for satire (Figure 4-1). If lawyers and the courts have always been so hated and made the butt of so many bad jokes, why do we still use them to engineer settlements of our most important disputes and conflicts? And why do we also rely on their abilities to structure agreements and undertakings to avoid legal problems in the first place?

Figure 4-1. *An all too typical view of the legal establishment.*
NON SEQUITUR © 1993 & © 2001 Wiley Miller. Dist. By UNIVERSAL PRESS SYNDICATE.
Reprinted with permission. All rights reserved.

The popularity of material lampooning the perceived foibles of the legal profession has spanned many centuries, involving many well-known denizens of the literary and artistic ranks. For instance, Charles Dickens provided a comprehensive critique of the advocacy system of justice in England during the 18th century, and William Hogarth provided extremely popular cartoons depicting its many failings during the same period.

> *The one great principle of the English Law is to make business for itself. There is no other principle distinctly, certainly, and consistently maintained through all its narrow turnings. Viewed by this light it becomes a coherent scheme, and not the monstrous maze the laity are apt to think it.*[1]

Trial by Combat

Lawyer jokes and cynical assessments of the legal system abound throughout recorded history, and a brief sprint through time may help to frame a discussion about expert witnesses. Though far from perfect, the legal system's current method of deciding important controversies through the process of requiring opposing parties to present their evidence and submit to the judgment of a judge or jury is actually far more civilized than the original competition from which it evolved. Trials in the Middle Ages involved actual physical combat between the accused and the accusers or between their champions, who were chosen to represent the interests of the parties. These trials often culminated in ritualized murder. Other forms of trial by compurgation[2] and ritual demonstrations of the will of God gradually gave way to the current process of presenting testimony from witnesses with knowledge of the facts and other forms of tangible and documentary evidence to be examined and considered by the jury or judge. As Charles Rembar has written, the western path has been slow but steady toward more humane exercises of authority.

> *It will upset some readers to hear that human beings have in the last one thousand years improved. But the graph of Western history shows a clear if crooked line— weaving, wayward, but in its main path undeniable—of morality ascending. Whether the line will reach high enough fast enough to save us from destruction is another matter. So is whether one should be disgusted by its current level. But we have come a long way from those centuries when most men of Christendom were slaves, and not just knighthood but intellectuals of the time, the churchmen, found ecstasy in massacre. . . .*[3]

---

1. Dickens, Charles. *Bleak House*. Oxford: Oxford University Press, 1998, p. 573.

2. Compurgation was an early common law method of trial in which the defendant was acquitted on the sworn endorsement of a specified number of friends or neighbors.

3. Rembar, Charles. *The Law of the Land, the Evolution of Our Legal System*. New York: Simon and Schuster, 1980, p. 30.

Eventually, jurors were selected who were supposed to be unbiased between the parties and otherwise competent to consider and decide the case based solely on the admissible evidence and the credibility that they gave to the witnesses called to testify. The *civil law* tradition that developed on the European continent relied primarily on a professional magistrate to conduct an independent investigation into the facts and to frame the issues for decision. The *common law* tradition that evolved in England and the United States depended far more on the opposing parties to frame the issues and select the witnesses to advance their respective cases before the judge and jury. The philosophy behind this common law advocacy system of justice was that the best chance for the jury to determine the facts was to allow the two sides to compete and to present different points of view and conflicting evidence in the ritual of the trial. The original trial by combat or ordeal has been replaced by trial by competing advocates. However, the basic philosophy of managing the trial from the bench to enable both sides to strike all the fair blows they can muster remains.

Evidence and the Advent of Testimony

Modern cartoons, television dramas, movies, novels, and articles are more likely to lampoon the advocacy system with sporting analogies, disaster scenes, exposures of corruption within the system, and gambling metaphors. These artistic devices are used to make fun of the techniques that admittedly don't make much sense when removed from their historical context and from the continuous evolution of more effective and equitable advocacy rules of engagement in modern litigation. Nevertheless, these oft maligned techniques of advocacy need to become second nature to technical witnesses if experts are to be effective in their own roles. A basic understanding of the historical roots of the current legal system of advocacy should enable the expert to appreciate some of the reasons for the continuing commitment of the legal system to allow the parties to frame and argue about the issues litigated before a jury. The crucial consequence of that choice is that all the parties are also entitled to discover all the evidence they can, and to present it as they see fit, by calling all the relevant and competent witnesses they can find to testify at trial.

Judges are empowered to protect the jury from the most outrageous and misleading tactics of legal advocates or their witnesses and even to throw out cases that are without an adequate factual or legal basis. In cases that involve complex technical issues or require the discovery of a great deal of evidence, including electronic or digital evidence, judges ordinarily allow the parties in civil litigation to frame the issues and conduct discovery without much interference. Today, in nearly every case in which technical issues are involved, both sides enlist experts before and after the complaint is filed to assist them in the discovery and proof stages of litigation. In complex criminal cases, the prosecution may take months or even years to assemble its evidence before filing any charges. Again, judges seldom intervene in that investigation process but are empowered to dismiss part or all of a criminal complaint or indictment once charges have been brought and the defense has challenged the legal or factual basis of the charges in pretrial litigation.

The procedural and evidentiary rules that evolved to filter out or admit physical evidence and testimony arose in part out of a fear that jurors might be prejudiced or unduly swayed by certain forms of evidence. The strict limitation on the ability of ordinary witnesses to give their opinions about the matters in controversy were put in place to prevent witnesses from influencing the jury merely because of their status or rhetorical abilities when they lacked relevant and material evidence about the facts of the case. These rules also were developed to give judges some discretion in the admission of blatantly false or totally unreliable evidence and to exclude obviously fraudulent witnesses.

New methods of proof also had to overcome a strong bias in society (and to some extent in the law) in favor of the use of torture to extract evidence. Ironically, torture was considered a significant advance over trials by combat, ordeal, or compurgation. These practices became most notorious during the inquisitions and political criminal trials that occurred throughout the Middle Ages and lasted well into the Renaissance. Based on modern depictions of courtroom dramas in novels and movies, individuals who have never prepared for or given testimony as an expert in a deposition or at trial may worry about more modern tortures such as invasive background investigations and humiliating cross-examination tactics!

It should be clear as we proceed to the present that throughout the evolution of the western common law legal tradition, and in western society at large, the tradition of resolving important, contested matters through the communication ritual of what has come to be known as formal testimony has long been recognized as a reliable method of proof. Testimony both outside the courtroom and within the litigation ritual of a jury trial is still framed by rituals that have changed little over the centuries, such as giving an oath in order to add to the solemnity and significance of the testimony and the trial.

Experts Replace Bishops and Knights as Key Witnesses

Ordinarily, witnesses in a trial are allowed to testify only about what they have personally perceived through one or more of their senses or about what they themselves have done or said. The basic rules of evidence are similar in all the states and in the federal courts. Those basic rules are set out in Appendix C, and this would be a good time to read through the Federal Rules of Evidence, especially Rules 701–706, which have to do with expert witnesses. Over time, the law decided to allow certain categories of witnesses to testify about more than just their actions and sense perceptions. As the complexity of American culture, its systems and its artifacts steadily increased, the law gradually recognized the need for specialized experts to explain these things to juries.

Experts are defined by the rules as those individuals who have applied themselves to understanding a specialized body of knowledge or who have developed techniques that would be difficult for a lay juror or judge to comprehend without the assistance of the expert. The expert provides this assistance to the fact finder by offering testimony to the court.

Unfortunately, as with many other good ideas about making science available to laypeople, by the end of the 1980s the consensus was that some lawyers had abused this exception to the general rule that prevented ordinary witnesses from giving their opinions about matters before the court. These lawyers called as expert witnesses people whose experience and knowledge did not really qualify them as experts. Some attorneys called witnesses to venture opinions based on false or flawed methods and techniques, in an attempt to help persuade judges and jurors of the merit of the theories of one side of a legal dispute, or to contradict the testimony of lay witnesses. The peculiar nature of litigation in the United States and other common law countries is a test of strength between opponents (which depends, to some extent, on the clever performance and occasional cunning of counsel). This is quite different from the ideal of the civil law system of other countries that features an open inquest or investigation by an impartial magistrate who selects what evidence to consider and which witnesses to see and hear.

The *Daubert* Line—Corrections in Course

The abuse of expert testimony was addressed in three decisions by the U.S. Supreme Court in the 1990s. These three decisions set out and clarified guidelines for federal judges to use in determining whether and when a particular witness should be allowed to testify as an expert. We are hard pressed to come up with another instance in the history of American jurisprudence of any single issue being selected three separate times for consideration and opinion by the Supreme Court in just a seven-year period. By any reckoning, this is a lot of action by the nation's highest court on a single issue in a relatively short amount of time.

The first decision, *Daubert v. Merrell Dow Pharmaceuticals, Inc.*, established the "gatekeeper" function for judges, in which the judge is empowered and charged with determining whether a given expert is allowed to testify in a given case. It established criteria for use by the judge when determining an expert's qualifications.

The second decision, *Kumho Tire Co., Ltd., et al. v. Carmichael et al.*, made it clear that the gatekeeper duties were required not only in cases where the expert opinion pertained to scientific methods but also in cases where technical expertise was involved. (In particular, this covers situations in which the expert renders an opinion based primarily on years of training and experience in the domain in question, which is not within the traditional sciences.) This effectively extended the reach of the *Daubert* gatekeeping functions to most of the world of IT expertise.

The third decision, *General Electric Company et al. v. Joiner et al.*, emphasizes that the discretion of the judge in making gatekeeper decisions is almost unlimited. It makes it very difficult for appellate courts to overturn the decision of a trial judge to exclude or admit expert testimony based on the gatekeeping criteria endorsed by those decisions.

Following these three opinions, all federal court and many state court judges have been bound by this line of cases and the tests for admitting expert testimony. Furthermore, judges in federal jurisdictions and in states that have adopted similar tests are now required to act as gatekeepers and to apply flexible standards in proactively determining whether to allow an expert witness to offer testimony in a given case. Any technical expert who considers assisting the court in understanding a technical issue should review these cases and the standards that have evolved in the courts in which he or she may be testifying. These decisions are set out in full in Appendix B and are also considered in greater detail in Chapter 8, which further explains the modern gatekeeping function of the courts.

The Rules of Engagement

When the opportunity arises to become an expert witness in a legal matter, you, as the technical expert, may quite naturally approach the role using time-tested, problem-solving processes you're accustomed to applying to technical tasks involving information systems. The first step in such a process might be, "Find the documentation for the system and read it."

Federal Rules

The documentation for the conduct of legal proceedings in the United States starts with the Federal Rules of Procedure in tandem with the Federal Rules of Evidence. Here is the first rule from the Rules of Evidence that the prospective expert witness needs to read and understand.

> ### Rule 702. Testimony by Experts
> *If scientific, technical, or other specialized knowledge will assist the trier of fact to understand the evidence or to determine a fact in issue, a witness qualified as an expert by knowledge, skill, experience, training, or education, may testify thereto in the form of an opinion or otherwise, if (1) the testimony is based upon sufficient facts or data, (2) the testimony is the product of reliable principles and methods, and (3) the witness has applied the principles and methods reliably to the facts of the case.*[4]

The Rules of Procedure outline the process followed in court for resolving legal disputes. There are two sets of Federal Rules of Procedure, one covering civil trials and

---

4. Federal Rules of Evidence. U.S. Government Printing Office, 2001, p. 13.
Available at *http://www.house.gov/judiciary/evid2001.pdf*.

another covering criminal trials. There are also local rules for each federal district, some of which apply to expert testimony. Step by step, the rules lay out the time line for trials and include scheduling and management of discovery and litigation. The Rules of Evidence document what things the combatants in a legal contest may legitimately provide the fact finder in order to support their claims.

The Rules of Procedure and Rules of Evidence are available from a plethora of sources, both in textual and digital form. Appendix C contains sections of some of the Rules that pertain to expert witnesses, the evidence they provide to the fact finder, and the procedures they must take into consideration while performing their duties.

State and Local Rules

It is important to note that although the Federal Rules of Procedure and Evidence are most often cited in court opinions and law review articles, much of the court duty an expert witness performs may occur in state and local courts or outside the courtroom proper in arbitration or public fact-finding hearings. This book focuses primarily on courtroom testimony. However, the skills discussed here are also important in those other contexts where sworn or formal oral testimony is taken. Improvement in those skills needed to testify effectively in court should hold you in good stead in those other forums as well. Each of these courtroom, arbitration, or formal hearing systems may have its own rules of procedure and evidence, which may add features to the legal terrain you need to consider when crafting and delivering your testimony. Always consult as early as possible with the attorney with whom you are working about the rules that apply in the relevant jurisdiction.

The Roles of an Expert Witness

Another fact associated with expert witness service is that there are several capacities in which a technical expert may serve the legal system. Many neophytes believe that the service they will be called to give is limited to stating their opinions on a technical matter in testimony before the court. They may believe that walking in, taking an oath, taking the stand, answering questions, and then leaving is basically all that's involved.

While this might suffice as a rough map for the stages of expert witnessing, the actual landscape of the legal process is, of course, much richer and more complex than this. The roles that a technical expert may be asked to take on in the course of litigation vary as well.

It's important to realize the diversity of expert roles and furthermore where to draw the boundaries between these roles since the behavioral constraints associated with different roles for experts vary according to the roles they serve. Remember, these constraints are defined by the rules of procedure and evidence alluded to above as well as court decisions clarifying those rules. This means that it is critical that you clearly understand from the outset of the expert witness assignment what role or roles you are to play and the kinds of conditions that may cause those clearly delineated roles to change during the course of the engagement. The case of *W. R. Grace & Co. v. Zotos International, Inc.*, which we discuss later in this chapter, outlines some of the serious problems that can occur when experts are called on to play multiple roles. Such assumption of multiple roles when the expert or the lawyer fails to consider all the complications such role shifting can create during the case can do real damage to the reputation of the expert or the lawyer who must practice another day before that judge or in that jurisdiction.

As with all of the reported cases discussed in this book, understand that we and the publishers are not criticizing any of the parties, attorneys, or witnesses in these cases we discuss. Our intention is to document the cases and resultant opinions of the courts in order that other expert witnesses might learn from them. It is also important for you to understand that the performances of the actors involved in these cases should not be harshly judged. Remember that published and reported judicial opinions and the issues decided in them can be overruled at any time, and different courts can reasonably rule in different ways on very similar issues.

The Consulting Expert

The first role a technical expert can assume in a legal action is that of a consultant or advisor. In this capacity, the expert provides a combination of training, review of existing technology, advice on strategy, assessment of the competition's expert and strategy going into court, and any number of other technology-related tasks. The technical expert may be treated as a member of the legal team. In this capacity, the expert is allowed (but as we shall see, not necessarily encouraged) to be an advocate on behalf of the client and to advise the attorney and other members of the legal team on strategic and tactical matters. These matters may extend well beyond the objective determination of the technical or scientific issues involved in the case. For technical experts who are accustomed to working with consulting clients, this is pretty much business as usual in that clients ask questions and request technical functions, and the expert responds with information, explanations, and advice. Consultants as well as those who function as experts in corporate environments will also find the presumption of confidentiality of communications between them and the rest of the legal team both familiar and comfortable.

The Court's Expert

A special case of the consulting expert that is becoming more common in modern cases involving information technology is that of a court's appointed or stipulated expert. In this role, the expert serves in a consultant capacity but performs his or her technical consulting for the court itself. This is especially valuable to judges presiding over major cases that involve complicated technical issues in which the competing parties and their respective experts present wildly divergent views. This situation is more common than you might imagine, especially in cases involving nascent technologies. An independent expert who understands the arguments posed by both sides and can explain the strengths and weaknesses of both arguments to the fact finder is of obvious value.

One example of a case in which a court's stipulated expert played a major role is a case in which Predictive Systems, a computer security consulting firm, was hired by the court to conduct a review of the security of the Bureau of Indian Affairs (BIA) network that housed the trust accounts for Native American trust beneficiaries. This particular example was more complex an arrangement than normal. In most cases, an expert is hired directly by the court to advise about some technical issue in the case. In the BIA situation, the court appointed a court monitor to advise the judge about a number of aspects of the Department of Interior's fiduciary duties as trustee for the billions of dollars in royalties and other forms of payment collected by the Department to be held in trust for Native American beneficiaries. One of the problem areas in the course of this lengthy lawsuit was the quality of the network security that the Department had installed to comply with earlier court orders mandating improvement in the state of computer security. In order to report to the court about the state of that security, the court monitor hired security experts at Predictive Systems to test the security of the systems that were in place at the Department and the BIA. That report had an enormous impact on the judge, who ordered the Department to disconnect the trust fund computer systems from the Internet until it could prove that its network security problems had been corrected. In complying with the judge's order, the Department disconnected all of its computer systems from the Internet, including its Web servers, thus extending the impact of the report to the day-to-day operation of the Department itself. Such cases serve as reminders that experts and the reports they submit to the court can have broad-ranging effects on both litigation and matters far beyond the scope of the lawsuits themselves.

The Testifying Expert

The third role that a technical expert can assume is the one most technologists think of first when the topic of serving as an expert witness comes up. As a testifying expert, the raw technical functions may be similar to those of a consulting expert (that is, training, explanations, analysis, opinions about technical issues in which the expert has some depth of knowledge), but the constraints are considerably different. As we discuss in more detail later in the book, there is an implicit ethical responsibility (enforced by the judicial gatekeeper function) for the testifying expert to be scrupulously impartial and objective.

Furthermore, as part of the provisions of the Rules of Evidence, there is no presumption of privilege that applies to most of the communications between the attorney and the testifying expert. That means that any communication, electronic or physical, is probably not confidential and hence subject to discovery by the opposing legal team. This adds a whole new dimension to the mind-set of a technical expert since it requires the expert to alter his or her work patterns in order to serve the needs of both the fact finder and the client.

The Expert as a Witness to Fact

A role that many technical experts will likely be asked to assume at some point in their careers is that of a witness to fact. In this capacity, the expert is asked to testify as a "normal" non-expert witness. This means that the expert is only expected to testify to events he or she personally experienced (that is, saw, heard, or felt), actions he or she took, or things he or she said. In this case, the expert's technical mastery of certain areas is not the central feature of testimony.

However, the understanding that the fact witness is also an expert in one or more areas is also bound to bias the fact finder's judgment of the credibility and demeanor of the witness as the testimony develops on direct examination and on cross-examination. You've already seen an example of this in Bill Gates's testimony in the Microsoft antitrust trial (Chapter 2). Although not called as an expert, Gates is undeniably an expert and perhaps, as to some of the issues that he testified about, he was the most expert of any witness who could be called. As such, he was presumably capable of answering in great detail a number of questions about the technical features of the products being discussed and other related matters. The fact that he chose not to play the role of knowledgeable and helpful expert apparently served only to convince the judge that his testimony was less trustworthy than it might have been had he chosen to display his expertise in his answers to the government's questions.

This kind of choice is obviously guided by counsel when you are in Gates's position of being CEO of a major corporation and therefore subject to having the other side claim that anything you testified about is admissible as an admission against a party's legal interests. Assuming that you are not in the role of a party or an agent of the party to the litigation, or otherwise responsible in some way for the actions of a party or potential party to litigation, the fact that you are still an expert is something to keep in mind any time you are called to testify, presumptively as a factual witness. There is no formula for guaranteeing effectiveness in this situation, but as Gates's testimony indicates, the expertise of witnesses accompanies them to the stand, whether they are formally qualified and offered to testify as experts or not.

The different hats an expert may wear can confuse the fact finder and in turn lead to some adverse conclusions as to why the witness is behaving the way he or she is.

When everybody knows the witness knows more than he or she is willing to testify about, reluctance by a witness to explain items such as the clear meaning of documents prepared by the witness begins to appear much less like a strategy to limit the damage on cross-examination and more like an attempt to frustrate the presentation of evidence to the fact finder. And the judge or the jurors may resent this.

As a witness you may feel that you cannot afford to go into areas in which you are clearly expert, for fear of putting yourself and thereby your company or the party paying your witness fee in harm's way. You may perceive that by opening yourself up to an even more searching cross-examination on two fronts (as was the case for Gates, the personification of the corporate party and at the same time a qualified expert in the subject matter), you would be treading on quicksand. This is especially difficult when you are subpoenaed and are not a party or even potentially a party to the dispute and therefore not represented by counsel. So what should you do? This may be the time to seek a second opinion from independent counsel who specialize in these kinds of potential conflicts. But it may also help to become more skilled as a witness, by doing some extra reading on what the courts have had to say about these kinds of situations in prior cases. This research may be of benefit to you regardless of whether you're called as a normal fact witness with an obvious and relevant expertise or as an expert for a fee.

On the Importance of Keeping Roles Straight

Now that you know there are at least four distinct roles a witness with expertise can play in litigation, you may wonder, "What difference does this make to me?" Again, the ground rules of the legal domain elevate this otherwise arcane point to some importance. As in the undertaking of other potentially conflicting roles, the price paid for failing to acknowledge and deal with their different requirements created by the law can be harsh. These conflicts can even jeopardize a favorable outcome for the client on whose behalf the expert is testifying. The following case alludes to the importance the law invests in the separation between testifying and consulting expert roles.

When Consulting Experts Are Asked to Testify

In the case *W. R. Grace & Co. v. Zotos International Inc.*, a dispute arose over the question of exactly which role a technical expert working with the defense was playing at different times in the lawsuit. At issue in the portions of the case you are about to read is whether a legal provision, called the *attorney work product doctrine*, is applicable when a consulting expert becomes a testifying expert in midstream and the attorneys attempt to protect the work product that applies to the consulting functions the expert performed.

The doctrine provides that the work product generated by an attorney and his or her team while preparing to present a case to the court is covered by the attorney/client privilege. This means that it is not subject to discovery as evidence by the opposing legal team. Generally, the materials created by a consulting expert who is not going to testify are privileged, that is, protected from discovery. This expectation of protection from discovery can change when the expert takes on conflicting roles. When the consulting witness is called to the stand, the fact finder needs certain information to do his or her job. In particular, the fact finder requires access to any evidence needed to evaluate the witness for bias and interest. The court first discusses the rule of procedure that applies.

The following excerpts from the opinion in this case will give you a feeling for the way courts create opinions. The judge authoring the opinion carefully constructs the arguments of the opinion, using constant references to controlling rules and prior case decisions as construction elements. Be forewarned, however, that unless you're particularly interested in the difference between the status of a consulting expert and that of a testifying expert witness, excessive exposure to the legal style found in this and most opinions is an excellent antidote to insomnia. So unless you are prepared to spend the time and energy to get the feel of how these opinions actually appear in the reports of these cases, this may be one of the sections of the book to return to when you are especially motivated to pursue the topic. With that in mind, here are excerpts from the opinion by one court concerning the issues raised when the boundaries between the roles of consulting and testifying experts become blurred.

> *First, as noted, while the 1993 amendment to Rule 26 regarding disclosure of information considered by a testifying expert in preparing his report does not, in terms, refer to Fed. R. Civ. P. 26(b)(3), the federal codification of the attorney work product doctrine, the broad scope of permissible disclosure as stated in the amended Rule 26(a)(2)(B) together with the Advisory Committee statement that the amendment's purpose is to require disclosure irrespective of "privileges" and "other" possible sources of protection from disclosure, render additional legislative guidance on the issue unnecessary.*
>
> *Second, the distinction established by Rule 26 between experts retained to testify, Fed. R. Civ. P. 26(b)(4)(A), thereby subjecting the experts to mandatory disclosure and deposition at the request of an opposing party, and those retained to provide technical assistance in the case, Fed. R. Civ. P. 26 (b)(4)(B), which limits discovery as to such experts, negates any notion that testifying experts can be considered a member of a party's "team." Indeed, even experts hired solely to provide assistance in anticipation of litigation or in preparation for trial are subject to discovery of "facts known or opinions held," permitted under Fed. R. Civ. P. 35(b), or upon a showing of "exceptional circumstances."*
>
> *Third, although consultation with counsel may assist an expert in achieving "clarity in the preparation of the required written report," such communications,*

including the attorney's mental impressions and legal theories, may nevertheless influence the expert's consideration of the issues in matters of substance as well as form. As one court has stated in regard to testifying experts, "the trier of fact has a right to know who is testifying." Intermedics, Inc. v. Ventritex, Inc., 139 F.R.D. 384, 396 (N.D.Cal. 1991) (construing pre-1993 Rule 26 to permit discovery of work product information provided to testifying expert).

Thus, there is no reason to exclude from disclosure attorney communications submitted to testifying experts, who the jury may believe carry a degree of independence, on the basis such experts are part of the defense "team" and that the communications may promote "clarity."

The availability of cross-examination at trial to thoroughly probe the basis and process of reasoning underlying an expert's opinion as stated in his report is not an adequate substitute for pretrial disclosure and evaluation of the specific information received by the expert from an attorney. Such discovery enables counsel, both through deposition of an expert and later cross-examination at trial, to expose risks of non-objectivity resulting from receiving attorney comments by an expert in the course of formulating his opinion. Preventing access to such information, even if constituting "core" work product, therefore impedes informed consideration of the case and proper evaluation of any expert's report included in summary judgment motions, for purposes of settlement and, ultimately, at trial. The court now turns to a review of the disputed materials.[5]

The passage from the court decision in this matter discusses certain tenets we've already mentioned. In particular, it covers the rationale for the attorney work product doctrine and the differentiation between a testifying expert and a consulting expert. Furthermore, it lays out some of the assumptions the court made and that other fact finders may make in future cases about the degree of independence associated with each of those expert roles.

Now back to the decision, as the court discusses the issues raised by the existence or nonexistence of prior drafts of the expert's reports and comments of counsel about them.

The materials provided for in camera review include copies of Barber's draft reports transmitted to Defendant's attorneys via facsimile, on September 28 and 30, 1999, together with Barber's request for the attorneys' comments. On each page of the type-written texts appear handwritten notations, presumably written by one of Defendant's attorneys to whom the drafts were sent for review and comments. Defendant states that only the notes of counsel on the September 30, 1999 draft report were communicated to Barber. Defendant's Memorandum at 20. Defendant

---

5. *W. R. Grace & Co. v. Zotos International, Inc.* 2000 U.S. Dist. LEXIS 18096, West Law 1843258. U.S. District Court for the Western District of New York, Case Number 98 Civil 8385(F). Decided on November 2, 2000.

also represents that three documents, constituting redrafts of Barber's draft reports, were transmitted from defense counsel to Barber, . . . thereby implying they were prepared by counsel to assist Barber in formulating his final report.

The court's review of the documents shows that although some of the revisions suggested and as redrafted by counsel appear to represent matters of form, others are plainly directed to matters of substance. For example, in the September 30th draft report, the section of the document addressing selection of remedial alternatives was then blank with an "In progress" notation only. However, in the September 30th and October 1st drafts, transmitted from Defendant's attorneys to Barber, the section includes two full paragraphs of text discussing the draft's conclusion that the remedy selected by Plaintiff was not consistent with the National Contingency Plan. Thus, the exchange of documents between counsel and Barber raises an issue of the extent to which Barber's final report represents Barber's own product or that of Defendant's attorneys.

This question cannot be evaluated by Plaintiff without disclosure of the earlier drafts prepared by Barber and forwarded to Defendant's counsel for review. As those drafts are, according to Barber, no longer available, the September 28th and 30th drafts, prepared by Barber and transmitted to defense counsel, shall be provided to Plaintiff. However, based on Defendant's representation, which the court accepts, that counsel's handwritten notes which appear on the drafts were not transmitted to Barber, such notations may be redacted prior to disclosure.

Further, the one page undated memorandum prepared by Mr. Tyson, one of Defendant's attorneys, to Mr. Smith regarding Barber's "outline," need not be disclosed as there is no indication it was transmitted to Barber for his consideration. In sum, Barber's drafts dated September 28th and 30th, 1999, in redacted form, along with the September 30th and the two October 1st draft reports prepared by Defendant's attorneys that were e-mailed to Barber for his review, shall be provided to Plaintiff.[6]

You may note that the decision to allow opposing plaintiff counsel to access the expert's (Barber's) notes and draft reports could create strategic problems at trial for the defense. In particular, the fact that substantive portions of Barber's opinions appeared to the court to have changed after it was determined that they weren't consistent with the defense's objectives could be argued by opposing counsel to suggest that Barber has less independence than counsel would urge the fact finder to accept in a testifying expert. Note that there is nothing wrong in general with changing one's opinions or reports, so long as these are disclosed. The key point is that they usually needn't even be disclosed so long as the expert is limited to serving as a consultant.

The court continues to discuss issues raised by the expert's diary entries.

A review of the documents submitted as copies of Barber's "dairy" [sic] entries in connection with his work on this case shows that they were made over the period

---

6. *W. R. Grace & Co. v. Zotos International, Inc.*

September 9, 1999 through November 17, 1999. Defendant states that it has pro-
duced a copy of the notes made by Barber prior to October 1, 1999 as relevant to the
basis for his opinions expressed in his final report dated October 1, 1999. As to entries
made after that date, Defendant states they represent information exempt from dis-
covery except pursuant to Fed. R. Civ. P. 26 (b)(4)(B) as Barber also served as a con-
sultant expert to Defendant in assisting Defendant in preparation for trial including
evaluation of Plaintiff's expert's report. . . .

Upon reviewing the documents, the court finds the Barber diary entries for the
pre-October 1, 1999 period represent statements of facts and information considered
by Barber in formulating his opinions in this matter, and as such shall be produced
to Plaintiff in unredacted form to the extent not previously provided. As to entries
after October 1, 1999, the court finds that except for one entry made on October 22,
1999, the information is related to Barber's evaluation of Plaintiff's expert's report
and deposition testimony, and accordingly, is not discoverable. However, the text of
that entry beginning with the phrase "For deposition" and ending with the phrase
"concentrations of hazardous substances (metals)" should be disclosed. Although
written during the time frame when Barber was serving primarily as an expert con-
sultant, the court finds the entry is directed to an issue then expected to arise in con-
nection with Barber's deposition testimony regarding the conclusions stated in his
report. Therefore, the court finds such information is relevant to Barber's formula-
tion of his opinions for purposes of discovery, and should be disclosed.[7]

This section deals with the blending of roles between consulting and testifying
experts. The expert, Barber, apparently kept a diary of his observations and thoughts
about the site he was asked to evaluate. The court asserts here that what matters is the
actual function Barber served, not his official label at the time, asserting that those
things that he did as an expert (that is, those things that affected his testimony as an
expert witness) should be discoverable, and those things he did that were confined to
his role as an expert consultant to the defense should not. So "time bracketing" of
expert roles is not always recognized by the court as a legitimate means of defining
roles and privileges.

The court continues to discuss the memoranda from Barber to the defendant's
attorneys made after October 1, 1999.

Plaintiff contends that because Barber was retained as both a testifying expert and
to assist Defendant in preparing for trial, the blending of these roles is to be construed
against Defendant thus rendering all of Barber's communications with Defendant's
attorneys after filing of his report on October 1, 1999, discoverable under Defendant's
obligation to supplement. . . . Defendant argues that an inspection of the disputed
documents demonstrates they were prepared solely to assist defense counsel in
preparing to depose Plaintiff's expert and are therefore immune from disclosure as
work product.

---

7. *W. R. Grace & Co. v. Zotos International, Inc.*

Documents which have "no relation to the expert's role as a [testifying] expert need not be produced but . . . any ambiguity as to the role played by the expert when reviewing or generating documents should be resolved in favor of the party seeking discovery." B.C.F. Oil Refining, Inc., supra, at 62 (directing disclosure of documents where it was "not clear" whether reviewed by expert solely in capacity of consultant or "whether they informed his expert opinion as well."); Grace A. Detwiler v. Offenbecher, 124 F.R.D. 545 (S.D.N.Y. 1989) (no disclosure required of documents reviewed by expert for purpose of preparing questions of prospective trial witness, however, stating that documents reviewed by expert in role as consultant and later reviewed in capacity as testifying expert are discoverable); Beverage Marketing Corporation v. Ogilvy & Mather Direct Response, Inc., 563 F. Supp. 1013, 1014 (S.D.N.Y. 1983) (noting possibility that expert retained to testify and to assist attorney "outside of the subject of his testimony" may obtain attorney work product protection as to latter function "if delineation were clearly made.").[8]

In cases where these conflicts are unavoidable (for example, courts in different jurisdictions with different case precedents that appear to control the resolution of these discovery battles and dictate different outcomes for very similar factual predicates), the expert must seek the updated advice of trial counsel as to how to handle any changes in the expert assignment immediately. Beyond the issue of the need to disclose different statements or reports made by the expert in various stages of the expert assignment, the question of preserving the documents or e-mails produced or shown to the expert in the course of playing these overlapping and potentially conflicting roles can often take center stage. Usually opposing counsel will recognize that these issues are best dealt with by entering into a stipulation and agreement as to how both sides will handle the inevitable creation of materials that both sides should be able to agree will be considered privileged and therefore undiscoverable, regardless of their obligations under the rules that would otherwise control the situation. The court also had to deal with the loss or destruction of certain documents sought in discovery.

It is undisputed that, acting under instructions of Defendant's attorneys, Barber got "rid" of earlier drafts in his possession when his final report was filed on or about October 1, 1999. . . . According to Barber's deposition testimony, Defendant's counsel's instruction was given to Barber about two to three weeks prior to Barber's scheduled deposition on November 23, 1999. According to Plaintiff, disposal of the documents occurred following the filing of Barber's report on October 1, 1999 and subsequent to the scheduling of the deposition on October 28, 1999. . . . The record does not specifically reveal whether this action was accomplished by electronically deleting the applicable files on Barber's word processor or whether actual hard copy documents were physically destroyed or discarded without retaining copies. In any event, Plaintiff contends that as Barber admitted he acted at Defendant's counsel's instruction so as not

---

8. *W. R. Grace & Co. v. Zotos International, Inc.*

"to confuse things," such conduct creates an inference that the discarded material was likely detrimental to the defense, constituting a violation of Defendant's duty of disclosure pursuant to Rule 26, and requiring a sanction. . . .

In opposing Plaintiff's request for sanctions, Defendant states that Plaintiff did not formally seek any documents from Barber's file until November 16, 1999, after the date Barber estimates he disposed of the drafts. . . . While not specifically mentioning "drafts" of Barber's reports, Plaintiff's letter request for documents, dated November 16, 1999, sought "portions of [Barber's] file, including any notes or other work product." . . . Defendant also asserts that, as Barber's routine practice was to discard such draft materials, there is no basis to find that the draft reports would have remained available to Plaintiff even absent Defendant's attorney's direction to dispose of the drafts. . . . However, no affidavit from Barber supporting this statement has been submitted by Defendant and Defendant does not argue that Barber's draft reports do not come within Plaintiff's pre-deposition request for Barber's "work product."

Courts have held that drafts of reports prepared by testifying experts are subject to disclosure pursuant to Fed. R. Civ. P. 26 (a)(2)(B). See B.C.F. Oil Refining, Inc., supra, at 60 (holding any "material consulted or generated by the expert in connection with his role as an expert, must be produced."). Courts have even extended the scope of the rule to allow disclosure of drafts of reports or memoranda experts have generated as they develop the opinions they will present at trial. . . .

"Spoliation is the destruction or significant alteration of evidence, or the failure to preserve property for another's use as evidence in pending or reasonably foreseeable litigation." (Citation omitted.) Whether to impose sanctions for spoliation of discoverable evidence lies within the court's discretion. . . . Courts must consider whether the party accused of the spoliation or destruction had a duty to preserve requested documents, . . . whether the party acted willfully, negligently or in bad faith, and the degree of prejudice inflicted upon the party seeking the discovery as a result of the spoliative conduct at issue. . . .

While violation, through spoliation, of a court order directing production of discoverable evidence will support sanctions, the absence of such an order does not prevent sanctions based upon the court's inherent authority to control the litigation. . . . The sanction chosen must achieve deterrence, burden the guilty party with the risk of an incorrect determination, and attempt to place the prejudiced party in the evidentiary position it would have been in but for the spoliation. . . . An adverse inference instruction to the jury may be imposed based upon a finding of gross negligence by the party responsible for the spoliation. . . . A party found guilty of spoliation may also be directed to reconstruct evidence or be precluded from giving testimony regarding the destroyed evidence. (Citation omitted.)

Although Plaintiff's written request covering Barber's draft reports was served after Barber destroyed the drafts of his final opinion, drafts of a testifying expert's reports have long been held to be subject to discovery in preparation for a deposition of the expert. . . .

Disclosure of draft reports or other material containing a testifying expert's preliminary conclusions, . . . "can guard against the possibility of a sanitized presenta-

*tion at trial, purged of less favorable opinions expressed at an earlier date." . . . Nor
is there any basis for a contention that preliminary drafts of Barber's reports are protected from discovery under the attorney work product rule as such documents are
prepared by an expert, not a party's attorney. . . . Further, the Second Circuit has held
that when litigation is pending, parties have an obligation to preserve relevant evidence. . . . Accordingly, the court finds Defendant had a duty to preserve and maintain Barber's draft reports for possible disclosure upon Plaintiff's request.*

*The record establishes that the draft reports at issue were intentionally destroyed
at counsel's direction to avoid "confusion." Such admitted purpose supports an inference that any desire to avoid "confusion" stemmed from a possibility that disclosure
of Barber's draft reports would reveal damaging inconsistencies between the earlier
drafts and Barber's final report harmful to Defendant's position. As the Second
Circuit has stated, "it is a well-established and long-standing principle of law that a
party's intentional destruction of evidence relevant to proof of an issue at trial can
support an inference that the evidence would have been unfavorable to the party
responsible for its destruction." . . . Defendant's contention that Plaintiff's expert also
deleted earlier drafts of his report, is irrelevant as Defendant has made no motion to
compel as to these materials. In any event, Plaintiff stated that the expert's draft
reports were electronically retained and are available to Defendant.*

*While the record establishes a potential basis for the sanctions requested by
Plaintiff, the court is unable to determine the extent to which Plaintiff can demonstrate any degree of actual prejudice, a criteria necessary to determine the proper
sanction. Specifically, Plaintiff has noted, that if Barber's drafts were prepared on a
computer, there may exist a procedure by which the draft reports at issue can be
retrieved from Barber's computer's electronic storage system notwithstanding
Barber's attempted deletions. . . . Further, as the court has directed the disclosure of
Barber's draft reports contained in Defendant's attorneys' files, which were submitted to defense counsel for review prior to completion of the final version of the report,
any potential for prejudice that may result from the sanctionable destruction of the
other draft reports at issue may be ameliorated.*

*Finally, regardless of whether the deleted draft reports can be retrieved from
Barber's computer, it may also be possible to reconstruct their content insofar as they
were inconsistent with Barber's final report, through a further deposition of Barber
limited to such issue. . . . Thus, the court must reserve final decision on Plaintiff's
request for sanctions until the outcome of additional discovery directed to whether
the documents at issue may nevertheless be available or the relevant information
reconstructed, and the degree of any resultant prejudice to Plaintiff.*[9]

The role the expert fulfills colors what he or she is and is not allowed to do with
draft reports and notes. Here, the court first alludes to the "spoliation of evidence," a
serious problem that carries the risk of penalties in the form of sanctions and unhelp-
ful inferences or presumptions that the jury can make about missing evidence and the

---

9. *W. R. Grace & Co. v. Zotos International, Inc.*

methods of its disposal. Note further the court's explanation of the spoliation features the problem that the expert's role was not established and maintained from the outset; it is extremely difficult to bracket the roles an expert plays over the course of a trial in a way that allows him or her to be both consulting and testifying expert. In this case, the court stops short of levying a sanction against the client Barber was retained to serve. Every expert and his or her attorney should strive to avoid the threat of such sanctions by following careful plans and practices to avoid problems from developing during the course of the assignment.

The Complex Art of Expert Testimony

The effective interaction between a trial lawyer and the chosen expert can amount to an independent art form. Most of the available literature for this sort of collaboration is found by analogy to traditional mentor crafts and skills such as the theatrical arts, and specifically the relationship between director and actor. This literature often fails to capture the richness of the unique nature of the partnership formed by a lawyer and an expert who become engaged in litigation. The lawyer and expert often combine skills from what may appear to each to be diametrically opposed philosophies and principles of professional practice. Nevertheless, in an open give-and-take they must both suspend judgment about who is mentor at any given point and learn to teach each other. This fluid collaborative style is needed to allow both to present the clearest picture and to create the most compelling story about the true state of affairs at the crux of the case.

One metaphorical way for both participants to think about this joint venture in the beginning is for the lawyer to imagine that he or she is a recognized master, teaching a martial art to someone whose survival depends on learning how to defend himself or herself and also how to attack an opponent. This opponent is assumed to be extremely skilled and intent on harming or killing both the opposing attorney and expert participants and the party whose interests they are representing. Simultaneously, the expert must be constantly ready to reverse roles from student to master and to become engaged in teaching the substance of his or her art to the lawyer, who now takes on the role of student in order to learn those aspects of the technology or science in question that need to be communicated to the fact finder. This ability of each participant to flow through the transition from master to student and back again will result in both being capable of constructing a strong and convincing account of the facts and furthermore presenting that account to a judge or a jury.

A Game within a Game

But even this metaphor for the complexity of the professional interaction and teamwork is overly simplistic. At times the lawyer and expert must act as if they are facing mortal combat and at the same time preparing to turn this fight into a dramatic pres-entation. It is crucial that any potential expert witness who wishes to become compe-tent must first understand that in the courtroom or during a deposition, there will be moments when the skills the expert learned from the lawyer will help determine the outcome of the case. The expert, while maintaining an objective stance throughout the process, has a personal interest in the case going as well as it can since his or her rep-utation is also on the line. The result of this ritualized conflict may well depend on the ability of the expert to respond to both expected and unanticipated challenges or to perform a particular move in the heat of battle that wins a significant point or even tips the entire contest.

Similarly, the lawyer must have a kind of local knowledge of the technical concepts and facts. This specialized knowledge may only be completely intelligible through the use of the scientific methods or technical language explained in the opinions of the expert. In order to persuade the judge and jury of the point at issue at any given time in the litigation, the lawyer must be able to capture and communicate its essence to the audience when the expert is offstage. This knowledge and facility to explain technical points allows the lawyer to defeat the efforts of the opposing counsel to confuse or contradict key issues in the case and to destroy the effectiveness of the opposing expert's opinions when they are clearly off the mark.

Even as this metaphorical life-and-death battle is being fought before the jury, both the expert and the lawyer must have worked out their own elaborate and precise system of linguistic control and pacing of the testimony through exhaustive prepara-tion. While it is true that this aspect of the performance remains invisible to the jurors and to the judge, there is nothing insidious about the fact that the attorney and the expert must understand what the other is doing at all times. The use of the terms "con-trol" and "pacing" is not intended to mean any more or less than a certain comfort level that has been reached between the lawyer and the testifying expert. This process can be considered as a kind of mutual teaching and learning shared between these two participants in the perfection of a kind of special language game. The complexity that each of the participants may feel in preparing for deposition or trial may be somewhat akin to the experience of someone who is only moderately fluent in the language of a native speaker who is making an important speech while the listener is being provid-ed with an expert simultaneous translation.

The lawyer and the expert must come to understand that they will always feel a need to say more about a technical concept that is being translated by the expert for the fact finder. But this is the impossible goal of a perfect translation, and in the court-room there is practically never enough time to realize this dream. It is crucial that the expert and the lawyer come to agreement about what amount of testimony is enough to make clear the meaning that must be communicated. The truth is that any transla-tion, as Ortega y Gasset has said, always tries to say more than it can and always ends in saying too little of what is intended or too much of what we might wish to remain silent about.[10]

The expert and the lawyer (and through their successful performance, the fact finder) must become as comfortable as they can with what is being said in the context of the case that is being presented. The expert comes to understand what the case is all about in order to be clear on just why the technical testimony is important. The lawyer learns enough about the technicalities and the expert's area of competence to be able to help the expert to more effectively translate his or her expertise for the fact finder. In the final analysis, the fact finders are going to have to decide whether to trust the expert, based on what they have learned about the expert and his or her expertise and what they can comprehend about the issues addressed in the testimony. The judge and the jurors will not be able to become experts themselves. They will have to come to believe in the translation offered by the expert. A successful presentation allows the fact finders to trust in the expertise of the witness and to apply his translation of the scientific and technical concepts and findings to the issues that the fact finders must decide.

This level of comfort in conversing allows the lawyer and the expert to ensure that neither gets in the other's way or catches the other off-guard during the actual testimony. The members of the lawyer–expert team must coordinate their moves without telegraphing any of them (or revealing the essence of their strategy) to their opponents. Again, none of this teamwork should be considered to be some sort of paralinguistic programming or subconscious communication between the expert and the attorney. Nor is it meant to subvert in any way the important rules of evidence or procedure by creating some secret code or system of signaling between the lawyer and the expert. To the contrary, these rules must be followed to the letter in order to ensure the smooth and comprehensible presentation of the evidence by enabling the court, opposing counsel, and the fact finders to understand the questions put to and the answers received from the expert.

Tony Wolf, a martial arts expert who directs fight sequences for the entertainment industry, provides another example of this strange sort of ritualized cooperation under stress when presenting dramatically what is otherwise almost identical to adversarial combat. Wolf describes his role as a fight tutor and distinguishes that role from the very different tasks of a martial arts master: "actors work co-operatively, as partners, to tell a story; fighters work competitively, as opponents, in a contest."[11]

---

10. Ortega y Gasset, José. *Man and People.* New York: Norton, 1957. See especially his Chapter 11, "What People Say: Language, Toward a New Linguistics."
Discussed in Becker, A. L., *Beyond Translation: Essays toward a Modern Philology* (Ann Arbor, MI: University of Michigan Press, 1997).

11. Wolf, Tony. "Ne'er the Twain—Some Thoughts on the Martial Arts/Performing Arts Dichotomy." Accessed July 21, 2002, at *http://www.thehaca.com/essays/twain/htm.*

With the presentation of expert testimony in court, both of these levels of interaction are constantly in play. It reaches a crescendo at trial before the jury when in a very real sense the opposing counsel and experts called by the other side may attempt to destroy or seriously undermine the testimony of the expert. Recent changes in the litigation ritual have created another moment of crescendo in the pretrial skirmishes that now often determine whether a particular expert will be qualified to testify as an expert witness and whether the methods and opinions of the expert are suitably reliable for presentation to a jury. These changes have increased the salience of the need to prepare for a knock-down, drag-out fight, while at the same time ensuring that the performance will be credible and comprehensible to the fact finder. As the role of the expert has become ever more essential in technical cases, while at the same time subject to increased controversies and challenges, the dual purposes of competitive performing and conveying the truth required by the adversary system of justice must be constantly borne in mind in the combination of attorney and expert skills throughout the litigation process.

Setting the Tone for the Lawyer–Expert Relationship

Sonya Hamlin, a celebrated expert on jury behavior, includes a chapter on the handling of expert witnesses in her book for lawyers, *What Makes Juries Listen Today*.[12] In that chapter, she takes some time discussing the importance of a lawyer giving the expert his or her due. After all, Hamlin asserts, it's important that the attorney show the proper respect for the accomplishments of any expert that counsel would consider for the crucial role of explaining the technical issues in the case.

When advising lawyers how to proceed to build constructive, creative relationships with experts, Hamlin begins with the basics of how first impressions can make or break associations. According to Hamlin, small and simple things like the best place for a meeting between a trial attorney and a potential expert are well worth considering. Should it be at the attorney's office or on the expert's home turf? Or is some neutral, more social setting preferable? While Hamlin goes into what sort of food and drink should be served by the lawyer (if the first meeting is in the lawyer's office), the selection of food and drink is clearly not the primary point she is making. Nevertheless, from the perspective of a beginning expert witness, how the lawyer handles these initial ceremonies and settings can have a significant influence on the expert's decision to pursue the assignment. At times, such simple factors can be as important to the beginning expert witness as the substance of the issues or the reputation of the lawyer. This is because the care with which the lawyer handles these social

---

12. Hamlin, Sonya. *What Makes Juries Listen Today.* Little Falls, NJ: Glasser Legal Works, 1998.

amenities and the approach that the lawyer takes in getting to know the expert can speak volumes as to the experience and capabilities of the attorney. A capable attorney who is skilled in building good relationships with experts takes pains to give the expert a chance to share not only his or her expertise but also any anxieties or concerns that he or she may have about acting as an expert in general on in a particular case.[13]

Dreams and Nightmares—Take Your Pick

To be in a better position to contemplate how to go about taking on an expert witness assignment, consider the following two imaginary scenarios. Although these encapsulations are idealized extremes that would be unlikely to occur as they appear here, particular parts of these dreams probably happen to some lucky or unlucky expert witnesses almost every day.

An Expert's Dream

The expert entered the courtroom and walked down the aisle toward the witness stand. She had expected to be anxious about passing by the jury, but it relieved her to make eye contact with two or three of the jurors. She was aware that they would be watching her, sizing her up, and now that it was beginning it wasn't so bad. They were seated in two rows, and there was a computer monitor between every two jurors.

When she arrived at the witness stand, the plaintiff's attorney gestured for her to step up and be sworn in by the bailiff. She recognized the judge from the earlier motion hearing and noticed that he was looking at the computer screen on his bench. He seemed to be very relaxed. She had been impressed with his handling of the motions that the respondent's attorney had presented in his attempt to keep her from testifying several weeks ago. That seemed like a lifetime ago. There had been a furious attempt to settle the case, but it had all fallen through in the last ten days. Now the trial was underway and the expert was about to give her testimony. She knew her performance would be critical to the success of the plaintiff's case.

As she took the oath she remembered to check her breathing. She realized that she was breathing a bit too fast and that her heart was beating faster than normal. She was in good shape, and she had taught herself how to measure the movement of her diaphragm as she breathed in and out and to let go of actually counting her inhalations once she felt the rhythm return. She started to smile to herself, remembering that the attorney had told her over and over again that everything depends on the breath. As an athlete, she had been amused at his insistence that she practice breathing and speaking, but she had even agreed to see a voice coach after she became involved in the

---

13. Hamlin, *What Makes Juries Listen Today.*

case. The drills the lawyer had taught her and the advice from her voice coach had worked at the deposition and at the motion hearing, so she knew they would work now. She began to relax into her seat. She took a look at the entire jury and also at the lawyers and their client's representative. She saw the opposing experts seated in the front of the spectator section. She was about to begin her testimony.

She took a drink of water. The expert was feeling good and thought for a moment about how long she might be testifying. She reminded herself that she knew the material as well as anyone could be expected to understand it, and she had gone over her reports and the reports of all the other experts a dozen times, thinking about how they did or did not support the issues in the case. She had practiced her testimony and rehearsed with the attorney at length; she believed she could listen and answer for as long as it would take to make her points clear. She was prepared not to be frustrated with whatever tactics the respondent chose to make her testimony sound unclear or confused.

This was the moment for which she and the attorney had prepared. She understood how important it had been to prepare exhaustively, and she knew she was conditioned and prepared to communicate her expertise in the course of her examinations by the attorneys or the judge. She knew that her credibility was even more important than the demonstration of her competence. She believed that, as in most situations, her credibility would naturally become apparent during her effort to communicate her knowledge and understanding of the technical issues in the case.

She smiled to herself when she recalled the first meeting with the attorney to discuss the case and to consider whether she would become a consultant or, as it turned out, the testifying expert witness. Through most of her professional career she had little interest in how the courts functioned. During her work for the government and at the university she had heard only bad things from her peers who had gotten caught in the litigation machine. She had formed an opinion that being at the mercy of a bunch of lawyers was not a good thing. The books she had read and the movies she had seen about trials did nothing to shape that opinion in any positive way.

However, as she began to publish papers and then her book, she was asked to debate the important questions that were on the cutting edge of her field. She had enjoyed the speaker circuit and the discussions of broader social issues that these technical problems and their solutions raised. In the process, she realized that her acknowledged expertise was becoming a sought-after commodity in the legal world. She had agreed to testify before committees and to serve on panels of experts, but she had declined all inquiries about her willingness to testify as an expert in court.

When the attorney first attempted to hire her to be a consulting expert, she had been intrigued about the issues involved and for the first time had asked him for the names of other experts who had worked on cases that he had taken to trial. He had immediately e-mailed her a list of five experts, together with their vitas and contact information. He encouraged her to contact them to find out how they felt about their experiences as expert witnesses.

She contacted two of the experts, one a scientist and the other a technical expert, in areas far afield from her own expertise. Before she called them, she did a little digging and found that they were well-respected authorities in their areas of expertise. She began to make inquiries and discovered that the lawyer was considered to be one of the best trial attorneys in the state. At this stage, she still thought of trial attorneys as the hired guns, portrayed in the media and the movies as people willing to do anything to persuade judges and jurors of the righteousness of their cases. She was not quite sure whether that reputation represented an asset or a deficit. Still, it appeared that this lawyer knew what he was doing in the courtroom and that his choice of experts was first class. The expert began to think that those two things might go together.

After talking to the experts who had worked with the lawyer, she was impressed with their reports of rewarding experiences. Only one of the experts had testified at trial, and the jury was not allowed to vote because the case settled in the client's interest after the expert completed his testimony. The other case had settled before trial, again to the benefit of the attorney's client.

Based on the recommendations of these two experts and her own research and informal discussions with friends who knew trial lawyers, she decided to meet the attorney at his office. She was not prepared for the first conversation. He again quickly explained what he believed his case was about and very generally what he believed her expertise could contribute to the presentation. He told her that she was one of two or three experts on his list. He understood that she had never testified in a case that was being litigated and that she might have lots of questions. He also understood that she might need some intensive preparation for the role of expert witness if they were able to come to terms.

After some more pleasantries about the litigation process in general, he suggested that she consider being retained initially as a consulting expert. He explained that this would not obligate her to give any testimony, but that if after becoming involved in the issues in the case she decided that she could handle the job as the testifying expert, he could then disclose that fact and prepare her further for the role of witness. She had the feeling that he had already decided he wanted her to sign on as the testifying expert but that he wanted her expertise to be part of the trial team he was assembling, whether or not she decided to testify.

She asked who else he was considering and was again impressed with his other two choices. She knew them both to be competent experts and thought she had heard about a big case in which one of them had testified. The lawyer told her that he had read a number of her publications and that he had lots of questions prepared for her if she agreed to join the team. He told her that the legal team really needed her expertise to prepare discovery requests, to develop an examination strategy for the opposing experts (once they were disclosed), and to consider additional testing and analysis of the preliminary results and evidence already collected in his due diligence investigation.

That's when the interview took an unexpected turn. The lawyer asked her what she did for fun. They began talking about sports, about discipline, and about the inner game of competitive activities of all kinds. Within a week after reviewing the preliminary materials, the expert had agreed to join the team.

Contrast this view from the stand with the following, which represents a much more cynical account of an expert witness's experience in court, portrayed as a bad dream.

An Expert's Nightmare

The expert was having a horrible day. "Is there such a thing as a positive outcome when you're on the witness stand?" he idly wondered as he felt the sweat drip from his brow. Funny, it didn't seem that hot in the courtroom when he had entered a few short moments before. It seemed like he'd been on the stand an eternity, though he had not yet been sworn in by the bailiff. He found himself fidgeting and glanced up to see a jury member looking at him with an expression of concern on her face. "Geez, do I look that bad?" he wondered. "How am I going to survive when they start asking me questions?"

The expert's ordeal had started several months before when he was summoned by the county's Director of Information Systems. "We've got a problem on our hands," announced the Director. "The head of the Revenue Department has been apprehended after attempting to cash a check for $175,000 drawn on his personal bank account. They audited the county books this morning and the funds appear to have come from the county tax accounts. The police are coming over right now to collect evidence from your system. Work with them to collect the evidence and explain anything they don't understand about how the system operates."

"Great, freaking great," thought the expert when the front door opened to reveal a couple of uniformed police officers. They went through the formalities of announcing that they were investigating a theft of public assets and that they wanted assistance in locating relevant evidence on his system. As he walked into his office, the expert cursed the day he agreed to be the system and security administrator of the county's accounting servers. Once the police had given him a list of items they wished to see from the system, he logged into his administrator account and started copying files and logs to removable media and generating hard copies of access and payment logs.

He offered the media to one of the police officers, who responded, "What do you expect us to do with this?"

"I thought you might want to take the disks back to the office and review them as part of your investigation," he said.

"We don't have a system at our office that can read the disks, and even if we did, we don't know anything about what the disks can tell us. We need you to handle this for us," the officer replied.

The expert spent the next month working double-time, doing his regular job as well as assisting the police in their investigation. Because the police officers didn't understand the technology, they didn't have any idea of how to do even simple things, aside from applying chain of custody procedures to the files and printouts he generated for them. Despite these obstacles, he was able to point out log entries for account accesses and funds transfers that appeared to have been performed by the suspect. The police were able to take this evidence to the District Attorney, and he obtained an indictment from the Grand Jury.

"Oh no," thought the expert when he was summoned by the District Attorney after the indictment was handed down.

"You're going to be the County's prime expert witness in this case," declared the District Attorney. "And don't try to get out of this—it's your job as a county employee to support us, and we expect you to deliver great testimony that will win a conviction."

And so the expert found himself in court on a warm spring day, tired, nervous, and stressed from the workload associated with the investigation. To make matters even worse, he recognized the face of a prominent security expert sitting behind the defense counsel and defendant, conferring with them as his testimony proceeded. "They're going to challenge everything I say. This is going to be hell."

New Technologies and Modern Legal Disputes Require More Experts

Because of the mass adoption by American society over the last century of automotive technology, much of the legal system is dedicated at any given time to handling disputes that arise concerning the operation, maintenance, or loss of cars and trucks. Some might even suggest that our law enforcement communities at the state and local levels are primarily concerned with handling the investigation, prosecution, or informal resolution of social problems involving drivers and owners of automobiles or the persons or their property that were damaged as a result of a collision. These were the generally acknowledged priorities, at least until the drug war and the war on terrorism.

Information technology is proving to be similar in many ways to the automobile in terms of its treatment under the law. Both were extended a grace period by the legal system until they had evolved and become an established part of modern life. Thus far there have been only a few lawsuits alleging damages due to the use and abuse of information and other new technologies. When cars were first introduced, the risks were simply considered to be assumed by all who chose to use them or who placed themselves in harm's way and were injured when the automobiles or their drivers failed to act as expected. These legal grace periods allowed the new technology industries to develop without being constantly faced with liabilities for their failed products or the deviant uses of those products. This same state of grace has been one reason that software vendors were allowed to release products known to have large numbers of defects and proven to have extraordinary vulnerabilities to security failures in network environments. But this initial grace period in imposing standards of liability is fairly typical of the introduction of new technologies that are more or less rapidly adopted by society.

As society becomes increasingly dependent on these new technologies, the legal system, through legislation or through court-imposed responsibilities or both, gradually begins to assign the risks of failure or anticipated deviant uses to the various parties involved in the chain of causation and responsibility. Eventually, there is sufficient carnage that with the passage of laws and a number of court decisions that impose liability, insurance companies figure out a way to quantify the risks of liability and share those risks across an affected community of interest. The hope is that the correct apportionment of responsibility will motivate technology developers and users to improve performance and safety. This is seen by society as a means of managing the risk associated with new technologies without curtailing their benefits or their rapid advancement and proliferation. The recognition of a new technology's risk factors by society at large, or by the insurance industry in particular, marks the point in the evolution of that technology that the courts begin to experience growing levels of litigation. It is also at about this time that trial lawyers and the courts recognize the need for trained experts to explain how these technologies work (or don't work) in order to decide the growing number of cases as expeditiously and accurately as possible.

The Expert Trend

Throughout the twentieth century there was one constant trend in the litigation of cases involving new technologies—that is, the increased use of technical and scientific expert witnesses. During that period, auto mechanics, accident reconstruction specialists, engineers of all kinds, and hundreds if not thousands of other specialty technical experts were required to testify in hundreds of thousands of cases. As a result of this enormous reservoir of expert experience, a number of formal and informal rules have been developed outlining what parties involved in litigation may be allowed to do with and to expert witnesses. These rules bring some order to the expectations that those parties have with regard to the litigation of their cases. These rules—written and unwritten—also furnish some guidelines to enhance the preparation of experts who are following in the tradition of earlier experts in their chosen fields. At times these rules can be generalized to benefit experts serving in other fields that are unrelated to the traditional areas of expertise.

There are books that the expert auto mechanic can look to for edification as to the role that he or she will be assuming as an expert in this area, and of course there is always *My Cousin Vinny*. Books for experts in other fields of expertise relate to the technologies that have come to play a major role in how our society functions and therefore passed through the same stages of assimilation as the automobile. For example, health care professionals have experienced an explosive growth in the number of lawsuits that allege both human and technical failures resulting in death or injury in almost every conceivable combination of technical errors or malpractice. Construction failures have also generated a large number of experts who frequently testify about the poor construction of bridges, highways, and buildings and also about their failures or collapses. Industrial process engineers testify when accidents or catastrophes occur in those contexts. Since World War II, both the private and commercial airplane industries have needed to identify experts to testify in hundreds of cases that are litigated based on claims of technical or human failures, or both.

A Wake-Up Call for IT Professionals

The main reason for producing this book at this time is to begin to acquaint IT professionals with the fact that there will be a growth in demand for IT expert witnesses in the very near future. That is intuitively obvious to everyone connected with the litigation process who has watched the growth of this industry over the past 30 years. What may be less intuitive even to experts in this field is the distinct possibility that the number of IT experts needed to assist the legal process as expert witnesses or consultants may soon approach the total number of experts used in cases involving some aspect of automotive technologies and construction engineering combined. This is not yet being discussed much outside the legal system, but the writing is beginning to appear on the wall—and the wall of the future of forensics is pretty clearly electronic.

We continue to experience growth in the number of legal disputes brought before the court. These disputes require IT expertise to assist the courts and jurors in understanding the complex issues faced in lawsuits involving (among other things) system or software application failures. For many years there has been a growing amount of civil litigation involving intellectual property (IP) challenges. These cases involve challenges to the IP rights to both hardware and software and typically become lengthy litigation battles with a number of experts called by each side of the lawsuit. Lawyers have become known for specializing in bringing patent and copyright infringement lawsuits and in defending those actions. Thus far, this has been the main playground for IT expert witnesses. But as the cases reviewed will demonstrate, even in substantive IP cases, arguments over the discovery and destruction of electronic evidence that is relevant to the underlying lawsuits tend to take on a life of their own and require the services of additional technical expert witnesses in expensive discovery-related litigation.

Today, we are beginning to see high-stakes lawsuits that allege failures in the development, implementation, or performance of enterprise software applications for commercial use. At the end of 2001, there were a growing number of these suits in the litigation pipeline, and the total financial damages alleged were in the billions. At the same time a number of law review and legal periodical articles have discussed the concept of "downstream liability" in accidents or intentional acts of malfeasance that allegedly harm another party one or more steps removed from the actor and the immediate target or platform[14] of an attack. The premise of downstream liability is that the immediate target or platform is then used to stage an attack on a further-removed but network-connected target or innocent bystander. Liability is asserted because security flaws on the immediate target are prerequisites for the successful attack of the secondary target. Security experts are beginning to assess the likelihood of serious terrorists, rather than mere "script kiddies," attempting to take advantage of these targets of opportunities to create serious problems for individual targets and the network as a whole.

The *Real* Y2K Disaster

Even though the Y2K millennium bug did not develop into the catastrophe that the most vocal alarmists predicted, it did something else that may affect the momentum of IT progress. It alerted the entire legal profession to the potential for large numbers of claims due to the negligent design, use, and failure to repair known problems in software applications and systems. Lawyers are paid to devise new analogies from previous proven causes of action that have evolved in the legal response to earlier technological revolutions. Once attorneys see a basis for the reasonable claims of their clients for damages based on proven analogies, rest assured they will seek out the best experts they can find to help them plead and prove their cases. The defendants likewise will have little choice but to recruit experts who are willing to testify in opposition to the plaintiff's case or to defend a criminal prosecution.

Assuming that the legal system will increasingly be involved in IT-related conflicts, the questions we hope to raise are these: Just who will these experts be? Will they bother to educate themselves as to the written and unwritten rules that define the role of a technical expert in the 21st century, or will they wing it like Mona Lisa Vito was forced to do by her desperate fiancé? Will they study the professional and ethical rules of their specialized areas of technical expertise, or will they just learn by doing and hope for the best? Will they be independent and objective, or will they be pliant and conforming to the subtle and not so subtle pressures of the adversary system of justice, becoming sus-

---

14. *Platform* is used here to refer to the specific operating system or computer on which a process (for example, an attack) runs.

ceptible to the affinity interest described by Brodsky? How will they conduct themselves in their approaches to understanding the facts involved in a particular case and in their application of traditional or new methods to reach a solution to both old and new IT problems? Will they blindly accept direction from others, including lawyers, or will they come to their own objective conclusions when rendering their reports and opinions for use by counsel or in connection with testimony in court?

IT experts will play a crucial role in assisting the prosecution and defense of cases involving these technologies. The way courts decide these cases is often determined by the quality and quantity of the expert assistance that judges and juries receive from the various expert witnesses. When a critical mass of cases has been decided, there can be a spill-over effect on the industry. While the tort model attempts to contribute to better and safer products without making them unaffordable to the public or specialized users due to the risk of liability, this ideal is predicated on experts providing their consultation and testimony to get the facts and the appropriate risk factors right.

Getting these things right within the rules of the game of litigation is a challenge that the best and most highly motivated experts must be willing to accept if our system of conflict resolution is to succeed and to consistently reach the right decisions. On the other hand, like Gresham's Law,[15] if the majority of so-called IT experts are not properly trained, completely committed to being objective, and highly motivated to getting it right, poor expert contributions to the process can lead to ever poorer expert performances and wrong decisions. Poor expert performances and clearly wrong decisions may also lead to a fully warranted feeding frenzy in the media, decrying the irrational, inequitable, or inefficient resulting outcomes of the litigation process.

This could in turn lead to the unfortunate influence of inadequately informed state and federal legislators and regulators who feel obligated to do something about the problem the media is hyping. Legislation and regulation of industry under these kinds of pressures could lead to shortsighted solutions that do more harm than good. So, our argument runs, if only for the public good, it would be a very good thing indeed for IT professionals to seriously consider getting involved sooner rather than later. But even beyond a patriotic pull or the commitment to *pro bono publico* service, it is highly likely that most IT professionals will be drafted by their companies or subpoenaed by some attorney as potential witnesses. Sooner or later they will be forced to give testimony, whether they want to or not.

---

15. "The theory holding that if two kinds of money in circulation have the same denominational value but different intrinsic values, the money with higher intrinsic value will be hoarded and eventually driven out of circulation by the money with lesser intrinsic value." (Definition from *The American Heritage Dictionary of the English Language*, Fourth Edition, Houghton Mifflin Company, 2000.)

With Omnipresent Digital Evidence, What Case *Isn't* an IT Case?

Beyond wondering who these experts who will respond to future challenges will be, perhaps the more interesting question becomes: Are we already at the point of no return in needing experienced IT experts for nearly every major civil case? Might this need for experts in system and application failure cases soon extend to any case that involves the discovery of massive amounts of evidence produced and maintained by complex computer systems, regardless of whether or not the underlying facts of the case involve IP or IT issues?

While it will be quite interesting to watch the developments of IT-related lawsuits in the coming years, many if not most major commercial cases already involve complicated strategic and practical planning and execution of electronic evidence discovery plans. These measures are needed to assure the attorneys who are handling the litigation that they are getting all the relevant evidence they need. Recent studies estimate that well over 90 percent of business information that has evidentiary value is currently being produced by computers. No one in the legal community seriously doubts the importance of doing discovery of electronic evidence such as e-mail after the devastating use that was made of the thousands of e-mails uncovered by the federal government in the antitrust suit against Microsoft. Today most of the important evidence in commercial litigation and increasingly in other civil and criminal cases comes from computers.

The federal courts have already begun to experiment with the appointment of special masters and consultants to the court who are experts in IT. There is a growing need for experts to advise attorneys not only on how to discover the electronic evidence they need to frame their claims and prosecute their lawsuits but also on how to get their own electronic evidence in shape in advance of litigation in order to provide complete discovery economically to their opponents. A number of companies have begun to carve out a niche in serving companies and law firms as expert consultants and system designers for litigation-ready record-keeping operations. We recommend a periodic review of the constantly updated collection of materials relating to the explosion of technical and procedural issues generated by the increasing dependency of the justice system on electronic evidence.[16]

Technical Experts and Routine Legal Functions

While the attention devoted to discovery of electronic evidence may be a mixed blessing to lawyers and their clients in litigation, it will open up an enormous new area for

---

16. Ken Withers maintains such a collection of data online at *http://www.KenWithers.com.*

scrutiny by IT professionals. Experts will also be called to opine as to the reasonableness and timeliness of the routine purging of things like e-mails and drafts of documents that are automatically and often unknowingly kept by applications that are widely used by companies to prepare and store their business documents.

Beyond the strategic decisions to prepare for litigation and to conduct routine discovery of millions of documents, the question of authenticity of this data will require expert analysis where there is reason to believe that data has been altered, destroyed, or hidden. In a later chapter, we examine one early reported case that has become a landmark of sorts, in which a computer forensic expert won a duel of technical experts that ultimately helped resolve several key issues in the case. In a subsequent case we examine the problem of determining what has happened inside a computer and how that should be interpreted in deciding whether evidence has been destroyed or whether parties should be sanctioned for interfering in the discovery process. Unfortunately, not many cases go into enough detail in their reported opinions to give us any useful standards for gauging how future courts are likely to decide these issues. So long as this is the case, we can expect more rather than less protracted litigation of the same or similar issues until the appellate process or the legislative process establishes standards that can be economically and equitably enforced.

So, we find ourselves in a situation in which it is reasonable to assume that liability for IT failures will soon require technical experts to assist lawyers, judges, and jurors to understand the underlying technologies. At the same time we already find ourselves confronting the problem of determining the existence and authenticity of vast amounts of discoverable digital evidence. This evidence has been created (often unwittingly) and maintained by complex applications in various operating systems and stored in both connected and unconnected, highly complex storage systems in all sorts of networked environments. Precious little of prevalent IT has been designed with the evidentiary needs of the legal system in mind. Courts are being forced to become increasingly involved in electronic discovery due to the complexity and expense involved in complying with rules and traditions that were paper-based. Courts will increasingly depend on independent experts in order to avoid creating a new tier of litigation rituals to decide on the reasonableness and appropriate cost allocations for the problems presented by the discovery of electronic evidence and the forensic examination of original media.

We are rapidly approaching the point where it will be difficult to imagine a competent, adequately financed lawyer bringing a lawsuit without having in-house or consultant IT experts to advise on the electronic discovery issues that the lawyer must anticipate and handle.

Chance, Coincidence, or Causation— Who Cares?

For centuries, lawyers have found themselves in the prediction business. Their predictions range from the respective likelihood of success for different litigation strategies, to the chances that a jury will find their client credible (or at least more sympathetic than the other party), to the outcome in the appellate courts of a legal matter of first impression. Like lawyers, forensic experts have also been encouraged by their clients and principals to predict the future or to assign probabilities as to how complex technical systems may have behaved in the past.

Americans are in love with scientific explanations for everyday occurrences. Unfortunately, those things that are accepted as scientific fact are often warped by the romantic beliefs and hopes of the public, to the detriment of good science. Furthermore, humans seem to be on a never-ending quest for techniques for making accurate predictions, for everything from weather to commodity markets.

Molecular biologists have not, as far as we know, identified a "prediction gene," but the quest to predict seems as deeply instinctive to the human condition as language, self-consciousness, and artistic expression. Unlike these other characterizing traits, however, the instinct to predict has not always been expressed in effective performance. Oracles, prophets, and stock market forecasters have been accorded a status in society that is commensurate with the promise—not the delivery—of tomorrow revealed.

Scientists today seek to turn prediction into a reputable profession. They bring impressive tools to the quest: powerful theoretical understanding of fundamental processes; advanced monitoring technologies that digitize nature in all its rich profusion; supercomputers that crunch gigabyte-sized databases and spit out a vision of the future. Indeed, these days, science without prediction hardly seems like science at all.

Still, even the most sophisticated scientific predictions are plagued with uncertainties. But unlike predictions based on entrails or the stars, these uncertainties can be quantified (although quantifications of uncertainty are often themselves highly uncertain). We may therefore ask: What characteristics of a scientific prediction will allow us to make a decision that is better than the one we would have made without the prediction? (Of course, the answer to this question, too, may be highly uncertain.)[1]

The tendency of the public to color perceptions of scientific and technical fact in accordance with myth or current fad can be disastrous to the objective decision-making process that is the hallmark of an equitable settlement of a legal dispute. The courts in our technological society acknowledged this long ago by establishing the special role of an expert witness to guide the fact finder through complex concepts and processes that relate to the issues being litigated and to serve as a scientific or technical conscience for the court. In this chapter, we discuss the circumstances that defined the role of the expert witness, outlining some examples of "junk sciences" that have been foolishly accepted by both society and the courts, and then rejected from time to time during the past century. We suggest that some of these same growing pains are apt to be in store for IT experts and their chosen fields of expertise in the twenty-first century as they distinguish themselves from the charlatans, quacks, and unqualified experts who (if history is any judge of what to expect in the future) will nonetheless offer their bogus expert opinions to the highest bidders.

Dealing with Experts in the Age of Scientific Progress

When expertise is prized, there will always be those who seek to anoint themselves as experts, even if they don't actually qualify for the designation. It seems that regardless of the complexity of the scientific or technical domain, there is always a rogues' gallery of pretenders there to take advantage of naïve souls who need assistance in dealing with challenges that arise. In the legal arena, where experts can determine the outcome of multimillion dollar cases, the importance of filtering the true experts from those who are pretenders to the title increases.

Fortunately, there are sanity checks for these determinations. Courts have devised a number of tests to determine whether an expert is correct in his or her assessment of the field of expertise and his or her qualifications to perform as an expert within

---

1. Sarewitz, Daniel, Roger A. Pielke, Jr., and Radford Byerly, Jr., eds. *Prediction: Science, Decision Making, and the Future of Nature.* Washington, DC: Island Press, 2000, p. 10.

that field. The process used to determine these qualifications has changed drastically during the last decade in the federal courts and in more than half of the state courts. (We deal in detail with these new rules and techniques for admitting a particular expert's testimony and opinions in Chapter 8, which is concerned with expert screening by the courts and the evolving judicial gatekeeping techniques.)

But first we need to understand the context in which the Supreme Court decided to make judges more responsible for preventing charlatans from testifying as expert witnesses in court. These mountebanks were especially notorious for testifying about pseudoscience in personal injury and defective product litigation cases before juries.

Frye v. U.S.: Distinguishing Pseudoscience from Science

In 1923, the D.C. Circuit Court of Appeals heard *Frye v. U.S.*, a case involving the admissibility of a novel scientific method for testing a defendant in a murder case for signs of deception. The defendant's attorney engaged an expert witness who argued that the truthfulness of the defendant on a particular point could be reliably determined by measuring the defendant's systolic blood pressure during the course of an examination. The theory was that telling the truth is spontaneous, requiring no effort on the part of the subject. Therefore, the systolic blood pressure of the defendant would rise initially, then gradually fall, provided he or she were telling the truth. Were the defendant lying, his or her blood pressure would rise during the course of the examination. This theory might be familiar to those who have dealt with modern polygraph or lie detector examinations.

The government prosecutors objected to the admission of the defendant's expert and also objected to the defendant's attorney's offer to have the expert examine his client before the jury. The lower court sustained both objections, excluding the expert testimony. The defendant appealed this decision to the Appeals Court, arguing that the proffered expert's testimony was within the limits defined by the rules of evidence governing expert testimony and should therefore be admissible.

The Appeals Court responded by upholding the lower court's decision, declaring that this early application of lie detection technology did not meet the standards of scientific acceptability. The *Frye* decision includes a passage that is key to one of the challenges the court faces in a technological age—how to determine when a scientific discovery makes the leap from hypothesis to established technique.

> *Just when a scientific principle or discovery crosses the line between the experimental and demonstrable stages is difficult to define. Somewhere in this twilight zone the evidential forces of the principle must be recognized. While courts will go a long way in admitting expert testimony deduced from a well-recognized scientific principle of discovery, the theorem from which the deduction is drawn must have gained general acceptance in the particular field from which it comes.*[2]

---

2. *Frye v. U.S.*, 293 F. 1013, at 1014 (1923). See Appendix A for the text of this case.

Keeping Quacks and Their Technologies at Bay

The *Frye* decision was an early attempt to establish a formula for courts to weed out the charlatans and the quacks from those experts who were traditionally allowed to give opinions about matters relevant to the resolution of lawsuits. As we shall see, the fact that the case dealt with lie detection technology raised other problems touching on the traditional province of the jury to determine issues of credibility, above and beyond the question of the acceptance of lie detection by any established scientific community. The concepts of just what was scientific and technical, in the sense of being adequately tested and standardized by recognized authorities and experts, were not so easy to grasp at the time when *Frye* became the standard used by courts to measure an expert's expertise. But to understand the other kinds of quacks masquerading as experts that courts worried about in the first quarter of the last century, and to make clear just how much (or how little) times have changed, consider a few of the "medical technologies" that many members of the general public purchased during this period.

- The Spectro-Chrome was marketed in the 1920s and '30s and steadily found demand throughout the United States. It consisted of a hood, a lamp, and a set of color slides. Patients were instructed to sit in the nude during appropriate moments of the stages of the moon and bathe in the different colored lights. The therapy was advertised as providing a proper balance of the four basic colors to which the body is responsive. When the patient was diagnosed as lacking a certain color or having too much of a color, the Spectro-Chrome treatment was prescribed. Lemon color, for example, helped build strong bones, green light was germicidal, scarlet was a genital stimulant, and purple was antimalarial.[3]
- The Radioendocrinator was comprised of two small pads charged with radium and then attached to the body by an adapter. It sold during the 1920s for $150. It was recommended for various treatments that helped the patient by ionizing the endocrine system and by increasing hormone production. Essentially, it was supposed to invigorate the patient, in addition to generally halting or slowing the process of aging.[4]
- The inventor of the Radioclast purported that it neutralized abnormal vibrations and allowed diseased organs to be cured by returning them to their

---

3. McCoy, Bob. *Quack: Tales of Medical Fraud from the Museum of Questionable Medical Devices.* Santa Monica, CA: Santa Monica Press, 2000.

4. "The Radioendocrinator (ca. 1930), Radioactive Quack Cures." Oak Ridge, TN: Oak Ridge Associated Universities, 2000. Accessed July 23, 2002, at *http://www.orau.com/ptp/collection/quackcures/radend.htm.*

normal vibration rates. One version of the device sold for $945 and did contain many radio parts, but they were apparently not connected in any way that produced much of anything, let alone healing vibrations. This and other similar devices were invented and sold to thousands during the 1920s and '30s by Dr. Albert Abrams, who was at one time the elected vice president of the California State Medical Society and a respected expert in neurology. The American Medical Association refused to investigate him, viewing his theories and devices too absurd to be taken seriously.[5]

These examples of the pseudomedical sciences at their finest should suffice to demonstrate why courts were concerned that not all doctors had the good health of their patients and customers in mind. There are hundreds of other examples of such "advances in medical technology," all designed and delivered to the public by doctors who asserted that the devices were good for what ailed you.

Expertise in the Face of Technological Trends

Were the courts being too conservative in their reluctance to embrace new scientific movements as valid, just to avoid the obvious quacks and charlatans? There are many examples of situations in which common acceptance is not an indicator of validity. With this realization, acknowledged professional communities of interest that demanded scientific integrity with enforced standards and peer review of new tools and techniques began to make sense.

Bumping Heads with Phrenology

Consider one quaint historical example of what today might simply be called "junk science" and thrown out of court—the practice of phrenology during the nineteenth century. Phrenology was widely accepted 150 years ago as an effective science for predicting behavior and understanding attitudes, based on the physical attributes of an individual's skull as correlated with certain faculties located in identifiable areas in the bodies of all individuals. Pierre Schlag's entertaining exegesis of the history of law and phrenology argues that as two fascinatingly complex, self-reflexive systems of knowledge, both phrenology and the common law had a lot in common during the first half of the nineteenth century.[6] In those days, these self-identified and largely self-authenticated professional communities of interested experts and practitioners both claimed

---

5. McCoy, Quack.

6. Schlag, Pierre. "Commentary: Law and Phrenology." *Harvard Law Review* 110, 1997, p. 877.

to base their theories and practices on the scientific method. With the authority of science to support their claim to special knowledge, both the practitioners of law and of phrenology could to some degree claim to be the new and improved replacements for discredited traditions that predated both the common law and phrenology. The claim to a scientific basis gave these two bodies of knowledge and practice the social support and power that the ancient practices of astrology had maintained for hundreds of years as the tradition of choice for providing its clients with the precious commodity of prediction.

Distinguishing Astrology from Astronomy and the Rule of Law

Throughout history, western society has sought reliable methods for predicting the future behavior of individuals and rationalizing past events. Before the acceptance of the scientific method, only astrologers could persuasively make use of mathematics and quantitative methods to predict the future and to offer expert risk assessment services and authoritative advice on how best to take advantage of social opportunities.

> *At the most abstract level, astrologers ancient and early modern carried out the tasks that twentieth-century society assigns to the economist. Like the economist, the astrologer tried to bring the chaotic phenomena of everyday life into order by fitting them to sharply defined quantitative models. Like the economist, the astrologer insisted, when teaching or writing for professional peers, that astrology had only a limited ability to predict the future. Formally speaking, after all, astrology concerned itself with the interplay of general forces rather than the outcome of a single configuration of them. The very number of questions that could be posed about any given horoscope ran into the thousands, ensuring that any given prediction had a tentative character. Like the economist, the astrologer proved willing in practice, when powerful clients demanded it, to predict individual outcomes anyhow. Like the economist, the astrologer generally found that the events did not match the prediction; and like the economist, the astrologer normally received as a reward for this confirmation of the powers of his art a better job and a higher salary.[7]*

However, lawyers also engaged in the business of prediction and especially in the prediction of failures and insuring against them through contracts to protect a client's interest in the future against anticipated and unanticipated setbacks. Common law practitioners gradually recognized that they did not need the scientific imprimatur for the legal system to maintain its methods of practice and its accumulated knowledge in order to sustain itself as an honored and certified profession of acknowledged expertise. Besides, by inventing and then imposing "the rule of law" it had a monopoly on the

---

7. Grafton, Anthony. *Cardano's Cosmos: The Worlds and Works of a Renaissance Astrologer.* Cambridge, MA: *Harvard University Press*, 1999, p. 10.

power of the state and the use of force if necessary to carry out its decisions and thereby to make good on its predictions.

Although horoscopes abound to this day, by the nineteenth century astrology had gradually lost its traditional control over the study of the motions and makeup of the heavenly bodies. Some of this study became the scientific pursuit and expertise of astronomers. This separation of functions between astrology and astronomy, together with the evolution of other sciences, the practical applications of technical expertise, and the establishment and growth of professions such as law and medicine, led to astrology losing most of its social force.

Why Wasn't Phrenology the Kind of Expertise the Courts Wanted?

Before we consider what forensic economists have to offer the courts, let's pause for a brief historical moment and reflect on the fact that there were practicing expert phrenologists aplenty in the nineteenth century. Furthermore, according to the publicists and practitioners of phrenology, their claims to expert knowledge and techniques were largely based on the scientific method. For many years these experts and their field of expertise seemed to have all the trappings of other recognized sciences. In the United States the phrenology movement also served as a kind of catchall for people looking for a scientifically based system to replace the confidence that people had formerly placed in astrology as a way of predicting their futures and rationalizing their pasts. At the same time, phrenologists offered a framework to doctors, lawyers, and therapists of all kinds to deal with mental illness.

Society ultimately realized that there was no significant supporting data for the basic assumptions of the phrenologists. Today no one takes phrenology seriously as a method of predicting future behavior or accounting for a person's conduct over time. As Pierre Schlag argues in his critique of phrenology:

> *Despite all of these conceptual refinements, despite the cautious case analysis, and despite its sundry practical applications, phrenology failed to live up to its ambitions. The simple explanation is that Gall and the other phrenologists had their ontology wrong. The fundamental faculties (as such) did not exist. They were not linked to the size of cranial organs. Further, the cranial organs did not bear any relation to cranial prominences. For all of their detailed inquiries, their sorting of countless cases, and their remarkable attempts to synthesize their research into fundamental faculties, principles, or laws, the phrenologists failed.*
>
> *The interesting question is how was this failure occasioned? What precisely enabled the phrenologists to fail in such a spectacular way? Put another way, the question is, "How did the phrenologists manage to sustain their failure for the better part of a century?" The question deserves close inquiry because phrenology was not just any kind of disciplinary failure.*

It was a grand failure that attracted countless adherents—including some very intelligent men. It was a failure that sustained professional associations, symposia, treatises, and journals. The phrenologists assembled an elaborate structure of detailed information and thus, phrenology became a kind of expert domain. The question arises, what enabled all of this detailed expertise to flourish, even though its fundamental ontology and its grounding structure were deeply flawed?

The question is particularly salient because some of the phrenologists were quite sincere in their ambition to establish a genuine science—one informed by careful empirical observation of cases. Unlike their predecessors, the speculative philosophers and the metaphysicians, the phrenologists were committed to and did indeed perform countless case studies and case analyses. Given such sustained encounters with empirical data—the real world of human comportment—how did phrenologists fail to recognize that their own hypotheses, their own methodological presuppositions, were not true? After inspecting so many craniums, how did they fail to realize that the cranioscopic hypothesis was wrong?

These questions are of interest not only for those who seek to understand the evolution of phrenology, but also for those who seek to understand the development of other expert disciplines. The answers have much to do with the ways in which the phrenological paradigm was constructed. It was an amalgamation of animisms and reifications; of self-referential complexity, of self-legitimations and folk beliefs. The internal organization of phrenology gave its practitioners what they wanted most: the belief that they knew something and that this something was useful—even good. It also gave them an elaborate construct that could be deployed to deny conflicting evidence and to counter opposition—without dealing seriously with either.[8]

Perhaps you have some objection to the historical example of phrenology as so much stuffing in a book that is supposed to be about the modern predicament of technical experts. Modern experts would never be tempted to use such obviously fraudulent rationales to serve their purposes or to explain mysterious patterns of behavior, right? Perhaps you believe that nineteenth-century society was uniformly misled by men who were simply deluded and desperate to believe in their powers to predict the behavior of others. Thus, phrenology might be considered inappropriate as a warning to technical experts and lawyers of this enlightened age.

In that case, reconsider Grafton's analogy between astrologers and economists to gain some more recent perspective on the current dilemma that courts and juries face when asked to sort out sound science from the myriad of pseudosciences or specialized knowledge that is not based on any generally recognized scientific methods or testing procedures that exist today. Consider for a moment the number of things (for instance, stock market behavior) for which we rely on economists to predict or explain with their theories and quantitative analyses. Furthermore, we consistently rely on them to offer their opinions on the ultimate issues that need to be determined by expert predictions in many types of litigation.

8. Schlag, "Commentary," pp. 894–895.

Modern Examples of Questionable Forensic Science Claims

What do economic experts and handwriting experts have in common? Do they have a science to offer to the marketplace, or is it simply that no market exists for their science outside the courts?

The Economists

Forensic economists served as expert witnesses throughout the twentieth century. They are most often encountered in litigation as experts on the causation and calculation of economic damages. More recently they have played an important role in restraint of trade and antitrust cases such as the Justice Department's high-profile civil prosecution of Microsoft. Just as the practice of phrenology did a century before, forensic economists have developed a highly technical discipline. The general acceptance of forensic economics is reflected in numerous broad and deep academic programs at major universities that grant B.A., M.A., and Ph.D. degrees in the discipline. The past 20 years have marked the formation of national associations of forensic economists and academies of economic experts. Commercial forensic economists conduct research and publish scholarly journals and books on a regular basis. However, the professional economics associations organized for forensic purposes as a rule neither regulate nor certify their practitioners. Insurance defense attorneys maintain that they have no choice but to counter the irresponsible economic experts so often called by their brothers and sisters of the plaintiffs' bar. Samuel Day describes the situation:

> *The defense decision to use a forensic economist is critical in terms of the potential impact on a jury's verdict. A solid, well-reasoned analysis from a forensic economist can be the saber that strikes the fatal blow to a plaintiff's damage claim. An untested analysis based primarily on theory and assumption from a forensic economist can be the express elevator to a substantial plaintiff's verdict.* [9]

Day argues convincingly that the new standards of reliability being imposed by the courts open up new opportunities for defense lawyers to challenge unqualified plaintiff's experts, but make the game much less certain to predict when challenges can and will be made by both parties to the opposing experts and how the legal system can weed out the bad experts.

> *Faith in market forces operating within the litigation industry, which in turn is based on the advocacy of competing parties and their lawyers, has been suggested as an operational necessity given the current state of such a profession.*

---

9. Day, Samuel. "Use of Forensic Economists in Commercial Litigation: A Defense Perspective." *Defense Counsel Journal*, October 1999, pp. 552–560.

> *... Thus, it is left to the attorneys and their clients to regulate the field by market forces—unethical experts will not be hired and zealous advocacy on the part of experts will be identified and discredited in the courtroom.*[10]

The Handwriting Experts

Interestingly, the use of the market metaphor has led David Faigman, a highly regarded commentator on the problems of expert testimony, to a decidedly different conclusion about its efficacy to weed out the bad experts in the field of handwriting analysis. Faigman has suggested that with regard to the validity of handwriting expert testimony, the failure of experts who practice the art of handwriting identification to progress to the establishment of any sort of scientific reliability of their techniques is due primarily to a single cause: market failure.

> *There are a number of aspects of nineteenth-century methods of handwriting identification that seem to be problematic. Most striking, perhaps, is how unscientific the process appears. The experts all knew what results would confirm the hypotheses they were testing. Experimenter bias, usually avoided at all costs in empirical research, was palpable here. The experts also approached the samples looking for confirming instances and were quick to discount or dismiss differences as "adapted for disguise."*
>
> *The practice of searching a multitude of exemplars for similarities actually turns the scientific method on its head. These experts seemed to take the view that if you have a hundred points of comparison and five constitute "matches" this observation supports the conclusion that the two samples came from the same hand. A less biased method would ask what percentage of matches would be expected if the person did not write the disputed document. A comparison of this number to the number discovered would provide a more accurate statement concerning likely authorship.*
>
> *Unlike many other sciences, the primary market for handwriting experts is the law. Neither do they compete among themselves to discover new insights about handwriting comparison, nor do their discoveries have value to other fields. They are a discrete and insular sect of self-validating specialists. They are not trained in the scientific method and they have little clue how to test their claims of expertise. So long as their customers, the courts, keep buying the old model there is no need to come up with anything new. It is as if they began making the Edsel and over the years nondiscriminating car buyers just kept plunking down money for the same old car.*[11]

If it turns out, as seems likely, that many of the forensic uses of IT expertise will remain within the litigation industry, are we facing the same dilemma that appears to occur in other areas of technical expertise? If IT experts are not required to be scien-

---

10. Day, "Use of Forensic Economists in Commercial Litigation."

11. Faigman, David. *Legal Alchemy: The Use and Misuse of Science in the Law.* New York: W. H. Freeman, 1999, pp. 4–5.

tific until they get to court, or at least until they prepare their expert reports, in what sense can we expect to see scientific or technical standards for IT forensic methods and evidence developed through acceptable scientific methods, or adequate testing and peer-reviewed techniques produced outside the litigation industry?

You may still assume that the foregoing examples are all either ancient history or of little relevance to the brave new world of IT forensics. Or you might believe that these concerns about determining the scientific methods of economists and with their potential biases as hired experts are just plain old sour grapes from authors who lost their money in the stock market and are looking for expert economists to blame for their investment follies. Perhaps it seems that these issues are now so obvious that the lessons learned from these marginally relevant accounts of the use of expertise to sell predictions have already been assimilated and are being dealt with by the courts.

However, the real point of this discussion is that IT in general and the hundreds of potential branches of expert knowledge about its interconnected technologies and techniques are all either subject to legal dispute or essential to determining what the electronic evidence means in a case where IT stands between the relevant evidence and the parties' understanding of its existence or significance. Not only that—it often takes a series of experts from different technical specialties to set the stage for the key IT expert to explain what happened in a network environment and what the evidence collected from that environment means.

There will inevitably be a number of rounds of challenges from lawyers once such expertise becomes an issue in a piece of litigation. No practitioner of a discipline based on IT engineering should take for granted that their particular area of expertise will be accepted by the adversary or by the court. Worse yet, the techniques information technologists assume are appropriate and generally accepted by their peers are likely to be almost incomprehensible to the judge who is trying the case and hearing the technical details for the first time, without some additional help from a special master or court-appointed expert.

As lawyers and courts learned to apply new standards to the qualification of scientific and technical experts and to the admission of opinions from fields that have been customarily accepted by the courts and the litigants as scientific, some unexpected and quite serious bumps have been encountered. These bumps suggest what may be in store for expert witnesses who are called to testify about their qualifications and the collection of methodologies they use to understand and solve problems in the behavior of software applications, operating systems, intrusion detection systems, and complex computer and communications network transactions. Even if the expert is successful in explaining his or her qualifications and methodologies, there is still no guarantee that the expert will be allowed to give any or all of the opinions concerning the facts he or she has been asked to investigate and analyze. This is especially true if the judge is lost in the technobabble of the expert or the confusion injected by opposing experts and counsel. The courts are now looking for preliminary proof of the scientific methodology that was used, before experts will be allowed to testify about their findings in the absence of a demonstration that their conclusions are in fact based on clearly acceptable scientific methods.

The Fingerprint Analysts

Consider the recent challenges mounted against the "science" of fingerprint analysis (Figure 5-1). With the possible historical exception of mug shot identifications and the recent acceptance of DNA testing technologies, fingerprint comparison is perhaps the most significant and certainly the most frequently used physical evidence and theory for the expert identification of a criminal suspect. It is also quite frequently used as evidence of identification on any number of issues in many civil cases. Because court decisions and revised rules of evidence have established certain new criteria for the acceptance of a field or a technical method as scientific, criminal defense attorneys have for the first time challenged this evidence as not being the least bit scientific. This is a profoundly important issue to the entire criminal justice system. It could also have enormous impact on the conclusive identification of individuals through new biometric authentication techniques.

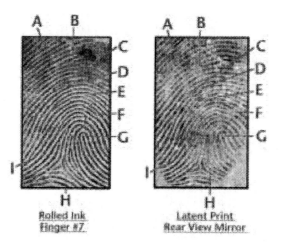

Figure 5-1. *Fingerprint-matching criteria as taught to investigators and forensics experts. (From Keogh, E., "An Overview of the Science of Fingerprints," Anil Aggrawal's Internet Journal of Forensic Medicine and Toxicology 2(1). Accessed July 23, 2002, at http://anil299.tripod.com/vol_002_no_001/papers/paper005.html.)*

Relying on the revised criteria, defense attorneys and their experts have begun to systematically challenge the opinion of a "dactyloscopist." Fingerprint experts are no longer automatically entitled to the presumption that their methods are scientific. Opinions are today being challenged based on unproven and unverifiable "scientific" theories. These theories assert that a properly collected, preserved latent print, when compared with and matched by the expert to a known print of the suspect, is to a scientific probability that of the suspect.[12]

One Court's Changing Attitude about Fingerprint Forensic Evidence

The traditional acceptance of "qualified" fingerprint expert witness opinions about the identity of the maker of fingerprints, based on a comparison of unknown prints with known prints of the individual to be identified or ruled out, has come under attack in state and federal courts throughout the United States since the *Daubert* and *Kumho Tire* decisions.

This move to challenge the "science" of fingerprint identification has pushed law enforcement to take a new and very different approach in the presentation of expert forensic evidence, at least in those courts where the defense attorneys have been paying attention to these new developments. Today, due to these ongoing challenges, the prosecutor is most likely to qualify the expert by asking for an expert opinion based on experience and training. Furthermore, the prosecutor will attempt to demonstrate to the court that the methods of collecting, comparing, and critiquing fingerprint evidence used by the expert are sufficiently sound and repeatable to support the admission of the opinion of that expert. But courts are for the first time beginning to draw some lines between the ability of a trained expert to present the evidence of identity or matching patterns and the ability to offer an expert opinion about how significant that evidence is in relation to an ultimate issue in the case, such as in-court identification of the defendant as the individual who made the prints left at the scene of the crime.

A crisis arises for traditional fingerprint comparison evidence when a properly qualified dactyloscopist is asked to render an expert opinion based on his or her observations as to whether the latent print was made by the same individual who made the known print. (This dactyloscopist has likely testified for years on the assumption that the theory and research behind the comparison of two fingerprints by a qualified expert entitles him or her to answer as a scientist.) The traditional follow-up question from the prosecutor is to ask the expert to opine as to whether or not there is a match "to a scientific certainty" and in accordance with the traditional "scientific" hypothesis of the fingerprint identification field. In effect, the lawyer is asking the expert to render an expert opinion, ostensibly based on scientific methods, that

---

12. Cole, Simon. *Suspect Identities: A History of Fingerprinting and Criminal Identification*. Cambridge, MA: Harvard University Press, 2001.

identifies the maker of the suspect print as the defendant, to the exclusion of all others. In other words, the guy who is charged is clearly guilty because the expert can identify his fingerprints on the gun and assure the jury that no one else in the world could have left those prints!

The Judge Presents His Initial Decision

Since the *Daubert* line of cases, courts have been asked to draw back from the tradition of allowing federal and state fingerprint analysts to render such opinions. Consider the following initial opinion rendered by Federal District Judge J. Pollak (in the Eastern District of Pennsylvania) in *U.S. v. Plaza, Acosta and Rodriguez*, which was decided in January 2002. At issue was whether the classic fingerprint identification methodology, abbreviated as ACE-V (an acronym for analysis, comparison, evaluation, and verification), qualifies as a scientific discipline to the extent that fingerprint examiners can deliver expert opinions regarding the identity of the person who makes a particular fingerprint. Quoting from the court's opinion:

> *Pursuant to the foregoing discussion, it is the court's view that the ACE-V fingerprint identification regime is hard to square with* Daubert.
>
> *The one* Daubert *factor that ACE-V satisfies in significant fashion is the fourth factor: ACE-V has acceptance within the American fingerprint examiner community. But the caveat must be added that, in the court's view, the domain of knowledge occupied by fingerprint examiners should be described, in Rule 702 terms, by the word "technical," rather than by the word "scientific," the word the government deploys.*
>
> *Given that* Kumho Tire *establishes that the* Daubert *analysis is applicable to "technical" as well as "scientific" knowledge, it may be thought that this court's characterization of the knowledge base of fingerprint examiners as "technical" rather than "scientific" is a semantic distinction which is of no practical consequence. However, as discussed above, the court finds that ACE-V does not adequately satisfy the "scientific" criterion of testing (the first* Daubert *factor) or the "scientific" criterion of peer review (the second* Daubert *factor). Further, the court finds that the information of record is unpersuasive, one way or another, as to ACE-V's "scientific" rate of error (the first aspect of* Daubert's *third factor), and that, at the critical evaluation stage, ACE-V does not operate under uniformly accepted "scientific" standards (the second aspect of* Daubert's *third factor).*[13]

In the court's initial ruling, things looked pretty gloomy for those relying on the ability of the expert to render an expert opinion about the identity of who may have

---

13. *United States of America v. Carlos Ivan Llera Plaza, Wilfredo Martinez Acosta, and Victor Rodriguez.* United States District Court for The Eastern District of Pennsylvania: Cr. No. 98-362-10, 11, 12. Decided January 7, 2002. Cited as 179 F. Supp. 2d 492, and also reported at 57 Fed. R. Evid. Ser. 983, and at 2002 WL 27305 (E. D. Pa.).

left the evidentiary prints, based on the traditional way of interpreting fingerprint-based identification in this case. *Daubert* lays out a set of checks that the fingerprint identification methodology must meet, and in the court's initial opinion, the judge found that this technical expertise satisfied only one of those criteria. However the court stopped short of asserting that the failure of the methodology to satisfy the *Daubert* criteria should be used to prevent the admission of fingerprint testimony entirely.

> *Since the court finds that ACE-V does not meet* Daubert's *testing, peer review, and standards criteria, and that information as to ACE-V's rate of error is in limbo, the expected conclusion would be that the government should be precluded from presenting any fingerprint testimony. But that conclusion—apparently putting at naught a century of judicial acquiescence in fingerprint identification processes—would be unwarrantably heavy-handed. The Daubert difficulty with the ACE-V process is by no means total. The difficulty comes into play at the stage at which, as experienced fingerprint specialists Ashbaugh and Meagher themselves acknowledge, the ACE-V process becomes "subjective"—namely, the evaluation stage. By contrast, the antecedent analysis and comparison stages are, according to the testimony, "objective": analysis of the rolled and latent prints and comparison of what the examiner has observed in the two prints. Up to the evaluation stage, the ACE-V fingerprint examiner's testimony is descriptive, not judgmental.*[14]

The court initially agrees with the defense that fingerprint experts should be limited in their opinions about what their forensic methods enable them to conclude.

> *Accordingly, this court will permit the government to present testimony by fingerprint examiners who, suitably qualified as "expert" examiners by virtue of training and experience, may (1) describe how the rolled and latent fingerprints at issue in this case were obtained, (2) identify and place before the jury the fingerprints and such magnifications thereof as may be required to show minute details, and (3) point out observed similarities (and differences) between any latent print and any rolled print the government contends are attributable to the same person. What such expert witnesses will not be permitted to do is to present "evaluation" testimony as to their "opinion" (Rule 702) that a particular latent print is in fact the print of a particular person. The defendants will be permitted to present their own fingerprint experts to counter the government's fingerprint testimony, but defense experts will also be precluded from presenting "evaluation" testimony. Government counsel and defense counsel will, in closing arguments, be free to argue to the jury that, on the basis of the jury's observation of a particular latent print and a particular rolled print, the jury may find the existence, or the non-existence, of a match between the prints.*[15]

---

14. *U.S. v. Plaza, Acosta and Rodriguez,* January 2002.

15. *U.S. v. Plaza, Acosta and Rodriguez,* January 2002.

In reaching its initial decision (limiting the expert to simply describing the comparisons without making a positive identification of the defendant if the expert found that the prints match), the court alludes to taking its cue from a previous case involving an analogous forensic discipline, handwriting analysis. Note the court's systematic consideration of the *Daubert* and *Kumho Tire* criteria in this initial opinion.

In arriving at this disposition of the competing government and defense motions and supporting memoranda, this court has derived substantial assistance from the thoughtful approach taken by Judge Gertner, of the District of Massachusetts, in dealing with the comparable problem of handwriting evidence. In United States v. Hines, *55 F. Supp. 2d 62 (D. Mass. 1999), Judge Gertner wrote as follows:*

"The Harrison [Diana Harrison, an FBI document examiner] testimony may be divided into two parts: Part 1 is Harrison's testimony with respect to similarities between the known handwriting of Hines, and the robbery note. Part 2 is Harrison's testimony with respect to the author of the note, that the author of the robbery note was indeed Hines.

When a lay witness, the girlfriend of the defendant for example, says 'this is my boyfriend's writing,' her conclusion is based on having been exposed to her paramour's handwriting countless times. Without a lay witness with that kind of expertise, the government is obliged to offer the testimony of 'experts' who have looked at, and studied handwriting for years. These are, essentially, 'observational' experts, taxonomists—arguably qualified because they have seen so many examples over so long. It is not traditional, experimental science, to be sure, but Kumho's gloss on Daubert suggests this is not necessary. I conclude that Harrison can testify to the ways in which she has found Hines' known handwriting similar to or dissimilar from the handwriting of the robbery note; part 1 of her testimony.

Part 2 of the Harrison testimony is, however, problematic. There is no data that suggests that handwriting analysts can say, like DNA experts, that this person is 'the' author of the document. There are no meaningful, and accepted validity studies in the field. No one has shown me Harrison's error rate, the times she has been right, and the times she has been wrong. There is no academic field known as handwriting analysis. This is a 'field' that has little efficacy outside of a courtroom. There are no peer reviews of it. Nor can one compare the opinion reached by an examiner with a standard protocol subject to validity testing, since there are no recognized standards. There is no agreement as to how many similarities it takes to declare a match, or how many differences it takes to rule it out.

I find Harrison's testimony meets Fed. R. Evid. 702's requirements to the extent that she restricts her testimony to similarities or dissimilarities between the known exemplars and the robbery note. However, she may not render an ultimate conclusion on who penned the unknown writing."

For the foregoing reasons:

A. This court will take judicial notice of the uniqueness and permanence of fingerprints.

B. The parties will be able to present expert fingerprint testimony (1) describing how any latent and rolled prints at issue in this case were obtained, (2) identifying, and placing before the jury, such fingerprints and any necessary magnifications, and (3) pointing out any observed similarities and differences between a particular latent print and a particular rolled print alleged by the government to be attributable to the same persons. But the parties will not be permitted to present testimony expressing an opinion of an expert witness that a particular latent print matches, or does not match, the rolled print of a particular person and hence is, or is not, the fingerprint of that person.[16]

On Further Reflection, the Judge Changes His Mind

What happened approximately two months after the court rendered its opinion is remarkable in a number of ways. Because the initial well-reasoned opinion was a distinct departure from the practice of state and federal courts for over a century, there was a great deal riding on the precedential value of such an opinion for both defendants and prosecutors. Accordingly, the government immediately filed a motion requesting a rehearing, in part because of the dramatic difference that such a precedent would make on the investigation and prosecution of criminal cases throughout the criminal justice system. The court granted the motion for a rehearing and agreed to allow both the government and the defense to supplement the record with additional evidence and additional testimony from expert witnesses in reviewing the initial decision the court had made in the case.

For the beginning expert, the comparison of the initial opinion of this highly respected federal judge with his own subsequent reversal of that opinion should impress the reader with the importance of particular experts and their testimony on the ultimate outcome of difficult decisions. The point of covering these two opinions, coming to such different conclusions about the admissibility of crucial expert testimony in a criminal case, is to demonstrate something about the process that thoughtful judges and jurors go through when attempting to grasp the complexities of what experts have to say about important technical or scientific issues that relate to the evidence to be considered in the case. These two different results make it even more obvious how important it is to determine whether an expert will be allowed to say things like, "The defendant made the prints at the scene of the crime," as opposed to being limited to saying only that the known print has these characteristics and the unknown print has those characteristics, leaving it up to the jurors to decide whether they think the defendant did or did not make the prints. For IT experts, a similar situation exists when an expert is asked whether he or she thinks that the person sitting at the com-

---

16. *U.S. v. Plaza, Acosta and Rodriguez,* January 2002.

puter with a certain address and phone connection sent the virus or worm to the victim's system. Following the reasoning of the court's initial ruling in the fingerprint case, the IT expert would be allowed to testify only that he or she found certain evidence on the first computer and certain other evidence on the target system.

After hearing from additional experienced experts who could persuade with authority, from both the government and the defense (and after taking account of another legal system's experience with and endorsement of the same method that was used in this case), the court became convinced that, at least for FBI trained and experienced experts, the criteria established by the gatekeeping decisions were adequately met by the techniques that these particular expert examiners used in this case.

In other words, what had led the judge to doubt those methods and to limit the FBI expert's testimony in the first opinion was more than overcome by the additional evidence and persuasiveness of the new experts produced at the second hearing. The totality of the evidence before the court persuaded the judge that the *Daubert* and *Kumho Tire* standards had been met by the use of the methods approved by British courts for many years, so long as those methods were applied by FBI qualified experts. This still leaves open the question of what standards of other experts who are not trained by the FBI will be accepted by other courts, if and when their use of similar or other fingerprint identification and comparison methods are offered and challenged.

Here in the court's own words are the concluding sections of the second opinion.

(iii) In the January 7 opinion, the aspect of the Daubert inquiry into "the existence and maintenance of standards controlling the technique's operation," . . . that was of greatest concern was the acknowledged subjectivity of the fingerprint examiner's stated opinion that a latent print and a known exemplar are both attributable to the same person. Government witnesses Meagher and Ashbaugh both described the "match" opinion as "subjective," and defense witness Dr. David Stoney agreed. I concluded that "[w]ith such a high degree of subjectivity, it is difficult to see how fingerprint identification—the matching of a latent print to a known print—is controlled by any clearly describable set of standards to which most examiners prescribe." On further reflection, I disagree with myself. I think my assessment stopped with the word "subjective" when I should have gone on to focus on the process the word describes. There are, to be sure, situations in which the subjectiveness of an opinion properly gives rise to reservations about the opinion's reliability. . . . But there are many situations in which an expert's manifestly subjective opinion (an opinion based, as Sergeant Ashbaugh said of the opinions of fingerprint examiners, on "one's personal knowledge, ability and experience") is regarded as admissible evidence in an American courtroom: a forensic engineer's testimony that a bottom-fire nailer's defective design caused an unintended "double-fire," resulting in injury to the plaintiff, Lauzon v. Senco Products, 270 F.3d 681 (8th cir. 2001); an electrical engineer's testimony that fire in a clothes drier was caused by a thermostat malfunction, Maryland Casualty Co. v. Therm-O-Disc, 137 F.3d 780 (4th Cir., 1998);

a marketing researcher's testimony as to consumer interpretations of advertising claims, the testimony being based on a market survey of consumers, Southard Sod Farms v. Stover Seed Co., 108 F.3d 1134 (9th Cir., 1997) . . . . In each instance the expert is operating within a vocational framework that may have numerous objective components, but the expert's ultimate opining is likely to depend in some measure on experiential factors that transcend precise measurement and quantification. As compared with the degree of subjectiveness inherent in one or more of the foregoing examples of expert opinion testimony, the subjective ingredients of opinion testimony presented by a competent fingerprint examiner appear to be of substantially more restricted compass. The defined characteristics of such testimony are illumined by the following exchange in the House of Lords on March 11, 2002:

"Lord Lester of Herne Hill asked Her Majesty's Government:

"Further to the Written Answers by Lord Rooker on 25 February (WA 172-73), what are the objective criteria and prescribed verification procedures for fingerprint identification used in evidence in criminal trials. [HL3041]

"Lord Rooker: To determine whether or not a crime scene mark and a fingerprint impression have been made by the same person, the fingerprint examiner must carry out a process of analysis, comparison and evaluation by determining whether in each impression friction ridge features are of a compatible type; they are in the same relative positions to each other in the ridge structure; they are in the same sequence; there is sufficient quantitative and qualitative detail in each in agreement; and there are any areas of apparent or real discrepancy. The examiner must address all these issues before declaring that both mark and impression have been made by the same person.

"The next stage is verification. The examiner's conclusion must be verified independently by two other officers who must both be fingerprint experts. Any mark/impression identification notified to investigating officers and presented in court will have, and must have, been subject to the above procedures."

In sum, contrary to the view expressed in my January 7 opinion, I am now persuaded that the standards which control the opining of a competent fingerprint examiner are sufficiently widely agreed upon to satisfy Daubert's requirements.

(3) Completing the Daubert/Kumho Tire Assessment

Having re-reviewed the applicability of the Daubert *factors through the prism of* Kumho Tire, *I conclude that the one* Daubert *factor which is both pertinent and unsatisfied is the first factor—"testing."* Kumho Tire, *as I have noted above, instructs district courts to "consider the specific factors identified in* Daubert *where they are reasonable measures of the reliability of expert testimony." . . . Scientific tests of ACE-V—i.e., tests in the* Daubert *sense—would clearly aid in measuring ACE-V's reliability. But, as of today, no such tests are in hand. The question, then, is whether, in the absence of such tests, a court should conclude that the ACE-V fingerprint identification system, as practiced by certified FBI fingerprint examiners, has too great a likelihood of producing erroneous results to be admissible as evidence in a courtroom setting. There are respected authorities who, it appears, would render such a verdict.*

In a recent OpEd piece in The New York Times, *Peter Neufeld and Barry Scheck, who direct Cardozo Law School's Innocence Project, have this to say:*

"No one doubts that fingerprints can, and do, serve as a highly discriminating identifier, and digital photographic enhancement and computer databases now promise to make fingerprint identification more useful than ever before. But to what degree incomplete and imperfect fingerprints can be reliably used to identify individuals requires more scientific examination. . . . Forensic science has rarely been subjected to the kind of scrutiny and independent verification applied to other fields of applied and medical science. Instead, analysts testifying in courts about fingerprint analysis, bite marks, handwriting comparisons and the like have often argued that in their field the courtroom itself provided the test. . . . As the National Institutes of Health finance basic scientific research, the National Institute of Justice should put money into verification and validation before a technique of identification is admitted into court." . . .

As explained in Part II of this opinion, I have found, on the record before me, that there is no evidence that certified FBI fingerprint examiners present erroneous identification testimony, and, as a corollary, that there is no evidence that the rate of error of certified FBI fingerprint examiners is unacceptably high. With those findings in mind, I am not persuaded that courts should defer admission of testimony with respect to fingerprinting—which Professors Neufeld and Scheck term "[t]he bedrock forensic identifier of the 20th century"—until academic investigators financed by the National Institute of Justice have made substantial headway on a "verification and validation" research agenda. For the National Institute of Justice, or other institutions both public and private, to sponsor such research would be all to the good. But to postpone present in-court utilization of this "bedrock forensic identifier" pending such research would be to make the best the enemy of the good.

IV

English and American trial courts have accepted fingerprint identification testimony for almost a century. The first English appellate endorsement of fingerprint identification testimony was the 1906 opinion in Rex v. Castleton, *3 Cr. App. R. 74. In 1906 and 1908, Sergeant Joseph Faurot, a New York City detective who had in 1904 been posted to Scotland Yard to learn about fingerprinting, used his new training to break open two celebrated cases: in each instance fingerprint identification led the suspect to confess . . .—important early indices of the reliability of fingerprint identification techniques when responsibly practiced. The first American court of last resort to consider the admissibility of such evidence was the Illinois Supreme Court: in* People v. Jennings, *96 N.E. 1077 (1911), the court concluded that such evidence was admissible and affirmed appellant's murder conviction. The identification testimony in* Jennings *came from William M. Evans and Michael P. Evans of the Chicago Police Department's Bureau of Identification; Inspector Edward Foster of the Dominion Police in Ottawa, who "had studied the subject at Scotland Yard"; and Mary E. Holland, who "began investigation of finger print impressions in 1904, studied at Scotland Yard in 1908, passed an examination on the subject, and started the first bureau of identification in this country for the United States government at Washington." Id. at 1082. The court ruled:*

"From the evidence in this record we are disposed to hold that the classification of finger print impressions and their method of identification is a science requiring study. While some of the reasons which guide an expert to his conclusions are such as may be weighed by any intelligent person with good eyesight from such exhibits as we have here in the record, after being pointed out to him by one versed in the study of finger prints, the evidence in question does not come within the common experience of all men of common education in the ordinary walks of life, and therefore the court and jury were properly aided by witnesses of peculiar and special experience on this subject. Id. at 1083.

"The Jennings *opinion and Sergent Faurot's cases illustrate the extent to which American fingerprint identification programs depended, in their infancy, on lessons learned from Scotland Yard." . . .*

In due course—as much of the testimony of Stephen Meagher, David Ashbaugh and Allan Bayle, and also the pronouncements of the Court of Appeal in Buckley and of Lord Rooker in the House of Lords, suggest—the techniques of North American fingerprint identification specialists appear to have reached a level of sophistication paralleling that of their English counterparts.

The opinion of the Court of Appeals in Buckley adumbrated the fingerprint identification regime which Her Majesty's Government has now put into force—an ACE-V regime which, stripped of any required minimum number of Galton points, corresponds almost exactly with the ACE-V procedures followed by the FBI. . . . It is to be expected that English trial judges, in accordance with Buckley, (1) will require a showing (or an agreement of the parties) that (a) a fingerprint examiner called as an expert witness is properly credentialed and (b) any prints presented in evidence will, at least arguably, possess the characteristics referred to by Lord Rooker as predicates for determining the existence, or the non-existence, of a match; and (2) will, subject to such a showing (or agreement of the parties), permit the examiner to give testimony before the fact-finder. The ACE-V regime that is sufficiently reliable for an English court is, I conclude, a regime whose reliability should, subject to a similar measure of trial court oversight, be regarded by the federal courts of the United States as satisfying the requirements of Rule 702 as the Supreme Court has explicated that rule in Daubert *and* Kumho Tire.

Conclusion

Motions for reconsideration are not favorites of the law. It is an important feature of a judge's job to arrive at a decision and then move on to the next issue to be decided, whether in the pending case or the case next to be addressed on the judge's docket. This judicial convention has special force for trial judges, for if a trial judge's ruling is mistaken it can, and if need arises will, be corrected on appeal. But there are occasions when a motion for reconsideration has its uses. This is such an occasion.

By agreeing to reconsider my prior ruling, I had the opportunity to acquire information not previously presented, or that I had not fully digested, on the record made in another courtroom more than two years ago. Through the efforts of government counsel, Stephen Meagher, heretofore a name in a transcript, became a real person, and through his live testimony I was able to get a substantially more rounded picture of the procedure—the FBI's ACE-V process of fingerprint identification—whose degree of reliability for expert evidentiary purposes it is my responsibility to determine. And, through the efforts of defense counsel, I had the opportunity to learn from Allan Bayle, a senior English fingerprint specialist, that one aspect of the FBI's system—the annual proficiency testing of FBI fingerprint examiners—may have shortcomings. But I also learned from Allan Bayle's testimony two more important truths: namely, that the ACE-V process employed by New Scotland Yard is essentially indistinguishable from the FBI's ACE-V process, and that this formidably knowledgeable and experienced veteran of the Yard—the legendary and actual source of the systematic and comprehensive utilization of fingerprint identification as an instrument of law enforcement—believes in ACE-V without reservation. Reopening the record also led me to educate myself about the legal framework with respect to the receipt in evidence of expert fingerprint identification testimony that has just been put into effect in England by Her Majesty's Government. That new legal framework—which departs very significantly from the regime I had read about in the Mitchell record—turns out to be substantially the same as the legal framework that our government, in the case at bar, has contended is appropriate for FBI fingerprint identification evidence.

Based on the foregoing considerations, I have concluded that arrangements which, subject to careful trial court oversight, are felt to be sufficiently reliable in England, ought likewise to be found sufficiently reliable in the federal courts of the United States, subject to similar measures of trial court oversight. In short, I have changed my mind. "Wisdom too often never comes, and so"—as Justice Frankfurter admonished himself and every judge—"one ought not to reject it merely because it comes late." Henslee v. Union Planters Bank, *335 U.S. 595, 600 (1949) (Frankfurter, J., dissenting); cf.,* Wolf v. Colorado, *338 U.S. 25, 47 (1949) (Rutledge, J., dissenting).*

Accordingly, in an order filed today accompanying this opinion, this court GRANTS the government's motion for reconsideration of the January 7 order; VACATES the January 7 order; DENIES the defendants' Motion to Preclude the United States from Introducing Latent Fingerprint Evidence; and GRANTS the government's Motion in Limine to Admit Latent Prints.

At the upcoming trial, the presentation of expert fingerprint testimony by the government, and the presentation of countering expert fingerprint testimony by any of the defendants . . . will be subject to the court's oversight prior to presentation of such testimony before the jury, with a view to insuring that any proposed expert witness possesses the appropriate expert qualifications and that fingerprints offered in evi-

dence will be of a quality arguably susceptible of responsible analysis, comparison and evaluation.[17]

Scientific Methods Are No Guarantee

Broad-based challenges to the tradition of assuming that an experienced expert in a particular forensic detection and identification field like fingerprint comparisons will be allowed without objection to testify as to his or her expert opinion will continue. More scientifically reliable forensic identification methods will still be countered by attacking the competence and credibility of the forensic evidence handlers over the length and breadth of the chain of custody of the evidence. Indeed, this strategy was used to great success by the O. J. Simpson defense team. At the time of Simpson's trial, there was no good way to challenge the scientific basis for establishing identity by an accurate DNA analysis. Therefore, the defense chose not to challenge the DNA evidence on the basis of whether the DNA of the samples matched that of Simpson. Unlike the current turmoil about fingerprint comparison techniques, DNA analysis appears by consensus to be amply based on very strong scientific research and valid statistical methods.

The members of the Simpson legal "Dream Team" simply accepted the science of DNA identification and the probabilities that essentially excluded all but the defendant as the source of the blood found at the murder scene and at his home. They assumed the certainty of the DNA analysis, and then focused on casting reasonable doubt on the evidence collection and comparison procedures that were used. The doubts created about the motives and credibility of law enforcement forensic experts and evidence handlers in the field served as the foundation of the defense's claim that the defendant was being framed by racist Los Angeles police investigators. This claim became the core defense and the major thrust of the case in the cross-examination of the State's expert witnesses, ultimately leading to Simpson's acquittal.

Thus, it seems that forensics in general faces challenges from two directions. One set of challenges comes from the *Daubert* and *Kumho Tire* scientific method series of hurdles erected by the Supreme Court to test expert witnesses and their methods and opinions. When the tools and techniques are sufficiently sophisticated and authenticated to pass the Supreme Court test for scientific reliability, the experts are still

---

17. *United States of America v. Carlos Ivan Llera Plaza, Wilfredo Martinez Acosta, and Victor Rodriguez.* Nos. Cr. 98-362-10, 98-362-11, 98-362-12, decided on March 13, 2002. The opinion is cited as 188 F. Supp. 2d 549, and also reported at 58 Federal Rules of Evidence Service 1. The entire opinion is included in Appendix A.

subject to a second attack on the lack of training and experience or the failures of the individuals who are in the chain of custody of the evidence that is to be examined by the experts.

Learning from Pseudoscientists

So how does all of this apply to expertise about computer systems? To a judge with an average layperson's understanding of how computers and software are supposed to work, the question of whether a given piece of code behaved as it was supposed to on a given occasion would appear to be a scientifically provable process. The problem for the IT expert and the sponsoring trial attorney is that reality dictates that software applications run on hardware and that hardware runs in an often indeterminate environment. It takes a great deal of time to devise the kinds of tests capable of instigating and diagnosing a particular software problem. It can also be argued that the primary limitation on our remarkable advances in the computing power of hardware is that software can't be developed quickly enough to accommodate advances in speed and complexity of hardware as it is delivered to the market and therefore will always generate new uncertainties.

Hence, even knowledgeable schoolchildren who work on computers note that old software runs quite predictably on the hardware for which it was designed, but that in order to allow the software to continue to run on more modern systems, changes in operating systems are required. So, unless we are talking about static combinations of a particular application and a particular operating system, configured in a particular way to run on a particular piece of hardware, subjective opinions as to how an application should perform in a more complex and unpredictable network environment are going to be the rule rather than the exception. So much for scientific theories and the ability to generalize experimental determinations! In the future, lawyers and their experts will enjoy creating and attempting to resolve doubts about the ability to predict the behavior of newer or older applications. Challenging experts as to their opinions about operating systems, running on newer and faster hardware than those they were designed for, or running in complex, constantly changing processors and network configurations should be as interesting as cross-examining the government witness in the Simpson case.

To take but one example, consider the case in which a plaintiff alleges injury due to a critical software application failure. Expert testimony about software testing and the reliability of a particular application will at some level of the testing or analysis fall back to the subjective, based on the experience and knowledge of the particular expert. At this time, with IT expertise so largely subjective, the storytelling and other communication skills of the expert witness are apt to be the difference between judicial confusion and clarity. And although that may sound good to teachers and storytellers, here's the rub.

This inescapable reality also throws open the gate to a Daubert challenge (which will be discussed in greater detail in Chapter 8 on the gatekeeping function of the court). This requires that the potential expert and the attorney be ready and able to persuade a judge that the expert should be allowed to give his or her opinion, regardless of whether it is totally scientific or only as scientific as the current state of the technology allows. The rub is that this expertise is based today in large part on the subjective opinions of the witness, but it must still be sufficiently reliable under the gatekeeping standards to be admitted along with objective, more clearly scientific opinions. This doesn't mean that software engineers shouldn't be qualified by courts to apply their expertise to a problem in order to help the fact finder decide an important issue in the case. However, it is not going to be easy for a computer-phobic judge to clearly comprehend where the science stops and the art begins. Judges considering complex computer forensic evidence will certainly need and seek out all the help IT experts can offer. Furthermore, it will require a great deal of soul searching on the part of the IT community to acquire clarity on why these areas of expertise are sufficiently different from phrenology and astrology to pass legal muster. This is vital if IT experts are to be allowed to apply their proven techniques and methods in their attempts to aid fact finders. Should the IT community decide that IT experts are in the same boat as the forensic fingerprint experts and the forensic economists, IT experts should be prepared to give convincing reasons why their communities of interest should be counted as a source of qualified expertise and why they possess a legitimate mastery of the technology.

Considering the current state of the art of software testing and the subjectiveness of attempts to analyze the performance of a critical application when there is an allegation of failure, you can see that the qualification and admission of expert testimony about these things is going to be at least as close a call as we are now seeing in the challenge to fingerprint evidence. However, IT does not have the benefit of 100 years of operating assumptions that the art and science of fingerprint comparison was beyond question as to its underlying theory that no two fingerprints are alike. What we face with IT forensic expertise in things such as software testing is a piece of code that theoretically is determinative. Between that theoretical substance and the form of the testing and analysis, an enlightened attorney will find a growing shadow of suspicion that the opinions of the technical expert are not yet adequately based on scientific methods and are therefore subject to consistent legal challenges.

When Science Turns into Art and Vice Versa

Once you understand how pseudoscience can become interspersed in the bigger picture of an expert's legitimate investigation that uses both scientific methods and nonscientific methods, it is a bit easier to understand why judges have been tempted in the past to leave it up to the lawyers and their experts to fight it out in open court before the jury. But this is no longer an option. Courts are understandably reluctant to return to the tradition of letting in the good, bad, and ugly experts. Ultimately, the key to dealing with technical disputes may lie in listening to IT graybeards like David Bailey (who was in charge of computer security at Los Alamos National Laboratory when the world's largest computer system was being developed) who like to tell stories and share advice about how things should be done to get the best results. Standing alone, outside of the context of a carefully choreographed expert witness's testimony, these teaching stories can appear to be but idiosyncratic tales. Without more stories, based on their experiences and the successful practice of their art and founded on scientific proof of the theories and methods, expert storytellers run the risk of being dismissed by technophobic judges. For example, Bailey likes to explain the problem for experts who must testify about what happened in a complex computer system by pointing out that to be most effective, the expert must prepare to testify by doing exhaustive computer software application testing. And there is a very significant difference between amateur and expert levels of effective, exhaustive testing. To fully understand that difference, we may be reduced to the individual experience of a given expert who has also benefited from the collective wisdom of the most experienced members of the professional community. Such an expert distinguishes testing by amateurs as testing things in an intuitive and superficial way until the tester is exhausted. Experts, on the other hand, test the software until they have thoroughly exhausted the software. For Bailey, being able to explain to a judge or a jury the difference between testing that exhausts the software and testing that exhausts the expert really defines the true expert.[18] It also exposes the amateur and his or her failure to do adequate testing to be qualified as an expert.

This is quite similar to the ways in which martial artists distinguish between the teacher and the student. Many martial arts experts assert with Eugen Herrigel that the confidence of amateurs is the envy of all true experts. But the beginning student has only enthusiasm, without the mastery. And so the confidence of the student (in the battle of experts) is also the greatest single advantage of the true expert over less accomplished practitioners. Socrates had his own peculiar spin on the same problem when he acknowledged in his debates that he knew only that he knew nothing. The winner in the round of expert witness qualification is most likely to be the diligent practitioner who uses proven techniques based to the largest degree possible on the scientific method. The use of these techniques clearly demonstrates the years of training and experience that justify both objective and subjective proofs presented in the entire context of the testimony. The greatest advantage goes to the expert who can explain and teach the accumulated knowledge of the field of expertise simply, and apply proven techniques with clearly demonstrated results.

---

18. Bailey, David. Personal communication, August 2001, Albuquerque, New Mexico.

A Case in Point

Let's anticipate for a moment the testimony of an expert in a criminal computer fraud case. Suppose that in the case in question, a suspect is accused of placing software on a victim's computer system that disrupts the operation of the system, thereby resulting in the disruption of the victim's business. We might infer, based on the fingerprint challenges currently underway in the courts, the areas that may be used in an effort to impeach the ultimate conclusions of a technology expert brought in to investigate the incident. In such cases, an expert will attempt to correlate digital evidence collected from both the victim's and the defendant's computer systems, demonstrating a cause-and-effect relationship between the actions of the defendant and the resulting damage to the victim's system. The whole point of a fingerprint expert's testimony regarding the comparison of a known fingerprint with one discovered during the criminal investigation has, until recently, been to tell the jury that the same person did or did not make both prints. After reading both of the fingerprint case opinions, you should suspect that these experts can anticipate being challenged as to their training, methods, and all the rest of the evolving gatekeeping tests. Similarly, the IT expert might be asked about and allowed to testify as to how he or she thought the evidence left on the logs in the victim's computer system could be explained. Is it the expert's opinion that the electronic evidence proves that the actions of a human who was at the defendant's residence, where phone tolls indicated that the attack calls had originated, left these traces in the logs and tolls? Or, alternatively, could this evidence be explained as the result of an automated program or some other mechanism outside the control of the defendant? We predict that it will not be long before attorneys in civil cases and criminal cases will be challenging such IT expert opinions. One basis for the challenges will be that the techniques used by IT experts have not been subjected to the scientific and technical scrutiny required by the *Kumho* and *Daubert* cases and equivalent state standards for determining the reliability of scientific and technical methods.

What may well be in store for experts in this field is the consistent challenge of an opposing expert that their claims of scientific proofs simply don't measure up to what the challenging expert is prepared to demonstrate are or should be generally accepted standards. For these reasons, the successfully impeached expert will not be allowed to opine, for example, that a particular person at a given location caused the logs to be created. Such a limitation on how far an expert will be allowed to reach could mean, in this example, that IT experts often are only allowed to testify about what the recovered logs demonstrated was going on in the machinery at a particular time, but not about whom the expert may reasonably have determined was responsible for this anomalous behavior. As with the recent decisions in the fingerprint arena, IT expert witnesses may find themselves in the position of setting the stage for forming an opinion but being forced to leave the rendering of the ultimate opinion to the fact finders to formulate themselves. This makes IT experts more like glorified fact witnesses. It means that they must carefully explain all the evidence that would give the expert confidence in the conclusion that the expert is not allowed to state, while leaving it to the attorney to argue what, based on the work of the expert and all the facts in evidence, the ultimate opinion must be. However, for the reasons outlined above, IT experts may be precluded from rendering that ultimate opinion as to the scientific probability or certainty of an identification or of a relevant but technically and scientifically unsubstantiated chain of causation. Such a move makes the distinction between the testing expert and the exhausted amateur in Bailey's teaching story all the more telling in deciding whether a given expert should be allowed to render an ultimate opinion.

The Expert Storyteller

At this point, you may be wondering how this discussion will lead you toward better service as an expert witness. Think about how you will deal with the responsibility of explaining your area of expertise to the lawyer, the judge, the opposing experts, and the jurors. As shown in this chapter, one traditional forensic specialty after another has faced the challenge of the *Daubert* line of reasoning. Either you put forward the proof of the scientific method and testing that allows for the opinion that the attorney seeks to have the expert give, or you must be content to leave the opinions up to the fact finders to make, based on the facts presented by the experts and other ordinary witnesses, as well as the arguments of counsel.

The greatest technical experts known for their abilities to explain the most complex details of a technology to inexperienced people, like trainees who need to use the technology safely and effectively in their work, have at least two things in common. First, they have a deep understanding of their area of expertise, gained through a lifetime of study and experience. Second, they are gifted teachers and storytellers. This is where the partnership between the expert witness and the trial lawyer comes full circle. As the expert teaches and trains the lawyer about the technical issues at stake, the trial lawyer is often of most assistance to the expert in passing on the many arts of communication the lawyer has been forced to learn, practice, and perfect in his or her career in the courtroom.

Law lives on narrative, for reasons both banal and deep. For one, the law is awash in storytelling. Clients tell stories to lawyers, who must figure out what to make of what they hear. As clients and lawyers talk, the client's story gets recast into plights and prospects, plots and pilgrimages into possible worlds. If circumstances warrant, the lawyers retell their client's stories in the form of pleas and arguments to judges and testimony to juries. Next, judges and jurors retell the stories to themselves or to each other in the form of instructions, deliberations, a verdict, a set of findings, or an opinion. And then it is the turn of journalists, commentators, and critics. This endless telling and retelling, casting and recasting is essential to the conduct of the law. It is how law's actors comprehend whatever series of events they make the subject of their legal actions. It is how they try to make their actions comprehensible again within some larger series of events they take to constitute the legal system and the culture that sustains it.[19]

The expert's testimony has become one of the single most important parts of any serious litigation in which technical issues are involved. It is about to become the central issue in much of the pretrial litigation over electronic evidence in discovery. It will certainly be the deciding evidence when one side challenges the other's experts or the basis or scope of one or more crucial technical opinions. Our thesis is simply put: How well a new expert can expect to do is directly dependent on how hard he or she is willing to work to find the words and the images to explain technical issues in simple stories. Getting clear on the big picture of the litigation and then deciding on the best narrative structure are crucial first steps. Finding simple analogies, developing clear graphics and other images, and demonstrating a willingness to explain what fits and what doesn't is a basic recipe for success as an expert witness.

In the exceptionally fast-paced, fluid world of IT systems, we may feel far removed from the need to create compelling narratives. However, the legal process ineluctably pulls us back to the need for narrative in order to understand just what went wrong (or what did not). To continue to consider the example of litigation over an alleged critical software failure, it seems likely that at least for the immediate future the establishment of recognized institutional authorities and accepted standards of testing and quality assurance for most systems will trail behind the litigation of large numbers of particular system failures.

Many important new standards for software and the design and operation of complex computer systems are likely to come from the resolution of judges and jurors of the competing stories contained in the reports, depositions, and trial testimony of experts. These de facto standards, while focusing on the case at hand, will evolve into more general standards from the collected stories and reports from preceding cases. It behooves an aspiring software expert to learn how to use Lexis/Nexis or Westlaw, the two primary legal information resources, to keep abreast of the stories that courts report in their published opinions of real cases. It also seems fitting that IT professionals should at least acquaint themselves with the ritual of giving expert testimony, just in case such a fate should befall them. The opportunity to testify as an expert may be the most significant contribution to the establishment of proper and adequate standards for IT that a particular expert can make at this time.

Based on our experiences and on conversations with experts from a number of different IT disciplines, we have found that the relationship between an experienced and successful litigator and a genuine expert witness can provide professional rewards

---

19. Amsterdam, Anthony G., and Jerome Bruner. *Minding the Law.* Cambridge, MA: Harvard University Press, 2000, p. 7.

for both participants on a level that is hard to match in most other aspects of their respective practices. But as this brief sampling of the history of bogus science and dubious prediction techniques should make clear, patience is needed when preparing to explain why and how complex technologies work and how well they work. This patience in preparation and presentation will pay great dividends when IT experts are called to testify about their chosen expertise. Ultimately, this slow but steady approach will become crucial when they are asked to critique questionable methods and opinions of other experts, who claim to have the magic that entitles them to state their opinions but, on closer examination, often lack the scientific methods to adequately explain the facts.

Ethical Rules for Technical Experts

There are a number of ways to characterize the different legal and ethical rules that apply to experts who become involved in the litigation process. One way is to consider first the ethical rules that define and establish professionalism for trial attorneys and judges and then examine how those rules are passed on to the experts who testify. The legal professional and ethical rules, with only minor variations from state to state, are designed to be self-imposed, subject to enforcement and discipline by the trial courts or appellate courts during the course of litigation. Furthermore, these rules, which are universally adopted by attorneys and judges, are enforced by ethics and disciplinary committees that deal with infractions reported outside of the course of a particular litigation. Another approach to understanding might be to step through the traditional rules and assumptions about how ordinary witnesses should be treated when they become caught up in the legal system and compare those descriptions with the way things are handled when experts are called as witnesses, as described in the following quote from Samuel R. Gross.

> *Imagine how adversarial fact finding would function under the following regime: the lawyers on each side of a dispute, acting in secret, choose people from an almost indefinitely large array and designate them as the witnesses; these witnesses are paid handsomely for their testimony; lawyers can preemptively hire witnesses in order to keep them from testifying when their honest testimony might help the other side; many witnesses make a business of testifying, and advertising their services; the attorneys control the information and the issues on which their witnesses testify; wit-*

nesses are allowed to testify to matters beyond their personal knowledge and to eval-uate, as well as to present information; the existing rules of pre-trial discovery are curtailed so that the identity and the evidence of many potential witnesses can be concealed from the opposing party; the usual rules of evidence are inapplicable at trial; and, finally, the subject matter of the testimony by these witnesses is intrinsi-cally confusing, if not incomprehensible, to judges and jurors.

Odd as it may seem, this is an accurate thumbnail sketch of the present mode of using expert information in American courts.[1]

Some technical experts are formally bound by the ethics and professional codes of conduct of their own professions (by dint of membership in certain organizations or certifications granted by others). In the absence of such codes, many experts can be convinced that they need to comply with such measures on a strictly voluntary basis. In this chapter, we'll define and then contrast various sets of ethics rules for different professional communities of interest. We'll also consider rules of conduct for judges and attorneys and explore how those rules apply to the experts who testify.

A significant problem for IT expert witnesses is that there may not be any gener-ally recognized body of ethics rules applied to and enforced by the members of the IT professional communities of interest. Furthermore, even when a particular expert belongs to an IT professional community that has ethics rules, those rules may not relate (directly or even indirectly) to the duties of such an expert when acting as a witness in litigation. Because of this, experts may find themselves looking to the lawyers who hire them for guidance, not only about the formal and informal rules of procedure but also for the ethical guidelines that govern the litigation process. Such guidelines call for complying with the letter and the spirit of the established rules of procedure for litigation. Many of the generally understood and fairly intuitive rules about the conduct of discovery that takes place with regular witnesses and docu-ments are suspended when it comes to experts.

A Failure Analysis: Examples of Ethics-Challenged Experts

Perhaps the best way to demonstrate how the failure of foundation components affects the stability of structures is to use the time-honored technique of failure analy-sis. The entire edifice of trial by advocacy relies on the common-sense rules of profes-sional ethics and the cardinal principles of professional conduct. Here our failure analysis will consist of analyzing what happens when the violation of these ethical

---

1. Gross, Samuel R. "Expert Evidence." *University of Wisconsin Law Review*, vol. 1991, p. 1113.

rules causes the structure of an apparently successful litigation to fail. We'll begin by examining two cases in which the courts found that the experts failed to act ethically. In these cases the failure of the technical experts to testify truthfully cost the parties that employed them judgments of over $100 million. In each case, the expert had determined that a patent or family of patents was valid and enforceable against another party that had been alleged to have wrongfully benefited from the infringement of the original patents. These were, in essence, high-stakes legal duels in which the persuasive testimonies of the respective technical experts were the keys to the kingdom—and to the large judgments rendered by the respective juries.

While these stories require you to consider the proceedings that gave rise to the questionable testimony of the experts in some detail, in doing so you can also better understand how experts can yield to the temptation to become advocates. Remember that by becoming an advocate, the expert witness violates basic ethical rules. Although limiting your perspective to one side of the controversy might appear to resolve ethical conflicts and might furthermore make it far easier to deliver the most persuasive testimony, these advantages come at a premium. For the price of advocacy is most often surrendering your ability to deliver the most truthful and useful information. In particular, you sacrifice your ability to deliver appropriate information both during discovery, for the benefit of the attorneys for the other side, and also at trial, for the benefit of the fact finders.

You might naively believe that telling the truth is a concept that any qualified expert can comprehend without a special code of instruction. However, in the heat of the legal battle, the expert can begin to believe that winning is all that matters. Furthermore, this flawed premise may spawn the attitude that it is up to the people on the other side to do their own due diligence to determine whether the expert is testifying truthfully. Such beliefs set the stage for the kinds of disasters these two stories describe.

By understanding the context of patent infringement litigation, you can follow the path of the experts in these two patent cases and in the process learn a good deal about how both diligent discovery techniques and blind luck can combine to reveal the false testimony of a technical expert witness. In both stories, the experts were the key witnesses in their respective cases. In the first story, the questionable testimony concerned the circumstances surrounding a crucial test. The expert's opinion that led to the $100 million verdict against the defendant was based on this testing. In the second story, unknown to the court or the attorneys for the defendant, the plaintiff's expert was conducting a parallel expert witness engagement—and simultaneously rendering a conflicting expert opinion on similar issues that had arisen in another pending patent infringement case. The expert, however, testified in his deposition that this was not the case and repeated this testimony at trial.

On the Importance of Knowing Where You Are (and Aren't)

The legal system strives for finality in the resolution of disputes. This does not mean that individual lawsuits that set at stake millions of dollars, the continued existence of business enterprises, or the lives of criminal defendants do not take their sweet time in getting to that final stage of resolution. However, along the way, significant burdens are placed before a party who wishes to reopen something that has been resolved by trial. So it is with great reluctance that a court orders a new trial; usually this happens only in cases of the most significant error or prejudice to one of the parties. Such a situation occurred during the case of *Viskase Corporation v. American National Can Corporation.* The expert who testified falsely has died since the trial in that case and his name will not be mentioned in the telling of this sad tale. Instead the deceased will be referred to only as "the chemist" or "the expert."

In this case there was a battle of the experts as to the proper method of testing to determine whether the defendant's material was an infringing use of the patented material of the plaintiff. Therefore, the nature and accuracy of the testing became extremely important as the basis for the testimony of the plaintiff's expert. Since the defendant's position through their own expert was that the plaintiff's approach to testing was wrong, the credibility of the plaintiff's expert and the appropriateness and accuracy of the testing procedures used became crucial to the outcome of the case. This problem is more common than one might think. Remember our discussion in Chapter 5 of the problems encountered when distinguishing between chance, coincidence, and causation with relation to exhaustive testing.

In this case, the jurors apparently approved of the methods used by the plaintiff's expert and believed this witness more than the other expert who testified for the defendant. The jurors ultimately found that the defendant had infringed on the plaintiff's patents and awarded over $100 million to the plaintiff. After trial, lawyers for the defendant obtained evidence for the first time that documents they had requested during pretrial discovery had not been produced, and they asked the trial judge to allow them to investigate. In the course of the postverdict investigation of the allegations that the plaintiff's expert and counsel had not provided all the relevant documents concerning the testing, the trial judge, Elaine Bucklo, made the following findings.

> [The judge] agreed to allow ANC [the defendant] to take the deposition of the person who reportedly claimed, contrary to trial testimony, to have actually performed certain tests. That deposition appeared to confirm ANC's suspicions, if what the deponent[2] had said was true. [The court] then suggested that if Viskase wanted to clarify the matter that it take depositions of personnel at the testing laboratory who

---

2. The witness giving testimony in a deposition.

could confirm or deny the apparently conflicting testimony with regard to altered documents. Viskase agreed and took several depositions. ANC [then] filed a supplemental motion arguing that Viskase not only did not produce relevant documents before trial but that [their expert] testified falsely at trial regarding the tests upon which his opinion regarding infringement of the films was based.[3]

In order to determine whether a new trial would be required, the trial judge reconsidered in some detail the expert testimony at the trial concerning the testing that was done.

After stating his background, [the plaintiff's expert, a chemist] began his testimony by explaining to the jury the basic chemistry involved in as well as some history of polyethylenes and the relationship of long chain branching to linear polyethylenes. He also discussed an analysis of long chain branching in a linear polymer at the National Bureau of Standards. [The expert] then explained that there were two principal testing techniques for determining long chain branching. The first was magnetic resonance imaging (an MRI, with which the jury may well have been familiar), but [the expert] said this test would have limited ability to detect the level of long chain branching at issue in this litigation. The second method was gel permeation chromatography or GPC-DV testing. [The expert] explained the test and testified that it was very accurate.[4]

The court found that at this point in his testimony the witness was questioned further.

[The expert] was asked whether he supervised any GPC-DV tests on the Affinity PL 1840 resin. He stated that he did. . . . After stating that this test was better than the other test he had mentioned, he stated that his recommendation was that they use the best GPC-DV testing available in the United States. [The expert] was again asked if he supervised tests on Affinity PL 1840, and he again said yes. . . . In response to a question as to where he supervised these tests, [he] stated that he wanted an outside independent evaluation of any long chain branching that might be in Affinity, and that he chose Jordi Associates. He was again asked if he supervised these tests. After stating "yes" a third time, . . . Viskase attempted to move into evidence a document described as "the testing that you supervised at Jordi Associates." . . . ANC objected on hearsay grounds. Viskase counsel attempted to lay a foundation, asking the expert whether he was "there when the tests described in this Viskase Trial Exhibit No. 167 were performed?" . . . The expert responded as follows:

A: *Yes. I believe this was the second visit. I drove some distance to go there, and I asked to be present while the injections were made. The column was eluted, the detector*

---

3. *Viskase Corporation v. American National Can Corporation.* U.S. Dist. Ct. N. D. Ill, ED, 979 F Supp. 697, 700, 1997, U.S. Dist.

4. *Id.*, 700.

responded. But I also asked to leave, and I asked them to send me, without my previous notification, what their results were so that there would be no indication that I in any way would influence the results that were to be presented. . . .

Following this testimony, Viskase again sought admission of the test results. [The court] sustained ANC's objection. [The expert] again testified that he observed the testing at Jordi Associates, . . . that he was there when the tests were done, that he was there when the samples were prepared, and when they were injected, and when they eluded from the GPC-DV. . . . Following another objection, [the expert] testified as follows:

A: Well, I'll just speak the truth, your Honor. This was faxed to me after I left, and I asked that that be done because I did not want to be looking over their shoulders at the time they did the computation, plain and simple, in the interest of objectivity and honesty. . . .

[The expert] was then asked if he calculated long chain branching in Affinity PL-1840 based on the results he obtained from the Jordi testing. ANC objected that no such documentation had been provided them. [The expert] was again asked whether he observed the results of the Jordi testing while he was at Jordi. [The expert] responded that he saw the samples elude from the columns and saw the detector responses and base line return. He added, "I saw the stability of the base line. I saw the recorder of the two detector outputs and saw the information entered into their software computer program." . . . [The expert] was then asked what level of long chain branching he observed, to which he answered that he saw no detectable level. . . . He was essentially asked the same question, and gave the same response "based upon our observations at Jordi Associates" a minute later. . . . The expert compared the level of long chain branching that he "saw" with the level detected on the National Bureau of Standards sample, and testified that the Affinity resin was linear.[5]

Following this testimony, the court found that the expert

. . . testified about the various ANC products and the fact that they infringed Viskase's patents due to the absence of long chain branching in the resin. On cross-examination, [the expert] again was asked to describe what he saw. He responded that:

"With Dr. Wong, I asked him to make up the solution and do the injections and watch the recorder trace over time. . . . So we make up solutions carefully. I watched that process. That has to be truly in solution, and we have to be very careful we don't degrade the material because you have to dissolve it at high temperature, and you have to put antioxidant in the polyethylene to make sure you are getting the right answer. Then after a period of time, it can be minutes to an hour or so, then with a hypodermic syringe or other device, you withdraw a sample and inject it into the gel permeation chromatograph when the

---

5. *Id.*, 700–701.

base line is stable. I watch the base line stability, and that is very important for precise determination. So the base line was stable in the recorder charts, and I watched that. . . . "

At this point in the cross-examination, ANC referred to the report from Jordi Associates that [the court] had not allowed in evidence, asking [the expert] about the fact that the report had said "maybe" the Affinity resin had long branching. [The expert] was further referred to the part of the report that in fact stated that in order to correctly determine whether the samples were linear or branched, full statistical analysis would be required. [He] admitted that he did not do such an analysis.

At a conference before trial began on the following morning, responding to a suggestion made by [the judge] the day before that a solution to the hearsay problems of the Jordi testing exhibit could be to bring in someone from Jordi, Viskase reported that no one from Jordi would be able to testify. Counsel from Viskase (Mr. Frankel) stated, however, that "in terms of the actual tests, [the expert chemist] was present from start to finish." . . . After discussion, [the judge] again ruled that the Jordi report itself could not be put in evidence without a foundation from Jordi, but that [the expert] could state his opinion based on the testing if it had been established that the report was the kind reasonably relied upon by experts.

On redirect, Viskase counsel asked [the expert] "when the sample is injected and the trace comes out and the data go into the computer, is there any intervention possible by you or Jordi at that point?" . . . [The expert] answered, "No intervention is possible, and they have extensive experience in running branching determinations, so we use their standard protocol." . . . [He] then reiterated once more that he was present during the testing, adding:

> "There are certain things that one can actually see by eye. As I mentioned earlier, it's hypersensitive to temperature and other variations. So I could watch the recorded baseline to see if it was stable by my previous experience of having run hundreds of GPC in companies and at university. So I was aware of the sensitivity, I was aware of the standards they had run, and the perspective in which these determinations were made. . . . "

On redirect examination, [the expert] was also asked about the fact that the Jordi report had indicated that the Affinity resins might be branched. [He] explained that he wanted to know what Jordi thought about the alpha values coming out of the computer, and that he had come to a different conclusion. Both on redirect and recross, [he] was asked about the correlation between alpha values and long chain branching.

The post-trial depositions of Jordi employees and principals established that much of what [the judge] quoted from [the expert's] testimony is false. . . . All of the Jordi people agreed that [the expert] was not present for any of the testing to which he testified at trial. Neither was the testing done by Dr. Wang (described above by the expert as "Dr. Wong") who would ordinarily have been the person at Jordi to do the tests. During the summer in which the expert wanted the tests done, Dr. Wang was away. No one else at Jordi was capable of doing these tests so Jordi brought in an out-

sider, Trevor Harvard. Mr. Harvard performed the tests at Jordi and then took the computer home and made the report. "His report was sent to [the expert]. [The expert] believed Mr. Harvard had set an erroneous base line and asked that it be changed. Mr. Harvard would not make any change but everyone at Jordi agreed that Mr. Harvard had made an error. When Dr. Wang returned he was able to correct the error, and the tests were recalculated. With input from the expert as to the style in which he wanted the final report (some reports of samples of other resins were removed), a final report was prepared and sent to [the expert]. The alpha values in the final report for Affinity were not changed with respect to one of the two samples. The alpha value of the second sample changed by virtue of the recalculation from .627 to .638."[6] . . .

Viskase concede[d] that [the expert] was not present at the tests he stated he supervised although it argued that he 'may' have been at a subsequent test. Even this statement is based on testimony by one Jordi employee who thought [the expert] might have been looking over his shoulder at sometime when he was looking at his computer. Assuming the employee's vague recollection was correct, no one argues that what the expert was observing was the test he testified about in court. (Viskase Corporation v. American National Can Corporation, footnote 2.)

Furthermore, the court found that from all of the evidence as well as his own observations of the expert at trial, it was clear that he could not have simply been mistaken in his memory.

The Court found that

ANC had a right to the discovery it sought. Clearly, the Jordi Associates' documents, and those sent to [the expert] by Jordi (which included the draft report) were within the control of Viskase. Indeed, in ANC's discovery requests, Viskase specifically was defined to include any 'consultants.' In these circumstances, courts have held that a party has the right to assume that discovery responses are accurate and complete. . . . Furthermore, some of the missing documents compared the two resins used by the parties. With regard to those tests, commissioned by [the expert] in May 1995, [he] testified at his deposition that he had never done such a comparison. [The judge] conclude[d] that Viskase should not be able to benefit from ANC's failure to vigorously pursue discovery under these circumstances.[7]

The court also carefully analyzed the next two requirements for the relief that the defendants were seeking pursuant to Rule 60; namely, that the new evidence was not merely cumulative or impeaching, and that it was material.

The court determined that the two types of evidence at issue . . . the missing documents and the false trial testimony could be considered together, and that the docu-

---

6. *Viskase Corporation v. American National Can Corporation.*

7. *Viskase Corporation v. American National Can Corporation*, 703.

Rule 60 of the Federal Rules of Civil Procedure states in part that "On motion and upon such terms as are just, the court may relieve a party or a party's legal representative from a final judgment, order, or proceeding for the following reasons:

1. mistake, inadvertence, surprise, or excusable neglect;
2. newly discovered evidence which by due diligence could not have been discovered in time to move for a new trial . . . ;
3. fraud . . . , misrepresentation, or other misconduct of an adverse party;

    . . .

6. any other reason justifying relief from the operation of the judgment."

ments themselves would have been useful principally for impeachment purposes. "Thus the principal question is whether [the expert's] false trial testimony with respect to his participation in the Jordi tests was material."[8] The judge described how the problem of the expert's false claim that he was present during the testing might have been avoided without the loss of essential evidence in the following portion of the opinion.

> *ANC argues that the fact that [the expert chemist] was not actually present at the tests relied on by him at trial was material because he would not otherwise have been allowed to testify about the results of the tests. Viskase counters that Fed. R. Evid. 703 allows an expert to testify to his opinion even if the underlying data are not admissible. Rule 703 does allow an expert's opinion, even though based on inadmissible data, so long as the facts relied on by the expert are of the type "reasonably relied upon by experts in the particular field in forming opinions or inferences upon the subject. . . ." The initial problem in this case was that Viskase attempted to introduce [the expert's] opinion through the introduction of the Jordi report, which Viskase attempted to authenticate by testimony that [the expert] had actually supervised tests. For much of [the expert's] testimony, Viskase attempted to introduce the actual results based entirely on reliance of the supposed fact that [he] had personally supervised the tests. In fact, Viskase might have avoided the issue by asking for [the expert's] opinion, ascertaining that it was based on tests that he commissioned, and that those tests were the type of tests reasonably relied upon by experts in his field. . . . "[M]ight," because [the expert] testified that the testing was "hypersensitive" and he generally testified that the persons doing the testing required considerable training.[9]*

8. Id., 703.

9. Id., 704.

The court found that based on the record, "it would appear that experts in [the chemist's field] would not rely on GPC testing without knowledge of who had done the testing."[10] The court further reasoned that the expert might have testified:

> . . . that he was satisfied that Jordi Associates did have the requisite training and that, based on his knowledge of the kind of work they did, experts in his field would rely on their tests. This would have been a sufficient basis upon which [the chemist] could have rendered his opinion. At that point, with leave of court, [the chemist] might have been able to testify to the information contained in the Jordi report, even though it was otherwise inadmissible hearsay. . . . But Viskase did not directly pursue this route. Instead, it sought to demonstrate the reliability of the Jordi testing through testimony of [the expert's] direct involvement in that test. Because that was the foundation upon which it sought admission of the basis for [the expert's] opinion, his testimony is material. . . . It is material in a second respect also. [The court] described [the expert's] testimony in some detail above not only to illustrate the number of times he testified falsely during the course of his testimony but also to attempt to provide some sense of that testimony. [His] repeated statements of his personal involvement may well have influenced the jury in deciding whether to credit his testimony, and theory, over ANC's theory of significant long chain branching. Contrary to Viskase's argument in the present motion, Viskase offered almost no other testimony that would support its claim that Affinity is a linear polyethylene. The expert's testimony was the central part of Viskase's infringement case with respect to the Affinity films.[11]

In another footnote to the opinion, the court found that based on the record,

> . . . Viskase did not directly ask [the expert] until redirect, over ANC's objection, whether the tests were the type reasonably relied upon by experts in the field. . . . Prior to dealing with the specific Jordi test, Viskase did on direct elicit testimony that this was one of two tests used and that this type of test was the more reliable. Thus, it probably introduced sufficient evidence upon which to base an opinion. But when he turned to the specific test at Jordi Associates, [the expert's] entire testimony was based on his alleged personal participation.[12]
>
> The last requirement under Rule 60(b)(2) is that the evidence would probably have produced a new result. . . . This requirement, as noted earlier, does not exist under Rule 60(b)(3). [The court could not say] whether if [the expert] had testified truthfully the outcome would have been different. It makes no difference. It might have been different and since [the court] concluded his testimony was materially false, ANC has satisfied its burden under Rule 60(b)(3), Fed. R. Civ. P.

---

10. Id., 704.

11. Id., 704.

12. *Viskase Corporation v. American National Can Corporation,* footnote 6, at 704.

Viskase nevertheless argues that even if the expert testified falsely, under Metlyn Realty Corp. v. Esmark, Inc., *763 F.2d 826 (7th Cir. 1985), it cannot be held responsible for the testimony of an outside expert. The court in* Metlyn *upheld the district court's decision not to reopen a judgment entered on a settlement more than a year after the judgment became final, where it was found that an expert had testified falsely about some matters, including his credentials. But as ANC argues, in that case the district judge had approved a settlement, and after holding a hearing on the newly discovered evidence concluded that he would have nevertheless approved the settlement. That is far different from considering the impact of false testimony from the party's main witness on a jury.*[13]

Furthermore, the court found that:

Viskase agrees that it would be bound by an expert's false testimony if it or its attorneys knew the testimony was false. While it is not possible to know in this case whether Viskase's counsel knew that the expert was not present at the tests that led to the Jordi report, they surely knew there must have been additional documents and that there were additional tests conducted. Both the invoices directed to Viskase counsel and the expert's notes document counsel's knowledge of these facts. Based on this evidence the court concluded that Viskase cannot escape responsibility for their expert's false testimony.[14]

Finally, the court found that Rule 60(b)(6) allows relief from judgment for "any other reason justifying relief." The court also noted that the verdict that was the subject of the motion pursuant to Rule 60 was in excess of $100 million, and although a final judgment is desirable for parties and courts alike, a $100 million judgment should not be based on the facts found by the court in this case.

Thus, ANC's motion for a new trial on infringement as it related to Affinity-based films, willful infringement with respect to those films, and damages on all of Viskase's claims was granted by Judge Bucklo on September 29, 1997. She also ruled that the expert chemist would not be allowed to testify at any new trial.[15]

In July 2001, the Federal Circuit Court affirmed Judge Bucklo's order for a new trial due to the false testimony of the expert witness, holding in part:

A Viskase expert witness (now deceased) testified that he had been present and personally observed the tests that were performed by an independent laboratory con-

---

13. Id., 704–5.

14. Id., 705.

15. Other related litigation citations, including the opinion quoted here, include: *Viskase Corporation v. American National Can Corporation.* 947 F. Supp. 1200 (N.D. Ill. 1996) (claim interpretation and infringement); 979 F. Supp. 697, 45 USPQ2d 1675 (N.D. Ill. 1997) (new trial); 18 F. Supp. 2d 873 (N.D. Ill. 1998) (infringement); No. 93 C7651 (N.D. Ill. July 1, 1999) (final judgment).

cerning the linear or branched structure of the Affinity very low density ethylene copolymers. In post-trial discovery (an unusual event, flowing from new information) it was learned that he was not present during any of the tests. The district court commented that the witness had lied "at least 15 times" about his role in this testing. Based on this perjury, the district court vacated the judgment of literal infringement and granted a new trial.

It is not disputed that Viskase was not aware of the perjury. ANC states that the perjured testimony was critical to the verdict, while Viskase argues that the test data themselves were not challenged, only whether this witness personally watched the tests. Although Viskase suggests that the jury verdict could now be reinstated, we agree with the district court that the jury verdict was irretrievably tainted and was properly set aside.[16]

So it would appear from this opinion that for want of a truthful expert, a $100 million judgment was set aside. The foregoing lengthy recounting of the court's spiral of factual and legal reasoning may require more than one coffee break to follow the twists and turns of how it was discovered and why it is so crucial to the judge's decision to grant a new trial. To the extent you can work your way through this example, you will gain a great deal of insight into the way expert testimony is connected with the process of discovery of the expert's work and opinions and how those pretrial proceedings relate to the actual trial and then to any posttrial review of errors in the process that are brought to the attention of the trial judge.

Lightning Strikes Again: The Case of the Ethically Conflicted Expert

As the manuscript for this book was nearing completion, we learned of a recent opinion reversing another jury verdict of over $100 million in a second case. This case illustrates the pitfalls of an expert who was unable to decide what his duty was when it came to testifying truthfully in one case about what he may or may not have been doing in another expert witness assignment. This story comes from another patent infringement case, *Cardiac Pacemakers, Inc. et. al. v. St. Jude Medical, Inc. et. al.* that was tried in June 2001. The case involved allegations of infringement of a patent that was applicable to a medical device. The case resulted in a verdict awarding the plaintiffs $140 million in royalties. After consideration of numerous postverdict motions from both sides of the litigation, the trial judge determined that there must be a new trial and set aside the verdict for the plaintiffs.

In considering the defendants' motions for sanctions against the plaintiff for the deception of the chief expert witness for the plaintiffs, the court found that the expert

---

16. *Viskase Corporation v. American National Can Corporation.* 261 F.3d 1316;
2001, U.S. App. LEXIS 17039.

admitted deliberately lying at trial and during his deposition so as to conceal matters that went to the heart of both his credibility and the merits of the case. The court found that the expert's deception seriously undermined the integrity of the proceedings leading up to, during, and after the trial. While the court took some actions during the trial in an attempt to remedy the problem of deception by the expert when it appeared, the court ultimately determined that those actions were insufficient to ensure a fair trial for the defendants. The court also determined, based on the evidence summarized below, that the measures taken to remedy the deceptive testimony at trial were based on the premise that the expert might have been honestly mistaken. After the trial the expert admitted that he deliberately deceived the defendants during discovery and the jurors and judge during the trial.

The court fashioned the following remedy in its reconsideration of the problems presented by the deception of the expert witness:

> *Accordingly, in the event that this court's final judgment in favor of defendants were to be set aside on appeal, St. Jude would be entitled to a further remedy for Dr. Bourland's deception. St. Jude would be entitled to a new trial on all issues as to which it did not prevail, as well as a financial sanction to compensate St. Jude for the additional expenses of a new trial, including attorney fees, it incurs as a result of Dr. Bourland's deception and CPI's failure to disclose it. St. Jude is also entitled now to a financial sanction to compensate it for the expenses and attorney fees it has already incurred in uncovering and seeking relief from that deception.*[17]

In what follows, the opinion of the court is summarized to help you understand what caused the trial judge to throw out a $140 million verdict and grant a conditional new trial due to the unethical conduct of a witness at trial.

> *Dr. Bourland was the single most important witness for plaintiffs. Dr. Bourland is a biomedical engineer, with a doctorate in physiology and a bachelor's degree in electrical engineering. He has been a faculty member at Purdue University since 1974. Dr. Bourland has been involved in researching and developing cardiac rhythm management devices since he was an undergraduate in the mid-1960s.*
>
> *Dr. Bourland testified as CPI's principal infringement witness. He testified as to both the '472 and '288 patents. He studied both patents, their claims, and the court's construction of disputed terms in those claims. He also examined defendant's devices and their accompanying technical manuals. Dr. Bourland opined that all of the accused defendant's devices infringed both patents. He opined on the issue of equivalents and about the written description issue under the '472 patent. Without Dr.*

---

17. *Cardiac Pacemakers, Inc. et al. v. St. Jude Medical, Inc. et al.* S.D. Ind., No. IP 96-1718-CH/K, February 13, 2002, p. 124. This Entry on Postverdict Motions can be reviewed at 2002 WL 392499 (S.D. Ind.) and on the Web at: *www.insd.uscourts.gov/opinions/ip961718.pdf* (visited April 1, 2002).

Bourland's testimony, St. Jude would have been entitled to judgment as a matter of law finding that neither patent had been infringed.

In pretrial reports and in the briefing on motions for summary judgment, Dr. Bourland also considered and addressed issues of validity, including obviousness and the written description requirement as applied to the '472 patent. At trial, however, CPI chose not to ask him about obviousness issues.

While Dr. Bourland was working for CPI on this case, he was also working as an expert witness for the third principal ICD manufacturer, Medtronic in another case called Moore v. Medtronic. *Dr. Moore sued Medtronic for royalty payments allegedly due under a license agreement concerning other ICD patents. In his work for Medtronic, Dr. Bourland prepared a report addressing issues of patent infringement and validity on issues closely related to those presented here. . . .*

When Dr. Bourland's report in the Moore *case came to light, it became apparent that his approaches to and opinions about some of the same patents . . . and nearly identical issues in this case and in the* Moore *case were very different. . . .*

The specific issue that caused the trouble was Dr. Bourland's testimony about the extent of other work he had done as an expert witness. The undisputed evidence, including Dr. Bourland's own testimony in a post-trial deposition, establishes that Dr. Bourland deliberately lied during his pretrial deposition and during his trial testimony in this case, and in a post-trial affidavit. Plaintiffs themselves concede: "Plaintiffs do not seek to excuse or minimize Dr. Bourlands' actions." . . . Dr. Bourland's sworn testimony before, during, and after trial was deliberately false.[18]

Dr. Bourland, in his pretrial deposition, "volunteered" that he had been "involved in some litigation within the last five years that involves some of the manufacturer's devices. . . ." He was asked what litigation it was. He answered: "There were actually two suits that were involved and both of those have now been resolved." The testimony continued:

Q: And who was the litigation involving Medtronic against?
A: There was one that was in the case of Charms versus Medtronic. *And there was a second one in the case* Moore versus Medtronic. *But I was not an expert—did not go to the point of having depositions taken in that.*
Q: Did you provide any expert reports?
A: Don't believe we got that far. . . .

The last answer was false. When he gave this deposition testimony in this case, Dr. Bourland had completed two expert reports in the Moore *case that had already been provided to opposing counsel in that case.*

After the trial in this case, Dr. Bourland explained that when he gave his pretrial deposition, he had not merely "forgotten" about those reports:

Q: Was your answer false?

---

18. Id., 116–117.

A: It was false, and the reason was, I felt it would have been a violation of confidence to reveal what was going on in the case A to the attorneys in case B.

Q: Okay. Meaning that, your answer was not mistaken, it was deliberate based on your understanding of the confidentiality order?

A: I was very reluctant to share the proceedings in one case with another. And the answer is yes, I did not feel I should answer that question and reveal what was going on in the other case. . . .

Q: Do you believe that your confidentiality obligation requires you to lie under oath?

A: I do not.

Q: But that's what you did, isn't it?

A: I was faced with a moral dilemma, and that is, I violate one obligation or I violate the other. And I chose to not reveal what was going on in a case that was in potential competition to the one underway. . . .

The "moral dilemma," however, had obviously not prevented Dr. Bourland from at least telling CPI's and St. Jude's lawyers about the existence of the cases. Why the mere existence of the reports should be so sensitive is something Dr. Bourland has not explained.

After studying Dr. Bourland's principal report in the Moore case, the court sees no legitimate basis for a court to treat it as confidential at all. See generally Union Oil Co. of California v. Leavell, *220 F.3d 562, 567-68 (7th Cir. 2000) (discussing circumstances in which court may properly seal records). Dr. Bourland discussed a number of patents and prior art—all of which were public documents—and reported on the results of his examination of Medtronic devices that were available on the market for sale, scrutiny, and even reverse engineering.

The evidence thus demonstrates that Dr. Bourland made a deliberate decision during his pretrial deposition in this case to lie rather than disclose the truth about his work in Moore v. Medtronic. *CPI points out that Dr. Bourland and CPI were not required by Fed. R. Civ. P. 26(a)(2) to disclose the fact of his work in the Moore case, let alone the report itself. For hired experts, the rule requires a listing of cases in which the witness has given trial or deposition testimony. It does not mandate such a listing of all cases in which the expert has consulted or provided a report. At the risk of emphasizing the obvious, however, those limits on Rule 26(a)(2) cannot possibly excuse a deliberate decision to give a false answer to a direct question in a deposition.

Dr. Bourland testified in the pretrial deposition that he believed the Moore *case* had been resolved. He later testified that his belief was based on a telephone call he had received from Medtronic's attorneys in the case. Before trial in this case, however, Dr. Bourland learned that the Moore case had not been resolved. In May and early June 2001, he was preparing for his deposition in the Moore case, in addition to preparing for trial in this case. Dr. Bourland did not correct this mistake, either when he had an opportunity to review his deposition testimony or later.[19]

---

19. Id., 117–119, footnote 37.

The opinion continues to discuss Dr. Bourland's deception during trial.

During the afternoon of June 14, 2001, the expert witness was being introduced to the jury. He gave the following testimony:

Q: Now, Dr. Bourland, you're here to testify as an expert witness in this lawsuit now, correct?
A: That is correct.
Q: Have you ever been an expert witness before?
A: One time many, many years ago, but it was not a patent infringement suit.
Q: So you don't do this for a living?
A: No, sir. I certainly do not. . . .

The obvious intent and effect of this testimony was to present the expert witness as an intellectually honest academic rather than a professional expert witness. The expert then began explaining why, in his view, defendant's devices infringed two of the patents at issue in this case. His direct examination was not complete when the court recessed for the evening.

Listening in the courtroom audience that afternoon was an attorney for Dr. Moore in Moore v. Medtronic. After the court recessed, Dr. Moore's lawyer spoke with counsel for the plaintiffs in this case and provided a copy of an expert witness report that the expert had written in the Moore case.

The next morning, before Dr. Bourland had completed his direct examination, counsel for St. Jude provided a copy of the Moore report to CPI's counsel and stated their intent to use the report in their cross-examination. As a result, neither Dr. Bourland nor CPI's counsel were surprised when the report was used in cross-examination. During cross-examination, Dr. Bourland was asked:

Q: Did you overlook a more recent case in which you were retained as an expert witness?
A: Actually, no. When he asked the question, I thought he asked me had I been in court as an expert witness, and so I must have misunderstood the question. I apologize if I misled you.
Q: I thought that's what had happened. . . .

That explanation appeared to be plausible at the time, for CPI's question on direct about whether he had been "an expert witness" had not been precise. CPI's counsel had already suggested the "forgetfulness" explanation during discussion of the proposed exhibit before Dr. Bourland took the stand the morning of June 15th.

After trial, however, Dr. Bourland confessed that this benign explanation was false:

A: Prior to trial, I very much limited my conversation to [CPI's attorneys] about the other lawsuit, because I thought that would be a violation of the confidentiality agreement that I had in—involving those suits.
Q: Was that the reason you did not mention the Moore or the Charms case in your direct testimony at trial?
A: That is correct.

Q: So you didn't forget that you were involved in the Moore *and the* Charms *case on the 14th of June, did you?*

A: I felt like I would be violating a confidence if I discussed one area of litigation in the context of the other. I thought that would be a violation of an agreement that I had made with the other court.

Q: I understand. My point is, that you didn't forget about the Moore *case or the* Charms *case, you chose not to reveal them because of what you thought was your obligation under the confidentiality order, correct?*

A: That is correct. . . .

In addition, Dr. Bourland also later admitted that in the one case he did mention during his direct trial testimony, he had never testified in court. . . . Thus, Dr. Bourland's explanation on cross-examination, which CPI has continued to advocate long after Dr. Bourland himself had abandoned it—that he had "misunderstood" the question from plaintiff's lawyer—was thoroughly false. . . .

It is now as plain as could be that Dr. Bourland did not merely forget the second case or the report when he testified on direct. He made a deliberate decision not to answer truthfully. Then, when confronted on cross-examination, he deliberately offered a false excuse for the supposed "misunderstanding" on direct.

Moreover, Dr. Bourland's professed concern about his obligations under other protective orders is of dubious credibility. He never bothered to check his views on this "moral dilemma" by, for example, actually checking the protective orders or consulting a lawyer. . . . If his professed concern were deemed credible, it might be of interest to other authorities who have responsibility for dealing with perjury, such as federal prosecutors. But whether Dr. Bourland's asserted but ill-considered excuse is honest or not has no bearing on this case or the prejudice his action caused to St. Jude or to the integrity of this proceeding.[20]

The court went on to find that even if a $140 million verdict was returned, the problems with the expert's ethical dilemma continued.

When the jury returned its verdict, the major damage was done but Dr. Bourland's deception continued. St. Jude sought and was granted permission to conduct post-trial discovery with Dr. Bourland regarding his actions and testimony. In response to a request to take Dr. Bourland's deposition, CPI's counsel helped Dr. Bourland prepare an affidavit that he signed on July 11, 2001. . . . That affidavit was not a successful effort to be honest. . . .

Dr. Bourland explained his failure to disclose the Moore reports during his deposition on the ground that he thought the question had applied to the Charms case and not to the Moore case. That is not how the transcript reads, though it is not unusual for witnesses to misunderstand questions. When questioned in the July 18th deposition, Dr. Bourland repeated that explanation at first. When asked again, however, he abandoned the "misunderstanding" explanation:

---

20. Id., 122–123.

Q: And in the Moore case, you prepared, as of March 24th, two reports?

A: Yes, I have.

Q: Was your answer false?

A: It was false, and the reason was, I felt it would have been a violation of confidence to reveal what was going on in the case A to attorneys in case B. . . .

Thus, when pressed even mildly, Dr. Bourland did not claim to have misunderstood the question as limited to the Charms *case. The explanation that he and CPI's lawyers provided in the post-trial affidavit collapsed just a week after they offered it under oath.*

Perhaps most striking in the affidavit is its concluding assertion: "At no time did I ever intend to conceal the fact that I had prepared expert reports in the Moore *case and had served as an expert in that matter during the pendency of this case." . . . Dr. Bourland admitted during his deposition taken just one week later, on July 18th, that he had in fact intended to conceal both the report and his work in the* Moore *case.*[21]

Of particular interest to beginning experts is the court's admonishment in this case that:

[I]n the event of a genuine conflict between a protective order and a witness's obligation to testify in another case, of course, the conflict may be raised with the courts in question and a resolution will be found. The expert's self-help method for resolving his professed "moral dilemma" has nothing to recommend it.[22]

The court found that the false testimony of the expert had two results, neither of them positive for the integrity of the proceeding. "The overall effect was to deny the defendants a fair trial and to undermine the integrity of this proceeding."[23]

One of the problems that is always present for an advocate who is presenting an expert hired by the party to testify is avoiding the brand of the hired gun. Here the court observes:

First and most basic, Dr. Bourland's false direct testimony enabled CPI to present Dr. Bourland to the jury as more of an honest academic researcher than as a "hired gun" expert witness. That deceptive presentation helped enhance Dr. Bourland's credibility before the jury. After trial, however, Dr. Bourland also testified that, despite his testimony that he does not testify as an expert for a living, income from such work was "a substantial amount" of his earned income for the year 2000.[24]

---

21. Id., 125–126.

22. Id., 123, footnote 37.

23. Id., 126.

24. Id., 126.

The court continued to observe that a second effect of the false testimony was even more important. This cuts to the heart of the role of technical experts in technically complex cases.

CPI's infringement theories in this case required some long (too long) intellectual stretches. It was up to Dr. Bourland to do the stretching and to convince the jury to follow him. The same can be said of CPI's approach to the written description issue under the '472 patent.

Regarding the "determining means" element in the '288 patent claims, CPI and Dr. Bourland had to argue that the relatively sophisticated "binning" algorithm in St. Jude's ICDs was equivalent to the "determining means" described in the '288 patent, which in this case combined the use of a cardiac rate detector with the so-called "probability density function" (PDF) detector. The two types of devices performed the same general function—any ICD must have some mechanism for detecting the heart's rhythm and determining when therapy is needed. It was up to Dr. Bourland to convince the jury that these different means for accomplishing that function were equivalent to one another. On that issue, Dr. Bourland apparently was not successful. The jury found that particular '288 patent was not infringed.

Dr. Bourland was more successful with the '472 patent. His testimony laid the essential foundation for the jury's verdict awarding CPI $140 million. He provided the testimony, for example, that the more sophisticated "H-bridge" switches in St. Jude's products were equivalent to the simpler "switch means" disclosed in the '472 patent. . . . He also provided essential testimony to support CPI's theory that the software or "firmware" programmed into St. Jude's devices was equivalent to the "initiating means" disclosed in the '472 patent. . . . Dr. Bourland's testimony was essential to allow CPI to avoid judgment as a matter of law on infringement of the '472 patent.

Dr. Bourland's report in the Moore *case offered an extensive basis for impeaching his testimony in this case. It also offered an extensive basis for attacking CPI's defense of the validity of the '472 and '288 patents.*

Dr. Bourland testified in this case that St. Jude's determining means were equivalent to the rate-plus-PDF determining means in the patent even though the rate-plus-PDF system was less reliable, resulting in more unnecessary shocks for the patient. He testified that rate-plus-PDF was interchangeable with rate-only. . . . He also testified on cross-examination that the use of rate-plus-PDF resulted in unnecessary shocks to patients. . . . He added that the change away from use of PDF "dramatically reduced" the incidence of unnecessary shocks. A moment later, though, apparently after realizing the effect of that concession, he back-pedaled and claimed there was no "dramatic difference." . . .

Dr. Bourland eventually agreed "that the use of rate alone, as St. Jude uses rate, gives many fewer shocks than the use of PDF alone, or the use of PDF with rate." . . . Nevertheless, he still did his best to minimize the different results. . . . He even went to the impossible length of asserting that, as long as the two types of devices both identify arrhythmias, the reliability of their results has nothing to do with the patent issues. . . .

> *"In other words, Dr. Bourland struggled on the witness stand to portray St. Jude's rate-only algorithm as an equivalent of the '288 patent's less reliable determining means with rate-plus-PDF. The jurors did not buy this testimony. But in light of their finding of infringement of the '472 patent, they obviously did not reject Dr. Bourland as an outright liar willing to say almost anything to help CPI win."[25]*

With full use of the Moore report, Dr. Bourland's efforts would have appeared very different. . . . [I]n the Moore case, Dr. Bourland took a far narrower approach to a very similar equivalence problem involving the means used in ICDs to identify an arrhythmia and the appropriate electrical therapy. In contrast to his testimony in this case, he opined in Moore that the reliability of the determining means' results was critical to equivalence. . . .[26]

More generally, on the issue of equivalence, Dr. Bourland's testimony in this case repeatedly took the simplistic approach that, as long as a St. Jude's device contained structure that performed the same function as the claimed means in the '472 or '288 patents, the St. Jude device contained equivalent structure. In the Moore report, Dr. Bourland was far more discriminating. He recognized in that report that merely performing the same function was not sufficient, and he went on to analyze the "way" and "result" elements of the most familiar "function-way-result" approach to analyzing equivalence issues. . . .

The court said at trial that timely disclosure of the Moore report would have been very helpful to St. Jude and probably would have enabled "very effective" cross-examination of Dr. Bourland on the equivalence issue. . . . The court stands by that view. In an attempt to minimize the effects of Dr. Bourland's deception, CPI points out that St. Jude did in fact obtain a copy of Dr. Bourland's expert report in the Moore case at the end of his first day of testimony, and then did relatively little with it in cross-examining him. This point is factually correct but misses the actual effects. First, St. Jude was expecting Dr. Bourland to testify on issues of validity as well as issues of infringement. At the end of the first day of Dr. Bourland's testimony, the St. Jude lawyer who would cross-examine him learned for the first time that Dr. Bourland would not be addressing validity issues. . . . That attorney had to spend that night restructuring and reorganizing his planned cross-examination of Dr. Bourland. It simply is not realistic in a case of this complexity to expect attorney Rackman both to have done that essential work and to have digested a 35-page expert report and planned a cross-examination using the report. That is why Rule 26 of the Federal Rules of Civil Procedure requires so much advance disclosure of expert materials. Those reasons apply with great force in a high-stakes patent case. . . .

---

25. Id., 128–129.

26. Id., 129–130.

Second, the issues are complex. As talented as all the lawyers in this case are, digesting the Moore *report and preparing to use it effectively before a jury would have taken much more time than Rackman had, especially with a witness as smart as Dr. Bourland, and especially without an opportunity to take his deposition to ask detailed questions about the report. CPI's lawyers themselves made this point about the complexity of the issues in explaining their failure to raise during trial any of the objections they first made after trial to St. Jude's demonstrative exhibits addressing Dr. Bourland's contradictions. . . .*[27]

The court went beyond the determination that the expert had deceived the jury, deceived the court, and deceived the defendants and that he did so deliberately on matters that went to the heart of his credibility and to the heart of the case. The court analyzed in considerable detail what if any role or responsibility CPI and its lawyers had for these deceptions by Dr. Bourland. There is much in the court's analysis of the interaction between CPI, its lawyers, and Dr. Bourland, but for our purposes the focus remains on the actions of Dr. Bourland himself in his reports, depositions, affidavits, and testimony and the serious consequences that at least one judge attached to the conduct described in the opinion in this case.

This case illustrates many key elements of expert witness ethical responsibilities. The dependence of the fact finders on the expert witness to guide them through the nuances of determining patent infringement is clear in this case. This dependence defines the landscape in which a breach of ethics on the part of the expert witness can have major negative impacts on the outcome of a case. The court's decision in this case articulates these issues and the ways in which courts are inclined to punish experts and the parties who engage them for failures to comply with the rules and ethical tenets of expert witnesses. Finally, the case serves to illustrate that the expert cannot offload the responsibility for objectivity and ethics on the assumption that the advocacy ritual will be able to sort everything out.

Determining Master–Servant Relationships in Litigation

Many legal ethics rules are intended to honor a master-servant relationship between the client and the attorney. This relationship defines the central motivation for an attorney's actions in the course of litigation, and as the expert is often considered a part of the attorney's team, he or she must not interfere with this interaction. Furthermore, an expert witness must first recognize which master he or she will be serving from the very beginning while considering an assignment from an attorney or an appointment by the court in a criminal or civil case.

---

27. Id., 129–133.

Criminal Prosecution

In a criminal case, the expert will ordinarily be contacted by the prosecutor, a defense attorney, or, on rare occasions, the trial judge. In state and federal criminal cases, the prosecutor has almost unbridled discretion to begin and end a criminal prosecution and to decide which witnesses and which evidence will be presented at trial. Although many states give increasing attention to the rights of victims and their families, by and large the prosecutor calls all the shots, and there is no other client besides the abstraction of "the government" or "the people." This tradition of prosecutorial discretion in the management of criminal cases is quite different from the traditions and ethical rules that govern the handling of civil cases.

When a government prosecutor seeks to hire a private expert, there will almost always be an issue of how the expert will be paid and whether it is appropriate to charge more or less than the usual fee for expert witness services. The immediate need is to come to some agreement that the fee or lack thereof is clearly established and deemed acceptable to all parties. Both the prosecutor and the witness need to be candid about projected time and costs and decide whether there are adequate funds available to pay the reasonably anticipated costs. In many state and local jurisdictions, the prosecution is expected to rely on salaried state or federal experts and has little, if any, budget for private expert witnesses.

Civil Litigation

In civil litigation, the client hires an attorney or trial team and is ultimately responsible for paying for the services of an expert witness, unless the agreement entered into by the expert makes the attorney ultimately responsible. Regardless of the terms of the expert's contract, in civil cases it is the client and the client alone who has the right to call all the key shots while bringing a cause of action and during the course of litigation. In many cases, the client will also be involved in setting the goals of the litigation and on occasion will even become personally involved in the selection of experts and in strategy meetings with the expert after he or she is chosen and hired. Clients often attend depositions and hearings as well.

Beyond the selection and payment of the expert, the client is ordinarily involved in establishing the objectives of the litigation, at least to some extent. This client involvement may be evident to the expert before the lawyer hires the expert, and it may continue throughout the litigation. Regardless of the client's actual presence or absence during civil discovery and trial preparation, a retained expert must understand that it is the ethical responsibility of the lawyer to carry out the objectives of the client. Furthermore, these strict ethical restraints placed on the relationship between attorney and client in the civil arena make it very important for the expert to determine just what the rules of engagement are likely to be. The expert should establish this before accepting an assignment from a particular lawyer and client. The expert also needs to clearly understand how the demands of different stages of litigation will require the lawyer to change tactics in order to honor this ethically mandated allegiance to the client.

> *It is the client who chooses. The lawyer's task is to protect the client's autonomy from the threat posed by the complexity and alien nature of the legal system. If the choice is to litigate, to go to trial, the lawyer becomes less the philosopher and more the fighter, or at least the very single-mindedly loyal diplomat. He or she puts partisanship, fellowship, competitiveness, and ambition at the service of presenting the most morally and factually compelling version of a client's story. Or perhaps I should say "position," because the narrative will be the result of a set of conversations in which the story that the client claims to be true is confronted by the lawyer's judgment about what is factually plausible and morally compelling. The result of this effort is the presentation of a case as imagined and researched with the care that only the most delicate conscience and rigorous intelligence could muster. It is even guided by a kind of fair-mindedness, the imagined perspective of an impartial juror. By providing this energetic form of partisanship, the legal system says something like the following: There is really a great deal to say on behalf of any person, and of most causes. We sometimes don't imagine so because of the main enemy of human compassion, sloth. We cannot count on compassion's overcoming sloth, but desire for victory, for status, for public display, and for wealth can defeat even that formidable adversary.*[28]

Balancing the Demands of Expertise

In today's society, in order to successfully assume these multiple roles of advisor and advocate, counselor and crusader, the attorney often needs the assistance of recognized experts from other fields. In particular, given the fact that so much evidence resides on computer systems, the attorney will likely need the advice of technical experts regarding the optimal techniques for obtaining evidence from computer networks, assuming that it can be obtained—and obtained at a reasonable cost. The attorney may also require technical assistance in determining the significance of such evidence.

As we will see with other ethical, procedural, and evidentiary rules, the rules governing the conduct of attorneys and experts are not isolated from each other. In fact, from time to time, the expert will have to deal with the fact that these rules are often at odds with each other. Furthermore, these rules will interact in competing and occa-

---

28. Burns, Robert P. *A Theory of Trial.* Princeton, NJ: Princeton University Press, 1999, pp. 79–80.

sionally antagonistic or even contradictory ways. Without an understanding of the full complexity of the adversary system of justice, these conflicts will often make little sense to the neophyte expert. For this reason, the wise expert will obtain a basic understanding of all the rules, including the ethical rules that constrain the professional behavior of the attorney, before encountering the ineluctable conflicts in duties and responsibilities that can be created by conflicting rules. Modern courts and jurors are likely to assume that experts have their own ethical rules, both within their own professional communities of interest (such as licensed CPAs and structural engineers) and possibly even specific rules as to their conduct as expert witnesses within those specialized practices (as is the case with forensic psychologists and certain other professionals who often find themselves in court).

Judges and jurors, and for that matter everyone else, probably should assume that anyone representing themselves as belonging to a professional community of interest that takes responsibility for advising others about crucial matters that require special knowledge, training, and experience would have a clear set of ethical principles. Furthermore, anyone entitled to be recognized as an expert and qualified to give expert opinions concerning important matters in a court of law ought to be the first to agree that he or she recognizes clear ethical principles and rules that govern his or her conduct when performing expert duties.

Ethical Principles for Information Technologists

If the attorney is required to honor the interests of his or her client and to act within the ethics of the legal profession, the objective expert technologist is also required to honor the spirit and tradition of scientific integrity when applying scientific methods as part of his or her expert duties and responsibilities. You might legitimately wonder how scientific integrity is defined and interpreted, especially given the dynamic nature of scientific progress. For starters, let's consider the consensus of communities of technical and scientific experts.

There are many professional organizations for technologists whose members are likely prospects for expert witness duties. Most of these organizations provide codes of ethics as guidance for their members. Consider the common tenets of several codes of ethics from the major professional organizations whose members are IT practitioners.

An Overview of Professional IT Organizations

The following organizations are chartered to advocate the scientific and technical theory and practice of networking, engineering, and computing sciences, from which many information technologists are drawn. Hundreds of specialty professional organizations deal with IT; however, most have codes of ethics that are in harmony with those published by the organizations that follow.

The Institute of Electrical and Electronic Engineers (IEEE)

The IEEE, founded in 1884, advocates the scientific and technical theory and practice of electrical engineering and the allied engineering areas of electronic, radio, and information technologies. As it publishes many of the peer-reviewed journals related to computer hardware, networking, and software engineering, it serves as one of the primary professional communities for information technologists.

The Association for Computing Machinery (ACM)

The ACM, which was founded in 1947, is the first educational and scientific computing society. Like the IEEE, it promotes scientific advancement in the area of computing technologies and publishes peer-reviewed technical journals. Although the ACM also publishes a code of ethics for computing professionals that includes a code of professional conduct, the ACM code varies in structure from that of the IEEE.

The Codes of Ethics

Several common threads run through professional codes of ethics and codes of conduct for technology professionals. We have selected several key components to these codes for review here.

- **Technology is important to modern society.** For much of the civilized world, technology permeates everyday existence. In particular, information technologies can be involved in delivering water, electricity, and other necessities of life to households. It also drives the financial and economic infrastructures on which society relies. It is important for technologists to understand that their professional responsibilities have significant impacts on the world at large.
- **Technologists must take care not to endanger the life, health, safety, and welfare of the public.** In a world where technology can save lives, regulate transportation, control manufacturing assembly lines, and meter electricity, it can just as easily wreak havoc, deny needed life supports to innocent parties, and result in massive casualty. Thus, it is easy to understand how the incidental failure of technology can have catastrophic effects on members of society. It is the responsibility of technologists to take great pains to ensure that their technical activities do not endanger the public. This might be considered the technologist's equivalent of the Hippocratic Oath—a commitment to do no harm in the course of performing professional duties.
- **Technologists should demonstrate competence and due care in their technical duties.** This rule means that technologists should be both prepared for

their technical duties and careful in the execution of those duties. Lapses on either front can lead to catastrophic results.

- **Technologists must maintain and update their technical skills.** It is the nature of technology to be dynamic, but in IT the speed of progress is measured in hours and days, not months and years. This means that technologists must continuously update their technical skills, using both informal and formal means, as new research findings, products, and ideas are reported.

- **Technologists should avoid conflicts of interest.** Employers and clients value technology professionals for being objective and independent in their technical findings. A conflict of interest occurs when a technologist has private or personal interests that conflict (or sometimes, merely appear to conflict) with this objectivity and independence. At the very least, a technologist, when encountered with a situation in which the possibility of a conflict exists, should inform the parties involved and allow them to participate in mitigating the situation.

- **Technologists should be honest and forthright in their dealings with others.** In general, technologists should be honest. As in the previous point, this requirement of honesty and forthrightness is necessary to preserving the objectivity and independence that represent a technologist's value to a client.

- **Technologists should be honest about their limitations, acknowledging errors and correcting them.** Although this is in fact a special case of the prior rule, this tenet is especially critical for technologists. Over time the reach of technology grows to the extent that mastery of all areas of technology by a single person is simply impossible. A technologist's value depends on the ability to be objective about what he or she does and does not know. This is especially important when, as often happens in litigation, the technologist is dealing with a technology outsider who is likely to be unable to make an independent determination of the technologist's real capabilities beyond a superficial review of his or her educational credentials or professional résumé. The second portion of this rule, that of acknowledging errors and correcting them, is also important for any expert practitioner. First, it isn't reasonable to expect perfection of any human. Therefore errors are expected in any production environment. That said, part of professional responsibility calls for checking one's work product for errors and correcting those errors when identified. In intuitive terms, this rule essentially deals with the attributes of a mature person, who has integrity and takes responsibility for his or her actions.

- **Technologists should refrain from discriminating against individuals based on race, religion, age, gender, or national origin.** Although this rule is a reflection of civil rights philosophies in place in much of the civilized world, it is one of the most demanding of the ethics requirements of technologists—for this rule applies not only to the interpersonal interactions of a technologist (for instance, his or her selection of a project team or relationships with clients and peers) but also to the intended application of the work product. A technologist who is asked to write a performance appraisal system that automatically downgrades the scores of one ethnic group must, by the terms of this ethics code, refuse that task. Furthermore, a technologist who is asked to develop a promotional Web site for a hate group must also refuse the task.

- **Technologists should give proper credit to others for their work and honor property rights, including copyrights and intellectual property.** The original intent of this rule was likely to enforce standards of academic honesty when reporting original work. Given the nature of the information economy, it takes on even more significance these days. Many of the most precious assets of modern corporations involve intellectual property. Therefore, this rule calls for technologists to exercise care in handling the intellectual property of others, recognizing the property rights associated with knowledge-based assets.
- **Technologists should help the public understand technology and support the professional development of peers.** This rule covers the responsibility of technologists in the community at large. Note that this rule actually promotes the participation of technologists as expert witnesses, given the educational role that duty requires.

Other Pertinent Rules

In addition to the common ethics rules above, many other professional values are promoted as suitable for technologists. These include protecting client information as confidential, respecting individual rights to privacy, complying with laws, agreeing to access systems only when authorized, and honoring contractual commitments.

A special case of ethics rules is in the form of a Request for Comments (RFC) published by the Internet Society, the body that governs the operation of the Internet. This document outlines the acceptable, ethical use of the Internet.

The expert may belong to a community of interest that has set forth a specific set of ethical guidelines or rules or has endorsed those of other professional organizations. Regardless of whether there is a specific set of ethical rules, the cross-examining attorney is likely to probe this area to attempt to determine just what sort of ethical code the expert acknowledges and then develop lines of questions that further probe whether the practices in the case at hand are consistent or inconsistent with those general ethical principles that the witness has committed to in his or her answers.

Beyond the ethics of a particular community of professional interest, generally accepted rules or recommended standards developed by various professional groups govern the conduct of their members when asked to testify as expert witnesses. These generally accepted ethics guidelines will also form the basis of questioning by opposing counsel.

Model Ethical Rules and Recommendations for Expert Witnesses

As the importance of technical expert witnesses in litigation has grown, some specialized ethics rules and recommendations have been published to guide them. In particular, the Academy of Experts, headquartered in London, was formed by a group of lawyers and technical experts in order to champion the use of independent experts in settling legal disputes. As part of this objective, the Academy offers training, promulgates standards for expert witnesses, and provides a forum in which legal personnel and experts can exchange views.

The Academy of Experts Code of Practice

The Academy of Experts publishes a Code of Practice for Experts. Some of the rules in the code are restatements of the rules we listed above. However, some rules are peculiar to the legal process.

1. The expert has a duty to serve the court or tribunal.
2. The expert has a secondary duty to serve the best interests of those engaging him or her.
3. The expert should not be compensated on contingency. (That is, the expert should not receive compensation that depends on the outcome of the trial—to do so would represent an undue interest in the outcome of the trial, thereby compromising the expert's objectivity.)
4. The expert should arrange for appropriate insurance coverage in order to protect his or her client.
5. The expert shall exercise restraint in publicizing his or her practice, assuring that the publicity is accurate and not misleading in any way.[29]

Recommended Practices for Design Experts

Although it is not an IT-centric manual, *Recommended Practices for Design Professionals Engaged as Experts in the Resolution of Construction Industry Disputes*, has much information that is readily adaptable to the IT expert. The manual, published by

---

29. Paraphrased from the Academy of Experts' Code of Practice for Experts. Accessed July 29, 2002, at *http://www.academy-experts.org/defaultin.htm.*

the Associated Soil and Foundation Engineers (ASFE), is endorsed by a number of professional organizations. Robert Ratay lists recommended practices for design experts based on the ASFE information as follows.

1. *The expert should avoid conflicts of interest and the appearance of conflicts of interest.*
2. *The expert should undertake an engagement only when qualified to do so and should rely upon other qualified parties for assistance in matters which are beyond the expert's area of expertise.*
3. *The expert should consider other practitioners' opinions relative to the principles associated with the matter at issue.*
4. *The expert should obtain available information relative to the events in question in order to minimize reliance on assumptions, and he or he should be prepared to explain any assumptions to the trier of fact.*
5. *The expert should evaluate reasonable explanations of causes and effects.*
6. *The expert should strive to ensure the integrity of the tests and investigations conducted as part of the expert's services.*
7. *The expert witness should testify about professional standards of care only with knowledge of those standards which prevailed at the time in question, based upon reasonable inquiry.*
8. *The expert witness should use only those illustrative devices or presentations which simplify or clarify an issue.*
9. *The expert should maintain custody and control over whatever materials are entrusted to the expert's care.*
10. *The expert should respect confidentiality about an assignment.*
11. *The expert should refuse or terminate involvement in an engagement when fee is used in and attempt to compromise the expert's judgment.*
12. *The expert should refuse or terminate involvement in an engagement when the expert is not permitted to perform the investigation which the expert believes is necessary to render an opinion with a reasonable degree of certainty.*
13. *The expert witness should strive to maintain a professional demeanor and be dispassionate at all times.*[30]

Recommendations for Structural Engineer Expert Witnesses

David Thompson and Howard Ashcraft, who outlined the ASFE recommendations for design professionals listed above, also outlined additional recommendations for forensic structural engineers who act as expert witnesses, including the recommendations listed that follow.

---

30. Ratay, Robert T., ed. *Forensic Structural Engineering Handbook*. New York: McGraw-Hill, 2000.

Qualifications

Engineering expert witnesses should guard against agreeing to take on matters that are not clearly within their areas of proven expertise. This can be determined by asking two questions: first, "Is this the type of work you routinely do?" and second, "If you were the client, would you hire yourself to do this work or would you hire someone with more experience?"[31] There is clearly a duty to advise a client and the client's attorney of any problems or limitations that you feel will impede in any way your ability to perform as an expert. This duty is part and parcel of being a credible expert, before, during and after accepting any assignment. The standard of integrity and avoiding any appearance of conflict of interest require complete disclosure of any limitations you may have to handle a particular assignment.

Options

Any technologist who serves as an expert witness should remember that there are almost always potential or actual competing theories that can explain an event or a failure. Good experts accept the responsibility of carefully considering all the other opinions and theories in addition to finding support for their own. Experts should never rule out a theory or opinion without considering all the assumptions that form the basis of competing theories and assessing their validity. These expert practices enable the witness to explain even more clearly why his or her own theory and opinion is entitled to greater weight than the options offered by other experts or authorities.

Assumptions

Experts should reveal their assumptions earlier rather than later in testimony.

> *Experts have crumbled under skilled cross-examinations when forced to admit their opinion is based on unstated assumptions. If the opposing party can prove these assumptions were false, the expert's credibility and opinions are destroyed. If the assumptions are limited or clearly stated, however, debate over basic facts is less damaging. At worst, the debate becomes a difference of opinion rather than an attempt by the expert to deceive the judge or jury.[32]*

Level of Inquiry

Technology design specialists need to draw up a work plan with the client that takes a standard shape and deals with the client's needs with the descriptive tools appropriate

31. Thompson, David, and Howard Ashcraft. "The Expert Consultant and Witness." In *Forensic Structural Engineering Handbook,* Robert T. Ratay, ed. New York: McGraw-Hill, 2000, p. 16.

32. Thompson and Ashcraft, "The Expert Consultant and Witness," p. 16.

to the context. When accepting an assignment, expert witnesses are agreeing that the testimony they will give about their beliefs based on their expertise is true and also helpful to a fair decision on at least some of the issues in a case. Unless there will be ample resources to allow the expert to reach an opinion, the expert should not accept the assignment.

Integrity

This is really the sum of all the other recommendations, guidelines, and rules of ethical conduct. The expert brings technical competence and integrity to the stand. As Thompson and Ashcraft suggest, without equal portions of both, the expert is worthless.

Standard of Care

It is worth remembering that engineers are liable in professional malpractice actions if their services fall below the accepted standard of care in a particular jurisdiction.

> *A design professional is liable when a breach of the standard of care causes damage. Because the trier of fact (judge, jury, or arbitrator) does not know the standard of care and may not be able to analyze the technical issues involved with causation, most courts require expert testimony on these issues. Breach of the standard of care is ordinarily proved by testimony of experts who are conversant with the applicable standard.*[33]

There are additional factors to consider:

1. *The need to guard against using only personal standards when asked to testify about standards of care,*
2. *The need to confirm that the expert was practicing at the time of the incident that the alleged failure to adhere to the standards in existence took place,*
3. *The need to take special pains to investigate the consensus of experts about an issue where there do not readily appear to be any clearly stated or recognized standards of care, and*
4. *The recommendation that as a general rule, an expert should "not testify about the standard of care unless [the expert has] performed similar work under similar circumstances."*[34]

A Cautionary Note

It is tempting for an aspiring IT expert to focus on the possibility of being called as an expert to testify on the standard of care in connection with information technology or

---

33. Thompson and Ashcraft, "The Expert Consultant and Witness," p. 17.

34. Thompson and Ashcraft, "The Expert Consultant and Witness," p. 17.

information security issues. Presumably, in some of these cases it is alleged that another expert or organization has failed to live up to those standards. However, it is important to understand that it is also possible for the expert to be liable for gross negligence in performing the duty of an expert witness. Recent cases have held that different types of expert witnesses can be liable for negligent performance of their duties where it can also be shown that their client or another party was damaged as a result of that negligence. This is a rapidly developing area of malpractice law. If you need an additional reason to become familiar with the ethical rules that relate to expert witness practice, this potential liability should be sufficient incentive.

Any forensic expert, regardless of his or her specialty, should become thoroughly familiar with the ethical and forensic standards and rules of conduct that relate to that specialty before considering accepting an assignment as an expert. Information technologists have been slow to push for licensing and other formal recognition of professional status. Nevertheless, as more and more IT and information security experts are called to assist the courts, those courts will begin to fashion standards of care that apply not only to the objects of the forensic expert's analysis but also to the competence and performance of forensic experts themselves. These standards will likely apply to IT experts practicing in the capacity of a recognized expert, with or without the traditional trappings of legislatively or socially recognized and licensed professionalism.

Ethical Standards for Attorneys

As mentioned before, many of the ethical imperatives facing lawyers involve their responsibility to their clients. However, this responsibility is not infinite. Attorneys may—indeed must—advocate on behalf of their client's interests, but attorneys may not encourage or allow their clients to testify falsely when answering interrogatories, responding to requests for written admissions, giving a deposition, or testifying on direct or cross-examination at trial. Neither may the lawyer counsel or assist any other witness to testify falsely.

This strict prohibition against presenting false testimony is also primary to the legal ethos. The attorney cannot allow an expert to stretch the truth under the claim that it is solely up to the expert to determine what is or is not the truth. Furthermore, the rationale that this is somehow an exception to the absolute prohibition from knowingly assisting any witness to shade the truth is fatally flawed. Although the special powers afforded an expert witness by the court allow the expert great discretion to determine what constitutes truth within his or her expertise, this doesn't nullify the attorney's responsibility under the ethics code. Therefore, regardless of the expert's privilege, the rule that absolutely prohibits a lawyer from assisting a witness in testifying falsely still applies.

Model rules for expert witnesses make this same rule as clear as a bell. Abuse of these clear ethical rules for lawyers and the suggested rules for experts can lead to what would clearly be perjury by any non-expert witness. Both the bench and the bar have pushed for greater control during litigation. *Daubert* and its progeny empowering courts to take a more active role in the qualification of experts and the admission of their opinions can be seen as a direct reaction to the perceived pattern of abuse of this fundamental rule.

An equally fundamental ethical rule that affects attorney conduct is the absolute requirement of attorney–client confidentiality. Another related rule exists to protect what is called the attorney work product from disclosure to and discovery by the opposing party. This rule exists to protect the mental processes and strategic planning of counsel from being given to the other side. It harks back to the fundamental commitment to advocacy by opposing parties and is often invoked by a party to prevent what is considered unfair advantage to a party that seeks discovery of the other party's work product when the party seeking to discover could do the work itself. But the attorney work product privilege goes only so far and is of little help to the technical expert required to take the stand at a deposition, hearing, or trial. A novice might naïvely and mistakenly believe that the attorney work product privilege should cover what the attorney and the testifying expert discuss. This is not necessarily the case in federal courts where Rule 26 covers the disclosure of all matters that formed the basis of the expert's opinion. It is also not the case in those state courts that have either adopted the federal rules of procedure or have case law that requires all communications concerning the expert's work to be discoverable.

Attorney–client confidentiality is almost always honored by the court unless there has been a waiver by some act of the client or the attorney, and this same confidentiality umbrella is most often extended to cover conversations and communications between and among the attorney's team, including other attorneys, paralegals, support staff, and consulting experts who will not be identified or called to testify. Importantly, no such privilege is generally extended to conversations between the attorney or the trial team and the testifying expert. While there are confusing and contradictory decisions relating to this question of under what circumstances communications with a consulting expert are or are not subject to discovery, it is prudent to assume that, unless the expert is acting solely as a consulting expert, anything that the attorney or anyone else says to the testifying expert is not protected by attorney–client confidentiality, the attorney work product, or any other legally recognized privilege. An expert who is hired to give a formal opinion and to testify in a civil or criminal case should assume that any conversations, communications, and documents are fair game for opposing counsel to inquire into in deposition and at trial.

Going to the Movies for More Examples

To state the general rule against influencing the testimony of witnesses is a simple matter. To determine how it applies when it comes to developing testimony for a deposition or at trial is tricky business. As W. William Hodes points out in a series of law review articles,[35] some esteemed members of the bench and bar decry litigation tactics that come anywhere near the line that can be drawn between perjury and the objective testimony of witnesses. The technique of subtly (and not so subtly) influencing a witness is known to litigators as "horseshedding" the witness. In this section you can once again benefit from the price of a couple of video rentals and begin to appreciate some of the ethical problems encountered in the use and abuse of expert witnesses.

In particular, the controversial issues surrounding the practice of horseshedding are presented in two legal classics, *The Verdict* and *Anatomy of a Murder*. These important issues are presented in different ways. *The Verdict* focuses on the struggle of a civil lawyer to find the expert he needs to expose the conspiracy of silence and the false testimony of experts for the civil defendants, while *Anatomy of a Murder* involves the relationship between a defense attorney and the defendant. In addition to thinking about where the line should be drawn between appropriate and unethical witness preparation as represented in these movies, you should also realize that real jurors, who are also movie fans, may be looking at any expert witness performance with prejudices colored by these classic scenes. While the memory of the scenes we are about to consider may no longer be conscious to those real jurors, the bias or prejudice they may have formed against lawyers or expert witnesses because of these kinds of movies can play a part in how they view what they see in their service as jurors in a real case. These and similar dramatizations portray the methods used by lawyers to blur the line between ethical but still highly questionable tactics in the representation of a client and the legitimate preparation of the testimony of any witness.

The Verdict, directed by Sidney Lumet and based on the novel by Barry Reed and the screenplay by David Mamet, was released in 1982. It stars Paul Newman as the plaintiff's attorney and James Mason as the insurance defense lawyer for two doctors who have been sued for malpractice. The film received five Academy Award nominations. Although this film is worth a look on its merits, it is especially suitable fare for anyone interested in exploring the games associated with using expert witnesses in litigation. *The Verdict* is one of a number of pictures that portray the judicial system as thoroughly corrupt in all its many twists and turns, even as it holds out hope that a jury will still be able to figure out the truth.

The film tells the story of a down-and-out alcoholic trial lawyer with only one client and only one chance to turn his failing practice and life around. Paul Newman's client has been injured, left in a vegetative state by a botched delivery that also took the life of her child. The culprit is an overworked anesthesiologist in a Catholic hospital

---

35. Hodes, William W. "The Professional Duty to Horseshed Witnesses—
Zealously, within the Bounds of the Law." *Texas Tech Law Review* 30(1343), 1999.

in Boston. A well-meaning bishop is talked into letting the masterful James Mason (in the role of the hospital's legal counsel) push the hapless Newman to trial in order to make a last-minute settlement at the lowest possible cost to the Church.

Enraged after he visits his comatose client in the hospital, Newman decides to turn down the lowball settlement offer and fight the good fight. He believes he has an ace in the hole with a dream expert who is willing to buck the medical establishment and tell the truth about the defendant's incompetence, which he describes as criminal. Now, if you've thought about being an expert in a real case, you might ask yourself what an accomplished physician and respected expert is thinking by signing on to be a member of a drunken, down-and-out attorney's litigation team. Apparently the expert does give it some thought and ultimately abandons the plaintiff's case, heading for the Bahamas, where he cannot be subpoenaed on the eve of the trial.

Newman's replacement expert has problems that are played up at trial, and he ends up actually helping the defendant by his demeanor and answers in the course of the cross-examination by Mason. What makes the film essential viewing for our purposes are the scenes when Mason and most of his law firm prepare the defendant to testify. The viewer is shown a magnificent conference room. Around an enormous hardwood table sit enough high-paid associates to staff the combined forces of the O. J. Simpson defense table, the *Harvard Law Review*, and a Congressional hearing with the full committee in attendance. Video cameras capture every word and gesture of the witness for future critique. Pens and pencils are poised over legal tablets to create the perfect questions and answers for their mentor. The expert witness hardly gets a word out before either Mason or one of his minions corrects the wrong impression that a candid answer might create, letting the expert know what he should have said and how to say it most persuasively in order to win the case.

Perhaps the most famous cinematic witness preparation scene of all time takes place between James Stewart, playing the defense attorney, and his client, played by Ben Gazzara, who has been charged with murder in the 1959 film, *Anatomy of a Murder*. This classic film, based on a book by a Michigan Supreme Court judge, was also nominated for a number of Academy Awards.

There is a large and growing legal literature debating the ethics of what has come to be called in the legal trade "the speech" but what is really a variation of what we have been discussing as horseshedding the witness. As with the schooling of a criminal defendant in *Anatomy of a Murder*, the preparation of an expert witness in a civil or criminal case raises a number of difficult ethical issues for both the lawyer and the expert. All of these ethical issues revolve around just how far the lawyer can go to prepare the expert to get the facts and the issues right, in order to prevail against an opponent who is presumed to be doing his or her best to script the opposing expert to persuade the judge and jurors that their opinions are entitled to carry the day in court.

The horseshedding that takes place in *Anatomy of a Murder* involves a defense attorney coaching his client to beat a murder rap with an insanity defense. The main courtroom action in *The Verdict* offers dramatic insights into how the rules of evidence and procedure (stretched to the breaking point to carry the story) relate to what attorneys and experts can ethically do when preparing testimony and how those rules are abused during the actual process of preparing for and putting on the experts at trial.

So, the audience and the jury in *The Verdict* are forced to endure the mismatch between the polished performance of the thoroughly corrupted defendant doctor and the honest but ineffectual substitute expert called at the last minute to the stand by the plaintiff to prove that there was medical malpractice. Mason impeaches the expert as to his qualifications and experience by pointing out that he often testifies for injured plaintiffs against their doctors. The suggestion is that he has become a 74-year-old professional plaintiff's witness and that this has become his practice and also how he makes his living. Not content to let Mason pin the plaintiff's expert through a devastating cross-examination, the judge jumps into the ring and finishes off the expert with a few off-the-wall evidentiary rulings that would make a directed verdict in favor of the defendant all but certain in the real world.

Now, it is certainly true that not all advocates are equally skilled, and those less skilled tend to lose in litigation. It also happens that some judges do take sides when they should be objective between the parties, their attorneys, and their expert witnesses. For our purposes, these movies depicting the abuse of the rules of evidence and procedure by a judge and the unethical schooling of experts by a masterful manipulator suggest the kinds of questions an expert might also want to ask about the presiding judge and opposing counsel during any given case.

The Verdict helps us recognize and learn to laugh at the obvious weakness in the system. Of course, it's far easier to laugh when these abuses are dramatically carried out in order to set up the miracle that allows justice to prevail and the jury to reach the right verdict. It also makes it possible to escape a cynical view of the process, while keeping in mind the obvious flaws and pressure points that are subject to systematic abuse or failure.

The Verdict also helps us understand the different and sometimes conflicting roles that experts can wind up playing in litigation. It is essential for the expert to grasp at the outset of any expert witness engagement what role or roles he or she may be called to play. No single rule or concept is more important in the shaping of the presentation of the testimony of witnesses at trial than the rule that forbids fact witnesses from testifying about their opinions.

The first expert we see is the defendant doctor being told what to say and how to say it. Although the good doctor is certainly going to be qualified as an expert when he testifies for the defense, if he is called as a witness by the plaintiff, which is often done in personal injury litigation, he will be treated like any other ordinary witness by the plaintiff. In this case there are several reasons for this treatment. The doctor is being sued, so he is a party to the litigation and cannot escape the fact that he plays the role of both a party and a fact witness, in that he was present and responsible for the treatment that the plaintiff received during her surgery. This means that the plaintiff's lawyer can go into just about anything, including everything that the doctor, as a factual witness, knows about the actual incident, without giving up his expertise to render an opinion.

The distinction between fact and expert witnesses is one of the most fundamental rules that shapes the conduct of litigation. Factual witnesses are ordinarily not allowed to give their opinions, while experts can. This enormous difference between the way the rules of evidence treat the testimony of the ordinary witness, who is restrained from opining about much of anything, and that of a qualified expert to render opinions has required the modern jury trial to be remodeled around the handling of experts in discovery and at trial. The *Daubert* and *Kumho Tire* guidelines and the recent changes to federal and state rules of evidence and procedure all reflect this core importance of (and litigation's increasing dependence on) the testimony of experts.

In *The Verdict*, because the expert doctor is also testifying as both a factual witness and a party opponent, the judge may need to be creative in deciding how to admit the doctor's opinion about whether his actions and the actions of the surgical team measured up to or exceeded the standard of care, which is the ultimate issue in the case. What is interesting about the facts portrayed in this story is what the audience knows happened when the defendant's lawyers rehearsed the doctor for his testimony. What the audience would like to see come out at the trial is the doctor's objective assessment of the quality of care he delivered to the plaintiff. This issue could be explored if the defendant were allowed to testify as an expert. However, because of the attorney–client privilege, this issue probably could not be broached if he were testifying simply as the client/defendant and not as a testifying expert. This is because the fundamental rule that protects the confidentiality of attorney–client conversations and certain other materials that may be developed by the lawyer in preparation for the trial will usually trump the need to fully cross-examine a non-expert witness about what may have influenced his or her testimony.

However, the minute the witness is qualified as an expert, these matters may be explored with the court's permission in order to fully examine the basis of the expert's opinion. It is almost always a mistake for an expert to believe that anything that is discussed with an attorney in preparation of an expert report or other aspect of the assignment will be considered privileged by the rules of evidence. One expert legal scholar, David Malone, who has published a number of valuable resources for both litigators and expert witnesses,[36] puts the basic principle somewhat facetiously in his lit-igation training sessions to the effect that the only written document that a lawyer needs to independently prepare, sign and give to the testifying expert is the check for services rendered."[37] The point Malone stresses is simply that whatever the lawyer gives to the expert is most likely to be considered as discoverable and to be fair game for examination during deposition or trial testimony. This being the case, ethics aside, for the attorney and the expert to engage in the kind of behavior that *The Verdict* pre-sents so effectively for our entertainment may also be subject to discovery.

Because the law attempts to protect both of these interests, it is most likely that in a real case such as this the court would not allow the plaintiff to breach the attor-ney–client privilege and attempt to force the doctor to answer questions about what he was told by or has discussed with his attorney, merely because the defendant was a potential testifying expert. However, if the defendant sought to qualify the doctor as an expert for the purpose of giving his expert opinion as to his own or another doc-tor's negligence, the court would probably allow the plaintiff to inquire into what was discussed and rehearsed in preparation for his testimony as an expert witness. The real lesson here for the beginner is simply that the law attempts to facilitate the presenta-tion of all the relevant evidence, without unnecessarily or unfairly compromising any important rights or interests of individuals involved in litigation. The expert needs to be clear on the roles that he or she may be asked to play at the beginning of the rela-tionship, so that appropriate communication channels and methods can be used by both the expert and the trial team throughout the litigation.

Advocacy by experts, whether prodded by the horseshedding of the lawyer or due solely to the expert's frolic, is almost always a mistake and can easily lead to disaster when competent counsel with adequate information about what is really going on approaches the witness to cross-examine.

The last move by the lawyer played by Paul Newman in *The Verdict* that we want to mention is the equally pathetic scene in which the plot treats the audience to an example of what happens when a lawyer who cannot afford to pay for an expert to testify to the truth makes the fatal mistake of retaining a well-meaning, semi-retired doctor who is really just an expert for hire. While in real life an honest expert may be available due to his or her own decision to specialize as a forensic expert or because he or she can no longer find interesting employment as a doctor, in the movie, the fact that the expert has a good heart does not save his credibility when the highly skilled opposing counsel succeeds in showing a demonstrable bias toward testifying

---

36. For example, see Malone, David M., and Paul. J. Zwier, *Effective Expert Testimony*. Notre Dame, IN: *National Institute for Trial Advocacy*, 2000.

37. Malone, David. From his comments at a litigation training session in Albuquerque, NM.

for injured plaintiffs and little recent clinical experience other than preparing to testify in court. As if that were not bad enough, the expert has none of the qualifications and credibility to get beyond the jury's suspicions as to his bias and lack of current practical experience about the practice of medicine. To make matters even worse, he is not competent to testify effectively and makes extremely damaging if not devastating admissions on cross-examination. Taken together with the examples of the defense lawyers feeding the defendant doctor not only his lines but also his entire expert persona, *The Verdict* gives us a series of vignettes that can serve as object lessons as to what to avoid in any relationship that the beginning expert may consider forming with the attorney and client involved in civil litigation.

To end our visit to the movies, suffice it to say that *The Verdict* and to some extent *Anatomy of a Murder* have given movie-going audiences some food for thought in the form of classic stories of how the lip service we all pay to the ethical principle that the justice system is based on the search for truth is easily compromised by the deft corruption of the experts called to help the jury understand complex issues. In fact, these stories do perform a service by putting us on our guards that the temptation to corrupt the principle of truth seeking through a trial by turning the objectivity of competent retained experts into the biased advocacy of paid witnesses is a very serious threat in any trial. One reason that cynics use terms like "hired guns" and "prostitutes" to refer to the purchase of qualified experts to render biased testimony is that the experts who agree to give a biased opinion (or end up rationalizing the presentation of biased testimony) without revealing that fact to the court and the jury are in fact selling a commodity or service that is not supposed to be sold.

These Hollywood stories take for granted that there is a certain amount of cynicism concerning the potential for this kind of corruption already in the minds of their audiences. In neither movie is this cynicism overcome by the safeguards of the system. In both stories the bad guys attempt to get away with murder again—but this time in terms of their abuses of the expert witness opportunities the system offers. Unlike these cinematic cases, the unethical injection of bias into the approaches and findings of experts are not always so easy to discover. There are serious institutional and procedural problems with the way expert witness testimony is sometimes allowed to be solicited, prepared, influenced, and presented, all without necessarily giving any clue to the fact finder or to the opposing counsel that an apparently objective and well-qualified expert has been completely compromised and has in fact become a biased witness.

Pushing the Ethical Boundary

There is a long tradition and extensive philosophical literature in support of allowing parties to test each other's theories and proof, including their expert's qualifications, methods of testing or analyzing the evidence, and contradictions or mistakes in their testimony. The procedural and evidentiary rules that must be followed today in all state and federal jurisdictions that support this tradition of trial by competitive advocacy do not ordinarily allow for the dramatic surprises in litigation that make movies so entertaining.

There is an inherent paradox here in that when experts are attempting to explain and teach a judge or a jury about a complex technical or scientific process or concept, the need to use analogies and metaphors means that there is going to be ambiguity in any expert presentation that is truly helpful to the fact finder.

Because expert testimony is not so much a science as an art, it will always be subject to a critique that undue influence is being exerted on the fact finder through the use of rhetorical techniques like the persuasive use of apt analogies and clarifying metaphors. But testimonial tactics that are subject to linguistic analysis and rhetorical criticism through cross-examination ought not be confused with intentionally attempting to present false or misleading expert testimony. When the basic rule that requires the attorney to shape his or her case to carry out the client's purposes is juxtaposed with the rule that forbids an attorney to assist in any way with the presentation of false or intentionally misleading testimony by any witness, we begin to see why these rules of conduct must be considered in tandem if they are to be understood at all.

For a ritual based on advocacy and competitive storytelling, the strategic decisions made by the trial team, and in part carried out by the expert witness, will seldom be easy to place with confidence at any great length from the line that separates zealous advocacy from objective expert opinion. Some legal scholars claim that attorneys should steer completely clear of this line. W. William Hodes and other legal scholars have argued that in reality the entire process of witness preparation is directed in one way or another at influencing a witness's testimony and presenting the client's situation in a completely truthful but more favorable light. When these two ethical rules are read together it makes no sense to use the rule that can be read to forbid influencing a witness's testimony to favor the client in such a conservative fashion that it cancels the attorney's ability to act as a competent advocate for the client. Such a constrained application could nullify the justifiable basis for hiring a competent advocate in the first place—to present the client's lawful interests within the context of all the ethical rules, and to present the client's claims in the most favorable light possible, in order to persuade the judge or jury. But for a moment, before we close this chapter, think once more about the way some trial lawyers handle the preparation of ordinary, fact witnesses to report under oath what they have done, seen, or heard to the fact finders.

With respect to distortion of the truth through omission, the rules of engagement in our real-world adversary system contemplate that each side will put its own best foot forward. The advocate's goal, after all, is to present a winning case, not a neutral report that covers all of the bases and makes the maximum contribution to revelation of the truth. If there is evidence that weakens the case, the other side will be only too pleased to bring it forward. Thus, the choice of what material to present and what to omit is a crucial aspect of every litigating lawyer's overall advocacy effort, and the resulting "courtroom truth" need not match every chapter and every verse of objective truth. For this reason lawyers never counsel witnesses to tell "the whole truth." Witnesses are instead told—as they should be—to tell the truth in response to whatever questions are asked. The lawyer will then be careful to ask only such questions as will elicit truthful-but-favorable answers. If the other side's lawyer fails to ask questions that will result in truthful-but-unfavorable answers, that is the other side's misfortune, for which the proper remedy is a suit for legal malpractice, not an attack on the first lawyer. . . .

The adversary system maintains somewhat of a schizophrenic position regarding discussions about proposed testimony that results in changes in the testimony that is actually given. Everyone agrees, for example, that an expert witness may be taught to avoid the use of technical terms, or to avoid mannerisms that might displease a jury. And a lay witness may be urged to use words that have accepted meanings in the context of a particular case, or not to use slang or derogatory terms. On the other hand, most authorities hold that it is improper to "influence" the way in which a lay witness will testify, including influencing his choice of words. But the distinction is vacuous. . . . In my view, it may be permissible to go even further, given the premise that the presentation of even factual testimony is a matter of advocacy, not reportage. Suppose, then, that suggestions from counsel enhance the effectiveness of the witness's communication, without enhancing its accuracy. So long as the material eventually presented is still truthful, and at least not less accurate than the pre-horseshedding version, why should that be beyond the bounds of law? Legal ethics is hard. You must try to find the line between what is permitted and what is not, and then get as close to that line as you can without crossing over to the bad side. Anything less is less than zealous representation—which already leaves you on the bad side of the line. Whatever distance is left to travel up to that illusive line is territory that belongs to the client and has been wrongfully ceded away. . . .

Play that formula out in the context of horseshedding, and you have ethical lawyering in a nutshell. Arming the client with pertinent legal information and trusting the client to make good and legitimate use of it demonstrates loyalty and zealousness. Recognizing that at some point a loyal servant can be manipulated into becoming an accomplice in crime is honoring the bounds of law. And knowing how to flirt with that boundary but not cross over it is true professionalism.

True professionalism takes not only loyalty and the skill to find those boundary lines, but also courage. Professional lawyers must not only have the courage to make hard and close choices, but also the courage to stand up for the choices that they made. Lawyers have essentially only one job—to represent clients zealously, within the bounds of law. But not everyone—not even everyone within the legal profession—will praise lawyers for a job well done.[38]

---

38. Hodes, "The Professional Duty to Horseshed Witnesses," pp. 1360–1361, 1363–1364, and 1367.

Note the contrast between the role of the attorney, whose ethical responsibility to serve as a zealous advocate for his or her client may lead the attorney to obscure key points (that are harmful to the client's case) in his arguments before the court, and the expert, who has an equally vital responsibility to explain the technical evidence to the fact finders in a clear and objective fashion. Even as you are cognizant of the attorney's responsibility to push the boundaries, you must also understand that your responsibility as an expert witness is to be immovable in the truth. It is only in this interplay between advocate and expert that the best decision becomes accessible to the fact finders.

The Responsibility of the Expert Witness

Professional expert witnesses who are called on to provide critical testimony in life-and-death struggles require the same character strengths attorneys need. How experts decide to shape their testimony must comply with the ethics and ethos of both their profession and the legal system of justice. This means that experts must be qualified, objective, scrupulously honest, forthright, unbiased, and prepared to deliver their testimony in a clear and convincing fashion. To do any less does a disservice to the court and the client alike.

However, technical acumen is not enough. Like good lawyers, good expert witnesses must possess not only the requisite knowledge and skills but also the courage of their ethical convictions. They must also have the resolve to explain their meaning clearly and convincingly to those who must decide the outcome of these courtroom struggles. This may mean that the ethical expert must persevere with the knowledge that another expert or opposing counsel may not feel constrained by these same ethical principles or rules of professional conduct.

Enhancing Objectivity in a World of Bias

Dan Poynter has written extensively about a great number of things, including how to be an effective expert witness. His *Expert Witness Handbook* has been a popular read for experts of all kinds since 1987. It is particularly relevant to technical experts. Poynter suggests that any potential expert witness or litigation consultant should establish a consistent process for formalizing the business relationship the expert has with the attorney and the client. That relationship most often begins with a call or a letter from an attorney looking for an expert to consult on or testify in a case that is often fairly well along the litigation path. Beginning experts should understand what trial lawyers are looking for in forensic witnesses. Poynter describes what a typical attorney is looking for. Attorneys want an expert recognized as an authority in a particular field or located in a particular geographical location where the trial will take place (or both) who has the winning combination of the following criteria:

- expertise in the relevant subject areas;
- competence in the field;
- integrity;
- the ability to communicate specialized knowledge to lay people;
- locally situated; and
- whenever possible, "court-wise."[1]

Poynter points out that this initial selection process is a two-way street, with the expert investigating the potential client and attorney while the attorney is doing his or

---

1. Poynter, Daniel. *Expert Witness Handbook*. Santa Barbara, CA: Para Publishing, 1987, p. 32.

her due diligence on the qualifications and character of the expert, well before they actually meet to discuss forming a relationship. Poynter also counsels caution when considering the acceptance of a new case.

> *A great part of your decision to accept or reject the case should depend on your judgment about the case and how the calling attorney addresses it. Is the caller trying to push you toward a favorable conclusion? Is the caller unreasonable to work with? If, at any time, you realize the client-attorney is incompetent, unreasonable or dishonest, sever the relationship.*[2]

Poynter warns that attorneys all too often approach potential experts in the following way:

> *The attorney will call, give a few basic details and say, "Based on what you have heard, what do you think?"*
> ***Expert:*** *"I will send you my curriculum vita, other materials, and fee schedule. If you like what I send, send me a $500 retainer fee and all the paperwork. I will let you know within a few days if I will take the case."*[3]

Poynter advises that the expert not give an opinion. Instead, he or she should tell the caller what additional information he needs.

> ***Attorney:*** *"Well, are you interested in the case?"*
> ***Expert:*** *"I can't tell you. Send the information (complaint, interrogatories, depositions, equipment, police report, coroner's report, witness statements, etc.) and the retainer. I will evaluate them, report to you and will tell you if I am interested in the case." (Be firm.)*[4]

Assessing the Expert–Attorney Relationship

David Liddle is one of the pioneers of the IT age. During the course of a career he began as a member of the original engineering team at Xerox's Palo Alto Research Center (PARC) in the early 1970s, Liddle started a successful computer company and served as CEO for a prominent research firm for almost a decade before joining a venture capital group in Silicon Valley. He appeared as an expert witness in two major civil cases in the 1990s. One of those cases was *Lotus v. Borland*, still considered one of the most important decisions concerning the fundamental nature of IT intellectual property rights. Liddle (who testified for Borland) obviously impressed opposing counsel in that case with his mastery of the technology as well as his court wisdom, for, after that case was litigated through the U.S. Supreme Court, he was asked by the attorney for Lotus to act as an expert witness in a subsequent case. The second case was ultimately tried

2. Poynter, *Expert Witness Handbook*, p. 31.

3. Poynter, *Expert Witness Handbook*, p. 32.

4. Poynter, *Expert Witness Handbook*, p. 33.

before a jury, and again, the side for which Liddle served as the key technical expert witness prevailed in the lawsuit.

Liddle, an expert pilot, likens the initial contact between the expert and the attorney—the mutual background investigation, the expert's familiarization with the issues and facts of the case, and the decision by the witness to accept or reject a particular case—to the process of preparing to take off in an airplane. While this is only one of many analogies that might assist an expert in formalizing relationships with attorneys, it has worked well for Liddle.

Liddle likes to fly his own jets, and he flies a lot. While he seldom agrees to act as an expert witness, he believes, based on his experiences in major cases, that drawing an analogy between accepting an assignment as an expert witness and preparing to take off as an aircraft pilot is useful. It prompts him to use expert witness checklists like checkout procedures for a pilot to ensure that he identifies any reasons not to begin the engagement. These checklists also ensure that he is very well prepared for the unexpected after accepting an assignment and that he is able to decide whether to safely abort the "flight" at any given stage, walking away from the responsibility of being an expert witness without harming his reputation or unfairly compromising the interests of any party to the litigation.

Using Liddle's analogy of aviation checklists, once the expert has met with the attorney and requested that the attorney provide the relevant material needed to analyze the case, the expert should consult his or her first checklist. It is important, in order to gain maximum benefit from this analogy, to differentiate the checklist from a "to do" list. This checklist offers a reminder of what the expert already knows he or she needs to do in a given situation. It does not offer a set of instructions for making a systematic decision based on inadequate information in a crisis mode. A comprehensive "preflight" list is an essential tool that helps the expert perform consistently at all stages of the activity.

There are additional reasons why experts might want to be cautious and systematic when checking out an offer before deciding whether to become involved in litigation. Gary Summers, a principal at Silicon Valley Expert Witness Group[5] (SVEWG) in Mountain View, California, provides assistance to attorneys who require the services of technical experts. When an attorney calls about such assistance, SVEWG's procedure is to advise the attorney not to provide any information about the strategy being pursued in litigation but to limit the initial contact to such things as the names of the parties involved, the basis of the lawsuit, and a general description of the technology at issue in the case. Large consulting groups like SVEWG have a number of technical experts on staff who are available to consult or to become expert witnesses themselves. They also draw on several hundred proven experts as subcontractors to provide

---

5. See *http://www.SVEWG.com.*

lawyers with the most qualified expert in a particular technical area. The problem is that such an organization gets new calls every day, sometimes from opposing parties who are both looking for a qualified expert to assist their side of the case. In order to avoid any suggestion of a conflict of interest, Summers and his partners have learned that it pays to simply avoid getting into the details of the case or any discussions whatsoever as to the strategic thinking of the lawyers.

After taking the basic information, SVEWG does its own research and decides whether to recommend one of the in-house experts or one or more of the subcontracting experts who may be available and interested in applying for the assignment. Assuming everything checks out during the research, the consulting firm then contacts two or three experts and provides their names and a brief résumé to the law firm. It is then up to the law firm to contact the applicants for interviews.

While SVEWG runs a very active placement service for technical experts throughout the country, its policies and procedures for the initial contact by attorneys should be carefully considered by the occasional and first-time expert as well. It is not unknown for a lawyer to attempt to discuss his or her case with as many qualified experts who specialize in a small technical niche as possible. While this may be completely above board in an effort to assemble a profile of experts who may later be considered or to attempt to collect as much free expert advice as possible in a short time, it may also serve to create potential challenges to any later attempt by the contending party to retain the services of the contacted experts. This can have the effect of potentially disqualifying experts who made the simple mistake of being polite while they listened to a lawyer talk about a lawsuit or some of the key issues in the case in a single phone call.

It is probably no accident that Dan Poynter, who has been renowned as a technical expert in the fields of parachuting and skydiving since 1973, also likes checklists. He is a prolific writer—his book on expert witnesses is one of over two dozen books he has written, and he has written several hundred magazine articles as well. Each of the chapters in his book for expert witnesses contains useful checklists. Poynter includes several basic queries in his formula for evaluating your suitability as an expert for the case and evaluating the merit of the case itself.

1. *Are you competent to render an opinion in this particular area?*
2. *Do you need more information?*
3. *What are the weaknesses of the case and can they be diluted or overcome?*
4. *What are the strengths of the case?*
5. *Do you want to run more tests?*
6. *Do you want to prepare some demonstrative evidence?*
7. *Do you need some reference material?*
8. *Can you suggest a reading list to educate the client-attorney?*
9. *Is the calling client-attorney being candid?*[6]

---

6. Poynter, *Expert Witness Handbook*, p. 36.

Poynter recommends that if you find you are not receiving all the information requested or if you have any doubt about the ethical status of the case, you should reject it.

Using Liddle's and Poynter's approaches is the first step toward deciding whether to take on an expert witness assignment. It is also the first step toward ensuring the requisite objectivity you must exhibit as an expert witness throughout the assignment. Beyond taking the advice of Summers to avoid unnecessary conflicts of interest from the very first contact with the attorney, you can address many of the issues that seem to crop up later (and that can endanger your objectivity) by being both methodical and cautious in your initial decision to serve in a case.

A Different Style of Reporting

Many technical experts first learned to write reports while students in secondary schools and college. They learned to write based on a linear process in which they structured their ideas in outline form, fleshed out that outline with additional information (citing sources where necessary), and went through a number of draft versions, tweaking and polishing the document until it was complete. Despite this almost universal preparation in secondary schools and at university, many technologists still do not like to write. They dislike the rigor of the writing process and prefer to spend their time in the more interesting creative processes of design and implementation of new technology. Although documentation of one's results is considered essential, especially when those results are part of a commercial product, this part of the technical process is often badly neglected or gladly delegated to others.

The law, however, expects expert witnesses to write reports for the court, outlining their opinions on the matters about which they are testifying. In the eyes of the law, the expert's testimony is allowed by the court only to the extent that the expert adequately documents the basis for it in a report and makes it available to the opposing party before the trial.

This discovery process alters the classic writing process outlined above because the forensic writing process and the rules of disclosure can lend the opposing counsel ample fodder for cross-examination. The key to understanding how the legal process requires you to document your expert opinions lies in Rule 26.

Rule 26 and Its Effect on Expert Testimony

Rule 26 of the Federal Rules of Procedure is entitled "General Provisions Governing Discovery; Duty of Disclosure." It includes the rules relating to the discovery of evidence and outlines such items as the information lawyers must divulge about the witnesses who will testify at trial and the time limits they must observe when responding to discovery requests. It includes some surprises, as well—for instance, it includes the provision that anyone who has knowledge of what evidence should be subject to discovery as well as the location of that evidence is obligated to convey that information to the party who needs the evidence. As is the case with much of the Federal Code, Rule 26 has been amended to include provisions dealing with electronic evidence discovery.

This ongoing process of amendment raises an important point. You should not rely on the current or past authority of the statutory provisions referenced and quoted in this book. These rules and statutes are constantly subject to revision and are in fact almost always being debated about and then revised from time to time. Equally important are the constant changes in the interpretation of the different provisions of these rules that different courts are constantly issuing. Any cases or portions of cases quoted, cited, or discussed in this book are also subject to being overturned and reversed or reinterpreted in different ways by other courts in other jurisdictions. You should request from the attorney with whom you're working or from your own private counsel any advice as to the current state of the law regarding any rule or legal authority that is of concern to you.

Rule 26 has an entire section in which it deals with the special circumstances of expert testimony. Here is what the rule says on that topic.

(2) Disclosure of Expert Testimony.

In addition to the disclosures required by paragraph (1), a party shall disclose to other parties the identity of any person who may be used at trial to present evidence under Rules 702, 703, or 705 of the Federal Rules of Evidence.

Except as otherwise stipulated or directed by the court, this disclosure shall, with respect to a witness who is retained or specially employed to provide expert testimony in the case or whose duties as an employee of the party regularly involve giving expert testimony, be accompanied by a written report prepared and signed by the witness. The report shall contain a complete statement of all opinions to be expressed and the basis and reasons therefore; the data or other information considered by the witness in forming the opinions; any exhibits to be used as a summary of or support for the opinions; the qualifications of the witness, including a list of all publications authored by the witness within the preceding ten years; the compensation to be paid for the study and testimony; and a listing of any other cases in which the witness has testified as an expert at trial or by deposition within the preceding four years.

These disclosures shall be made at the times and in the sequence directed by the court. In the absence of other directions from the court or stipulation by the parties, the disclosures shall be made at least 90 days before the trial date or the date the case is to be ready for trial or, if the evidence is intended solely to contradict or rebut evidence on the same subject matter identified by another party under paragraph (2)(B), within 30 days after the disclosure made by the other party. The parties shall supplement these disclosures when required under subdivision (e)(1).[7]

---

7. Federal Rules of Civil Procedure, Rule 26(a)(2).

Before the 1993 amendments to Rule 26 of the Federal Rules of Civil Procedure and the *Daubert* line of decisions, technical expert witness reports were often intentionally drafted with the assistance of trial counsel or a member of the litigation team with one goal in mind: to yield the barest of bone to the other side. In effect, the legal team considered the artful finessing the Rule 26 report requirement to be a finer point of litigation strategy. This served to preserve all the strategic options concerning the expert's actual trial testimony and to give up as little of the expert's information as possible before depositions or other testimony were taken at the expense of the other party. Courts tended to endorse this kind of behavior on the theory that parties should not have to do or pay for expert work for their opponents in discovering all the relevant facts and preparing for trial. Later, when reports were required before the depositions of the opposing experts were taken, the same philosophy of a high-stakes game of advocacy dictated that neither side would be required to tip its hand in the report. So, counsel ordinarily set a goal for early discovery efforts about the other side's expert testimony: to obtain sufficient facts to be able to take the expert's deposition and then find out as much as possible through a thorough examination of the expert under oath. This strategy delays (at least until the deposition) the full divulgence to the other side of the scope and the limits of the expert's qualifications, methods, theories, research, testing, and ultimate conclusions or opinions.

Today, many experienced trial attorneys still attempt to limit the amount of material created in the process of working with an expert witness who will testify. This is accomplished by taking precautions not to generate unnecessary correspondence or e-mail messages about the discussions that take place in the process of preparing the expert's report. Another technique for minimizing discoverable expert-generated evidence is to use the telephone as much as possible for communications between legal counsel and expert. When the time comes for drafting the Rule 26 report or exchanging any formal letters for record-keeping purposes (such as the record of what documents or other material have been given to the expert to review or returned by the expert to the attorney), the telephone is still used as much as possible. All preliminary discussions of what should or should not go into any written correspondence or into the one and only final copy of the report that will be disclosed are generally oral and unrecorded. As indicated previously, opposing counsel often make informal or formal agreements to treat certain communications between them and their experts as not subject to disclosure in order to economize on these otherwise essential safety precautions against creating unnecessary disclosures of the expert's process of analysis and preparation.

When Not to Document Process

There are also excellent practical reasons to limit the number and size of written or electronic documents created while generating the Rule 26 report. You can expect experienced trial counsel to attempt to access all drafts of reports and opinions in pretrial discovery. You can understand why these would be relevant to the fact finder at trial. However, counsel will then use every inconsistent statement contained in any document so discovered in an attempt to probe the reasons for changes between initial reactions and the final opinions expressed in the official report. Jack Grimes, an experienced technical expert in California, has described a situation that required him to spend a number of painful hours during his deposition explaining to a cross-examining attorney why Grimes had made some marginal notes in another expert's report.[8]

Grimes had been provided a report prepared by the opposing expert. He carefully reviewed the report in order to come to some understanding of the opinions and analysis of the opposing expert. Unfortunately, as he reviewed the report, Grimes made notations with words and symbols, highlighting, question marks, and emphasis punctuation on almost every line of the multipage report, as was his custom prior to this experience.

According to Grimes, the process of attempting to remember just what he was thinking when he made each of those notations and marks on the report, what significance they had to him when he made them, and what importance he gave them now, was one of the most excruciating deposition experiences he has had to endure as an expert witness. Because of this incident, he asserts that it is better practice to simply avoid creating these kinds of notations in discoverable documents in the course of your preparation as a testifying expert.

As we will see from some of the cases discussed below, the same general lesson has been learned by experts and their counsel when it comes to creating diaries, detailed work or billing records, and multiple draft versions of the report itself. One technique that many trial attorneys have adopted when they are unable to negotiate a mutual waiver of disclosure for these sorts of routine records is to alter the way they communicate with their expert witnesses when collaborating on the preparation of the report that will be disclosed to opposing counsel and their experts for review. The report is put into written or electronic form only when the expert is fully satisfied with the final draft. Once the report is put into written or electronic form, it is subject to disclosure and discovery by the other side.

These cloak-and-dagger tactics may seem bizarre to the novice expert. You may think this level of care devoted to avoiding the creation of unnecessary records or documents that will be discoverable during the course of litigation seems excessive. However, the experiences of experts like Jack Grimes are worth considering and discussing with the attorney in some detail before you begin your assignment. This may help prevent problems later due to confusion about what should have been preserved or exactly what needs to be disclosed to the other side.

---

8. Grimes, Jack. Personal communication, November 2001.

Think of the avoidance of unnecessary records or documents as controlling unnecessary expense in deposition time. Think of it as making it easier to focus on the significant issues that are ultimately the basis of the expert's findings and opinions to be offered to the fact finder. This is straightforward process optimization applied to the legal process, and the potential savings go beyond considerations of time and money. Among other things, the aggravation associated with dealing with obstacles of your own creation can be significant, especially when these obstacles primarily come from old habits of practice. These habits may be perfectly reasonable research techniques in the laboratory, but they are usually poorly applied in the context of litigation. New habits that eliminate these time and energy drains allow experts to be more effective witnesses. They can render opinions and conclusions based on the actual research, testing, and thought they applied to the case, rather than having to prepare to explain largely irrelevant and diverting artifacts of the process.

Note that this process optimization is another situation in which you can use Liddle's checklist approach to good effect. Continually improving on this checklist of things you already know can help you more carefully and comprehensively plan and carry out the specific tasks you will encounter in almost every new case, such as the preparation of a Rule 26 report.

If this level of planning and orchestration seems contrived, remember the fundamental function of expert witnesses. The point of hiring and presenting an expert in litigation is to bring objective expertise that actually helps explain issues and facts that are too complex for the average judge or juror to easily understand. Anything that gets in the way of this goal will be assiduously avoided by an experienced trial lawyer and also by an experienced expert like Jack Grimes. There is nothing wrong with tactics that minimize the creation of discovery materials that are not required by the rules and that interfere with the purpose of being an expert witness in the first place. Indeed, like everything else involved in the litigation game, some attorneys are quite willing to make trade-offs in order to enhance one or more of the goals of presenting a particular expert. This goal enhancement often comes at the expense of providing seemingly unnecessary document discovery, or offering generous opportunities to interview the expert at an early stage of the process, or generating and disclosing additional documents or even early drafts of reports to the other side. Often early and mutually beneficial settlements result from such open and effusive discovery of the expert's qualifications and evolving work product.

Most of these trade-offs are also designed by the attorney to enhance the appearance of the objectivity and competence (and therefore the credibility) of the chosen expert, should the case end up in trial. It is crucial that the expert determine just what legal strategy is being used before getting involved, so that the expert can decide whether he or she will be able to perform his or her duties according to the particular rules of engagement and in accordance with ethical and professional standards.

The Case of the Mystery Client

Perhaps a war story about one attorney's strategy to both encourage settlement and enhance the expert's appearance of objectivity will indicate the tremendous range of strategies from which a lawyer can select when sculpting his or her approach to a given case. Ross Mayfield is a technical expert who has many years of IT and digital forensics experience. A well-known trial attorney approached Mayfield with an unusual request: to consider a hypothetical scenario concerning certain evidence that had been deleted in what the client felt were suspicious circumstances. The attorney went over the facts that needed to be investigated by Mayfield in order to offer an expert opinion in the case.[9] Some of the same sorts of evidentiary issues that were discussed in the landmark case of *Gates v. Bando* (described in detail in Chapter 9) were involved in this case as well.

Mayfield thought about the scenario as described by the attorney and considered his own experience and training. He concluded that he was amply qualified to undertake the assignment, provided everything that he was expected to do had been covered in the attorney's overview and the materials that he had been shown. Then it occurred to him that the attorney had not indicated which party in the dispute was his client. Mayfield called the attorney to say he thought he could handle the assignment but that he would need to know for which party he would be working. This is important information in order to be sure that the expert has no apparent or real conflicts of interest in taking on the case for a particular party.

That's when the attorney's strategy became clear. If it would not make any difference to Mayfield which party the attorney represented, the attorney told him that it would be best in this particular case if Mayfield would simply act as a neutral expert. This required some discussions that made it clear to both the attorney and Mayfield that there would be no potential conflict for Mayfield to become involved. Of course, he had clearly been hired and would be paid by one of the parties, who would remain unidentified throughout Mayfield's employment. Mayfield had never encountered this kind of request for his services, and it threw him off balance momentarily until he had a chance to think about it. Having resolved the conflicts issues with some extra effort, the idea of not knowing which party had hired him began to appeal to him since it allowed him to act almost as if he were a neutral consultant to the fact finder, even though he would be hired and paid by one of the contending parties.

Mayfield asked the attorney if this assignment meant that he would do his investigation, make a call, and then let the chips fall where they may when Mayfield's findings were reported to the fact finder. The attorney answered that this was exactly what he had in mind, then went on to explain that in this way he believed that the objec-

---

9. Mayfield, Ross. Personal communication, November 2001.

tivity of the expert opinion and any subsequent testimony would be preserved in every way. This assurance of objectivity would exist despite the obvious fact that one of the two parties (the unidentified party who was actually the attorney's client) was paying for the expert analysis.

Mayfield accepted this assignment, and after doing the work and issuing his report to be disclosed to counsel for both parties, he met with the attorneys for each party and explained his report. After receiving additional information from the parties, he revised his report slightly and testified before an appointed arbitrator. After his testimony, the case was resolved. As it turned out, the case was resolved in favor of the party who had paid Mayfield's bill for services rendered.

Establishing Objectivity

Although most experts will not see this strategy used in very many cases in which they are asked to serve, it is one example of the strategies that attorneys devise to place the objectivity of their experts uppermost in the minds of the fact finders. These strategies can also serve to minimize challenges based on the amount of money that a party is paying the expert and arguments that the expert is just another overpaid hired gun. Perhaps more importantly, the "mystery client" strategy also eliminates challenges based on written correspondence between expert and attorney that can be interpreted as suggesting that the expert is conditioning his or her opinions in favor of the paying party. This potential for opposing counsel to create the appearance of bias can affect the outcome of the case regardless of whether or not the communications in question actually influenced the investigation, thinking, or opinions of the expert in the final analysis.

The point is simply that to a certain extent, an expert's objectivity can be preserved, enhanced, or seriously eroded simply by the way the attorney and the expert orchestrate the preparation and discovery process. The more effectively this orchestration is done, the more the court and the jurors are likely to feel that the expert has not become biased or become an advocate witness. This process of creating as much professional distance and objectivity as possible before an opinion is reached can to a large extent be controlled by the expert by having a strict protocol for evaluating the issues and evidence associated with the case. The expert needs to independently consider the basic materials and issues that the attorney seeking to hire the expert has prepared before sitting down with the attorney and discussing the expert's preliminary views at that first meeting.

In other words, before getting to the reporting stage, in order to avoid the obvious attack by the opposing attorney in deposition or at trial that the "hired gun" is just doing what he or she has been asked to do, the ritual of interaction between the attorney and the expert should follow some simple rules. For example, in order for the expert to be seen as investigating a serious problem on his or her own and coming to an independent opinion, whenever possible (after the initial request from the attorney), sharing information about the case should begin with the presentation of a set of documents for the expert to review, before the attorney and the expert start discussing strategies of analysis and presentation.

No statement of the theories about the technical issues in the case should precede these initial disclosures to the expert. As Liddle and Poynter suggest, the expert needs to determine whether he or she is qualified and interested in the issue to be resolved. Only after the expert conducts the initial review and then expresses interest in serving as an expert should he or she advise the attorney of his or her preliminary views. Certainly at that point the attorney will need to determine whether the expert's analysis is going to yield helpful information, but these results may be helpful in many ways, independent of the substance of the initial views.

For example, it may be most helpful to know that at least this qualified expert doesn't agree with the attorney's initial theory. This realization at the earliest possible moment in the case may allow for the most favorable settlement for the party or enable the lawyer to avoid throwing good money after bad due to a misperception of the technical issues in the case. Should the expert be interested but undecided as to what the available facts and the current research indicate with regard to the problem that has been presented, the attorney will need to consider whether there is additional evidence available. Furthermore, the attorney will also need to determine whether extensive research, experimentation, or testing need to be done, whether this expert is the most competent available, and whether the available budget will suffice to get the job done.

Rule 26 Reports and First Impressions

These general suggestions raise another question of how the lawyer decides on the appropriateness of the particular expert for a given case. Should the attorney decide to designate the expert as the testifying witness, at some point the expert will need to write a Rule 26 report of his or her expert opinion and disclose it to the other side. Today, that report has taken on a heightened importance due to the new twist in the litigation ritual represented by the *Daubert* gatekeeping challenge, discussed in more detail in Chapter 8.

The expert's Rule 26 report is likely to be one of the first things a judge considers when asked to decide a question of an expert's qualifications or the admissibility of some or all of the proffered testimony. It also may be the attorney's first and best chance to let the judge know just how competent and helpful the expert is. A psychological principle states that first impressions are extremely important to the ultimate decisions made about credibility and meaning. This suggests that a great deal of thought should go into the expert's report and the events that lead up to and frame the drafting of that document. Writing the report to highlight the objectivity of the expert and other experts the witness may have relied on can also enhance the likelihood that the ultimate opinions of the witness will survive a serious *Daubert* challenge. This attention paid to enlightening the judge with regard to the technical and professional qualifications of the expert can also increase the possibility of the expert opinion surviving any challenge pursuant to Rule 26 that alleges an inadvertent breach in complying with the duties that are set out in that rule.

The Role of Expert Opinions and Reports: Learning by Example

We have selected several cases to discuss here in some detail to enable you to gain a broader understanding of the role that expert reports play in the overall strategy of litigation. These cases also illustrate the reasoning process used by several courts to evaluate allegations of failures on the part of the expert and/or the attorney to play by the rules or to provide sufficient expertise to enable the party to proceed further with a claim in the controversy and to ensure the objectivity of expert evidence.

Experts Need to Write Their Own Rule 26 Reports

Contrast what Ross Mayfield did when he began investigating the problem of deleted evidence, without knowing which side had hired him, with what was reportedly done in the case of *In Re Jackson National Life Insurance Company Premium Litigation*, a 1998 decision about the sufficiency of the Rule 26 report submitted by the plaintiff's expert witness.

In this case, Jackson National moved for an order striking the testimony of an expert witness. Plaintiffs opposed the motion and provided excerpts of the expert's testimony in another pending federal court matter. The court conducted a hearing on the motion and at the conclusion of the hearing, the court made oral findings, including the following:

(a) The expert's report in the present case is substantially derived from his report in another case;

(b) the language of the expert's report in the case was provided by plaintiffs' counsel;

(c) the language of the expert's report in the case is substantially similar to that used by another expert witness in a third case pending in the state courts of Louisiana;

(d) the substantial similarity among the three expert witness reports derived from the authorship of their common language by plaintiffs' counsel;

(e) the expert witness' report in the present case was not "prepared by" him, in violation of Fed. R. Civ. P. 26(a)(2);

(f) the expert testified untruthfully at his deposition in this case concerning the authorship of the language in his report, and the attempts of defense counsel to discover the truth of the matter were unjustifiably impeded by instructions to the witness not to answer, made by plaintiffs' counsel in violation of Fed. R. Civ. P. 30(d)(1); and

(g) plaintiffs have not borne their burden under Fed. R. Civ. P. 37(c) to show that the violation of Rule 26(a)(2) was harmless.

Based on these and other findings, the Magistrate granted the motion of Jackson National Insurance Co. to preclude the testimony of their expert as an expert witness and precluded plaintiffs from presenting his testimony in any of these actions.[10]

This is the story of an expert witness called to testify in a case. In the opinion, the judge outlines a situation that appears to violate the tenets regarding objectivity that we've covered in this chapter. First, the expert's Rule 26 report has been contested because the evidence shows that the expert's report is virtually identical to a Rule 26 report he submitted in a completely different case. Things take a truly strange turn when the fact comes to light that the expert's report in that second case is identical to a Rule 26 report submitted in a third case—a report submitted by a different expert! The common theme among all three cases and reports is the attorney who, it is alleged, provided the contents of all three reports to the experts. To avoid confusion in the following opinion, the names of the respective experts have been removed.

This is a clear violation of Rule 26, which requires the expert to prepare and sign the report. Finally, to add insult to injury, the expert, when asked during a deposition in this case about the authorship of his report, according to the court failed to answer truthfully. When the opposing counsel attempted to get to the truth, the expert's counsel directed the expert not to answer. In conclusion, the magistrate judges, citing the following rule, excluded the expert and his testimony from the case.

> *Rule 30(d)(1). Any objection during a deposition must be stated concisely and in a non-argumentative and non-suggestive manner. A person may instruct a deponent not to answer only when necessary to preserve a privilege, to enforce a limitation directed by the court, or to present a motion under Rule 30(d)(4).*[11]

Finally, in a procedural finale, the Magistrate Judge asserted that the expert and plaintiff counsel failed to demonstrate that the Rule 26 violation fell within defined exclusions to the rules of discovery, and that the plaintiff should therefore be subject

---

10. *In Re Jackson National Life Insurance Company Premium Litigation.* U.S. District Ct., W.D. Michigan, S. Div., No. 5:96-MD-1122. Decided September 1999 by Hon. U.S. Magistrate Judge Joseph G. Scoville, 1999 WL 33510008 (W.D. Mich. Sept. 29, 1999); 1999 U.S. Dist. LEXIS 17153.

11. Federal Rules of Civil Procedure, Section V, Rule 30(d)(1).

to the penalties associated with Rule 26 violations, namely the exclusion of the expert's testimony and imposed sanctions.

(c) Failure to Disclose; False or Misleading Disclosure; Refusal to Admit.

(1) A party that without substantial justification fails to disclose information required by Rule 26(a) or 26(e)(1), or to amend a prior response to discovery as required by Rule 26(e)(2), is not, unless such failure is harmless, permitted to use as evidence at a trial, at a hearing, or on a motion any witness or information not so disclosed. In addition to or in lieu of this sanction, the court, on motion and after affording an opportunity to be heard, may impose other appropriate sanctions. In addition to requiring payment of reasonable expenses, including attorney's fees, caused by the failure, these sanctions may include any of the actions authorized under Rule 37(b)(2)(A), (B), and (C) and may include informing the jury of the failure to make the disclosure.

(2) If a party fails to admit the genuineness of any document or the truth of any matter as requested under Rule 36, and if the party requesting the admissions there-after proves the genuineness of the document or the truth of the matter, the request-ing party may apply to the court for an order requiring the other party to pay the reasonable expenses incurred in making that proof, including reasonable attorney's fees.[12]

The plaintiff appealed the decision. The decision continues with the district court judge's review, paraphrased in the following excerpt.

On September 29, 1999, Magistrate Judge Joseph G. Scoville issued an order pre-cluding testimony by plaintiffs' expert. . . . Plaintiffs have appealed the ruling. Magistrate Judge Scoville's ruling is premised upon three findings. First, he found that plaintiffs violated Fed. R. Civ. P. 26(a)(2)(B) by providing defendant with an expert witness report that had not actually been "prepared" by the witness. Second, he found that [the expert] testified untruthfully in his deposition concerning the authorship of the language of the report and that plaintiffs' counsel unjustifiably impeded defendant's counsel's search for the truth of the matter. Third, he conclud-ed plaintiffs had failed to show their violation of Rule 26(a)(2) was harmless.

The magistrate judge's ruling on a nondispositive matter will be affirmed unless it is shown to be "clearly erroneous or contrary to law." . . . Factual findings are reviewed for clear error, while conclusions of law are reviewed de novo. . . . In review-ing the factual findings, the evidence must be considered in the light most likely to support the magistrate judge's decision. "A factual finding will only be clearly erro-neous when, although there may be evidence to support it, the reviewing court on the entire evidence is left with the definite and firm conviction that a mistake has been committed." . . .

Applying this standard of review after duly considering the parties' briefs and exhibits, oral arguments of counsel, and the record of proceedings before Magistrate

---

12. Federal Rules of Civil Procedure, Section V, Rule 26(c)(1) and 26(c)(2).

Judge Scoville, including the transcript of his thorough bench ruling, the Court finds no error in his factual findings. The record clearly supports the finding that the language of [the expert's] report, including the formulation of his opinions, was not prepared by him, but was provided to him by plaintiffs' counsel. Granted, Rule 26(a)(2) contemplates some assistance of counsel in the preparation of an expert's report. . . .

However, undeniable substantial similarities between [the expert's] report and the report of another expert prepared with assistance from the same counsel in an unrelated case, demonstrate that counsel's participation so exceeded the bounds of legitimate "assistance" as to negate the possibility that [the expert] in this case actually prepared his own report within the meaning of Rule 26(a)(2). Plaintiffs' failure to furnish defendant with a report prepared by [the expert], constitutes a violation of Rule 26(a)(2). . . .

The Court also concurs with the magistrate judge's finding that [the expert] testified untruthfully in his deposition. Plaintiff's counsel's attempts to assign arguably truthful meaning to [the expert's] testimony are not persuasive. [The expert] witness, with advice of counsel, clearly gave incomplete and misleading answers to legitimate questions concerning the authorship of his report.

Magistrate Judge Scoville further concluded that plaintiffs' violation of Rule 26(a)(2) warranted exclusion of [the expert's] testimony pursuant to Fed. R. Civ. P. 37(c)(1) unless plaintiffs were able to show their violation was harmless. Finding that plaintiffs had not carried this burden, he imposed the exclusionary sanction. Plaintiffs object, contending defendant suffered no prejudice as a result of counsel's participation in the preparation of [the expert's] report. Since [the expert] was made available for deposition, plaintiffs contend, defendant was able to avoid any harm that might flow from the supposed Rule 26(a)(2) violation.

Again, the Court cannot find the magistrate judge clearly erred in finding the violation had not been shown to be harmless. In other cases, Rule 26(a)(2) has been found to have been "technically" violated in that the expert's report had not been signed by the expert and included, in addition to the expert's own opinions, portions that were prepared by counsel. The violation was deemed harmless, however, because the report did contain portions actually prepared by the expert and because the expert, in deposition, frankly explained what portions of the report were his.

Here, in contrast, the Court is presented with something more than a mere "technical violation." First, it has been established that the language of [the expert's] report was originally prepared by plaintiffs' counsel. The report does not contain a statement of [the expert's] opinions in his own words. Moreover, [the expert's] deposition, rather than affording opportunity to remedy any prejudice, actually compounded the violation. When confronted with questions about the report's authorship, [the expert] gave misleading and evasive answers. It is this conduct by the expert witness, and plaintiffs' counsel, in the deposition, reflecting a cavalier or stubborn disregard for the Rules of Civil Procedure and the integrity of the judicial process which, in the Court's opinion,

*justifies the sanction imposed. The magistrate judge did not abuse his discretion in
ordering [the expert's] testimony excluded.*[13]

Lessons Learned

As a result of the reviewing court's analysis, the plaintiff's appeal was denied and the
order precluding the plaintiff from calling the expert or using his report was affirmed,
leaving the plaintiff high and dry. We can draw at least three conclusions from this case.

1. It is a mistake and unprofessional to allow the attorney to draft your report.
   An expert is responsible under the rules for performing his or her own independent analysis and developing his or her own independent conclusions.
   This is especially important when, as the case demonstrates, an attorney may
   be drafting nearly identical reports for other experts in other cases. These
   identical reports would be available to opposing counsel through basic discovery techniques or, as also happens, through blind luck discovery. There
   may be nothing wrong with having the secretarial staff in the attorney's office
   prepare the final report based on your independent findings and conclusions,
   and such a process may never be challenged by opposing counsel. However,
   "independent" means what it says, and when the expert does not actually prepare the report, clearly there is an opportunity to inquire about the process of
   preparation and about who did what and when. Also, when this is the chosen
   process, the problems of multiple drafts need to be considered and dealt with
   appropriately since all drafts of an expert's report are generally made available to the opponent in discovery and may be inquired into during deposition and testimony at trial.
2. Never testify in a misleading or evasive way (let alone untruthfully) about the
   independence or authorship of your report (or anything else) during your
   deposition or at any other time.
3. Don't write your report like a judicial opinion. That said, you do need to
   learn to read judicial opinions in order to understand what the most significant reader of your report may be looking for. You can also gain insight on
   how judges fit facts with rules and previous decisions to reach a decision.

Lies and Statistics

You might infer from the *Jackson National Life Insurance* case that the temptation of
attorneys to treat their experts as ventriloquists' dummies is immense, especially in
high-dollar cases. And it is just this kind of disastrous impression that those who have

---

13. *In Re Jackson National Life Insurance Company Premium Litigation*, 46 Fed. R.
Serv. 3d (Callaghan) 201, 2000 U.S. Dist. LEXIS 1318. (W.D. Mich. Feb. 8, 2000).

thought and written about the art of expert witness testimony are concerned about when they warn their readers of the dangers of moving the slightest distance from a presentation that makes it clear that the expert is objective and not under the management or control of the lawyer. Paul Meier has listed a number of concerns about practices that can lead to disaster. As an experienced expert witness and accomplished statistician, Meier has written that "The phenomenon of 'shopping for witnesses' is well recognized by the courts, and it contributes to the wary attitude they have about experts in general. The shopping is done by the lawyers, however, and is thus not subject to exposure in the actual testimony."[14]

Meier worries that because of the advocacy rules of engagement, the professional integrity of the expert witness may not be adequately protected by the lawyer who hires the expert or by the court. He set out a series of corrupting influences that may be inherent in the context of providing expert testimony. The expert cannot escape the fact that the lawyer is his or her source for instructions on how the litigation game must be played. It is difficult to resist the role of advocate that some lawyers may attempt to assign to the expert, and this will be even more difficult when the expert agrees completely with the lawyer's theory of the issues that the expert's testimony is being sought to address.

In his article Meier addressed the new importance that statistical evidence had been given by the courts in the mid-1980s. As a statistician, he was aware of a new problem for statistical experts that he called "aggrandizement." As an example of this process that he perceived was well under way by 1986, with regard to a growing judicial embrace of statistical significance testing, both courts and academia (economic experts in particular) had begun to endorse the magical properties of multiple regression analysis. As a consequence of this new-found favor in academic circles and in the courts, Meier expressed his concerns that:

> . . . the statistician is strongly tempted to give the definitive rather than a qualified answer to the key questions. He will be tempted to ignore or to minimize those qualifications that he might emphasize in a more academic setting, he may fail to emphasize the existence of schools of thought other than his own, and he may lay claim to overly broad scope for the inferences he draws.[15]

In Meier's view, additional corrupting influences that result from the adversarial nature of the presentation of expert testimony include what he terms "bribery," in the sense of being paid only to assist the lawyer's view of the case; "flattery," as described below; "co-option," as when the case is introduced by the advocate or the expert is asked to critique the opposing expert's opinion from the point of view of the theory of the employing party. Experts also are faced with the forced adoption of a gladiato-

---

14. Meier, Paul. "Damned Liars and Expert Witnesses." *Journal of the American Statistical Association* 81(394), 1986, p. 269.

15. Meier, "Damned Liars and Expert Witnesses," p. 273.

rial role with the interrogating attorney for the adversary, against whose rhetorical attacks the expert feels he or she must defend; and they can be influenced by strongly held personal views that may subtly and not so subtly influence the decision to accept an assignment and to color testimony that could and probably should be far more nuanced in order to strike a blow for what the expert perceives to be a just cause. Consider with Meier how he personally experienced the use of flattery from a respected and highly skilled attorney to get him to accept an expert witness assignment.

> *I well recall an occasion on which I was asked to consult in a case at a time that was not especially convenient. I explained that I really could not participate on this occasion. The lawyer, with whom I had worked before and for whom I had a great deal of respect, pled the sorry state of statistical testimony in the courts in general, and in the instant case in particular. He read from the transcript some particularly egregious quotes from the statistical expert for the other side, and he urged the importance for the future of statistics in the domain of public affairs of having corrective testimony. That being a viewpoint I could only share, and tacitly mindful of our shared opinion that I was the ideal candidate to champion the honor of the profession, I reluctantly agreed to testify.[16]*

Too Little, Too Late, Too Bad

In addition to frowning on the attorney writing the expert's report, courts quickly run out of patience when the report or its appropriate and necessary supplements are submitted too late to meet the disclosure deadlines under the rules. In the case of *Baker v. Indian Prairie Community Unit, School District No. 204*, et al., the issue was timeliness of supplemental expert opinions coupled with a failure to comply with the *Daubert* standard in both the initial and the supplemental expert opinions. In *Baker*, the defendants moved to strike the expert affidavits and exclude the testifying experts, and the court agreed. The court's opinion also offers some insight into the process that one court went through in determining that the expert lacked a reliable theory or method for rendering the opinion that his attorney hoped to introduce as evidence but sought too late to disclose.

The Issue of Timeliness

Quoting from the opinion, the court restates the arguments put forth by both parties to this dispute.

> *ServiceMaster and Vlamis contend that numerous opinions and data contained in Wakeley's and Holland's affidavits are untimely and should be stricken. Rule 26(a)(2)(B) requires expert witnesses to prepare a written report containing a complete statement of all opinions to be expressed, the basis and reasons therefor, and the data or other information considered by the expert in forming the opinions as well as*

---

16. Meier, "Damned Liars and Expert Witnesses," p. 274.

a list of exhibits to be used, the expert's qualifications, the expert's compensation, and a list of other cases in which the expert testified in the last four years. A party's failure to comply with Rule 26(a) results in an "automatic and mandatory" exclusion of expert testimony "unless the party to be sanctioned can show that its violation of Rule 26(a) was either justified or harmless." [citations omitted] The Bakers have not shown that their failure to timely disclose all of Wakeley's and Holland's opinions was either justified or harmless, and the arguments raised by the Bakers in response to the timeliness issue are without merit.

The Bakers first claim, without any citation to authority, that it is "patently unfair and prejudicial to the plaintiff to prevent him from consulting with his experts and obtaining from them updated, modified or even new opinions and data in response to Motions for Summary Judgment filed after the expert disclosure date." . . . The expert disclosure deadlines do not prohibit the Bakers from thereafter consulting with their experts but do establish firm dates for disclosure of experts and expert opinions. The Bakers' assertion that expert disclosure deadlines do not prevent them from later offering new expert opinions is frivolous. Deadlines play an important role in the Court's ability to manage and control its docket, and the Court has the ability to establish and enforce its deadlines. . . .

The Bakers also maintain that the affidavits of Wakeley and Holland merely supplement their prior reports. Although Rule 26(e) provides that a party has a duty to "supplement or correct" its prior disclosures if it learns that the prior information "is incomplete or incorrect," the statements at issue are new conclusions which do not merely correct or complete prior opinions of Wakeley or Holland. For example, Wakeley's report contained one opinion: minor Baker demonstrated a level of hazard perception and risk awareness entirely consistent with his age and level of development. In his affidavit, Wakeley concludes not only that Baker acted reasonably and rationally for his age but also that the dangers associated with sledding down the hill and over the snow pile were not obvious to a twelve-year-old boy and that the risk involved is not similar to the risk involved in a fall. Wakeley's opinions concerning the obviousness of the risk and whether the risk encountered by minor Baker were similar to a fall are new and offered for the first time after Defendants' summary judgment arguments on the exact same issues.

Finally, the Bakers contend that Defendants cannot show any prejudice as a result of the new expert opinions because: (1) "this is a summary judgment proceeding;" (2) if summary judgment is denied, Defendants "will have ample opportunity to obtain appropriate expert opinions;" and (3) Defendants chose not to take depositions of the Bakers' experts. The Bakers appear to misunderstand the Federal Rules of Civil Procedure and the role of expert reports.[17]

---

17. *Baker v. Indian Prairie Community Unit, School District No. 204, et al.*, 1999 WL 988799 (N.D. Ill. Oct 27, 1999) (No. 96C 3927); also reported at 1999 U. S. Dist. Lexis 17221.

In this case, involving a lawsuit over a minor's injuries, there is a dispute over a procedural issue, namely whether the plaintiffs' experts' opinions could be excluded from consideration because they were submitted to the courts after the established deadlines. The court alluded to the fact that the plaintiffs were, in their arguments, exhibiting a lack of understanding of the relevant Rules of Civil Procedure.

The court continues

> *The sanction of exclusion applies at summary judgment as well as at trial. Rule 37(c)(1) explicitly provides that untimely disclosures may not be used "at a trial, at a hearing, or on a motion." Moreover, Defendants need not wait until after a ruling on summary judgment to discover all of Wakeley's and Holland's opinions and data where the Court set an expert opinion disclosure deadline prior to the dispositive motion deadline. Rule 26(a) requires expert reports to be "detailed and complete" and "not sketchy, vague or preliminary in nature." [citations omitted] A complete expert report includes "the substance of the testimony which an expert is expected to give on direct examination together with the reasons therefor." . . . The requirement of a complete expert report minimizes the need for expert depositions. "The report must be complete such that opposing counsel is not forced to depose an expert in order to avoid ambush at trial; and moreover the report must be sufficiently complete so as to shorten or decrease the need for expert depositions and thus to conserve resources." . . .*
>
> *Although correct, the Bakers' argument that Defendants chose to stay expert depositions until after the Court rules on summary judgment misses the point. Defendants did not move to stay expert depositions until after the Bakers' expert opinion disclosure deadline. After reviewing Wakeley's and Holland's reports, Defendants concluded it was unnecessary to engage in expensive expert depositions prior to moving for summary judgment on certain issues, including the issue of whether the risks encountered by minor Baker were "open and obvious." Defendants were entitled to assume that Wakeley's and Holland's reports were complete. Defendants are now unfairly prejudiced by the Bakers' reliance on new and untimely expert opinions in response to summary judgment. The Bakers' failure to inform Defendants of their experts' latest opinions denied Defendants the opportunity to depose Wakeley and Holland prior to moving for summary judgment. One of the primary goals of the federal civil discovery rules and Rule 26(a) is to "eliminate surprise." The Court will not allow the Bakers to ambush Defendants with new expert opinions after the expert opinion disclosure deadline and after they filed for summary judgment.*[18]

The court also noted that it had granted the Bakers numerous extensions in this matter, including extensions of the discovery deadlines. If the Bakers needed more

---

18. *Baker v. Indian Prairie Community Unit, School District No. 204, et al.*, at p. 2 of the opinion.

time to work with their experts and obtain expert opinions, they should have filed an appropriate motion before the expert opinion disclosure deadline rather than waiting until after the defendants filed for summary judgment to come forward with new opinions in their experts' affidavits.

This case can teach the expert a bit about the kinds of skirmishes that go on even before the deposition of the expert is taken. From time to time a glance at the actual text of Rule 26 and the other Rules of Civil and Criminal Procedure that are referred to may make more sense of what the courts are discussing in the entire context of that rule. Rule 26 is set forth in full in Appendix B.

Lessons Learned

Interestingly enough in the *Baker* case, the defendant benefited as much by not doing certain things as by doing them. For instance, by not taking the deposition of the challenged expert and simply moving on the inadequacy of the expert's report and the untimely attempts to supplement the report, after the deadlines and extensions had passed, the defendant managed to steer the decision as to the admissibility of the expert's evidence (essentially a kind of *Daubert* challenge, which will be discussed in detail in the next chapter) to a motion for summary judgment.

A summary judgment against a plaintiff in a civil lawsuit can mean that based on all the available evidence for a particular claim that has been pled, the court determines that the plaintiff cannot prevail. Since the plaintiff against whom the summary judgment is rendered cannot proceed further with that claim against the defendant, the plaintiff loses.

A Little More, a Little Later Doesn't Help

A similarly successful expert challenge occurred in the case of *Brumley v. Pfizer, Inc.*, decided in June 2001. In this case, the plaintiffs sued the pharmaceutical firm Pfizer after a family member used the popular drug Viagra and subsequently suffered a fatal heart attack. The plaintiffs engaged Dr. Gerald Polukoff, a well-qualified cardiovascular specialist, as an expert witness. As in *Baker*, the challenge to the expert came before the court on a motion for summary judgment against the plaintiffs. The expert witness had also submitted a subsequent opinion in addition to his original Rule 26 disclosure, in a belated attempt to counter the defendant's *Daubert* challenge. In this case Dr. Polukoff's deposition was taken prior to the hearing and used as part of the basis for the motion to preclude the expert from testifying. The court's analysis as reported in the opinion in this case follows.

> *In their summary judgment response, Plaintiffs offered the opinion of Dr. Gerald Polukoff that linked the popular drug Viagra to cardiac risk. Dr. Polukoff had produced a Rule 26 report in February of 2001. That initial report stated that "Viagra*

(Sildenafil) and sexual intercourse triggered the untimely death of [the decedent] because Viagra (Sildenafil) enables sexual activity in patients at increased risk to cardiovascular events and death."

Dr. Polukoff also executed an April 5, 2001 affidavit in response to Defendant's motion for summary judgment. That affidavit restates the opinion contained in the Rule 26 report that [the decedent's] death resulted from his participation in vigorous sexual activity enabled by Viagra, but the affidavit also adds the following, previously undisclosed, opinion:

"Viagra causes a marked increase in sympathetic activation. Increased sympathetic activation is associated with myocardial ischemia, myocardial infarction, malignant and fatal arrhythmias and sudden cardiac death; therefore, [the decedent] would have survived sex were it not for his ingestion of Viagra on the night of his death."[19]

Note that plaintiff expert Dr. Polukoff's opinion originally stated that because Viagra enabled the plaintiff's cardiac-challenged family member to engage in sexual intercourse, it was complicit in his death. When the defendant moved to dismiss the case, Dr. Polukoff and the plaintiff counsel responded by submitting another expert statement that restated his original opinion and added to it another opinion. This added opinion extends the arguable role of Viagra in the fatal event in question, asserting that Viagra actually contributed to causation.

Pfizer moved to exclude the second opinion on the grounds that it was not previously disclosed as required by Rule 26 and because the opinion did not have a valid scientific foundation. The court held a *Daubert* hearing to consider the defendant's objections to the expert testimony and second opinion.

Note in reviewing the following ruling that Dr. Polukoff's problem-solving process isn't unreasonable by any pragmatic standard for information technologists.

At the hearing and during his deposition, Dr. Polukoff testified that he discerned a direct link between the use of Viagra and increased cardiac risk after reading a report authored by Brady Phillips [on sympathetic activation] . . . . Dr. Polukoff theorized that he can "extrapolate [Phillips's] findings and apply them to our findings and our understanding that our patients with coronary artery disease are at risk for death or infarction with sexual activity, and that this risk may actually be exacerbated or heightened with common use of sildenafil." . . .

The Phillips report demonstrated that Viagra produced a rise in catecholamine levels in the volunteers who participated in his study. At the Daubert hearing, Dr. Polukoff asserted that the rise in catecholamine levels in the Phillips report "demonstrates the mechanism by which there's people dropping dead with Viagra. It's a sen-

---

19. *Brumley v. Pfizer, Inc.* Reported at 200 F.R.D. 596, 598, 50 Fed. R. Serv. 3d 627, Prod. Liab. Rep. (CCH), p. 16, 124 (S.D. Tex. 2001) and at 2001 U.S. Dist. LEXIS 8130, (S.D. Tex. Jun 7, 2001).

*tinel paper." Dr. Polukoff opined that catecholamines are "clearly known to alter car-
diovascular outcome . . . adversely." Although he posited that the catecholamine levels in the report were elevated over levels that would be observed in people at rest, he
acknowledged that they were not abnormal for someone engaged in physical activity. Importantly, he could not cite any studies nor could he identify or quantify what
are normal or abnormal levels of catecholamines.[20]*

This is, for IT practitioners, familiar ground. Much of the information and thought
process that comes into play in everyday operational practice is based on anecdotal
information and simple deductive process. If a particular agent is present when bad
things happen, it is natural that we consider the possibility that some blame or association may be attributable to that agent. Here, Dr. Polukoff embraced Phillips's study as
explaining the correlations he saw between the use of Viagra and subsequent cardiac-
related deaths. One of the core questions that arose in connection with Dr. Polukoff's
assertions at the *Daubert* hearing was the role of catecholamines in this lethal association. Flaws in his logic became apparent on cross-examination, when inconsistencies
were uncovered. (For instance, although he attributed the cardiac episodes that followed Viagra use to elevated catecholamine levels, he couldn't quantify what levels of
catacholamine were considered normal.) Consider that in many IT matters, experts
may anticipate being able to testify as to how and why certain system events took place
based on deductive process, absent metrics, and other quantifiers. This may leave them
open to the same cross-examination process Dr. Polukoff endured.

Dr. Polukoff then made another common move that invites challenge by taking a
section of a research finding out of context, assuming that it alone was sufficient to
illustrate a point. Unfortunately, during cross-examination he was compelled to admit
that the research study he relied on didn't go as far as he did in making the case that
Viagra contributed to the death in question. Again, it doesn't take much imagination
to predict that there will be many IT experts whose initial, reasonable findings are successfully contested under cross-examination, using similar lines of questioning and
reasoning.

> *Dr. Polukoff then concentrated on the following language from the Phillips study:
> "Nevertheless, it is reasonable to assume, first, that increased sympathetic drive may
> contribute to the initiation of cardiovascular events, and second, that cardiovascular
> events, particularly arrhythmias and myocardial infarction, that occur in the setting
> of a high level of sympathetic activation are likely to have poorer outcomes." . . . Dr.
> Polukoff agreed that the Phillips study did not actually demonstrate that Viagra has
> an adverse effect on cardiac risk, nor did it claim to do so. Nowhere does the Phillips
> Report conclude that the increased catecholamine levels actually have a detrimental
> effect on heart functioning in healthy or diseased cardiovascular systems. Rather, the
> study suggested that these are important subjects for future study.*

20. Id., pp. 598–599.

When asked whether there are any studies, apart from the Phillips Report, that demonstrate an adverse effect of Viagra on the heart, Dr. Polukoff stated, "The studies that have been done to date that look at patients with ischemic heart disease and coronary artery disease and Viagra are short-term studies without long-term follow-ups, small populations, and have inconclusive data."[21]

There was a secondary debate over an allegation that Pfizer failed to advise cardiac patients of the potential ill effects of Viagra on those with significant cardiac problems. Fast forward now beyond the problem of Timely Rule 26 Reports to another core issue of this proceeding—the court's application of the *Daubert* line of criteria to this expert witness. Consider this portion of the *Brumley* opinion as an introduction to the subject of how courts apply the gatekeeping standards first enunciated in the *Daubert* case (see Chapter 8). In reading the following *Daubert* criteria, consider the generalization of the court's reasoning to similar IT issues. There is much that IT experts take for granted about the admissibility of practices and problem-solving procedures from IT that may not fare any better under a serious *Daubert* challenge. Consider the court's application of *Daubert* to the testimony of Dr. Poukoff.

The Court Applies the Daubert Standard

Plaintiffs contend that Pfizer defectively marketed Viagra and that the use of Viagra was both a proximate cause and a producing cause of [the decedent's] death. Their principal evidence in support of these claims is the expert testimony of Dr. Gerald Polukoff, M.D., Ph.D., who is an adjunct member of the faculty of the Utah School of Medicine and who is certified by the American Board of Internal Medicine with a subspecialty in cardiovascular disease. There is no dispute between the parties that Dr. Polukoff is qualified as an expert in the field of medicine.

Pfizer challenges Dr. Polukoff's April 5, 2001 affidavit on two separate grounds. First, Pfizer contends that his opinion, linking the pharmacological effect of Viagra to heightened cardiac risk, does not satisfy the requirements of Daubert. Second, the affidavit was not timely disclosed in accordance with the Court's Scheduling Order and Fed. R. Civ. P. 26.

A. Admissibility under Daubert

. . . Daubert supplies a four-part test for scientific opinions: (1) whether the theory or technique in question can be and has been tested, (2) whether it has been subjected to peer review and publication, (3) its known or potential rate of error along with the existence and maintenance of standards controlling the technique's operation, and (4) the degree of acceptance within the relevant scientific community. Although the Daubert court emphasized that this test is not the only means to examine expert testimony, the Court finds that it is appropriate in this case.

Before turning to the four factors, the Court summarizes Dr. Polukoff's opinion. Although he stated his opinion in terms of sympathetic nerve activity in his April

---

21. Id., 599.

2001 affidavit, it is clear that he now views Viagra's effect on catecholamine levels as adversely affecting sympathetic nerve activity, in turn resulting in cardiac risk; as Dr. Polukoff testified, the Phillips report "demonstrates the mechanism" by which Viagra subjects the heart muscle to increased sympathetic nerve activity. Dr. Polukoff's opinion is that Viagra increases the levels of catecholamines in the blood, which increases sympathetic nerve activity, which has an adverse effect on the heart, which in turn results in increased cardiac risk in patients with ischemic heart disease.

Testability

There is no question that Dr. Polukoff's theory can be tested; the problem is that it has not been tested. Dr. Polukoff acknowledges that the Phillips study does not, itself, demonstrate that Viagra has any adverse effect on the functioning of healthy or diseased cardiovascular systems.

Plaintiffs respond in two ways. First, they asserted during argument that the mere fact of testability makes Dr. Polukoff's opinion admissible. The "testability" requirement is a threshold requirement aimed at excluding pseudoscience from the courtroom. A theory that is untestable is unfalsifiable and of no practical value in the courtroom. (See Foster, Kenneth R. and Peter W. Huber, Judging Science: Scientific Knowledge and the Federal Courts, *Ch. 3 [MIT Press, 1997]). But to stop the analysis at testability would allow in any theory, even one universally recognized as wrong, merely because it is falsifiable. Moreover, the requirement that a theory be subject to testing is only one prong of a two-part requirement: the question is whether the theory "can be* (and has been) *tested."* . . .

Plaintiffs' second response is that Dr. Polukoff's opinion is a valid extrapolation from the data in the Phillips study. The problem is that not even Dr. Polukoff could confidently demonstrate that any extrapolation is possible from the Phillips study. In spite of the suspicion that the Phillips report may have raised, Dr. Polukoff could not offer any testimony regarding safe levels of catecholamines, nor could he cite to any report that supports a conclusion that the levels in the Phillips report were unsafe. Plaintiffs cannot use the Phillips study to support a conclusion that the study itself does not make. (citations omitted) The "analytical gap" between the Phillips study and Dr. Polukoff's conclusion is simply too great. . . . The strong temporal relationship between [the decedent's] first use of Viagra and his sudden death, without more, does not make Dr. Polukoff's opinion any more reliable. . . .

The Court concludes that Dr. Polukoff's opinion simply is not supported by any real world observations or experimental scrutiny. Although Dr. Polukoff may have identified an area of real concern and an avenue for fruitful study, he has not demonstrated that his opinion is reliable in the sense required to make it admissible.

Peer Review and Publication

As shown above, no test of Dr. Polukoff's theory has been the subject of a published article. In fact, Dr. Polukoff stressed repeatedly that studies to demonstrate or refute his theory have not been done. Dr. Polukoff acknowledged at the Daubert *hearing that the only studies that have been reported have concluded that there was no indication that Viagra created any increased cardiac risk. Dr. Polukoff discussed at length a study by Dr. Richard Conti, who surveyed patients with a history of ischemic heart disease. The Conti study did not detect any adverse cardiovascular effects of sildenafil. Dr. Polukoff, however, contends that the meaning of this and other studies is diminished either because they do not focus on patients with ischemic heart disease, or because they relied on self-reporting by patients who had been prescribed Viagra. In essence, Dr. Polukoff concluded that Viagra is unsafe because no study has tested whether it is safe for patients with ischemic heart disease who engage in sexual activity.*

Dr. Polukoff may have pointed out an important void in the scientific literature, but the lack of proof of a drug's safety does not prove it is dangerous. It may be advisable to assume that Viagra is dangerous for patients with ischemic heart disease, given the lack of evidence to the contrary, but in a lawsuit where the plaintiff bears the burden of proving that a drug is dangerous, the Court cannot assume that element of the plaintiff's claim.

Rate of Error

Given that Dr. Polukoff's opinion has failed the first two factors of the Daubert analysis, the Court concludes that the third factor simply does not apply. The Court cannot assess the "known rate of error" for a theory that has no empirical foundation.

Acceptance within Scientific Community

Dr. Polukoff testified that the American Heart Association and the American College of Cardiology have developed recommended guidelines for physicians who prescribe Viagra to patients with heart disease, including those who use nitrates. Dr. Polukoff emphasized that these associations developed these guidelines in the face of the real world challenge of advising patients who suffer from both erectile dysfunction (ED) and coronary artery disease (CAD). Dr. Polukoff noted that a large percentage of ED sufferers also are CAD sufferers, and the compelling importance of sexual activity to one's quality of life has resulted in overwhelming demand for Viagra from those patients for whom it may be contraindicated. The consensus appears to be that it is dangerous for certain CAD patients to take Viagra, but that patients who are informed of all of the risks should be entitled to make a decision whether those risks are acceptable.

The Court concludes that this is some evidence that a degree of risk to CAD patients has become acceptable to physicians within the medical community, but it is not evidence that Viagra poses any greater danger than is acknowledged in the insert that Pfizer included with the medication. The fact that the medical community may have developed an approach to a demand from patients does not count as evidence of an acceptance of a very specific theory that Viagra's effect on the sympathetic nerve system exacerbates cardiac risk in patients with ischemic heart disease.

Conclusion

The Court concludes that Plaintiffs have not sustained their burden of demonstrating the reliability of Dr. Polukoff's opinion.[22]

---

22. Id., pp. 601–3.

Here, for IT experts, there is a lesson to be learned: although you may have extraordinary, rock-solid credentials as an expert (in this case, Polukoff is a medical professor, board-certified internist, and cardiologist with many years of applicable experience), you must still be able to demonstrate that the opinions you express in testimony are provable using a rigorous process of proof that is now required by the courts. In other words, the qualifications are necessary but quite insufficient under the new regime for allowing expert opinions to be given from the witness stand.

Turning once again to the issue of timeliness in making written expert evidence available in litigation, the court continued its opinion.

B. Timely Disclosure of Dr. Polukoff's Opinion

Separate and apart from the admissibility of Dr. Polukoff's testimony under Daubert, *Pfizer argues that Dr. Polukoff's April 5, 2001 affidavit, submitted after the end of discovery, is materially different from his Rule 26 expert report submitted on February 15, 2001. Therefore, the April 5, 2001 affidavit was not timely disclosed as required under Fed. R. Civ. P. 26, and Pfizer seeks to exclude the testimony contained in the affidavit to the extent it goes beyond the opinions stated in his Rule 26 report. . . .*

Plaintiffs retained Dr. Polukoff on February 14, 2001, and he issued his Rule 26 report the next day. A review of the report and the affidavit shows that the affidavit adds a new theory of causation that was not contained in Dr. Polukoff's Rule 26 report. . . . Moreover, at the Daubert *hearing, Dr. Polukoff stated the additional opinion that the language of the Viagra package insert was inadequate to inform [the decedent's] physician of the risk of patients with coronary artery disease; this opinion was not contained in his Rule 26 report. . . . Nevertheless, given the request to exclude all testimony that "goes beyond the initial report," the Court will exclude the opinion regarding the package insert as well.*

Since Rule 26 requires "a complete statement of all opinions to be expressed," Dr. Polukoff's new opinions fail to comply with Rule 26 because his Rule 26 report did not contain those opinions. Therefore, the Court finds that Dr. Polukoff's April 5, 2001 affidavit is untimely under Rule 26 to the extent that it goes beyond the opinions in his report, as is his opinion regarding the package insert. The Court strikes both his opinion regarding the pharmacological effects of Viagra and his opinion that the package insert was inadequate, and any other opinion that was not contained in the initial Rule 26 report.

Plaintiffs also violated Rule 26, and the Joint Discovery/Case Management Plan by proffering Dr. Polukoff for deposition on April 6, 2001, the last day of discovery. Under this Court's Scheduling Order, discovery ends two weeks after the deadline for dispositive motions. . . . The deadline for summary judgment motions in this case was March 15, 2001. The belated deposition of Dr. Polukoff forced Pfizer to file supplemental pleadings in order to effectively address Dr. Polukoff's deposition testimony and the opinions contained in his April 5, 2001 affidavit which were not in his initial Rule 26 report. The only reason discovery cutoff is two weeks after the dead-

line for dispositive motions is to enable a plaintiff to conduct discovery for a sum-
mary judgment response. The discovery deadline is not intended to enable a party to
withhold expert witnesses until the last minute so as to hinder the other party from
filing a proper summary judgment motion. . . . Therefore, due to the untimeliness of
Dr. Polukoff's affidavit as well as Plaintiffs' discovery abuse by not proffering him for
deposition in a timely manner, the Court finds that the opinions in the affidavit
should be excluded, pursuant to Rule 26, to the extent they go beyond the opinions
contained in Dr. Polukoff's Rule 26 report.[23]

So the final outcome of this case is that the court excluded Polukoff's testimony from the case for two separate reasons, first because some of his most significant conclusions were not made available for discovery before the deadlines for such submissions, and second because his conclusions were not sufficiently supported to pass the *Daubert* tests for admissibility.

Preparing Effective Reports

Given the importance of complying with the *Daubert* requirements in those jurisdictions where it is the rule, it makes some sense to consider whether to include information that satisfies the court that the expert is not only competent to testify, under all of the *Daubert* criteria, but also that the theories and methods chosen by the expert are supported by all the indices of reliability, including falsifiability, testing, peer review, and general acceptance by the relevant communities of expertise and interest. This is certainly a reasonable thing to do if counsel and the expert agree that there is anything novel or against the grain of any competing theories or methods that may be raised by the opposing counsel in a challenge before trial. It may not make as much sense in a situation where there is no doubt as to the reliability of the methods or theories.

Passing on the decision as to whether to include the *Daubert* elements in the Rule 26 report, the question of how to make the report accessible and persuasive to the judge remains. We have reviewed a number of Rule 26 reports that experts have shared with us during the process of researching this book. We (and the authors of those reports) have concluded that the same skills taught to technical writers need to be revisited by the authors of some, if not all, Rule 26 reports. Beyond the standard structure of recognized high-quality technical reports, the expert needs to consider that the likely audience is starting out as anything but technically sophisticated. The role of the expert with the advice of counsel is to educate the judge about the technical issues and about the technical basis for the proposed opinions concerning one or more aspects of the case, while clearly displaying the work and opinions of the expert.

23. Id., pp. 603–4.

Steering a Steady, Objective Course

From the expert's first exposure to the attorney seeking the expert's participation in the case through the selection process, the formulation of the expert opinion and documentation of that opinion in a Rule 26 report, and on to the actual courtroom experience, the expert must remain focused on some key concepts. As mentioned before, the expert must be objective. The expert must also be meticulous in concert with the attorney to comply with all procedural requirements and submit reports before deadlines expire. The expert must practice good science, not yielding to the temptation to assert untested or unsubstantiated theories as official expert opinion. With these foundational values satisfied, we can proceed to the often counterintuitive constraints and idiosyncrasies of the courtroom.

The Gatekeeper:
Judicial Control of
Expert Witnesses

At this point you understand what an expert witness is, what sets the expert witness apart from other types of witnesses, and what major obligations an expert witness has to the client and to the court. Now it's time to delve into more advanced topics. As mentioned before, a particular set of cases changed the manner in which expert witnesses participate in the legal process. These cases have profound impact on legal strategy for both civil and criminal litigation, and any technologist who wishes to be a competent expert witness should be familiar both with the cases themselves as well as the complications they introduce to the legal process.

The Metaphor of the Gatekeeper

While preparing this book, we interviewed many experienced trial attorneys and expert witnesses. With few exceptions, these interview subjects are in agreement on one thing: one of the most dramatic changes in the practice of litigation over the past 20 years has been induced by a line of Supreme Court decisions about expert witnesses. These cases served to shift the balance of power from the jury to the judge in determining the use of expert witnesses. Starting with *Daubert v. Merrell Dow Pharmaceuticals, Inc.* in 1993 and continuing with a subsequent series of cases over the next decade, the U.S. Supreme Court, lower federal courts, and state appellate courts made it clear that, at least in the federal courts and about half of the state courts, the trial judge must act as a gatekeeper, or filter, for experts. The judge acting in this capacity is charged with considering the competence of an expert witness, as well as the relevance and reliability of that expert's methods and theories, to determine whether the expert's participation in the case should be allowed.

This additional role for the judiciary represents a tectonic shift in the balance of power within the court system. Before *Daubert* and its follow-on cases, juries were usually allowed to determine the effect of expert testimony on issues considered at trial. Starting with *Daubert*, the trend has steadily moved toward empowering trial judges to decide cases or to force settlement of costly appeals by exercising their gatekeeping powers at the pretrial stage. This is where procedures allow opposing parties to request a hearing at which they can challenge the admission of expert testimony.

It is not clear whether this shift toward greater control by the courts over what experts are allowed to testify about will pick up speed or will continue in its current direction. It is possible that the enormous amount of time and money commonly invested in preparing for and presenting these *Daubert* challenge hearings will become a problem in and of itself. Indeed, when considering the impediments to the economical and equitable management of litigation, excesses in presenting challenges to expert testimony may become as worrisome as the perceived evils of allowing too much pseudoscience into evidence under the old *Frye* doctrine. Perceived deficiencies in *Frye*, of course, led to the coining of the term "gatekeeper" in the first place.

The stress of several more years of testing the flexibility of a constantly changing set of general standards of reliability of scientific and technical expertise may well instigate additional changes to stem the problems associated with excesses in mounting *Daubert* challenges. Such changes might drive the various specialized technical disciplines to codify a large number of universally recognized standards. These may be sufficient to serve the courts in a similar way as the *Frye* test served licensed or generally recognized scientific and technical disciplines before the *Daubert* line of decisions. In the meantime, especially in IT and information security (Infosec) areas, it may be difficult to get any two experts to agree on appropriate standards, tools, and techniques. Furthermore, it is highly probable that any experts in these areas will be challenged by peers who are as recognized as or better recognized than the expert being challenged. Without court-appointed neutral experts with equivalent credentials and experience to advise the judge, the outcome of many of these hearings will be in question and may often require unnecessary, expensive litigation to resolve. It will also be difficult for counsel to understand how best to generate a record that is adequate to persuade the trial court of the righteousness of a challenge to opposing experts while effectively defending the qualifications and reliability of his own expert and his opinions.

The Effect of Gatekeeping on Expert Witnesses and the Court

Despite the novelty of expert testimony in litigation early in the twentieth century, by the close of the century experts were called to testify in a large number of cases. As mentioned in prior discussions, abuses in such a rapidly changing system became apparent, and the *Daubert* measures were prescribed as a way to curb those abuses. Today, nearly ten years after the *Daubert* case was litigated, the judicial system finds itself facing another tidal wave of technical experts. Thanks to the proliferation of paperless businesses, complete with online storage of business records, IT and Infosec techniques and tools are involved in the discovery and analysis of evidence in many legal disputes. This dependence on a new generation of experts and their techniques may not have been in clear view when the Supreme Court decided to limit the abuses of Rule 702 by tapping the trial judge as the gatekeeper for the court.

IT tools and techniques affect the most common of societal interactions, including computerized record keeping, electronic commerce, and individual communications through global networks. The complexity of the tools and techniques as well as the dizzying pace of technological advances imply that at a minimum, the litigation of almost every kind of case requires a computer expert for the discovery of electronic evidence of all kinds. It is also needed at trial to authenticate and explain some of the electronic evidence of both human actions and the behavior of critical applications, systems, and computer networks. This requirement will be augmented by new waves of expert testimony and techniques to assist the fact finder, driven by the evolution of technology and scientific advances.

The gatekeeping solution applied to the kinds of problems presented by pre-*Daubert* medical, engineering, and other traditional experts may well have been an appropriate control mechanism for the issues involving expert witnesses for hire and their occasional pseudoscientific opinions. However, the evolution of IT has introduced additional complications. The evolving gatekeeper approach may be helpful for addressing individual situations in which adversaries attempt to use dubious expert testimony to strengthen their cases. However, this solution may not scale to a world in which almost every case involves a technical expert, even if simply to discover and analyze the relevant digital evidence.

Historical Gatekeeping and the Needs of the Current Legal System

An analogous requirement for gatekeeping predates *Daubert* by at least a century. This kind of gatekeeping may have originated with a similar requirement for keeping competing economic forces separate long before the twentieth century. By the time cattle and sheep ranching were confronted with expanding mining and oil industries that needed access to their mines and wells throughout the country (but especially in the west), fences and gates were installed to allow for the separation of the competing uses of the same open range. When railroad and motor vehicle transportation became essential for the economic development of the region and the country, constantly opening and closing cumbersome gates at every fence became both expensive and extremely dangerous. This sort of gatekeeping became a liability and the cause of continuous conflict between competing users of the plains.

The solution to this problem in the nineteenth and early twentieth centuries in the United States was an adaptation of the simple cattle guard, used for centuries in Great Britain and elsewhere in Europe to keep livestock out of church cemeteries and gardens (Figure 8-1). The elegance and economy of this invention and its successful application by various cultures to quite different situations and demands is also evidenced by its continued use today. Many guard designs were put into service, and opinions differ about which is most effective and economical. In essence, the combination of a cattle guard together with a gate was designed and implemented to allow relatively rapid access and egress for trains and later on for motor vehicles, while maintaining a boundary between two sections of land or herds of cattle belonging to separate owners.

Figure 8-1. *A cattle guard—a common filter mechanism that still serves to selectively contain cattle and other livestock while allowing vehicles to pass across boundaries with little impediment.*

IT experts may soon be asked to assist the courts in coming up with tools that amount to a better cattle guard. Such a solution would allow the court to consider electronic evidence and digital evidence of computer application and network behavior without the need to stop or seriously slow down discovery of the relevant evidence in both civil and criminal litigation. Meanwhile, things are likely to get more intense as IT and Infosec expert witnesses find themselves challenged in *Daubert* hearings in many cases for which they are called to testify. This chapter is designed to help prepare you for such a challenge. It is also intended to assist you in advising attorneys on challenging an opposing expert who is unqualified or who offers bogus expert testimony.

Judges may occasionally determine that in cases of great technical complexity (in particular, cases that have great amounts of disputed electronic evidence), not all issues are subject to resolution by the application of the scientific method. For example, the *Gates Rubber Company v. Bando Chemical Industries, Ltd.* case, discussed in detail in Chapter 9, had issues that arose within a proceeding parallel to the initial intellectual property lawsuit. Resolving these issues took several years, hundreds of separate depositions and motion hearings, and cost the client many millions of dollars.

Challenges to Technical Expert Witness Evidence

We have attempted to keep case citations to a minimum in the previous chapters. However, in order to fully understand the role of the successful expert witness in litigation as it is practiced today, an aspiring expert witness should read at least the three key Supreme Court opinions that currently define the way expert witnesses are regarded by the Court. You'll find the opinions for all three of these cases in Appendix A. Reading and thoroughly understanding these cases will give you some idea of how a trial judge might determine the qualifications of experts and the admissibility of their testimony and opinions.

As you read these cases, remember that they are all cases from the federal bench. Many but not all states have adopted rules of evidence patterned after the federal rules, and embraced the standards set forth in *Daubert* and its progeny. If you're involved in testifying in a state court, legal counsel will need to review the controlling appellate court decisions that set out those different standards. However, in all the federal courts and a growing number of state courts, the expert needs to understand the application of the controlling rules of evidence, primarily Rule 702 of the Federal Rules of Evidence or its state counterpart, and the current standards that must be applied by the trial judge in the event of a challenge to a technical expert witness by the opposing party.

Once the competence of an expert or the relevance or reliability of the evidence the expert presents is challenged, a challenge hearing will occur. In this hearing the judge will determine whether the expert will be allowed to testify at all or, if allowed, whether limitations will be placed on what the expert may testify about. It's critical that the expert prepare for this hearing. The expert must be able to educate the judge and explain how the expert's work on a specific case and his or her experience and knowledge qualify and entitle the expert to render an expert opinion on all the matters within his or her expertise and relevant to that particular case. In order to accomplish this goal, the expert and the attorney must be crystal clear in their understanding of the gatekeeping standards a given judge will apply.

The shift from the traditional *Frye* standard that was marked by the initial announcement of the gatekeeping function has produced unanticipated consequences. Subsequent cases have made it clear that the same standards of reliability, drawn loosely from the Supreme Court's interpretation of the scientific method, will be applied whether the expert evidence is from a recognized area of scientific or technical expertise or from some sort of new discipline.

Furthermore, when a judge has ruled that an expert will or will not be allowed to testify about a particular issue in the case, generally speaking that ruling is dispositive and not subject to being overturned by a higher court unless the judge can be shown to have abused his or her discretion. That burden of proof has been interpreted and applied by the appellate courts and the U.S. Supreme Court so that any reasonable disqualification of an expert by the trial court is extremely difficult for an attorney to overcome.[1]

The practical impact of the gatekeeping process has been a relocation of one of the critical points of a trial. This means that cases are now frequently won or lost at the hearing when an expert witness is challenged. Because so much is now riding on winning or losing challenge hearings, the litigation practice involving expert witnesses has quickly been transformed to focus on preparing experts to satisfy the gatekeeping standards and preparing challenges to attempt to disqualify the opposing experts or their testimony. The litigation game used to be played close to the vest in anticipation of settlement or taking one's chances before a jury. Today, ever-increasing amounts of time and resources are poured into preparing for and presenting evidence at these hearings.

The failure to take seriously the need to convincingly carry the burden of proof that an expert is or is not qualified to testify, or that his or her methods or theories are or are not reliable or relevant to the issues in the case, can result in the reviewing court reversing a jury verdict in favor of one of the parties and awarding the victory to the opposing party. Such decisions have been made on the grounds that the judge abused his or her discretion by allowing an unqualified expert or an unreliable expert opinion to be presented to the jury. In *Weisgram v. Marley Company*,[2] the Supreme Court not only reversed a jury verdict but dismissed the action entirely. This left the winning party in the original action out in the cold, its apparent victory nullified. Furthermore, the court denied the party a second chance to call additional experts who might be better qualified to give their expert opinions in a retrial.

---

1. See *Joiner v. General Electric Company* in Appendix A.

2. *Weisgram v. Marley Company*, 120 S. Ct. 1011 (2000).

Through this series of decisions, the courts have placed attorneys and their proffered experts on very clear notice that when they are challenged, they had best appear in a challenge hearing equipped with all the information required for a judge to properly qualify the witness. In particular, the judge must understand why this particular expert should be allowed to testify about a particular method or technique. The judge must also understand why this expert should be empowered to reach an expert opinion about causation or some other issue within the witness's expertise. Conversely, attorneys attempting to invalidate an expert whom they perceive as being unqualified or as offering irrelevant or unreliable expert testimony must prepare for the challenge with the understanding that the other side will be sparing no available resources to defend their expert. The lawyers for whom the challenged expert works must construct a record that will not only persuade the judge of the expertise of their witness but satisfy an appellate court as well, should they prevail before the jury. It is a well-known fact among litigators that the vast majority of civil and criminal cases settle before trial. The gatekeeping challenge stage of the proceedings as the point where settlement decisions are likely to be made by the parties.

The Classic Case of Dr. John Snow

Every expert who understands the importance of being able to demonstrate and explain scientific or technical evidence with images as well as words should study three books written and published by Edward R. Tufte: *The Visual Display of Quantitative Information*[3]; *Envisioning Information*[4]; and *Visual Explanations: Images and Quantities, Evidence and Narrative*.[5] We will have much more to say about Tufte's suggestions for making and using effective visual aids in reports and in connection with expert witness testimony in Chapter 10. Tufte also offers an excellent historical example together with a graphic illustration of what gatekeeping is all about.

In *Visual Explanations*, Tufte analyzes the famous map that John Snow prepared to explain his theory and his account *On the Mode of Communication of Cholera* in the epidemic in London in 1854. Tufte calls Snow's work classic medical detection, "with an eloquent and precise language of evidence, number, comparison,"[6] and he supplies a number of modern visual displays of some of Snow's data that further elucidate the information that Snow collected and included in the map.

---

3. Tufte, Edward R. *The Visual Display of Quantitative Information*, 2nd ed. Cheshire, CT: Graphics Press, 2001.

4. Tufte, Edward R. *Envisioning Information*. Cheshire, CT: Graphics Press, 1990.

5. Tufte, Edward R. *Visual Explanations: Images and Quantities, Evidence and Narrative*. Cheshire, CT: Graphics Press, 1997.

6. Tufte, *Visual Explanations*, p. 30.

Snow used his map to explain his theory of cause and effect. He graphically illustrated the argument of his text by showing the proximity of cholera deaths to the location of the Broad Street well and pump (Figure 8-2).

This is an early example of excellent but also novel scientific theories and methods
and equally excellent ways of communicating those theories and methods. It serves our
purpose as a classic example of what modern courts are looking for in their post-
Daubert, gatekeeping capacity. Snow believed that cholera was transmitted by polluted
drinking water; in this case, the source of the 1854 epidemic was proven to be the water
taken from the Broad Street well and pump station. Snow's theory of transmission
through water was not the only theory competing for acceptance by the scientific and
medical communities at the time. Some mid-nineteenth-century "scientists" speculat-
ed that cholera, like other contagions, was disseminated through the air in the form of
"miasmas." So both collecting the proof and presenting it in a persuasive way were
required for the scientific and medical communities to accept Snow's theory.

Snow stuck to his theory, and as Tufte explains, he not only had a good theory
about causation but he also developed some excellent methods and a discipline to

Figure 8-2. *Dr. John Snow's famous map plots the occurrence of deaths in the 1854 cholera
epidemic of London. (From Snow, John, On the Mode of Communication of Cholera,
2nd ed. London: C. F. Cheffins, 1854.)*

gather enough relevant information with "a shrewd intelligence about evidence, a clear logic of data display and analysis."[7] Tufte discusses the difference to a scientist like Snow between just having good descriptive narratives and also creating sound causal explanations. Snow recognized the need to collect all the data concerning all the cholera deaths in London during the time the contagion raged. Snow also looked for and found an appropriate context to determine the cause of those deaths. "Instead of plotting a time-series, which would simply report each day's bad news, Snow constructed a graphical display that provided direct and powerful testing about a possible cause-effect relationship."[8] This display, depicted in Figure 8-2, featured black marks, each corresponding to a fatality plotted on a street map of London. The resulting display disclosed the location of the suspect well and pump in a cluster of deaths.

Snow went on to investigate and answer questions raised by his data and highlighted by his visual display. For example, he found excellent reasons why no workers at a nearby brewery were killed. As Tufte observes, it seems they were saved by the beer they drank instead of imbibing the water from the nearby pump. The lack of expected fatalities was explained in a way that strengthened the theory. Another nearby workhouse had its own pump on site, and the resulting lack of cholera deaths of those who drank only from the in-house pump again served to confirm the theory that cholera had spread through water taken from the Broad Street pump.

Like a post-*Daubert* court, Snow carefully considered alternative explanations and apparent contrary cases he saw in his collected data. He made a concerted effort to understand these apparent contradictions. As Tufte puts it:

> Sometimes it can be difficult for researchers—who both report and advocate their findings—to face up to threats to their conclusions, such as alternative explanations and contrary cases. Nonetheless, the credibility of a report is enhanced by a careful assessment of all relevant evidence, not just the evidence overtly consistent with explanations advanced by the report. The point is to get it right, not to win the case, not to sweep under the rug all the assorted puzzles and inconsistencies that frequently occur in collections of data.[9]

By considering all of this apparently contrary evidence, Snow was actually able to discover several additional cases that strongly supported his theory even though they had at first appeared inconsistent with it.

Finally, as with the contemporary application of the *Daubert/Kumho* standards in considering the merits of a particular application of the scientific method, Snow was careful nearly 150 years ago to consider the rate of error and to assess possible mis-

---

7. Tufte, *Visual Explanations*, p. 30.

8. Tufte, *Visual Explanations*, p. 30.

9. Tufte, *Visual Explanations*, p. 32.

takes in the inclusion of numbers that he reported in his map. However, Tufte points out that the visual arguments made in Snow's map could have been even more persuasive had Snow included additional significant data comparisons when drawing his map. Nevertheless, we can see from this example of a wonderfully effective teaching visual image that the goals of judicial gatekeeping are pretty straightforward.

Critics of the gatekeeping function are right to express concern that the shifting balance of power can move too far from the core feature of the judicial system and its fundamental reliance on the advocacy of attorneys to enable a reasonable jury to decide the issues. But as the Snow example shows, the goals of clarifying scientific and technical methods and distinguishing them from pseudoscience are worth pursuing, though they are nothing new. The results of discipline and diligence in proving and disproving scientific and nonscientific theories are something the legal process should endeavor to further in its embrace of expert testimony as essential to resolving conflicts. The contemporary effort to ensure competence and reliability is clearly consistent with the classical methods of science and forensic detection exhibited by Snow's work. Charlatans will continue to slip through the gate on occasion, and from time to time a judge will surely fail to let a qualified expert testify about a reasonably reliable method or technique. But for now, the best advice we can offer to experts is to test your own qualifications, competence, theories, and methods and to prepare to be tested by others in deposition and trial pursuant to the *Daubert* standards. It should be some comfort to consider that at least one expert had all of this figured out a century and a half ago.

Putting Yourself in the Judge's Shoes

As an expert attempts to predict the decision process that a judge will use in a challenge hearing, it is helpful to consider the advice that legal scholars give judges and other fact finders on gatekeeping processes. One of the best resources to begin with is the chapter by Margaret A. Berger in the second edition of the *Reference Manual on Scientific Evidence*, a manual compiled for use by the U.S. federal courts. Professor Berger describes the purpose of her chapter as follows:

> *The object is not to suggest that evidence is or ought to be admissible or excluded in any particular case. Instead, this paper is designed to assist judges in structuring inquiries necessary for making rulings on objections to expert evidence in pretrial proceedings, in connection with motions for summary judgment, or in connection with judgments as a matter of law at trial where the legal sufficiency of evidence is challenged.*[10]

10. Berger, Margaret A. "Evidentiary Framework." *Reference Manual on Scientific Evidence*, 1st ed. Federal Judicial Center, 1994, p. 43. Accessed on July 27, 2002, at *http://www.fjc.gov.*

In her article for the first Manual on Scientific Evidence, Berger addressed four broad categories that seem to capture the central concerns that permeate judicial opinions about the admission of both scientific and technical expert evidence before and after the publication of all the Supreme Court opinions discussed in this chapter.

1. Is the expert qualified?
2. Is the expert's opinion supported by scientific reasoning or methodology?
3. Is the expert's opinion based on reliable data?
4. Is the expert's opinion so confusing or prejudicial that it should be excluded pursuant to Evidence Rule 403? (That rule gives judges discretion to consider these issues regardless of how relevant a piece of evidence is.)

By beginning to think about how judges (many of whom read Berger's chapter that was published after *Daubert* but before the Supreme Court decisions in *Joiner* and *Kumho*) think about gatekeeping challenges to experts and their evidence, you can adapt to the changing standards that will be applied in the various jurisdictions. In other words, by tracing the evolution of the Supreme Court opinions together with the evolution of the analysis of the significance of those decisions by one of the most distinguished legal scholars in this area, you can better understand how to anticipate the demands that judges may place on the organization and presentation of expert evidence in support or in defense of an expert challenge.

Both before and after the first edition of the *Manual*, many legal scholars considered what the Supreme Court may have had in mind when it crafted the *Daubert* opinion and announced that henceforth the federal trial bench would sit as gatekeepers determining whether experts with novel scientific theories or techniques would be allowed to testify before a jury. The Supreme Court itself addressed the use of its metaphor and the "gatekeeping" role of the trial judge at the end of the *Daubert* opinion:

> [T]he goals of science and the law differ. While acknowledging some similarities between the scientific and legal endeavors, the opinion recognizes that there are important differences between the quest for truth in the courtroom and the quest for truth in the laboratory. Scientific conclusions are subject to perpetual revision. Law, on the other hand, must resolve disputes finally and quickly. . . .
>
> [A] gatekeeping role for the judge, no matter how flexible, inevitably on occasion will prevent the jury from learning of authentic insights and innovations. That, nevertheless, is the balance that is struck by Rules of Evidence designed not for the exhaustive search for cosmic understanding but for the particularized resolution of legal disputes.[11]

---

11. *Daubert v. Merrell Dow Pharmaceuticals, Inc.*, 113 S. Ct. 2786 (1993), at 2798–99.

Early academic legal analysts concentrated on other passages in the *Daubert* opinion that suggested that the main purpose of the opinion was to relax the traditional standard that had been in place since the 1930s, with the standard that the Court read into the more recently passed Federal Rules of Evidence, and to allow new science to be admitted as evidence so long as the proponent could satisfy the judge that it was scientifically reliable and relevant to the case.

In practice, something quite different has actually taken place. After several years of different interpretations by the lower federal courts and legal scholars as to whether or not gatekeeping was a judicial obligation in nonscientific cases, and after contradictory applications of the gatekeeping standards set out in *Daubert*, the Supreme Court clarified the application of the gatekeeping function in technical expert witness cases as well as scientific evidence cases with its opinion in *Kumho Tire Co. v. Carmichael*. The *Kumho Tire* decision made it clear that gatekeeping was to take place regardless of whether or not the expert testimony involved purely scientific methods or technical areas of expertise. The objective of the gatekeeping requirement in both scientific and nonscientific evidence cases is:

> [T]o ensure the reliability and relevancy of expert testimony. It is to make certain that an expert, whether basing testimony upon professional studies or personal experience, employs in the courtroom the same level of intellectual rigor that characterizes the practice of an expert in the relevant field.[12]

The *Joiner v. General Electric* case had already made it clear that the trial judge had almost unbridled discretion to determine whether the expert and his or her evidence measured up to those standards. When the expert failed to make the grade, it did not matter what the jury thought about the evidence—the appellate court's duty was to throw out the evidence if it was below the announced standards. If the appellate court found no abuse by the trial court, the appellate court's duty was to uphold the discretion of the trial judge in throwing out the expert and the evidence unless there was an apparent abuse of discretion in the record leading up to the trial judge's decision. There is also authority for the proposition that where an inadequate record was made by the proffering party, it was simply too little too late once the opportunity for a challenge hearing had come and gone, regardless of what any subsequent proof demonstrated about the competence of the disqualified expert.

Again addressing the significance of *Daubert* in light of subsequent Supreme Court decisions on the subject of the admissibility of expert witness testimony, Berger contributed a new chapter to the second edition of the *Reference Manual on Scientific Evidence*.[13]

---

12. *Kumho Tire Co. v. Carmichael*, 119 S. Ct. 1167 (1999), at 1176.

13. Berger, Margaret A. "Supreme Court's Trilogy on Admissibility of Expert Testimony." *Reference Manual on Scientific Evidence*, 2nd ed. Federal Judicial Center, 2000. Accessed on July 27, 2002, at *http://www.fjc.gov*.

The *Kumho* decision suggested that trial courts have a number of procedural devices at their disposal to ensure the proper exercise of discretion in making pretrial determinations of expert evidence admissibility that may be dispositive and nearly immune from review except for abuse of that discretion. Berger identified a number of these procedures that are consistent with *Daubert/Joiner/Kumho*.

> The Court explained in Kumho *that applying the abuse-of-discretion standard to determinations of how to test an expert's reliability gives the trial judge broad latitude "to decide whether or when special briefing or other proceedings are needed to investigate reliability." The standard also allows the trial court to make other choices about how to respond to a request to exclude expert testimony, and to use mechanisms that would provide the court with needed information in making its relevancy and reliability determinations.*
>
> *In civil cases, a court might respond to a* motion in limine *by refusing to undertake any reliability-relevancy determination until the moveant has made a prima facie showing of specific deficiencies in the opponent's proposed testimony. Although the burden of persuasion with regard to showing the admissibility of expert testimony is clearly on the proponent, shifting the burden of production to the party seeking to exclude the expert testimony may at times be expeditious and economical. As the Court noted in* Kumho, *quoting from Federal Rule of Evidence 102, "the Rules seek to avoid 'unjustifiable expense and delay' as part of their search for 'truth' and the 'just determination' of proceedings."*
>
> *Certainly, a trial court need not hold a full pretrial hearing in every case, and, indeed, the trial judge in* Kumho *did not. However, in complex civil litigation that has the potential to affect numerous persons, the trial court may conclude that extensive evidentiary hearings are the most efficacious way for the court to inform itself about the factors it will have to take into account in ruling on admissibility. The facts of the case and the consequences of losing the* in limine *motion will determine the extent of the opportunity the proponent of the expert must be given to present its case.*
>
> *Trial judges also have discretion to avail themselves of the techniques Justice Breyer described in his concurring opinion in* Joiner: *using court-appointed experts, special masters, and specially trained law clerks, and narrowing the issues in dispute at pretrial hearings and conferences.*[14]

Expanding the Standards of *Daubert*

Nearly half of the states have either adopted rules of evidence similar or identical to the Federal Rules of Evidence or adopted the gatekeeper obligations for trial judges as set out in *Daubert* and *Kumho*. One of those states is Texas, which has both adopted similar rules of evidence and applied the *Daubert* standards for admitting expert witness testimony as announced in the Texas Supreme Court decision of *E. I. Du Pont de*

14. Berger, "Supreme Court's Trilogy on Admissibility of Expert Testimony," p. 37.

Nemours and Co., Inc. v. Robinson.[15] In that case the Texas Supreme Court added two more factors to consider when determining the reliability of expert evidence. So, in Texas, judges start with at least six categories that they are apt to be interested in and about which experts are apt to be challenged:

1. The extent to which the theory relied on by the expert has been or could be tested
2. The extent to which the tools or techniques used by the expert ultimately rely on the subjective interpretation of the results of those techniques by the expert
3. Whether or not the theory and methods have been subjected to peer review and publication in recognized professional literature
4. Whether the potential rate of error of the technique has been or could be measured
5. Whether or not the relevant scientific or technical community of interest has generally accepted the theory, techniques, tools, and methods as valid and reliable
6. What nonjudicial uses have been made of the same theory, techniques, or methods

This expansion of the four core criteria originally announced by the U.S. Supreme Court in *Daubert* and endorsed as flexible criteria to be applied as appropriate in a given case (or to be expanded or contracted depending on the particular facts and issues involved) is consistent with the approach recommended by the Court in *Kumho Tire*. IT experts should expect these and other additional criteria to be considered by opposing experts and attorneys in depositions and in motions to exclude during a challenge hearing.

In his Center for Legal Education seminar, "Excellence with Experts," legal expert David M. Malone has suggested eight criteria to add to the original four *Daubert* tests.

1. Non-litigation purpose: Was the methodology created for purposes other than lawsuits?
2. Explanatory ability: Was the methodology sufficient to explain the important facts or observations?
3. Sufficiency and reliability of data employed: Was the information used by the expert quantitatively and qualitatively sufficient?
4. Internal consistency: Was the expert's analysis internally consistent?
5. Adherence to methodology in the particular examination or analysis?
6. Support in the literature: Is there a body of literature dealing with the particular topic or technique?

15. *E. I. Du Pont de Nemours and Co., Inc. v. Robinson*, 923 S. W. 2d 557.

7. Adequate credentials: Are the expert's credentials and professional stature well-established?
8. Logical derivation of theory: Is the theory an outlier with respect to other methods of analysis?[16]

Perhaps this mini-survey of additional criteria that lend themselves to a *Daubert* challenge, increasing the number of points from four to six to eight, will impress on you that a great deal of imagination and insight is necessary in order to withstand a *Daubert* challenge. Such challenges will come on any one or all of an increasing number of suggested fronts. Conversely, in order to assist the trial attorney in his or her challenges of the opposing party's unqualified experts, speculative methods, or invalid theories, you need to use similar creative and inquisitive processes, brainstorming with your trial counsel to come up with appropriate lines of questions. These questions should be designed to seek out the kinds of gaps that could exclude an opposing expert or portions of their expert testimony as the result of a successful *Daubert* challenge hearing. This brainstorming process is critical, so we'll take a closer look in the next section.

Brainstorming Strategies and Scenarios to Prepare for *Daubert* Challenges

A useful model constructed around an environmental pollution and toxic tort scenario may be helpful for IT experts who are preparing for a *Daubert* challenge. Jack V. Matson develops this model, based on the *Robinson* case, by creating a hypothetical transcript, complete with abbreviated testimony by opposing experts, and then discusses the probable outcome of a *Daubert* challenge. In order for the plaintiff's medical and toxicological experts to be able to render an expert opinion, they must rely on the development of facts and expert opinions as to the significance of those facts by two or three separate experts from specialized disciplines. The respondent can succeed by challenging either of two foundation experts as unqualified or as having relied on theories or methods that do not measure up to the *Daubert/Kumho/Robinson* standards.[17]

This challenge strategy is helpful for IT and Infosec technical experts in that the structural attributes of the cases encountered are likely to be very similar. It is likely, given the degree of complexity and specialization in the current IT world, that a daisy chain of foundation experts will be required to develop all the essential facts and to

---

16. Malone, David M. "Excellence with Experts." Seminar, Center for Legal Education.

17. Matson, Jack V. *Effective Expert Witnessing*, 3rd ed. Boca Raton, FL: CRC Press, 1999, p. 71.

apply their own separate but perhaps overlapping expertise to the initial analysis of the foundation problems. This will certainly be necessary in many cases involving alleged critical software application failures or liability due to security protection mechanism failures that cause damage to innocent third parties who are connected through a corporate network or even through the Internet. Even a routine network attack trace-back analysis that requires different application, operating system, and network configuration expertise may represent similar challenges to legal teams attempting to construct a straightforward and logical proof of causation.

The point to remember is that a technical expert must understand the big picture while competently constructing the finer-grained technical opinions. This challenge is similar to that encountered in the course of designing and implementing reliable systems. You must design and develop a credible opinion, applying reliable and valid theories and methods throughout the entire process. This process must be robust enough to withstand the scrutiny of different experts, testing techniques, and new assumptions. Whether you are doing part of the foundation work or building the ultimate causation opinion atop that foundation work, you must bear in mind the need to check on the work of other experts to determine that there are no gaps that will set you up for a *Daubert* challenge. This requirement might sound familiar to Infosec experts—it is analogous to security vulnerability testing!

In most cases, once the reports of the respective experts have been prepared and disclosed to the opposing attorney and experts, you can expect the other side to perform a systematic examination of most of the following areas during a deposition. As another legal scholar, Robert Whitney, points out, the goal is to build a record of gaps in inadequate qualifications, unsound foundation, invalid methodology, suspect reasoning, or even speculative reasoning. The areas of inquiry that Whitney suggests should be expected and prepared for include those listed below.

1. *A precise explanation of each step in the expert's reasoning, methodology, or application of principles leading up to each conclusion;*
2. *The factual bases and assumptions used by the expert;*
3. *The sources of fact bases or assumptions;*
4. *Other fact sources which were available but not used (e.g., especially when expert relies on facts from his client);*
5. *Standard, principle or reasoning which allows expert to rely on his client for important assumptions;*
6. *Whether the method or reasoning consists of a testable hypothesis;*
7. *If so, whether it has been tested and the results;*
8. *What the test was, whether it can be reproduced, and whether there are other test protocols that have been used or described in professional literature to test this hypothesis;*
9. *Whether the expert knows if authoritative texts or periodicals are published in the expert's field;*

10. *Publications used in expert's education, practice, or teaching;*
11. *Whether publications are peer-reviewed;*
12. *What publications support the expert's work in the case;*
13. *Whether the expert's work in this case is subject to peer review;*
14. *What professional standards apply to expert's work;*
15. *How, if at all, standards apply to expert's work;*
16. *How does expert explain departure from any standards;*
17. *Whether expert's method, reasoning, and application of principles are generally accepted and why;*
18. *All sources—publications, standards, others—which one could look to in order to test expert's work here;*
19. *The relationship of the technique to the methods which have been established to be reliable;*
20. *The qualifications of the expert to meet standards or methodology or both;*
21. *The non-judicial uses to which the method has been put;*
22. *Whether the testimony is based "directly on legitimate, preexisting research unrelated to the litigation";*
23. *Objective sources for each step in the methodology; or*
24. *Objective sources for each factual assumption.*[18]

As might be clear to you after reviewing Whitney's list of issues, preparation for each stage of the trial is vital to your success. Experts should expect the opposition to put both their qualifications and their processes under serious stress during the course of a *Daubert* challenge before a high-stakes trial. Consider the *Daubert* challenge, should one occur, to be a separate trial.

A Hypothetical *Daubert* Disqualification

As you read the *Daubert* and *Kumho Tire* decisions and the discussions of the gatekeeper function, you may wonder how the trial process changes with the introduction of the *Daubert* hearing. In this section, we include a fictional account of a civil suit in which competing experts are asked to attest to the results of forensic examinations and analyses of data collected from systems involved in a theft of intellectual property. This account is oversimplified—we acknowledge that the unqualified expert is truly clueless—and is intended only to demonstrate the procedural flow of a *Daubert* challenge.

The Scenario

A prominent software firm ("XYZ Software") discovered proprietary plans and slogans from its confidential marketing plan being used by a competitor ("ABC

---

18. Whitney, Robert. "A Practicing Lawyer's Guide to the Application of Daubert and Kumho." *American Journal of Trial Advocacy*, 23(241), 1999, pp. 252–253.

Software"). When XYZ management received a tip that Jack H., a system administrator for ABC Software, was boasting in a hacker chat group that he had designed and used a new attack tool to gain access to a critical file on XYZ's system, XYZ's staff investigated, then filed a civil suit against ABC, alleging that Jack H. had attacked the system and accessed XYZ's confidential marketing plan.

The Issues of the Case

The expert witnesses will address the primary issues of this case as listed below.

1. Is that portion of the evidence recovered in digital form from the computer systems in question reliable—that is, was it collected and protected from alteration in an adequate fashion?
2. What does the data collected show about the causation of the plaintiff's loss? Is there compelling evidence that ABC Software (the respondent in this action) or its representative, Jack H., is responsible for the theft of proprietary data from XYZ Software (the plaintiff in this action)?

Synopses of the Experts' Rule 26 Reports

Three experts are offering testimony on this case. A court-appointed expert is handling the issues of computer-related discovery. He has collected all data from the affected computer systems and made copies of that data available to both parties in the case, thus addressing the issue of data reliability. Both the plaintiff and the respondent have experts who have analyzed the data provided by the discovery expert. Their reports outline their findings as well as the methods they used to arrive at those findings.

Highlights of the Rule 26 Report from the Court-Appointed Discovery Expert

The following excerpts summarize the discovery expert's Rule 26 report.

- "I am John Smith, a senior computer research scientist employed at a national laboratory operated by a large university. I have baccalaureate and master's degrees in electrical engineering and, prior to my employment with the lab, served twenty years as a Secret Service Agent, the last five of them as a forensics specialist in the computer lab."
- "The data is complete—I used a popular commercial forensics software tool suite to make images of all the disk drives on all relevant systems within the plaintiff and respondent organizations."

- "The data has not been altered since its initial capture—I used a crypto-graphic checksum to counter this possibility and furthermore transferred the checksummed data to a read-only storage medium."
- "The data has also been adequately protected from deletion; again, the cryptographic and other measures I've already taken protect the data from this threat as well."
- "I delivered cryptographic checksums to both experts after tamper-proofing the data. I asked both experts to regenerate and compare checksums again in order to demonstrate that both plaintiff and respondent received identical data sets from both systems and to demonstrate that the data had not changed since I first archived it from the original systems."

Highlights of the Rule 26 Report from the Plaintiff's Expert

The following excerpts summarize the Rule 26 report filed by the plaintiff's expert.

- "I am Isadora Walker, a senior scientist employed by Anzuru, Inc. I have baccalaureate and master's degrees in computer science and electrical engineering plus twenty years of experience in IT, with ten of those years spent in the IT security field. I have eight years of experience in computer forensics and five years of experience conducting investigations of computer and network security incidents. I am a Certified Fraud Examiner. I am recognized by my peers as an expert in the area of computer and network forensics and investigation, and I have written two books on those topics."
- "I performed an investigation of the events surrounding the transfer of XYZ Software's files to the systems of ABC Software."
- "I performed this investigation using the evidence taken from the file servers, workstations, and security systems of both ABC Software and XYZ Software by the court's discovery expert."
- "Based on my analysis, I have found evidence that Jack H., a system administrator for ABC Software, created and used a data-driven attack tool to access and copy XYZ Software's marketing plan from their systems. These figures [Figures 8-3 and 8-4] illustrate the main points of my investigative protocol, using an analogy of a physical file for the computer file in question here. In the first, I describe the process of gathering information that indicates the "tracks" left by a data file on the move. In the second, I describe the synchronization of data file movements across multiple systems on the network, by using time clock synchronization."
- "My analysis results were gained using a stable, documented investigative protocol developed and published by my firm, Anzuru, Inc."

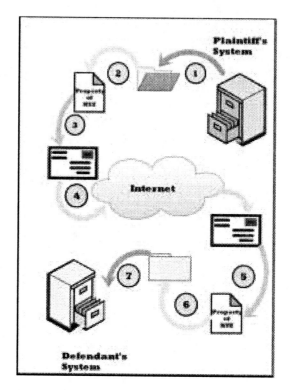

Figure 8-3. *In this figure, the plaintiff's expert draws an analogy between the theft of a computer file and the theft of a physical file.*

Highlights of the Rule 26 Report from the Respondent's Expert

The following excerpts summarize the Rule 26 report filed by the respondent's expert.

- "I am Tim Geraldo, a consultant for IT Experts Limited. I have fifteen years of forensics experience and twelve years of investigative experience."
- "I performed an analysis of evidence collected by the court's discovery expert from ABC Software's systems as well as the file server in question at XYZ Software. The evidence I considered in my analysis includes the disk drive images from both systems and the logs from the XYZ enterprise intrusion detection and firewall servers."
- "I conducted an inspection of the firewall and intrusion detection system logs for the XYZ Software enterprise systems. This inspection turns up no illicit approaches from ABC Software's IP address range, nor from Mr. H's personal system."

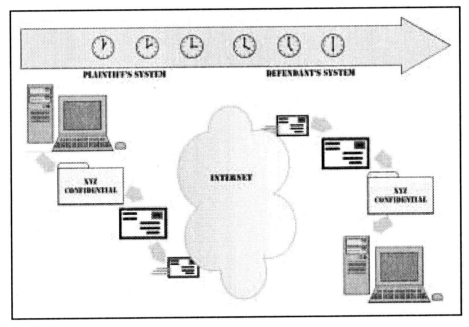

Figure 8-4. *In this figure, the plaintiff's expert describes the time clock synchronization that allows her to track movement of the file across separate systems.*

- "Though I acknowledge that a copy of the disputed information was found on ABC Software's file servers, according to XYZ's own security systems, it is my opinion that Mr. H. was not responsible for taking that information from XYZ."

The Issues Surrounding the Qualification of the Experts

Expanding on the requirements of Rule 702, the issues germane to the qualifications of the expert witnesses include those listed below.

1. What are the qualifications of the expert?
   a. Educational degrees and training
      i. In computer science or engineering
      ii. In computer security
      iii. In computer forensics
   b. Professional experience
      i. In computer science or engineering
      ii. In computer security
      iii. In computer forensics

  c. Membership in professional societies
   i. In computer science
   ii. In computer security
   iii. In computer forensics or investigation
  d. Specialized employment related training
   i. Specific training
   ii. Date of training
  e. Technical skills
   i. Programming
   ii. System administration
   iii. Computer security
   iv. Computer forensics or investigation
2. Is the expert's testimony based on sufficient facts or data?
3. Is the testimony the product of reliable principles and methods?
4. Has the witness applied the principles and methods reliably to the facts of the case?

The Issues in Dispute

The issues on which the experts differ in opinion speak to the central issue of the case, establishing the cause of the transfer of XYZ Software's proprietary information to ABC Software. XYZ Software (the plaintiff in this case) asserts that ABC software's representative is responsible for the transfer; ABC asserts that its representative had nothing to do with it. The disagreements pertain to the investigative methodology used to establish the cause of the transfer.

After deposition of both experts, the specific points of disagreement are articulated as follows.

- What is the appropriate context of the evidence yielded by the systems that best allows an analysis suggesting or proving the cause of the file transfer?
  - The plaintiff's expert asserts that the context must be the operating system for each system involved in the transfer.
  - The respondent's expert asserts that the proper context is the log file output of the security devices for the plaintiff site from which the files were transferred.
- How should the evidence be organized in order to perform an analysis of it?
  - The plaintiff's expert asserts that the evidence should be organized by time and filename.
  - The respondent's expert asserts that there is no organization required beyond that already inherent in the result logs from the firewall and intrusion detection systems.

- What analysis strategy should drive the methodology for establishing cause?
  — The plaintiff's expert asserts that the data file in question should be key here and that its movements should be tracked over the time interval in question.
  — The respondent's expert asserts that one should isolate how the file was transferred and then inspect the security device logs for evidence that a hacking incident took place at that time.
- What caused the transfer of the plaintiff's proprietary data file to the respondent's system?
  — The plaintiff's expert asserts that the data shows that John H., an employee of ABC Software, took the file by using a custom data-driven attack tool.
  — The respondent's expert asserts that no file transfer took place as a result of a network incident. He asserts that the file was transferred to ABC's systems by other means.
- Is there any additional evidence that corroborates this account of the incident?
  — The plaintiff's expert asserts that the files recovered from the rest of the data show evidence that John H. wrote and deployed the attack tool.
  — The respondent's expert asserts that since no attack took place, there is no corroboration of interest.

The Structure of the *Daubert* Challenge

You may have deduced by now that there appears to be a huge discrepancy between the analyses of the plaintiff's expert and the respondent's expert. It appears that there may also be a significant problem in qualifications. If you were advising the plaintiff's attorney, how would you advise him to prepare in order to devise a case for a *Daubert* challenge of the respondent's witness?

You can do several things to question the qualifications of a proffered IT or Infosec expert. In this case, let's first zero in on the educational and training background of the respondent's expert.

- Does he have a degree or advanced college coursework in computer science or computer engineering? Does he have advanced degrees? (For many years IT and Infosec drew on people with little formal training in computer science or computer engineering because there were few academic programs. Given the level of understanding of computers this expert needs to do this analysis, a lack of coursework or degree would today raise a red flag within the community of interest and therefore should be fair game to challenge.)

- What specific training does he have in firewalls and intrusion detection systems?
- Is this training up to date?
- Was it on a specific firewall and/or intrusion detection system?
- Were the systems on which he was trained the systems used in both installations? (There's a fair difference between the different firewall and intrusion detection products on the market. If he doesn't have an understanding of the systems in place in both installations, he may be unable to adequately analyze the logs from these systems.)

Next, let's target his experience in IT and in security.

- What security training does he possess? (Depending on the training source and specific course, his training may be irrelevant or out of date. For instance, security training that covers the applicable regulations for a particular environment may not be relevant to this investigation.)
- What courses has he taken, from whom, and how long ago? (Security curricula age quickly. If it has been more than five years since he took his last course, that's a red flag.)
- With what operating systems has he worked? How long has he worked with each? (It's important to establish that he understands the systems in place in both the plaintiff and respondent organizations.)
- Does his experience include programming? If so, in what languages and on what operating systems has he programmed? (This isn't critical until we get into the question of automated attacks.)
- Does he hold a certification in security? If so, which one does he hold?
- Does he hold a certification in software engineering or systems administration?
- Is he a member of any professional organizations for IT or security? If so, which ones? Has he agreed to abide by their rules of ethics?

Now let's proceed on his qualifications in software and systems forensics and investigation.

- What experience does he have in software and systems forensics and investigation?
- What training does he have in software and systems forensics and investigation?
- Does he possess any certifications in the software and systems forensics and investigation areas? If so, which ones?
- What software packages were used in the analysis of the disk drive images and system logs from the systems?
- Has he been trained in the use of these packages?

Finally, let's examine the investigative and forensics processes he used to reach his conclusions in this case.

- What investigative process did he use? Where did it come from?
- What process did he use to decide whether Jack H. had taken the intellectual property in question from the plaintiff's system?

The processes related to the latter question will tend to fall into two general approaches:

1. Investigating whether the security monitoring software detected a problem and assuming that if no problem was detected, then none existed.
2. Looking at the information that both systems contain and trying to discern exactly what happened. This requires coming up with hypotheses of attack and testing them to see if the artifacts of the hypothesized attacks are present on the systems.

The first of these approaches fits well with the intrusion detection and firewall log review approach the respondent's expert seems to have used. However, that approach is problematic for several reasons:

- It makes a lot of assumptions about the configuration of the intrusion detection and firewall system—all of them can be configured to deliberately ignore certain attacks.
- It makes a lot of assumptions about the ability of the firewall and intrusion detection systems themselves to withstand attack. In particular, some firewalls and intrusion detection systems are subject to attacks that selectively delete system logs.
- It presumes that the firewall and intrusion systems themselves are configured to reflect current notions of attack. As new attacks surface daily, this is a challenge for operational personnel, and few actually keep their systems current.

Note that a recurring theme when questioning qualifications is that training on a particular topic is not in and of itself sufficient. The training must also be *current*. Given the pace of new operating systems and hardware, experts must keep up with the technology in order to deliver analyses that are of sufficient quality to meet client and court needs.

As you will see in *Gates v. Bando*, covered in Chapter 9, the failure to stay current with technology can result in a decision that penalizes your client when the opposing expert has a better idea that is rapidly becoming (or most likely to become) a new standard for your technical community of interest. In *Gates*, the trial judge ruled against a plaintiff because an expert retained by that party relied on old technology to acquire evidence from a hard disk drive. When the respondent's expert pointed out that the technique used to acquire the evidence was out of date and actually resulted in some of the evidence being deleted, the judge ruled that the failure to use the more modern technique (disk image transfer) nullified the claim of the plaintiff, resulting in a large judgment covering legal costs and fees. Had *Gates v. Bando* taken place after the *Daubert* decision, the issues in contention between the parties and their respective experts would likely have been resolved much earlier in the litigation and at far less expense at a gatekeeping challenge hearing.

The Challenge Itself

This is a mock motion that requests a *Daubert* gatekeeper hearing. Note the points that are used as the basis to challenge the qualifications and methodology of the respondent's expert, Geraldo.

THE XYZ SOFTWARE COMPANY'S MOTION FOR A GATEKEEPER HEARING FOR RESPONDENT'S EXPERT TIMOTHY L. GERALDO.

TO THE HONORABLE JUDGE O. W. HOLMES:

THE XYZ SOFTWARE COMPANY ("XYZ"), A DELAWARE CORPORATION, a plaintiff herein, moves this court, pursuant to Federal Rule 702, to perform its "gatekeeper role" and exclude the testimony of respondent's expert Timothy L. Geraldo ("Geraldo") for the reasons that Geraldo is not qualified and further that his testimony is neither relevant nor reliable, and in support thereof would show the Court the following.

I. Background

Respondent seeks to introduce Geraldo's testimony on the following issues:

1. That the logs generated by the security systems protecting the plaintiff's computer networks and systems do not reveal access by Mr. Jack H., an employee of the respondent,
2. That such access was the only way that Mr. H. could have acquired the plaintiff's data files in question, and
3. That the absence of such access implies that Mr. H. could not have acquired the plaintiff's data files in question and hence should not be culpable for any damage resulting to the plaintiff from the theft of those files.

Geraldo is not qualified to render the opinions on the meaning or trustworthiness of the security system logs, on the means available for gaining illicit access to computer files, or on whether the lack of certain log entries exonerates the respondent. He has neither the professional background nor the requisite skills, knowledge, experience, and training to render the opinions offered in those areas.

Geraldo's opinions are not reliable as they are not based on solidly supported scientific or recognized technical grounds. His methodology is faulty, his analysis software unproven, and his underlying data is at best incomplete and unreliable. His opinions are not helpful to the trier of fact, as they are based on speculation, guess, conjecture, and assumption.

II. Evidence in Support of Motion

1. Excerpted portions of the depositions of miscellaneous witnesses
2. Geraldo's C.V.
3. Geraldo's report, dated February 1, 2001
4. Geraldo's deposition

III. Arguments and Authorities

A. The Pitfalls of Expert Testimony

As businesses rely increasingly on computer technologies to conduct commercial transactions, the proportion of business records that are maintained in computer systems connected by networks has grown commensurately. When disputes occur, expert testimony is almost always needed in order to explain the ramifications of storing these records and other evidence on computer systems and networks.

In any area of commercial promise, savvy operators set up shop to capitalize on the new market. In the realm of computer expert testimony this is the case. Unfortunately, the desire to serve the fact finder's need for expert explanations of computer and network evidence does not necessarily equate to the ability to serve those needs in a credible way. As in other scientific and technical areas of expertise, professionals, when faced with the prospect of generous payments for expert witness services, may be tempted to testify to certain facts regardless of their technical merit.

B. This Court Is the Gatekeeper

The Supreme Court, recognizing the problems associated with experts and opinions, responded by imposing the role of "gatekeeper" upon the trial judge, initially in *Daubert v. Merrell Dow Pharmaceuticals, Inc.*, 509 U.S. 579 (1993), then extended to other technologists in *Kumho Tire Co., Ltd. v. Carmichael*, 526 U.S. 137, 149 (1999).

Rule 702 asserts that in order to offer expert testimony, the following conditions must be met:

1. The witness must be qualified as an expert by knowledge, skill, experience, training, or education, and furthermore,
2. the testimony is based upon sufficient facts or data,
3. the testimony is the product of reliable principles and methods, and

4. the witness has applied the principles and methods reliably to the facts of the case.

C. *Burden Rests with the Proponent of Expert Testimony*

When an objection is raised to expert testimony, the proponent of that expert bears the burden of demonstrating the admissibility of that testimony.

1. The offering party must demonstrate that the expert has knowledge, skill, experience, training, or education regarding the specific issue before the court which would qualify that expert to give his opinion on the particular subject. The mere fact that the individual possesses some general skills not possessed by people generally will not mean that such expertise will assist the trier of fact. The issue is whether the particular expert truly has sufficient specialized knowledge about the actual subject about which he is offering an opinion.

2. Should the qualification hurdle be satisfactorily crossed, the next requirement for admissibility of expert testimony is that the proposed testimony is relevant. The proposed testimony must be sufficiently tied to the facts of the case such that it will assist the trier of fact in rendering its verdict.

3. Finally, the proposed expert testimony must be reliable. Unreliable testimony does not assist the trier of fact and under Rule 702 is therefore inadmissible. Among other things, the trial judge may consider these factors in making the gatekeeper determination of admissibility:

   a. Whether the theory has been subjected to peer review and/or publication
   b. The technique's potential rate of error
   c. Whether the underlying theory or technique has been generally accepted as valid by the relevant scientific community
   d. The nonjudicial uses that have been made of the theory or technique

The reliability of an expert's opinion depends directly on the quality of his methodology. The core question to be addressed in this component of determining the admissibility of the expert testimony is whether the opinion at trial would withstand the same scrutiny that it would among the expert's professional peers.

In determining the reliability, the court must focus on the principles and methodology used by the expert, not the truth or falsity of the conclusion. There is a distinct difference between the reliability of the underlying techniques or theory and the credibility of the witness. Although the expert may be very believable, his opinion may be based on flawed methodology and thus inadmissible. Furthermore, the opinion may be unreliable because the foundational data is unreliable. Therefore, at a minimum, in order for an expert opinion to be considered reliable, it must be based on both sound data and sound methodology. In other words, expert testimony cannot be based on mere speculation or guesswork.

GERALDO KNOWS LITTLE ABOUT THE COMPUTER SYSTEMS, THE
SECURITY SYSTEMS, OR THE PROCESSES INVOLVED IN INVESTIGATING
COMPUTER ATTACKS OF THE SORT HE'S TESTIFYING ABOUT, BUT HE'S
SURE THE RESPONDENT DIDN'T HAVE ANYTHING TO DO WITH THE
ATTACK IN QUESTION.

Respondents have retained Geraldo to render opinions on the interpretation
of computer data for the purpose of determining how a confidential business
plan was transferred from the computer system of the plaintiff, the legitimate
owner of that plan, to the respondent's computer system. Geraldo, by his own
admission, has no formal education in computers or networks; no specific experience in programming or administering such systems; no training, beyond ele-
mentary courses, in computer technology or computer security; and no formal
training in system forensics or investigation of computer security incidents.

D. Geraldo Is Not Qualified to Render an Opinion on the Interpretation
of Computer Data

Respondents are unable to satisfy even the initial requirement of Rule 702 that
requires that their expert be qualified by knowledge, skill, experience, training, or
education regarding the specific issue before the Court. Geraldo is clearly unqualified to deliver an opinion regarding an area in which he has no training, education, and little, if any, knowledge or experience.

1. **Geraldo Has Little Knowledge of Computers**

   Geraldo, by his own admission, is not a computer scientist nor engineer
   by education. He has minimal experience in computers, and that he does
   have is not on the types of systems involved in this case. His training in
   computers has been limited to beginner's-level courses. His formal education is limited to an undergraduate degree in business, with no college-
   level coursework in computer or networking technology beyond an entry-
   level course.

2. **Geraldo Has Little Knowledge of Computer or Network Security**

   Geraldo's training in computer security has been limited to vendor training for specific security equipment (again, not on the types of security
   equipment involved in this case) or courses addressing regulatory requirements, not technical topics.

3. **Geraldo Has No Training and Limited Experience in Computer**
   Forensics and Investigation

   Perhaps the most worrisome aspect of Geraldo's lack of qualifications is the
   fact that he has no training and minimal experience in the forensic analysis
   and investigation of computer systems. Indeed, even in the investigation
   about which he has been asked to testify, he has relied on other parties to pro-

vide advice, interpretations of evidence, even analytical tools. His forensics experience has been limited to operation of a data recovery software tool.

E. Geraldo's Opinions Are Not Reliable

Respondents have retained Geraldo to testify that their representative was not responsible for the transfer of plaintiff's confidential computer data files to the respondent's computer system. His opinions are based on his analysis of evidence discovered on the computer systems of both plaintiff and respondent. As the following analysis establishes, Geraldo's opinions (1) are based on unsound methodology and (2) are dependent on subjective interpretation.

1. The methodology is unsound.

   By his own admission, Geraldo's analysis of the computer system information was as follows:

   a. Ask for help from friends on the Internet.

      Although this problem-solving approach is popular among those who spend a great deal of time connected to the Internet, there are several problems associated with it. In fact, the concerns mirror those that are articulated in this challenge.

      i. The qualifications of those offering advice and tools are unknown.

      ii. There is no guarantee that the recommendations obtained reflect sound scientific or technical process.

      iii. There is absolutely no guarantee that the recommendations obtained are objective—because the interactions on the Internet are in large part anonymous, there is no way of assuring that someone with a vested interest in the outcome of the analysis isn't offering advice biased toward a particular finding.

   b. Come up with a theory for how an attacker would take a file from the plaintiff's system and transfer it to the respondent's system (that might be logged by the security devices on the network).

      This is problematic from a variety of perspectives.

      i. It limits the number of possible explanations for how the file in question may have been transferred between the two systems.

      ii. It limits the information considered to that most easily accessed by the investigator.

      iii. It bases the outcome of the entire investigation on the logging capabilities of the security devices without first establishing whether they are reliable.

      iv. It also begs the question of whether the logging capabilities of the security devices were configured to capture any evidence of file transfers at all.

   c. Inspect the security device logs for file transfer operations of the file in question.

     This further compromises the quality of the investigation.

     i. It limits the scope of the inspection of the evidence to a single type of operation.

     ii. It limits the object of the inspection to a file known by a particular name, choosing to ignore the possibility that the attacker may have simply renamed the file in question.

   d. Conclude that the absence of log entries showing file transfers of the file in question indicates that the respondent was not responsible for theft of the file.

     i. This is akin to the oft-quoted joke about the drunk looking for his keys under a lamppost (despite the fact that he'd lost the keys in another location) because the light was better there.

     ii. Even were the assumption that the file transfer didn't take place over the network correct, it would not imply that the respondent was not responsible. It would simply imply that the file was not transferred over the network—nothing more, nothing less.

2. The opinion is dependent upon subjective interpretation.

Geraldo's opinions are based on his uncalled-for assumptions and his unsubstantiated subjective interpretation of the evidence he has chosen to consider and on which he wishes to base his blatant surmise and unwarranted speculation. He has done nothing to exclude other possible scenarios for the transfer of the files from plaintiff's to respondent's computer. As he admits that he did not use any semblance of a peer-reviewed or authoritative investigative process in order to arrive at his conclusion that the respondent was not responsible for the transfer of the plaintiff's file, he is not offering expert testimony to the court; he is offering personal opinion.

In order to understand how ludicrous Geraldo's methodology is, consider this case as an analogy for an incident in which a missing physical data file (contained within a file folder within a file cabinet) was discovered in a file cabinet inside the respondent's facility. An investigator is brought in to determine how the file went from its original location within the plaintiff's building to the point at which it was discovered within the respondent's facility.

Suppose the investigator asserts that the custodian of the file cabinet in which the plaintiff's file was discovered is obviously innocent of any involvement with that file transfer. When queried about his investigative method, the investigator states the following:

"I discovered that the plaintiff's building has a guard desk and a burglar alarm. If the respondent was responsible for taking that file, he must have hand-carried it out of the plaintiff's building. Therefore, he must have either signed in at the guard desk, gone to the file repository, and taken the file out, or else he broke in through a door or window, thereby setting off the burglar alarm. So I checked the guard logs to see if the respondent's name appeared there. It didn't. Then I checked the burglar alarm records to determine whether an alarm had been set off and if so, whether the respondent was apprehended. There were no burglar alarm records for the entire week before the file was discovered at the respondent's location."

It is clear that artificially and unrealistically constraining the possible avenues via which the file could have been transferred for investigation is a fatal flaw in any investigative technique. And it is no less a problem when the file in question is composed of bits and bytes, not paper and ink.

For all the reasons cited above, Geraldo's testimony is not reliable and should not be admissible. Therefore it should be excluded by the court.

F. Geraldo Did Not Employ the Same Level of Intellectual Rigor That Characterizes the Practice of an Expert in His Field

The objective of the gatekeeping requirement is to ensure the reliability and relevance of expert testimony. It is ultimately designed to make certain that an expert, regardless of whether he is basing his testimony on professional studies or experience, employs in the courtroom the same level of intellectual rigor that characterizes the practice of an expert in the relevant field. In failing to conduct a comprehensive examination of the evidence, considering all possible explanations for how an attack might have occurred against the plaintiff's system, Geraldo failed to employ that appropriate level of intellectual rigor, and the Court should strike his testimony under Rule 702.

IV. Conclusion

Geraldo's testimony fails to satisfy any of the requirements of expert witnesses as specified under the authorities of *Daubert* or *Kumho*. His lack of computer experience and qualifications only served to confuse the issues that should have been but were not properly investigated in his analysis of the facts and collection of data referred to in his report. His expert investigation and the contents of his report appear to have been conducted primarily in order to comply with the wishes of the plaintiff's counsel who engaged him. This clearly violates even nominal requirements for any expert witness.

What Happens Now?

After the challenge is filed, a *Daubert* hearing is held. At that point, the judge has a number of options:

- He can hold the hearing and make the decision on the challenge at that point.
- He can reserve decision until later in the trial.
- Should the topic be deemed sufficiently complex, the court can appoint an independent expert to advise the court or even a special master to consider the scientific issues and report to the court.

Ultimately the judge will rule on the challenge to the expert, determining whether the expert is qualified and whether the proffered testimony will be allowed in whole or in part at the trial. Should the expert be disqualified as a witness, or should a crucial part of the expert's conclusions or opinions be excluded as evidence, the case may be subject to dismissal as to part or all of the pending claims at another hearing similar to those reported in the cases discussed in Chapter 7.

Looking Forward to the Gatekeeping Challenge

If we are correct in suggesting that the round of gatekeeping challenge hearings is here to stay in both civil and criminal litigation, it behooves a beginning technical expert to accept the responsibility to understand and to fulfill the evolving standards that courts in the various jurisdictions are developing to test expert qualifications, methods, and opinions. One of the things that has most puzzled beginning technical experts until recently has been the lack of published literature as to just what the courts expect from experts.

This should not be considered an additional burden to either an accomplished or a beginning expert witness. The applications of scientific method and technical expertise to solve controversial social problems is not something that must be reinvented because of the *Daubert* decision or the development of gatekeeping standards. The whole purpose of providing technical expertise to the court or to the jury is to assist the fact finders in understanding the facts of the case. The temptation to consider accepting an expert witness assignment when you are not completely qualified to answer the questions that need to be answered will always exist. By understanding the applicable standards for performing as a qualified forensic expert in litigation, you should find it easier to decide whether to accept an assignment in the first place. If you know when you begin an assignment how much time and other resources will be needed in order to satisfy a fair and reasonable judge that you are qualified to give the expert testimony that the trial attorney seeks to introduce at the trial, you will avoid many of the predictable pitfalls of a *Daubert* challenge.

The Magic of Testimony: Communicating with the Fact Finder

Taking a Page from the Jury Consultant

Sonya Hamlin is a widely recognized consultant who counsels trial lawyers on the fine points of communicating with juries. In addition to the tips and techniques for lawyers in her book, *What Makes Juries Listen Today*,[1] she included a chapter on expert witnesses. That chapter is an excellent place for new technical experts to start addressing (and overcoming) their natural fears of appearing in the formal setting of a courtroom.

Although Hamlin wrote her book primarily for the benefit of trial lawyers, it is just as useful to the beginning expert who wants to know what to expect from the legal process. With a focus on how the jury will perceive the presentation of expert testimony at trial, Hamlin gives the expert witness the benefit of understanding how trial lawyers are currently being taught to deal with the preparation and presentation of experts. Furthermore, Hamlin's writings offer insight as to what one well-regarded expert in the field of litigation consulting believes is most effective in the presentation of experts and their opinions to a lay jury in a modern trial.

---

1. Hamlin, Sonya. *What Makes Juries Listen Today*. Little Falls, NJ: Glasser Legal Works, 1998.

In addition to comprehensive books for trial lawyers that are useful for the beginning technical expert witness, there are a number of books and articles about the art and science of jury work. One such work is *Stack and Sway: The New Science of Jury Consulting*.[2] Written by Neil Kressel, a social psychologist, and Dorit Kressel, a lawyer, the book discusses various methods that attorneys and their consultants use to predict who will make the best jurors and whom to exclude. Staging mock trials is one method used for this purpose in important cases, just as mock testimony by key witnesses is used to critique their rehearsal and to attempt to gauge their effect on different types of practice jurors.

Both lawyers and witnesses can benefit from discussions of these kinds of techniques. They can learn how to testify more effectively, how to decide which demonstrative exhibits work better, and how to work together to keep the jury interested in the presentation of evidence of all kinds through expert testimony. For those who remain doubting Thomases about the effectiveness of the jury system of justice, Kressel and Kressel have concluded after their study and their experiences that jurors do decide cases according to the facts. If lawyers and witnesses fail to effectively communicate the facts of the case, then sympathy and bias for the attorneys and experts of one side over the other may mean that a miscarriage of justice will occur.

The Paradox of Case Studies and Trial Preparation

Motivated neophytes, especially if they have attained the status of expert in another knowledge domain, usually rely on a set of standard processes to come up to speed in the new area they hope to master. IT experts who seek to prepare for expert witness duty may find that attempts to study the trial performances of other IT experts are stymied by a lack of data. Why are there so few IT expert trial performances to study?

By their nature, jury deliberations are secret. Jury interviews and books by former jurors can be candid or self-serving rationalizations of a group decision of which the writer may or may not be proud. You can find a recent example of such an account of one jury trial, told by the foreman of the jury who acquitted a man charged with stabbing his victim to death, in *A Trial by Jury*.[3] This account may be of particular interest to scientific experts because the author has published books about the history of science and therefore writes about the trial process as viewed through a scientist's eyes. Because of the inherent bias associated with these accounts, they are interesting but not necessarily optimal learning models for trial preparation. Furthermore, of those IT cases that have actually made it to court, a significant number of the resulting pro-

2. Kressel, Neil J., and Dorit F. Kressel. *Stack and Sway: The New Science of Jury Consulting*. Boulder, CO: Westview Press, 2002.

3. Burnett, D. Graham. *A Trial by Jury*. New York: Knopf, 2001.

ceedings have been sealed by the court to protect the intellectual property rights of the parties.

Therefore, novice expert witnesses may find it difficult to use the case study method to aid them in preparing for testimony. We have used a variety of approaches in this book to compensate for this paucity of empirical data. In addition to an occasional reference to the work of litigation consultants such as Hamlin, we have also used the generalizations of several experienced trial lawyers and judges who provide insights about the dynamics of the court environment. These legal experts shared their perceptions of what jurors expect from lawyers and experts in the course of a trial. In synthesizing the collective wisdom of experienced denizens of the legal world, we define an approach to preparing for testimony at trial that is consistent with the best practices articulated by these and other acknowledged practitioners and teachers cited from time to time along the way.

Why Should You Prepare for a Case That Will Never Get to Trial?

Perhaps less than 5 percent of the cases for which expert witnesses prepare actually proceed to a jury trial. Thus you may wonder, "Why is there so much emphasis on the need to be prepared to testify before a jury?"

The answer to this reasonable question is found in the very nature of testimony. At the most general level of analysis, testimony is simply an individual's communication considered in connection with some subject or issue that needs to be discussed or decided. Much of this book addresses the formalities that the legal system has constructed around the context for the various formats for testimony in a legal proceeding. The most dramatic form of testimony is often the sworn testimony of a party or other key witness in a civil or criminal jury trial.

However, expert witnesses must understand a fundamental fact: the most dramatic testimony is not necessarily the most important testimony that takes place in a trial. For that matter, the most important testimony may not even be that testimony that takes place for the first time during a trial. This point was exemplified by the testimony of Bill Gates as discussed in Chapter 2. The most important testimony in a trial may actually be taken during a deposition that is then admitted in segments by the opponent of the party or witness who was deposed before the trial.

Note, also, the following irony: it is far less likely that the case will be pushed to trial if the opponents realize relatively early in the process that the expert and the attorney are more than prepared to testify at trial. Thus, the best experts are seldom pushed to trial because opponents know that they are always prepared (and furthermore continuously preparing) to perform as persuasive experts should the case fail to settle before trial. If you believe that this sounds like a strategy befitting a high-stakes poker game, you are correct. Regardless of the degree of certainty that a case will settle before trial, the lawyer and the expert must still go through all the preparation that would be required in order to go to trial. To do otherwise yields a critical strategic advantage to their opponent.

Learning by Example

When developing skills to testify in court, as in other complex processes, observing an actual performance is often the best way to understand what happens in a legal proceeding. In the absence of a greater number of publicly available video transcriptions of testimony such as Bill Gates's deposition, the next best thing are the accounts of experts and the fact finders who determined the credibility of those experts and their testimony. In this chapter, in order to explain the formal process of expert testimony, we will consider excerpts from a lengthy opinion by a federal trial judge who had to choose between two technical experts in a landmark intellectual property case, *Gates Rubber Company v. Bando Chemical Industries, Ltd., et. al.* This opinion is unusual in at least two regards. First, it states exactly and in some detail why the judge accepted and relied on the testimony of the expert for the respondent, rather than relying on the plaintiff's expert. Second, the judge, after articulating a belief that standards should exist for certain issues, actually sets out the standard that he feels should be applicable in cases such as this.

The fact finder outlines the detailed reasoning process that led him to accept the qualifications and opinions of one expert, Dr. Robert Wedig, over those of another. He furthermore explains that he invested a certain amount of trust in that expert's analysis and conclusions, based on his regard for the expert's experience and training. Expert qualifications are considered by both lawyers and experts to be very important, and in this case the fact finder reaffirms that widely accepted belief. Note that the judge is also clearly cognizant of the purposes of forensic expert testimony. The opinion neatly follows the path of how experts can and do assist the fact finder in (1) understanding the facts relevant to an issue in the case and (2) thinking through the ramifications of those facts. This case illustrates why it is primarily the expert's job to correctly apply any technical or scientific methods to the relevant facts in the case and clearly explain the theories behind those methods in order to help the fact finder reach an appropriate conclusion.

The judge also echoes another major accomplishment of the best technical expert witness testimony when he establishes a standard that is generally applicable beyond the needs of the case at hand. This opinion sets out the standard that the judge feels should be applied in both this and future cases in which digital forensic examinations of computer evidence are required. As a result, *Gates v. Bando* has become a landmark decision, defining legal standards for examining computer evidence that remain relevant to this day.

How Does the Court Deal with the Absence of Recognized Standards?

At the time the matter that gave rise to the *Gates v. Bando* opinion discussed here was heard, there were few standards and essentially no decided cases that dealt with the precise issue raised, that is, how best to retrieve data from a computer disk drive. Interestingly enough, the standards that the judge applied have become the general standards in computer forensic examinations and would be endorsed today by all computer forensic experts. But at the time of the case, based on the court's opinion, at least the opposing expert apparently felt comfortable in taking a slightly different tack in his testimony to the court. This is a normal situation in cases involving evidence presented by opposing experts, who use slightly different investigative or testing methods in relation to IT issues. Note that once the litigation process identifies and applies generally accepted and applied standards, some of the ambiguity of relying on testing or investigative methods is eliminated by requiring all experts to proceed in roughly identical ways. Until such standards exist, the litigation process is routinely subject to some significant inconsistencies in results rather than as the exception to the rule.

As you read through the portions of the opinion excerpted here, you can clearly see that the fact finder in this case had little difficulty in determining which of the competing experts made the most sense to him. He acknowledges the needs of a forensic technical expert to address the ability of two different tools or techniques to obtain the most evidence, both in quantity and quality, to bring to the attention of the fact finder.

Although the published decision is many pages longer than the quotes included in this chapter, it behooves new experts to review the entire opinion to see how crucial the testimony of the competing experts proved to be. This case involved literally hundreds of depositions and motions, with many separate hearings for testimony by witnesses and arguments of counsel, all followed by repeated rulings of the court. It lasted several years before it was finally settled. As with many serious intellectual property cases that are litigated, all the records of this litigation, save the opinion cited here, have been sealed or destroyed, presumably by the agreement of the parties to protect intellectual property interests. One of the general problems that new experts face in their attempts to learn from the successes and failures of their peers is that the majority of IT expert witness testimony recorded in hearings and depositions has taken place in litigation over intellectual property disputes and consequently has been sealed or destroyed. Thus much of that potential treasure trove is unavailable for review and study.

The *Gates v. Bando* Case

In the case of *Gates Rubber Company v. Bando Chemical Industries*, the original lawsuit involved the claim by the plaintiff that the defendant had violated its intellectual property rights by wrongfully obtaining and using a computer software application called Life in Hours. In the course of civil discovery, the plaintiff developed evidence that relevant information had been deleted from the defendant's data storage. The plaintiff hired a computer expert to obtain a copy of the hard drives of some of the defendant's employees' computers to demonstrate to the court with forensic computer evidence that someone working for the defendant had destroyed information stored on the hard drives during the course of litigation.

Quoting from the opinion:

> *Gates alleges in this claim that Ron Newman stole a computer program called Life in Hours when he left his employment with Gates. For purposes of sanctions, Gates alleges in this claim that Newman did two things: (1) removed evidence of Life in Hours from his computer at the Denver facility of Bando American, Inc. (the Denver computer), and (2) attempted to delete word processing files which contained evidence that he had used this program in his activities at Bando. These two claims must be addressed separately, because each separate action by Newman has a different effect.*
>
> *(1) Deletion of Life in Hours. Newman learned on February 6, 1992, that he had been named as a defendant by Gates. In his deposition testimony, Newman admitted that this program was installed in the computer which he used at the Denver Bando facility. He testified that upon learning of the allegations in the Amended Complaint he took immediate efforts to remove it. He copied the Life in Hours to a floppy disk, and then deleted the files from his hard drive. Finally, he deleted reference to the program from his entry menu. The following day, Newman gave the disk to the attorney who was retained by Bando. Gates argues that Newman, at the time he copied Life in Hours to a disk, never intended to give it to an attorney. Nevertheless, he did. A copy of the disk was provided to Gates in discovery.*
>
> *(2) Gates argues that Newman's deposition testimony establishes that he has admitted that he "destroyed" evidence. Bando argues that Newman acted reasonably, and that by downloading to a disk he preserved, rather than destroyed, evidence. I agree with Bando.*[4]

Here we have a problem that obviously requires an expert to assist the fact finder in determining what makes sense based on evidence over which the parties are squabbling. The fact finder also needs assistance in determining whether what the non-expert actor did to the computer and to the electronic evidence, or potential evidence, was reasonable, unreasonable, negligent, or worse. So, the stage is set in this sanctions litigation (which is but a part of the larger intellectual property case) for each side to summon an expert to take a look at the events each side claimed occurred, to conduct some tests to see what might have been done to the computers and the data, and to render their respective opinions on these issues to the court.

---

4. *Gates Rubber Company v. Bando Chemical Industries, Ltd., et al.*, 167 F.R.D. 90, 1996, U.S. Dist. LEXIS 12423. Decided May 1, 1996.

The experts presented the court with two conflicting versions of what the various pieces of electronic evidence signified. While there are few published court opinions that go into the reasoning process and the method of weighing the qualifications of opposing technical computer experts (and sweeping generalizations are therefore ill advised), this case has been cited by other courts since it was decided several years ago. It offers at least one judge's opinion as to what he was looking for in assessing competing expert testimony about computer forensic methods. Again quoting from the opinion:

> *Bando's expert on matters associated with computer science was Robert Wedig, who holds a Ph.D. in computer science from Stanford. Wedig's credentials, experience and knowledge were impressive, and I relied upon his opinions. Gates failed to obtain a similar expert in timely fashion. Gates did offer the testimony of Robert Voorhees, the technician who was hired by Gates to copy the hard drive of the computer at Bando's Denver facility. His credentials, experience and knowledge were nowhere near those of Dr. Wedig, and I placed much less weight on his testimony than on Wedig's.*[5]

Presenting the Expert's Qualifications

While reading the last paragraph of the *Gates v. Bando* decision, you might wonder what credentials, experience, and knowledge might strike the fact finder as "impressive." Although Wedig's résumé is not included in the opinion, we present below its main content as it stood in December 2001. It was essentially the same at the time he testified several years before, except for his more recent activities.

Robert G. Wedig, Ph.D.
December 2001

Education

B.E.E.	Electrical Engineering, University of Dayton, 1977.
M.S.	Electrical Engineering, University of Southern California, 1979.
Ph.D.	Electrical Engineering, Stanford University, 1982.

Professional Experience

1/86–present	Independent Consultant. Wedig Consulting. Cupertino, CA.
8/82–12/85	Assistant Professor of Electrical and Computer Engineering. Carnegie-Mellon University, Pittsburgh, PA.
9/79–6/82	Research Assistant, Instructor, and Teaching Assistant. Computer Systems Laboratory, Stanford University, Stanford, CA.

---

5. *Gates Rubber Company v. Bando Chemical Industries.*

| 4/77–9/79 | Processor Design Engineer. Hughes Aircraft Company, Fullerton, CA. |
| 9/74–4/77 | Application Programmer. University of Dayton, Dayton, OH. |

Awards

1983–1985   IBM Faculty Development Award.
1980–1982   IBM Predoctoral Fellowship.
1977–1979   Hughes Aircraft Masters Fellowship.

Professional Societies

Tau Beta Pi, IEEE, ACM, PATCA

Research Interests

High Performance Processor Design, VLSI Architectures, Language

Oriented Machine Design, Educational Computing, Artificial Intelligence Machines, GaAs Processors and Digital Circuit Analysis.

Invited Presentations

"The Directly Interfaceable Parallel I/O Chip," Professional Seminar, Xerox Palo Alto Research Center, April 1981.

"Advances in Computer Architecture," Program for Technical Managers, Carnegie-Mellon University, April 1983.

"The GaAs Realization of a Production System Machine," Hawaii International Conference on System Sciences, January 1986.

"GaAs Computer Architectures," NCR Corporation, April 1986.

"Software and Hardware Techniques for Stack Management," Hawaii International Conference on System Sciences, January 1987.

"A Performance Analysis of Automatically Managed Top of Stack Buffers," NCR Corporation, June 1987.

"Concurrency in Single Chip Processors," NCR Corporation, September 1987.

Professional Activities

Session Leader of GaAs Processor Session, Hawaii International Conference on System Sciences, January 1986.

Minitrack Chairman of Hardware Track, Hawaii International Conference on System Sciences, January 1988.

Committee Member, Asilomar Microcomputer Workshop, 1986–2001.

Program Chairman, Asilomar Microcomputer Workshop, 1998.

Committee Member, HOT Interconnects Symposium, 2000–2001.

Publications

1. Wedig, R. G., "Dynamic Detection of Concurrency in DO-Loops Using Ordering Matrices," Technical Report 209, Stanford University, May 1981.
2. Wedig, R. G., A "Phenomenal" Chip for Toy Design, *VLSI Design*, Vol. 2, No. 3, 1981, pp. 51–52.
3. Wedig, R. G., "Dynamic Detection of Concurrency in DEL Instruction Streams," Technical Report 231, Stanford University, February 1982.
4. *Detection of Concurrency in Directly Executed Language Instruction Streams*, Ph.D. dissertation, Stanford University, June 1982.
5. Wedig, R. G. and Flynn, M. J., "Concurrency Detection in Language-Oriented Processing Systems," *Proceedings of the 3rd International Conference on Distributed Computing Systems*, IEEE, October 1982, pp. 805–810.
6. With Flynn, M. J., Huck, J. C. and Wakefield, S. P., "Performance Evaluation of Execution Aspects of Computer Architectures," *Proceedings of the International Workshop on High Level Language Computer Architectures*, University of Maryland and the Office of Naval Research, December 1982.
7. Wedig, R. G., "The Detection of Concurrency Using Structured Control Flow," *Proceedings of the International Workshop on Computer Systems Organization*, IEEE Computer Society, March 1983, pp. 28–35.
8. Wedig, R. G., "A Language-Oriented Approach for Implementing Branches: Structured Control Flow," *Proceedings of the International Workshop on High-Level Computer Architecture*, University of Maryland, May 1984, pp. 3.1–3.7.
9. Wedig, R. G. and Rose, M. A., "The Reduction of Branch Instruction Execution Overhead Using Structured Control Flow," *Proceedings of the 11th Annual International Symposium on Computer Architecture*, IEEE Computer Society, June 1984, pp. 119–125.
10. Wedig, R. G., "Using ISPS to Teach Computer Architecture," *Proceedings of the National Educational Computing Conference*, ACM, June 1984.
11. With Forgy, C., Gupta, A. and Newell, A., "Initial Assessment of Architectures for Production Systems," *Proceedings of the National Conference on Artificial Intelligence*, AAAI, August 1984.
12. Wedig, Robert G. and Lehr, Theodore F., "The GaAs Implementation of a Production System Machine," *The Proceedings of the 19th Annual Hawaii International Conference on System Sciences*, IEEE Computer Society, January 1986.

13. With Anoop Gupta and Charles Forgy, "Parallel Algorithms and Architectures for Rule-Based Systems," *Proceedings of the 13th Annual International Conference on Computer Architecture*, IEEE, June 1986.

14. With Augustus K. Uht, "Hardware Extraction of Low-Level Concurrency from Serial Instruction Streams," *Proceedings of the 15th Annual International Conference on Parallel Processing*, ACM, August 1986.

15. Wedig, Robert G., "Software and Hardware Techniques for Stack Management," *The Proceedings of the 20th Annual Hawaii International Conference on System Sciences*, IEEE Computer Society, January 1987.

16. With Theodore F. Lehr, "The GaAs Implementation of a Production System Machine," *IEEE Computer*, April 1987.

17. With Timothy Stanley, "A Performance Analysis of Automatically Managed Top of Stack Buffers," *Proceedings of the 14th Annual International Conference on Computer Architecture*, IEEE, June 1987.

18. Wedig, R. G., *High Level Language Computer Architectures*, Elsevier Science, New York, NY, 1988, chapter 6.

[Wedig also lists his experiences in the roles of neutral expert and expert witness or consultant to the court or to a mediator, as well as his appearances in court or in deposition in litigated cases. For example, he lists his appearance in the Gates rubber case as follows: "*Gates Rubber v. Bando America*, Expert for the Defense, United States District Court, District of Colorado, November 1994."][6]

Although you may feel after reviewing Wedig's résumé that your résumé is a bit anemic in comparison, don't worry. It is important, however, to always have a current résumé prepared in advance whenever you are applying for or being considered for expert witness assignments.

Meanwhile, back to the opinion from *Gates v. Bando*. The court continues:

Wedig confirmed what is generally known by all computer users, that the process of copying from hard drive to floppy disk does not result in the loss or deletion of data, and "no information is lost." Gates argues as follows: this is true only if Newman downloads everything; Newman is a liar; therefore, Wedig's conclusions are faulty.

There is no evidence that Newman "lied" about everything, and even Gates relies upon his testimony when it suits Gates' purposes to do so. Whether Newman is a "liar" or not, when a party preserves material, as Newman did here, and provides

---

6. Résumé provided by Dr. Robert Wedig via personal communication, December 2001.

that material to an opponent as part of a discovery obligation, as Bando did here, I find that it would be unreasonable to infer that material was destroyed unless there is some evidence which leads to such an inference. I am persuaded that Newman preserved, rather than destroyed, evidence when he copied from hard drive to disk.

This order would be unduly complicated if I discussed each detail of the technical disputes which surrounded the downloading of Life in Hours to disk, and each detail of the various files which were lost or recaptured from Newman's word processing files. However, one particular dispute should receive attention. During the injunction proceedings which were conducted before Judge Sparr, counsel for Bando introduced into evidence a disk and printout of a directory which purported to be a copy of the disk and directory which had been downloaded by Newman. The directory of the disk provided to Gates contained 45 file entries, while the directory provided to the court contained only 44 file entries. The missing file is LHX.SEC.DAT. Counsel for Bando at that time, James Lowe, stated to the court that he did not know how this could have happened. Gates argued that this was an intentional effort to mislead the court, for which Bando should be sanctioned.

I am satisfied with the explanation which was offered by Wedig, though the explanation was extremely technical. In fact, according to Wedig, the missing file was present in deleted form on the disk provided to the court. Wedig offered a detailed explanation on the mechanics of how this one file would be deleted inadvertently when another portion of the program was run by someone.[7]

The Devil Is in the Details

In the course of litigation, for many fact finders, be they judge or juror, the details will make all the difference in how they comprehend the big picture. And as often as not, trial lawyers who interview jurors learn (to their delight or dismay) that one or two of the details not adequately explained by one of the testifying experts made all the difference in the decision. It is even more mortifying to an attorney to learn that the unfavorable verdict was due in part to details that were not argued in a clear and comprehensible way by the lawyer, after the expert had explained them for hours or days on end. It is not unusual for the expert testimony to occur weeks before the bungled summation by counsel at the end of the trial. What may have been clear enough in the details of the expert's testimony can become muddled when the lawyer forgets to include every piece of the puzzle at the close of the evidence in final argument.

Often, the most crucial element of an expert's performance on the stand is the effort to communicate to the fact finder that he has taken the time, both during his investigation, and on the stand testifying, to explain what may seem to be a nit picking, far fetched, or extremely abstract point that was testified to by the opposing expert or is likely to be argued in closing by the other side.

---

7. *Gates Rubber Company v. Bando Chemical Industries.*

At this point in *Gates v. Bando*, the plaintiff's counsel had a series of points they were arguing, based on the technical evidence produced by their expert. It would have been easy for Bando's legal counsel simply to argue that there were insufficient facts to justify the conclusion that Gates was advocating. However, the respondent chose to ask their expert to undertake far more. It is clear from the court's opinion that in this case, Wedig acted out the role of the archetypal objective and meticulous technical expert. He greatly impressed the judge by actually taking the time to look carefully at both the disk from which the file was allegedly deleted and the disk that was in fact provided to the court as evidence. He then went on to explain in some technical detail how he could account for all the facts he discovered. This painstaking investigation and testimonial performance combined to allow the fact finder, without any advocacy from the witness, to understand the facts and the expert explanations. It furthermore allowed the fact finder to do this without reaching the conclusion sought by the plaintiff in this litigation—that someone had intentionally destroyed a great deal of relevant evidence or sought to deceive the plaintiff or the court about the nature of the deletions that did in fact take place.

With this in mind, let's return to the court opinion.

> *In addition to the Wedig explanation, I fail to see how Bando would be benefited, or Gates harmed, by the fact that the court copy reflected one less file, while the copy received by Gates contained all of the files. Gates received full discovery, and if any harm resulted from the confusion surrounding the disk which was introduced into evidence, Judge Sparr implicitly resolved the problem in his injunction ruling of June 24, 1992, which was in favor of Gates.*
>
> **(2) Destruction of Word Processing Files.**
>
> *Newman admitted during his deposition testimony that at about the same time that he downloaded Life in Hours to a disk he "cleaned up" his word processing files by deleting certain materials which he had previously stored on his computer. He stated that he did not erase any materials which were relevant to this litigation. The lawyers for defendants argue that Gates is not harmed by Newman's acts because all files were recaptured in some manner: some files were preserved on disk; some were provided to Gates as "hard copy" (i.e., the printed letters or memos which were deleted from the hard drive); and others were shown to have been deleted in the ordinary course of business prior to the initiation of the litigation by Gates.*
>
> *Gates argues, correctly, that the court cannot rely upon the opinions of Newman as to whether the materials which he deleted are relevant or not to this case. Gates argues further that Bando cannot demonstrate that Newman's files were deleted prior to litigation, or were recaptured. On this subject, Bando presented the testimony of Wedig. Gates attacked the testimony similarly to above: the opinions of Wedig are only as accurate as the truthfulness of Newman.[8]*

---

8. *Gates Rubber Company v. Bando Chemical Industries.*

The Parties May Be Held Responsible for Their Experts' Performances

The following analysis by the court demonstrates as clearly as a single case can that the weight that a fact finder may assign to the qualifications, experiences, and methods of one expert, as opposed to those of another, can ultimately contribute to the positive outcome of a case. In particular, the weight assigned to the qualifications may serve to persuade the court or a jury that the expert's opinions are better grounded in his or her expertise and should make the difference in ultimately finding for one party over another. Where the expert can detect and clearly describe actual errors in the methods of the opposing expert to the satisfaction of the court, it can erode or erase the reasoning of the attorneys as to other issues in the case as well.

Here the court considered the argument of Gates that the conclusions of the technical expert, Wedig, could only be considered if the court first believed the testimony of another witness named Ron Newman, who testified for Bando. The court, however, was convinced by Wedig's testimony that the entire argument of the plaintiff was subject to doubt. This doubt was warranted by the failure of the plaintiff's expert to perform as Wedig testified he should have in order to preserve all the evidence that needed to be considered by the fact finder to reach a reasonable decision, including the decision on Newman's credibility as a witness.

There is a very reasonable basis for the fact finder to hold the attorney and the party responsible for vouching for an expert whose opinions, methods, or investigations don't make sense. The judge and the jury understand that experts are available and that most often the parties and their attorneys can select one that is going to help them present their side of the case. When the contrast between opposing experts, either in their qualifications or in the integrity of their investigation or testimony, becomes glaring, as the court apparently found in this case, the suspicion that other claims made by that party need closer scrutiny can begin to cascade. This is why any expert needs to carefully consider the wisdom of accepting an assignment that will place him or her in a position where his or her experience or training is significantly inferior to the experts who are likely to be called by the opposing party.

Sometimes Experts Have to Judge Other Experts—and Find Them Wanting

The court continues with its opinion in *Gates v. Bando.*

> *The accuracy of Wedig's testimony does not depend exclusively upon the truthfulness of Newman. During the sanctions hearing, I was presented with testimony which related to what might be dubbed the "inside" of the Denver computer. The two experts, Voorhees and Wedig, agreed that deleted files remain on the hard drive, and*

only disappear in pieces, in a random fashion, as other data is written over the files. In view of this fact, in an order of February 10, 1992, Judge Sparr granted to Gates the opportunity to copy the hard drive in the Denver computer in order to obtain as much information as was available with regard to deleted files. Gates retained Voorhees as its technician to do the copying, and he attempted to do this through the use of a program called Norton's Unerase. Proper use of the program could yield information, or partial pictures, about files which were once present on the computer's hard drive, but were deleted.

Gates argued that Voorhees did an adequate job of copying the Denver computer. Wedig persuaded me, however, that Voorhees lost, or failed to capture, important information because of an inadequate effort. In using Norton's Unerase, Voorhees unnecessarily copied this program onto the Denver computer first, and thereby overwrote 7 to 8 percent of the hard drive before commencing his efforts to copy the contents.

Wedig noted that information which is introduced into a computer is distributed, in a random manner, to space which is not being used, or to space which contains a deleted file and is therefore available for use. To use Norton's Unerase, it was unnecessary for Voorhees to copy it onto the hard drive of the Denver computer. By doing so, however, the program obliterated, at random, 7 to 8 percent of the information which would otherwise have been available. No one can ever know what items were overwritten by the Unerase program.

Additionally, Voorhees did not obtain the creation dates of certain of the files which overwrote deleted files. This information would have assisted in determining the deletion date of some files. If a deleted file has been overwritten by a file which was created prior to the Gates litigation, for example, Bando would be relieved of suspicion as to that file. Thus, failure to obtain the creation dates of files represented a failure to preserve evidence which would have been important to Bando in its efforts to resist Gates' motions for default judgment

Wedig pointed out that Voorhees should have done an "image backup" of the hard drive, which would have collected every piece of information on the hard drive, whether the information was allocated as a file or not. Instead, Voorhees did a "file by file" backup, which copies only existing, non-deleted files on the hard drive. The technology for an image backup was available at the time of these events, though rarely used by anyone.[9]

Experts Often Quarrel for Legitimate Reasons

Almost ten years have passed since the discovery in *Gates v. Bando* was conducted. Today, absent absolute necessity or an emergency, qualified IT forensic experts would not consider working on the original storage media. What may have been unusual practice ten years ago is now considered standard procedure by forensic experts when dealing with a personal computer hard drive or other storage media. The same essen-

---

9. *Gates Rubber Company v. Bando Chemical Industries.*

tial set of problems as evidenced in *Gates v. Bando* will almost always exist to some extent for technical experts when dealing with newer technologies or newer tools and techniques. Again, a primary factor will be the absence of generally accepted standards that have been published and used by other courts.

In the absence of accepted standards, what may be standard practice for a given community of experts will be challenged by another community of experts with slightly or significantly different qualifications, experience, or knowledge about the particular problem or the hardware or software at issue. Courts and jurors may be persuaded by arguments that an expert failed to apply the state of the art in tools and techniques to analyze a technical problem or to collect evidence. Attorneys may argue that an expert failed to apply the most modern techniques when conducting an experiment and then providing an opinion based on the interpretation of the results.

In the rapidly changing worlds of IT and information security, both the attorney and the expert must do some serious soul searching about the depth and breadth of their understandings of the technical problems that a given case presents before they settle on the strategies for that case. They must similarly consider their proposed solutions to those problems. Perhaps most importantly, they must then understand and often second-guess the reality that their strategies will be just as seriously challenged by the opposing experts and attorneys during deposition and trial testimony.

While the problem that Wedig had to address may seem relatively simple today, especially in light of ten additional years of experience in searching computer hard drives and data storage devices of all kinds in both criminal and civil cases, it suggests a larger, more fundamental problem. Very similar requirements for determining the most appropriate methods, tools, and techniques for attacking a technical problem can arise that are much subtler and extremely difficult to anticipate at the start of litigation.

In the *Gates* case, evidence either was or was not lost or destroyed, and qualified technical experts could and did differ in their judgments of the best practice for the preservation and analysis of the relevant and material digital evidence. These issues were ultimately resolved by selecting the best expert opinion about how particular digital forensic tools and techniques should have been applied in a given situation. However, the job of the judge or the juror can turn out to be much more difficult than it proved to be in this case. In particular, when there is a genuine, irreconcilable disagreement among equally qualified and experienced experts as to what tools and techniques to apply for more complex investigations of application or network activity, the fact finder's path may be muddier. The Australian philosopher C. A. J. Coady has discussed this problem at length in his writings. He has drawn on the work of George Smith, a fellow philosopher with an engineering background who has cited several reasons for the frequent clashes of experts in technological fields. Coady refers to these observations as follows:

One reason he [Smith] gives is the way in which quite different practices for achieving similar ends can exist in different businesses or fields. All of these practices may "work" and it may be a difficult and delicate matter of judgment which ones work better than which. Moreover, within any given practice, some procedure may be essential to the success of that practice, which would none the less be a disaster if operated within some other practice with the same or similar ends. Given past success, practitioners are liable to place great emphasis upon agreement about existing procedures within a practice, and where two companies, for instance, operate different practices with different crucial procedures, then experts familiar with one can easily be emphatic, even dogmatic, in their rejection of the other. There are parallels here with sporting skill. Anyone who has ever had lessons from coaches with different backgrounds in cricket or golf or tennis will recognize the problem. Relatedly, it is a common experience that changing some element of a player's style to conform more to a textbook may prove disastrous because of the integrated nature of his existing "practice".[10]

Again, in *Gates v. Bando*, the court placed a great deal of trust in the defendant's expert's opinions that, given the forensic nature of the practices being applied, there was no question as to which practice was most appropriate. The court concluded that the methods used by the plaintiff's expert fell below the mark for forensic purposes. This failure to measure up to the standards that Wedig testified should clearly have applied was held against the plaintiff on issues that went far beyond the determination of whether a particular piece of evidence had been wrongfully deleted.

The Rest of the Story

The court completes its decision on the sanction.

Wedig testified that Gates was collecting evidence for judicial purposes; therefore, Gates had a duty to utilize the method which would yield the most complete and accurate results. I agree with Wedig. In these circumstances, Gates failed to preserve evidence in the most appropriate manner. Gates' failure to obtain an image backup of the computer is a factor which I have weighed against Gates as I considered a number of the claims which Gates has asserted.

Gates argues that Bando had an equal opportunity to preserve evidence, and if Bando thought that an image backup was so important, it could have obtained such a result itself. I do not find this argument persuasive. Bando probably had very little idea that the copying of its Denver computer would spark a sanctions proceeding which would take several years, and cost several millions of dollars. Gates, on the other hand, has been the party which has been driving the controversy, and has sought to use the "absence" of evidence to its fullest advantage.

---

10. Coady, C. A. J. *Testimony*. Oxford, UK: Oxford University Press, 1994, pp. 289–290.

Therefore, I find that the duty was on Gates, and not Bando, to utilize the best technology available.

Gates also argues that a loss of 7 to 8 percent of the information available is insignificant. I disagree. If the roles had been reversed, and if Bando had been responsible for copying the hard drive in such a way that 7 to 8 percent of the information was lost, I have no doubt that the lawyers for Gates would find that the 7 to 8 percent loss was of critical, even fatal, importance. In fact, that is exactly the argument which Gates is making throughout these sanctions proceedings: some small portion of alleged evidence has been lost; no one knows what it is; therefore, Gates should be granted a default judgment.

I have weighed Gates' concern with the loss of data against its failure to preserve the evidence in the most complete manner available, and against the totality of discovery material which has been made available to Gates.

Some things remain clear. Newman did, in fact, delete word processing files. The deletion of the files was intentional, and was done after he had learned that he was named in the litigation. I find, however, that an accounting has been made of all of the deleted files, either by a showing that they were deleted prior to the initiation of this litigation, by a showing that they were recaptured, or by a showing that adequate substitutes in the form of hard copies have been provided.

Nevertheless, evidence of the destruction of word processing files has caused Gates to incur attorneys fees and costs which it would not otherwise have incurred. Gates was justified in its challenge to the adequacy of the computer record which was being provided by Bando, and the challenge necessarily resulted in the legal fees and costs which are associated with the filing of the motion for sanctions as to this claim, and with the discovery efforts which followed in the wake of the motion. I therefore find that Gates is entitled to the attorneys fees and costs which were incurred by it in the discovery efforts and the prosecution of this part (2) of the Newman claim.

Having observed these sanctions proceedings for several years, I am aware that it would be difficult, if not impossible, for Gates to separate from its total bill those fees and costs which are specific to the Newman claim. Discovery from each of the witnesses, for example, was frequently applicable to more than one of Gates' claims. In order to resolve this dilemma, I find that Gates is entitled to be awarded ten percent of the total amount of fees and costs which it incurred throughout the sanctions proceedings. The figure of ten percent no doubt exceeds the amount of fees and costs which Gates actually incurred on this claim, but any amount in excess of the true figure is awarded to Gates as a sanction.

Gates need not calculate the sum to which it is entitled. I find in later portions of this order that Gates was not justified in the filing and prosecution of the majority of its claims, and I award fees and costs to Bando in excess of ten percent. The figure of ten percent will be offset against any fees and costs awarded to Bando.[11]

---

11. *Gates Rubber Company v. Bando Chemical Industries.*

Expert Performances Can Make Enormous Differences in Outcome

You may by now realize that most of the issues discussed in this case were, to everyone involved in the original intellectual property lawsuit, a relatively trivial pursuit when they began. The search by a technical expert to find evidence of the spoliation of some amount of evidence that was presumably relevant to the underlying litigation ended in triggering a separate major piece of litigation. This parallel litigation lasted several years in its own right and contributed in a significant way to a multimillion-dollar costs claim awarded to the defendant in the sanctions lawsuit that threatened to engulf the original multimillion-dollar IP claims.

It is part of our thesis that attentive jurors, like the judge in this case, are constantly scanning the evidentiary horizon for standards they can use to measure competing testimony. This is especially true of expert testimony. Here, the judge essentially found that Wedig's testimony amounted to standards that were more reasonable than those that could be gleaned from the actions, opinions, and arguments that opposing counsel and competing experts could demonstrate. Beyond the issue of establishing reasonable standards, there is a more fundamental question. When equally qualified experts disagree in good faith about the conclusions that can reasonably be drawn from the common set of facts they have been asked to consider, what is going to enable the fact finder to make a sound decision? If this scenario sounds familiar, it also describes the problem that judges face in the *Daubert* challenge round of litigation, discussed in Chapter 8.

What Can an Expert Do to Reassure a Lay Judge or Juror?

We have seen how in this case the court first determined that both experts could testify. Then, acting as the fact finder, the judge had to choose between them without knowing the facts or the technology in the same way that the experts presumably did. So the big question for our purposes is this: Just how do experts manage to accomplish what Wedig did in the *Gates* case? How does the expert manage not only to convince the judge that he or she is qualified to testify as an expert but also to cause the fact finder to rely on his or her contested explanation and standards to decide the technical issues in the case?

The litigation experts surveyed generally agree that much of this comes down to a matter of framing that must be accomplished by the lawyer, beginning with the selection of the jurors. During the questioning (or voir dire) of the potential jurors, the lawyers (or in some cases only the judge) are allowed to interview the jurors during the selection process. During the interviews and from the beginning of the opening statement, the lawyers will try to introduce their experts and their technical evidence to the fact finders. Where technical issues will be important and where the opposing expert witnesses are both credible, the lawyer and the expert who are best able to frame the challenge for the fact finder may find that their framing efforts are rewarded. Our experiences instruct us that it is usually a mistake to encourage either the judge or the jury to think that he or she must become as knowledgeable as the expert in order to rely on one expert's opinion over that of another. Furthermore, the jurors must be prepared as early as possible to be willing to rely on the expertise of the expert, without feeling like they must master the expertise that it has taken the expert an entire career to master. It is an even more serious error for the expert and the attorney to believe that this "expertising" is ever possible to accomplish in the time allotted for the presentation of the expert's testimony in the formal ritual of the trial.

One way of thinking of the problem is to consider two extremely different contexts in which the same technical evidence could ultimately be presented but for which vastly different amounts of evidence and explanation would be required. For example, if the expert were presenting a paper to peers or defending a doctoral thesis before a graduate school committee, the fact finders would understand the presentation in the same way the expert did. Indeed, in these extreme examples, the fact finders would be expected to be even more expert than the speaker. Judges and jurors are not peers.

Some Rules of Engagement for Presenting Expert Testimony

In a jury trial it is assumed by the law and incorporated in the rules of procedure and evidence that the fact finders know very little if anything about what the expert is prepared to explain about some issue in the case involving technical evidence. The Federal Rules of Evidence relating to experts (including Rules 702, 703, and 705) all assume that jurors will be assisted the most by allowing experts to skip many of the formalities of proof that would otherwise be required of ordinary witnesses. Experts are therefore allowed and encouraged by the rules to testify about their conclusions without going into all the preliminary findings and without being required to rely solely on foundational facts that are themselves independently admissible as evidence.

These rules and customs that encourage expert witnesses to testify in this unusual way (as compared to other witnesses) and that enable jurors to cast votes of confidence for one expert as opposed to another in the jury's ultimate deliberations may not be intuitively obvious to jurors. Thus, the court needs to carefully explain these points to the jurors. The attorneys should also remind the jurors of these rules and customs at appropriate stages of the trial. In this way the jurors can accept the expert testimony without becoming concerned that they are not going to understand all the technical evidence in the same way that the expert (or even the attorney who has been working on the case for months or years) does. The same rules need to be revisited in the jury instructions at the conclusion of the case to remind the jurors that it is not their duty or their role to become experts, but only to choose between competing experts or to disregard all of the expert evidence.

The fact that the rules of evidence and procedure encourage and enable the fact finders to use experts to help them understand highly technical issues does not mean that the evidence is not ultimately going to be subjected to wide-ranging and probing cross-examination by opposing counsel. The expert is always subject to a searching cross-examination by opposing counsel after the expert has concluded his or her testimony. All the foundational facts and assumptions made by the expert or skipped over in the direct testimony by taking advantage of the special rules regarding the presentation of expert testimony are fair game once cross-examination commences.

But Shouldn't We Expect Judges and Jurors to Be Experts Too?

The context of expert testimony at trial is radically different than other contexts where the expert may be speaking to an audience of professional peers. As lecturer to his or her peers, the expert assumes that the attendees are already experts. In a trial the expert needs to make the opposite assumption. The law does not require—and indeed cannot require—the jurors to understand the testimony in the same way as the expert's peers are assumed to be able to do, without any need to apologize for that obvious fact. But many commentators have found this to be an apparent quandary, when we expect lay judges and jurors to decide which expert to believe, based only on their common sense interpretation of the competing performances of the witnesses and the arguments of the attorneys. Some have suggested that this dependence on lay juries is a fatal flaw in the system by allowing important social decisions such as the outcome of criminal and civil cases to be made in this fashion. These commentators have conveniently forgotten about the central role that testimony and the reliance on that testimony has always played in all aspects of social intercourse and critical decision making about the proper course of action for a group or community to take.

Coady, the philosopher, reminds us of the reality of how not only lay people but also the most sophisticated scientists rely on the testimony of others to do their work and to make important personal and professional decisions.

> *Even the more abstract sciences, such as astronomy and theoretical physics, are dependent in different ways upon testimony. A great deal of research work in physics, for instance, is collaborative in character (considered synchronically) and dependent upon a tradition of investigation (considered diachronically). As to the first, more than two-thirds of physicists surveyed in the United States in the 1960s said that*

most of their work was collaborative either with co-workers within their discipline or with workers in other disciplines [citation omitted]. Much of this collaboration presumably involves the acceptance of observations and calculations of colleagues, and even where the scientist works, as it were, by himself, he relies upon such accumulated funds of information as are contained in reputable tabulations or stored in computers or even embodied in the standard treatment of issues that he is not directly concerned with but needs to know about for the progress of his own work. Reliance upon previous experimental work in science can, of course, go seriously astray but it seems also to be a condition of progress since even where results are theoretically "replicable" it would be a practical absurdity for any given worker to replicate all the experimental and observational work upon which his own investigations depend. Indeed, it would often be literally impossible to do so, either because of an inevitable lack of time or lack of competence.[12]

Why Do Most People Respect Teachers and Authors?

What the expert is really engaged in while testifying is a lot like teaching. This is another reason why experts with academic credentials including classroom responsibilities for students tend to impress jurors more than experts who lack these credentials. But expert testimony is a kind of teaching that also requires the expert to be adept at translating some of many concepts that may be second nature to the expert but will certainly not be as easy for the jurors to grasp.

To the degree that the expert can satisfy the jurors that he or she has the requisite knowledge, experience, and credibility to explain matters so they make sense, it should not be a problem for the jurors to realize they can consider the evidence to help them understand the factual issues in the case even though they cannot understand the evidence in the same way the expert does. Part of the translation problem, then, is the ability of the expert, with the attorney's assistance, to grasp the way that his or her expertise can shed light on issues in the case. For that to happen effectively, the attorney, too, may need to be quite skilled in translating the technical issues and in understanding how to best explain them to fit into the big picture the attorney desires to develop during the course of the trial.

These translations must be kept simple and really must be shown or demonstrated to the jurors visually to give the jurors the best chance of comprehending most or all of the technical evidence. (See Chapter 10 for a discussion on visual exhibits.) As most trial experts would agree, the witness and the attorney are combining their talents to give the jurors new metaphors and almost a new language to talk about some of these technical issues that appear in the case. During deliberations these new metaphors and ideas and the way they do or do not fit into the overall case that the jurors are assembling for themselves and as a group will be revived and debated. The point of a trial is to give all the available relevant evidence to the fact finders, test the evidence through cross-examination and argument of counsel, and then allow the group to decide what the verdict should be.

What enables this system to work as well as it does is the set of rules applied by the court and recognized by the attorneys but sometimes not made sufficiently clear to the witnesses and the jurors. These rules are the presumptions and burdens assigned by the law in both civil and criminal cases which, when properly explained, make the fact finder's job simpler to accomplish. So, when one party such as the prosecutor for the state in a criminal case assumes the burden of proving all the elements of a criminal charge beyond any reasonable doubt, the jury can find the defendant not guilty even though they may all agree that the defendant is probably guilty, but just not guilty beyond a reasonable doubt. In this way, the presumption of innocence and the burden of proving guilt beyond a reasonable doubt control the discretion of the fact finders in deciding the case. As advocates like to argue in summation, if the burden of proof were any greater, the guilty would be unjustly set free; if the burden were any less, those not guilty would be in danger of conviction.

Presumptions and Burdens of Proof and Persuasion

Some jurors have reported after trials that problems arose when one or more jurors did not feel they were expert enough to decide the technical issues one way or another. This scenario is the source of great frustration for experts as well. It is the job of the attorneys and the court to set the jurors' minds at ease and to instruct them that the law assigns the burdens of production, persuasion, and proof. In a civil case the plaintiff has the burden of proving it more likely than not that he or she is right and has sufficient evidence to prove the case. It is not the responsibility of the jurors to become experts in those issues that require technical expertise to be understood. It is the court's job to make this division of labor crystal clear.

If it is the plaintiff's burden to prove something and the expert is an essential part of that proof, it is necessary that the jurors rely on that expert's evidence if the plaintiff is to successfully carry the burden of production of evidence and in turn carry the burden of persuasion based on that evidence. The jurors must simply listen to the expert and decide whether the testimony helped them with one or more of the issues in the case. If it is a toss-up and the plaintiff's expert has not proven a key issue as more likely the case than not, the plaintiff loses on that issue and on that claim, regardless of how knowledgeable the fact finders have become in some area of expertise.

Houdini as Expert Performer and Professional Skeptic

In our experience, it has helped to use metaphors and historical figures to make clear this crucial point about how presumptions and burdens of proof function as rules of decision. Some stories seem to work better for those first-time experts who still wonder how a juror or a judge can be expected to make a reasoned determination of complex technical or scientific theories and choose between the explanations of competing experts. The use of specific analogies and metaphors to help convey how the demonstration of real expertise does shift the burden of persuasion and proof about important, complex questions is completely up to the lawyer's choice of communication strategies in attempting to explain to the expert how these trial phenomena operate. We could think of other experts in history who worried about the correct application of their expertise and its abuse by charlatans, but let's take the metaphor of magic and the historical figure of Harry Houdini, born Ehrich Weiss. Nearly everyone recognizes Houdini as the world's best-known escape artist. Dramatic images of his performances are almost emblematic of the entire genre of performance artists as entertainers (Figure 9-1).

Figure 9-1. *Harry Houdini in one of his most popular roles: master escape artist and stage performer. (McManus-Young Collection, Library of Congress, ca. 1899.)*

The Magical Harry Houdini

Two excellent biographies follow Houdini's turn from a vaudeville magician to a respected analytical thinker and debunker of the hoaxes perpetrated by the spiritualists:

- Kenneth Silverman's *Houdini!!! The Career of Ehrich Weiss* (New York: Harper Collins, 1996)
- Adam Philips's *Houdini's Box: The Art of Escape* (New York: Pantheon Press, 2001)

Perhaps fewer people also recognize that Houdini is considered to have been one of the greatest performing stage magicians of all time. Professional magicians throughout the world honor the anniversary of his death (which happens to be on Halloween) with ritual and benefit performances. Probably far fewer people know that Houdini published manuals on the art of magic and had the world's largest collection of magic texts when he died.

Even fewer probably know that he waged a crusade for the last 20 years of his life against a related form of entertainment that turned into a widespread fraudulent practice called *spiritualism*, or communicating with the dead. In his efforts to make public the fraudulent practices of the spiritualists, which he considered as no better than a criminal confidence game, he was at some pains to distinguish what he called "honest magic" from spiritualism.

Houdini developed and performed tricks and created illusions that no one else could figure out or duplicate. He was without doubt the world's foremost expert at devising this kind of illusion. But Houdini was always careful to deny that his powers to mystify were based on any divine force or spiritual assistance. When he decided to apply his knowledge and experience to debunk the practices of spiritualists, no one could deny his expertise in the arts of deception, stagecraft, and the creation of entertaining illusions. But precisely because his reputation as an expert depended on his ability to fool an audience and to present illusions no one else could figure out, his expertise as a debunker of spiritualism was necessarily also somewhat suspect.

The point of this digression into the distinction between the expertise of magic and the confidence game of spiritualism through undisclosed techniques of stage magic by arguably the most expert magician of his time(if not of all time) is to attempt to dramatically demonstrate the different contexts that IT experts must become comfortable working within during their different litigation assignments and roles. When the expert is asked to plan the discovery of evidence and to help develop the attorney's strategic attacks on the credentials, expertise, methods, and conclusions of an opposing expert, the attitude of the skeptic is called for. As discussed in other chapters, this can be extremely problematic, as it is also very similar to the role of advocate and can nudge the objective expert toward becoming a member of the trial team. At first blush, it does not seem that the skeptic can be the preferred role of the testifying expert, whose honest and objective expert advice is supposed to be offered to the judge and the jurors to help them understand the facts, rather than focusing on developing a litigation strategy to advance a persuasive and winning argument against another expert. However, the role of the skeptic must remain a part of the preparation and effective performance of the testifying witness as well as the consulting expert.

Coming to Terms with the Different Roles of the Expert

Aggressively projecting the role of the skeptic, as Houdini did in his battle with the spiritualists, is probably not the ideal image of the objective, helpful, teaching, expert witness that is most likely to win the case. This is not to say that the role of the skeptic is not essential to the consulting, nontestifying expert or, appropriately juxtaposed, to the opposing attorney during contentious or misleading cross-examination. It is certainly a device that the trial lawyer needs to apply in argument to the jury, whenever the need to make skeptical points arises. The preferred place for skepticism is in the testifying expert's critical analysis of all the evidence, especially his or her own, in order to incorporate and adequately explain all reasonable counterarguments in the thesis that the expert is able to advance at trial. A classic example of this kind of skeptical preparation of one's own report and testimony is the report by John Snow, discussed in Chapter 8.

Houdini played the archetypal role of the skeptic for over 20 years as a tireless investigator of all claims by spiritualists that they had succeeded in communicating with the dead. He advocated against spiritualism constantly in testimony, articles, interviews, and books that he produced in a sustained effort to totally destroy the credibility of its practitioners. Just as Houdini had so successfully done throughout his professional life, spiritualists attempted to and did create illusions that persuaded their patrons, including such illustrious and passionate true believers as Sir Arthur Conan Doyle, that it was possible to communicate with the dead. Houdini's proofs were quite persuasive and did a great deal to limit the number of successful scams based on fraudulent practices by spiritualists during and after Houdini's life. His book *Magician Among the Spirits*, published in 1923, was widely read at the time of publication and is still available. In it he chronicles his investigations of dozens of claims of spiritualistic contacts with the dead and describes in great detail what he observed and how the deceptions were accomplished in each case.

Houdini the Skeptic Assigns the Burden of Proof

Houdini was not just an exceptionally skilled and knowledgeable magician; he also understood the psychology of audiences and exactly what it took to make an audience believe. He understood a thing or two about the law and often used it and its authorities to lend legitimacy to his performances. Some of his greatest triumphs as an escape artist were getting out of jail. He understood perfectly well the importance of appearing to have a completely open mind when he put forth his method of investigation and explained the way he arrived at his conclusions or his proofs that spiritualism had no scientific or objective evidence to support its claims of having made contact with the dead. In his book, Houdini described this approach and effectively shifted the burden of proof:

> *Sir Arthur Conan Doyle has repeatedly told the Spiritualists that I will eventually see the light and embrace Spiritualism. If the memory of a loved one, gone to the protection of the hands of the Great Mystifier means Spiritualism, then truly I do believe in it. But if spiritualism is to be founded on the tricks of exposed mediums, feats of magic, resort to trickery, then I say unflinchingly I do not believe, and more, I will not believe. I have said many times that I am willing to believe, want to believe, will believe, if the Spiritualists can show any substantiated proof, but until they do I shall have to live on, believing from all the evidence shown me and from what I have experienced that Spiritualism has not been proven satisfactorily to the world at large and that none of the evidence offered has been able to stand up under the fierce rays of investigation.*[13]

Understanding a thing or two about the law, Houdini also understood the power of presumptions and burdens to control the outcome of a debate between two competing camps that for whatever reason find themselves with a vested interest in persuading others of their contending claims. When one side has the burden of production of admissible evidence and fails to offer any to prove its case, it loses and the verdict goes to the other side. When the burden of production is met, as in the case of the spiritualists, but is completely destroyed and shown to be fraudulent in every instance that can be objectively examined and explained, then it fails to persuade with its evidence and again the verdict is awarded to the side without the burden of production. When it comes to the burden of persuasion in the court of public opinion, Houdini knew that the most persuasive expert was the one who could reasonably claim to be the most knowledgeable and who had applied that knowledge and experience with an open mind. He knew when to set aside skepticism and to appeal to his audience as an objective scientist and technical expert, making observations, conducting experiments, and explaining fully the phenomena under consideration (Figure 9-2).

Houdini therefore concludes his book with the following endorsement of the real reason that expert witnesses should not worry that their audiences, whether judges or jurors, cannot hope to gain sufficient expertise to completely understand the evidence in the same way as acknowledged experts do.

---

13. Houdini, Harry. *Magician Among the Spirits.* New York: Harper and Row, 1927, p. 270.

It is not for us to prove that the mediums are dishonest, it is for them to prove that they are honest. They have made a statement, the most serious statement in recent times, for it affects the welfare, the mental attitude and means a complete revolution of age-old beliefs and customs of the world. If there is anything to Spiritualism then the world should know it. If there is nothing to it, if it is, as it appears, built on a flimsy framework of misdirection, then too the universe must be told. There is too much at stake for a flighty passing, for unsubstantiated truths.[14]

Figure 9-2. *Poster for a lecture by Houdini, in his public service persona, on fraudulent mediums. (Oscar Teale Houdini scrapbook, Library of Congress, April 27, 1923.)*

The rules of the game of litigation control the outcome when the expert fails to contribute to carrying the burden placed on a party to the litigation. The judge or jurors need only be able to rely on or disregard the evidence of the expert. The law with its consistent assignment of burdens in like cases is responsible for creating the structure for the ultimate outcome that the vote of the fact finders dictates.

---

14. Houdini, *Magician Among the Spirits*, p. 270.

As a technical expert, there are not likely to be many opportunities at trial to confront another expert who is making an easily detected, demonstrably bogus claim for his or her chosen method or theory. It is not so easy for a technical expert to distinguish between a technique or method that he or she uses to explain a complex piece of behavior in a corporate computer network and a similar technique or method used by another well-qualified technical expert called by the other party. On the other hand, what Houdini was doing can be seen as similar in some ways to what certain technical experts find themselves doing when they become ensnared in cases where standards are nonexistent or not well settled. They are encouraged to be creative in their interpretation of what might have happened in order to shed doubt on or to shore up an amorphous set of facts by exposing the lack of substance in the proofs of the opposing expert with the burden.

Why Experts Can't Create Idiosyncratic Standards

The opinion in *Kumho Tire v. Carmichael* (see Appendix A) can certainly be read to have suggested that the tire expert in that case was imminently qualified (insofar as his extensive experience and knowledge were concerned). Hence he was entitled to testify as to his opinion about the general method of determining whether or not a particular tire was defective or whether its failure was caused by abusive use. When he chose to go beyond those generally recognized standards and to suggest that his own standard and method allowed him to be more precise, opining that the failure was due to a defect, the Supreme Court declined the invitation. It found no reason to allow a jury to consider his personal opinion when that opinion was totally lacking in any of the validating requirements for reliability announced in *Daubert* for the admission of expert testimony purportedly based on the scientific method and the general acceptance of methods applied by a particular expert in a given case.

Houdini was quite safe in his application of expertise because he understood that spiritualism and every one of its practitioners and all their many artifices were fraudulent. He challenged only sure things, and he knew all the spiritualists' tricks far better than they. But as a metaphor for the two decidedly different contexts that technical experts often find themselves in, Houdini's seemingly contradictory choice of public roles as expert performer of illusions and expert debunker of confidence men and women masquerading as spiritualists shows these often commingled expert roles (teacher and skeptic) in stark contrast.

Houdini was an expert in the arts of deception. What seems to have irked him to the point of rededicating his professional life work was not that others also attempted to deceive their audiences for fame and fortune but that they also claimed they had some sort of religious or spiritual power they used to reveal their contacts with the dead, instead of relying on and revealing only their artistry and powers to bring off an illusion. Houdini and other professional stage magicians performed stunts, which by definition succeeded only to the extent that the audience could not understand how the trick was done. In addition to their skills at selecting potent symbols and their degree of mastery of stagecraft, this secret of how the trick was done and whether it was really hard or simple to do was an important part of their art. In order to unmask the deceivers who practiced spiritualism, Houdini exposed how they created their effects and explained them with documentation and demonstrations whenever possible.

With any discussion of Houdini and his heuristic value for technical experts, it is always tempting to share available anecdotes provided by experts who have had to flee from attorneys whom they perceived to be looking more for an escape artist for their clients, rather than for an objective expert. If the apocrypha can be believed, this is probably most often the case where an injured plaintiff or a guilty defendant is desperately looking for any expert with a theory that will create a claim or some doubt about a crucial piece of evidence. Indeed, the case that started the national debate about experts with novel theories was the attempt in *Frye v. U.S.* (see Appendix A) to have an early form of the polygraph examination admitted on behalf of a defendant charged with murder. The Supreme Court attempted to limit when a novel scientific theory could be considered to be scientific enough, based largely on the general acceptance of such a new theory and method by the recognized community of interest.

Beware of Those Looking for the Perfect Expert

These concerted efforts by trial lawyers to find some helpful expertise to call to the stand on behalf of their clients and in support of their cases can be observed in the recent Supreme Court opinion in *United States v. Scheffer*. In this case, the Court upheld a ban on the use of polygraph experts in military courts, finding no violation of the rights of the defendant in that case by a judge who refused to allow defense counsel to call an expert witness to testify about the defendant's lack of deception in answering the questions put to him by a polygrapher. Ethical criminal defense lawyers who believe their clients are innocent certainly can feel justified in attempting to take advantage of a licensed polygraph expert's testimony that corroborates their client's account. This is reasonable given the degree to which law enforcement and the intelligence community rely on polygraph tests to screen applicants and to eliminate suspects in investigations. However, in *Scheffer* the Court was clearly concerned with the formal context of the trial itself and maintaining certain traditional limits in military trials on the kinds of technical expertise available to parties when it comes to issues like demonstrating the credibility of a witness with technical expert witnesses such as polygraphers.

The approach taken by the President in adopting Rule 707—excluding polygraph evidence in all military trials—is a rational and proportional means of advancing the legitimate interest in barring unreliable evidence. Although the degree of reliability of polygraph evidence may depend upon a variety of identifiable factors, there is simply no way to know in a particular case whether a polygraph examiner's conclusion is accurate, because certain doubts and uncertainties plague even the best polygraph exams. Individual jurisdictions therefore may reasonably reach differing conclusions as to whether polygraph evidence should be admitted. We cannot say, then, that presented with such widespread uncertainty, the President acted arbitrarily or disproportionately in promulgating a per se rule excluding all polygraph evidence. . . .[15]

It is equally clear that Rule 707 serves a second legitimate governmental interest: Preserving the jury's core function of making credibility determinations in criminal trials. A fundamental premise of our criminal trial system is that "the jury is the lie detector." Determining the weight and credibility of witness testimony, therefore, has long been held to be the "part of every case [that] belongs to the jury, who are presumed to be fitted for it by their natural intelligence and their practical knowledge of men and the ways of men."

By its very nature, polygraph evidence may diminish the jury's role in making credibility determinations. The common form of polygraph test measures a variety of physiological responses to a set of questions asked by the examiner, who then interprets these physiological correlates of anxiety and offers an opinion to the jury about whether the witness—often, as in this case, the accused—was deceptive in answering questions about the very matters at issue in the trial. Unlike other expert witnesses who testify about factual matters outside the jurors' knowledge, such as the analysis of fingerprints, ballistics, or DNA found at a crime scene, a polygraph expert can supply the jury only with another opinion, in addition to its own, about whether the witness was telling the truth. Jurisdictions, in promulgating rules of evidence, may legitimately be concerned about the risk that juries will give excessive weight to the opinions of a polygrapher, clothed as they are in scientific expertise and at times offering, as in respondent's case, a conclusion about the ultimate issue in the trial. Such jurisdictions may legitimately determine that the aura of infallibility attending polygraph evidence can lead jurors to abandon their duty to assess credibility and guilt. Those jurisdictions may also take into account the fact that a judge cannot determine, when ruling on a motion to admit polygraph evidence, whether a particular polygraph expert is likely to influence the jury unduly. For these reasons, the President is within his constitutional prerogative to promulgate a per se rule that simply excludes all such evidence.[16]

While more difficult to spot, the aspirant expert may want to carefully consider using some of Houdini's tricks (or at least a healthy dose of his skepticism) to aid in an escape from any attorney who is desperately seeking an expert to overcome existing scientific standards with a brand-new theory for liability or untested techniques for arriving at opinions. Some cases about birth defects possibly caused by Bendectin (a morning sickness drug) and many breast implant cases have failed to pass the *Daubert/Kumho* tests, but not for lack of expert witness efforts to persuade judges and

---

15. *U.S. v. Scheffer.* 523 U.S. 303 (1998), II-A.

16. *U.S. v. Scheffer.* 523 U.S. 303 (1998), II-B.

jurors of their own novel scientific theories and methods of proof of causation. And of course there will always be attorneys seeking experts to help their corporate clients escape from liability for their unreasonably dangerous products, creative accounting maneuvers, or negligent failures to secure a system that causes extensive downstream liability. Again, if the images of Houdini performing his illusions or unmasking deception collected here give the beginning expert pause about whether to proceed when asked to follow in the footsteps of the great magicians and to create an entrancing illusion for a crowd of twelve, the metaphor will have proven useful.

While such hazards of the trade can be avoided, the real point of this digression is to highlight the true magic of the trial, which turns out not to be based on either deception or illusion but on the simple and straightforward evolving legal strategy of applying reasonable presumptions and assigning clearly distinguished but sometimes flexible burdens of production, persuasion, and proof to the opposing parties. Experts can certainly expect to help a party meet its burden or assist in preventing the other side from meeting theirs. They are not responsible for and rarely capable of making independent experts of the judges and jurors they perform before.

Much of the criticism of the use of the *Frye* scientific community consensus standard to judge advances in technical and scientific expertise and the more recent *Daubert* set of standards has been based on confusion over just how the law can presume to include scientific and technical evidence without the need to have scientists also serving as judges and jurors. One answer to this criticism, as discussed in two articles appearing in the *Whittier Law Review*,[17] is that this often esoteric technical evidence is in fact relevant, and qualified experts are sufficiently helpful to judges and jurors who must choose between the evidence offered by the respective experts, based on what they can understand, without the need to become experts themselves.

Illinois Tool Works v. MetroMark Products: A Postscript to *Gates v. Bando*

For a second computer forensic case that provides an interesting counterpoint to the standard-setting battle of the experts in *Gates v. Bando*, consider the case of *Illinois Tool Works v. MetroMark Products*. In this case, there were allegations of willful obstruction of the discovery process—allegations that the court took quite seriously. As with the *Gates* case, the litigation over alleged discovery abuses took on a life of its own and resulted in the dedication of considerable expense and time to sorting out

---

17. (1) Golanski, Alani. "Why Legal Scholars Get Daubert Wrong: A Contextualist Explanation of the Law's Epistemology." *Whittier Law Review* 22(3), 2001, p. 653.
(2) Abramson, Bruce. "Blue Smoke or Science? The Challenge of Assessing Expertise Offered as Advocacy." *Whittier Law Review* 22(3), 2001, p. 723.

the charges and countercharges between the parties over what was originally a trade secret misappropriation and Lanham Act lawsuit between competitors.

By order of the court, the defendants were required to preserve the integrity of all computers in issue without any spoliation of any information they contained. *Spoliation* is simply another example of legal jargon for destroying or tampering with evidence (in this case, evidence of invoices contained in a computer) that could reasonably be expected to be relevant in a pending case or some likely future litigation. The plaintiff asserted this order was violated in connection with a computer in the defendants' possession, which failed to operate when produced for inspection just six days after the preservation order, despite functioning properly a few days earlier. The court held that certain aspects of the physical condition of the computer indicated it had been tampered with.

The saga concerning the computer was only one episode in what the court found to be a pervasive course of conduct by the defendants calculated to frustrate legitimate discovery. By requiring the plaintiff to file motions to compel in order to obtain documents that should have been voluntarily produced, the defendants had engaged in conduct sanctionable under the Federal Rules of Civil Procedure, Rule 37 (Fed. R. Civ. P. 37), section a, subsection 4, paragraph A. The court was left with the firm conviction that there was a purposeful effort to prevent the plaintiff from obtaining the information from the computer. Thus the court granted the plaintiff's motion for sanctions under Fed. R. Civ. P. 37 and awarded reasonable fees and costs incurred by the defendants' failure to comply with discovery.[18]

The original case was brought to resolve a relatively common commercial dispute. Both parties to the lawsuit were in the business of selling hot stamp and thermal imprinting equipment. Two individuals were first employed by Illinois Tool Works (the plaintiff in this action) and later took on employment with MetroMark Products and another competitor to Illinois Tool Works, Horizon Marking Systems, Inc. (the defendants in this action, along with the named individuals). The plaintiff alleged that these individuals (and the corporate defendants) misappropriated trade secrets, including the customer list, belonging to the plaintiff.

As a part of the original case, the plaintiff served a request for production of documents, explicitly including those stored as computer data. The defendants, while not objecting to the request, produced only a single invoice!

The plaintiff then filed a motion to compel with the court, to which the defendants' counsel responded by asserting that the defendants had "complied fully" with the document request. The court directed that the primary custodian of the documents (Heinzel) be made available for a deposition (conducted at Heinzel's expense)

---

18. *Illinois Tool Works, Inc. v. MetroMark Products, Ltd.,* No. 98-C-4244, 43 F. Supp. 2d 951, 1999, U.S. Dist. LEXIS 6579. Decided April 22, 1999. "Overview."

regarding the documents in question and furthermore directed that all parties act to preserve the integrity of all computers at issue in the matter without any spoliation of information contained within those computers.

The court was quite direct about its intentions in ordering the integrity of the computers preserved:

> *If it's "don't push the delete button" or if it's "don't change the C drive" or "don't pull the plug at the wrong time" or "don't take a sledge hammer to it," I don't want it spoiled in any way, okay, so don't limit it.*[19]

On the same day, a request was served by the plaintiff on the defendants to inspect all computers used by the defendants for the prior two years. The inspection was scheduled for the week following, at the offices of the plaintiff's attorneys.

To paraphrase a common aphorism, "stuff happens." And so it was in this sad tale, for one of the computers in question was produced for inspection at the appointed time in a most curious state. The system, already dented from a mishap that was claimed to involve a falling air compressor, was not operational at all by the time it was produced. It had, however, allegedly been functioning at the time the court issued the order to preserve the integrity of the computer. Furthermore, the defendants apparently asserted that in addition to the blow from the falling compressor, the computer itself had fallen to the floor on a number of occasions, and belatedly its custodian testified that he had also dropped it on the way to the production hearing. Nevertheless, it had still been used in its damaged state in connection with the business until the time for production.

The court said the following about the testimony of the custodian of the computer:

> *The Court does not find Mr. Heinzel's testimony about the alleged damage to Packard Bell computer, and its allegedly sporadic performance prior to October 29, 1998, to be entirely credible. Perhaps an air compressor fell on the computer in 1997. However, the Court finds it implausible that a desktop computer would simply "fall off" a desk even once—let alone four to five times—in less than two years. Mr. Heinzel offers no details that would explain how such a bizarre event could have repeatedly occurred. Moreover, the Court finds it implausible that Mr. Heinzel would continue to use the Packard Bell computer for business records into late 1998, as he admits he did, if the computer functioned as sporadically as he claims beginning in 1997. Defendants offer no explanation as to why they did not use one of the other computers to which they had access (Pl. Mem. Ex. F, Heinzel Dep. 12–13) or did not buy a replacement computer.*[20]

---

19. *Illinois Tool Works, Inc. v. MetroMark Products, Ltd.,* "B—The Court's October 23, 1998 Order."

20. *Illinois Tool Works, Inc. v. MetroMark Products, Ltd.* "C—The History of the Packard Bell Computer at Issue."

Even more curiously, when the system's hardware enclosure was opened by the defendants' computer expert, he found the cables connecting the motherboard to both hard and floppy disk drives were completely disconnected.

As in the *Gates* case, the court compared and contrasted the differing interpretations of the contending experts.

> *Plaintiff's expert, Ms. May, and defendants' expert, Mr. Goldberg, agree on many of the objective facts concerning the condition of the Packard Bell computer. Their principal disagreement lies in whether to infer from the physical condition an intent to compromise the integrity of the computer or its contents: Ms. May says yes, and Mr. Goldberg says no. Although the Court agrees with Mr. Goldberg that certain aspects of the computer's physical condition may be innocently explained, the Court concludes that certain aspects of the physical condition of the computer indicate an intent to tamper with it—particularly when considered in the overall context of the defendants' conduct in connection with discovery. There are a number of factors central to the Court's finding.*
>
> *First, the parties agree that the Packard Bell computer was operational as of October 25 and October 26, but was not operational on October 29 at the time of the inspection. . . . Mr. Goldberg later was able to access the information on the hard drive of the Packard Bell computer only by using extraordinary means: he made a copy of the hard drive, attached that copy of a hard drive to another computer, and ran a utility program to correct errors that had "corrupted" certain of the files on the hard drive—including certain invoice files that were responsive to plaintiff's requests (Def. Mem. Ex. D, Goldberg Deposition, at pp. 22-23).*
>
> *Second, there is no dispute that the cable that connected the hard drive to the mother board of the Packard Bell computer, as well as the cable connecting the floppy drive to the mother board, were both completely disconnected. . . . The connections are through interconnecting 40-pin (for the hard drive) and 34-pin (for the floppy drive) sockets which are designed to fit together snugly. The pins all must be in contact in order for each drive of the computer to function. Accordingly to Ms. May, it would be "almost impossible" to remove these cables completely through accidental jostling. Although Mr. Goldberg suggests that it is not difficult to undo the connections, the Court has been provided with a sample of the cable connection and finds that if the connections are properly made, the cables would not be easily dislodged completely from the mother board.*
>
> *Mr. Goldberg suggests that the cables nonetheless could have been dislodged by the computer being dropped if the cables had not been tightly connected when the computer was serviced by Best Buy in 1995, but in his deposition admitted that he was simply stating a "possibility" and has no knowledge as to whether the cables were firmly connected by Best Buy (Citing Def. Mem. Ex. D., Goldberg Dep. 79). Moreover, the Court finds that it is unlikely that both the cable to the floppy disk and the cable to the hard drive would have been improperly secured by the people at Best Buy (indeed, there is no evidence they were both disconnected in the 1995 servicing work). And, the Court further finds that even if the cables had been improperly con-*

nected, it is highly unlikely that neither [sic] cable would have been dislodged if the computer had been dropped four to five times prior to October 29, as Mr. Heinzel has sworn was the case. Mr. Goldberg also opined that the cable could become completely dislodged if it were caught in the computer cover, but admitted that if that happened he would expect the cable to be creased. However, he did not check the cable and could not say that it was creased (Citing Def. Mem. Ex. D, Goldberg Dep. 114, 141-42, 149-50). . . .

> *Defendants imply that this disconnection of the cables might have occurred after the October 29 inspection, when the computer was in the custody of plaintiff's counsel (Defs. Reply Mem. 3). However, defendants do not assert that the behavior of the computer on October 29 was inconsistent with the cables being disconnected at that time. Indeed, Mr. Goldberg's hypotheticals are designed to explain how that disconnection could have occurred accidentally while the computer was in defendants' hands. Defendants have offered no evidence to contradict the conclusion that the cables were disconnected as of the October 29 inspection. (Footnote 4)*

Third, *the Court notes that defendants' expert admits that approximately 80-100 files on the hard drive of the Packard Bell computer were "corrupt[ed]" (Def. Mem. Ex. C, Goldberg Rpt. at 5, subsection j)—and that some of those files contained invoices (Def. Mem. Ex. D, Goldberg Dep. 22–31). Mr. Goldberg opined that this kind of "corruption" of files normally would occur from a power failure while operating the computer or from improperly shutting down the computer (Def. Mem., Ex. C, Goldberg Rpt. at 5-6, subsection j). Mr. Heinzel admits operating the computer on October 25 and 26, and the record shows that he accessed the invoice files at that time. Thus, even Mr. Goldberg's opinion about the possible way in which the computer files were corrupted is consistent with defendants failing to exercise due care to preserve the integrity of the computer files—or worse (a fact that is not altered by Mr. Goldberg's ability later to repair the corrupted files).*

Fourth, *the inside of the computer was free of dust, which indicated that the back had recently been opened and the inside of the computer physically accessed (Pl. Mem. Ex. E, May Dec. P 9). Mr. Heinzel has sworn that he did not remove the computer cover (Def. Mem., Ex. E, Heinzel Aff. PP 14-15), but the only other explanation offered by defendants for the dust free condition of the entire of the computer is that it was cleaned when last worked on by Best Buy in 1995 (Def. Mem., Goldberg Rpt., Ex. C, at 5, subsection f). However, the last servicing by Best Buy preceded the October 1998 inspection by three years, and Mr. Goldberg admitted that he would usually expect to see dust collect inside a computer within a year after servicing (Def. Mem. Ex. D, Goldberg Dep. at 118.*

> *The Court finds that other aspects of the physical condition of the computer— while somewhat suspicious—are insufficient to independently require the conclusion that defendants attempted to tamper with the computer. For example, the fact that one of the two modems was disconnected from the power supply*

is consistent with the computer having been upgraded in 1995 to have a faster modem. The fact that the metal plate on the back is bent and the mother board was skewed, and the base slots were bent away from the metal plate, might be consistent with accidental damage from being hit by the compressor. With respect to the fact that the parallel port was disconnected from the metal plate with screws missing, neither Mr. Goldberg nor Ms. May was willing to say that this required an inference of tampering (Def. Mem. Ex. A, May Dep. 121; Goldberg Dep., Ex. D. 119-20)-and thus neither is the Court.[21] (Footnote 5)

Using the process so meticulously explained by Wedig in *Gates v. Bando*, the computer experts had made a copy of the hard drive, mounted the copy in another computer, and discovered 80–100 corrupted files. The defendant's expert was able to characterize the corruptions as those that might occur if there were a power failure during computer system operation or else improper power-down of the system. He was also able to use a utility to repair the corrupted files and found that some of them contained invoices. He furthermore found that the inside of the computer was free of dust, which indicated that the hardware enclosure of the computer had been recently opened.

The court summarized the defendant's expert testimony as follows:

Mr. Goldberg said that when he first examined the Packard Bell computer on February 28, 1999, he had turned [on] the computer and believed that it had short-circuited because of a popping sound and smell of smoke that he observed (Def. Mem. Ex. D, Goldberg Dep. at 18). Significantly, Mr. Heinzel did not indicate that he heard a popping sound or smelled smoke when he allegedly turned on the computer on the morning of October 29. Similarly, there is no evidence that the Packard Bell computer exhibited those characteristics when it was turned on at the offices of plaintiff's lawyers on October 29 at the time of the inspection.

When Mr. Goldberg was deposed on March 16, 1999, nearly five months after the inspection, defendants for the first time produced more than 800 pages of invoices that had been stored on the hard drive of the Packard Bell computer (Def. Mem. Ex. D, Goldberg Dep., 48, 123). Mr. Goldberg was able to access the information from the Packard Bell hard drive only by making a copy of the hard drive from the Packard Bell computer, attaching it to a different computer, and running a different version of the DOS operating system than was originally on the Packard Bell computer. . . . The invoices contained on the hard drive that were accessed by Mr. Goldberg span a period of five years, going back to 1994, . . . many of which had not been previously produced. This was contrary to the sworn testimony of Mr. Heinzel, who on October 29 testified that (a) the only invoices on the Packard Bell system other than the ones produced that morning for the period January 1997 through September 1998 were invoices from October 1998, and (b) other than October 1998 invoices, there were no

---

21. *Illinois Tool Works, Inc. v. MetroMark Products, Ltd.* "F—The Expert Analysis of the Condition of Packard Bell Computer."

other documents on the Packard Bell computer that had not already been produced in hard copy. . . .

Although Mr. Heinzel had accessed the invoices files on the Packard Bell computer as recently as October 25 and 26, he did not disclose the existence of those additional documents either in his October 29, 1998 or February 18, 1999 deposition sessions. Those additional documents were disclosed and produced only in the face of plaintiff's motion for sanctions. Defendants have not offered any reason for their failure to produce these documents earlier.[22]

All of these findings from the computer experts, and especially the defendants' own expert, were taken by the Court as evidence that the defendants had not complied with the court's order regarding preserving the integrity of the system. Furthermore, invoices were found on the computer system that indicated that the defendants had not delivered requested evidence to the plaintiff as required by the law.

When the Defendants' Expert Is Not the Defendants' Ally

For our purposes, the most interesting thing about this opinion is that the judge's findings can be viewed as resting primarily on the expert testimony from the defendants' computer expert, rather than the expert who testified for the plaintiff. In the course of this litigation, the defendants had also asked for sanctions against the opposing party, in part based on allegations that the plaintiff's expert witness had failed to do adequate testing and investigation to be able to render the opinion she had given in her report and alleged mistakes in connection with other issues contained in her report. Here is how the court summarized the defendants' allegations about the plaintiff's expert's conduct:

Defendants seek sanctions on the ground that plaintiff's motion allegedly is "full of baseless statements, half-truths and deceptions designed to mislead the Court into believing that the defendants had intentionally destroyed important documents." . . . In particular, defendants assert that plaintiff should be sanctioned because its expert, Ms. May, opined that files or programs had been deleted (when in her deposition she admitted that she had not run tests that would allow her to determine whether this had happened), and that a disconnected modem was operational on October 26 (when in her deposition she later said that she could not attest for certain which of the two modems was operational that day).[23]

Based on the opinion, what appears to have happened in this case is that the defendants' attorneys, regardless of what the defendants or their agents or others may

---

22. *Illinois Tool Works, Inc. v. MetroMark Products, Ltd.* "G—Recovery of Information from the Hard Drive."

23. *Illinois Tool Works, Inc. v. MetroMark Products, Ltd.* "II- B—The Court's October 23, 1998 Order."

have done to the computer and the data residing there, hired a competent and thorough expert to reexamine the computer and belatedly to extract whatever data could be found, consistent with the court's order. In other words, the defendants' attorneys and their expert witness found the missing evidence and explained how it came to be missing as best they could. The court found this explanation quite convincing and then promptly decided the case in favor of the plaintiffs, based in large part on the expert testimony of the defendants' own expert.

The court ultimately determined that sanctions were not in order because of any alleged mistakes by the plaintiff's IT expert. There are lessons to be learned from the court's recitation of the respective performances of the two experts. Here is how the court disposed of the allegations against the plaintiff's IT expert witness.

> *With respect to the defendants' claim that plaintiff's expert opined that files or programs had been deleted, Ms. May never squarely asserted in her declaration or her deposition that documents had been deleted. She opined that programs and files "were deleted or ceased to be functional" (Pl. Mem. Ex. E, May Dec. P 6) or were "otherwise corrupted." In fact, Ms. May's assertion that files had "ceased to be functional" or were "otherwise corrupted" is correct, as defendants' expert Mr. Goldberg acknowledged: he admitted that the Packard Bell computer was not operational on October 29, even though it operated on October 25 (Def. Mem. Ex. D, Goldberg Dep. 50-52), and he further admitted that 80 to 100 files—including certain invoice files—were "corrupt" (Goldberg Rpt. at 5). When defendants revealed that they were able to access all of the documents that apparently were on the hard drive of the Packard Bell computer, plaintiff acted responsibly and withdrew its request for the sanction of a default judgment based on spoliation of evidence.*

> *As to the question of the modem, Ms. May's declaration does not clearly say which modem she believed was operational in the few days prior to the October 29 inspection. However, neither modem was functioning on October 29, and Ms. May stated that one modem that was disconnected in a way that "could not have happened accidentally" (Pl. Mem. Ex. E, May Dec. P 8e). Defendants do not dispute that this modem was intentionally disconnected, but have offered an innocent explanation (that the Court has accepted)—that it was disconnected when an upgraded modem was installed.*

> *None of this—or the other criticisms defendants offer of plaintiff's expert declaration—amounts to conduct by plaintiff that is sanctionable. The Court strongly believes that a motion for sanctions should not simply be a reflexive response to a motion for sanctions by one's adversary. The basic premise of the declaration offered by plaintiff's expert is that the failure of the Packard Bell computer to operate properly on October 29, 1999 is attributable to conduct by Mr. Heinzel between October 23 and 29. The Court agrees with that premise. The fact that the Court does not agree with every assertion offered by plaintiff's expert in support of that premise does not make her declaration sanctionable—just as the Court does not find sanctions inde-*

pendently appropriate against defendants merely because the Court disagrees with certain assertions by their expert. . . .

> *Defendants also claim that plaintiff's expert declaration offers only "unsupported speculation" and thus, even if their request for sanctions is denied, the declaration should be totally disregarded. The Court disagrees. The Court has independently reviewed the declarations, reports and testimony of both experts, and the fact findings set forth above reflect the Court's determination as to the weight and credibility to be given to the various opinions and observations they offer.[24] (Footnote 8)*

The Outcome

What was the outcome of all this? The following portion of the court's opinion lays out the reasoning behind the judge's final decision.

> *The sequence of events described above leaves the Court with no doubt that sanctions against defendants are wholly appropriate. The saga concerning the Packard Bell computer is only one episode in a pervasive course of conduct by defendants that can only be described as calculated to frustrate legitimate discovery. Although the parties' briefing has understandably focused principally on issues concerning the Packard Bell computer that was a subject of the Court's October 23, 1998 preservation order, the Court emphasizes that the only reason that there was ever an order entered concerning the Packard Bell computer, and a dispute arose about what happened to the computer thereafter, is because of the defendants' failure to produce invoices that were clearly responsive to plaintiff's document requests.*
>
> *In their initial discovery response, defendants produced only a single invoice. Only when plaintiff continued to press did the defendants—grudgingly, and over a five-month period—finally produce the invoices they should have supplied in the first place:*
>
> *In response to plaintiff's motion to compel on October 23, 1998, defendants produced a literal handful of additional invoices and represented to the Court that they then had "complied fully" with the request (Pl. Mem. Ex. C, 10/23/98 Tr. 2). Defendants made this representation even though, at the time, there were more than 1,000 pages of unproduced invoices that were available on the hard drive [of] the Packard Bell computer. Plainly Mr. Heinzel did not simply "forget" that there were invoices on the hard drive, as he had been inputting those invoices into the hard drive as recently as September and October 1998.*
>
> *On October 29, 1998, when Mr. Heinzel appeared for the Court-ordered deposition as custodian of records, he suddenly was able to produce 332 pages of additional*

---

24. *Illinois Tool Works, Inc. v. MetroMark Products, Ltd.* "II-B-Defendants' Counter-Motion for Sanctions."

invoices from January 1997 through September 1998 (Pl. Mem. Ex. F, Heinzel Dep. 6–8), despite his counsel representing on October 23 that all the documents had been produced. At that deposition, Mr. Heinzel then testified on oath that the only additional invoices were from October 1998, and that there were no other documents on the hard drive of the Packard Bell computer that had not already been produced in hard copy. . . .

However, the court found that the sworn testimony by Mr. Heinzel also was less than credible. Nearly five months later, in March 1999, defendants produced an additional 800 pages of invoices obtained from the hard drive of the Packard Bell computer, many of which predated January 1997 and which had not previously been produced in any form. Again, it is implausible that Mr. Heinzel could have simply "forgotten" about these pre-1997 invoices when he testified on October 29 that nothing of that kind was on the Packard Bell computer, when just a few days prior to that deposition he had accessed the invoices files on the Packard Bell computer.

This additional group of 800 plus invoices was not produced by defendants until late March 1999, even though the Packard Bell computer had been returned to the defendants in late January or early February and defendants' expert had accessed the hard drive and the documents on it several weeks earlier.[25]

The Court next considered the application of Rule 37 and sanctions regarding the Court's order. Following that discussion, the opinion continues.

But there has been more than "mere inadvertence or negligence." Having reviewed the evidence carefully, the Court is left with the firm conviction that there was a purposeful effort to prevent plaintiff from obtaining the information from the Packard Bell computer. This is not a conclusion that the Court reaches lightly, but one that the Court felt was compelled by clear and convincing evidence, based on all of the expert testimony and the credibility of both experts and the lay witnesses about the handling of the data and the computers as evidence. For example:

Defendants' course of conduct demonstrates that they wished to avoid producing the invoices. Had defendants wished to make full disclosure, even after the Court's October 23, 1998 Order, defendants could have printed all of the invoices from the hard drive of the Packard Bell computer when Mr. Heinzel accessed them on October 25 and 26. Not only did defendants fail to do so, but in two deposition sessions Mr. Heinzel provided misinformation about what invoices in fact were on the hard drive.

The fact that both cables were completely dislodged from the hard drive and the disk drive, is simply not consistent with accidental conduct. Mr. Goldberg testified that if the internal cables had not been securely seated in the drives that an accidental dropping could dislodge them. But it asks too much to accept that (a) both of the internal cables were improperly connected in 1995, that (b) those internal cables did not become completely disconnected at any time when, according to Mr. Heinzel's

---

25. *Illinois Tool Works, Inc. v. MetroMark Products, Ltd.* "II-A—Plaintiff's Request for Sanctions."

testimony, the computer was hit by a compressor and knocked off his desk four to five times in the intervening three years, but (c) only became completely dislodged when Mr. Heinzel supposedly dropped the computer on his way to the offices of plaintiff's lawyer on October 29. Indeed, it asks too much to credit Mr. Heinzel's affidavit statement that he was so careless as to drop a computer he was bringing to Court-ordered inspection: particularly when Mr. Heinzel did not disclose that "accident" in his deposition testimony or in his conversations on the morning of the inspection, did not unequivocally disclose it to his own expert, and no one else witnessed that alleged occurrence.

Likewise, the absence of dust inside the computer further supports the finding that plaintiff tampered with the computer. Mr. Goldberg testified that he would normally expect dust within the computer within the space of a year, but this computer had not been serviced for some three years.

In short, the disconnection of the cables and the relatively dust free state of the interior of the computer are best explained as attempts to frustrate the ability to obtain information from the computer. This conclusion is further supported by defendants' overall stonewalling of information that existed on the hard drive of the computer, and Mr. Heinzel's shifting and evasive testimony on key points.[26]

Ultimately, the court found that the plaintiff's motion for sanctions should be granted and the defendants' cross-motion for sanctions denied. As is authorized by Rule 37(a)(4) and Rule 37(b)(2), the court imposed these sanctions against the defendants directly.

What Experts Can Learn from Court Opinions

In both *Gates v. Bando* and *Illinois Tool Works v. MetroMark*, the complex interactions between the computer experts and the judges as interpreters of presumptions and as fact finders are apparent. It is obvious in both cases that the courts understood what could and could not be reasonably construed from the computer-related evidence. Ultimately, the two judges found a way to determine what the most reliable evidence was in order to decide the respective cases.

These decisions demonstrate the variations in process that judges and jurors go through in weighing the qualifications and the testimony of the opposing experts. As you reflect on these cases, it is not so important that you decide which of the competing experts had the best day in court as it is for you to think through the processes that the fact finders used to understand what the evidence in the case was, based on all the testimony, including the testimony of the expert witnesses.

A critical point to remember if you decide to put yourself in the shoes of these respective experts is that your role as an expert is to assist the fact finder (the judge in

---

26. *Illinois Tool Works, Inc. v. MetroMark Products, Ltd.* "II-A—Plaintiff's Request for Sanctions," continued.

these cases) and that therefore your findings may or may not ultimately help the party on whose behalf you are appearing, depending on how all the evidence is viewed in the final analysis. Therefore, it is wise to make sure that the party and the attorney who have hired you to examine all the evidence and to render your opinion fully understand that your testimony may well be part of the basis for a decision in the case against the party who is paying your bills.

With this chapter and those that have gone before it, we've given you an idea of the *whos, whats,* and *whys* of expert witnesses. Now it's time to turn our attention to the hows, specifically how you can become a more effective witness. In the following chapters, we'll talk about the different aspects of effectively communicating with fact finders in a manner that enhances their decision-making abilities. We'll also provide you with exercises and resources to apply in establishing your own style and honing your own communication techniques.

The Role of
Visual Exhibits
in Expert Testimony

Thinking in Pictures: Sage Advice from the Pros

If asked to assert fundamental truths about expert testimony, experienced expert witnesses would likely put forth a range of beliefs synthesized from the lessons they have learned during their tenure in the litigation business. However, the following would surely be a common theme: the expert's perceived value to the client and the court is directly dependent on his or her ability to communicate expert opinions to the fact finders accurately, clearly, and in terms that are meaningful to them.

This point has not gone unnoticed in the legal community, and a sizable industry has evolved to service the needs for litigation support. In particular, several organizations specialize in the design and development of courtroom exhibits. In our research into this area, we found the litigation exhibit experts at The Focal Point, LLC (*http://www.thefocalpoint.com*), in Oakland, California. These experts spoke at length with us about their experiences and recommendations for the preparation of graphics for use by technical expert witnesses. They were willing to share what they have found to be the best methods for enhancing the effectiveness of expert witnesses charged with explaining key IT issues involved in litigation. Many of the suggestions offered within this chapter are based on their experiences in preparing expert witnesses and their trial attorneys to educate judges and jurors. With his and the firm's blessings, Christopher Ritter, an attorney and a partner with The Focal Point, agreed to discuss some of these ideas with us while he is preparing a book of his own.

The lessons in this chapter are based largely on the success of graphic designers, simulation architects, and trial consultants who work primarily with attorneys and their litigation assistants preparing for trial. This chapter suggests that lawyers and their litigation teams can benefit even more from the creative input of their technical experts, once those experts have become conversant with the general principles of graphic design. We believe that the ability of technical experts to help devise and use visual exhibits, including animations and simulations, is directly proportional to their ability to communicate complex technical concepts and processes to both judges and jurors in reports and testimony. Based on the experience of professionals such as Ritter and the staff at The Focal Point, we also believe that forensic experts need to become familiar with the ways that these images are used in modern trials to assist in presenting highly technical evidence.

We are not suggesting that expert witnesses need to learn all about the technical aspects of graphic design and production of good graphic exhibits. Rather, we are passing on the experiences of experts who have worked with highly skilled graphic design and production professionals and have learned the value of incorporating these tools and techniques into effective expert testimony. It will, however, be helpful for expert witnesses and the lawyers working with them to understand a little of the philosophy behind what graphics professionals and litigation exhibit consultants are trying to accomplish with these images.

The Basic Philosophy: Keep It Simple and Honest

The philosophy behind producing effective graphics for experts is to keep it simple and honest (KISH), which ought not to be confused with KISS, an acronym familiar to nearly everyone who has ever felt stupid about making something simple seem confusing. Christopher Ritter describes his own philosophy, developed over years of trying cases before joining the firm, in the following way:

> The first and foremost goal of any good graphics person is to make sure that the basic concepts are communicated to a target audience in as simple and honest a manner as possible. Simplicity without honesty is worthless and honesty without simplicity is equally useless.[1]

Ritter suggests an analogy that he has found on altars in Buddhist temples in Japan. Here, the statue of the Buddha sits between two other statues. On one side is a statue representing compassion. On the other side is a statue representing knowledge. The fact that the Buddha sits exactly midpoint between the two is intended to show that knowledge without compassion and compassion without knowledge are ineffective.

---

1. Ritter, Christopher. Personal communication, November 2001.

When jurors believe that the graphic is simple and honest, they will latch on to it, and in turn, they will latch on to the witness, party, or story of the case that makes use of this exhibit. Simplicity and honesty are the two standards that the expert should apply in setting up his direct testimony. When there is a need to underscore the technical and complex, many lawyers and experts who have worked with The Focal Point have learned through experience that it is often best to save it for cross-examination, rather than attempting to lay it all on in the direct examination. In cross-examination the expert can talk about all the detailed differences, distinctions, studies, etc. Waiting until then also can deter the other lawyer from attempting an aggressive or confusing cross-examination of the expert because the expert will control the technical explanation on cross. These decisions are examples of the kind of strategic thinking that lawyers are constantly doing, and the decisions can be aided immensely when, in addition to brief or detailed testimony from the expert, you have helpful graphics to make both simple and complex points visually arresting.

Of course, simple and honest exhibits still must pack in the essential message of the witness on direct examination. A good opposing attorney will simply pass on cross-examination, if he believes that the witness did not hurt his case on direct examination, or will hurt the case even more on cross. Beyond strategic considerations as to controlling cross-examination, with an effective presentation on direct, most of the jurors will have already accepted or rejected the expert's testimony. They are not going to change their mind just because the opposing counsel makes the expert go into brain-numbing technical explanations during cross-examination. In other words, if the expert and his attorney have done their jobs on direct, cross is not usually going to hurt the effectiveness and credibility of the expert—obviously there are exceptions, but this is a very broad general rule that seems to hold more often than not.[2]

Establishing Credibility by Teaching the Basics

It is also very helpful for experts who will be using these images to understand the various techniques the graphics person can and does use in order to make it easier for jurors to learn what the expert is attempting to explain. This understanding can help experts incorporate the images into their testimony. It can also assist lawyers in incorporating the images into their presentations of expert witnesses.

If the jurors are going to be able to understand anything about technical testimony, it will be the basics. This is also where the jurors can find some basis on which to judge an expert's testimony and whether to rely on his or her expertise to explain the things they don't comprehend. Hence, experts need to spend an appropriate amount of time in their testimony and through their exhibits establishing their credibility by teaching the basics.

---

2. Ritter, Christopher. Personal communication, November 2001.

To be effective, any graphic tool that you present to jurors must be user-friendly. If the jurors cannot understand the tool, you have wasted your time (and theirs). You can make visual tools user-friendly if you are careful to do four things.

1. **First, be succinct and use only everyday, real-world language.**
   This is not advocating that you "dumb down" your presentation. Remember, learning takes place in two stages: the jurors must first see the connection between familiar and unfamiliar; once this happens, the jurors can begin to process more complex facts. Certainly, whenever you are creating the core of the testimony, and as often as possible when you are adding to it, keep your concepts and the terms that advance them simple. You had the luxury of having years to understand the technicalities involved in your field and probably months to understand the important parts of the story of this case. The jurors do not have that privilege. They need all the help they can get.

2. **Find analogies in the real world that illustrate the principles you're advancing.**
   Creating analogies to the real world is a second place where you can actually teach and in so doing build credibility with the jurors. The best jurors are those who have some ammunition to argue your points for you in their deliberations with the rest of the jurors. Your well-developed analogy gives jurors something memorable they can use to argue the same or similar points during deliberations. Graphics that introduce visual analogies that can be used to follow the testimony are crucial when it comes time for the jurors to deliberate.

3. **Answer the question, "Compared to what?"**
   The answer to this question always provides some perspective or scale that jurors need. Later in this chapter, we present a detailed description of this technique to demonstrate how this works through the use of graphics in a case involving alleged radiation injuries and the amounts of exposure that should be expected to cause serious injury.

4. **Use graphics to add value.**
   After handling exhibits for trial lawyers in over a thousand cases during the past decade, the professionals at The Focal Point have found that there is an unexpectedly large value added to the careful planning and development of effective trial graphics. Beyond the value of the exhibits themselves, the process of illustrating key aspects of your case forces you to organize your presentation in a more coherent and persuasive manner. The final product (that is, the trial graphic itself) makes you more effective in litigation in many ways. This is true regardless of whether the graphic is "spontaneously" sketched on a whiteboard or displayed as a professionally prepared, computer-generated illustration projected on a 52-inch state-of-the-art flat-screen video monitor.

Another lesson that professional graphic designers find themselves teaching trial attorneys over and over also holds for at least the academically inclined technical expert. Based on their experiences in the classroom, experts may tend to think of the graphics shown in a lecture as simple aids to learning the subject discussed by the professor and covered by the students in their reading assignments. It is most likely that these experts think of their lectures and books (and not the visual aids) as the substance that will become facts for the student, recalled on the exam, and returned to in the next semester at another level of instruction. In court, however, the visual displays represent the substance of the expert's verbal contribution and the visual aids may be the things jurors remember most as they deliberate. Though the jurors may also remember the expert's words, they may do so more easily in association with the images presented to illustrate those words.

Turning Students into Teachers and Advocates

The most experienced and successful expert witnesses and trial attorneys come to appreciate that the most important rituals of persuasion in a trial often take place in the jury room, as vividly conveyed by the 1957 film *Twelve Angry Men*. Just as Henry Fonda's character in that film made use of a simple floor plan of the murder scene to gather the disintegrating jurors back into a group to continue their deliberations, so a contemporary juror will focus on an effective graphic introduced into evidence and use it to continue the process of persuasion that was begun by the expert's testimony. Legal scholars call these kinds of jurors "active jurors," and trial advocates refer to them as their "advocates in the jury room."

One of the reasons that *Twelve Angry Men* is so effective is that the story leads the audience to believe that the trial attorneys (or at least the defense attorney) failed to persuade the jury of much of anything during the presentation of evidence and that there is a strong circumstantial case against the defendant. The movie uses these premises to make Fonda the advocate for testing all the evidence in deliberations and allows the jurors to appear heroic in their independent review. The jurors come to a decision by first setting aside their preconceptions about the guilt of the defendant and then examining and relying on the evidence to guide their verdict.

With expert testimony it is probably safe to assume that even the most attentive and intelligent jurors may clearly understand only a small percentage of what the expert says. Consequently, the lawyer and the expert need to maximize the impact this limited testimony will have on the jurors. In the academic world the lecturer, with his or her greater level of expertise, gets to evaluate and grade those who listen, that is, the students. In trial, this scenario is turned on its head. Here the group with the least amount of specific information judges the believability of the more experienced person who does the testifying.

Thinking about Highly Complex Technical Processes as Pictures

Because good graphics are in essence pictures, they are pound for pound far richer in information than words or gestures. This is not to suggest that demeanor and gestures when used appropriately during testimony are not powerful communicators. Those components will be discussed in Chapter 11. But after all the evidence is in and the jury retires, images can also become icons for key portions of the story that the expert witness and the trial lawyer were attempting to tell. Seen in this way, good graphics can serve as visual stories, riddles, maps, memories, or recordings, but they can also become powerful rhetorical tools in the hands of a juror and ultimately in the minds of all the jurors. Thus, graphics complete the persuasion and commitment process that the expert who introduced the image began through his or her testimony.

We have already referenced Edward Tufte's classic works on graphic design and the use of visual evidence to present information and persuade viewers, in his analysis of Dr. John Snow's map-based explanation of the cholera outbreak in nineteenth-century London (see Chapter 8). If you are interested in this subject, you should sample some of the other fascinating books about how images tell stories for use in various rituals:

- *Reading Pictures: A History of Love and Hate*, by Alberto Manguel (New York: Random House, 2001)
- *The Power of Images: Studies in the History and Theory of Response*, by David Freedberg (Chicago: University of Chicago, 1989)
- *Good Looking: Essays on the Virtue of Images*, by Barbara Maria Stafford (Cambridge, MA: MIT Press, 1996)
- *The Object Stares Back: On the Nature of Seeing*, by James Elkins (New York: Simon and Schuster, 1996)

Introducing the Expert with Graphics in the Opening Statement

David M. Malone, in his trial advocacy training seminars and in the guide book he wrote with Paul Zwier, *Effective Expert Testimony*,[3] suggests that jurors often prejudge

---

3. Malone, David M, and Paul J. Zwier. *Effective Expert Testimony*. Notre Dame, IN: National Institute of Trial Advocacy, 2000.

the performances of experts in court by the way they are introduced by their respective attorneys. Unfortunately for both the attorneys and their experts, many jurors have reported that they began the trial by expecting to be bored silly by the experts, based on the way the lawyers described them. It may not be enough to attempt to frame the expert's presentation as an explanation by an accomplished teacher or scientist. As a first impression, most people tend to recall their best teachers when they decide what to expect from an expert with academic qualifications. But the recollections of the bad teachers jurors may have had, as well as their possible general dislike of boring academicians and scientists, can work to the detriment of the expert who is bound to classroom experience. A rigidly academic approach can sometimes make it difficult to persuade jurors with memories of bad teachers to give the expert the benefit of the doubt when he or she actually takes the stand to testify. This is merely to say that any metaphor for understanding expert testimony has its limits and cannot be slavishly followed by the practitioner.

One method for attempting to preempt or counteract these negative impressions and preconceptions about the expert witness is to use dramatic visuals in the opening statement when the lawyer first introduces the expert.

When you are thinking about your performance at trial as an expert witness, think about everything you are going to do from the point of view of a juror. A typical juror, while wanting to do the right thing, probably has another concern—he or she wants to avoid being bored. You may be a natural entertainer, or you may think of yourself as basically an introvert, after years of cloistered study or solitary field work. Some terrific experts may have spent a lifetime primarily researching, writing, and publishing. Others may have spent a career speaking in public. Regardless, when it comes to playing the role of witness, no expert can ignore the fact that he is performing for a very special audience whose individual members may have very different expectations. Like any other audience, jurors want respect. In particular, they want to feel as if the expert is prepared to proceed in a carefully orchestrated way that will take neither their attention nor their time for granted.

The Benefits of Using Graphics in the Opening Statement

One way to stimulate interest in what you have to say is to make sure (whenever it is allowed by the judge) that the attorney shows an arresting graphic when he or she introduces you during the opening statement. This can be a very basic bullet summary with or without much in the way of nonverbal graphics. For example, it can consist primarily of the highlights or headlines of your experience and expertise. Then, other equally interesting graphics should be shown and explained by you as you begin your testimony. Most jurors report that they are better able to follow complicated and highly technical expert testimony if they can see the processes and important concepts illustrated visually, at least in outline form, while the expert is explaining them. But first the jurors need a reason to listen to the expert. Thus, it makes sense to build expectations from the beginning rather than running the risk of having to overcome negative preconceptions later.

Opening Graphics Allow the Lawyer to Introduce the Expert as Part of the Big Picture

The opening statement is one of the very few times when the lawyer gets to stand up and tell the story of the case. This is the first opportunity for the attorney to talk directly to the jurors and give them an explanation without having to go through a witness. The rules of examination are question, answer, question, answer. While there is a very good reason for this, it is not the best way to introduce a topic to people, especially a complex or highly technical topic. In other words, using a graphic at the outset allows the lawyer to show the jurors a trailer for the entire movie of the case, not limiting them to viewing the story frame by frame.

Good Graphics Prepare the Jury Favorably for the Expert Presentation

If done well in the context of an opening statement, the trial graphics emphasize the teacher in the expert. This same aspect of teacher should come across when the expert uses the graphics later in the trial. Bear in mind that the use of the analogy of the teacher is not to suggest that the expert has no motive—he or she is, after all, paid by one of the parties to the lawsuit to prepare for and present testimony relevant to the case. So of course there is a motive: the teacher wants to persuade. All teachers want to persuade, just as all lawyers want to persuade. The expert as teacher must communicate just like any other witness, but because you, as the expert, can render your opinion, the letter and the spirit of the rules require that it be your facts, methods, and experiences that persuade the fact finder. Another difference in the kind of persuasion taking place during the trial testimony of experts is that most people listen to and trust both experts and teachers more than they do lawyers. So anything that lets you start teaching from the very beginning is almost by definition very important.

Good Graphics Indicate Preparation for and Respect for the Fact Finders

If you use effective visual aids throughout the presentation, the jurors (or at least some of them) will understand that you have taken the time to organize your work so that it is simple to follow during the actual testimony. These same jurors will see that you are showing a certain kind of respect by constructing and making available some graphic learning tools for the jurors to use. Jurors who are paying attention can see how you demonstrate these graphics and illustrate the various concepts as they are identified. Attentive jurors can then review the graphics and the facts they represent as you connect the concepts; then the jurors can confirm these concepts and the pattern of proof as you reach your conclusion. Equally important and greatly appreciated is the opportunity for jurors to have these visual aids available as you illustrate your summation and also in their deliberations to reconsider all the evidence and arguments in the case.

Think once again about the rule of evidence that allows experts (unlike any other kinds of witnesses) to give their opinions. To do this well, effective experts must also be concerned about having good graphics to help jurors understand complex concepts and processes. Just being allowed to render an opinion is not going to help the situation if the fact finders are completely lost. This is a risk, given that they must follow the nuances of the processes you are describing or the methods you used to come to your conclusions. Graphics enable the jurors to follow your entire presentation. Even though they may not be able to understand all of the science and technology you are describing, they will be able to see the logic of your method and why it has led you, as an expert, to the conclusion you reached. Without clear visuals to help the fact finders follow the trail, you are asking the jurors to take a greater leap of faith than necessary. The visual trail allows the jurors to follow a difficult reasoning process in a simplified way. Furthermore, it allows you to demonstrate that you prepared for your presentation to this audience rather than relying solely on your reputation as an expert to carry the day.

Many experts may not fully appreciate the process of dealing with prejudice on the part of a juror. In particular, they may be oblivious to the process of overturning a juror's bias for or against the advertised expertise of a particular expert witness. Both of these blind spots follow from a failure on the part of an expert to fully appreciate how he or she will be judged by the fact finder.

Expert witnesses also need to understand that a trial is nothing like the process of academic peer review. If anything, it is the direct opposite of peer review (which is a process that will often need to be explained to both judge and jurors as a part of the qualifying round in a *Daubert* challenge). A trial is a review by a group of people who were deliberately chosen for a variety of reasons, including the fact that they know less about the expert's specialty than he or she does. Because of this counterintuitive context, the process of creating an exhibit for an expert must seek to create an illustration that speaks to those who know next to nothing about the subject.

The most effective experts are those who take advantage of the simplifying skills of both a good lawyer and a good graphic artist, enlisting their help in reviewing the expert's testimony and pointing out what is clear and what is not.

Graphics Speak to Both the Judge and the Jury

As outlined in Chapter 8, it is also becoming increasingly important to attempt to educate the judge as early in the process as possible, perhaps even before the attorney has determined whether or not to challenge the opposing expert's opinions. Preparing effective graphics for the court is now an important part of preparing for trial, whether or not the court will ultimately entertain any *Daubert* challenge against you and your evidence. This means that clear and convincing graphics may become an even more important tool to be used within the formal Rule 26 report itself and at your deposition. Good graphics can more effectively convey the meaning of the report to a judge, who is considering whether to grant a hearing on a *Daubert* challenge motion. If your opponents mount such a challenge and if the judge decides to consider your qualifications and the competence of your expert opinion, the judge's decision may be based in large part on what is in that report and in your discovery deposition.

Designing Defensive Visual Exhibits

The expert may also be called on to assist the attorney in devising effective graphic exhibits to counter the opposing expert's opinions, regardless of whether or not the attorney believes that the exhibits will be admitted into evidence. The rules of evidence and advocacy allow counsel to impeach witnesses by using exhibits that are being offered only to impeach the previous testimony of that witness, with no intent to introduce the exhibit as substantive evidence. Similarly, graphic exhibits may be used to refresh the recollection of a conveniently forgetful witness and then be used again in closing argument by the attorney. The graphic can be used at that time to remind the jurors what it took to make the opposing expert admit that he had previously held another opinion that was helpful to the side with the pictures.

Because so much about the trial and the presentation of experts has to do with the different burdens of the opposing parties, we need to say a word about the burden that an attorney has to carry in order to introduce important visual aids such as summary charts, complex graphs, and much more sophisticated exhibits such as animations, films, and computer simulations. The way the courts generally handle the assignment of burdens and exercise their discretion as to whether or not the respective parties have fulfilled their burdens can be illustrated with an example.

Let's say the plaintiff wants to show an animation of a complex process, such as the recreation of an accident scene. Assume that this animation does not rely on some sophisticated proprietary software application (which could be called into question by the other side as too unreliable to be admitted into evidence). Let's also assume that the animation itself passes muster as an exhibit. For purposes of this example, this simply means that the animation is found to be sufficiently reliable to be shown to the jury during cross-examination. Furthermore, its persuasiveness as a recreation of an accident scene is due not to its ability to prejudice the fact finder against the other side but to its ability to illustrate what the side offering the animation maintains happened. Assume that the expert uses the off-the-shelf software application frequently and that it is subject to advance discovery and available for independent use and testing by the defendant. Then the plaintiff should be able to offer the computer-generated exhibit, if the expert can also say that he or she actually prepared the animation or consulted with a qualified graphic artist who can independently testify as to the steps taken in preparing the clip.

The expert will also need to be able to testify to other points. First, he or she needs to testify that the animation is a fair and accurate presentation of the results of the application's treatment of the data that the expert has used to analyze the problem and recreate the event. Then the expert needs to testify how the clip helps explain his or her expert testimony and gives the jurors a better understanding about how the accident happened under those facts reasonably assumed by the expert.

All of this foundation testimony may still only allow the jurors to view the animation as illustrative evidence during the witness's testimony. This is up to the judge, whose exercise of discretion is pretty much absolute. The effect of limiting the animation to illustrative evidence can be significant, depending on the nature of the case. Only if the animation is admitted as a substantive demonstration (that is, admitted by the court as evidence for all purposes in the case) can it be used by the jurors during deliberations.

Quite often, exhibits are agreed to by the parties or ruled on by the court without serious challenge. But the example above demonstrates the typical kinds of foundational criteria that are applied in order for the court to allow the expert to use something like an accident recreation animation in direct testimony, where the exhibit is subject to challenge and has not previously been admitted. The court also uses the same types of criteria to ultimately rule on whether the exhibit goes to the jury. It is helpful for the expert to think of this ritual of laying the foundation for a graphic in the same way that more complex, computer-generated exhibits are handled. A burden is initially placed on the offering party in order to present the visual aid during the expert's testimony. If all of this were done properly, most courts would at least allow the animation to be used for demonstrative purposes. The court would permit use of the animation under the theory that the illustration helps lay jurors understand the expert testimony being presented. Increasingly these complex computer-generated exhibits are being admitted, and often each side comes prepared with its own video or animated reenactment.

Follies with Visual Aids Can Be Disastrous

If, on the other hand, the party opposing the admission of a particular exhibit has its own expert who can demonstrate that some or all of the foundation testimony is sufficiently shaky or that the animation is not a reliable rendition of the foundational facts and concepts (or is negligently or even intentionally misleading), the animation may be precluded from admittance based on the defendant's challenge. Such a situation arose in the Microsoft antitrust case (see Chapter 2) when the defendant attempted to introduce a film purported to be a demonstration of the operation of an application or combination of applications at issue in the litigation. On cross-examination, it turned out that the film shown to the court had some serious problems, including images that did not appear to correspond with the defendant's foundational testimony of how the film was created.

Some journalists and legal commentators who followed the Microsoft trial felt so strongly about this single incident in a rather lengthy trial that they described it as a critical moment. Legal reporter Kate Marquess wrote that the video purported to show a computer running Microsoft Windows 98 both before and after Internet Explorer was removed from the operating system:

> In one section, a desktop icon disappears and then reappears on the computer screen. [Government counsel] Boies replayed the section slowly, pausing the tape at key points, to reveal that more than one machine was used for the demonstration. Microsoft's expert witness couldn't explain what happened.
>
> The tape was intended to bolster Microsoft's defense—that Windows 98 suffered from the removal of Internet Explorer—against the government's claims that bundling the products was anti-competitive. Instead, the video crushed the defense's credibility.
>
> Despite the Microsoft follies, many litigators insist videotape demonstrations are effective. But others say nothing convinces like a live demo of the technology in question."[4]

Because of these problems that can escape the notice of the creators of an exhibit, any attempt to introduce the visual demonstration must be carefully reviewed by the expert and the trial team attorneys. This care is needed in order to avoid creating an opportunity for a serious adverse impact on the credibility of the expert called to testify. Because so much may be riding on these computer-generated exhibits in the framing of the overall presentation of the testimony of a key expert, or in the presentation of the case by the attorneys, any potential adverse impact must be carefully scrutinized and guarded against. The impact can extend not only to the expert's credibility about the visual aid but also to the competence and credibility of the expert's testimony in general, and even to the credibility of the entire case presented by counsel.

---

4. Marquess, Kate. (ABA Network.) Accessed January 4, 2001, at *http://www.abanet.org/journal/jan01/fnet.html.*

The point here is that the burden is first on the party creating and offering the visual evidence. That party must lay a proper foundation that is not subject to successful impeachment and that assures the court that the expert's visual exhibit will be helpful to the jury and not overly prejudicial to the defendant. If the plaintiff succeeds in laying the proper foundation, the burden then shifts to the defendant to persuade the court otherwise. If the defendant cannot carry that burden, then the visual exhibit will at least be allowed for illustrative purposes and may end up being admitted by the court as substantive demonstrative evidence.

Courts Have Concerns about Computer-Generated Evidence

Increased use of computer-generated evidence such as simulations and animations has proved at least as troublesome as the early use of photographs proved to be in the nineteenth century. Courts still worry a great deal that these electronic demonstrations are exceptionally persuasive and also that they are susceptible to undetectable manipulation and alteration. The increased use of these electronic visual exhibits also tends to remove the expert from the traditional reach of verbal cross-examination. In a number of new ways, experts who are pressed during cross-examination are able to fall back on these powerful visual demonstrations to help them explain concepts and processes that they may not be as eloquent or persuasive at explaining with their words alone. In the end, assuming that the reliability of these computer-generated demonstrations can be shown by their proponents, it may turn out that both sides will be relegated to the increased use of competing computer-generated visual aids simply because they are more effective in explaining highly technical processes.

If indeed these new kinds of visual exhibits do help the jurors understand case issues, as appears likely, the techniques will be fully embraced by experts and attorneys alike. But this is still fairly new territory, and the continued resistance (perhaps not without good reason) to the demise of the more extensive if not exclusive use of verbal cross-examination techniques to attack the presentation of experts can be expected to continue. The trend now appears to be to allow into evidence more of these films, animations, and computer simulations, just as courts grudgingly learned to do with the highly suspicious images produced by the new technology of photography. There are some remarkable similarities to the halting acceptance of computer-generated evidence and photographs, which were only fully accepted after a lengthy initial period of allowing them to be used only for illustrative—but not substantive—evidentiary purposes.

Many of these new technologies lend themselves to being presented through trial graphics. All of these presentation techniques become apparent if you learn to see trial graphics not only as an end product but also as a process.

The Radiation Case Study from
The Focal Point Archives

Christopher Ritter tells the following story of the creation of one memorable exhibit for a litigation team that had a difficult problem. The team needed to convey a difficult technical point clearly and with the impact that the importance of the technical information deserved.

> You represent a nuclear power plant that has been accused of exposing nearby residents to small amounts of radiation. Specifically, people living near the plant, which is located in northern California (an area not overly sympathetic to nuclear power), allege that they are being exposed to an additional millirem of radiation per year. Your experts have convinced you that there is nothing harmful about the plant and that it poses no health problems to any one.
>
> Radiation sounds scary—justifiably so. You need to convince a jury of twelve that, if it exists, this amount of radiation (an extra millirem per year) poses no health problem to any of them. Ideally, you will find a way to let them know that, in everyday lives, people constantly and voluntarily expose themselves to this additional level of radiation, with no resulting harm.
>
> You need to come up with user-friendly data that (1) explains the concept succinctly in everyday language; (2) allows the jurors to answer the question, "Compared to what?"; (3) is memorable; and (4) hopefully, creates some "buzz" when you use it.
>
> You interview your radiation expert and ask him to tell you what it means to be exposed to one millirem of radiation.
>
> "No problem," he replies, "It's easy. I will just tell the jury that a millirem is one thousandth of the dosage of an ionizing radiation that will cause the same biological effect as one roentgen of X-ray or gamma-ray dosage."
>
> At this point, you should be afraid, very afraid. Your expert's proposed explanation tells your potential jurors nothing—absolutely nothing. Actually, it tells them worse than nothing. It tells them that you don't care enough to take the time to teach them or to give them information that they can understand.
>
> So, you keep probing with your expert. Put on a "beginner's mind" and start asking questions, listen carefully to the answers, and keep asking and listening until you know you have it. Is a millirem a lot or little? Even without the power plant, how long would it take for an individual to be exposed to a millirem of radiation? Would the expert be afraid of getting exposed to an additional millirem of radiation each year?
>
> Your expert starts giving you more useful information. He tells you that we are surrounded by virtually limitless sources of natural radiation (the sun, rocks, etc.). In fact, in a given year, an average person is exposed to 360 millirems of "background radiation" from these natural sources. This radiation is so common that the Nuclear Regulatory Commission deems exposures of 10 millirems at one time to be insignificant and not to be a threat to anyone's health.

These facts are better. With these facts you know that 1 millirem is 1/360th of what we get naturally each year. It is an amount approximately equal to what an average person gets in a single day. You also know that it is 1/10th of what the United States government deems to be an acceptable one-time dose. With this information you can provide the graphic depicted in Figure 10-1.

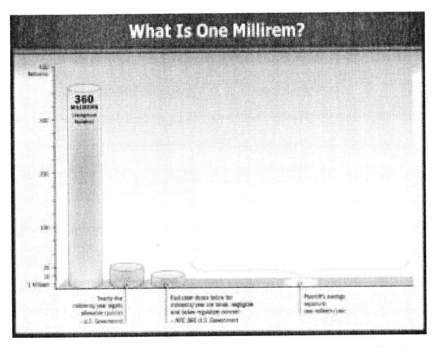

Figure 10-1. *Radiation example graphic, version 1. The first in the series of graphics demonstrating the effect of a radiation leak. (The Focal Point, LLC.)*

This graphic is good. It is better than mentioning roentgens of X-ray and gamma ray dosages—information that is helpful, but it does not really create a buzz. And, if there is any fact in this case that requires a buzz, this is one. You push your expert witness for more concrete examples of how we voluntarily expose ourselves to a millirem of radiation in our everyday life. You ask your expert when was the last time he voluntarily exposed himself to an additional millirem of radiation.

Your hard work, your pursuit of the facts with a beginner's mind pays off. It turns out that if you take an airplane trip from Sacramento (the nearest large town to where this case is venued) to Denver (a two-hour flight), you will be exposed to an additional millirem of radiation because there is more radiation at the altitudes that planes fly than on the atmosphere-sheltered ground. So you illustrate this point and add it to your trial graphic (Figure 10-2).

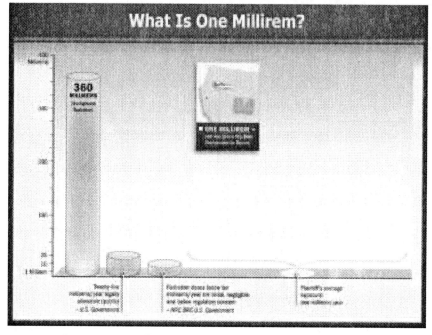

Figure 10-2. *Radiation example graphic, version 2. Adding a data reference point to the graphic. (The Focal Point, LLC.)*

You also find out that when people go up into the mountains to go skiing for a weekend, they expose themselves to an additional millirem of radiation; again, this is from the increased levels of radiation at higher altitudes. You know your jury can relate to this fact. Because they live in northern California, many of your jurors spend much of the winter either going or wanting to go up to Lake Tahoe to ski for the weekend. In fact, your jurors are so eager to do so that they often spend hours in bumper-to-bumper traffic just to get the opportunity to escape to nature and expose themselves to that additional millirem of radiation on the slopes. So you illustrate this point and add it to your graphic (Figure 10-3).

You also learn that smoking one cigarette in your lifetime exposes you to an additional millirem of radiation. If you live in a stone house for 6 days rather than in a wooden one, you get an additional millirem of radiation. You illustrate these points and add them to your trial graphic (Figure 10-4).

By now the jury understands what a millirem is. Your evidence is beginning to buzz. Then you offer the final point, the point that not only causes the jury to lean forward but also causes most of them to laugh—a sure sign that you have made your point. It turns out that if your significant other is like mine, he/she eats a lot of bananas. Bananas contain potassium, which is why my wife eats them. Potassium has various isotopes—at least one of which is slightly radioactive. People who eat bananas will eventually emit very low levels of these radioactive isotopes. And you know what? After six months of sleeping next to my wife, she will have emitted and

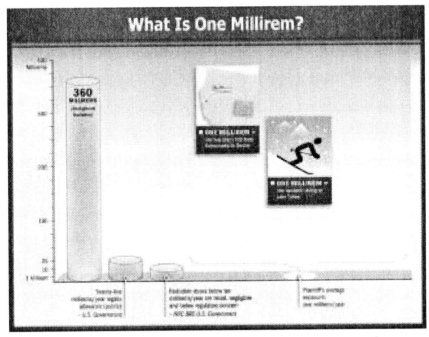

Figure 10-3. *Radiation example graphic, version 3. Adding yet another reference point to the graphic. (The Focal Point, LLC.)*

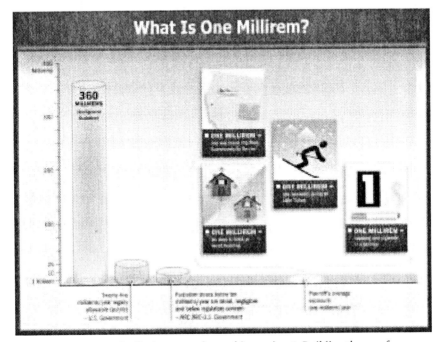

Figure 10-4. *Radiation example graphic, version 4. Building the case for understanding radiation exposure. (The Focal Point, LLC.)*

I will have been exposed to—you got it—an additional millirem of radiation. As you might suspect, this fact does not in any way compel me to seek the safety of sleeping on the couch!

You illustrate this final point and your graphic looks like Figure 10-5.

Now, your jury understands. Your jury is not bored with explanations of biological exposure to roentgens of X-rays. Your jury will appreciate the fact that you took the time to explain a key concept to them in an understandable manner. Your active jurors will remember and use this fact as ammunition throughout jury deliberations.[5]

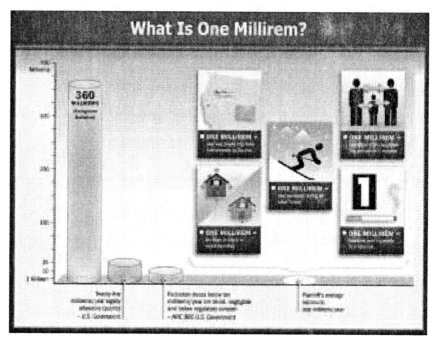

Figure 10-5. *Radiation example graphic, version 5. Voilà! A millirem of radiation exposure becomes clear to the jury. (The Focal Point, LLC.)*

What the Jurors Need

Ritter tells his clients, who are generally trial lawyers conducting trials that require expert witnesses, that they need to keep in mind at least three things when they are thinking about what will help the jurors or the judge as fact finders. The lawyer needs to provide the necessary tools to help the fact finders (1) understand the case, (2) be personally persuaded by it, and (3) (in the case of a jury trial) be equipped to persuade others to vote for the lawyer's client's case.

---

5. Ritter, Christopher. Personal communication, November 2001.

Jurors, especially curious, active jurors, want to "see" things in court. When they do, you have an increased chance that these jurors will be compelled to become "your jurors" and, in turn, they will be better able to persuade undecided jurors to do the same.

Furthermore, Ritter recommends that experts thinking about the most effective kinds of visual aids keep in mind three organizing concepts for graphic information as a tool for their use in connection with testifying on the stand.

1. **Explain the format of the exhibit or exhibits.**
   Explain the format you have chosen to illustrate your concepts, experiments, and conclusions with the graphics you have developed. Do this in your report, if possible, because the report may end up in evidence or may be shown to the jury in direct or cross-examination. Definitely do it in the beginning and whenever you shift the format of illustrations you use during the trial. In videotaped depositions it is equally important to get these images into your testimony.

2. **Explain the content of the visual.**
   What is the content of the graphic? Why did you choose that particular content? Is it a visual analogy offered only to get the judge or the jurors to recognize that these complex concepts are not that different from something we all understand? You need to be able to explain that the graphic or picture actually shows both how things are alike and, if appropriate, also how they differ.

3. **Put the exhibit in the proper context.**
   This is the key to getting the fact finders to use these images as tools in their reasoning and later in their advocacy during deliberations. You have to understand how the images build to the entire context of your testimony and to the story of the case. In other words, good images are prepared because they push the story or theme throughout the context of not only the expert's testimony but the testimony of opposing experts. These images should also allow the story to flow through the opening statement, if they are shown that early, and through the closing argument. Most importantly, these graphics add value to the case in the assistance they give to the judge in *Daubert* challenge hearings and in the deliberations of the jury after all the evidence is in.

Using Outlines for Technical Expert Testimony

The simple outline remains one of the most effective kinds of visual aids for a technical expert. It tracks all the principles we have already discussed.

The consultants at The Focal Point are convinced that for many experts, the biggest bang for the buck in graphics are simple outlines. The outlines have a couple of advantages. First, in order to create an effective outline, the lawyer and witness need to spend some time thinking about the testimony. In particular, they need to identify what is important, how to structure the presentation, and so on. This is something you cannot overdo. Second, you can use the outlines at crucial points in the testimony to wake up jurors and/or get them to concentrate for a few seconds on what you really care about. Generally, the following types of outlines are very helpful.

- The first is an overall outline of the areas the expert will cover in testimony (Figure 10-6). This graphic is used in the opening statement and at the beginning of the expert's testimony.

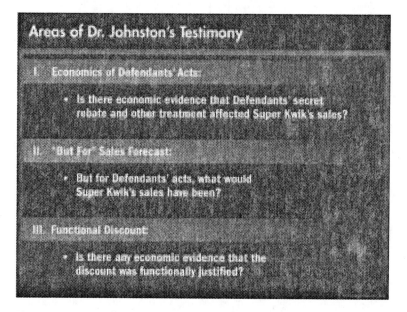

Figure 10-6. *Overall outline of the expert's testimony. (The Focal Point, LLC.)*

- The second type of outline summarizes the expert's conclusions. In Figures 10-7 through 10-9, the three functional areas named in the overall outline (Figure 10-6) are explained, along with conclusions associated with each.
- In some outlines, a final version of the presentation slide provides greater detail about what the issue is, what the conclusion is, why the expert is qualified to say this, and/or what evidence was used to come to that conclusion. In this case, the initial slide (Figure 10-6) could be simply redisplayed for this purpose.

These graphics are used at various points during the testimony. The idea is to wake up the jurors and have them focus on the fact that you have information about each of these topics. Jurors will deal with this information in a variety of ways. A less

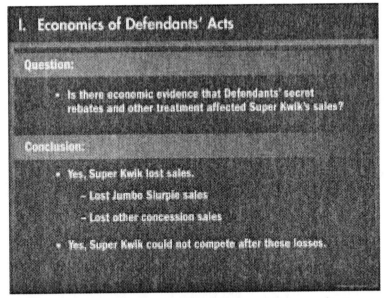

Figure 10-7. *Summarized explanation of the expert's first area of testimony. (The Focal Point, LLC.)*

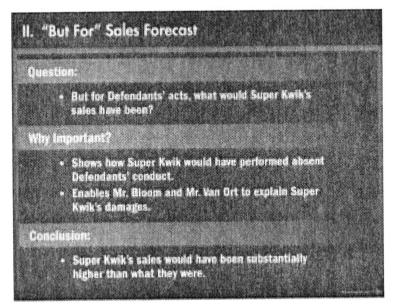

Figure 10-8. *Summarized explanation of the expert's second area of testimony. Note that this graphic directly addresses two pieces of information an expert needs to convey to the fact finder: (1) Why is the question important? and (2) What's the answer? (The Focal Point, LLC.)*

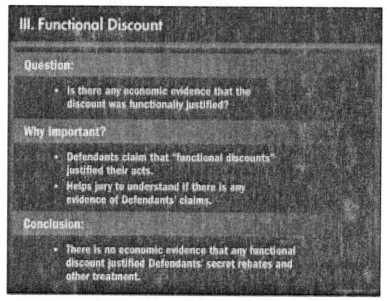

Figure 10-9. *Summarized explanation of the expert's third area of testimony. Note that this graphic explains the significance of the expert's findings on this point. (The Focal Point, LLC.)*

motivated juror is like a math teacher in junior high school who gives daily homework assignments and grades them merely by seeing if there is something in the answer box. It does not seem to really matter what is there, only that there is *something* there.

Many jurors want the same thing. For each expert's testimony they want to know that there are answers to the following questions:

- What is the topic?
- What is the answer?
- How is it that the expert is qualified to answer the question?
- What's the evidence?

For many jurors the *fact* that these questions are answered is as important as the answers themselves. Other jurors are willing to look at and think about the answers to these questions, provided you make it easy for them to get this information—which is what a simple outline graphic does.

Using a Scoreboard to Tie It All Together

The Focal Point experts also encourage attorneys to consider the space and the function of their graphics and the potential for one or more of them to be used like stadium scoreboards (Figure 10-10). This is a concept with which the judge and the jurors are all familiar. In a football stadium, a baseball park, or a basketball arena, they look to the scoreboard for both entertainment and important information, while helping them keep track of the game. More importantly, for our purposes, if the appropriate scoreboard exhibit can be created for the key expert, it can be left visible during much of the proceedings; jurors learn that it is part of the ritual space and can be relied on throughout the trial.

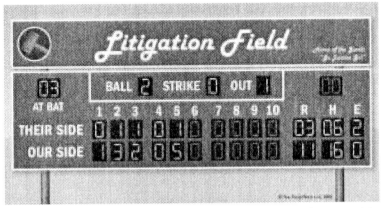

Figure 10-10. *An example of a scoreboard display. (The Focal Point, LLC.)*

These days, spectators often find the replay screen on the scoreboard and look to see what action they missed in the preceding play. Sometimes they watch the giant image to better follow the actual play, while keeping the action on the field in their peripheral vision. Contrast this ability of spectators to track the status of the game with that of spectators for a little league baseball game, where scoreboards are absent. Remember that the trial is also at heart a highly rehearsed and concentrated contest, and therefore not unlike a professional or college baseball game. Judges and jurors may be accustomed to following the action of the games they are interested in with one or more visual aids, sometimes preferring them to the real action over the course of the entire game. So, to the extent that you can hijack this familiar concept with one or more of your visuals to which you can keep returning during the course of a complicated explanation of technical concepts, you will have a better chance of keeping the majority of the jurors in their seats until the final inning.

Winning the Battle but Losing the War: The Risk of Argumentative Titles

It is also very important that particular images that are not designed to function much like scoreboards have a meaningful and fitting title that makes them memorable. The importance of a good title should not be ignored. Titles often require as much brainstorming by the expert and the attorney as the graphic images themselves. Regardless of what sort of graphic image or chart the expert needs to use, titles help a certain number of jurors understand the internal and external contexts of the illustration. Jurors can more easily recall a particular image and its content within the overall context of the presentation and argument if they can recall the title of the image.

Thus, consistent choices of titles, all different but related in style, type and tone, add a level of context to the series of images chosen by the expert and the trial lawyer to keep the jurors interested and to keep them oriented in time and space during the complex conceptualization required to understand the expert's testimony. The team is really trying to say something important not only about the exhibit and the content of that particular exhibit but also about why the jurors should remember this particular exhibit as it relates to the entire case much later, perhaps weeks later, when they attempt to resolve the case during deliberations.

The need for a memorable and significant title should not become confused with the goal of attempting to present all the evidence as an objective and unbiased expert witness. Titled images are an integral part of the presentation of an advocate's argument from the selection of the jury through the closing argument. This tension that must be maintained throughout the preparation and presentation of a trial is also present in the process of creating effective graphics and in the selection of titles that must not appear so argumentative that they erode the expert's credibility.

An approach that will make the expert's brainstorming with the trial attorney yield the maximum number of powerful images, whether argumentative or not, is to conceptualize potential visual exhibits with their titles as potential admissible evidence. Then examine them as if they were to be used only to illustrate an issue during the testimony and not offered as substantive evidence. Finally, consider whether the title is worth risking the exhibit's being admitted as evidence. If the title is too argumentative, the exhibit may not even be allowed while the expert is testifying. It might be limited in use to arguing the case—neither allowed during the witness's testimony nor admitted into evidence.

Admissible substantive evidence is the most desirable kind of evidence because it not only can be used by the expert during his or her testimony but also can be shown to other witnesses, used in opening and closing arguments by the attorney, and go to the jurors for use during deliberations. For most exhibits to qualify as admissible evidence, they must be authenticated—someone must confirm that the exhibits are what they are represented to be. If the expert or another foundation witness can authenticate the exhibit, the next issue is whether the information contained in the exhibit is based on otherwise admissible evidence. If this is not the case, assuming that the contents of the exhibit are a combination of otherwise admissible evidence and evidence that may not be admissible but is of the sort other experts in the field ordinarily rely on, then the exhibit can still be admitted by the judge and introduced as substance evidence.

Experts need to bear in mind the distinction between those visual exhibits that definitely do need to be admitted and those that can probably be used effectively and memorably during their testimony or by the attorney in argument, whether or not they are ever actually admitted into evidence. The problem with argumentative titles is that they can jeopardize the admissibility of a particular visual exhibit and possibly even cause it to be excluded from illustrative or demonstrative use by the expert.

Malone and Zwier succinctly summarize the different kinds of argumentative objections lawyers can make to the improper use of titles on expert visuals.

> When opposing, look carefully at the labels used on exhibits, and consider the appropriateness of the label to the particular use at trial. Do the labels argue? Not allowed on opening. Do they lead? Not allowed on direct examination. Do the labels mischaracterize? Not allowed on direct or cross. Do the labels represent as evidence things not entered into evidence? Not allowed on closing.[6]

All of these issues are primarily for the attorney to grapple with, but it certainly helps for the expert to have a firm grasp of them when it comes to handling the exhibits and testifying about the foundation for them on direct. These kinds of issues can also arise on voir dire (as we saw in the failed attempt by the prosecutor to keep Mona Lisa Vito off the stand in *My Cousin Vinny*) if the opposing attorney decides to object to the admission of a particular exhibit and, of course, on cross-examination of the expert during the trial, as occurred in the Microsoft case example discussed earlier in this chapter.

The performance of the expert with the visuals varies depending on the manner of display, but a few of the commonly used strategies for successful communication are briefly presented below.

Remember, the general rule is that experts should not be argumentative in their testimony. Titles, just like the images on which they appear, should not be argumentative either. But the titles should enable the witness to build the context established by the trial attorney's opening statement and the entire body of evidence in the case, and the titles should also assist the judge or the jurors to recognize, remember, and rebuild that context with the assistance of the trial lawyer's arguments in closing.

The debate about how to title expert exhibits should be engaged early by both the attorney and the expert, from the beginning of the process of preparing the report (and any responses to possible *Daubert* challenges) through the deposition testimony. When the time comes to submit the trial presentation graphics, everyone should be well satisfied that the exhibits and their titles are effective and admissible. Merely because graphic exhibits and their titles cannot be argumentative does not mean that they cannot and should not be persuasive.

---

6. Malone and Zwier, *Effective Expert Testimony*, p. 128.

Obviously, persuasion and a great deal of the determination of an expert's credibility depends on not appearing to be argumentative, despite the equally obvious fact that the expert is being presented as part of the context of an advocate's overall argument in presenting the case itself. The worst images create an impression in the mind of the jurors that the expected objective expert explanations (as exemplified by the exhibits) are, upon closer scrutiny, really no different than the anticipated zealous advocacy of the attorney. To make a difference, to be ultimately persuasive of the truth of their testimony, the experts and their exhibits need to be seen as different from the advocacy of the attorneys.

Ritter suggests the following strategy as a compromise that could conceivably give an aggressive advocate the best of both worlds and avoid an objection to either the use of an exhibit or a specific title on an exhibit during the expert's testimony:

> *Even if on the verge of testifying, the title is seen by the judge, the expert or attorney as being too argumentative, the problem is relatively easily fixed and/or the exhibit may simply be reserved and used later on in closing argument. So, if your title comes to seem too argumentative to you on the day of your testimony, what do you do? The simplest thing to do is to offer to cover up the title. This can be done very easily by: (1) merely covering the title with a strip of opaque paper; (2) having the person who printed the board prepare a blank strip that you can add over the original title; or (3) having the person who printed the poster prepare a strip with an alternative title on it. These solutions work well if the exhibit is used in opening or during witness testimony. They have the added advantage that you can often take these strips off during closing argument with a sudden flourish.[7]*

Authentication Tags for Visual Exhibits

In the art world, one painting that is considered by the consensus of the experts to be an authentic master work may be worth a million dollars, and an identical painting that cannot be authenticated (but may well be another master work) may be worth almost nothing at the fine art auction houses. Hundreds of effective techniques have been developed over the centuries to authenticate cultural artifacts and works of art from cultures throughout the world. Similar kinds of approaches for satisfying the judge and the jurors as to authenticity should be in the minds of both the lawyer and the expert witness when they develop their images and other visual exhibits.

Most people realize that sophisticated computer-generated evidence and digital images can be easily manipulated. Such images can also be erroneous due to programming or input errors. Thus judges and jurors can be quite reasonably concerned about the authenticity of this kind of evidence, especially because of its highly persuasive potential and therefore its potentially prejudicial effects. These facts have led

---

7. Ritter, Christopher. Personal communication, November 2001.

to lengthy challenges and expensive litigation over the authentication and admissibility of such exhibits. But the design or use of almost any paper-based graphic can also attempt either to deceive or to accurately represent what the creators reasonably believe to be truthful information. The pros at The Focal Point believe that it is always a good idea to include an "authentication tag" on the visual exhibit itself when this sort of overt authentication makes sense.

It is essential for the expert who will use the exhibit or at least the graphic designer who worked with the expert (if the challenge runs that far) to be able to give the provenance of all the data, designs, icons, visual analogies, and other graphic techniques when questioned about the exhibit. These approaches should be thought through well in advance of deciding what images to use and how much time it may take to satisfy the judge or a doubtful juror as to what went into the production of a particular image.

You can even use the different techniques for attesting to the authenticity of images in combination to reinforce the impression that you have indeed been meticulous. Used in this way, authentication of graphic exhibits can enhance your credibility by demonstrating that you have a broad base of experience in attempting to explain these issues and concepts and that you care enough about your work, your exhibits, and the jurors to let them know where the information included in the exhibits actually originated. Without this provenance, you are making an unwarranted assumption that the judge or jurors will understand what the exhibit is based on. Taking the additional step to visually authenticate the evidence provides another reason for the judge and jurors to accept the information depicted in it as straightforward and unaltered. Your description during testimony of the process of authentication is what's important here. The actual "authenticity tag" associated with a particular exhibit can be as simple as a brief citation at the bottom of the exhibit, a small picture of the document from which the text of the image was pulled, or the cover of the book from which the material came.

As with the *Daubert* tests for novel scientific evidence, the game of authenticating expert evidence graphic images is advanced through reliance on recognized authorities, referenced experiments, quoted reports (including the reports of the opposing expert), cited documents, quoted expert witness deposition testimony that relates to the expert's work, and cited peer review comments. This is really no more than adding a further layer of credibility, broadening the context of your testimony and at the same time contributing to the cohesiveness of the overall case for the party on whose behalf you are testifying. It also enhances the jurors' perception of your objectivity by including the flavor of a well-researched presentation. It is, moreover, a trial strategy that targets those jurors who may need this approach to enable them to become "active jurors" at the close of the evidence, when they move into deliberations. Ritter believes that these active jurors need as many additional tools as possible to articulate their understanding of all the expert testimony in order to effectively attempt to explain the concepts to jurors who don't quite understand them or who, because of unnecessary confusion, may still favor the opposing expert's conclusions.

Ritter's partner and one of the founders of The Focal Point, Andrew Spingler, consistently reminds clients (usually ones who are eager to try out the latest technical gizmo), "The medium should never drive the message." In other words, you do *not* begin by picking a particular method to display your trial graphic (for example, video, exhibit board, or animation) and then design the graphic to be shown that way. Instead, you first design the trial graphic—the best possible trial graphic—and then determine the ideal way to show it to the jury. Sometimes the best way to make your point is to use a simple blackboard. Other times, when the budget allows, expensive 3-D animation may be the ideal way to go. The point is, *after* you design the general parameters of your trial graphic, you need to know (1) what display options you have and (2) the various advantages that each display medium presents.

A lawyer needs all the help he or she can get when assisting the expert to look less like an advocate during testimony. If the expert appears to be an advocate, it detracts from the expert's role as an objective teacher. The lawyer is an advocate, but especially when he or she is attempting to stay out of the way of the expert's objective presentation to the jury, the lawyer's advocacy role is best advanced by enhancing the objectivity of the expert.

On the other hand, the jurors will probably expect to see some of the magic of these tools involved in the expert's advertised field of mastery. This does not mean that all of the graphic exhibits need to be comprised of flying toasters and dancing raisins. To have the best chance of reaching all the jurors, it may mean that the expert should present some magic in the form of computer-generated charts, computer visual sequences, or animations, as well as some old-fashioned charts, whiteboard drawings, and pointer presentations.

In the final analysis, whether enlarged outlines or complex computer-generated simulations are selected to enhance and explain the expert's testimony, more expensive technology will not improve a poorly designed graphic. If anything, expensive, eye-popping technology probably highlights how bad a poorly conceived graphic really is. This is definitely a case in which improved technology can make a bad thing incalculably worse.

Don't Forget Spontaneously Generated Visual Exhibits

By their very nature, spontaneously created trial graphics create a certain level of attention and intimacy that may not exist in other forms of display. A spontaneous graphic is created right in the courtroom with the jurors witnessing its creation. It did not exist prior to the expert walking over to the blackboard or flipchart. This creates a connection between the witness, the jurors, and the trial graphic that may not exist with prepepared graphics.

Of course, some "spontaneous" graphics are not entirely spontaneous. The graphics may be created in the courtroom in front of the jurors, but many of these graphics are conceived long before the trial lawyer ever arrives at court.

These spontaneous graphics require the same careful consideration that goes into trial graphics created by outside artists. As such, you should not hesitate to apply the same kind of brainstorming techniques to the creation of these spontaneous exhibits as you would to any other graphics. In fact, it should not surprise you that a portion of what some litigation graphic consultants do in client brainstorming sessions is to consider what trial graphics would be most effective if drawn by the lawyer or the witness in the courtroom rather than by a consultant on a computer.

Ritter and the team at The Focal Point have also observed how the skill of spontaneous exhibit creation has been incorporated by some trial lawyers into a powerful dimension of their storytelling at trial. We believe that experts who are willing to practice the art involved can use this same skill. Once again Ritter elaborates.

> There is a wonderful skill that certain lawyers have developed—the skill of incorporating their spontaneous drawing into their storytelling. Trial lawyers who are able to do this are able to describe a series of events while at the same time drawing out a map or some other illustration. Rather than completing the drawing all at once, these trial lawyers take their time slowly drawing the scene verbally and with actual pictures. When this technique is done well, it can be spellbinding on the jurors. I suspect that this technique is so effective for three reasons.
>
> First, it simultaneously appeals to two of the jurors' most important physical senses—vision and hearing—without overwhelming them with too much detail at any one time.
>
> Second, the fact that the jurors are watching the spontaneous creation of a trial graphic captures and holds their attention more than a prepepared exhibit board or other graphic would.
>
> Finally, your spontaneous performance is somewhat equivalent to that of a tightrope walker without a net; people are somewhat morbidly curious to see if you can pull it off.[8]

Above all, you need to be very careful when you create these on-the-fly graphics and any other visual aids. It is easy, in the heat of trial, to create a trial graphic that is a complete mess. Ritter has the following tips.

> Unless you have inherently neat handwriting, your words can appear messy. Unless you have carefully planned what you want to put into the graphic and where, you can forget where you want bits of information to go. So, unless it is a true emergency

---

8. Ritter, Christopher. Personal communication, November 2001.

and you are "dancing" to create some unforeseen exhibit, practice creating your graphic several times before you go to court. If it is crucial that the graphic be just a certain way, then prepare that graphic before you arrive at court.

When I suggest that you "prepare that graphic before you arrive at court," I am not suggesting that you must always pay to have a graphic artist prepare your exhibit for you. If your client's budget and/or time dictate that you draw on newsprint paper, there is no problem.[9]

Assuming that the exhibits you wish to use in connection with your testimony have either already been approved or ruled only conditionally admissible by the judge before trial, as will most often be the case, you should then carefully rehearse with the attorney how you will handle all those exhibits you will definitely be using during your testimony. In this rehearsal, you should decide when and where you should be to make the most effective use of the different types of visual evidence. Ordinarily, the attorney will be handing an exhibit to you on the witness stand and you will be able to examine, identify, and, to the degree necessary, authenticate the exhibit and tell how and why it was created. In some courts, the judge will allow you to leave the witness box and place yourself near display tools such as a computer projector, a large map, a whiteboard, or a flipchart.

This ability to place yourself near your display tools is very desirable and should be requested and rehearsed whenever the trial attorney believes the court will allow it. You will already be aware that the judge, opposing counsel, and all the jurors already have the preadmitted exhibits that you need to discuss. However, you do not want the jury to be examining these visuals in small printed copies or TV monitor projections, unless there are no other options. Even with preadmitted copies of large-scale exhibits or projections you wish to work with and explain, ideally, these smaller copies will not be used by the jury until after you have testified about the full-sized exhibit before the jury.

One serious problem with computer screens placed in front of each couple of jurors (as they are in many courtrooms) is that it is difficult, if not impossible, for the jury to simultaneously look at both these monitors and the expert who is explaining the evidence, its content, and its context all at the same time. This is also the case in a large-screen projection setup, which we encounter most of the time in state courts that do not already have individual computer monitors set up in the courtroom for the witness, judge, and jurors.

The goal should be to have the expert's credibility enhanced by the exhibits or the display of the graphics during the course of the expert's testimony. This is different from replacing the expert with a television program. As Ritter points out, it is also

---

9. Ritter, Christopher. Personal communication, November 2001.

helpful for the display of the information to appear to be a display of the expert's information. This can be more problematic with electronic displays, especially if they cannot be viewed simultaneously with the expert's discussion of these images. It is important to conjoin the expert with the images whenever possible.

Talk to the Jury, Not the Exhibit

Finally, no matter how simple or complex the visual is going to be, when you or you and the attorney are working in front of the exhibit, it is a mistake to talk to the exhibit. (Contrast Figure 10-11 with Figure 10-12.)

Figure 10-11. *Talking to the exhibit while using a visual aid.*
(Photo courtesy of Dan Pearlman, Brooke Gamble, and Fred Smith.)

David Malone counsels both attorneys and experts to bear in mind what he calls "The Three Ts": *touch, turn,* and *talk.* In other words, don't face the exhibit, except to locate a part of the visual to touch or point to. Don't talk to the exhibit; rather, turn from the exhibit and face or approach the jury. Use the exhibit to talk to the jury about the ideas or concepts that the exhibit illuminates or reinforces. Based on these fundamental rules for handling visual exhibits, the orchestration of the entire presentation is subject only to your creativity. For example, Malone recommends that "for special

Figure 10-12. *Talking to the jury while using a visual aid.*
(Photo courtesy of Dan Pearlman, Brooke Gamble, and Fred Smith.)

emphasis and drama, pause mid-sentence, turn, face the chart or screen, and write or reveal without speaking, then turn back and reestablish eye contact."[10]

Mesmerizing with Magnets

Almost as important as the selection of words to go into outlines and exhibits with lists of quotes is the method of handling and displaying those textual exhibits. David Malone recommends magnetic boards and describes his use of them with experts as follows:

> *Magnetic cards that stick up on a whiteboard are a very effective way to present words, category titles, and essential quotes. The process of adding, subtracting, and rearranging words and phrases is neat, quick, and simple. The attorney can emphasize the subject of particular testimony, give a heading to a listing of factors, or add a picture to a speaker's words without detracting from his own performance by relying on his own poor public penmanship. The attorney can also color-code the magnetic cards so related ideas are immediately associated with one another. In theory, Velcro stick-ups should work just as well, but they do not because they are not actually*

10. Malone and Zwier, *Effective Expert Testimony*, p. 133.

magic like magnetic cards. Magnetic tape with an adhesive back can be used to stick just about anything on a coated steel board.[11]

The choices of what medium to use and just how best to choreograph the different movements and actions of the expert and the attorney illustrate the complexity of the teamwork rehearsed long before the actual trial. These choices determine who will do what with the visual evidence, the timing of movements to and from the jury box, and the sharing of copies of exhibits with the jurors before or after the testimony about the visuals contained in the exhibit.

You can generally rely on the attorney to remove as much uncertainty as possible from planning the expert's actual testimony. In order to be able to make the best of a situation in which the judge will not allow the expert to show some of the prepared exhibits at trial that both the expert and the attorney were planning to use, it is a tremendous asset for an expert to be able to spontaneously illustrate the same points, processes, or concepts with less sophisticated images or diagrams. Even if they are not as dynamic or persuasive as the exhibits that have been excluded for whatever reason, the effort is still worth making.

A working knowledge and experience in preparing simple drawings and diagrams to help illustrate ideas is indispensable to be able to proceed without missing a beat when the judge rules that a particular graphic or series of visual exhibits may not be used. The expert and the trial attorney need to practice in advance the preparation and presentation of these sorts of exhibits just in case the professionally prepared exhibits are not allowed. Remember that the cardinal principle here is that showing and telling is almost always better than just telling. At the same time, unless you are very confident that the graphic evidence will not be subject to attack as misleading or confusing, it is probably best not to attempt to produce it at all.

Connecting the Links in the Chain

Edward Tufte is generally considered the master of graphic display of information, a characterization enthusiastically endorsed by The Focal Point and by trial experts like David M. Malone and other recognized authorities on the art of presenting expert testimony. Tufte asserts that the most effective use of visuals should never rely on the memory of the observer to connect a long series of images or charts. Whenever possible, the expert should short-circuit the memory process by juxtaposing as many comparisons that need to be made as possible between ideas or conditions, all contained in the same graphic exhibit.

Remember that the comparison is usually the most important lesson you are trying to teach. You can use the chain of graphic exhibits to accentuate this conclusion,

---

11. Malone and Zwier, *Effective Expert Testimony*, p. 133.

and you can use combination graphics to make the links stronger. This technique will work even though your testimony may have had to cover many independent premises before the conclusion can be dramatically and persuasively stated. With the right visual aids, your entire proof may be presented, highlighted, and reinforced, while keeping each exhibit simple and honest.

Demeanor and Credibility

We wish to advance an old-fashioned message in this chapter and to attempt to justify that message against extremely long odds. The oddsmakers are those who have noticed that winning at all costs seems to be the theme for most of the cases we hear about in the media. The common-sense message contained in this chapter is that judges and jurors in almost every case still pay a great deal of attention to a wide range of human behavior and nonverbal cues and clues when they assign credibility to any witness. They apply this reading of demeanor especially rigorously to an expert and to the lawyer interacting with the expert on direct or cross-examination. That message runs counter to the thesis of much of the modern interpretation of the deleterious effects of the perceived erosion of the law's claim to legitimacy. Many commentators have observed the apparent lessening of the capacity for critical judgment by judges and jurors, as evidenced in highly publicized trials such as the O. J. Simpson case. These commentators suggest that this is a general trend in litigation, driven by a number of factors. In particular, some of the factors consistently cited are the overwhelming influence of new modes of communication and the demands for fresh, nightly news, as well as the adjustments to these modern pressures made by witnesses, lawyers, judges, and the entire legal system.

Law in an Age of Sound-Bite Attention Spans

Perhaps the single image that many contemporary commentators and legal scholars point to when expressing concern for the impact of the media on high-profile litigation is O. J. Simpson trying on the glove found by Mark Fuhrman. Since we just endorsed the use of images in the courtroom to communicate technical concepts, we need to turn our attention to the influence on litigation that the media's use and abuse of trial exhibits and images that are often never even admitted into evidence can have on the way litigation is conducted today.

Richard K. Sherwin comments on recent changes in the legal system:

> *What goes on inside the courtroom is changing. Opening and closing statements are becoming shorter, snappier. And verbal speech is increasingly sharing court time with visual, multimedia displays as television and computer screens proliferate. As one attorney put it: "Our sound-bite society has an ever decreasing attention span, requiring points to be made quickly and succinctly. . . . An eye-catching graphic of a dramatic animation can seize the viewer/juror, with interest being the first step in understanding." The new goal is to let technology do the visualizing for the jury— through computer animation, computer graphics, and digital simulations of automobile, aviation, and maritime accidents; bodily injury processes; structural failures; and environmental damage patterns—even crime reenactments. In court as elsewhere, "seeing is believing." The question is, how is the reality we see being constructed?*[1]

What Sherwin describes in this passage from *When Law Goes Pop* is an important part of the interplay between the popular commercial media and the communication strategies of savvy lawyers. What we address in this chapter is the equally important role the presentation of *self* plays in the testimony of the expert witness and in the interactions of the witness with the sponsoring attorney, judge, jurors, and the opposing attorney. This presentation of self also comes into play indirectly through the witness's interactions with the opposing expert or experts. In high-profile cases, even the witnesses come under media pressure to behave according to the expectations of the larger society and the witnesses' often larger-than-life reputations.

But Sherwin (along with other contemporary commentators on modern litigation practices) has far more on his mind than just the increasing use of visual images and cinematic techniques and their potentially deleterious effects on the search for truth and justice in modern trials. There are several reasons for even greater concern. Among these reasons is the danger of adversely affecting the very nature of the legal story and the ability of witnesses and attorneys to make their stories believable to juries. Above all else, Sherwin considers trial lawyers to be storytellers and the story to be the key to communicating with the ultimate fact finder. Trial lawyers increasingly make their cases, especially high-profile cases, simultaneously to the fact finders and to the public at large through the popular media, both inside and outside the courtroom.

---

1. Sherwin, Richard K. *When Law Goes Pop*. Chicago: University of Chicago Press, 2000, p. 25.

... it behooves us to consider with great care the legal implications of significant shifts in our storytelling practices. Such changes may betoken a collective change of mind and culture. Today the institutions of law, politics, and journalism have been radically transformed by such a change. Postmodern ideas, new communication technologies, and the unrestrained demands of the marketplace are converging with tremendous synergistic impact. Meanings are thinning out as they collapse into the popular. We see this in law as legal meanings increasingly yield to the compelling visual logic of film and graphic images and by extension to the market forces that fuel their production. This is what happens when law, like politics, takes root in a culture of spectacle, when it mimics the communicative style and persuasive techniques of public relations.[2]

Sherwin and other modern theorists on the impact of media on modern trials have many important things to teach us about what technical experts can expect from the media and from media-savvy attorneys. We can expect these things whenever the public interest is significant enough for a case to become a big story. With this in mind, let's drop back to the level of routine cases that may or may not ever be picked up by the local or national media. Let's first consider what have traditionally been the hallmarks of demeanor that every child knows are important to how strangers interpret our intentions and receive our communications, and that trial lawyers attempt to prepare themselves and their experts to focus upon. These include such basic considerations as how to dress appropriately for court and how to relax when facing stressful events such as sworn testimony. Also included are exercises and suggested disciplines to better control the breath while testifying and to make the most effective use of the voice to communicate thoughts. A digital forensics expert should also know what to do with his or her hands while listening to a question or giving an answer and how to handle exhibits and visual aids while speaking to the issues they illustrate.

In our rush to ensure that we have a million-dollar computer-generated animation of the processes at issue in a case, we may forget, at our peril, a crucial and obvious point about the presentation of the expert by the sponsoring attorney. As important as these props are—and demonstrative exhibits certainly are essential to the success of technical testimony—the jurors are watching the demeanor of the lawyer during the entire trial. This sustained focus on the behavior and attitudes of the attorney is not entirely deflected when the expert arrives at the witness stand, but for better or worse, it certainly may be intensified and transferred to the witness when called to the stand to testify. The lawyer has been talking about the expert and the expert's testimony in one way or another since the opening statement. The jurors are waiting to see just who this all-important expert will turn out to be. They have been promised that this expert is an important witness and is going to be able to help explain some very important

---

2. Sherwin, *When Law Goes Pop*, from the Preface.

things in the case. The jurors have been told the story of the case since they were select-ed and have been told parts of that story in chunks by other witnesses who have already taken their turns on the stand. Just as a poor job of introducing the witness can cause the jurors to ignore important technical testimony, the careless behavior or difficult delivery of testimony by an important and presumably capable expert can easily dash the jurors' expectations. The most careful preparation and appropriate behavior on the witness stand may still not produce a performance that measures up to a particular juror's expectations of what an ideal expert witness should be. So be it. The real objec-tive here is not to win a beauty contest but to be perceived as a competent and credible human who is doing his or her level best to explain important issues to each and every juror.

Legal folklore has always recognized that the reality of the case being recreated in the courtroom hinges on the determination of the truth of a witness's testimony. This determination can be tangled by the lawyers who are fighting to control the percep-tion of that reality through their competing versions of the story of the case. In other words, the law assigns fact finders the responsibility of deciding the credibility of each of the witnesses and of the stories they tell. Tests for credibility have enjoyed variable levels of support from academics and commentators on the art of litigation over the years. But since time immemorial (or at least since writing preserves the discussion of these attributes) humans seem to have gauged credibility roughly along the lines of their reading, both individually and collectively, of the demeanor of a witness. Demeanor inside the courtroom can certainly be managed and manipulated. The jurors are also capable of recognizing this manipulation as a part of the human con-dition and necessary to the preparation of testimony and especially expert testimony for the formal presentation that a trial requires. Hence they can be expected to take this aspect of the observed indices of demeanor into account when considering the attitudes and behavior expressed by the witness in the courtroom. Experts who think they are not obligated to consider how their demeanor may influence the fact finders fail to take their own testimony seriously and fail to do their best to effectively com-municate the information and knowledge they possess about the issues in the case.

The law generally leaves these determinations of demeanor for the deliberative process, which is conducted in secret. So there is seldom a record made of a witness's nonverbal acts unless a comment is made by an attorney, the judge, or the witness. But it is significant that the law continues to take these matters very seriously. For instance, the law recognizes that the demeanor of a witness or a party as displayed outside of the court, even long before the trial, can be evidence of a crime or can affect the cred-ibility of the witness or party, should they take the stand.

For example, in New Mexico, should a defendant charged with murder attempt to flee from the scene of the crime or to escape from the jurisdiction, proof of that fact is allowed as evidence of criminal intent. Of course the concealment of, destruction of, or tampering with evidence is equally relevant and may itself become evidence of a separate charge. The point is that demeanor has always been considered important as evidence suggesting or disproving credibility; however, the common law has tended to leave the evaluation of this aspect of credibility to the collective wisdom of the jurors in the course of their deliberations or to the judge when a jury has been waived, without ever requiring the fact finder to report their findings concerning demeanor.

There is quite a bit of concern that some of the aspects of the gatekeeper function that flows from the *Daubert* line of cases seem to shift those ultimate issues of demeanor and credibility from the jurors to the discretion of the judge as he or she determines before the trial whether a particular expert should be allowed to testify. An appellate court generally will not overrule an issue that has been decided at trial, especially when it falls into the fact finder's traditional determination of the credibility of a witness. Jurors are still instructed that they may consider their observations of how a witness behaved on the stand when determining how much, if any, credibility to assign to an expert's opinion and, relative to other opinions or evidence in the case, how much weight to give to the evidence presented.

Playing for Effect

Sometimes the witness is making an excellent presentation and feeling in complete control of his or her demeanor on the stand when the unanticipated happens. This can come in a wide range of incidents, such as the deliberate, provocative actions of a party or an attorney in the courtroom, designed to upset or upstage the presentation of an expert witness that is going too well. At some point in their careers, most attorneys and their experts will experience bush-league tactics by opposing counsel or one of the members of the opposition's trial team. Examples of such tactics include the apparently accidental dropping of large exhibits, vessels of water, piles of papers, or even falling out of or knocking over chairs, blackboards, or easels during a particularly interesting and damaging piece of expert testimony.

When you are on the stand and these things happen, it becomes even more important to maintain control of your own demeanor during the histrionics or other outrageous conduct that may be taking place. Exerting this control might involve concentrating or remaining centered, relying on your ability to keep a disciplined body language, and maintaining your breathing. This should continue until the proper objections are made and ruled on by the judge and order is restored in the court.

Bernard Ewell, whom you may remember from Chapter 1 as an expert witness from another domain, recalls testifying as an expert for the prosecution in a criminal trial concerning allegations of art fraud against two defendants. During the cross-examination by the attorney for one of the two defendants, Ewell admitted that based on additional research and information, he had changed his opinion about the exact method of reproduction that was used to create the forged and fraudulent pictures. In reality this change of opinion reflected an improved analysis of the methods used to reproduce the art, not a change in Ewell's ultimate conclusions based on the analysis. His change in opinion left untouched the fact that either method would have produced fake pictures and worthless objects in the legitimate art market, where they were being sold as authorized multiples with investment potential as limited editions.

This case happened to be one of those "big story" cases, and television news crews were in the courtroom waiting for "visuals" to occur. The producers already had dozens of pretty pictures to run with the evening coverage of the case. Another crew from the news program *60 Minutes* was filming the trial to do a special on the bigger story of the Dali art scandal. This case played a small part in that program's coverage of the growing multimillion-dollar scandal. As Ewell recalls the incident, one of the defendants, upon hearing Ewell's testimony, broke into loud, hysterical sobs and threw himself across the defense table. Before the judge could succeed in removing the jurors from this display of emotion by one of the defendants, the other defendant jumped up and moved toward his codefendant in a touching display of anguish and sympathy, interrupting the fraternal comforting gestures just long enough to turn toward the expert with a look that registered his anger over this change in opinion. This vacillation between expressions of anger and care continued for a few moments, while the jury retired. The cameras had captured the nightly news footage, which reported that the key expert had changed a crucial opinion on the stand and lengthy commentary on the apparent emotional impact it had on the defendants.

Sometimes such reactions do happen spontaneously in the heat of the trial, and this certainly could have been one of those cases. But just as often such displays are well-rehearsed and practiced routines, designed to go into action in front of the cameras or the fact finders. The routines are intended to take advantage of a perfect dramatic moment that can be predicted in the testimony, based on the pretrial disclosures of information during discovery. For the prepared expert, it does not matter whether these dramatic episodes are spontaneous or rehearsed. Either way, as these displays unfold, at some point the fact finders are going to turn their attention to the expert and gauge the effect on his or her demeanor. The point of this digression is that once again the expert witness must be prepared to maintain an objective and professional demeanor at all times while testifying.

What Fact Finders Don't Like about the Demeanor of Experts and Attorneys

The Honorable Ortrie D. Smith, District Court Judge in Missouri, conducted a survey in 1999 to determine what impressed the jurors the most and the least about lawyers' performances. As part of that survey, Smith collected the comments of jurors. We have drawn on these comments about the demeanor of the trial attorneys to generalize those aspects of attorney demeanor that relate equally to the performance of technical experts in the courtroom.

Based on the survey analyzed by Judge Smith, jurors value performances in court from "lawyers who are professional, prepared and organized."[3]

> *Jurors see professionalism in a lawyer's sincerity, courtroom demeanor, delivery, self-confidence, and in courtesy to witnesses, opposing counsel and the Court. . . . Jurors also like lawyers who are prepared. Preparedness includes efficient use of exhibits, thorough knowledge of the subject matter, focusing on key issues, and moving smoothly from one topic to another. There is concentric circular overlap between professionalism, preparedness and organization. However, juries do appreciate lawyers who have exhibits ready, are familiar with the exhibits and audio-video equipment, who have their witnesses lined up and ready to go, and who help the judge keep the trial moving at a quick pace.[4]*

For the purposes of this chapter, we believe that the smooth functioning of the attorney and the expert in the presentation of technical expert testimony makes the results of this survey about what jurors like and dislike about trial attorneys very relevant to considerations of what constitutes proper and improper demeanor for the expert as well as for the lawyer.

Here are some of the collected comments about what was considered appropriate and attractive demeanor in presenting cases to the jurors surveyed.

- *He had a commanding presence.*
- *Her courtroom demeanor was very calm, very professional.*
- *He had a good courtroom presence and seemed to be sincerely concerned about his client.*
- *I liked his courtroom demeanor and his ability to make decisive points in a timely fashion.*
- *He was calm, even when the testimony was not going well.[5]*

Courtesy was also important and several particular courtesies were described as being appreciated by one or more of the jurors surveyed.

- *He was very polite.*
- *He treated opposing counsel with respect.*
- *He was very sincere, thorough and polite. He showed concern for opposing counsel.*

---

3. Smith, Ortrie D. "Essay from the Bench: Lawyer Performance from the Jury's Perspective." *University of Missouri at Kansas City Law Review* vol. 68, 1999, p. 185.

4. Smith, "Essay from the Bench," pp. 186–187.

5. Smith, "Essay from the Bench," pp. 186–187.

- *I liked his courtesy in the courtroom.*
- *He was very polite to the judge and the other attorney.*
- *I liked her respect and overall kindness to her clients and also to the defendant.*
- *He showed respect to each witness and was very professional.*
- *He was courteous and kind to all witnesses even during cross-examination.*
- *I was impressed by his courtroom demeanor. I was also impressed by his ability to get along with the other lawyer.*[6]

Perhaps more important than the positive reactions were some of the negative reactions that were recorded by jurors.

- *His sincerity didn't "shine through."*
- *He used ridiculous suggestions to try to put doubts in our minds or confuse us. It was very obvious what he was doing, almost to the point of insulting our intelligence.*
- *I was unimpressed because he overreacted.*
- *I didn't like his cheap carnival tricks 1) standing up, not saying anything then sitting down while opposing counsel was talking, and 2) moving paper around creating noise while opposing counsel was talking, and 3) moving his lips to form comments like "alright we got them" while opposing counsel was talking, and 4) giving the thumb-up sign while opposing counsel was talking, and 5) insulting witnesses, and 6) lying to confuse witnesses, and 7) pasty smile.*
- *His courtroom demeanor appeared to be inappropriate. He should not tell jokes, and especially those with racial overtones.*
- *I didn't like his overall arrogance, his down-talking to us as jurors and his insulting manner to the opposing party. I would never hire him for my lawyer. His client won in spite of him. [And, he] was very annoying. The only reason he won was that the plaintiff failed to prove he was discriminated against. It was not because of [the defendant's lawyer's] performance.*
- *I did not like the way she rolled her eyes during the opposing witnesses' testimony.*[7]

Responses to the survey also discussed the delivery of the attorneys.

- *The belittling of plaintiff's witnesses did not help their case. I felt insulted.*
- *Her habit of scratching is distracting.*
- *He was too animated with his gestures. I did not like the way he slammed down exhibits when he felt witnesses were not cooperating.*
- *He made gestures and comments (for the jury to see and hear) each time coming back from the side-bar. He would also give witnesses for the other side dirty looks as he would go to side-bars. This was unnecessary.*
- *He seemed aloof—as though he was superior.*

---

6. Smith, "Essay from the Bench," p. 188.

7. Smith, "Essay from the Bench," pp. 188–189.

- *His presentation seemed too nonchalant, like he knew he wasn't going to win anyway so what's the use.*[8]

The Unbroken Circle of Professionalism, Preparation, and Organization

It is worth noting that the jurors tended to think about the demeanor of the attorneys who performed before them as an aspect of professionalism. This attribution will certainly be equally the case when it comes to the fact finders' expectations of highly qualified expert witnesses. As the judge indicates in his discussion of the results of this survey, the aspects of courtroom performance tend to be mutually reinforcing or destructive of the overall evaluation by the jury.

This does not mean that they will necessarily hold a poor demeanor, lack of preparation, or disorganized presentation of testimony and visual aids against the party for whom the lawyers or experts serve. To the contrary, Judge Smith has found in his practice and years on the bench that jurors are conscientious about doing their duty and deciding cases based on their legal instructions and on the evidence produced in the trial. Nevertheless, the effectiveness of the process of communicating that evidence in a credible way from the witness stand is clearly enhanced by a professional, thoroughly prepared, and well-organized presentation of testimony.

Demeanor Professionals, Demeaning Professionalism

Before we launch into a discussion of the ways that a technical expert's demeanor can help or harm the effective communication of testimony, consider the star status that some entertainers have attained simply by perfecting the art of what we might today call extreme manipulations of appearance. In the old days it was called *grinning, gurning,* or *grimacing* and was popular during the seventeenth and eighteenth centuries. An example of such an entertainer is the subject of the sculpture depicted in Figure 11-1. Ricky Jay provides a delightful chapter about this marvelous form of entertainment in his book, *Jay's Journal of Anomalies.*

For grinning to become as successful a performing art as it did, it must have played on the basic assumption that there are definite limits of how much people can willfully change their normal appearances. These professionals could drastically alter their appearances to such a degree and with such variety that they became major stage attractions in addition to their usual haunts with the geeks, troglodytes, and whoever could pass as interesting freaks in circuses and menageries throughout Europe and America.

Jay discusses a number of accomplished grinners in his book. However, he found in his research that it was difficult to identify specific grimaciers because their names

---

8. Smith, "Essay from the Bench," p. 189.

Figure 11-1. *One of several grotesques in the Mirabell Garden in Salzburg, Germany, that was built in 1606 by Archbishop Wolf Dietrich for his mistress, Salome Alt. Archbishop Franz Anton Furst Harrach remodeled the gardens and added these sculptures around 1715. They are sometimes described as likenesses of actual dwarf actors who performed theatre in the garden and at other times as sculptures of grimmacing court jesters. Photographed by Fred Smith in October 2000.*

rarely appeared in the advertisements for their performances. He quotes from a fifteenth-century tract on grinning as to seven of the precepts of the grimacier's art, including the simple grimace, the compound grimace, the laborious grimace, the sad grimace, and several others.[9]

---

9. Jay, Ricky. *Jay's Journal of Anomalies: Conjurers, Cheats, Hustlers, Hoaxsters, Pranksters, Jokesters, Imposters, Pretenders, Side-Show Showmen, Armless Calligraphers, Mechanical Marvels, Popular Entertainments.* New York: Farrar, Strauss, and Giroux, 2001, p. 49.

Is Plastic Surgery an Issue Here—
Face Saving Notwithstanding?

There is a great deal of material in legal reference works about the significance of the face and technological (that is, surgical) advances and retreats in efforts to change what it discloses about a person. There is also a great deal written about the routine reading of a person's character and credibility based on the appearance of his or her face.

For example, James Hillman, in *The Force of Character and the Lasting Life*, has the following to say about the force of the face:

> *Not because of cosmetics and surgery is the face an aesthetic phenomenon, but because it is biologically so. Besides the muscles needed functionally to chew, kiss, sniff, blow, squint, blink, and twitch away a fly, most of the forty-five facial muscles serve only emotional expression. You don't need them to bring in food, to beat down an enemy, nurse an offspring, or perform sexual intercourse. The ventriloquist proves they are not needed for speaking. Nor are they essential to breathing, hearing, or sleeping. The extravagance of facial musculature is all for expression of major emotions, yes; but even more for such peculiar subtleties of civilization as supercilious contempt, wry irony, wide-eyed fawning, cool unconcern, smiling, and sneering.*
>
> *By means of these muscles, our faces make pictures. The psyche displays aesthetically its states of soul. Character traits become intelligible images; yet each expression is characteristically different, and the more complex the character, the more individual the expression.*[10]

Judge James P. Timony explains the difference in judging character out of court and pursuant to the rules of evidence in a trial:

> *In everyday life, we rely on our appraisal of a person's character in judging one's behavior. In order to ascertain whether a person performed an alleged act, it is often useful to know what kind of person he is. The trier of fact must ask himself if this particular person is the kind of person who would do such an act. In deciding whether to believe his story, we want to know his respect for truth and how fairly and accurately he observes, recites and narrates the events in question.*
>
> *At law, however, evidence about the character of a person to show that it is consistent with conduct at issue in the litigation is generally not admissible. Yet, character evidence is admissible for alternative purposes, specifically to show "motive, opportunity, intent, preparation, plan, knowledge, identity, or absence of mistake or accident."*
>
> *Character evidence may be used to impeach a witness on the theory that certain characteristics render that person more prone to testify untruthfully. For example,*

---

10. From the FORCE OF CHARACTER by James Hillman, copyright © 1999 by James Hillman. Used by permission of Random House, Inc. (Full citation: Hillman, James. *The Force of Character and the Lasting Life*. New York: Random House, 1999, pp. 138–139.)

general evidence of the trait of truthfulness or dishonesty of a witness is admissible on the issue of the credibility of the testimony. This form of impeachment evidence may be established by prior misconduct, including criminal convictions, or testimony that demonstrates a reputation for, or an opinion of, untruthfulness.[11]

Of course, demeanor also includes the way the expert goes about considering and responding to contrary opinions and contradictions. These may occur in his or her own testimony or in direct contradictions by the opposing experts, whose demeanor the jurors have already noted or will soon note when those experts testify. We generally don't think about these behaviors as demeanor evidence, but they are a crucial part of the overall attitude and behavior of the expert. Did the expert seem interested in the opposing experts and in their evidence? Did he or she attempt to shrug off these contrary or contradictory proofs? How clear were the distinctions the expert made between the facts he or she found crucial and those that were the focus of the opposing experts or the cross-examining attorney? How plausible were each of these explanations of the differences between the experts?

Timony discusses reports of scientific testing undertaken to determine what basis there is to assume that jurors (or judges, for that matter) are any good at determining credibility on the basis of observing demeanor. There is sparse scientific support for endorsing any one of the several traditional indices of witness demeanor as an indication of a witness's credibility. What is far clearer is that judges and jurors do in fact make these determinations and that they do in fact look at how witnesses, including experts, present themselves. It is also apparent that fact finders listen very carefully not only to the words and sentences that witnesses speak but also to the quality and overall effect of their voices.

Early in her career, Dr. Lillian Glass set out to determine how important voices were to a determination of credibility. Glass is a voice and speech expert who testifies in both state and federal courts about vocal analysis and when speech may be relevant to issues in litigated cases. She has published a number of books on effective use of the voice. In the research concerning the interaction of voice and appearance in credibility determinations, individuals were selected randomly and asked to rate the credibility of several pictured people. For each picture, the test subjects then listened to a voice that was arbitrarily matched with the picture (different voices for different pictures). The subjects then rated the same individuals as to their credibility. The qualities of the voices that were played and matched with individual pictures affected the degree of credibility the test subjects awarded the individuals pictured. How you say it—having a confident, articulate, and pleasant voice—rather than what you say can move a listener toward or away from considering you to be credible.

---

11. Timony, Honorable James P. "Demeanor Credibility." *Catholic University Law Review* 903 (2000). Used with permission of *Catholic University Law Review*.

Remember our old friends the phrenologists? (See Chapter 5.) Here's Hillman's take on their attempts to quantify demeanor:

Phrenology's mistake lay in trying to capture and measure invisible character in the visible face. Form as shaping principle and form as visible shape are co-relative, but not identical. The essential reality of one's image is more like an angel or a demon, not empirical, not measurable, not visible, only imaginable. Even J. K. Lavater of Zurich, the eighteenth-century founder of phrenology, insisted that it took a gifted imagination to apply his rules for reading character. Each face is different—not only because of its individuality, but because of its essential invisibility.[12]

Clarence Darrow "Examines" a Witness as to His Demeanor

As mentioned above, demeanor is often used as part of the evidence of a witness's credibility. Generally, demeanor includes the witness's dress, attitude, behavior, manner, tone of voice, grimaces, gestures, and appearance. Assessment of demeanor, therefore, depends on direct observation of the witness.

This direct observation can be as powerful as it is simplistic. For example, in one of the cases tried by renowned defense attorney Clarence Darrow, a key prosecution witness with a rather unappealing appearance was called to testify. In a classic example of the use of demeanor evidence, Darrow observed:

"[The witness] was a squat, heavy-set man of medium height. . . . His swollen face, bleary eyes, puffy eyelids, and reddish-purple nose marked the habitual drunkard. His shaggy . . . hair had been stranger to brush or comb for so long as to have become tangled and matted. His clothes . . . were covered with dirt and grease. His huge hands . . . were covered with grime."

Darrow's cross-examination of the witness consisted only of his request that the witness stand up and turn around for the jury.[13]

According to Imwinkelried, Darrow chose not to question the witness. His comment to the jury as he passed the witness was simply: "That's all. I just wanted the jury to get a good look at you." Today, most of the cases that reach the appellate courts that deal with demeanor evidence, according to Imwinkelried, involve the increased use of technology and expert witnesses who attempt to testify about traditional aspects of demeanor. These modern demeanor experts include polygraphers, psychologists, anthropologists, and psychiatrists. They have taken on questions such as deception,

---

12. From the FORCE OF CHARACTER by James Hillman, copyright (c) 1999 by James Hillman. Used by permission of Random House, Inc. (Hillman, *The Force of Character and the Lasting Life*, p. 140.)

13. Imwinkelried, Edward J. "Demeanor Impeachment: Law and Tactics." *American Journal of Trial Advocacy* vol. 9, 1985, p. 186.

recovered memories, and the ability to reliably report events witnessed under extreme stress in the few cases that still generate appellate opinions concerning the use and abuse of demeanor evidence.

Techniques for Fine-Tuning Your Courtroom Demeanor

Hopefully by now you are considering how to manage your demeanor before you venture into a courtroom. We now turn our attention to some proven techniques that may allow you to project a calm, centered demeanor that withstands efforts on the part of the adversary's counsel or the overall stress of the trial to pull you off center.

Controlling Demeanor Begins with Learning to Breathe and Relax

Communications expert Arch Lustberg has written a wonderful little book entitled *Testifying with Impact,* originally published by the U.S. Chamber of Commerce. In it he describes two essential ingredients to effective testimony: breathing and relaxation.

In order to relax, Lustberg recommends that you practice relieving tension under pressure by learning to tighten the muscles, then relax them. Repeat until the stress you're experiencing decreases.

> *The best, most complete exercise for reducing pressure is to stand and tense the toes. Drill them into the floor through the soles of your shoes. Tighten the calves. Move the tension up the thighs into the hips. Don't let up. Now tense your fingers. Then tense your forearms. Move the tightness up the arms into the chest and down into the stomach. Don't let up. Tighten the muscles of the head and neck. Your body should be shaking from tension as you raise your arms over your head and stretch as far as you can. Now, relax. Drop the arms. Loosen all those muscles you've just subjected to extreme tension. Feel the surge of well-being that overtakes the entire body. The blood seems to flow naturally again to all parts of the body. The whole process should take under ten seconds. In that time, you'll know nearly complete relaxation—all of it superimposed and controlled by you.*[14]

Learning to breathe correctly is the other essential ingredient to being able to testify effectively every time, but it must go hand in hand with the ability to relax. As Lustberg puts it:

> *You can't be relaxed if you breathe incorrectly. You can't breathe correctly if you're tense.*
>
> *So, the first step in effective communication—the foremost step in conquering tension—is proper breathing. The well-trained professional athlete, stage actor,*

---

14. Lustberg, Arch. *Testifying with Impact.* Washington, D.C.: U.S. Chamber of Commerce, 1985, pp. 13–14.

opera singer or musician demonstrates proper breathing techniques under stress and bears watching. If the method is correct, you won't notice the breathing. If it's wrong, you'll see the shoulders and upper chest move.

The best way to discover the correct breathing method is to lie down, close your eyes, place your fingers just under your rib cage (two to three inches above the navel), and concentrate on the rhythmic movement. On inhalation, the muscle under the fingers moves out. On exhalation, the muscle moves back in. The difficult part of this rhythm is that we've thought and been taught that inhalation means the muscle moves inward and that exhalation means the muscle moves outward. The diaphragm is the muscle located just under the lungs. When the diaphragm flattens, it creates a greater space in which the lungs can fill. When the diaphragm returns, air is literally pushed out of the lungs. . . .

If you've been doing it wrong for years, you can't correct it overnight. It requires effort—conscious effort. But the rewards are great. Proper breathing creates an almost instant feeling of well-being.[15]

Getting Centered with the Martial Arts

The Eastern martial arts, developed over many centuries, are based on the power of being centered in the present. The use of ritualized, systematic techniques, including techniques to relax and to control the breath, are practiced under the direction of a mentor or guru until they are experienced as natural gestures that accompany the exercise of the will. Developing these skills enables the student to master self-control to the point of being concerned solely with the problems presented in combat or other situations. These principles are extremely valuable to the expert who hopes to maintain focus and control while undergoing examination on the witness stand.

This centeredness and concentration seem simple enough in concept, and the practice of a martial art can appear deceptively easy. However, this art form in fact is difficult to attain and to maintain at the highest level of performance. Mastery of a martial art, like mastery of any art, requires conscious application of yourself to a specific discipline, to which you must remain devoted for as long as you practice it competitively. At the same time, such mastery requires the abandonment of many comfortable old habits of thought and action that students wish to cling to for their sense of security. We offer the following analogy to the martial arts only to add to what we said above about the need to think seriously about the physical side of testimony and how important your nonverbal acts, gestures, and overall demeanor are to the fact finders trying to weigh your testimony and your credibility as a witness.

By examining the principles of one of the most advanced forms of the martial arts, aikido, you can conceptualize a discipline akin to some of the skills and commitments required to excel as a witness. Consider aikido, then, as one of the most technically and

---

15. Lustberg, *Testifying with Impact*, pp. 10–12.

ethically advanced of the Eastern martial arts. *Ai* means to coordinate or harmonize; *ki* is the mental and physical energy or strength that comes from the centered and harmonized state of mind; and *do* means a way or method. Aikido is a martial art based on the philosophical concept of peace. In practice, the concept is that an attacker disturbs the harmony of the world by his or her attack, but that disturbance can be harmonized by skillfully using the attacker's nonharmonious thoughts, movements, and momentum against him or her.

To use this analogy to further our own study of what it takes to gain control over behavior on the witness stand, consider that an expert witness must also form some sort of mind-set that will represent to the fact finders the demeanor of a competent and objective expert who is prepared to answer questions, some of which may be extremely aggressive and nonharmonious with the presentation the expert intends to give. As an expert witness it is essential that you believe that you have some objective information to give to the fact finders that will help them understand some issues in the case being litigated. Since you're testifying for one of the contending parties, one way or another you are likely to be attacked directly on cross-examination by the questions of opposing counsel and indirectly by their experts through their testimony. Given what we have already discussed about *Daubert* challenge hearings, it should be clear that the attacks for which you need to prepare can come at several different stages of the litigation ritual. Whatever the form of the attack, or at whatever stage the attack on your competence or credibility takes place, it may be helpful to think through martial arts analogies.

The basic concept in defending yourself from the point of view of aikido is that once you have identified an attack, you must make sure that you are completely in the present and able to deal with what is happening then and there. If your goal as an expert is to do everything in your power to explain your expertise and your conclusions as they relate to the issues in the case, you must remain centered on those goals. A credibility or competence attack by another expert, the lawyer for the other party, or even a hostile judge may embarrass you personally or make you feel bad momentarily, but you must remain centered on the goal and continue to attempt to explain yourself and your findings with the confidence that the fact finders will understand your evidence. Some frivolous attacks must simply be gracefully endured without spending a lot of energy defending against them and without losing sight of your purpose in testifying.

When a defense must be mounted, the first thing to attend to is what is going on inside yourself. What is your state of mind while you are under attack? The basic martial arts concepts that apply to being in a courtroom have to do with staying centered, being calm, striving for objectivity, and maintaining an awareness of what is going on around you. All these concepts can be no more than feel-good buzz words or passive ideas unless you put them into an active practice and discipline with the understanding that consistent application of these basic ideas is the necessary foundation before you can realistically hope to defend against the varied forms and orchestrations of attack that can occur in a courtroom. You must remain centered both as a human being and as an expert witness, in relation to what you really want the jurors or the judge to know about you and your work on the case. Being centered, calm, and objective are not passive concepts in the practice of testifying as an expert. This is your role as an expert witness, and you are attempting to assist an important group of people charged with a serious responsibility to determine what is just in a particular case. But relaxation, breathing, and voice control techniques alone are not likely to be effective when the case is close and the lawyer and the opposing expert are highly skilled. To succeed under the most trying conditions, the character, objectivity, and credibility of the expert will be the deciding factors.

> *And consequently, by the "art" of archery he does not mean the ability of the sportsman, which can be controlled, more or less, by bodily exercises, but an ability whose origin is to be sought in spiritual exercises and whose aim consists in hitting a spiritual goal, so that fundamentally the marksman aims at himself and may even succeed in hitting himself.*[16]

The successful martial artist combines the skills of the hand and mind with the growth of his or her heart; and here we are focusing on the practices that can lead to this synthesis. This can be interpreted as integrating the masculine and the feminine, the aggressive and the merciful, or the logical and the emotional. Everyone knows that those are things that we must do in our lives to be effective members of our societies and to communicate effectively with others. But somehow when we enter a courtroom, we tend to forget these concepts and confuse who we are and what we are trying to accomplish with our abilities. Aikido as a philosophy and as a martial art can remind us that the people on the bench and in the jury box are no different than the people sitting around our living rooms and that we must communicate with them in similar ways. Experts who like tennis or chess have equally helpful analogies to apply to the art of testifying.

It may help to consider the aikido concept of centralization as the notion that you are in a circle and that you control that circle. You can think of this circle as your area of expertise, or alternatively as the things that you have done in working on the case. The other side is going to try to throw you out of your circle or attempt to stretch your circle to a size that you can no longer defend yourself effectively in the expanded space. Either you need to keep people and difficult issues where you can control them and what they can do to you and to your testimony, or you have to be able to eject them from the performance as soon as possible.

---

16. Herrigel, Eugen. *Zen in the Art of Archery*. New York: Random House, 1989, p. 4.

Another concept borrowed from martial arts is extension. The force of ki is a concept that has been put to work by martial artists as well as other artists, like athletes and musicians, who all know that you can alter your physical strength and abilities by using mental concepts to help you improve your skills. When you are waiting to testify or actually on the stand, it's natural to find yourself bombarded by sensations and thoughts about other cases you are working on, things that happened yesterday, and future events you are planning for or worrying about. If you can center yourself only on the specific thing that you have to accomplish during the testimony at the trial under way, you will increase the energy available for carrying out the acts and thoughts necessary for successful testimony. And this energy will not only be something you can feel and use—it will be transmitted in your thoughts, words, and actions in a way that the judge and jurors will perceive loudly and clearly. To borrow from Arch Lustberg once again, it will have an impact.

In the heat of cross-examination, perhaps our martial arts analogy fails to be as apt as others you can think of, since physical contact between the examining attorney and the witness simply is not allowed. However, the same techniques that work in actual contact martial arts competitions may still be instructive for the verbal combat that sometimes occurs in an aggressive cross-examination at trial or in a deposition. In aikido, immobilization means maintaining contact with the attacker by keeping the attacker under control and stopping this momentum or attack before it can do any damage. These techniques have to do with turning a person (or an argument) around so that his or her own force causes enough pain that your opponent can no longer continue to come at you and gives up the fight. Applying the concept of immobilization to testimony, your responses can stop the momentum of a line of questions and render them harmless. This is done by keeping the matters under examination within your circle of protection and demonstrating with your answers that you and your credibility have not been damaged.

It is in this area that the attorney who has sponsored your testimony and called you as a witness will have the necessary skills to protect your credibility and your testimony through timely objections or through appropriate questions on redirect examination at the conclusion of the opponent's attack. While it may prove helpful to think through analogies like the martial arts to gain confidence in the necessary skills you can develop, it is dangerous if you forget that the presentation of effective expert testimony requires even more practice with the other partner to the dance, the attorney.

Finally, projection is a technique you can use when you can't immobilize your attacker within the defense perimeter and also when you perceive that you can't maintain the necessary contact to either turn your opponents around or keep them out. In other words, when you can't control or immobilize the attackers, you need to get them out. Aikido concepts teach that you accomplish this best by using the attacker's momentum and direction of movement to cause him to keep right on going into irrelevant and harmless areas.

In many cases, immobilization techniques are even more effective because they tend to make the attacker look foolish to the judge or the jurors. You must be very careful when applying this technique, however, because the jurors and the judge don't really want to see witnesses playing the role of advocates and appearing to take on the attorney for the opposition. However, if calm and collected answers to ridiculous or irrelevant questions have the effect of humiliating the opposing counsel, it will be acceptable to the fact finders. But avoid moving from a philosophical application of the Eastern martial arts during testimony into the jousting lanes of trial combat. Always remember that these are analogies only and that advocacy is the job of the lawyer, not the expert.

Does the Current Adversary Ethic Threaten or Preserve the Legal System?

The history of the law and legal literature contains countless stories and discussions of the danger to the profession from a "win at all costs" excuse for a lack of ethical principles. Such a pure advocacy avoids or escapes from the bounds of a self-enforced professional cannon of ethics and strictly followed rules of professional conduct by practitioners. One famous story of the commitment of a barrister to the defense of his client at all costs to the interests of the greater society is that of Brougham's defense of Queen Caroline. Walter Bennett includes it in his attempt to reconsider the proper place of the extreme version of the traditional advocacy ethic for trial attorneys today.

> [T]he early nineteenth-century quotation from Henry Peter Brougham in his defense of Queen Caroline, that it is an advocate's "sacred duty . . . to save [one's] client at all hazards and costs . . . [even] if his fate it should unhappily be to involve his country in confusion," often cited as one of the founding creeds of the adversarial ethic, misperceives the ultimate danger. Under our system, the country will survive the confusion caused by zealous advocacy, as numerous over-lawyered, high-profile trials and independent counsel investigations have demonstrated. The question is, will the profession survive this increasing intensity, focus, and myopia? The answer to that is by no means certain.[17]

In this passage, Bennett, a lawyer, writer, trial attorney, and former trial judge who has also taught ethics and law at the University of North Carolina Law School, refers to the legal profession as an endangered professional society and community. While experienced and reasonable minds may and certainly do differ as to the importance of the adversarial ethic for trial lawyers, it should be clear that such an ethic cannot be center

---

17. Bennett, Walter. *The Lawyer's Myth, Reviving Ideals in the Legal Profession.*
Chicago: University of Chicago Press, 2001, p. 83.

stage in the forensic practice of the technical expert witness. The famous quote that Bennett cites from Brougham's defense of the Queen is the antithesis of the motto that should serve the ethical and objective expert witness. The expert's goal must be the opposite of confusion as to any aspect of his or her testimony or service in general, and in the eyes of the jury, the demeanor of the witness may be the key to being perceived as objective and credible rather than confusing or confounding.

Nonverbal
Communications

Our focus so far in this book has been on the substance of an expert's testimony and his or her intent in delivering that testimony. As teachers, businesspeople, and others whose livelihoods depend on effective communication can attest, it's not only what you say but how you say it that matters. Nonverbal messages are an essential component of communication. If the technical details of your communications are the *content* of your testimony, you might be tempted to consider nonverbal communication as the *context* of that testimony. This can certainly be the case. However, for purposes of practicing the art of expert witness testimony, you must recognize that fact finders are likely to consider nonverbal communications as significant as the technical details and the overall verbal explanations presented by the witness.

In this chapter, we explore a wide array of nonverbal communication modalities. We offer suggestions about factoring nonverbal communications into the rest of your communications skills in order to optimize your effectiveness in the courtroom.

Do Nonverbal Communications Really Affect an Expert's Performance?

Imagine that you are serving as a juror in a major murder trial. The defendant is a major media personality, and the victim his glamorous ex-wife. The circumstances of her death were murky at best, and the prosecution is introducing a great deal of evidence that requires a number of expert witnesses to explain its significance to the case. Due to the fame of the victim and defendant, the courtroom is packed, with television cameras and reporters everywhere. The prosecution systematically builds its case, introducing piece after piece of evidence. Each thread of physical evidence is tied together with expert testimony and then carefully woven into the fabric of the prosecution's argument that the defendant murdered his ex-wife in a particularly gruesome fashion. More forensic evidence is introduced to show that the defendant later took great pains to obscure his role in the crime.

The prosecution's case ultimately hinges on the testimony of a single expert, a prominent scientist who attests to the significance of a piece of evidence collected at the murder scene. The testimony is complex, with a lengthy direct examination and cross-examination of the witness. After several hours of rendering and explaining his opinion, the witness is becoming restless. He fidgets in his chair on the witness stand, glancing around in a distracted manner. And then he looks at his watch—not once, but several times during the course of just a few minutes.

What does this action on the part of the witness tell you and your fellow jurors? How does it affect your perception of the expert?

The answers to these questions may be different for individual jurors, and they may well depend on whether the expert is on the stand during direct or cross-examination when he studies his watch. If the witness is a well-known, highly paid professional expert, the jurors may read into his repeated glances at his watch that the witness is calculating how much money he is making by testifying and perhaps how he can manage to string out the questions and his answers to maximize his bill. Jurors know that experts get paid. However, jurors may react badly to situations in which the experts don't appear to be focused on their job, which is to help the jurors understand the evidence. If the expert witness is a public employee and this is part of his normal job, for which he is paid whether he testifies or just sits at his desk, the message is likely to be interpreted differently. When he looks at his watch during direct questioning, the message is likely to be interpreted by jurors as, "My time is too valuable to be wasting it here while these high-profile attorneys play to the media." Should the expert look at his watch while being cross-examined, the message is likely to be interpreted as, "I am feeling pressured. I don't want to have to explain all of this all over again, and I want this questioning to end soon." None of these messages are likely to inspire any trust in the expert's testimony on the part of the jurors. It may be that only one of the jurors will notice this gesture and will not raise it until later. However, if a juror brings up a negative message at a crucial time during the jury's deliberations, when the outcome of the case can rest on the jury's evaluation of the expert's credibility in order to accept or reject his opinions, the price for a simple gesture can be high.

We all recognize how important nonverbal communications are, whether those communications are consciously or subconsciously generated. But information technologies have revolutionized the ways in which we communicate with each other. E-mails, online messages, and chat rooms offer many the opportunity to communicate with others across vast distances, at little or no expense, with little perceivable delay.

These modes of communication also tend to compel us to focus on the content of a communication and to disregard the overall context in which it is delivered. For those whose livelihood is earned online, it is often easy to forget that in offline venues, the nonverbal context can overtake and even become the most important content, often nullifying the intended effect of verbal communications. Be it deliberate or inadvertent, an inappropriate nonverbal cue can introduce a level of doubt into the veracity or perceived relevance of a specific verbal communication.

In court, such doubt can undermine an otherwise strong case. Because IT professionals spend so much of their time in these digitally disengaged environments, the need to remind themselves of the importance of nonverbal communication skills in forensic practices may be greater than for other kinds of experts. We offer suggestions in this chapter to help you overcome this potential disadvantage that IT experts may find themselves saddled with. These suggestions are meant to be read in concert with the chapters on demeanor and the use of visual images.

Verbal and Nonverbal Communications: Which Is More Important for Credibility?

One of the earliest researchers exploring the topic of nonverbal communications was Albert Mehrabian, who performed his research at UCLA, where he is now professor emeritus of psychology. Mehrabian has published on the relative importance of nonverbal communication to the actual words communicated. While Mehrabian's more sophisticated mathematical correlations and variations were limited to situations in which the speaker was attempting to communicate emotions, some general numbers that came out of his research have been celebrated by the business community. These concepts have spawned several new species of communications experts and consultants.

Mehrabian is often cited as an authority for the assumption that less than 10 percent of what the audience uses to attribute credibility to a speaker and his or her remarks comes from the speaker's actual words. Mehrabian found that over 50 percent of the material that a listener uses to determine credibility comes from the listener's observations of the speaker's facial gestures, including the eyes, and body language. Almost 40 percent of the credibility factors a listener uses comes from the appreciation or lack thereof of the speaker's voice in speaking or remaining silent during the communication. In other words, 90 percent of a speaker's credibility is determined by the delivery of the message and less than 10 percent of the credibility is determined by the words spoken.[1]

---

1. Mehrabian, Albert. *Silent Messages: Implicit Communication of Emotions and Attitudes.* Belmont, CA: Wadsworth Publishing, 1971.

This was enlightening news to the business community in the 1960s and '70s, even though it sounds very familiar to us today. And were we writing a book solely for trial lawyers, we could safely assume that they are well aware of books by the likes of Sonya Hamlin and know just how important the delivery of expert testimony is. Similarly, if this were simply a book to teach techies how to give speeches, we could simply refer the technical expert to the countless books and audiovisual aids on that subject. Expert credibility demands careful consideration of nonverbal communication skills.

Lawyers and Technical Experts Generally Prefer to Read

Both members of the expert witness team that will ultimately produce and manage the expert testimony at trial suffer from a terrible curse. Attorneys and technical experts alike come to the task with training that doesn't necessarily prepare them to be excellent speakers. In fact, many of their exposures tend to curtail any natural or learned capacity to present themselves both credibly and persuasively. Lawyers and technical experts, for very different reasons and due to very different training and experiences, tend to generate a most unnatural investment in the words they have read and written about their subject areas of expertise, and of course about the particular case in which the testimony will be presented.

Both lawyers and technical experts can get so stuck on their words and ideas that they are reluctant to allocate practice time to pay the appropriate amount of attention to the other 90 percent of the communication equation. Ironically, most attorneys and, for that matter, most expert witnesses readily admit to understanding the importance of communicating through nonverbal channels. They would probably also acknowledge that to be effective, these techniques need to be pondered and practiced. The most significant problem for both of the players in this drama is that they tend to be very busy. Rather than spending time working with each other on the different aspects of testimony—including not only the words and the story line but also the nonverbal communication techniques—they end up preparing by themselves. This in turn tends to reinforce their dependence on words and phrases and encourages them to ignore liabilities and opportunities alike in their subconscious, nonverbal communication habits.

So what are the lawyer and the expert to do about this problem? Both need to constantly remind themselves and each other that creating effective testimony is a process. Their words, as important as they are, cannot be delivered to maximum effect without due consideration to other equally important elements of the communication process. In particular, the expert's ability to use his or her voice and overall nonverbal communication skills in the context of a performance is critical to his or her effectiveness as a witness. Also, carefully planned images add to the credibility and persuasiveness of the whole package. In other words, the images are not designed simply to drive home a word or phrase uttered from the witness stand but to also indicate that the entire performance of the expert has been designed to explain the relevant scientific or technical processes and conclusions to the fact finders.

Notes Don't Always Help Fact Finders
Remember What's Important

In another oddity of traditional legal practice, until very recently it was exceptionally rare for a judge to allow jurors to take notes during testimony given at trial. The non-verbal communication elements of testimony are easy to miss when your nose is in your notepad. And when given the opportunity to take notes, jurors tend to write down words and phrases, and these have a tendency to become the equivalent of sub-stantive evidence in their deliberations. Worse yet, jurors may argue over these words and phrases for hours and forget all about the importance of the demeanor of the wit-ness while he or she was testifying.

There is a cynical interpretation that could be drawn by someone who has not experienced the results both of allowing jurors to take notes and of denying jurors the opportunity to make a written record while receiving testimony. You might be inclined to feel that preventing note taking by jurors is simply another way to allow the attorneys to try to confuse the jurors with the attorneys' different interpretations of the evidence and their contradictory arguments at the close of the trial. You might object that not allowing the jurors to take their own individual notes deprives them of important evidence and makes it more difficult for them to do their jobs as judges of the facts. But, as with most traditions that have survived for centuries in the evolution of the jury system of trial, it turns out that in certain kinds of cases there are some psychologically sound reasons to limit the note taking to the judge and the attorneys.

Alton Lewis Becker, a linguist at the University of Michigan, has conducted a classroom experiment time and again to determine what happens when students write down what they think they have seen or heard in their presence. Becker asks his audi-ence to take out a piece of paper and a pencil and to carefully observe what he does and says at the podium. He instructs the students to begin making their observations when he says "start" and to continue observing carefully until he says "stop." Then, between the two verbal commands, Becker performs some simple act like climbing a flight of stairs and manipulating an object. The students write down their descriptions of what they observed in the lecture hall. These descriptions are then collected and read. In all the years that Becker has been conducting this experiment, there have never been two descriptions that were the same, and most of the time the descriptions of the scenarios acted out have varied widely within the group of observers.[2]

---

2. Becker, Alton Lewis. *Beyond Translation: Essays Toward a Modern Philology.*
Ann Arbor, MI: University of Michigan Press, 1995.

Becker has also conducted the following experiments over the years. The same rules from the first experiment apply, except that the students are not allowed to take notes and must describe what they see and hear orally. After the demonstration has been concluded, Becker asks the students in random order from around the lecture hall to orally describe what they have just seen or heard. Based on many reenactments of this experiment, Becker finds that after the third or fourth oral account of the demonstration, the rest of the audience members all simply report that they saw and heard what the previous speaker reported seeing and hearing. In other words, the infinite variety of the written accounts fairly quickly converges into a uniform consensus when students are forced into serial, oral reporting of their experiences in the absence of written notes.[3]

The act of writing seems to make a difference in what someone is willing to report as having been the case about a perceived action or utterance. Furthermore, think about having to take the notes while the words are being spoken in testimony, while the witness is gesturing about what he or she is attempting to communicate. This might evoke some deeper understanding of Mehrabian's insights on the importance of observing nonverbal behavior when the acts and utterances of another are especially critical. Given the importance of nonverbal cues, note taking may seriously interfere with a juror's normal process of comprehending the communications of others and assigning credibility to what they are saying or doing.

If this is at all reasonable, we come to the conclusion that the dedicated note taker may be missing up to 90 percent of the information being communicated in order to get 10 percent (the verbal component) completely correct. Individual jurors may have invested a great deal of their attention in their transcriptions of exactly what was said or demonstrated. Unfortunately, this investment might be made without allowing the juror the benefit of even observing what most of us need to consider when deciding whether those words or acts should be given any credibility whatsoever!

Fact finders have a real challenge before them as they juggle attempting to understand complex testimony, determining the credibility of the witness, and gauging whether the witness is knowledgeable as an expert. So, although the law seems to have hung on to an antiquated rule that interferes with jurors getting the best evidence, it may well be that in the rarefied atmosphere of the courtroom, the law is correct in attempting to limit the evidence that jurors actually consider in their deliberations to what is heard through testimony and admitted as documents or other exhibits. In other words, in this environment, it could be that the best way for individual jurors to both get the information and decide on how much credibility to assign to that information is to watch and listen, but leave the official note taking to the court reporter and the paralegals. This doesn't leave accuracy out in the cold—jurors are almost always instructed that they can request that testimony be read back to them during

---

3. Becker, *Beyond Translation.*

deliberations, so any desire for memory joggers can be satisfied.

Once you understand how important the nonverbal communication channels are to the individual fact finders, you are in a position to begin developing all of those nonverbal qualities that can assist you in your quest to be considered credible and persuasive by a judge or a juror.

How Important Is the Quality of the Voice?

More recent psychological and sociological research has actually confirmed and advanced the earlier work published by psychologists such as Albert Mehrabian and Lillian Glass (discussed in Chapter 11).

There is an argument that when verbal and nonverbal cues conflict or contradict each other in the mind of the observer, the nonverbal communications are weighted more heavily in determining whether to credit a particular witness. Clearly there is room for argument on both sides. The point is this: a witness who has some degree of control over his or her nonverbal communications will appear to be more credible than a witness who does not exhibit that control. This is especially true when the witness must contend with cross-examination under stress. This control is perceived as eliminating ambiguous communication cues. Ambiguity in communication tends to create cognitive dissonance in the listener, thereby canceling the credibility of the speaker.

Practicing control and improving your voice and your ability to use gestures and facial expressions naturally and consistently are good investments if you want to be a credible expert witness. These skills will cumulatively lend you advantages when attentive and intelligent fact finders assess your testimony. It will also enable you to focus on the questions presented to you on two planes—the actual words being asked and the context formed by where the line of questions is headed. You also need to learn how the audience is handling your testimony in the context of the examination and in the broader context of the case in general. You need to discern this feedback throughout the testimony or cross-examination without worrying consciously about keeping your breath, posture, facial expressions, and hands under control. Two clichés may be instructive as you prepare for testimony: "Actions speak louder than words," and "Practice makes perfect." Using feedback channels is discussed in Chapter 13.

Combining the Voice, Hands, and Body Language with the Words

In her writings, jury consultant Sonya Hamlin defines nonverbal communication as a physical extension of how you really feel and an expression of what else you may be thinking while you are speaking. "It's what else you do, unconsciously, with your body—with gesture, movement, posture and stance, hands and face—as you communicate a verbal message or when you listen."[4]

The most important point about all this for you to remember as an expert is that nonverbal communication is a physical phenomenon and not some abstract or metaphysical thing. People feel that they understand more about you by assessing how you appear and act, rather than by just listening to the words you say. And this bias for observing how you say things carries over into the rarefied atmosphere of formal testimony at trial. While it is true that the witness stand and the method of questioning severely limit the opportunities for action beyond the spoken word, the spoken word never occurs without other important behaviors accompanying it. Hamlin suggests that attorneys make lists of the things they do to help them explain important things to the people closest to them. This is a good exercise for potential expert witnesses as well. You should also think through the different things you do when in the company of loved ones as opposed to strangers to communicate your needs, wishes, or ideas.

The face, the eyes, the hands, and the posture of the body are all important tools to communicate significance, emotion, and credibility. Hamlin reminds us of old sayings that signify how we really make decisions about speakers and what is meant when we say things like, "He said he's telling the truth, but he didn't look or act like he really meant it." We don't necessarily need to articulate our thoughts or feelings much more than that to demonstrate that we were reading the speaker's behavior and adjusting our interpretation of the credibility of what was said accordingly.

Since it is neither possible nor advisable to attempt to avoid nonverbal communication, every effort must be made to enhance your natural abilities to communicate positively through these channels during testimony. Hamlin has a memorable way of summing up the importance of the most basic and essential forms of nonverbal communication: "After the face and eyes, hands are the most telling aspect of the human body."[5]

Hamlin discusses the potential for both positive and negative communication through the use of open hands, closed hands, hidden hands, hands in the pockets, various kinds of grips on objects, and the use of single and multiple finger positions while speaking or listening. As with the eyes, there are many sayings that confirm the importance we place on using our hands to communicate meaning. For instance, take such common descriptions of the outcome of a competition as, "He won hands down, or at least handily." To "handle" something is to take care of business. To be "handy" is to be useful. To "grasp" something is to understand it. And it is not just sayings about hands that give us a context for the way witnesses use their hands. The positions and

---

4. Hamlin, Sonya. *What Makes Juries Listen Today.* Little Falls, NJ: Glasser Legalworks, 1998, p. 193.

5. Hamlin, *What Makes Juries Listen Today*, p. 201.

movements of the hands yield information as well. We think of open hands as symbolic of many things, including openness to suggestion and a willingness to consider alternatives, as well as honesty. Finally, putting something "in the hands of an expert" is understood to be a practical thing—it's a matter of common sense to rely on special expertise to solve a problem for those who may be handicapped or just less handy!

What's in a Nonverbal Communication?

The area of nonverbal communications includes, as its name indicates, those communications other than spoken language. Such body language includes but is not limited to the following:

- Posture
- Eye contact
- Facial expressions
- Gestures
- Body orientation
- Positioning and proximity
- Vocal qualities
- Humor

This is a very short list, but together these aspects of nonverbal communication modes provide quite an array of factors that can either make or break your expert testimony. Let's explore each in more depth.

Posture

Bad news here—your mother was right, you really do need to stand up straight! Good posture conveys a sense of purpose and trustworthiness to audiences observing you. Standing erect, but not too rigidly, especially if you lean forward a bit, helps you appear to be approachable, reasonable, and congenial. Consider the effect of these qualities if you're hoping to convince fact finders of your mastery of your area of expertise as well as the reliability of your opinions are sound.

Eye Contact

Your attempts to make contact with the lawyers, judges, and jurors and to demonstrate that you want to communicate are often accomplished as much with your eyes as with your voice and spoken words. Good eye contact can signal that you are sincere and even that you appreciate the opportunity to explain something. Jurors naturally will attribute sincerity to witnesses who make intelligent and appropriate use of eye contact when speaking.

Sonya Hamlin suggests that with the eyes we can signal the recognition of others, their existence and importance, and our comprehension that they are willing to learn what we have to tell them. This kind of feedback can come into play in normal jury work only through nonverbal communication because the jurors are not allowed to interrupt the testimony with their own verbalized questions. They are allowed to ask questions through written notes. Often an expert will recall that a question came from a juror who communicated extreme interest in something the expert said through the eye contact made during testimony.[6]

Obviously, it is important to avoid the negative perceptions that can come from an inability, even when inadvertent, to make and maintain appropriate eye contact. To overcome the possibility of being seen as evasive, suspicious, or shifty, you should use your eyes to engage the fact finders when delivering your testimony. Again, since IT experts often spend much of their time communicating with others online, they can become uncomfortable with or lose proficiency in establishing and maintaining appropriate eye contact with live audiences.

Facial Expressions

Facial expressions are among the first things that infants notice and learn to interpret at an early age. One popular infant's toy consists of a set of panels portraying various facial expressions in iconic form. Many parents can attest to the level of interest babies exhibit when these panels are presented to them. A wide array of signals are conveyed in even simple facial expressions. A smile can convey happiness, affiliation, friendliness, and warmth. A scowl can provoke fear in an observer and can elicit elevated heart rates and other reactions from people nearby. A quizzical look (as in Figure 12-1) can allow you to cast doubt on even the most solid assertion, without uttering a single word.

Gestures

Many IT experts, conditioned by years of communicating through a keyboard, lose their natural tendency to gesture while they are speaking. Even when they are encouraged to gesture, their motions may be wooden and awkward. Gestures make presentations more interesting to audiences by capturing their attention and focusing it on appropriate points at appropriate times. Many cultures embed gestural indicators (think of these as the equivalent of acknowledgment signals in digital communication) as part of verbal communications protocols, so gestures may make it easier to communicate a point to a multiethnic audience. Certain gestures, such as nods or shakes of the head, are among the first communications we learn as infants. You can use such gestures to powerfully communicate key points to jurors and to indicate that

---

6. Hamlin, *What Makes Juries Listen Today*, p. 193.

Figure 12-1. *A measured quizzical look can cast doubt on a strong assertion with which you take issue. It tends to make the fact finders anticipate what you are preparing to say as soon as you have a chance to respond verbally. It also gives you an opportunity to collect your thoughts before speaking. (Photo courtesy of Dan Pearlman, Brooke Gamble, and Fred Smith.)*

you are paying attention to the jurors and the other actors in the courtroom. Since gestures are a critical aspect of an expert witness's performance, we'll discuss gestures again later in this chapter.

Body Orientation

In addition to maintaining good posture, performers need to face the audience. This creates a rapport that will help you build alliances with those jurors who will champion your opinion during the jury's deliberation. As outlined in Chapter 10 this is especially important when using visual displays to explain the key points of your opinion. As in conversational venues, turning your back on the jury or looking up or at the floor (as in Figure 12-2) tend to shut out the audience and indicate disinterest. On the other hand, such a gesture in the appropriate context of an outrageous cross-examination may register the proper disdain for the examiner's improper conduct.

Figure 12-2. *Looking at the floor can be interpreted as an indicator that you aren't interested in communicating with the jurors or as a polite and carefully calculated pause in responding to an outrageous comment by the lawyer that does not warrant a verbal response. This allows the fact finders to comprehend that you are mulling over your options rather than responding immediately in kind. (Photo courtesy of Dan Pearlman, Brooke Gamble, and Fred Smith.)*

Positioning and Proximity

Be sensitive to the court rules and cultural norms relevant to establishing an appropriate distance between you and the other occupants of the courtroom. This isn't usually a factor when communicating with the jury, but it might well be an issue when you are working with a visual display or other prop that brings you off of the stand and requires you to interact with counsel. There is a delicate balance between being appropriately close and being so close that you violate another person's space. If a person with whom you are interacting becomes uneasy, tapping his or her fingers or breaking eye contact with you, it may mean that you are violating his or her preferences regarding proximity.

Vocal Qualities

There are six critical elements of vocalization:

1. Loudness
2. Rhythm
3. Tone
4. Pitch
5. Inflection
6. Timbre

Again, conditioned by many years of communicating in keyboard and screen domains, many IT professionals and scientists also tend to speak in monotones. This bodes ill for any speaker hoping to impress a jury of his or her credentials and mastery of the topic in question. It is important to learn to vary the six qualities of your voice in order to optimize the effectiveness of your testimony. One of the major criticisms expressed by audiences of any sort is of speakers who speak in a monotone. Listeners perceive these presenters as boring and dull.

In educational settings, students report that they learn less and lose interest more quickly when listening to teachers who have not learned to modulate their voices. In cases where you must explain a complex technology or process to the jury, such loss of interest is a problem. Should an attorney realize that the best-qualified expert for a case suffers from a tendency to speak in a monotone, a modest investment in a good vocal coach may well be warranted.

Humor

Humor is often overlooked as a presentation tool. Laughter releases stress and tension for both speaker and audience. Though laughter should be well controlled in the courtroom (as a reflection of respect for the formality of the legal process), it remains a way of salvaging rapport with the jurors in extended or complex testimony. Humor is also extremely valuable as a risk control strategy. Should the unexpected befall you as a witness, humor can give you a powerful weapon to reestablish credibility in the face of a fiasco, building affinity with the jurors and the judge.

On the other hand, any conscious injection of humor by an expert is a precarious business. There is a distinct risk that jokes will not go over or will be viewed by jurors as inappropriate even when the humor arises inadvertently in the word play of routine testimony. Therefore, other than the natural humorous reaction to embarrassing or startling situations, the conscious injection of humor should probably be considered as a last resort. The point is not to fear such humor when it takes place naturally, as it will on occasion during testimony, but to allow it to run its course as a healthy and honest rendering of the situation and then quickly get back to work. The situation that Chris Stippich found himself in with his suit pants in tatters (described in Chapter 1) could only be effectively handled in good humor by the witness. By responding that way, Stippich won over the judge, the jury, and the opposing counsel, who all enjoyed the all-too-human moment in an otherwise formal presentation.

Gestures as Essential Components of Testimony and Communication

As indicated above, gestures are an especially important part of nonverbal communications in the courtroom. As such, let's delve a bit deeper into this area. Computational psychologist David McNeill provides an elegant taxonomy for classifying gestures:

> Gestures in this sense are idiosyncratic spontaneous movements of the hands and arms accompanying speech. An example is the hand rising upward while the speaker says "and he climbs up the pipe." Gestures (gesticulation) almost never occur in the absence of speech. "Language-like gestures" are similar in form and appearance to gesticulation but differ in that they are grammatically integrated into the utterance; an example is "the parents were all right, but the kids were [gesture]," where the gesture fills the grammatical slot of an adjective.
>
> In pantomime the hands depict objects or actions, but speech is not obligatory. This weakened speech presence locates pantomime in the middle of Kendon's continuum. There may be either silence or just inarticulate onomatopoetic sound effects ("whoops!" "click!" etc.). Moreover, successive pantomimes can create sequence-like demonstrations, and this is different from gesticulation where successive gestures do not combine. Emblems also occupy the middle area of Kendon's continuum. Which one—emblem or pantomime—belongs more to the right probably is arbitrary.
>
> Emblems are the familiar "Italianate" gestures, mostly insults but some of them praise, and virtually all attempts to control other people's behavior. Emblems have standards of well-formedness, a crucial language-like property that gesticulation and pantomime lack. For example, the OK sign must be made by placing the thumb and index finger in contact; using the thumb and second finger does not produce the OK sign. Thus emblems must meet standards of well-formedness. Emblems have as their characteristic use production in the absence of speech (indeed, this is probably their raison d'etre: they offer a way of getting around speech taboos.)[7]

McNeill allows us to see that gestural communication is rich and varied and involves much more than contextual cues. Gestures pack a great deal of power, especially when the audience grasps that the textual language you are using to communi-

---

7. McNeill, David. *Hand and Mind: What Gestures Reveal about Thought.*
Chicago: University of Chicago Press, 1998, pp. 37-38.

cate is less than complete. This is often necessary in expert technical testimony due to the nature of translating an alien field of expertise for use by a lay judge or jury.

Consider your use of gestures when you travel in countries where you have not mastered the spoken language. Many, indeed most, people react to such scenarios by cobbling together pantomime and single words, often successfully.

In situations when you are testifying about complex technological processes and concepts, you may be using what amounts to a foreign language to the judge and jurors. The use of gestures to augment your verbal explanations can help the fact finders understand your testimony.

Ultimately, It's in Your Hands

Renowned legal librarian and presentation skills expert Marie Wallace is a strong believer in the importance of hand gestures when delivering testimony or any sort of spoken communication. Wallace asserts that many speakers focus on the content of their messages, forgetting that the movement and cadence of hand motions can appreciably increase the understanding and retention of the messages.

There are numerous benefits associated with using hand gestures in your expert testimony.[8] Hand gestures allow you to

- Make better use of your time, by allowing you to say more in less time.
- Illustrate what you mean when you do not have visual displays.
- Add texture and dimension to your ideas. For instance, consider the difference in clarity between an expert who talks about a component which is "eighteen inches long" and the same expert who accompanies that measurement with hand gestures describing the length of the component.
- Uncover your personality and vitality.
- Signal your conviction and confidence. Consider the impact of a speaker who accentuates his points by snapping fingers, wagging a forefinger, or pounding his fist on a podium. These represent ways of saying, "Now pay attention!" "Listen to me!" "This is the truth!"

Some guidelines govern when you should consider using hand gestures. They can be used for the following purposes.

- Expressing emotion or attitude.
- Emphasizing importance, priority, or urgency.

---

8. The information here is based on Wallace, Marie, "It's in Your Hands." Law Library Resource Exchange, December 1, 1997. Accessed July 28, 2002, at *http://www.llrx.com/columns/guide11.htm.*

- Epitomizing action, relationship, or contrast. The positioning of hands can be used to dynamically step through an action, process, or set of states.
- Showing shape, direction, or location. Drawing shapes in the air can sometimes be a powerful way to convey a concept to jurors without resorting to visual displays.
- Signaling recognition, acceptance, departure, or approval. The use of "okay" or "thumbs up" emblems (using McNeill's terminology) is common for this purpose.
- Introducing humor. This can be done by deliberately using gestures that contradict the words being spoken. The discrepancy often creates an entertaining scenario.

Figure 12-3. *Consider the effect of hand positions in conveying the witness's emotion. Here, the apparent folding, tucking, and hiding of both hands, together with the witness's obvious yawning, can only signal negative things to the jurors. These negative communications may include boredom, weariness, or disdain for the entire process and the jurors themselves. Note that an expert who hides her hands can be just as unsettling to jurors as one who yawns in their faces. (Photo courtesy of Dan Pearlman, Brooke Gamble, and Fred Smith.)*

Working with Your Hand Gestures during the Course of Testimony

Stage fright is a fact of life for those who present to audiences, be they a couple of professional colleagues or a room full of strangers. It has been suggested that the number one fear that Americans have is not of a violent attack or an accident while driving but the fear of public speaking. One way to overcome this natural fear of performing in front of a live audience is to allow your hands to enter into the presentation, rather than trying to artificially restrain their natural tendency to help in communicating information and emotion. The extent to which you use hand gestures and the way in which you interweave them with your verbal presentation should vary during the course of your testimony. Here are some more rules of thumb.

Initially, you should plan to deliver your presentation with your hands relaxed at your sides. You may be surprised how much energy and focus it takes to keep your hands by your sides. Those who use their hands in an attempt to defuse their stage fright often make matters worse by revealing their anxiety through their uncontrolled or overcontrolled gestures.

Jurors often sense this anxiety and furthermore become anxious themselves when a witness makes inappropriate gestures. Such gestures include, but are not limited to, the following:

- Gripping the witness stand or lectern
- Fiddling with clothing
- Clenching hands together
- Clutching an object
- Touching a body part (pulling on an ear, wiping the brow, rubbing the chin, scratching the head)

Monitor yourself for such behaviors during testimony and when you find them, stop and place your hands by your side.

Learning to Use Gestures Effectively

Gestures can augment your effectiveness as a witness in court. They do not, however, come without some effort on your part. There are several things you can do to learn to use gestures in a natural, powerful way.

First, understand that gestures are a physical activity much like sports or dance—you don't learn to gesture strictly by reading about it. Though it's fine to do your homework with regard to how different people approach the topic of integrating gestures in presentations, eventually you must simply practice the gestures in front of a mirror. An even better way to improve your use of gestures is to videotape a presentation and have others join you in critiquing your performance, especially your use of nonverbal techniques. As Marie Wallace points out, "New gestures feel as strange to your body as new words do to your mouth; practice them until they are comfortable to you."[9]

You do need to do some additional homework before integrating gestures into particular presentations and testimony. You need to research the gesture scene worldwide since gestures that are accepted as innocuous in the United States may be considered offensive, even obscene, in other cultures. Given the increasing cultural diversity of the United States and many other countries, it pays to know which gestures are acceptable and which are not long before you include them in your presentations.

Although you may find many excellent speakers who use gestures to wonderful effect, you shouldn't attempt to imitate them without first trying them on to see how they fit your style. The best and most powerful gestures are those that are unique to you. Select gestures that make sense to you and mirror your presentation style.

Gestures are wonderful, but don't overdo them. Don't animate or mime your entire speech—focus on a few key areas that benefit from the animations. Avoid using the same gesture over and over again in a pumping action. Use gestures as structure, not decoration. And note that sometimes one-handed gestures are more powerful than two hands mirroring each other.

Finally, at the risk of repeating ourselves, when it comes to integrating gestures in your presentations, practice is key. If you simply do not have the time to go over the entire presentation, including the integration of gestures and graphic exhibits, with the trial attorney, find a friend to help critique your technique. If you don't have a friend available to help this way, then the videocamera can be your best friend during these practice sessions. Practice until the gestures become second nature—then find that friend who will serve as a sanity check to ensure that the gestures and your verbiage flow together seamlessly to form a powerful message. Finally, use the videocamera or tape recorder to ensure that your voice reinforces the image you project with your words, gestures, and movements.

Smile, Partner

As a final note, there is no surer way to inject energy into a courtroom and create a positive impression on the jurors than to simply smile (Figure 12-4). A smile can convey warmth, friendship, affiliation—all in an instant.

---

9. Wallace, "It's in Your Hands."

Figure 12-4. *A smile: the ultimate positive nonverbal communication.*
(Photo courtesy of Dan Pearlman, Brooke Gamble, and Fred Smith.)

Learning to Act the Part of an Expert Witness

All of the discussion in this chapter is intended to accomplish one thing: to get you to understand that a judge or a juror is basically another human being, one who needs to be entertained as well as informed in order to understand your message. Some exposure to the art and the craft of acting should be required not only for those who wish to become trial lawyers but also for those who wish to present key technical evidence in civil and criminal litigation. This blend of law and theatre isn't an abstract notion. For instance, Brooke Gamble, who served as the model for the photographs in this chapter that embody some of the words and ideas put forward, is an accomplished actress. Gamble left the stage to go to law school, and she is now a successful trial lawyer.

You needn't fear the stage of litigation just because you haven't been to acting school and learned how to be a professional entertainer. You need only realize how much easier it is to communicate complex technical ideas and concepts if you can master a few of the basic techniques of nonverbal communication. Like learning to use graphic images, establishing a process for learning and refining the nonverbal components of testimony will help you prepare a better overall performance. Using this process while maintaining your focus on delivering useful information to the judge or jury will help calm your natural fears about testifying. Polishing your performance skills through practice can result in delivering an entertaining and enlightening message to your audience. In this process you may surprise yourself at how much satisfaction comes from succeeding in the role of expert witness. In the final chapter of this book, three highly successful experts share some of their forensic experiences.

Putting It All Together: IT Expert Roles

Although we have used parables and war stories in previous chapters to illustrate the major issues facing IT expert witnesses, these have tended to be examples isolated from the larger continuum. In this chapter, we illustrate how three different IT expert witnesses dealt with the processes we've covered throughout this book.

Rebecca Mercuri: Testifying in Cases of National Importance

Dr. Rebecca Mercuri, a professor at Bryn Mawr College and an expert on electronic voting systems, understands the importance of good timing. She has served as an expert witness and investigator many times during her 20 years in IT, in cases addressing the full gamut of issues from patent disputes to murder. However, her fascination with voting technologies placed her in one of the most visible expert witness roles in recent years. Mercuri defended her dissertation at the University of Pennsylvania on October 27, 2000—just 11 days before the 2000 U.S. presidential election.

When the Initial Interview Consists of a Phone Call

On the Sunday following the election, with the outcome of the election still unclear, Mercuri received a phone call at her New Jersey home. The caller identified himself as the attorney for Vice President Gore. Gore's legal team requested that she prepare a sworn affidavit explaining the necessity for a manual recount of the ballots cast in Florida. She was also asked to stay on standby in case the court should require that she present the affidavit in person.

Mercuri worked through the night on the affidavit, presenting it at 7 A.M. for notarization and then delivering it to an attorney who hand-carried it to Florida for the court hearing on the recount. Although her affidavit was ultimately not used in the Florida case, it was presented later that week to the Eleventh Circuit Court of Appeals and was referenced in the brief to the U.S. Supreme Court.[1]

Qualifications

Mercuri has a rather novel twist on résumés and curricula vitae—she offers an interactive résumé on a Web site. Following is a condensed version of that résumé.[2]

Dr. Rebecca Mercuri's Résumé (Condensed)

Specialties

Voting technology risks and multimedia interactive computing (Web design and programming, computer graphics and animation, digital audio, real-time applications, educational software); computer security (risks analysis, software verification and validation, expert witness testimony); programming languages (assembly through 4th-generation compiler theory). Well-established research agendas and management skills. Strong ability to obtain project funding. Extensive teaching and lecturing experience.

Education

Ph.D., Computer and Information Science, University of Pennsylvania, 2001.

Master of Science in Engineering, University of Pennsylvania, 1990.

Master of Science in Computer Science, Drexel University, Department of Mathematics and Computer Science, 1989. G.P.A. 4.00.

Bachelor of Science in Computer Science, Pennsylvania State University, 1979.

Bachelor of Music in Classical Guitar, Philadelphia College of the Performing Arts (now the University of the Arts), 1977.

Expertise

Programming Languages: C, C++, Java, HTML, Perl, Pascal, Prolog, FORTRAN, BASIC, various assembly languages (RISC II, 68000, 80x86, Z-80, 6502).

Operating Systems: UNIX, Windows, PC/MS-DOS, CP/M, VMS.

---

1. Rosati, Juliana. "Rebecca Mercuri, BMC's Electronic Voting Expert." *The College News* (Bryn Mawr College, Bryn Mawr, PA), March 7, 2001. Accessed July 28, 2002, at *http://www.student.brynmawr.edu/orgs/cnews/current.html.*

2. Mercuri, Rebecca. Personal communication, May 2002, Bryn Mawr, Pennsylvania.

Hardware: Silicon Graphics, IBM PC family, Macintosh, Connection Machine, Sun-4, Apple II family, Z-80 family, VAX 11/780, DEC-20, IBM 360/370.

Job Experience: Academic

Faculty appointments have included:

- Full-time positions at Bryn Mawr College (current), The College of New Jersey (formerly Trenton State College), Drexel University, Mercer County College, and Delaware Valley College.
- Adjunct positions at the Pennsylvania State University, Immaculata College, and Eastern College.
- Guest and visiting lectures at MIT, Princeton University, Long Island University, and West Chester University.
- Contract workshop/seminars for the David Sarnoff Research Center, the United States Army, and the Federal Aviation Administration.

Job Experience: Industry

Notable Software, Philadelphia, PA-Owner and Senior Staff Consultant

- Tasks have required complete involvement with the software development lifecycle encompassing the phases of: concept development, project planning, proposal writing, funding, staffing, training, procurement, design and implementation, testing, documentation, marketing, and production.
- Focus of current projects is on multimedia, Web-based or PDA, interactive design.
- Software Quality Assurance tasks have included verification and validation of program code as well as in-depth analysis and input on System Requirements Documents, System Design Documents, System Test Documents, black-box and white-box testing.
- Expert witness work has involved investigation and testimony for civil, criminal and municipal cases.

AT&T Bell Laboratories, Holmdel, NJ

David Sarnoff Research Center, Princeton, NJ

A Wide Variety of Expert Experiences

Aside from her recent high-profile activity as voting system maven, Mercuri has spent a great deal of time in the expert witness trenches. Each assignment has brought her a new set of insights, with plenty of surprises along the way. Much of her advice is colored by those surprises.

As is clear from her rich and varied educational and professional exposures, Mercuri has a wide variety of expertise. She has served as an expert in the areas of computer security, microprocessor design, and computer architectures. Her multimedia software and systems consulting allowed her to blend her musical education with her avid interest in technology and produced one of her most interesting expert witness engagements.

In this case, a patent infringement dispute, the design of certain MPEG decoder chips used by a major computer manufacturer to support multimedia features was alleged to have infringed on a patent held by a third party. The technical and licensing issues were quite complex since the chip design involved basic components and add-ons required to implement essential functional specifications. The core argument of the plaintiff in the action centered on the MPEG standard, and the question ultimately focused on whether a public standard could be so tightly bound to a proprietary implementation that in essence all implementations based on the standard infringed on the patent. This case required the ability to read the computer code—for the specific patent in question, as well as all of the complex standard specification documents in order to determine their similarities and differences.

Mercuri's exposure to the grim reaper, in a suspected murder case, involved providing expert assistance to a New Jersey public defender's office in determining whether the accused was indeed the murderer. The murder involved a victim who was alleged to have been involved in pedophilia and trafficking in child pornography. Mercuri was asked to assist the legal team in recovering deleted files and searching for additional relevant data on each of the computers of the alleged murderer, another suspect, and the victim. Ultimately, the suspect received a plea bargain offer, in part on the basis of some of the recovered data.

On Testimony before Nonjudicial Fact Finders

Mercuri, by dint of her specialty in assessing risks associated with electronic elections, finds that her expertise is in demand in many novel venues. In particular, she testifies in matters related to voting technology disputes, proposed legislation, or procurements regarding voting systems. Instead of testifying before a court of law, she more often testifies before Congress or other legislative entities. These bodies usually have formal processes of testimony, similar to those of the judicial system. In particular, witnesses are expected to deliver full transcripts of their testimony to the body before testifying.

This represents a special case of testimony for technical experts—an extremely important case. The goals of educating fact finders in the legislative arena are very similar to those that the expert usually has when testifying in a court of law. Consider the following testimony Mercuri delivered to the U.S. House of Representatives Committee on Science.

Good morning. I am Dr. Rebecca Mercuri of Lawrenceville, New Jersey, an Assistant Professor of Computer Science at Bryn Mawr College in Pennsylvania, and President of Notable Software, Inc. (a New Jersey computer consulting firm). My testimony today represents my own opinions and not those of my employers or any professional organizations with which I am affiliated. Thank you for the opportunity to address your Committee on this important matter.

For the last decade, I have investigated voting systems, with particular emphasis on electronic equipment (hardware and software) used to collect and tabulate ballots. Through this research, I have identified numerous flaws inherent to the application of computer technology to the democratic process of elections. These flaws are both technologically and sociologically based, so a quick (or even long-term) fix is not readily apparent. For example, present and proposed computer-based solutions are not able to resolve (and in some cases even increase) the likelihood of vote-selling, coercion, monitoring, disenfranchisement, and fraud in the election process.

Some of the problematic issues with electronic balloting and tabulation systems are as follows:

- *Fully electronic systems do not provide any way that the voter (or election officials) can truly verify that the ballot cast corresponds to that being recorded, transmitted, or tabulated. Any programmer can write code that displays one thing on a screen, records something else, and prints yet another result. There is no known way to ensure that this is not happening inside of a voting system.*

- *Electronic balloting and tabulation makes the tasks performed by poll workers, challengers, and election officials purely procedural, and removes any opportunity to perform bipartisan checks. Any computerized election process is thus entrusted to the small group of individuals who program, construct and maintain the machines. The risk that these systems may be compromised is present whether the computers are reading punched cards or optical scanned sheets, or are kiosk-style or Internet balloting systems.*

- *Although (in many states) convicted felons and foreign citizens are prohibited from voting in U.S. elections, there are no such laws regarding voting system manufacturers, programmers and administrative personnel. Felons and foreigners can (and do!) work at and even own some of the voting machine companies providing equipment to U.S. municipalities.*

- *Each election season, newly deployed voting equipment fails to perform properly in actual use. Communities that rely on promises of security and accuracy when purchasing such systems run the severe risk that they will administer an election whose results may be contested. Even worse, system defects may be revealed years after an election, making all earlier results questionable.*

- *Electronic balloting systems without individual print-outs for examination by the voters do not provide a wholly independent audit trail (despite manufacturer claims to the contrary). As all voting systems (especially electronic) are prone to error, the ability to also perform a manual hand-count of the ballots is essential.*

- *Some electronic systems actually make the balloting process more lengthy, tedious and confusing, by requiring additional keypresses or transactions. The use of such devices has even been viewed, by some, as a modern-day literacy test.*

- *Encryption cannot be relied on to provide end-to-end privacy assurance. Nor can it assure the accuracy of ballot data recorded and tallies rendered. Cryptographic systems, even strong ones, can be cracked or hacked, thus leaving the ballot contents (and possibly also the identity of the voter) open to perusal.*

- *Internet voting (whether at polling places or off-site) provides avenues to the entire planet for malicious denial-of-service attacks. If the major software and hardware manufacturers in the United States are incapable of protecting their own companies from repeated Internet attacks, one must understand that voting systems (created by these firms or others) will be no better (and likely far worse) in terms of vulnerability.*

- *Off-site Internet voting also creates unresolvable problems with authentication, leading to possible loss of voter privacy, and increased opportunities for vote selling. Furthermore, Internet voting may make it easier for the techno-savvy elite to cast ballots, while potentially disenfranchising or at least creating a digital divide for the poor, elderly, rural, and disabled voters who do not have equal access to the Web.*

- *It is not possible to create a standardized voting system that could be used in all municipalities (as has been proposed by some members of Congress), without treading seriously on States' rights issues, and without mandating changes in many conflicting election code laws to provide conformity. (For example, in some States, one can cast a "straight party" ballot in a general election; some States require full-face ballots, etc.)*

These are but some of my concerns; many more appear in articles and papers I and other computer industry experts have written on this subject over the last few years. (Most of which are accessible via my Web site at http://www.notablesoftware.com/evote.html or http://mainline.brynmawr.edu/~rmercuri.) These concerns are not new—Roy Saltman noted many of these issues in his 1988 NBS report.

Now the computer industry has already established standards for secure system certification, mandated by Congress under the Computer Security Act of 1987. NIST typically administers this certification for devices purchased by the Department of Defense. Congress, though, exempted itself from compliance with the Act, hence they have never certified the accuracy and integrity of any computer-based voting systems used in Federal elections. This loophole must be changed. The existing standards are far from perfect, but they are the best assurance mechanism that the computer industry has at present. (It is important to understand that the Federal Election Commission does not now have voting system standards in place. Instead, the purchasers and vendors use an obsolete set of suggested practices that were never adopted by all of the States.)

To date, no electronic voting system has been certified to even the lowest level of the U.S. government or international computer security standards (such as the ISO Common Criteria or its predecessor, TCSEC/ITSEC), nor has any been required to comply with such. No voting system vendor has voluntarily complied with these stan-

dards (although voluntary compliance occurs within other industries, such as health care and banking), despite the fact that most have been made aware of their existence and utility in secure product development. There are also no required standards for voting displays, so computer ballots can be constructed to give advantage to some candidates over others.

I have long recommended that the NIST standards be applied to voting systems. As a part of my Doctoral Dissertation at the University of Pennsylvania, I performed a detailed evaluation of the Common Criteria against the features of voting systems. The painstaking description in the thesis provides an excellent starting point for the development of a voting standard. (I have provided the House Science Committee with a complete copy of my thesis; additional copies may be ordered from me via the contact information at the end of this testimony.) I have also formulated lists of questions that voting system vendors should be required to answer about their products. (Two of these lists are attached to this testimony—it should be noted that the answers are non-trivial and may require months of effort to produce validating documentation, as would be necessary for a Common Criteria evaluation.)

I would suggest that first a trial standard be developed, along with an assessment procedure. Then, voting systems (applying different state requirements) should be constructed and assessed against the standard to see what level of conformance is possible using current technologies. It is important that any new systems maintain a human-readable independent auditing mechanism, and that off-site voting not be used (for reasons mentioned above). All new systems must be subjected to real-world testing conditions (not simulations) to determine usability and discover risks.

In conclusion, I would like to remind the Committee that technology cannot and does not, at present, provide a solution to the balloting and tabulation problem. Our society has become increasingly enamored with computers, yet we all have experienced, first-hand, their (sometimes catastrophic) failures in products we use every day. The same is true for computer-based voting systems, but here, there are no warranties and insurance provided if we have problems with the results. It is therefore crucial that we continue to maintain and impose human checks and balances throughout our election process. This is the only way to insure that our democracy does not become one that is by the machines, of the machines and for the machines. Thank you.[3]

Obviously, in trials to the judge rather than to a jury or when a special master has been appointed by the court to attempt to resolve technical issues that are hotly disputed by the parties to a lawsuit, the practice of providing the fact finder with prepared testimony and then subjecting the expert to examination by the opposing attorney has much to be said for it. Bill Gates began his second appearance in the Microsoft

3. Mercuri, Rebecca. Testimony before the U.S. House of Representatives Committee on Science, Subcommittee on Environment, Technology, & Standards. Rayburn House Office Building, Washington, DC, May 22, 2001.

litigation with a lengthy piece of written testimony. Many attorneys may soon attempt to adapt this approach to the courtroom. Once again the ability to prepare a technical report will be at a premium for experts who are called on for such duty.

On Dealing with Logistic Issues

Based on the very different types of expert assignments she has accepted, Mercuri asserts that some of the biggest headaches associated with expert witness duty have to do with the nuts and bolts of the business relationship between expert witnesses and attorneys. By trial and error, she has learned how to avoid many of these problems and to structure her relationships with lawyers and their clients in more satisfactory ways. She recommends using a retainer arrangement[4] to cover the expert's fees and expenses. The retainer should be tracked, with a running account of hours and expenses drawn against the retainer. It is important to be very clear just what sort of record keeping (timesheets, diaries, notes, and so on) the attorney requires. It's also important to set up billing procedures so that the process information compiled by the expert is prepared in a form and retained in a way that does not create any discovery problems later in the litigation.

The retainer serves as a convenient way to structure tasks and also serves to define decision points in the course of the case. Mercuri reports that in several cases, when the retainer was exhausted with no breakthrough yielded by her investigation or analysis, the choice was made to close the case. In these cases, the retainer reduces the chance that the expert will not be compensated for work performed.

One such case with limited research funds involved a product liability case against a software manufacturer. The plaintiff alleged that the software produced by the defendant failed, causing damage to the plaintiff. Mercuri's investigation and analysis of the software and system convinced Mercuri that there had been postmarket alteration of the software, which nullified the damage claim.

Budgets will not always be sufficient to enable the expert to accomplish everything that he or she believes would be appropriate to thoroughly investigate the problems that are presented. Or, as another expert, David Bailey, puts it, sometimes he just never gets a chance to fully exhaust the software before he exhausts the funds made available for the testing process.[5] This is one of the reasons people in litigation must rely on the objective judgment of an expert to choose the best strategies within the budget to get the necessary work done in order to advise the lawyer and the client about the techni-

---

4. In such a retainer arrangement, the attorneys deposit funds to pay for the work before work is begun, and assignments are made on the basis of available funds remaining.

5. Bailey, David. Personal communication, August 2001, Albuquerque, New Mexico.

cal issues in a given case. Mercuri is very careful to consider how much she can accomplish within the available budget and whether her expertise and experience offer the right combination to get the job done under the given restrictions of time and money.

Surprises amidst Lessons

When asked about the biggest surprise she has gotten in the course of her expert witness duty, Mercuri replied:

> *I'm always surprised by how demanding expert witness work is. I consider myself to have a diverse set of skills, and I've devoted a lot of resources to developing those skills through continuing education and a variety of complimentary professional engagements. However, I have discovered that in many expert witness engagements, those skills are not only used, but tested in a way that I would never have anticipated outside of the forensic context.*[6]

She has also found that with the notoriety and public exposure yielded by her role in resolving the questions surrounding the 2000 presidential election, her biggest challenge now is selecting which engagements to accept.

> *A considerable amount of the voting technology work I do is pro bono, so I try to choose my engagements carefully. Lately I look for engagements that will have the greatest legislative impact, though I find myself doing a lot of amicus briefs and advocacy work in conjunction with disputes over failures of voting systems. These help to demonstrate precedents that I can later cite in other reports and in forensic testimony about similar issues.*[7]

Donald Allison: Finding Feedback Loops to Improve Performance

Donald Allison had a distinct advantage in getting into the IT expert witness game. His wife is an expert witness and neuropsychologist with extensive medical and legal experience who both whetted his appetite for trying it and then advised him on how to succeed as an effective forensic expert. Based on his wife's experience, Allison knew all about the need to avoid jargon and to keep things simple before he got involved as an expert witness. His wife also advised him to find and use real-world analogies to describe technical concepts, even after the concepts had been simplified and the jargon and acronyms eliminated from his vocabulary for forensic purposes. She also made him a believer in making eye contact with the judge and the jurors whenever he

---

6. Mercuri, Rebecca. Personal communication, April 26, 2002, Pacific Grove, California.

7. Mercuri, personal communication, April 26, 2002.

explained an answer and to do the same thing when listening to the attorney's questions.

You might think that all beginning experts get the same advice, whether it comes from a mentoring spouse with professional experience or the first lawyer who solicits the experts' services. You are probably right in thinking that these basic concepts are covered by almost anyone who wants the expert to do a good job and understands that the expert lacks any experience as a forensic witness. However, hearing about these basic requirements in an orientation speech or from time to time while preparing to testify is not enough. These simple pieces of advice are crucial to everything else that needs to be learned, but they tend to be left out of the practice sessions. However, it is these basic habits that the beginning expert needs to learn and practice repeatedly in order to succeed the very first time he or she testifies.

Allison's own expertise has been built on some accelerated learning, through the teaching stories of his expert witness wife, and then again and again in his own practice, giving him an exceptionally solid foundation on which to quickly build up the more sophisticated techniques of testifying. As it turned out, he had a second distinct advantage that helped him quickly adapt to forensic work and find it a comfortable transition, due to years of teaching groups of military systems users and managers about how IT systems work. The combination of an IT career that required him to hone his teaching skills, as indicated in the abbreviated résumé that follows, together with his expert wife's mentoring made his entry relatively painless and provided him with many of the tools to succeed.[8]

Résumé of Donald Eugene Allison

Summary

Information Assurance (IA), Cybercrime, and Critical Information Management consultant. Accomplished leader with multinational computer, network, and applications security and forensics analysis experience for government and commercial clients. Technical-legal expertise. Senior Management training and briefing experience.

Professional Experience

Senior Principal Engineer, design of the Missile Defense Agency Failure Review Board.

---

8. Résumé and other information in this section (unless otherwise noted) provided by Donald Allison, personal communication, February 2002, Foxwoods, Connecticut.

Computer crime investigator trained in forensics examinations of digital evidence. Consulting services in coordination with civil, domestic and criminal investigations. Specialized training in legal proceedings, evidence collection, operating systems, hardware and software.

Senior Principal Engineer, Information Assurance for the Missile Defense Agency, Test and Assessment Directorate. Led IA Program definition, development, implementation, and management.

Modeling and Simulation Lead for the Office of Secretary of Defense Joint Test and Evaluation program. Designed and managed international collection operations.

Technical Advisor to Commander, United States Atlantic Command for Joint Services training. Extensive training operations for senior military Leaders.

Briefed Joint Chiefs of Staff, Congressional subcommittees, senior military leaders, and board-level executives.

Critical Information Management consultation for military and commercial clients.

Operations Research Team Leader. Management of multinational operations including scientific visualization, data mining, advanced simulations, risk management, information management.

Project Manager under contract to NASA's Goddard Space Flight Center. Complete IT life cycle project management.

Employment

2000–2002, Computer Forensics Consultant, self-employed, Richmond, VA

1998–2002, Computer Sciences Corporation, Senior Principal, Arlington, VA

1993–1998, Sonalysts, Inc., Senior Partner, Virginia Beach, VA

1988–1993, Johns Hopkins University Applied Physics Laboratory, Laurel, MD

1985–1988, ST Systems Corporation, Greenbelt, MD

1984–1985, Skidaway Institute of Oceanography, Savannah, GA

Education and Professional Qualifications

High Technology Crime Investigation Association

Regional Computer Forensics Group

Certified Expert Witness

The Florida State University, MS Meteorology, 1984

The Pennsylvania State University, BS Meteorology, 1982

Awards-NASA Graduate Fellowship

Other Experience

Top-Secret Clearance

International Information Assurance operations

Digital forensics investigations: network and stand-alone systems

Incident Response

Strong network, computer, and communications experience

Strong tactical, operational and strategic planning/execution experience

Management of multinational projects with the United Kingdom, Germany, Spain, Italy, Japan, South Korea, and Russia

Allison has handled a number of expert assignments since he became interested in providing expert testimony. Most of those assignments have cast him in the role of digital forensic expert, attempting to explain the existence of certain discovered data that forms the basis of a civil or criminal lawsuit.

In the process of considering and accepting these assignments, conducting his tests and investigations, preparing to testify, and giving deposition and trial testimony, Allison has become convinced that there are a series of feedback loops that any expert witness can recognize and use to improve his or her performance as an expert witness. Five such feedback loops are discussed briefly in the subsections below.[9]

Deciding Whether to Accept an Assignment

The first feedback loop can be found in the process of negotiating whether to accept or decline a solicitation to become involved as an expert witness. Although Allison is well aware of the different kinds of roles that experts can and do play in the litigation process, he is initially looking for feedback from the attorney who has requested his involvement. What Allison has learned to do is similar in some ways to the analogous process of checking out an airplane before deciding to take off, as suggested by David Liddle in an earlier chapter. For Allison the most important thing is more often than not the kind of feedback he receives from the attorney (or, in some cases, from the party as well) when they discuss the approach Allison intends to take with the expert assignment. Thoroughly discussing the amount of time and the resources that the attorney or the party can provide to enable Allison to do the kind of job he feels is required is crucial feedback during the process of deciding whether to become involved.

---

9. Allison, Donald. Personal communication, April 2002, via telephone.

Conducting the Investigation and Reaching Conclusions

All of these issues come back again and again in the second stage of involvement, after the expert accepts an assignment and begins to examine the systems and applications that were involved. This second feedback loop necessarily must build on the first. It requires constant communication between the expert and the attorney to ensure that the work that needs to be done by the expert does get done in a timely fashion and that there are adequate resources and enough time to enable the expert to accomplish his or her mission. Allison has discovered that while almost never is there adequate time and money to do everything he would like to do to prepare to render his expert opinion and to testify, there needs to be a clear plan, based on agreed estimates of adequate time and resources, to cover the necessary ground for him to both reach and defend his conclusions.

This second feedback loop has taken on an increased importance due to the rapidly changing nature of the kinds of problems presented by digital forensics in litigation. In Allison's field, which is essentially the discovery and analysis of digital evidence, the focus of forensic experts who have testified has been on a relatively static data picture. In several of the expert assignments he has accepted, Allison has found that digital evidence problems have traditionally revolved around a seized computer or set of computer media and, as in the *Gates v. Bando* scenario, the experts' attempts to preserve, analyze, and opine as to the significance of the existing data.

Cases involving digital evidence bring up issues that test the limitations of current technology and investigative techniques. In particular, as noted in the *Mitnick* case we covered earlier, it is difficult to reliably link the digital evidence recovered from a computer system to the events that occurred on the system to produce that evidence. Part of the challenge of testifying as an expert in cases involving digital evidence is understanding what you can use as a baseline for going forward with an investigation. In other words, how can you be sure that the data you are using as the basis for your investigation has not been altered? Given the acknowledged problems in securing computer systems, in most situations in which computers are connected to live networks (such as the Internet) it's virtually impossible to rely on any single source of data to reconstruct what may have happened at a particular time on that system. Therefore, the forensic expert needs to test all the systems and applications to see how they behave now and to be able to say how they may have behaved at the time in question. This represents a change in the state of the art in digital forensics moving away from a static forensic examination of data that is accepted as authentic to the need to determine what if anything can be believed at all (and increasingly to the description of the most probable behavior of those applications and systems as a somewhat subjective matter). This has made it even more likely (human nature being what it is in situations of great uncertainty) that the expert will feel the tug of affinity toward the side that has hired him, as described by Brodsky in Chapter 1.

Preparing to Testify at Depositions and Trial

The expert needs the experience of the trial attorney to understand why the rituals of testimony are the way they are and why things like depositions are so different from testimony before a judge at a hearing or a nonjury trial. When a jury of six or twelve is present, for Allison the experience of testifying is as different from the experience of giving a deposition as any two things can be. To prepare for these different rituals requires a good working relationship with the litigator and the trial team. In cases where he serves as the key expert witness, with a backup team of other experts, Allison has found his interaction with the other experts is a crucial component, whether or not the other experts are actually called as witnesses. He asserts that there are very few situations in which he does not feel the necessity of consulting with other experts in order to feel confident about his approaches in handling the facts and in the conclusions he ultimately reaches.

Preparing to testify requires the expert to have on hand an available network of expertise to rely on when making findings and rendering expert opinions. What has surprised Allison the most about the entire process of contested litigation is just how different depositions are. For him the deposition has always seemed to be much more difficult to do well than testifying before a judge or a jury has proved to be. His experiences with depositions have been short periods of actual testimony interspersed with lengthy debates between the lawyers about things that tend to be mind numbing to technologists. Unless the depositions are videotaped, the manners and actions of the attorneys tend to be much less conducive to getting at the substance of the expert's testimony than the same attorney's behavior in court and especially in the presence of the jury.

In one criminal case, Allison found himself falling into the affinity trap described by Brodsky. The case involved the prosecution of a defendant charged with trading in child pornography, and the images that Allison was asked to retrieve and to trace were horrific. As he moved beyond the technical examination of the computers and the data of the defendant and began to prepare for his testimony at the suppression hearing (during which the defense attorney would essentially get to take a shot at Allison's qualifications and conclusions in an effort to exclude the evidence he had found[10]), Allison found himself being tugged to "help" the prosecutor develop explanations that went beyond the quantity and quality of the evidence that could be located and described on the defendant's computer. This began to turn into arguments about the intent of the defendant—something beyond Allison's range of competence as an IT expert witness.

Allison was fortunate in this case to be working with an experienced prosecutor who carefully explained why she needed the most objective expert she could find in

---

10. In many computer crime cases such a suppression hearing serves the same purpose as a *Daubert* challenge hearing.

order to ensure that the jurors did not get confused about what the evidence on the computer was, how it got there, and what had happened to it since it had been stored in that computer or media associated with the computer. She made it clear that Allison's role was strictly limited to presenting the technical evidence and giving his opinions about the state of the evidence. It was her job to make arguments to explain why the jurors could find that the defendant had intentionally obtained and stored the contraband on his computer. Allison could only hurt the case if he came across to the jury as a hired-gun advocate. This all made sense at the time, and after his talk with the prosecutor, it made preparing to testify much easier as well.

What actually happened at the trial made the advice he had gotten from the prosecutor even more valuable. During Allison's cross-examination, the defense attorney was inquiring about how much time Allison had spent looking at these horrific images. At one point the lawyer made a dramatic gesture in front of the jury and said something to the effect that Allison must have liked looking at the pornography if he spent that much time looking at it. Had Allison not been as well prepared as he was, carefully instructed to stick to the technical evidence and avoid even the appearance of advocating for the government, the temptation to say any number of things in response to this insulting question might have gotten the best of him. Instead, he remained silent, staring at the attorney, until first one and then another and then several of the jurors began to chuckle and finally to laugh at the attorney—quite obviously in support of Allison for holding his ground and not stooping to join the desperate defense attorney in the gutter of his thoughtless question. The real confirmation that Allison was doing the right thing came when he chanced to glance at the prosecutor, who was nodding knowingly in his direction, as the judge gaveled the court back to order.

Testifying at Trial

Allison has found that depositions are often boring and tend to be quite confusing to a technical witness because of the number of seemingly irrelevant objections by counsel and other interruptions in the narrative and the exposition of difficult ideas and concepts. For Allison it is actually much easier to testify at trial or in hearings where the context is conducive to a narrative or flowing presentation of the evidence. At trial, in the course of telling your story, it is crucial to key on the subtle and not so subtle cues you get from your audience if you are going to make adjustments in your presentation to help your audience understand what you are trying to teach or explain. Everyone has his or her own style, and for Allison, overcoming his overly logical and technical approach to most everything took hours and hours of practice. What he learned was that although his style is probably still very similar to what it has always been, he has been able to develop several new skills that seem to help him communicate better with the diverse kind of audience that a jury presents.

He always has to assume that several of the jurors have a difficult time understanding technical concepts. They are also unlikely to be as motivated as the military trainees he is used to teaching. He has had to pay attention to all the jurors and to select more or less basic analogies and examples to be able to feel his way along the different understanding curves that different jurors appear to follow. This is also true for different judges, who may be quite sophisticated or completely ignorant of a particular forensic reality that Allison must try to explain as part of his expert testimony.

As in the criminal child pornography case described above, many of the cases that Allison takes on involve an argument between an employee and his or her supervisor or employer about whether someone has planted the trade secrets or the pornography on his or her computer. If Allison cannot get the judge or the jurors to the point of at least understanding what it means for the computer to be operating normally and for a normally operating computer to have this kind of evidence stored or manipulated on it, then the case can become a crap shoot. When the jurors are asked to decide these issues, after the arguments that opposing counsel makes about what the defendant personally did or didn't do with or know about that computer and that particular data, they need to be able to recall your examples and explanations.

An expert witness must learn to establish constant feedback loops with the trial attorney during not only direct examination but also cross-examination to be able to have confidence in the attorney making any objections and arguments that need to be made at any time during the expert's testimony. This also gives the expert the freedom to pay close attention to the opposing attorney during cross-examination and to the jurors or the judge, in order to monitor how the testimony is coming across to all these members of his or her audience. If good direct expert testimony is somewhat like a serious conversation between two good friends, then good cross-examination from the point of view of the expert must at least be described as something else. It doesn't seem like a good idea to appear to be the good friend of the cross-examiner, but a serious conversation is certainly called for. Based on Allison's experience, it is hard to characterize just what kind of an interaction will develop with the opposing counsel, other than to guard against creating the appearance of being either a biased witness or just another paid advocate. In the child porn case, good preparation and feedback from his attorney enabled Allison to appear professional by maintaining his objectivity in the midst of overwhelming temptations to do otherwise, thus rendering the opposing counsel a laughingstock.

Soliciting Participants' Feedback after the Trial

The expert should always consult after trial with the trial attorney to determine whether it is acceptable to discuss his or her performance with the jurors. The possibility of an appeal and certain rules and rulings by the court may make this impossible in the short term. But without doubt, some of the best instruction an expert witness or a trial attorney can have often comes from judges and jurors who are willing to comment on the performance of the witness or attorney.

In addition to the fact finders who actually rendered the judgment in the case, other participants in the trial may be willing to go over the testimony and how it affected them. If the attorneys for both sides don't object, much can be learned by the expert witnesses for both sides by exchanging candid appraisals of each others' performances. When you are looking for feedback after the trial, don't forget to talk to the bailiffs and court reporters. It may be worth spending the time and money on a cup of coffee to get the impressions of these attentive, experienced, and usually objective observers. It is likely that they have seen far better performances and also far worse, and at least you can try to get them to share those stories if they are uncomfortable with talking to you about your own performance.

In a good working relationship between expert and attorney, both parties are going to want to know how they did from the perspective of the other participant in the presentation of expert testimony. Where the expert has been able to sit in on some or all of the other relevant testimony, these observations can be invaluable to the trial lawyer who wants to improve his or her ability to get the most from experts. The same sort of benefits are in store for the expert, if the trial lawyer will find the time to discuss in some detail all the ways the expert's testimony had an impact on the trial and the verdict. If this feedback loop continues to help both the expert and the lawyer improve their communication skills, it is very likely that there will be new opportunities to testify in other cases in which expert services are needed.

Eugene Spafford: Continued Education in the Legal Domain

Few active practitioners in the area of information security have matched the name recognition and accomplishments of Professor Eugene Spafford, Director of the Center for Education and Research in Information Assurance and Security (CERIAS) and full professor of computer sciences at Purdue University. Spafford is widely published in both security and software engineering and is a popular teacher, advisor, and speaker.

Since Spafford is internationally recognized as a seasoned IT expert in computer security and software engineering, we asked him to share his experiences as an expert witness.

The Initial Interview

Spafford is usually contacted by the attorney representing a party in the case at hand. Since he receives a large number of these approaches, Spafford has developed a process for deciding whether to participate in a specific case.

I am willing to provide up-front phone time for free to get a "feel" for the case. Unless I believe that the party involved is acting in good faith, and unless I am convinced I can bring something to the table, I don't take the assignment.[11]

A specialty focus has evolved for Spafford's expert witness services, with much of his efforts applied to questions involving theft of trade secrets and patent or copyright infringement. Although he deliberately shies away from serving as an expert witness in criminal cases, he has testified for the government in federal antitrust cases.

He also reports that at times attorneys representing both parties in a particular case contact him requesting his services. This is a special case of the problem that arises when an attorney contacts more than one expert to try to find out as much as he or she can about the subject matter or to be able to argue later that the experts he or she contacted but did not select are conflicted from representing the other side. Here, because of Spafford's reputation as an expert, both sides believed he would be the right choice for their respective cases. The details of such a situation and the creative actions taken by Spafford to resolve such a potential conflict in a case are outlined later in this chapter.

Qualifications

Spafford has, as do many IT experts, a significant Web presence, with résumé and curriculum vitae accessible through his Web site. He routinely refers those inquiring about his qualifications to his "narrative vita," posted to the Web site, reserving the full (18-page) academic vita for use in qualification (as in *Daubert* challenges). The highlights of Spafford's narrative vita follow. Spafford feels that using a narrative format helps prospective clients quickly assess his qualifications and determine whether he is a good fit for their specific needs.[12]

Narrative Vita, Eugene H. Spafford (condensed)

Position

Eugene Spafford is a professor of Computer Sciences, a professor of Philosophy, and Director of the Center for Education and Research in Information Assurance and Security (CERIAS).

---

11. Spafford, Eugene H. Personal communication, March 24, 2002, West Lafayette, Indiana.

12. Spafford, Eugene H. "Narrative Vita, Eugene H. Spafford." November 1999. Accessed July 28, 2002, at *http://www.cerias.purdue.edu/homes/spaf/narrate.html*.

Background

Dr. Spafford received his B.A. degree with a double major in Mathematics and Computer Sciences from the State University College at Brockport (1979, NY). Upon graduation, he was honored with a SUNY College President's Citation. He then attended the School of Information and Computer Sciences (now the College of Computing) at Georgia Institute of Technology, holding both a Georgia Tech President's Fellowship and a National Science Foundation Graduate Fellowship. He received his M.S. in 1981, and the Ph.D. in 1986 for his design and implementation of the original Clouds reliable, distributed operating system kernel, and for his contributions as one of the original members of the Clouds design team. Next, Dr. Spafford spent a year and a half as a research scientist with the Software Engineering Center at Georgia Tech. His duties there included serving as a principal software engineer with the Mothra software testing project.

At Purdue: Teaching

In 1987, Professor Spafford joined the academic faculty of the Department of Computer Sciences at Purdue University. At Purdue, he has taught courses in operating systems, compiler and language design, computer security, computer architecture, software engineering, networking and data communications, and issues of ethics and professional responsibility. In recent years, Professor Spafford has twice been cited as one of the 10 best undergraduate instructors in the School of Science.

Research

Dr. Spafford's primary research is on issues relating to information security, with a secondary interest in the reliability of computer systems, and the consequences of computer failures. In addition to work in computer and network security, this involves research into issues of computer crime and issues of liability and professional ethics. His work in security has resulted in several oft-cited papers and a number of books, as well as the development of the COPS and Tripwire security programs for UNIX-tools used world-wide for assistance in the management of system security.

Spaf's involvement in information security led, in early 1992, to his formation at Purdue of the COAST Project and Laboratory, of which he was the director. This was an effort to develop workable security technology and practical tools. In May 1998, Purdue University formed the Center for Education and Research in Information Assurance and Security (*CERIAS*) and appointed Spaf as its first Director. This university-wide center is addressing the broader issues of information security and information assurance, and draws on expertise and research across all of the academic disciplines at Purdue.

Because of its structure, and the incorporation of the COAST group in its activities, the CERIAS is the largest and most broadly structured academic research center in the world in its field.

In addition to his security research, Spaf has been an active researcher with the Software Engineering Research Center (SERC)—an NSF University/Industry Cooperative Research Center, located jointly at several universities including Purdue. His research in the SERC included continuing work with testing technology, including the Mothra II testing environment; and with investigation of new approaches to software debugging, including development of the Spyder debugging tool.

Dr. Spafford has also conducted research on issues relating to increasing the reliability of computer systems and the consequences of computer failures. This includes work with distributed computing systems (the Messiahs project).

Dr. Spafford is currently cochair of the ACM's U.S. Public Policy Committee, USACM, cochair of the ACM's Advisory Committee on Security and Privacy, and is one of ACM's two representatives on the Board of the Computing Research Association; he has served as chairman of ACM's Self-Assessment Committee and of its ISEF Awards Committee, as well as served as a charter member of the Technical Standards Committee. He is a member of the Computer Society of the IEEE. He is also a member of the Usenix Association and serves as that organization's campus representative at Purdue.

Over the past few years, Professor Spafford has served in an advisory or consulting capacity on information security and computer crime with several U.S. government agencies and their contractors, including the NSF's CISE division, FBI, National Security Agency, U.S. Attorney's Office, the Secret Service, and the U.S. Air Force. He has also been an advisor to several Fortune 500 firms, and state and national law enforcement agencies around the world. Spaf was a member of the Defense Science Study Group V and was a member of the science study group supporting the U.S. Government's Infosec Research Council. He is currently a member of the Air Force Scientific Advisory Board. He is a past member of the Board of Directors of the National Colloquium on Information Systems Security Education.

On the Importance of Objectivity and Focus

Spafford's points regarding objectivity reinforce the arguments made throughout this book, namely that the role of experts is to act as truth tellers to those involved in the legal process, scrupulously avoiding taking on any advocacy role. In Spafford's words:

> *Experts should help clarify matters of fact. The attorneys are the advocates who are supposed to convince and argue. Experts are much better if they stick strictly to the*

facts and don't try to persuade. In fact, once under oath, I act as if I am an impartial third party. If the attorneys who hired me are well prepared, they will ask the right questions to bolster their case—I don't need to interject my own material or steer the testimony. If the other side asks questions with difficult answers, I am truthful—again, if I have worked with the attorneys who hired me they know it is coming and have planned it in their strategy.[13]

He also provides some specific strategies for those dealing with software and engineering issues associated with intellectual property disputes. Most of his recommendations focus on the use of quantification and objective comparisons to demonstrate key points. Regardless of how impressive the qualifications and experience of a given expert are, jurors want to know the facts. If the expert has discovered facts that help answer a technical question, jurors expect the expert to use these facts to help them understand the issue on which the expert is opining. As one example, Spafford cites a case in which he compared the actual productivity of a software development team to industry averages. In the case, which centered on a question of software theft, the defendants claimed code production rates that were over 15 times the industry norm. The fact finders apparently accepted this anomaly data, along with other evidence of theft, and returned a judgment in favor of the plaintiff.

Spafford sees the use of metrics as key to gaining a competitive advantage in testimony since they reduce the likelihood of any strong attack on cross-examination by forcing the opposing attorney to deal with measurable quantities rather than abstract theories. Quantifying the testing results and the conclusions that the expert has reached allows the expert to return to those measurable things on redirect examination by his or her attorney, in order to clear up any confusion that cross-examination creates. Furthermore, Spafford asserts that the metrics seem to carry great weight even with jurors who have little understanding of IT. "It is very difficult for an opposing expert to gainsay metrics and structural comparisons. It is also very helpful in keeping one's objectivity to have such measures instead of being unduly influenced by the parties."[14]

You might say, "Now wait a minute. This seems to suggest that I should be focusing on providing rather dry research evidence to nontechnical people, instead of giving them my opinion as to whether something is true or valid. Doesn't this abdicate my responsibility as an expert?" Not so, asserts Professor Spafford. "An expert should have cultivated enough experience to have a 'gut feel' for things, but without some repeatable evidentiary measures to back it up it is opinion, and then you are in the space of convincing the jury that your opinion is more valid than someone else's."[15]

---

13. Spafford, personal communication, March 24, 2002.

14. Spafford, personal communication, March 24, 2002.

15. Spafford, personal communication, March 24, 2002.

Spafford also has some advice on how to handle the temptation to take a partisan stance in one's expert testimony:

> *Always remember that people are involved on both sides. In general, the parties are in court because they believe something strongly and need a "referee." That doesn't make either side good or bad. The attorneys are paid to represent their client, and again it is not a matter of good versus evil (well, usually not). But for the timing of a phone call, you could have been hired by the other side! As such, don't get caught up in "us versus them" mentality, or the "we're good, they're bad" mind-set. You are there to testify to fact. Let the judge and/or jury decide the bigger issues.*
>
> *If you find evidence damaging to your client, or you can't find evidence supporting your client's case, be up-front about it. State it early. Don't try to hide it or "cook" it. Knowing about problems in advance can help shape the attorneys' arguments, and may actually lead to a settlement that is less expensive than a drawn-out fight with embarrassing revelations in store on the stand.*[16]

On the Importance of Flexibility of Role

Spafford notes that there have been situations in which although he was initially approached to be an expert witness in an action, his ultimate role was quite different. Furthermore, the unanticipated role turned out to provide a more optimal outcome for all involved.

Case 1: When an Expert Becomes a Mediator

In the first case, Spafford was approached by both parties to an intellectual property dispute:

> *Company A made a specialty product that involved hardware sensors designed to a government specification and custom analysis software. Some of A's employees left and formed Company B that soon began to compete in the same space. Company A executives were concerned that the people [who] left were using the software they developed while working at A as a basis for the analysis software at B. Thus, this would have been a trade secret violation (among other things). Company B made some counterclaims about interference with their business, false claims, etc.*[17]

Spafford became involved when the attorney for Company B contacted him. Spafford spoke with the attorney for about 30 minutes to acquaint himself with the case but didn't agree to take the case immediately. The attorneys for Company A then contacted Spafford and asked him to be their expert in the matter.

---

16. Spafford, personal communication, March 24, 2002.

17. Spafford, personal communication, March 24, 2002.

Based on what he heard in the initial conversations with counsel, Spafford saw an alternative to a full court engagement and decided to suggest to both attorneys that he act as an independent mediator. The attorneys agreed and talked with the judge, who decided to appoint Spafford as a special master. In this role, Spafford agreed to take on the duty of reviewing the evidence (sealed code for both parties plus transcripts of all discovery interviews) and making a decision.

After conducting an analysis of the code provided to him, Spafford discussed his findings with the attorneys and the parties to the dispute. Spafford's expert analysis of the software enabled him to demonstrate to the parties what the software itself showed with regard to the question of theft.

> He was able to show, through use of functional flow diagrams and other structural analysis, that the programs company B was using were not similar to those at A in design or language. The similarities came about because of the language in the federal standards and sensor types they used, which were (of necessity) common to both systems. However, one system was in Fortran and one was in C, one was table-driven and the other used embedded constants, etc.[18]

The outcome was favorable, thanks to Spafford's ability to explain what the software did and did not show.

> Company A's executives (who really were not too angry with the company B folks as they had known each other for years—the executives were simply exercising their fiduciary duty for the corporation) accepted that the software was substantially different. Both sides agreed to drop that component from the suit. I also helped mediate some of the issues involving the non-compete issues.
>
> At that point, my service to the court was done, and I dropped from the case.[19]

Spafford believes that this was a successful resolution of certain IT and intellectual property issues, and his success in mediation was greatly enabled by his expert skills. He was compensated the full amount that he would have collected as an expert for either party. The companies involved in the action split his fee. Furthermore, they told him that his service as a special master had resulted in large cost savings for the parties to the suit. "I was told by the lawyers that I saved their clients something on the order of several hundred thousand dollars by removing that issue from contention (and potentially protracted litigation). I do not know what happened next, but I believe that the remaining issues were then settled out of court."[20]

---

18. Spafford, personal communication, March 24, 2002.

19. Spafford, personal communication, March 24, 2002.

20. Spafford, personal communication, March 24, 2002.

Case 2: The Expert as Technology Tutor for the Judge

You may remember that one of the roles the expert can play is that of an advisor to the fact finder. Spafford tells of a case in which attorneys requested that he take on that advisory role in order to resolve a security-related software dispute.

> *I had one other instance where the two sides asked me to prepare a tutorial for the judge in a complex case involving security software at a firewall. I wasn't a special master, per se, but the judge appointed me as his expert, rather than for the two sides. This was suggested by the lawyers for one firm, and the other agreed. Again, they split my fee. After I delivered the tutorial and answered questions for the judge (no jury was involved in the trial), I was on call for a while in the event the judge needed further information.[21]*

Note the advantages associated with Spafford's service as an advisor to the judge. This arrangement not only saved a great deal of time and money but also forced the lawyers to focus on what remained in dispute. Furthermore, Spafford's assistance gave the judge greater confidence that the technical issues were being clarified in as objective a way as possible.

Lessons Learned

A nice restatement of many of the points made throughout this book are contained in Spafford's recommendations to those IT experts who follow him in expert witness roles. It's only fitting that they serve to consolidate the main points of the book.

- *Spend time talking the issues through with the attorneys so you are clear on the issues of law, and they are clear on the issues of technology.*
- *Learn not to make unnecessary notes so they aren't a matter of discovery.*
- *Don't volunteer to explain answers when being deposed or in court. If an explanation is needed, the attorneys will ask. Brief is better than verbose.*
- *It is not a bad thing to state, on the stand or in deposition, that you can't remember a number or point you made. You can ask to review your deposition or code exhibit or another item to refresh your memory. That is much better than to guess and get caught by the other side—that looks like you either don't know what you are talking about or, worse, trying to lie.*
- *Last of all, speak slowly and clearly for the court report/transcriptionist, judge, and jury. There is no rush. Making certain they hear what you are saying and understand is much more important than finishing quickly![22]*

---

21. Spafford, personal communication, March 24, 2002.

22. Spafford, personal communication, March 24, 2002.

Packing Your Bags and Embarking on Your Own Adventure

And so we come to the end of our journey. We hope that the information we have presented in this book has given you some insight into what goes into the performance of a technical forensic expert. Some of the stories collected here and in previous chapters may serve you best when you decide that a particular request for expert services interests you. Others may give you a general overview about what the experience of being an expert witness entails.

If you had suggested several years ago to the three experts who have shared their stories in this concluding chapter that they would find the experience of working with lawyers on forensic problems to be one of the most enriching experiences of their careers, one or more of them would have called you crazy. They offer their testaments here as examples of the many ways that providing this important service can reward the technical expert. We hope you'll try testifying as an expert witness when the opportunity arises. If you have already developed your skills in performing forensic tasks, we hope that these stories will lead you to pursue other stories and to add your own to the community of technical experts who have taken the plunge.

You may well come away from reading this book believing that you have no interest whatsoever in serving as an expert witness. If so, given the likelihood that litigation will touch your professional life in one way or another, this realization may also be of some value to you as you plan your career. The concepts we have outlined for more effective expert witness testimony should prove useful in other areas of your professional and private life, regardless of whether you choose to take the stand as an expert. Many of the skill sets—from learning to communicate with clarity and credibility to dealing successfully with stressful situations in competitive environments of all kinds—will enhance your success as you climb the career ladder of your choice and otherwise deal with the challenges of communicating both within and without your areas of expertise.

However fervent your initial desire may be to avoid the legal domain, it's important to remember that you may not always have the option to refuse the duty that we all share of giving testimony when it is necessary to resolve a conflict that lands in court. As litigation increases and as ever more important and critical operations move to computer systems and networks, the probability increases that you may be called into service as a witness.

In closing, we urge you to remember that law is a separate and distinct professional specialty with an extremely rigorous set of educational requirements—and for good reason. The law can seem quirky, illogical, complex, inconsistent, and even unfair. But it is also powerful, and the legal system has the ability to deal with serious missteps in a harsh and unforgiving fashion. So it is extremely important that you not attempt to navigate the legal system without the best counsel you can acquire to work with on assignments or to advise you in your general practice as a forensic expert. Nothing in this book is meant to substitute for or second-guess the legal advice you receive in connection with your assignments or from your own competent legal advisors in your own expert enterprise. The law is a dynamic system. Courts make new decisions, parties file new cases, and appeal old ones. Legislatures pass new laws and amend or repeal old ones every day. Never assume that a legal decision is valid unless you first ascertain that it hasn't changed. Throughout the book, we have tried to emphasize the importance of working with or retaining competent counsel and learning to cooperate with them to navigate a safe and optimal course through both enjoyable and treacherous waters.

APPENDIX

Major Cases

Frye v. U.S.
No. 3968 D. C. Circuit Court of Appeals, decided December 3, 1923
Associate Justice Vanorsdel

A single assignment of error is presented for our consideration. In the course of the trial counsel for defendant offered an expert witness to testify to the result of a deception test made upon defendant. It is asserted that blood pressure is influenced by change in the emotions of the witness, and that the systolic blood pressure rises are brought about by nervous impulses sent to the sympathetic branch of the autonomic nervous system. Scientific experiments, it is claimed, have demonstrated that fear, rage, and pain always produce a rise of systolic blood pressure, and that conscious deception or falsehood, concealment of facts, or guilt of crime, accompanied by fear of detection when the person is under examination, raises the systolic blood pressure in a curve, which corresponds exactly to the struggle going on in the subject's mind, between fear and attempted control of that fear, as the examination touches the vital points in respect of which he is attempting to deceive the examiner.

In other words, the theory seems to be that truth is spontaneous, and comes without conscious effort, which is reflected in the blood pressure. The rise thus produced is easily detected and distinguished from the rise produced by mere fear of the examination itself. In the former instance, the pressure rises higher than in the latter, and is more pronounced as the examination proceeds, while in the latter case, if the subject is telling the truth, the pressure registers highest at the beginning of the examination, and gradually diminishes as the examination proceeds.

Prior to the trial defendant was subjected to this deception test, and counsel offered the scientist who conducted the test as an expert to testify to the results obtained. The offer was objected to by counsel for the government, and the court sustained the objection. Counsel for defendant then offered to have the proffered witness conduct a test in the presence of the jury. This also was denied.

Counsel for defendant, in their able presentation of the novel question involved, correctly state in their brief that no cases directly in point have been found. The broad ground, however, upon which they plant their case, is succinctly stated in their brief as follows:

The rule is that the opinions of experts or skilled witnesses are admissible in evidence in those cases in which the matter of inquiry is such that inexperienced persons are unlikely to prove capable of forming a correct judgment upon it, for the reason that the subject-matter so far partakes of a science, art, or trade as to require a previous habit or experience or study in it, in order to acquire a knowledge of it. When the question involved does not lie within the range of common experience or common knowledge, but requires special experience or special knowledge, then the opinions of witnesses skilled in that particular science, art, or trade to which the question relates are admissible in evidence.

Numerous cases are cited in support of the rule. Just when a scientific principle or discovery crosses the line between the experimental and demonstrable stages is difficult to define. Somewhere in the twilight zone the evidential force of the principle must be recognized, and while courts will go a long way in admitting expert testimony deduced from a well-recognized scientific principle or discovery, the thing from which the deduction is made must be sufficiently established to have gained general acceptance in the particular field in which it belongs.

We think the systolic blood pressure deception test has not yet gained such standing and scientific recognition among physiological and psychological authorities as would justify the courts in admitting expert testimony deduced from the discovery, development, and experiments thus far made.

The judgment is affirmed.

Daubert v. Merrell Dow Pharmaceuticals, Inc.

U.S. Supreme Court
DAUBERT v. MERRELL DOW PHARMACEUTICALS, INC., 509 U.S. 579 (1993)
509 U.S. 579
WILLIAM DAUBERT, ET UX., ETC., ET AL., PETITIONERS v. MERRELL DOW
PHARMACEUTICALS, INC.
CERTIORARI TO THE UNITED STATES COURT OF APPEALS FOR THE NINTH
CIRCUIT
No. 92-102
Argued March 30, 1993
Decided June 28, 1993

Petitioners, two minor children and their parents, alleged in their suit against respondent that the children's serious birth defects had been caused by the mothers' prenatal ingestion of Bendectin, a prescription drug marketed by respondent. The District Court granted respondent summary judgment based on a well-credentialed expert's affidavit concluding, upon reviewing the extensive published scientific literature on the subject, that maternal use of Bendectin has not been shown to be a risk factor for human birth defects. Although petitioners had responded with the testimony of eight other well-credentialed experts, who based their conclusion that Bendectin can cause birth defects on animal studies, chemical structure analyses, and the unpublished "reanalysis" of previously published human statistical studies, the court determined that this evidence did not meet the applicable "general acceptance" standard for the admission of expert testimony. The Court of Appeals agreed and affirmed, citing *Frye v. United States*, 54 App. D.C. 46, 47, 293 F. 1013, 1014, for the rule that expert opinion based on a scientific technique is inadmissible unless the technique is "generally accepted" as reliable in the relevant scientific community.

Held:
The Federal Rules of Evidence, not Frye, provide the standard for admitting expert scientific testimony in a federal trial. Pp. 4–17.

(a) Frye's "general acceptance" test was superseded by the Rules' adoption. The Rules occupy the field, *United States v. Abel*, 469 U.S. 45, 49, and, although the common law of evidence may serve as an aid to their application, id., at 51–52, respondent's assertion that they somehow assimilated Frye is unconvincing. Nothing in the Rules as a [509 U.S. 579, 2] whole or in the text and drafting history of Rule 702, which specifically governs expert testimony, gives any indication that "general acceptance" is a necessary precondition to the admissibility of scientific evidence. Moreover, such a rigid standard would be at odds with the Rules' liberal thrust and their general approach of relaxing the traditional barriers to "opinion" testimony. Pp. 4–8.

(b) The Rules—especially Rule 702—place appropriate limits on the admissibility of purportedly scientific evidence by assigning to the trial judge the task of ensuring that an expert's testimony both rests on a reliable foundation and is relevant to the task at hand. The reliability standard is established by Rule 702's requirement that an expert's testimony pertain to "scientific . . . knowledge," since the adjective "scientific" implies a grounding in science's methods and procedures, while the word "knowledge" connotes a body of known facts or of ideas inferred from such facts or accepted as true on good grounds. The Rule's requirement that the testimony "assist the trier of fact to understand the evidence or to determine a fact in issue" goes primarily to relevance by demanding a valid scientific connection to the pertinent inquiry as a precondition to admissibility. Pp. 9–12.

(c) Faced with a proffer of expert scientific testimony under Rule 702, the trial judge, pursuant to Rule 104(a), must make a preliminary assessment of whether the testimony's underlying reasoning or methodology is scientifically valid and properly can be applied to the facts at issue. Many considerations will bear on the inquiry, including whether the theory or technique in question can be (and has been) tested, whether it has been subjected to peer review and publication, its known or potential error rate and the existence and maintenance of standards controlling its operation, and whether it has attracted widespread acceptance within a relevant scientific community. The inquiry is a flexible one, and its focus must be solely on principles and methodology, not on the conclusions that they generate. Throughout, the judge should also be mindful of other applicable Rules. Pp. 12–15.

(d) Cross-examination, presentation of contrary evidence, and careful instruction on the burden of proof, rather than wholesale exclusion under an uncompromising "general acceptance" standard, is the appropriate means by which evidence based on valid principles may be challenged. That even limited screening by the trial judge, on occasion, will prevent the jury from hearing of authentic scientific breakthroughs is simply a consequence of the fact that the Rules are not designed to seek cosmic understanding but, rather, to resolve legal disputes. Pp. 15–17.

951 F.2d 1128 (CA9 1991), vacated and remanded.

BLACKMUN, J., delivered the opinion for a unanimous Court with respect to Parts I and II-A, and the opinion of the Court with respect to Parts II-B, II-C, III, and IV, in which WHITE, O'CONNOR, SCALIA, KENNEDY, SOUTER, and THOMAS, JJ., joined. REHNQUIST, C.J., filed an opinion concurring in part and dissenting in part, in which STEVENS, J., joined, post, p. ___.

Michael H. Gottesman argued the cause for petitioners. With him on the briefs were Kenneth J. Chesebro, Barry J. Nace, David L. Shapiro, and Mary G. Gillick.

Charles Fried argued the cause for respondent. With him on the brief were Charles R. Nesson, Joel I. Klein, Richard G. Taranto, Hall R. Marston, George E. Berry, Edward H. Stratemeier, and W. Glenn Forrester.

---

*Briefs of amici curiae urging reversal were filed for the State of Texas et al. by Dan Morales, Attorney General of Texas, Mark Barnett, Attorney General of South Dakota, Marc Racicot, Attorney General of Montana, Larry EchoHawk, Attorney General of Idaho, and Brian Stuart Koukoutchos; for the American Society of Law, Medicine and Ethics et al. by Joan E. Bertin, Marsha S. Berzon, and Albert H. Meyerhoff; for the Association of Trial Lawyers of America by Jeffrey Robert White and Roxanne Barton Conlin; for Ronald Bayer et al. by Brian Stuart Koukoutchos, Priscilla Budeiri, Arthur Bryant, and George W. Conk; and for Daryl E. Chubin et al. by Ron Simon and Nicole Schultheis.

Briefs of amici curiae urging affirmance were filed for the United States by Acting Solicitor General Wallace, Assistant Attorney General Gerson, Miguel A. Estrada, Michael Jay Singer, and John P. Schnitker; for the American Insurance Association by William J. Kilberg, Paul Blankenstein, Bradford R. Clark, and Craig A. Berrington; for the American Medical Association et al. by Carter G. Phillips, Mark D. Hopson, and Jack R. Bierig; for the American Tort Reform Association by John G. Kester and John W. Vardaman, Jr.; for the Chamber of Commerce of the United States by Timothy B. Dyk, Stephen A. Bokat, and Robin S. Conrad; for the Pharmaceutical Manufacturers Association by Louis R. Cohen and Daniel Marcus; for the Product Liability Advisory Council, Inc., et al. by Victor E. Schwartz, Robert P. Charrow, and Paul F. Rothstein; for the Washington Legal Foundation by Scott G. Campbell, Daniel J. Popeo, and Richard A. Samp; and for Nicolaas Bloembergen et al. by Martin S. Kaufman.

Briefs of amici curiae were filed for the American Association for the Advancement of Science et al. by Richard A. Meserve and Bert Black; for the American College of Legal Medicine by Miles J. Zaremski; for the Carnegie Commission on Science, Technology, and Government by Steven G. Gallagher, Elizabeth H. Esty, and Margaret A. Berger; for the Defense Research Institute, Inc., by Joseph A. Sherman, E. Wayne Taff, and Harvey L. Kaplan; for the New England Journal of Medicine et al. by Michael Malina and Jeffrey I. D. Lewis; for A Group of American Law Professors by Donald N. Bersoff; for Alvan R. Feinstein by Don M. Kennedy, Loretta M. Smith, and Richard A. Oetheimer; and for Kenneth Rothman et al.

OJ JUSTICE BLACKMUN delivered the opinion of the Court.

In this case, we are called upon to determine the standard for admitting expert scientific testimony in a federal trial.

I

Petitioners Jason Daubert and Eric Schuller are minor children born with serious birth defects. They and their parents sued respondent in California state court, alleging that the birth defects had been caused by the mothers' ingestion of Bendectin, a prescription antinausea drug marketed by respondent. Respondent removed the suits to federal court on diversity grounds.

After extensive discovery, respondent moved for summary judgment, contending that Bendectin does not cause birth defects in humans and that petitioners would be unable to come forward with any admissible evidence that it does. In support of its motion, respondent submitted an affidavit of Steven H. Lamm, physician and epidemiologist, who is a well-credentialed expert on the risks from exposure to various [509 U.S. 579, 2] chemical substances.[1] Doctor Lamm stated that he had reviewed all the literature on Bendectin and human birth defects—more than 30 published studies involving over 130,000 patients. No study had found Bendectin to be a human teratogen (i.e., a substance capable of causing malformations in fetuses). On the basis of this review, Doctor Lamm concluded that maternal use of Bendectin during the first trimester of pregnancy has not been shown to be a risk factor for human birth defects.

Petitioners did not (and do not) contest this characterization of the published record regarding Bendectin. Instead, they responded to respondent's motion with the testimony of eight experts of their own, each of whom also possessed impressive credentials.[2] These experts had concluded that Bendectin can cause birth defects. Their conclusions were based upon "in vitro" (test tube) and "in vivo" (live) animal studies that found a link between Bendectin and malformations; pharmacological studies of the chemical structure of Bendectin that purported to show similarities between the [509 U.S. 579, 3] structure of the drug and that of other substance known to cause birth defects; and the "reanalysis" of previously published epidemiological (human statistical) studies.

The District Court granted respondent's motion for summary judgment. The court stated that scientific evidence is admissible only if the principle upon which it is based is "'sufficiently established to have general acceptance in the field to which it belongs.'" 727 F.Supp. 570, 572 (S.D. Cal. 1989), quoting *United States v. Kilgus*, 571 F.2d 508, 510 (CA9 1978). The court concluded that petitioners' evidence did not meet this standard. Given the vast body of epidemiological data concerning Bendectin, the court held, expert opinion which is not based on epidemiological evidence is not admissible to establish causation. 727 F.Supp., at 575. Thus, the animal cell studies, live animal studies, and chemical structure analyses on which petitioners had relied could not raise, by themselves, a reasonably disputable jury issue regarding causation. Ibid. Petitioners' epidemiological analyses, based as they were on recalculations of data in previously published studies that had found no causal link between the drug and birth defects, were ruled to be inadmissible because they had not been published or subjected to peer review. Ibid.

The United States Court of Appeals for the Ninth Circuit affirmed. 951 F.2d 1128 (1991). Citing *Frye v. United States*, 54 App. D.C. 46, 47, 293 F. 1013, 1014 (1923), the court stated that expert opinion based on a scientific technique is inadmissible unless the technique is "generally accepted" as reliable in the relevant scientific community. 951 F.2d, at 1129–1130. The court declared that expert opinion based on a methodology that diverges "significantly from the procedures accepted by recognized authorities in the field . . . cannot be shown to be 'generally accepted as a reliable technique.'" Id., at 1130, quoting *United States v. Solomon*, 753 F.2d 1522, 1526 (CA9 1985). [509 U.S. 579, 4]

The court emphasized that other Courts of Appeals considering the risks of Bendectin had refused to admit reanalyses of epidemiological studies that had been neither published nor subjected to peer review. 951 F.2d, at 1130–1131. Those courts had found unpublished reanalyses "particularly problematic in light of the massive weight of the original published studies supporting [respondent's] position, all of which had undergone full scrutiny from the scientific community." Id., at 1130. Contending that reanalysis is generally accepted by the scientific community only when it is subjected to verification and scrutiny by others in the field, the Court of Appeals rejected petitioners' reanalyses as "unpublished, not subjected to the normal peer review process, and generated solely for use in litigation." Id., at 1131. The court concluded that petitioners' evidence provided an insufficient foundation to allow admission of expert testimony that Bendectin caused their injuries and, accordingly, that petitioners could not satisfy their burden of proving causation at trial.

We granted certiorari, 506 U.S. 914 (1992), in light of sharp divisions among the courts regarding the proper standard for the admission of expert testimony. Compare, e.g., *United States v. Shorter*, 257 U.S. App. D.C. 358, 363–364, 809 F.2d 54, 59–60 (applying the "general acceptance" standard), cert. denied, 484 U.S. 817 (1987), with *DeLuca v. Merrell Dow Pharmaceuticals, Inc.*, 911 F.2d 941, 955 (CA3 1990) (rejecting the "general acceptance" standard).

II

A

In the 70 years since its formulation in the Frye case, the "general acceptance" test has been the dominant standard for determining the admissibility of novel scientific evidence at trial. See E. Green & C. Nesson, *Problems, Cases, and Materials on Evidence* 649 (1983). Although under increasing [509 U.S. 579, 5] attack of late, the rule continues to be followed by a majority of courts, including the Ninth Circuit.[3]

The Frye test has its origin in a short and citation-free 1923 decision concerning the admissibility of evidence derived from a systolic blood pressure deception test, a crude precursor to the polygraph machine. In what has become a famous (perhaps infamous) passage, the then Court of Appeals for the District of Columbia described the device and its operation and declared:

> *"Just when a scientific principle or discovery crosses the line between the experimental and demonstrable stages is difficult to define. Somewhere in this twilight zone, the evidential force of the principle must be recognized, and while courts will go a long way in admitting expert testimony deduced from a well-recognized scientific principle or discovery, the thing from which the deduction is made must be sufficiently established to have gained general acceptance in the particular field in which it belongs." 54 App. D.C., at 47, 293 F., at 1014 (emphasis added).*

Because the deception test had "not yet gained such standing and scientific recognition among physiological and psychological authorities as would justify the courts in admitting expert testimony deduced from the discovery, development, and experiments thus far made," evidence of its results was ruled inadmissible. Ibid.

The merits of the Frye test have been much debated, and scholarship on its proper scope and application is legion.[4] [509 U.S. 579, 6] Petitioners' primary attack, however, is not on the content, but on the continuing authority, of the rule. They contend that the Frye test was superseded by the adoption of the Federal Rules of Evidence.[5] We agree.

We interpret the legislatively enacted Federal Rules of Evidence as we would any statute. *Beech Aircraft Corp. v. Rainey*, 488 U.S. 153, 163 (1988). Rule 402 provides the baseline:

> *"All relevant evidence is admissible, except as otherwise provided by the Constitution of the United States, by Act of Congress, by these rules, or by other rules prescribed by the Supreme Court pursuant to statutory authority. Evidence which is not relevant is not admissible."*

"Relevant evidence" is defined as that which has "any tendency to make the existence of any fact that is of consequence to the determination of the action more probable or less probable than it would be without the evidence." Rule 401. The Rule's basic standard of relevance thus is a liberal one.

Frye, of course, predated the Rules by half a century. In *United States v. Abel*, 469 U.S. 45 (1984), we considered the pertinence of background common law in interpreting the Rules of Evidence. We noted that the Rules occupy the field, id., at 49, but, quoting Professor Cleary, the Reporter, explained that the common law nevertheless could serve as an aid to their application:

> *"'In principle, under the Federal Rules, no common law of evidence remains. "All relevant evidence is admissible, except as otherwise provided. . . ." In reality, of course,*

*the body of common law knowledge continues to exist, though in the somewhat
altered form of a source of guidance in the exercise of delegated powers.'" Id., at
51–52.*

We found the common law precept at issue in the Abel case entirely consistent
with Rule 402's general requirement of admissibility, and considered it unlikely that
the drafters had intended to change the rule. Id., at 50–51. In *Bourjaily v. United States,*
483 U.S. 171 (1987), on the other hand, the Court was unable to find a particular com-
mon-law doctrine in the Rules, and so held it superseded.

Here there is a specific Rule that speaks to the contested issue. Rule 702, governing expert testimony, provides:

> *"If scientific, technical, or other specialized knowledge will assist the trier of fact to
> understand the evidence or to determine a fact in issue, a witness qualified as an
> expert by knowledge, skill, experience, training, [509 U.S. 579, 8] or education, may
> testify thereto in the form of an opinion or otherwise."*

Nothing in the text of this Rule establishes "general acceptance" as an absolute
prerequisite to admissibility. Nor does respondent present any clear indication that
Rule 702 or the Rules as a whole were intended to incorporate a "general acceptance"
standard. The drafting history makes no mention of Frye, and a rigid "general acceptance" requirement would be at odds with the "liberal thrust" of the Federal Rules and
their "general approach of relaxing the traditional barriers to 'opinion' testimony."
Beech Aircraft Corp. v. Rainey, 488 U.S., at 169 (citing Rules 701 to 705). See also
Weinstein, Rule 702 of the "Federal Rules of Evidence is Sound; It Should Not Be
Amended," 138 F.R.D. 631 (1991) ("The Rules were designed to depend primarily
upon lawyer-adversaries and sensible triers of fact to evaluate conflicts"). Given the
Rules' permissive backdrop and their inclusion of a specific rule on expert testimony
that does not mention "general acceptance," the assertion that the Rules somehow
assimilated Frye is unconvincing. Frye made "general acceptance" the exclusive test for
admitting expert scientific testimony. That austere standard, absent from, and incom-
patible with, the Federal Rules of Evidence, should not be applied in federal trials.[6]

B

That the Frye test was displaced by the Rules of Evidence does not mean, however, that
the Rules themselves place no limits on the admissibility of purportedly scientific evidence.[7] Nor is the trial judge disabled from screening such evidence. To the contrary,
under the Rules, the trial judge must ensure that any and all scientific testimony or evidence admitted is not only relevant, but reliable.

The primary locus of this obligation is Rule 702, which clearly contemplates some
degree of regulation of the subjects and theories about which an expert may testify. "If
scientific, technical, or other specialized knowledge will assist the trier of fact to

understand the evidence or to determine a fact in issue," an expert "may testify thereto." (Emphasis added.) The subject of an expert's testimony must be "scientific . . . knowledge."[8] The adjective "scientific" implies a grounding in the methods and procedures of science. Similarly, the word "knowledge" [connotes more than subjective belief or unsupported speculation]. The term "applies to any body of known facts or to any body of ideas inferred from such facts or accepted as truths on good grounds." *Webster's Third New International Dictionary* 1252 (1986). Of course, it would be unreasonable to conclude that the subject of scientific testimony must be "known" to a certainty; arguably, there are no certainties in science. See, e.g., Brief for Nicolaas Bloembergen et al. as Amici Curiae 9 ("Indeed, scientists do not assert that they know what is immutably 'true'—they are committed to searching for new, temporary theories to explain, as best they can, phenomena"); Brief for American Association for the Advancement of Science et al. as Amici Curiae 7–8 ("Science is not an encyclopedic body of knowledge about [509 U.S. 579, 10] the universe. Instead, it represents a process for proposing and refining theoretical explanations about the world that are subject to further testing and refinement" (emphasis in original). But, in order to qualify as "scientific knowledge," an inference or assertion must be [derived by the scientific method]. Proposed testimony must be supported by [appropriate validation]— i.e., "good grounds," based on what is known. In short, the requirement that an expert's testimony pertain to "scientific knowledge" establishes a standard of evidentiary reliability.[9]

Rule 702 further requires that the evidence or testimony "assist the trier of fact to understand the evidence or to determine a fact in issue." This condition goes primarily to relevance. "Expert testimony which does not relate to any issue in the case is not relevant and, ergo, nonhelpful." 3 Weinstein & Berger 70202., p. 702–18. See also *United States v. Downing*, 753 F.2d 1224, 1242 (CA3 1985) ("An additional consideration under Rule 702—and another aspect of relevancy—is whether expert testimony proffered in the [509 U.S. 579, 11] case is sufficiently tied to the facts of the case that it will aid the jury in resolving a factual dispute"). The consideration has been aptly described by Judge Becker as one of "fit." Ibid. "Fit" is not always obvious, and scientific validity for one purpose is not necessarily scientific validity for other, unrelated purposes. See Starrs, *Frye v. United States* "Restructured and Revitalized: A Proposal to Amend Federal Evidence Rule 702," 26 *Jurimetrics J.* 249, 258 (1986). The study of the phases of the moon, for example, may provide valid scientific "knowledge" about whether a certain night was dark, and if darkness is a fact in issue, the knowledge will assist the trier of fact. However (absent creditable grounds supporting such a link), evidence that the moon was full on a certain night will not assist the trier of fact in determining whether an individual was unusually likely to have behaved irrationally on that night. Rule 702's "helpfulness" standard requires a valid scientific connection to the pertinent inquiry as a precondition to admissibility.

That these requirements are embodied in Rule 702 is not surprising. Unlike an ordinary witness, see Rule 701, an expert is permitted wide latitude to offer opinions, including those that are not based on firsthand knowledge or observation. See Rules 702 and 703. Presumably, this relaxation of the usual requirement of firsthand knowledge—a rule which represents "a 'most pervasive manifestation' of the common law insistence upon 'the most reliable sources of information,'" Advisory Committee's Notes on Fed. Rule Evid. 602, 28 U.S.C. App., p. 755 (citation omitted)—is premised on an assumption that the expert's opinion will have a reliable basis in the knowledge and experience of his discipline.

C

Faced with a proffer of expert scientific testimony, then, the trial judge must determine at the outset, pursuant to [509 U.S. 579, 12] Rule 104(a),[10] whether the expert is proposing to testify to (1) scientific knowledge that (2) will assist the trier of fact to understand or determine a fact in issue.[11] This entails a preliminary assessment of whether the reasoning or methodology underlying the testimony is scientifically valid, and of whether that reasoning or methodology properly can be applied to the facts in issue. We are confident that federal judges possess the capacity to undertake this review. Many factors will bear on the inquiry, and we do not presume to set out a definitive checklist or test. But some general observations are appropriate.

Ordinarily, a key question to be answered in determining whether a theory or technique is scientific knowledge that will assist the trier of fact will be whether it can be (and has been) tested. "Scientific methodology today is based on generating hypotheses and testing them to see if they can be falsified; indeed, this methodology is what distinguishes science from other fields of human inquiry." Green, 645. See also C. Hempel, *Philosophy of Natural Science* 49 (1966) ("[T]he statements constituting a scientific explanation must be capable of empirical test"); K. Popper, *Conjectures and Refutations: The Growth of Scientific Knowledge* 37 (5th ed. [509 U.S. 579, 13] 1989) ("[T]he criterion of the scientific status of a theory is its falsifiability, or refutability, or testability").

Another pertinent consideration is whether the theory or technique has been subjected to peer review and publication. Publication (which is but one element of peer review) is not a sine qua non of admissibility; it does not necessarily correlate with reliability, see S. Jasanoff, *The Fifth Branch: Science Advisors as Policymakers* 61–76 (1990), and, in some instances, well-grounded but innovative theories will not have been published, see Horrobin, "The Philosophical Basis of Peer Review and the Suppression of Innovation," 263 *JAMA* 1438 (1990). Some propositions, moreover, are too particular, too new, or of too limited interest to be published. But submission to the scrutiny of the scientific community is a component of "good science," in part because it increases the likelihood that substantive flaws in methodology will be detected. See J. Ziman, *Reliable Knowledge: An Exploration of the Grounds for Belief in Science* 130–133 (1978); Relman & Angell, *How Good Is Peer Review?*, 321 New Eng.J.Med. 827 (1989). The fact of publication (or lack thereof) in a peer reviewed journal thus will be a relevant, though not dispositive, consideration in assessing the scientific validity of a particular technique or methodology on which an opinion is premised.

Additionally, in the case of a particular scientific technique, the court ordinarily should consider the known or potential rate of error, see, e.g., *United States v. Smith*, 869 F.2d 348, 353–354 (CA7 1989) (surveying studies of the error rate of spectrographic voice identification technique), and the existence and maintenance of standards controlling the technique's operation, see *United States v. Williams*, 583 F.2d 1194, 1198 (CA2 1978) (noting professional organization's standard governing spectrographic analysis).

Finally, "general acceptance" can yet have a bearing on the inquiry. A "reliability assessment does not require, although [509 U.S. 579, 14] it does permit, explicit identification of a relevant scientific community and an express determination of a particular degree of acceptance within that community." *United States v. Downing*, 753 F.2d, at 1238. See also 3 Weinstein Berger 70203., pp. 702–41 to 702–42. Widespread acceptance can be an important factor in ruling particular evidence admissible, and "a known technique which has been able to attract only minimal support within the community," Downing, 753 F.2d, at 1238, may properly be viewed with skepticism.

The inquiry envisioned by Rule 702 is, we emphasize, a flexible one.[12] Its overarching subject is the scientific validity—and thus the evidentiary relevance and reliability—of the principles that underlie a proposed submission. The focus, of course, must be solely on principles and methodology, not on the conclusions that they generate.

Throughout, a judge assessing a proffer of expert scientific testimony under Rule 702 should also be mindful of other applicable rules. Rule 703 provides that expert opinions based on otherwise inadmissible hearsay are to be admitted only if the facts or data are "of a type reasonably relied upon by experts in the particular field in forming opinions or inferences upon the subject." Rule 706 allows the court at its discretion to procure the assistance of an expert of its own choosing. Finally, Rule 403 permits the exclusion of relevant evidence "if its probative value is substantially outweighed by the danger of unfair prejudice, confusion of the issues, or misleading the jury. . . ." Judge Weinstein has explained: "Expert evidence can be both powerful and quite misleading because of the difficulty in evaluating it. Because of this risk, the judge, in weighing possible prejudice against probative force under Rule 403 of the present rules, exercises more control over experts than over lay witnesses." Weinstein, 138 F.R.D., at 632.

III

We conclude by briefly addressing what appear to be two underlying concerns of the parties and amici in this case. Respondent expresses apprehension that abandonment of "general acceptance" as the exclusive requirement for admission will result in a "free-for-all" in which befuddled juries are confounded by absurd and irrational pseudoscientific assertions. In this regard, respondent seems to us to be overly pessimistic about the capabilities of the jury and of the adversary system generally. Vigorous cross-examination, presentation of contrary evidence, and careful instruction on the burden of proof are the traditional and appropriate means of attacking shaky but admissible evidence. See *Rock v. Arkansas*, 483 U.S. 44, 61 (1987). Additionally, in the event the trial court concludes that the scintilla of evidence presented supporting a position is insufficient to allow a reasonable juror to conclude that the position more likely than not is true, the court remains free to direct a judgment, Fed. Rule Civ. Proc. 50(a), and likewise to grant summary judgment, Fed. Rule Civ. Proc. 56. Cf., e.g., *Turpin v. Merrell Dow Pharmaceuticals, Inc.*, 959 F.2d 1349 (CA6) (holding that scientific evidence that provided foundation for expert testimony, viewed in the light most favorable to plaintiffs, was not sufficient to allow a jury to find it more probable than not that defendant caused plaintiff's injury); *Brock v. Merrell Dow Pharmaceuticals, Inc.*, 874 F.2d 307 (CA5 1989) (reversing judgment entered on jury verdict for plaintiffs because evidence regarding causation was insufficient), modified, 884 F.2d 166 (CA5 1989). These conventional devices, rather than wholesale exclusion under an uncompromising "general acceptance" test, are the appropriate safeguards where the basis of scientific testimony meets the standards of Rule 702.

Petitioners and, to a greater extent, their amici exhibit a different concern. They suggest that recognition of a screening role for the judge that allows for the exclusion of "invalid" evidence will sanction a stifling and repressive scientific orthodoxy, and will be inimical to the search for truth. See, e.g., Brief for Ronald Bayer et al. as Amici Curiae. It is true that open debate is an essential part of both legal and scientific analyses. Yet there are important differences between the quest for truth in the courtroom and the quest for truth in the laboratory. Scientific conclusions are subject to perpetual revision. Law, on the other hand, must resolve disputes finally and quickly. The scientific project is advanced by broad and wide-ranging consideration of a multitude of hypotheses, for those that are incorrect will eventually be shown to be so, and that in itself is an advance. Conjectures that are probably wrong are of little use, however, in the project of reaching a quick, final, and binding legal judgment—often of great consequence—about a particular set of events in the past. We recognize that, in practice, a gatekeeping role for the judge, no matter how flexible, inevitably on occasion will prevent the jury from learning of authentic insights and innovations. That, nevertheless, is the balance that is struck by Rules of Evidence designed not for the exhaustive search for cosmic understanding, [509 U.S. 579, 17] but for the particularized resolution of legal disputes.[13]

IV

To summarize: "General acceptance" is not a necessary precondition to the admissibility of scientific evidence under the Federal Rules of Evidence, but the Rules of Evidence—especially Rule 702—do assign to the trial judge the task of ensuring that an expert's testimony both rests on a reliable foundation and is relevant to the task at hand. Pertinent evidence based on scientifically valid principles will satisfy those demands.

The inquiries of the District Court and the Court of Appeals focused almost exclusively on "general acceptance," as gauged by publication and the decisions of other courts. Accordingly, the judgment of the Court of Appeals is vacated, and the case is remanded for further proceedings consistent with this opinion.

It is so ordered.

Footnotes

[Footnote 1] Doctor Lamm received his master's and doctor of medicine degrees from the University of Southern California. He has served as a consultant in birth-defect epidemiology for the National Center for Health Statistics, and has published numerous articles on the magnitude of risk from exposure to various chemical and biological substances. App. 34–44.

[Footnote 2] For example, Shanna Helen Swan, who received a master's degree in biostatistics from Columbia University and a doctorate in statistics from the University of California at Berkeley, is chief of the section of the California Department of Health and Services that determines causes of birth defects, and has served as a consultant to the World Health Organization, the Food and Drug Administration, and the National Institutes of Health. Id., at degree 113–114, 131–132. Stuart A. Newman, who received his bachelor's in chemistry from Columbia University and his master's and doctorate in chemistry from the University of Chicago, respectively, is a professor at New York Medical College, and has spent over a decade studying the effect of chemicals on limb development. Id., at 54–56. The credentials of the others are similarly impressive. See id., at 61–66, 73–80, 148–153, 187–192, and Attachments 12, 20, 21, 26, 31, and 32 to Petitioners' Opposition to Summary Judgment, in No. 84-20, 3-G(I) (SD Cal.).

[Footnote 3] For a catalog of the many cases on either side of this controversy, see P. Giannelli & E. Imwinkelried, *Scientific Evidence* 1–5, pp. 10–14 (1986 and Supp. 1991).

[Footnote 4] See, e.g., Green, *Expert Witnesses and Sufficiency of Evidence in Toxic Substances Litigation: The Legacy of Agent Orange and Bendectin Litigation*, 86 Nw.U.L.Rev. 643 (1992) (hereinafter Green); Becker & Orenstein, *The Federal Rules of Evidence After Sixteen Years—the Effect of "Plain Meaning" Jurisprudence, the Need for an Advisory* [509 U.S. 579, 6] *Committee on the Rules of Evidence, and Suggestions for Selective Revision of the Rules*, 60 Geo. WashL.Rev. 857, 876–885 (1992); Hanson, James, *Alphonzo Frye is Sixty-Five Years Old; Should He Retire?*, 16 West St.U.L.Rev. 357 (1989); Black, *A Unified Theory of Scientific Evidence*, 56 Ford.L.Rev. 595 (1988), Imwinkelried, *The "Bases" of Expert Testimony: The Syllogistic Structure of Scientific Testimony*, 67 N.C.L.Rev. 1 (1988); *Proposals for a Model Rule on the Admissibility of Scientific Evidence*, 26 Jurimetrics J. 235 (1986); Giannelli, *The Admissibility of Novel Scientific Evidence: Frye v. United States, a Half-Century Later*, 80 Colum.L.Rev. 1197 (1980); *The Supreme Court, 1986 Term*, 101 Harv.L.Rev. 7, 119, 125–127 (1987).

Indeed, the debates over Frye are such a well-established part of the academic landscape that a distinct term—"Frye ologist"—has been advanced to describe those who take part. See Behringer, *Introduction, Proposals for a Model Rule on the Admissibility of Scientific Evidence*, 26 Jurimetrics J., 237, 239 (1986), quoting Lacey, *Scientific Evidence*, 24 Jurimetrics J. 254, 264 (1984).

[Footnote 5] Like the question of Frye's merit, the dispute over its survival has divided courts and commentators. Compare, e.g., *United States v. Frye* is superseded by the Rules of Evidence, Williams, 583 F.2d 1194 (CA2 1978) cert. denied, 439 U.S. 1117 (1979) with *Christophersen v. Allied-Signal Corp.*, 939 F.2d 1106, 1111, 1115-1116 (CA5 1991) (en banc) (Frye and the Rules coexist), cert. denied, 503 U.S. 912 (1992), 3 J. Weinstein & M. Berger, Weinstein's Evidence 70203., pp. 702–36 to 702–37 (1988) (hereinafter Weinstein & Berger) (Frye is dead), and M. Graham, *Handbook of Federal Evidence* 703.2 (3d ed. 1991) (Frye lives). See generally P. Giannelli & E. Imwinkelried, *Scientific Evidence* 1–5, n. 28–29 (citing authorities).

[Footnote 6] Because we hold that Frye has been superseded and base the discussion that follows on the content of the congressionally enacted Federal Rules of Evidence, we do not address petitioners' argument that application of the Frye rule in this diversity case, as the application of a judge-made rule affecting substantive rights, would violate the doctrine of *Erie R. Co. v. Tompkins*, 304 U.S. 64 (1938).

[Footnote 7] THE CHIEF JUSTICE "do[es] not doubt that Rule 702 confides to the judge some gatekeeping responsibility," post, at 4, but would neither say how it does so nor explain what that role entails. We believe the better course is to note the nature and source of the duty.

[Footnote 8] Rule 702 also applies to "technical, or other specialized knowledge." Our discussion is limited to the scientific context because that is the nature of the expertise offered here.

[Footnote 9] We note that scientists typically distinguish between "validity" (does the principle support what it purports to show?) and "reliability" (does application of the principle produce consistent results?). See Black, 56 Ford.L.Rev. at, 599. Although "the difference between accuracy, validity, and reliability may be such that each is distinct from the other by no more than a hen's kick," Starrs, *Frye v. United States* "Restructured and Revitalized: A Proposal to Amend Federal Evidence Rule 702," 26 *Jurimetrics J.* 249, 256 (1986), our reference here is to evidentiary reliability—that is, trustworthiness. Cf., e.g., Advisory Committee's Notes on Fed.Rule Evid. 602, 28 U.S.C. App., p. 755. ("'[T]he rule requiring that a witness who testifies to a fact which can be perceived by the senses must have had an opportunity to observe, and must have actually observed the fact' is a 'most pervasive manifestation' of the common law insistence upon 'the most reliable sources of information.'" (citation omitted)); Advisory Committee's Notes on Art. VIII of Rules of Evidence, 29 U.S.C. App., p. 770 (hearsay exceptions will be recognized only "under circumstances supposed to furnish guarantees of trustworthiness"). [In a case involving scientific evidence, evidentiary reliability will be based upon scientific validity.]

[Footnote 10] Rule 104(a) provides:

"Preliminary questions concerning the qualification of a person to be a witness, the existence of a privilege, or the admissibility of evidence shall be determined by the court, subject to the provisions of subdivision (b) [pertaining to conditional admissions]. In making its determination, it is not bound by the rules of evidence except those with respect to privileges." These matters should be established by a preponderance of proof. See *Bourjaily v. United States*, 483 U.S. 171, 175–176 (1987).

[Footnote 11] Although the Frye decision itself focused exclusively on "novel" scientific techniques, we do not read the requirements of Rule 702 to apply specially or exclusively to unconventional evidence. Of course, well-established propositions are less likely to be challenged than those that are novel, and they are more handily defended. Indeed, theories that are so firmly established as to have attained the status of scientific law, such as the laws of thermodynamics, properly are subject to judicial notice under Federal Rule Evidence 201.

[Footnote 12] A number of authorities have presented variations on the reliability approach, each with its own slightly different set of factors. See, e.g., Downing, 753 F.2d, at 1238–1239 (on which our discussion draws in part); 3 Weinstein & Berger 70203., pp. 7021 to 7022 (on which the Downing court in turn partially relied); McCormick, *Scientific Evidence: Defining a New Approach to Admissibility*, 67 Iowa L.Rev. 879, 911–912 (1982); and *Symposium on Science and the Rules of Evidence*, 99 F.R.D. 187, 231 (1983) (statement by Margaret Berger). To the extent that they focus on the reliability of evidence as ensured by the scientific validity of its underlying principles, all these versions may well have merit, although we express no opinion regarding any of their particular details.

[Footnote 13] This is not to say that judicial interpretation, as opposed to adjudicative factfinding, does not share basic characteristics of the scientific endeavor: "The work of a judge is in one sense enduring, and in another, ephemeral. . . . In the endless process of testing and retesting, there is a constant rejection of the dross and a constant retention of whatever is pure and sound and fine." B. Cardozo, *The Nature of the Judicial Process* 178–179 (1921).

CHIEF JUSTICE REHNQUIST, with whom JUSTICE STEVENS joins, concurring in part and dissenting in part.

The petition for certiorari in this case presents two questions: first, whether the rule of *Frye v. United States*, 54 App. D.C. 46, 293 F. 1013 (1923), remains good law after the enactment of the Federal Rules of Evidence; and second, if Frye remains valid, whether it requires expert scientific testimony to have been subjected to a peer review process in order to be admissible. The Court concludes, correctly in my view, that the Frye rule did not survive the enactment of the Federal Rules of Evidence, and I therefore join Parts I and II-A of its opinion. The second question presented in the petition for certiorari necessarily is mooted by this holding, but the Court nonetheless proceeds to construe Rules 702 and 703 very much in the abstract, and then offers some "general observations." Ante, at 12.

"General observations" by this Court customarily carry great weight with lower federal courts, but the ones offered here suffer from the flaw common to most such observations—they are not applied to deciding whether particular testimony was or was not admissible, and therefore they tend to be not only general, but vague and abstract. This is particularly unfortunate in a case such as this, where [509 U.S. 579, 2] the ultimate legal question depends on an appreciation of one or more bodies of knowledge not judicially noticeable, and subject to different interpretations in the briefs of the parties and their amici. Twenty-two amicus briefs have been filed in the case, and indeed the Court's opinion contains no fewer than 37 citations to amicus briefs and other secondary sources.

The various briefs filed in this case are markedly different from typical briefs, in that large parts of them do not deal with decided cases or statutory language—the sort of material we customarily interpret. Instead, they deal with definitions of scientific knowledge, scientific method, scientific validity, and peer review—in short, matters far afield from the expertise of judges. This is not to say that such materials are not useful or even necessary in deciding how Rule 702 should be applied; but it is to say that the unusual subject matter should cause us to proceed with great caution in deciding more than we have to, because our reach can so easily exceed our grasp.

But even if it were desirable to make "general observations" not necessary to decide the questions presented, I cannot subscribe to some of the observations made by the Court. In Part II-B, the Court concludes that reliability and relevancy are the touchstones of the admissibility of expert testimony. Ante, at 10–11. Federal Rule of Evidence 402 provides, as the Court points out, that "[e]vidence which is not relevant is not admissible." But there is no similar reference in the Rule to "reliability." The Court constructs its argument by parsing the language "[i]f scientific, technical, or other specialized knowledge will assist the trier of fact to understand the evidence or to determine a fact in issue, . . . an expert . . . may testify thereto. . . ." Fed. Rule Evid. 702. It stresses that the subject of the expert's testimony must be "scientific . . . knowledge," and points out that "scientific" "implies a grounding in the methods and procedures of science" and that the word "knowledge"connotes more than subjective belief or unsupported speculation." Ante, at 9. From this it concludes that "scientific knowledge" must be "derived by the scientific method." Ante, at 10. Proposed testimony, we are told, must be supported by "appropriate validation." Ante, at 10. Indeed, in footnote 9, the Court decides that "[i]n a case involving scientific evidence, evidentiary reliability will be based upon scientific validity." Ante, n. 9.

Questions arise simply from reading this part of the Court's opinion, and countless more questions will surely arise when hundreds of district judges try to apply its teaching to particular offers of expert testimony. Does all of this dicta apply to an expert seeking to testify on the basis of "technical or other specialized knowledge"— the other types of expert knowledge to which Rule 702 applies—or are the "general observations" limited only to "scientific knowledge"? What is the difference between scientific knowledge and technical knowledge; does Rule 702 actually contemplate that the phrase "scientific, technical, or other specialized knowledge" be broken down into numerous subspecies of expertise, or did its authors simply pick general descriptive language covering the sort of expert testimony which courts have customarily received? The Court speaks of its confidence that federal judges can make a "preliminary assessment of whether the reasoning or methodology underlying the testimony is scientifically valid, and of whether that reasoning or methodology properly can be applied to the facts in issue." Ante, at 12. The Court then states that a "key question" to be answered in deciding whether something is "scientific knowledge" "will be whether it can be (and has been) tested." Ante, at 12. Following this sentence are three quotations from treatises, which not only speak of empirical testing, but one of which states that the "'criterion of the scientific status of a theory is its falsifiability, or refutability, or testability'" Ante at 12–13.

I defer to no one in my confidence in federal judges; but I am at a loss to know what is meant when it is said that the scientific status of a theory depends on its "falsifiability," and I suspect some of them will be, too.

I [do not doubt that Rule 702 confides to the judge some gatekeeping responsibility] in deciding questions of the admissibility of proffered expert testimony. But I do not think it imposes on them either the obligation or the authority to become amateur scientists in order to perform that role. I think the Court would be far better advised in this case to decide only the questions presented, and to leave the further development of this important area of the law to future cases.

Kumho Tire, Ltd. v. Carmichael

KUMHO TIRE CO., LTD., et al. v. CARMICHAEL et al.
CERTIORARI TO THE UNITED STATES COURT OF APPEALS FOR THE ELEVENTH CIRCUIT
No. 97-1709.
Argued December 7, 1998
Decided March 23, 1999

When a tire on the vehicle driven by Patrick Carmichael blew out and the vehicle overturned, one passenger died and the others were injured. The survivors and the decedent's representative, respondents here, brought this diversity suit against the tire's maker and its distributor (collectively Kumho Tire), claiming that the tire that failed was defective. They rested their case in significant part upon the depositions of a tire failure analyst, Dennis Carlson, Jr., who intended to testify that, in his expert opinion, a defect in the tire's manufacture or design caused the blow out. That opinion was based upon a visual and tactile inspection of the tire and upon the theory that in the absence of at least two of four specific, physical symptoms indicating tire abuse, the tire failure of the sort that occurred here was caused by a defect. Kumho Tire moved to exclude Carlson's testimony on the ground that his methodology failed to satisfy Federal Rule of Evidence 702, which says: "If scientific, technical, or other specialized knowledge will assist the trier of fact . . . , a witness qualified as an expert . . . may testify thereto in the form of an opinion."

Granting the motion (and entering summary judgment for the defendants), the District Court acknowledged that it should act as a reliability "gatekeeper" under *Daubert v. Merrell Dow Pharmaceuticals, Inc.*, 509 U.S. 579, 589, in which this Court held that Rule 702 imposes a special obligation upon a trial judge to ensure that scientific testimony is not only relevant, but reliable.

The court noted that *Daubert* discussed four factors—testing, peer review, error rates, and "acceptability" in the relevant scientific community—which might prove helpful in determining the reliability of a particular scientific theory or technique, id., at 593–594, and found that those factors argued against the reliability of Carlson's methodology. On the plaintiffs' motion for reconsideration, the court agreed that *Daubert* should be applied flexibly, that its four factors were simply illustrative, and that other factors could argue in favor of admissibility. However, the court affirmed its earlier order because it found insufficient indications of the reliability of Carlson's methodology.

In reversing, the Eleventh Circuit held that the District Court had erred as a matter of law in applying *Daubert*. Believing that *Daubert* was limited to the scientific context, the court held that the *Daubert* factors did not apply to Carlson's testimony, which it characterized as skill- or experience-based.

Held:

1. The *Daubert* factors may apply to the testimony of engineers and other experts who are not scientists. Pp. 7–13.

(a) The *Daubert* "gatekeeping" obligation applies not only to "scientific" testimony, but to all expert testimony. Rule 702 does not distinguish between "scientific" knowledge and "technical" or "other specialized" knowledge, but makes clear that any such knowledge might become the subject of expert testimony. It is the Rule's word "knowledge," not the words (like "scientific") that modify that word, that establishes a standard of evidentiary reliability. 509 U.S., at 589–590. *Daubert* referred only to "scientific" knowledge because that was the nature of the expertise there at issue. Id., at 590, n. 8. Neither is the evidentiary rationale underlying *Daubert*'s "gatekeeping" determination limited to "scientific" knowledge. Rules 702 and 703 grant all expert witnesses, not just "scientific" ones, testimonial latitude unavailable to other witnesses on the assumption that the expert's opinion will have a reliable basis in the knowledge and experience of his discipline. Id., at 592. Finally, it would prove difficult, if not impossible, for judges to administer evidentiary rules under which a "gatekeeping" obligation depended upon a distinction between "scientific" knowledge and "technical" or "other specialized" knowledge, since there is no clear line dividing the one from the others and no convincing need to make such distinctions. Pp. 7–9.

(b) A trial judge determining the admissibility of an engineering expert's testimony may consider one or more of the specific *Daubert* factors. The emphasis on the word "may" reflects *Daubert*'s description of the Rule 702 inquiry as "a flexible one." 509 U.S., at 594. The *Daubert* factors do not constitute a definitive checklist or test, id., at 593, and the gatekeeping inquiry must be tied to the particular facts, id., at 591. Those factors may or may not be pertinent in assessing reliability, depending on the nature of the issue, the expert's particular expertise, and the subject of his testimony. Some of those factors may be helpful in evaluating the reliability even of experience-based expert testimony, and the Court of Appeals erred insofar as it ruled those factors out in such cases. In determining whether particular expert testimony is reliable, the trial court should consider the specific *Daubert* factors where they are reasonable measures of reliability. Pp. 10–12.

(c) The court of appeals must apply an abuse-of-discretion standard when it reviews the trial court's decision to admit or exclude expert testimony. *General Electric Co. v. Joiner*, 522 U.S. 136 , 138–139. That standard applies as much to the trial court's decisions about how to determine reliability as to its ultimate conclusion. Thus, whether *Daubert*'s specific factors are, or are not, reasonable measures of reliability in a particular case is a matter that the law grants the trial judge broad latitude to determine. See id., at 143. The Eleventh Circuit erred insofar as it held to the contrary. P. 13.

2. Application of the foregoing standards demonstrates that the District Court's decision not to admit Carlson's expert testimony was lawful. The District Court did not question Carlson's qualifications, but excluded his testimony because it initially doubted his methodology and then found it unreliable after examining the transcript in some detail and considering respondents' defense of it. The doubts that triggered the court's initial inquiry were reasonable, as was the court's ultimate conclusion that Carlson could not reliably determine the cause of the failure of the tire in question.

The question was not the reliability of Carlson's methodology in general, but rather whether he could reliably determine the cause of failure of the particular tire at issue. That tire, Carlson conceded, had traveled far enough so that some of the tread had been worn bald, it should have been taken out of service, it had been repaired (inadequately) for punctures, and it bore some of the very marks that he said indicated, not a defect, but abuse. Moreover, Carlson's own testimony cast considerable doubt upon the reliability of both his theory about the need for at least two signs of abuse and his proposition about the significance of visual inspection in this case. Respondents stress that other tire failure experts, like Carlson, rely on visual and tactile examinations of tires. But there is no indication in the record that other experts in the industry use Carlson's particular approach or that tire experts normally make the very fine distinctions necessary to support his conclusions, nor are there references to articles or papers that validate his approach.

Respondents' argument that the District Court too rigidly applied *Daubert* might have had some validity with respect to the court's initial opinion, but fails because the court, on reconsideration, recognized that the relevant reliability inquiry should be "flexible," and ultimately based its decision upon Carlson's failure to satisfy either *Daubert*'s factors or any other set of reasonable reliability criteria. Pp. 13–19. 131 F. 3d 1433, reversed.

Breyer, J., delivered the opinion of the Court, in which Rehnquist, C. J., and O'Connor, Scalia, Kennedy, Souter, Thomas, and Ginsburg, JJ., joined, and in which Stevens, J., joined as to Parts I and II. Scalia, J., filed a concurring opinion, in which O'Connor and Thomas, JJ., joined. Stevens, J., filed an opinion concurring in part and dissenting in part.

KUMHO TIRE COMPANY, LTD., et al., PETITIONERS
v. PATRICK CARMICHAEL, etc., et al.
ON WRIT OF CERTIORARI TO THE UNITED STATES COURT OF APPEALS
FOR THE ELEVENTH CIRCUIT [March 23, 1999]

Justice Breyer delivered the opinion of the Court.

In *Daubert v. Merrell Dow Pharmaceuticals, Inc.*, 509 U.S. 579 (1993), this Court focused upon the admissibility of scientific expert testimony. It pointed out that such testimony is admissible only if it is both relevant and reliable. And it held that the Federal Rules of Evidence "assign to the trial judge the task of ensuring that an expert's testimony both rests on a reliable foundation and is relevant to the task at hand." Id., at 597. The Court also discussed certain more specific factors, such as testing, peer review, error rates, and "acceptability" in the relevant scientific community, some or all of which might prove helpful in determining the reliability of a particular scientific "theory or technique." Id., at 593–594.

This case requires us to decide how *Daubert* applies to the testimony of engineers and other experts who are not scientists. We conclude that *Daubert's* general holding— setting forth the trial judge's general "gatekeeping" obligation—applies not only to testimony based on "scientific" knowledge, but also to testimony based on "technical" and "other specialized" knowledge. See Fed. Rule Evid. 702. We also conclude that a trial court may consider one or more of the more specific factors that *Daubert* mentioned when doing so will help determine that testimony's reliability. But, as the Court stated in *Daubert* , the test of reliability is "flexible," and *Daubert's* list of specific factors neither necessarily nor exclusively applies to all experts or in every case. Rather, the law grants a district court the same broad latitude when it decides how to determine reliability as it enjoys in respect to its ultimate reliability determination. See *General Electric Co. v. Joiner*, 522 U.S. 136, 143 (1997) (courts of appeals are to apply "abuse of discretion" standard when reviewing district court's reliability determination). Applying these standards, we determine that the District Court's decision in this case—not to admit certain expert testimony—was within its discretion and therefore lawful.

I

On July 6, 1993, the right rear tire of a minivan driven by Patrick Carmichael blew out. In the accident that followed, one of the passengers died, and others were severely injured. In October 1993, the Carmichaels brought this diversity suit against the tire's maker and its distributor, whom we refer to collectively as Kumho Tire, claiming that the tire was defective. The plaintiffs rested their case in significant part upon deposition testimony provided by an expert in tire failure analysis, Dennis Carlson, Jr., who intended to testify in support of their conclusion.

Carlson's depositions relied upon certain features of tire technology that are not in dispute. A steel-belted radial tire like the Carmichaels' is made up of a "carcass" containing many layers of flexible cords, called "plies," along which (between the cords and the outer tread) are laid steel strips called "belts." Steel wire loops, called "beads," hold the cords together at the plies' bottom edges. An outer layer, called the "tread," encases the carcass, and the entire tire is bound together in rubber, through the application of heat and various chemicals. See generally, e.g., J. Dixon, *Tires, Suspension and Handling* 68–72 (2d ed. 1996). The bead of the tire sits upon a "bead seat," which is part of the wheel assembly. That assembly contains a "rim flange," which extends over the bead and rests against the side of the tire. See M. Mavrigian, *Performance Wheels & Tires* 81, 83 (1998) (illustrations). [Graphic omitted; see printed opinion.] A. Markovich, *How To Buy and Care For Tires* 4 (1994).

Carlson's testimony also accepted certain background facts about the tire in question. He assumed that before the blowout the tire had traveled far. (The tire was made in 1988 and had been installed some time before the Carmichaels bought the used minivan in March 1993; the Carmichaels had driven the van approximately 7,000 additional miles in the two months they had owned it.) Carlson noted that the tire's tread depth, which was 11/32 of an inch when new, App. 242, had been worn down to depths that ranged from 3/32 of an inch along some parts of the tire, to nothing at all along others. Id., at 287. He conceded that the tire tread had at least two punctures which had been inadequately repaired. Id., at 258–261, 322.

Despite the tire's age and history, Carlson concluded that a defect in its manufacture or design caused the blow-out. He rested this conclusion in part upon three premises which, for present purposes, we must assume are not in dispute: First, a tire's carcass should stay bound to the inner side of the tread for a significant period of time after its tread depth has worn away. Id., at 208–209. Second, the tread of the tire at issue had separated from its inner steel-belted carcass prior to the accident. Id., at 336. Third, this "separation" caused the blowout. Ibid.

Carlson's conclusion that a defect caused the separation, however, rested upon certain other propositions, several of which the defendants strongly dispute. First, Carlson said that if a separation is not caused by a certain kind of tire misuse called "overdeflection" (which consists of underinflating the tire or causing it to carry too much weight, thereby generating heat that can undo the chemical tread/carcass bond), then, ordinarily, its cause is a tire defect. Id., at 193–195, 277–278. Second, he said that if a tire has been subject to sufficient overdeflection to cause a separation, it should reveal certain physical symptoms. These symptoms include (a) tread wear on the tire's shoulder that is greater than the tread wear along the tire's center, id., at 211; (b) signs of a "bead groove," where the beads have been pushed too hard against the bead seat on the inside of the tire's rim, id., at 196–197; (c) sidewalls of the tire with physical signs of deterioration, such as discoloration, id., at 212; and/or (d) marks on the tire's rim flange, id., at 219–220. Third, Carlson said that where he does not find at least two of the four physical signs just mentioned (and presumably where there is no reason to suspect a less common cause of separation), he concludes that a manufacturing or design defect caused the separation. Id., at 223–224.

Carlson added that he had inspected the tire in question. He conceded that the tire to a limited degree showed greater wear on the shoulder than in the center, some signs of "bead groove," some discoloration, a few marks on the rim flange, and inadequately filled puncture holes (which can also cause heat that might lead to separation). Id., at 256–257, 258–261, 277, 303–304, 308. But, in each instance, he testified that the symptoms were not significant, and he explained why he believed that they did not reveal overdeflection. For example, the extra shoulder wear, he said, appeared primarily on one shoulder, whereas an overdeflected tire would reveal equally abnormal wear on both shoulders. Id., at 277. Carlson concluded that the tire did not bear at least two of the four overdeflection symptoms, nor was there any less obvious cause of separation; and since neither overdeflection nor the punctures caused the blowout, a defect must have done so.

Kumho Tire moved the District Court to exclude Carlson's testimony on the ground that his methodology failed Rule 702's reliability requirement. The court agreed with Kumho that it should act as a *Daubert*-type reliability "gatekeeper," even though one might consider Carlson's testimony as "technical," rather than "scientific." See *Carmichael v. Samyang Tires, Inc.*, 923 F. Supp. 1514, 1521–1522 (SD Ala. 1996). The court then examined Carlson's methodology in light of the reliability–related factors that *Daubert* mentioned, such as a theory's testability, whether it "has been a subject of peer review or publication," the "known or potential rate of error," and the "degree of acceptance . . . within the relevant scientific community." 923 F. Supp., at 1520 (citing *Daubert*, 509 U.S., at 592–594). The District Court found that all those factors argued against the reliability of Carlson's methods, and it granted the motion to exclude the testimony (as well as the defendants' accompanying motion for summary judgment).

The plaintiffs, arguing that the court's application of the *Daubert* factors was too "inflexible," asked for reconsideration. And the Court granted that motion. *Carmichael v. Samyang Tires, Inc.*, Civ. Action No. 93-0860-CB-S (SD Ala., June 5, 1996), App. to Pet. for Cert. 1c. After reconsidering the matter, the court agreed with the plaintiffs that *Daubert* should be applied flexibly, that its four factors were simply illustrative, and that other factors could argue in favor of admissibility. It conceded that there may be widespread acceptance of a "visual-inspection method" for some relevant purposes. But the court found insufficient indications of the reliability of "the component of Carlson's tire failure analysis which most concerned the Court, namely, the methodology employed by the expert in analyzing the data obtained in the visual inspection, and the scientific basis, if any, for such an analysis." Id., at 6c. It consequently affirmed its earlier order declaring Carlson's testimony inadmissible and granting the defendants' motion for summary judgment.

The Eleventh Circuit reversed. See *Carmichael v. Samyang Tire, Inc.*, 131 F. 3d 1433 (1997). It "review[ed] ... de novo " the "district court's legal decision to apply *Daubert*." Id., at 1435. It noted that "the Supreme Court in *Daubert* explicitly limited its holding to cover only the 'scientific context,'" adding that "a *Daubert* analysis" applies only where an expert relies "on the application of scientific principles," rather than "on skill- or experience-based observation." Id., at 1435–1436. It concluded that Carlson's testimony, which it viewed as relying on experience, "falls outside the scope of *Daubert,*" that "the district court erred as a matter of law by applying *Daubert* in this case," and that the case must be remanded for further (non-*Daubert*-type) consideration under Rule 702. Id., at 1436.

Kumho Tire petitioned for certiorari, asking us to determine whether a trial court "may" consider *Daubert*'s specific "factors" when determining the "admissibility of an engineering expert's testimony." Pet. for Cert. i. We granted certiorari in light of uncertainty among the lower courts about whether, or how, *Daubert* applies to expert testimony that might be characterized as based not upon "scientific" knowledge, but rather upon "technical" or "other specialized" knowledge. Fed. Rule Evid. 702; compare, e.g., *Watkins v. Telsmith, Inc.,* 121 F. 3d 984, 990–991 (CA5 1997), with, e.g., *Compton v. Subaru of America, Inc.,* 82 F. 3d 1513, 1518–1519 (CA10), cert. denied, 519 U.S. 1042 (1996).

II

A

In *Daubert*, this Court held that Federal Rule of Evidence 702 imposes a special obligation upon a trial judge to "ensure that any and all scientific testimony . . . is not only relevant, but reliable." 509 U.S., at 589. The initial question before us is whether this basic gatekeeping obligation applies only to "scientific" testimony or to all expert testimony. We, like the parties, believe that it applies to all expert testimony. See Brief for Petitioners 19; Brief for Respondents 17.

For one thing, Rule 702 itself says:

"If scientific, technical, or other specialized knowledge will assist the trier of fact to understand the evidence or to determine a fact in issue, a witness qualified as an expert by knowledge, skill, experience, training, or education, may testify thereto in the form of an opinion or otherwise." This language makes no relevant distinction between "scientific" knowledge and "technical" or "other specialized" knowledge. It makes clear that any such knowledge might become the subject of expert testimony. In *Daubert*, the Court specified that it is the Rule's word "knowledge," not the words (like "scientific") that modify that word, that "establishes a standard of evidentiary reliability." 509 U. S., at 589–590. Hence, as a matter of language, the Rule applies its reliability standard to all "scientific," "technical," or "other specialized" matters within its scope. We concede that the Court in *Daubert* referred only to "scientific" knowledge. But as the Court there said, it referred to "scientific" testimony "because that [wa]s the nature of the expertise" at issue. Id., at 590, n. 8.

Neither is the evidentiary rationale that underlay the Court's basic *Daubert* "gatekeeping" determination limited to "scientific" knowledge. *Daubert* pointed out that Federal Rules 702 and 703 grant expert witnesses testimonial latitude unavailable to other witnesses on the "assumption that the expert's opinion will have a reliable basis in the knowledge and experience of his discipline." Id., at 592 (pointing out that experts may testify to opinions, including those that are not based on firsthand knowledge or observation). The Rules grant that latitude to all experts, not just to "scientific" ones.

Finally, it would prove difficult, if not impossible, for judges to administer evidentiary rules under which a gatekeeping obligation depended upon a distinction between "scientific" knowledge and "technical" or "other specialized" knowledge. There is no clear line that divides the one from the others. Disciplines such as engineering rest upon scientific knowledge. Pure scientific theory itself may depend for its development upon observation and properly engineered machinery. And conceptual efforts to distinguish the two are unlikely to produce clear legal lines capable of application in particular cases. Cf. Brief for National Academy of Engineering as Amicus Curiae 9 (scientist seeks to understand nature while the engineer seeks nature's modification); Brief for Rubber Manufacturers Association as Amicus Curiae 14–16 (engineering, as an "applied science," relies on "scientific reasoning and methodology"); Brief for John Allen et al. as Amici Curiae 6 (engineering relies upon "scientific knowledge and methods").

Neither is there a convincing need to make such distinctions. Experts of all kinds tie observations to conclusions through the use of what Judge Learned Hand called "general truths derived from . . . specialized experience." Hand, *Historical and Practical Considerations Regarding Expert Testimony*, 15 Harv. L. Rev. 40, 54 (1901). And whether the specific expert testimony focuses upon specialized observations, the specialized translation of those observations into theory, a specialized theory itself, or the application of such a theory in a particular case, the expert's testimony often will rest "upon an experience confessedly foreign in kind to [the jury's] own." Ibid. The trial judge's effort to assure that the specialized testimony is reliable and relevant can help the jury evaluate that foreign experience, whether the testimony reflects scientific, technical, or other specialized knowledge.

We conclude that *Daubert*'s general principles apply to the expert matters described in Rule 702. The Rule, in respect to all such matters, "establishes a standard of evidentiary reliability." 509 U.S., at 590 . It "requires a valid . . . connection to the pertinent inquiry as a precondition to admissibility." Id., at 592. And where such testimony's factual basis, data, principles, methods, or their application are called sufficiently into question, see Part III, infra, the trial judge must determine whether the testimony has "a reliable basis in the knowledge and experience of [the relevant] discipline." 509 U.S., at 592.

B

The petitioners ask more specifically whether a trial judge determining the "admissibility of an engineering expert's testimony" may consider several more specific factors that *Daubert* said might "bear on" a judge's gate-keeping determination. These factors include:

— Whether a "theory or technique ... can be (and has been) tested";
— Whether it "has been subjected to peer review and publication";
— Whether, in respect to a particular technique, there is a high "known or potential rate of error" and whether there are "standards controlling the technique's operation"; and
— Whether the theory or technique enjoys "general acceptance" within a "relevant scientific community." 509 U.S., at 592–594.

Emphasizing the word "may" in the question, we answer that question yes.

Engineering testimony rests upon scientific foundations, the reliability of which will be at issue in some cases. See, e.g., Brief for Stephen Bobo et al. as Amici Curiae 23 (stressing the scientific bases of engineering disciplines). In other cases, the relevant reliability concerns may focus upon personal knowledge or experience. As the Solicitor General points out, there are many different kinds of experts, and many different kinds of expertise. See Brief for United States as Amicus Curiae 18–19, and n. 5 (citing cases involving experts in drug terms, handwriting analysis, criminal modus operandi, land valuation, agricultural practices, railroad procedures, attorney's fee valuation, and others). Our emphasis on the word "may" thus reflects *Daubert*'s description of the Rule 702 inquiry as "a flexible one." 509 U. S., at 594 . *Daubert* makes clear that the factors it mentions do not constitute a "definitive checklist or test." Id., at 593. And *Daubert* adds that the gatekeeping inquiry must be "'tied to the facts'" of a particular "case." Id., at 591 (quoting *United States v. Downing*, 753 F. 2d 1224, 1242 (CA3 1985)). We agree with the Solicitor General that "[t]he factors identified in *Daubert* may or may not be pertinent in assessing reliability, depending on the nature of the issue, the expert's particular expertise, and the subject of his testimony." Brief for United States as Amicus Curiae 19. The conclusion, in our view, is that we can neither rule out, nor rule in, for all cases and for all time the applicability of the factors mentioned in *Daubert*, nor can we now do so for subsets of cases categorized by category of expert or by kind of evidence. Too much depends upon the particular circumstances of the particular case at issue.

Daubert itself is not to the contrary. It made clear that its list of factors was meant to be helpful, not definitive. Indeed, those factors do not all necessarily apply even in every instance in which the reliability of scientific testimony is challenged. It might not be surprising in a particular case, for example, that a claim made by a scientific witness has never been the subject of peer review, for the particular application at issue may never previously have interested any scientist. Nor, on the other hand, does the presence of *Daubert*'s general acceptance factor help show that an expert's testimony is reliable where the discipline itself lacks reliability, as, for example, do theories grounded in any so-called generally accepted principles of astrology or necromancy.

At the same time, and contrary to the Court of Appeals' view, some of *Daubert*'s questions can help to evaluate the reliability even of experience-based testimony. In certain cases, it will be appropriate for the trial judge to ask, for example, how often an engineering expert's experience-based methodology has produced erroneous results, or whether such a method is generally accepted in the relevant engineering community. Likewise, it will at times be useful to ask even of a witness whose expertise is based purely on experience, say, a perfume tester able to distinguish among 140 odors at a sniff, whether his preparation is of a kind that others in the field would recognize as acceptable.

We must therefore disagree with the Eleventh Circuit's holding that a trial judge may ask questions of the sort *Daubert* mentioned only where an expert "relies on the application of scientific principles," but not where an expert relies "on skill- or experience-based observation." 131 F. 3d, at 1435. We do not believe that Rule 702 creates a schematism that segregates expertise by type while mapping certain kinds of questions to certain kinds of experts. Life and the legal cases that it generates are too complex to warrant so definitive a match.

To say this is not to deny the importance of *Daubert*'s gatekeeping requirement. The objective of that requirement is to ensure the reliability and relevancy of expert testimony. It is to make certain that an expert, whether basing testimony upon professional studies or personal experience, employs in the courtroom the same level of intellectual rigor that characterizes the practice of an expert in the relevant field. Nor do we deny that, as stated in *Daubert*, the particular questions that it mentioned will often be appropriate for use in determining the reliability of challenged expert testimony. Rather, we conclude that the trial judge must have considerable leeway in deciding in a particular case how to go about determining whether particular expert testimony is reliable. That is to say, a trial court should consider the specific factors identified in *Daubert* where they are reasonable measures of the reliability of expert testimony.

C

The trial court must have the same kind of latitude in deciding how to test an expert's reliability, and to decide whether or when special briefing or other proceedings are needed to investigate reliability, as it enjoys when it decides whether that expert's relevant testimony is reliable. Our opinion in *Joiner* makes clear that a court of appeals is to apply an abuse-of-discretion standard when it "review[s] a trial court's decision to admit or exclude expert testimony." 522 U.S., at 138–139. That standard applies as much to the trial court's decisions about how to determine reliability as to its ultimate conclusion. Otherwise, the trial judge would lack the discretionary authority needed both to avoid unnecessary "reliability" proceedings in ordinary cases where the reliability of an expert's methods is properly taken for granted, and to require appropriate proceedings in the less usual or more complex cases where cause for questioning the expert's reliability arises. Indeed, the Rules seek to avoid "unjustifiable expense and delay" as part of their search for "truth" and the "jus[t] determin[ation]" of proceedings. Fed. Rule Evid. 102. Thus, whether *Daubert*'s specific factors are, or are not, reasonable measures of reliability in a particular case is a matter that the law grants the trial judge broad latitude to determine. See *Joiner*, supra, at 143. And the Eleventh Circuit erred insofar as it held to the contrary.

III

We further explain the way in which a trial judge "may" consider *Daubert*'s factors by applying these considerations to the case at hand, a matter that has been briefed exhaustively by the parties and their 19 amici. The District Court did not doubt Carlson's qualifications, which included a masters degree in mechanical engineering, 10 years' work at Michelin America, Inc., and testimony as a tire failure consultant in other tort cases. Rather, it excluded the testimony because, despite those qualifications, it initially doubted, and then found unreliable, "the methodology employed by the expert in analyzing the data obtained in the visual inspection, and the scientific basis, if any, for such an analysis." Civ. Action No. 93-0860-CB-S (SD Ala., June 5, 1996), App. to Pet. for Cert. 6c. After examining the transcript in "some detail," 923 F. Supp., at 1518–519, n. 4, and after considering respondents' defense of Carlson's methodology, the District Court determined that Carlson's testimony was not reliable. It fell outside the range where experts might reasonably differ, and where the jury must decide among the conflicting views of different experts, even though the evidence is "shaky." *Daubert*, 509 U.S., at 596. In our view, the doubts that triggered the District Court's initial inquiry here were reasonable, as was the court's ultimate conclusion.

For one thing, and contrary to respondents' suggestion, the specific issue before the court was not the reasonableness in general of a tire expert's use of a visual and tactile inspection to determine whether overdeflection had caused the tire's tread to separate from its steel-belted carcass. Rather, it was the reasonableness of using such an approach, along with Carlson's particular method of analyzing the data thereby obtained, to draw a conclusion regarding the particular matter to which the expert testimony was directly relevant. That matter concerned the likelihood that a defect in the tire at issue caused its tread to separate from its carcass. The tire in question, the expert conceded, had traveled far enough so that some of the tread had been worn bald; it should have been taken out of service; it had been repaired (inadequately) for punctures; and it bore some of the very marks that the expert said indicated, not a defect, but abuse through overdeflection. See supra, at 3–5; App. 293–294. The relevant issue was whether the expert could reliably determine the cause of this tire's separation.

Nor was the basis for Carlson's conclusion simply the general theory that, in the absence of evidence of abuse, a defect will normally have caused a tire's separation. Rather, the expert employed a more specific theory to establish the existence (or absence) of such abuse. Carlson testified precisely that in the absence of at least two of four signs of abuse (proportionately greater tread wear on the shoulder; signs of grooves caused by the beads; discolored sidewalls; marks on the rim flange) he concludes that a defect caused the separation. And his analysis depended upon acceptance of a further implicit proposition, namely, that his visual and tactile inspection could determine that the tire before him had not been abused despite some evidence of the presence of the very signs for which he looked (and two punctures).

For another thing, the transcripts of Carlson's depositions support both the trial court's initial uncertainty and its final conclusion. Those transcripts cast considerable doubt upon the reliability of both the explicit theory (about the need for two signs of abuse) and the implicit proposition (about the significance of visual inspection in this case). Among other things, the expert could not say whether the tire had traveled more than 10, or 20, or 30, or 40, or 50 thousand miles, adding that 6,000 miles was "about how far" he could "say with any certainty." Id., at 265. The court could reasonably have wondered about the reliability of a method of visual and tactile inspection sufficiently precise to ascertain with some certainty the abuse-related significance of minute shoulder/center relative tread wear differences, but insufficiently precise to tell "with any certainty" from the tread wear whether a tire had traveled less than 10,000 or more than 50,000 miles. And these concerns might have been augmented by Carlson's repeated reliance on the "subjective[ness]" of his mode of analysis in response to questions seeking specific information regarding how he could differentiate between a tire that actually had been overdeflected and a tire that merely looked as though it had been. Id., at 222, 224–225, 285–286. They would have been further augmented by the fact that Carlson said he had inspected the tire itself for the first time the morning of his first deposition, and then only for a few hours. (His initial conclusions were based on photographs.) Id., at 180.

Moreover, prior to his first deposition, Carlson had issued a signed report in which he concluded that the tire had "not been . . . overloaded or underinflated," not because of the absence of "two of four" signs of abuse, but simply because "the rim flange impressions . . . were normal." Id., at 335–336. That report also said that the "tread depth remaining was 3/32 inch," id., at 336, though the opposing expert's (apparently undisputed) measurements indicate that the tread depth taken at various positions around the tire actually ranged from .5/32 of an inch to 4/32 of an inch, with the tire apparently showing greater wear along both shoulders than along the center, id., at 432–433.

Further, in respect to one sign of abuse, bead grooving, the expert seemed to deny the sufficiency of his own simple visual-inspection methodology. He testified that most tires have some bead groove pattern, that where there is reason to suspect an abnormal bead groove he would ideally "look at a lot of [similar] tires" to know the grooving's significance, and that he had not looked at many tires similar to the one at issue. Id., at 212–213, 214, 217.

Finally, the court, after looking for a defense of Carlson's methodology as applied in these circumstances, found no convincing defense. Rather, it found (1) that "none" of the *Daubert* factors, including that of "general acceptance" in the relevant expert community, indicated that Carlson's testimony was reliable, 923 F. Supp., at 1521; (2) that its own analysis "revealed no countervailing factors operating in favor of admissibility which could outweigh those identified in *Daubert*," App. to Pet. for Cert. 4c; and (3) that the "parties identified no such factors in their briefs," ibid. For these three reasons taken together, it concluded that Carlson's testimony was unreliable.

Respondents now argue to us, as they did to the District Court, that a method of tire failure analysis that employs a visual/tactile inspection is a reliable method, and they point both to its use by other experts and to Carlson's long experience working for Michelin as sufficient indication that that is so. But no one denies that an expert might draw a conclusion from a set of observations based on extensive and specialized experience. Nor does anyone deny that, as a general matter, tire abuse may often be identified by qualified experts through visual or tactile inspection of the tire. See Affidavit of H. R. Baumgardner 1–2, cited in Brief for National Academy of Forensic Engineers as Amici Curiae 16 (Tire engineers rely on visual examination and process of elimination to analyze experimental test tires). As we said before, supra, at 14, the question before the trial court was specific, not general. The trial court had to decide whether this particular expert had sufficient specialized knowledge to assist the jurors "in deciding the particular issues in the case." 4 J. McLaughlin, Weinstein's Federal Evidence § ;702.05[1], p. 702–33 (2d ed. 1998); see also Advisory Committee's Note on Proposed Fed. Rule Evid. 702, Preliminary Draft of Proposed Amendments to the Federal Rules of Civil Procedure and Evidence: Request for Comment 126 (1998) (stressing that district courts must "scrutinize" whether the "principles and methods" employed by an expert "have been properly applied to the facts of the case").

The particular issue in this case concerned the use of Carlson's two-factor test and his related use of visual/tactile inspection to draw conclusions on the basis of what seemed small observational differences. We have found no indication in the record that other experts in the industry use Carlson's two-factor test or that tire experts such as Carlson normally make the very fine distinctions about, say, the symmetry of comparatively greater shoulder tread wear that were necessary, on Carlson's own theory, to support his conclusions. Nor, despite the prevalence of tire testing, does anyone refer to any articles or papers that validate Carlson's approach. Compare Bobo, "Tire Flaws and Separations," in *Mechanics of Pneumatic Tires* 636–637 (S. Clark ed. 1981); C. Schnuth et al., "Compression Grooving and Rim Flange Abrasion as Indicators of Over-Deflected Operating Conditions in Tires," presented to Rubber Division of the American Chemical Society, Oct. 21–24, 1997; J. Walter & R. Kiminecz, "Bead Contact Pressure Measurements at the Tire-Rim Interface," presented to Society of Automotive Engineers, Feb. 24–28, 1975. Indeed, no one has argued that Carlson himself, were he still working for Michelin, would have concluded in a report to his employer that a similar tire was similarly defective on grounds identical to those upon which he rested his conclusion here. Of course, Carlson himself claimed that his method was accurate, but, as we pointed out in *Joiner*, "nothing in either *Daubert* or the Federal Rules of Evidence requires a district court to admit opinion evidence that is connected to existing data only by the ipse dixit of the expert." 522 U.S., at 146.

Respondents additionally argue that the District Court too rigidly applied *Daubert*'s criteria. They read its opinion to hold that a failure to satisfy any one of those criteria automatically renders expert testimony inadmissible. The District Court's initial opinion might have been vulnerable to a form of this argument. There, the court, after rejecting respondents' claim that Carlson's testimony was "exempted from *Daubert*-style scrutiny" because it was "technical analysis" rather than "scientific evidence," simply added that "none of the four admissibility criteria outlined by the *Daubert* court are satisfied." 923 F. Supp., at 1522. Subsequently, however, the court granted respondents' motion for reconsideration. It then explicitly recognized that the relevant reliability inquiry "should be 'flexible,'" that its "'overarching subject [should be] . . . validity' and reliability," and that " *Daubert* was intended neither to be exhaustive nor to apply in every case." App. to Pet. for Cert. 4c (quoting *Daubert*, 509 U.S., at 594–595). And the court ultimately based its decision upon Carlson's failure to satisfy either *Daubert*'s factors or any other set of reasonable reliability criteria. In light of the record as developed by the parties, that conclusion was within the District Court's lawful discretion.

In sum, Rule 702 grants the district judge the discretionary authority, reviewable for its abuse, to determine reliability in light of the particular facts and circumstances of the particular case. The District Court did not abuse its discretionary authority in this case. Hence, the judgment of the Court of Appeals is Reversed.

KUMHO TIRE COMPANY, LTD., et al., PETITIONERS v. PATRICK CARMICHAEL, etc., et al.
ON WRIT OF CERTIORARI TO THE UNITED STATES COURT OF APPEALS FOR THE ELEVENTH CIRCUIT [March 23, 1999]

Justice Scalia, with whom Justice O'Connor and Justice Thomas join, concurring.

I join the opinion of the Court, which makes clear that the discretion it endorses—trial-court discretion in choosing the manner of testing expert reliability—is not discretion to abandon the gatekeeping function. I think it worth adding that it is not discretion to perform the function inadequately. Rather, it is discretion to choose among reasonable means of excluding expertise that is fausse and science that is junky. Though, as the Court makes clear today, the *Daubert* factors are not holy writ, in a particular case the failure to apply one or another of them may be unreasonable, and hence an abuse of discretion.

KUMHO TIRE COMPANY, LTD., et al., PETITIONERS v. PATRICK CARMICHAEL, etc., et al.
ON WRIT OF CERTIORARI TO THE UNITED STATES COURT OF APPEALS FOR THE ELEVENTH CIRCUIT [March 23, 1999]

Justice Stevens, concurring in part and dissenting in part.

The only question that we granted certiorari to decide is whether a trial judge "[m]ay . . . consider the four factors set out by this Court in *Daubert v. Merrill Dow Pharmaceuticals, Inc.*, 509 U.S. 579 (1993), in a Rule 702 analysis of admissibility of an engineering expert's testimony." Pet. for Cert. i. That question is fully and correctly answered in Parts I and II of the Court's opinion, which I join.

Part III answers the quite different question whether the trial judge abused his discretion when he excluded the testimony of Dennis Carlson. Because a proper answer to that question requires a study of the record that can be performed more efficiently by the Court of Appeals than by the nine Members of this Court, I would remand the case to the Eleventh Circuit to perform that task. There are, of course, exceptions to most rules, but I firmly believe that it is neither fair to litigants nor good practice for this Court to reach out to decide questions not raised by the certiorari petition. See *General Electric Co. v. Joiner*, 522 U.S. 136, 150–151 (1997) (Stevens, J., concurring in part and dissenting in part).

Accordingly, while I do not feel qualified to disagree with the well-reasoned factual analysis in Part III of the Court's opinion, I do not join that Part, and I respectfully dissent from the Court's disposition of the case.

Joiner v. General Electric Company

GENERAL ELECTRIC CO. et al. v. JOINER et ux.
CERTIORARI TO THE UNITED STATES COURT OF APPEALS FOR THE ELEVENTH CIRCUIT
No. 96-188.
Argued October 14, 1997—Decided December 15, 1997

Synopsis

After he was diagnosed with small-cell lung cancer, respondent Joiner sued in Georgia state court, alleging, inter alia, that his disease was "promoted" by his workplace exposure to chemical "PCBs" and derivative "furans" and "dioxins" that were manufactured by, or present in materials manufactured by, petitioners. Petitioners removed the case to federal court and moved for summary judgment. Joiner responded with the depositions of expert witnesses, who testified that PCBs, furans, and dioxins can promote cancer, and opined that Joiner's exposure to those chemicals was likely responsible for his cancer. The District Court ruled that there was a genuine issue of material fact as to whether Joiner had been exposed to PCBs, but granted summary judgment for petitioners because (1) there was no genuine issue as to whether he had been exposed to furans and dioxins, and (2) his experts' testimony had failed to show that there was a link between exposure to PCBs and small-cell lung cancer and was therefore inadmissible because it did not rise above "subjective belief or unsupported speculation." In reversing, the Eleventh Circuit applied "a particularly stringent standard of review" to hold that the District Court had erred in excluding the expert testimony.

Held:

   1. Abuse of discretion—the standard ordinarily applicable to review of evidentiary rulings—is the proper standard by which to review a district court's decision to admit or exclude expert scientific evidence. Contrary to the Eleventh Circuit's suggestion, *Daubert v. Merrell Dow Pharmaceuticals, Inc.*, 509 U.S. 579, did not somehow alter this general rule in the context of a district court's decision to exclude scientific evidence. *Daubert* did not address the appellate review standard for evidentiary rulings at all, but did indicate that, while the Federal Rules of Evidence allow district courts to admit a somewhat broader range of scientific testimony than did pre-existing law, they leave in place the trial judge's "gatekeeper" role of screening such evidence to ensure that it is not only relevant, but reliable. Id., at 589. A court of appeals applying "abuse of discretion" review to such rulings may not categorically distinguish between rulings allowing expert testimony and rulings which disallow it. Compare *Beech Aircraft Corp. v. Rainey*, 488 U.S. 153, 172, with *United States v. Abel*, 469 U.S. 45, 54. This Court rejects Joiner's argu-

ment that because the granting of summary judgment in this case was "out-come determinative," it should have been subjected to a more searching standard of review. On a summary judgment motion, disputed issues of fact are resolved against the moving party—here, petitioners. But the question of admissibility of expert testimony is not such an issue of fact, and is reviewable under the abuse of discretion standard. In applying an overly "stringent" standard, the Eleventh Circuit failed to give the trial court the deference that is the hallmark of abuse of discretion review. Pp. 4–5.

2. A proper application of the correct standard of review indicates that the District Court did not err in excluding the expert testimony at issue. The animal studies cited by respondent's experts were so dissimilar to the facts presented here—i.e., the studies involved infant mice that developed alveologenic adenomas after highly concentrated, massive doses of PCBs were injected directly into their peritoneums or stomachs, whereas Joiner was an adult human whose small-cell carcinomas allegedly resulted from exposure on a much smaller scale—that it was not an abuse of discretion for the District Court to have rejected the experts' reliance on those studies. Nor did the court abuse its discretion in concluding that the four epidemiological studies on which Joiner relied were not a sufficient basis for the experts' opinions, since the authors of two of those studies ultimately were unwilling to suggest a link between increases in lung cancer and PCB exposure among the workers they examined, the third study involved exposure to a particular type of mineral oil not necessarily relevant here, and the fourth involved exposure to numerous potential carcinogens in addition to PCBs. Nothing in either *Daubert* or the Federal Rules of Evidence requires a district court to admit opinion evidence which is connected to existing data only by the ipse dixit of the expert. Pp. 6–9.

3. These conclusions, however, do not dispose of the entire case. The Eleventh Circuit reversed the District Court's conclusion that Joiner had not been exposed to furans and dioxins. Because petitioners did not challenge that determination in their certiorari petition, the question whether exposure to furans and dioxins contributed to Joiner's cancer is still open. Pp. 9–10.

78 F.3d 524, reversed and remanded.

Rehnquist, C.J., delivered the opinion for a unanimous Court with respect to Parts I and II, and the opinion of the Court with respect to Part III, in which O'Connor, Scalia, Kennedy, Souter, Thomas, Ginsburg, and Breyer, JJ., joined. Breyer, J., filed a concurring opinion. Stevens, J., filed an opinion concurring in part and dissenting in part.

Opinion
[December 15, 1997]
Chief Justice Rehnquist delivered the opinion of the Court.

We granted certiorari in this case to determine what standard an appellate court should apply in reviewing a trial court's decision to admit or exclude expert testimony under *Daubert v. Merrell Dow Pharmaceuticals, Inc.*, 509 U.S. 579 (1993). We hold that abuse of discretion is the appropriate standard. We apply this standard and conclude that the District Court in this case did not abuse its discretion when it excluded certain proffered expert testimony.

I

Respondent Robert Joiner began work as an electrician in the Water & Light Department of Thomasville, Georgia (City) in 1973. This job required him to work with and around the City's electrical transformers, which used a mineral-based dielectric fluid as a coolant. Joiner often had to stick his hands and arms into the fluid to make repairs. The fluid would sometimes splash onto him, occasionally getting into his eyes and mouth. In 1983 the City discovered that the fluid in some of the transformers was contaminated with polychlorinated biphenyls (PCBs). PCBs are widely considered to be hazardous to human health. Congress, with limited exceptions, banned the production and sale of PCBs in 1978. See 90 Stat. 2020, 15 U.S.C. § 2605(e)(2)(A).

Joiner was diagnosed with small cell lung cancer in 1991. He[1] sued petitioners in Georgia state court the following year. Petitioner Monsanto manufactured PCBs from 1935 to 1977; petitioners General Electric and Westinghouse Electric manufactured transformers and dielectric fluid. In his complaint Joiner linked his development of cancer to his exposure to PCBs and their derivatives, polychlorinated dibenzofurans (furans) and polychlorinated dibenzodioxins (dioxins). Joiner had been a smoker for approximately eight years, his parents had both been smokers, and there was a history of lung cancer in his family. He was thus perhaps already at a heightened risk of developing lung cancer eventually. The suit alleged that his exposure to PCBs "promoted" his cancer; had it not been for his exposure to these substances, his cancer would not have developed for many years, if at all.

Petitioners removed the case to federal court. Once there, they moved for summary judgment. They contended that (1) there was no evidence that Joiner suffered significant exposure to PCBs, furans, or dioxins, and (2) there was no admissible scientific evidence that PCBs promoted Joiner's cancer. Joiner responded that there were numerous disputed factual issues that required resolution by a jury. He relied largely on the testimony of expert witnesses. In depositions, his experts had testified that PCBs alone can promote cancer and that furans and dioxins can also promote cancer.

They opined that since Joiner had been exposed to PCBs, furans, and dioxins, such exposure was likely responsible for Joiner's cancer.

The District Court ruled that there was a genuine issue of material fact as to whether Joiner had been exposed to PCBs. But it nevertheless granted summary judgment for petitioners because (1) there was no genuine issue as to whether Joiner had been exposed to furans and dioxins, and (2) the testimony of Joiner's experts had failed to show that there was a link between exposure to PCBs and small cell lung cancer. The court believed that the testimony of respondent's experts to the contrary did not rise above "subjective belief or unsupported speculation." 864 F. Supp. 1310, 1329 (ND Ga. 1994). Their testimony was therefore inadmissible.

The Court of Appeals for the Eleventh Circuit reversed. 78 F.3d 524 (1996). It held that "[b]ecause the Federal Rules of Evidence governing expert testimony display a preference for admissibility, we apply a particularly stringent standard of review to the trial judge's exclusion of expert testimony." Id. at 529. Applying that standard, the Court of Appeals held that the District Court had erred in excluding the testimony of Joiner's expert witnesses. The District Court had made two fundamental errors. First, it excluded the experts' testimony because it "drew different conclusions from the research than did each of the experts." The Court of Appeals opined that a district court should limit its role to determining the "legal reliability of proffered expert testimony, leaving the jury to decide the correctness of competing expert opinions." Id. at 533. Second, the District Court had held that there was no genuine issue of material fact as to whether Joiner had been exposed to furans and dioxins. This was also incorrect, said the Court of Appeals, because testimony in the record supported the proposition that there had been such exposure.

We granted petitioners' petition for a writ of certiorari, 520 U.S. _____ (1997), and we now reverse.

II

Petitioners challenge the standard applied by the Court of Appeals in reviewing the District Court's decision to exclude respondent's experts' proffered testimony. They argue that that court should have applied traditional "abuse of discretion" review. Respondent agrees that abuse of discretion is the correct standard of review. He contends, however, that the Court of Appeals applied an abuse of discretion standard in this case. As he reads it, the phrase "particularly stringent" announced no new standard of review. It was simply an acknowledgement that an appellate court can and will devote more resources to analyzing district court decisions that are dispositive of the entire litigation. All evidentiary decisions are reviewed under an abuse of discretion standard. He argues, however, that it is perfectly reasonable for appellate courts to give particular attention to those decisions that are outcome-determinative.

We have held that abuse of discretion is the proper standard of review of a district court's evidentiary rulings. *Old Chief v. United States*, 519 U.S. ____, ____ n.1 (1997) (slip op., at 1–2, n.1), *United States v. Abel*, 469 U.S. 45, 54 (1984). Indeed, our cases on the subject go back as far as *Spring Co. v. Edgar*, 99 U.S. 645, 658 (1879) where we said that "cases arise where it is very much a matter of discretion with the court whether to receive or exclude the evidence; but the appellate court will not reverse in such a case, unless the ruling is manifestly erroneous." The Court of Appeals suggested that *Daubert* somehow altered this general rule in the context of a district court's decision to exclude scientific evidence. But *Daubert* did not address the standard of appellate review for evidentiary rulings at all. It did hold that the "austere" Frye standard of "general acceptance" had not been carried over into the Federal Rules of Evidence. But the opinion also said:

"That the Frye test was displaced by the Rules of Evidence does not mean, however, that the Rules themselves place no limits on the admissibility of purportedly scientific evidence. Nor is the trial judge disabled from screening such evidence. To the contrary, under the Rules the trial judge must ensure that any and all scientific testimony or evidence admitted is not only relevant, but reliable." 509 U.S., at 589 (footnote omitted).

Thus, while the Federal Rules of Evidence allow district courts to admit a somewhat broader range of scientific testimony than would have been admissible under Frye, they leave in place the "gatekeeper" role of the trial judge in screening such evidence. A court of appeals applying "abuse of discretion" review to such rulings may not categorically distinguish between rulings allowing expert testimony and rulings which disallow it. Compare *Beech Aircraft Corp v. Rainey*, 488 U.S. 153, 172 (1988) (applying abuse of discretion review to a lower court's decision to exclude evidence) with *United States v. Abel*, supra at 54 (applying abuse of discretion review to a lower court's decision to admit evidence). We likewise reject respondent's argument that because the granting of summary judgment in this case was "outcome determinative," it should have been subjected to a more searching standard of review. On a motion for summary judgment, disputed issues of fact are resolved against the moving party— here, petitioners. But the question of admissibility of expert testimony is not such an issue of fact, and is reviewable under the abuse of discretion standard.

We hold that the Court of Appeals erred in its review of the exclusion of Joiner's experts' testimony. In applying an overly "stringent" review to that ruling, it failed to give the trial court the deference that is the hallmark of abuse of discretion review. See, e.g., *Koon v. United States*, 518 U.S. ____, ____ (1996)(slip op., at 14–15).

III

We believe that a proper application of the correct standard of review here indicates that the District Court did not abuse its discretion. Joiner's theory of liability was that his exposure to PCBs and their derivatives "promoted" his development of small cell lung cancer. In support of that theory he proffered the deposition testimony of expert witnesses. Dr. Arnold Schecter testified that he believed it "more likely than not that Mr. Joiner's lung cancer was causally linked to cigarette smoking and PCB exposure." App. at 107. Dr. Daniel Teitelbaum testified that Joiner's "lung cancer was caused by or contributed to in a significant degree by the materials with which he worked." Id. at 140.

Petitioners contended that the statements of Joiner's experts regarding causation were nothing more than speculation. Petitioners criticized the testimony of the experts in that it was "not supported by epidemiological studies . . . [and was] based exclusively on isolated studies of laboratory animals." Joiner responded by claiming that his experts had identified "relevant animal studies which support their opinions." He also directed the court's attention to four epidemiological studies[2] on which his experts had relied.

The District Court agreed with petitioners that the animal studies on which respondent's experts relied did not support his contention that exposure to PCBs had contributed to his cancer. The studies involved infant mice that had developed cancer after being exposed to PCBs. The infant mice in the studies had had massive doses of PCBs injected directly into their peritoneums[3] or stomachs. Joiner was an adult human being whose alleged exposure to PCBs was far less than the exposure in the animal studies. The PCBs were injected into the mice in a highly concentrated form. The fluid with which Joiner had come into contact generally had a much smaller PCB concentration of between 0–500 parts per million. The cancer that these mice developed was alveologenic adenomas; Joiner had developed small-cell carcinomas. No study demonstrated that adult mice developed cancer after being exposed to PCBs. One of the experts admitted that no study had demonstrated that PCBs lead to cancer in any other species.

Respondent failed to reply to this criticism. Rather than explaining how and why the experts could have extrapolated their opinions from these seemingly far-removed animal studies, respondent chose "to proceed as if the only issue [was] whether animal studies can ever be a proper foundation for an expert's opinion." Joiner, 864 F. Supp. at 1324. Of course, whether animal studies can ever be a proper foundation for an expert's opinion was not the issue. The issue was whether these experts' opinions were sufficiently supported by the animal studies on which they purported to rely. The studies were so dissimilar to the facts presented in this litigation that it was not an abuse of discretion for the District Court to have rejected the experts' reliance on them.

The District Court also concluded that the four epidemiological studies on which respondent relied were not a sufficient basis for the experts' opinions. The first such study involved workers at an Italian capacitor[4] plant who had been exposed to PCBs. Bertazzi, Riboldi, Pesatori, Radice, & Zocchetti, "Cancer Mortality of Capacitor Manufacturing Workers," 11 *American Journal of Industrial Medicine* 165 (1987). The authors noted that lung cancer deaths among ex-employees at the plant were higher than might have been expected, but concluded that "there were apparently no grounds for associating lung cancer deaths (although increased above expectations) and exposure in the plant." Id. at 172. Given that Bertazzi et al. were unwilling to say that PCB exposure had caused cancer among the workers they examined, their study did not support the experts' conclusion that Joiner's exposure to PCBs caused his cancer.

The second study followed employees who had worked at Monsanto's PCB production plant. J. Zack & D. Munsch, "Mortality of PCB Workers at the Monsanto Plant in Sauget, Illinois" (Dec. 14, 1979)(unpublished report), 3 Rec., Doc. No. 11. The authors of this study found that the incidence of lung cancer deaths among these workers was somewhat higher than would ordinarily be expected. The increase, however, was not statistically significant and the authors of the study did not suggest a link between the increase in lung cancer deaths and the exposure to PCBs.

The third and fourth studies were likewise of no help. The third involved workers at a Norwegian cable manufacturing company who had been exposed to mineral oil. Ronneberg, Andersen, Skyberg, "Mortality and Incidence of Cancer Among Oil-Exposed Workers in a Norwegian Cable Manufacturing Company," 45 *British Journal of Industrial Medicine* 595 (1988). A statistically significant increase in lung cancer deaths had been observed in these workers. The study, however, (1) made no mention of PCBs and (2) was expressly limited to the type of mineral oil involved in that study, and thus did not support these experts' opinions. The fourth and final study involved a PCB-exposed group in Japan that had seen a statistically significant increase in lung cancer deaths. Kuratsune, Nakamura, Ikeda, & Hirohata, "Analysis of Deaths Seen Among Patients with Yusho—A Preliminary Report," 16 *Chemosphere*, Nos. 8/9, 2085 (1987). The subjects of this study, however, had been exposed to numerous potential carcinogens, including toxic rice oil that they had ingested. Respondent points to *Daubert*'s language that the "focus, of course, must be solely on principles and methodology, not on the conclusions that they generate." 509 U.S., at 595. He claims that because the District Court's disagreement was with the conclusion that the experts drew from the studies, the District Court committed legal error and was properly reversed by the Court of Appeals. But conclusions and methodology are not entirely distinct from one another. Trained experts commonly extrapolate from existing data. But nothing in either *Daubert* or the Federal Rules of Evidence requires a district court to admit opinion evidence which is connected to existing data only by the ipse dixit of the expert. A court may conclude that there is simply too great an analytical gap between the data and the opinion proffered. See *Turpin v. Merrell Dow Pharmaceuticals, Inc.*, 959 F.2d 1349, 1360 (CA 6), cert. denied, 506 U.S. 826 (1992). That is what the District Court did here, and we hold that it did not abuse its discretion in so doing.

We hold, therefore, that abuse of discretion is the proper standard by which to review a district court's decision to admit or exclude scientific evidence. We further hold that, because it was within the District Court's discretion to conclude that the studies upon which the experts relied were not sufficient, whether individually or in combination, to support their conclusions that Joiner's exposure to PCBs contributed to his cancer, the District Court did not abuse its discretion in excluding their testimony. These conclusions, however, do not dispose of this entire case.

Respondent's original contention was that his exposure to PCBs, furans, and dioxins contributed to his cancer. The District Court ruled that there was a genuine issue of material fact as to whether Joiner had been exposed to PCBs, but concluded that there was no genuine issue as to whether he had been exposed to furans and dioxins. The District Court accordingly never explicitly considered if there was admissible evidence on the question whether Joiner's alleged exposure to furans and dioxins contributed to his cancer. The Court of Appeals reversed the District Court's conclusion that there had been no exposure to furans and dioxins. Petitioners did not challenge this determination in their petition to this Court. Whether Joiner was exposed to furans and dioxins, and whether if there was such exposure, the opinions of Joiner's experts would then be admissible, remain open questions. We accordingly reverse the judgment of the Court of Appeals and remand this case for proceedings consistent with this opinion.

Notes

1. Joiner's wife was also a plaintiff in the suit and is a respondent here. For convenience, we refer to respondent in the singular.

2. Epidemiological studies examine the pattern of disease in human populations.

3. The peritoneum is the lining of the abdominal cavity.

4. A capacitor is an electrical component that stores an electric charge.

Breyer, J., concurring

Justice Breyer, concurring.

The Court's opinion, which I join, emphasizes *Daubert's* statement that a trial judge, acting as "gatekeeper," must "'ensure that any and all scientific testimony or evidence admitted is not only relevant, but reliable.'" Ante, at 5 (quoting *Daubert v. Merrell Dow Pharmaceuticals, Inc.*, 509 U.S. 579, 589 (1993)). This requirement will sometimes ask judges to make subtle and sophisticated determinations about scientific methodology and its relation to the conclusions an expert witness seeks to offer—particularly when a case arises in an area where the science itself is tentative or uncertain, or where testimony about general risk levels in human beings or animals is offered to prove individual causation. Yet, as amici have pointed out, judges are not scientists and do not have the scientific training that can facilitate the making of such decisions. See, e.g., Brief for Trial Lawyers for Public Justice as Amicus Curiae 15; Brief for *The New England Journal of Medicine* et al. as Amici Curiae 2 ("Judges . . . are generally not trained scientists").

Of course, neither the difficulty of the task nor any comparative lack of expertise can excuse the judge from exercising the "gatekeeper" duties that the Federal Rules impose—determining, for example, whether particular expert testimony is reliable and "will assist the trier of fact," Fed. Rule Evid. 702, or whether the "probative value" of testimony is substantially outweighed by risks of prejudice, confusion or waste of time. Fed. Rule Evid. 403. To the contrary, when law and science intersect, those duties often must be exercised with special care.

Today's toxic tort case provides an example. The plaintiff in today's case says that a chemical substance caused, or promoted, his lung cancer. His concern, and that of others, about the causes of cancer is understandable, for cancer kills over one in five Americans. See *U.S. Dept. of Health and Human Services, National Center for Health Statistics, Health United States 1996–97* and *Injury Chartbook* 117 (1997) (23.3% of all deaths in 1995). Moreover, scientific evidence implicates some chemicals as potential causes of some cancers. See, e.g., *U.S. Dept. of Health and Human Services, Public Health Service, National Toxicology Program, Seventh Annual Report on Carcinogens,* pp. v–vi (1994). Yet modern life, including good health as well as economic well-being, depends upon the use of artificial or manufactured substances, such as chemicals. And it may, therefore, prove particularly important to see that judges fulfill their *Daubert* gatekeeping function, so that they help assure that the powerful engine of tort liability, which can generate strong financial incentives to reduce, or to eliminate, production, points towards the right substances and does not destroy the wrong ones. It is, thus, essential in this science-related area that the courts administer the Federal Rules of Evidence in order to achieve the "end[s]" that the Rules themselves set forth, not only so that proceedings may be "justly determined," but also so "that the truth may be ascertained." Fed. Rule Evid. 102.

I therefore want specially to note that, as cases presenting significant science-related issues have increased in number, see Judicial Conference of the United States, Report of the Federal Courts Study Committee 97 (Apr. 2, 1990) ("Economic, statistical, technological, and natural and social scientific data are becoming increasingly important in both routine and complex litigation"), judges have increasingly found in the Rules of Evidence and Civil Procedure ways to help them overcome the inherent difficulty of making determinations about complicated scientific or otherwise technical evidence. Among these techniques are an increased use of Rule 16's pretrial conference authority to narrow the scientific issues in dispute, pretrial hearings where potential experts are subject to examination by the court, and the appointment of special masters and specially trained law clerks. See J. Cecil & T. Willging, *Court-Appointed Experts: Defining the Role of Experts Appointed Under Federal Rule of Evidence* 706, pp. 83–88 (1993); J. Weinstein, *Individual Justice in Mass Tort Litigation* 107–110 (1995); cf. Kaysen, "In Memoriam: Charles E. Wyzanski, Jr.," 100 *Harv. L. Rev.* 713, 713–715 (1987) (discussing a judge's use of an economist as a law clerk in *United*

States v. United Shoe Machinery Corp., 110 F. Supp. 295 (D Mass 1953), aff'd, 347 U.S. 521 (1954)).

In the present case, the New England Journal of Medicine has filed an amici brief "in support of neither petitioners nor respondents" in which the Journal writes:

"[A] judge could better fulfill this gatekeeper function if he or she had help from scientists. Judges should be strongly encouraged to make greater use of their inherent authority . . . to appoint experts . . . . Reputable experts could be recommended to courts by established scientific organizations, such as the National Academy of Sciences or the American Association for the Advancement of Science."

Brief for *The New England Journal of Medicine* 18–19; cf. Fed. Rule Evid. 706 (court may "on its own motion or on the motion of any party" appoint an expert to serve on behalf of the court, and this expert may be selected as "agreed upon by the parties" or chosen by the court); see also Weinstein, supra, at 116 (a court should sometimes "go beyond the experts proffered by the parties" and "utilize its powers to appoint independent experts under Rule 706 of the Federal Rules of Evidence"). Given this kind of offer of cooperative effort, from the scientific to the legal community, and given the various Rules—authorized methods for facilitating the courts' task, it seems to me that *Daubert*'s gatekeeping requirement will not prove inordinately difficult to implement; and that it will help secure the basic objectives of the Federal Rules of Evidence; which are, to repeat, the ascertainment of truth and the just determination of proceedings. Fed. Rule Evid. 102.

Opinion of Stevens, J.

Justice Stevens, concurring in part and dissenting in part.

The question that we granted certiorari to decide is whether the Court of Appeals applied the correct standard of review. That question is fully answered in Parts I and II of the Court's opinion. Part III answers the quite different question whether the District Court properly held that the testimony of plaintiff's expert witnesses was inadmissible. Because I am not sure that the parties have adequately briefed that question, or that the Court has adequately explained why the Court of Appeals' disposition was erroneous, I do not join Part III. Moreover, because a proper answer to that question requires a study of the record that can be performed more efficiently by the Court of Appeals than by the nine members of this Court, I would remand the case to that court for application of the proper standard of review.

One aspect of the record will illustrate my concern. As the Court of Appeals pointed out, Joiner's experts relied on "the studies of at least thirteen different researchers, and referred to several reports of the World Health Organization that address the question of whether PCBs cause cancer." 78 F.3d 524, 533 (CA11 1996). Only one of those studies is in the record, and only six of them were discussed in the District Court opinion. Whether a fair appraisal of either the methodology or the conclusions of Joiner's experts can be made on the basis of such an incomplete record is a question that I do not feel prepared to answer.

It does seem clear, however, that the Court has not adequately explained why its holding is consistent with Federal Rule of Evidence 702,[1] as interpreted in *Daubert v. Merrell Dow Pharmaceuticals, Inc.*, 509 U.S. 579 (1993).[2] In general, scientific testimony that is both relevant and reliable must be admitted and testimony that is irrelevant or unreliable must be excluded. Id., at 597. In this case, the District Court relied on both grounds for exclusion.

The relevance ruling was straightforward. The District Court correctly reasoned that an expert opinion that exposure to PCBs, "furans" and "dioxins" together may cause lung cancer would be irrelevant unless the plaintiff had been exposed to those substances. Having already found that there was no evidence of exposure to furans and dioxins, 864 F. Supp. 1310, 1318–1319 (ND Ga. 1994), it necessarily followed that this expert opinion testimony was inadmissible. Correctly applying *Daubert*, the District Court explained that the experts' testimony "manifestly does not fit the facts of this case, and is therefore inadmissible." 864 F. Supp., at 1322. Of course, if the evidence raised a genuine issue of fact on the question of Joiner's exposure to furans and dioxins—as the Court of Appeals held that it did—then this basis for the ruling on admissibility was erroneous, but not because the district judge either abused her discretion or misapplied the law.[3]

The reliability ruling was more complex and arguably is not faithful to the statement in *Daubert* that "[t]he focus, of course, must be solely on principles and methodology, not on the conclusions that they generate." 509 U.S., at 595. Joiner's experts used a "weight of the evidence" methodology to assess whether Joiner's exposure to transformer fluids promoted his lung cancer.[4] They did not suggest that any one study provided adequate support for their conclusions, but instead relied on all the studies taken together (along with their interviews of Joiner and their review of his medical records). The District Court, however, examined the studies one by one and concluded that none was sufficient to show a link between PCBs and lung cancer. 864 F. Supp., at 1324–1326. The focus of the opinion was on the separate studies and the conclusions of the experts, not on the experts' methodology. Id., at 1322 ("Defendants . . . persuade the court that Plaintiffs' expert testimony would not be admissible . . . by attacking the conclusions that Plaintiffs' experts draw from the studies they cite").

Unlike the District Court, the Court of Appeals expressly decided that a "weight of the evidence" methodology was scientifically acceptable.[5] To this extent, the Court of Appeals' opinion is persuasive. It is not intrinsically "unscientific" for experienced professionals to arrive at a conclusion by weighing all available scientific evidence—this is not the sort of "junk science" with which *Daubert* was concerned.[6] After all, as Joiner points out, the Environmental Protection Agency (EPA) uses the same methodology to assess risks, albeit using a somewhat different threshold than that required in a trial. Brief for Respondents 40–41 (quoting EPA, *Guidelines for Carcinogen Risk Assessment,* 51 Fed. Reg. 33992, 33996 (1986)). Petitioners' own experts used the same scientific approach as well.[7] And using this methodology, it would seem that an expert could reasonably have concluded that the study of workers at an Italian capacitor plant, coupled with data from Monsanto's study and other studies, raises an inference that PCBs promote lung cancer.[8]

The Court of Appeals' discussion of admissibility is faithful to the dictum in *Daubert* that the reliability inquiry must focus on methodology, not conclusions. Thus, even though I fully agree with both the District Court's and this Court's explanation of why each of the studies on which the experts relied was by itself unpersuasive, a critical question remains unanswered: When qualified experts have reached relevant conclusions on the basis of an acceptable methodology, why are their opinions inadmissible?

Daubert quite clearly forbids trial judges from assessing the validity or strength of an expert's scientific conclusions, which is a matter for the jury.[9] Because I am persuaded that the difference between methodology and conclusions is just as categorical as the distinction between means and ends, I do not think the statement that "conclusions and methodology are not entirely distinct from one another," ante, at 9, is either accurate or helps us answer the difficult admissibility question presented by this record.

In any event, it bears emphasis that the Court has not held that it would have been an abuse of discretion to admit the expert testimony. The very point of today's holding is that the abuse of discretion standard of review applies whether the district judge has excluded or admitted evidence. Ante, at 5. And nothing in either *Daubert* or the Federal Rules of Evidence requires a district judge to reject an expert's conclusions and keep them from the jury when they fit the facts of the case and are based on reliable scientific methodology.

Accordingly, while I join Parts I and II of the Court's opinion, I do not concur in the judgment or in Part III of its opinion.

Notes

1. Rule 702 states: "If scientific, technical, or other specialized knowledge will assist the trier of fact to understand the evidence or to determine a fact in issue, a witness qualified as an expert by knowledge, skill, experience, training, or education, may testify thereto in the form of an opinion or otherwise."

2. The specific question on which the Court granted certiorari in *Daubert* was whether the rule of *Frye v. United States,* 54 App. D. C. 46, 293 F. 1013 (1923), remained valid after the enactment of the Federal Rules of Evidence, but the Court went beyond that issue and set forth alternative requirements for admissibility in place of the Frye test. Even though the *Daubert* test was announced in dicta, see 509 U.S., at 598–601 (Rehnquist, C. J., concurring in part and dissenting in part), we should not simply ignore its analysis in reviewing the District Court's rulings.

3. Petitioners do not challenge the Court of Appeals' straightforward review of the District Court's summary judgment ruling on exposure to furans and dioxins. As today's opinion indicates, ante, at 10, it remains an open question on remand whether the District Court should admit expert testimony that PCBs, furans and dioxins together promoted Joiner's cancer.

4. Dr. Daniel Teitelbaum elaborated on that approach in his deposition testimony: "[A]s a toxicologist when I look at a study, I am going to require that that study meet the general criteria for methodology and statistical analysis, but that when all of that data is collected and you ask me as a patient, 'Doctor, have I got a risk of getting cancer from this?' That those studies don't answer the question, that I have to put them all together in my mind and look at them in relation to everything I know about the substance and everything I know about the exposure and come to a conclusion. I think when I say, 'To a reasonable medical probability as a medical toxicologist, this substance was a contributing cause,' . . . to his cancer, that that is a valid conclusion based on the totality of the evidence presented to me. And I think that that is an appropriate thing for a toxicologist to do, and it has been the basis of diagnosis for several hundred years, anyway." Supp. App. to Brief for Respondents 19.

5. The court explained: "Opinions of any kind are derived from individual pieces of evidence, each of which by itself might not be conclusive, but when viewed in their entirety are the building blocks of a perfectly reasonable conclusion, one reliable enough to be submitted to a jury along with the tests and criticisms cross-examination and contrary evidence would supply." 78 F.3d 524, 532 (CA11 1996).

6. An example of "junk science" that should be excluded under *Daubert* as too unreliable would be the testimony of a phrenologist who would purport to prove a defendant's future dangerousness based on the contours of the defendant's skull.

7. See, e.g., Deposition of Dr. William Charles Bailey, Supp. App. to Brief for Respondents 56 ("I've just reviewed a lot of literature and come to some conclusions . . . .").

8. The Italian capacitor plant study found that workers exposed to PCBs had a higher-than-expected rate of lung cancer death, though "the numbers were small [and] the value of the risk estimate was not statistically significant." 864 F. Supp. 1310, 1324 (ND Ga. 1994). The Monsanto study also found a correlation between PCB exposure and lung cancer death, but the results were not statistically significant. Id., at 1325. Moreover, it should be noted that under Georgia law, which applies in this diversity suit, Joiner need only show that his exposure to PCBs "promoted" his lung cancer, not that it was the sole cause of his cancer. Brief for Respondents 7, n. 16 (quoting Brief for Appellants in No. 94-9131 (CA 11), pp. 7–10).

9. The Court stated in *Daubert*: "Vigorous cross-examination, presentation of contrary evidence, and careful instruction on the burden of proof are the traditional and appropriate means of attacking shaky but admissible evidence. . . . Additionally, in the event the trial court concludes that the scintilla of evidence presented supporting a position is insufficient to allow a reasonable juror to conclude that the position more likely than not is true, the court remains free to direct a judgment, Fed. Rule Civ. Proc. 50(a), and likewise to grant summary judgment, Fed. Rule Civ. Proc. 56. . . . These conventional devices, rather than wholesale exclusion under an uncompromising 'general acceptance' test, are the appropriate safeguards where the basis of scientific testimony meets the standards of Rule 702." 509 U.S., at 596.

U.S. v. Carlos Ivan Llera Plaza, Wilfredo Martinez Acosta, and Victor Rodriguez

IN THE UNITED STATES DISTRICT COURT
FOR THE EASTERN DISTRICT OF PENNSYLVANIA
UNITED STATES OF AMERICA
v.
CARLOS IVAN LLERA PLAZA,
WILFREDO MARTINEZ ACOSTA,
and
VICTOR RODRIGUEZ
Cr. No. 98-362-10, 11, 12:
OPINION Pollak, J. March 13, 2002

In the government's list of witnesses expected to be called at the upcoming trial, on drug and murder charges, of defendants Carlos Ivan Llera Plaza, Wilfredo Martinez Acosta and Victor Rodriguez, there are four Federal Bureau of Investigation (FBI) fingerprint examiners and one FBI fingerprint specialist. To bar the testimony of these anticipated witnesses, the defendants filed a Motion to Preclude the United States from Introducing Latent Fingerprint Identification Evidence. The government responded with a Combined Motion in Limine to Admit Latent Print Evidence and Response to [Defendants'] Motion to Preclude the Introduction of Latent Fingerprint Identification Evidence. The principal question posed by the defendants' motion and the government's counter-motion was whether, as the government contended, fingerprint identification evidence is sufficiently reliable to meet the standards for expert testimony set by Rule 702 of the Federal Rules of Evidence as explicated by the Supreme Court in *Daubert v. Merrell Dow Pharmaceuticals, Inc.*, 509 U.S. 597 (1993) and reaffirmed in *Kumho Tire Co., Ltd. v. Carmichael*, 526 U.S. 137 (1999). A logically antecedent—but far less difficult—question was whether, as the government also contended, the uniqueness and the permanence of fingerprints are matters that have been so clearly established as to be proper subjects of judicial notice pursuant to Rule 201 of the Federal Rules of Evidence. Resolution of these linked questions required consideration of evidence as to (1) the theoretical basis of fingerprint identification and (2) the procedures by which someone familiar with fingerprints (which, for the purposes of this opinion, include palmprints) arrives at a judgment that a fingerprint impressed on some surface (a so-called "latent" print) by an unknown person and thereafter found by and "lifted" from that surface by law enforcement technicians is— or is not—a print which "matches" a known person's "known exemplar" fingerprint (a so-called "rolled" print), thereby signifying that the person who made the latent print is—or is not—the person who made the rolled print. By stipulation of the parties, the evidence with respect to these questions consisted of a copy of the transcript of a five-day hearing addressed to the same question presided over by my colleague Judge Joyner, in 1999, in *United States v. Mitchell*, Cr. No. 96-407. While no new evidence was presented before me, the parties in the case at bar supplemented the *Mitchell* materials with extensive briefs.

On January 7, 2002, I filed an opinion and order addressed to the defendants' motion and the government's counter-motion.

First, I concluded that, as the government had contended, it was beyond reasonable dispute that the fingerprints of each person (a) are unique to that person and (b) are (barring some serious and deeply penetrating wound to the hand that substantially alters or defaces the surface of one or more of the fingers or of the palm) permanent from birth to death. I therefore ruled that, pursuant to Rule 201, I would, for the purposes of the up-coming trial, take judicial notice of the uniqueness and permanence of fingerprints. In agreeing to take judicial notice of the uniqueness and permanence of fingerprints, I was in effect, accepting the theoretical basis of fingerprint identification—namely, that a showing that a latent print replicates (is a "match" of) a rolled print constitutes a showing that the latent and rolled prints are fingerprints of the same person.

Second, I considered whether the ACE-V fingerprint identification system employed by the FBI sufficiently conforms to the *Daubert* standards of reliability laid down by the Court as guidelines in determining the admissibility of expert testimony under Rule 702. First I described the four fingerprint examination procedures—"analysis," "comparison," "evaluation," and "verification,"—for which "ACE-V" is an acronym: "analysis" by an initial fingerprint examiner of the observably distinctive patterns of a latent print; "comparison" by the examiner of the latent print patterns with those of a rolled print; "evaluation" by the examiner of these compared patterns with a view to determining whether the prints are, or are not, impressions made by the same finger or palm; and "verification" by a second examiner who repeats the analysis, comparison and evaluation steps in order to verify, or not, the initial examiner's finding. Next I identified the four *Daubert* factors of scientific reliability relied on by both the government and the defendants as touchstones of Rule 702 admissibility: (1) whether the technique on which the proffered expert testimony is premised "can be (and has been) tested"; (2) whether the technique has been "subjected to peer review and publication"; (3) "the known or potential rate of error . . . and the existence and maintenance of standards controlling the technique's operation"; and (4) "general acceptance." 509 U.S. at 593-84. Based on the *Mitchell* record, I came to the following conclusions with respect to ACE-V's conformity to the *Daubert* factors:

The one *Daubert* factor that ACE-V satisfies in significant fashion is the fourth factor: ACE-V has attained general acceptance within the American fingerprint examiner community [footnote omitted]. But the caveat must be added that, in the court's view, the domain of knowledge occupied by fingerprint examiners should be described, in Rule 702 terms, by the word "technical," rather than by the word "scientific," the word the government deploys.

Given that *Kumho Tire* establishes that the *Daubert* analysis is applicable to "technical" as well as "scientific" knowledge, it may be thought that this court's characterization of the knowledge base of fingerprint examiners as "technical" rather than "scientific" is a semantic distinction which is of no practical consequence. However, as discussed above, the court finds that ACE-V does not adequately satisfy the "scientific" criterion of testing (the first *Daubert* factor) or the "scientific"criterion of "peer review" (the second *Daubert* factor). Further, the court finds that the information of record is unpersuasive, one way or another, as to ACE-V's "scientific" rate of error (the first aspect of *Daubert*'s third factor), and that, at the critical evaluation stage, ACE-V does not operate under uniformly accepted "scientific" standards (the second aspect of *Daubert*'s third factor).

These conclusions did not, however, lead to a determination that fingerprint identification testimony could play no role whatsoever. The substance of my ruling was as follows:

The *Daubert* difficulty with the ACE-V process is by no means total. The difficulty comes into play at the stage at which, as experienced specialists Ashbaugh [David Ashbaugh, of the Royal Canadian Mounted Police] and Meagher [Stephen Meagher of the FBI] themselves acknowledge, the ACE-V process becomes "subjective"—namely, the evaluation stage. By contrast, the antecedent analysis and comparison stages are, according to the testimony, "objective": analysis of the rolled and latent prints and comparison of what the examiner has observed in the two prints. Up to the evaluation stage, the ACE-V fingerprint examiner's testimony is descriptive, not judgmental. Accordingly, this court will permit the government to present testimony by fingerprint examiners who, suitably qualified as "expert" examiners by virtue of training and experience, may (1) describe how the rolled and latent fingerprints at issue in this case were obtained, (2) identify and place before the jury the fingerprints and such magnifications thereof as may be required to show minute details, and (3) point out observed similarities (and differences) between any latent print and any rolled print the government contends are attributable to the same person. What such expert witnesses will not be permitted to do is to present "evaluation" testimony as to their "opinion" (Rule 702) that a particular latent print is in fact the print of a particular person. The defendants will be permitted to present their own fingerprint experts to counter the government's fingerprint testimony, but defense experts will also be precluded from presenting "evaluation" testimony. Government counsel and defense counsel will, in closing arguments, be free to argue to the jury that, on the basis of the jury's observation of a particular latent print and a particular rolled print, the jury may find the existence, or the non-existence, of a match between the prints.

I.

The government moved for reconsideration of the ruling. The government felt that its prosecutorial effectiveness, both in the case at bar and in other cases in which fingerprint identification could be expected to play a significant role, would be seriously compromised by the preclusion of opinion testimony at the "evaluation" stage "that a particular latent print is in fact the print of a particular person." Arguing that the analysis underlying the ruling was both factually and legally flawed, the government contended that the ruling was "at odds with Rule 702 of the Federal Rules of Evidence, and should be reconsidered and reversed." In aid of its motion for reconsideration the government sought leave to enlarge the record through the presentation of evidence that FBI fingerprint examiners achieve conspicuous accuracy on annual fingerprint identification proficiency tests.

In the defendants' view, reconsideration was not called for: there was no suggestion that the additional evidence the government wished to adduce (the proposed factual presentation relating to the FBI proficiency tests) was new, or had previously been unavailable; and it was not contended that the controlling legal principles, as laid down by the Supreme Court and the Court of Appeals for the Third Circuit, had been reconfigured since this court's January 7 decision. Further, the defendants argued, citing the Third Circuit's decision in *United States v. Kithcart*, 218 F.3d 213 (2000), that it would be error for this court to conduct an evidentiary hearing in aid of a motion for reconsideration.

Kithcart, so it seemed to me, was without application. In *Kithcart* the Third Circuit, on an initial appeal, had concluded that the district court should reexamine a suppression motion which the district court had previously denied. On remand, the district judge (a judge to whom the case had been assigned after the original judge had been elevated to the Third Circuit) conducted an evidentiary hearing to hear witnesses the government had not called at the prior suppression hearing and, on the basis of the enlarged record, adhered to the prior ruling denying the motion to suppress. On a renewed appeal, the Third Circuit held that it had been error for the newly assigned district judge, on remand, to hear testimony; the remand order, the Third Circuit explained, had contemplated that the suppression motion would be reconsidered by the district court on the original record unless the government, on remand, offered an adequate explanation why it had not presented the additional witnesses at the prior hearing—a showing the government, on remand, did not make. *Kithcart*, in sum, involved a construction by the appellate court of its procedural directive to a district court. No such scenario was presented in the case at bar.

Although *Kithcart* offered no support for the defendants' contention that I should decline to reconsider the January 7 ruling, the defendants were on sound ground in contending that neither of the circumstances conventionally justifying reconsideration—new, or hitherto unavailable, facts or new controlling law—was present here. It seemed to me, nonetheless, that there was a factor peculiar to this case which militated in favor of agreeing to reconsider the January 7 ruling. That factor was that the record underlying the January 7 opinion did not consist of testimony by witnesses I had actually seen and heard; my field of vision was a transcript of testimony presented in another courtroom more than two years ago. Therefore, it seemed prudent to hear such live witnesses as the government wished to present, together with any rebuttal witnesses the defense would elect to present.

Accordingly, I agreed to reconsider the January 7 ruling. The parties required a period of time to prepare for the evidentiary hearing requested by the government. The hearing was held on February 25, 26 and 27.

II

The Witnesses

At the hearing five witnesses gave testimony. The government presented two witnesses: Stephen Meagher, Unit Chief of Latent Print Unit 3 of the Forensic Analysis Section of the FBI Laboratory; and Kenneth O. Smith, Senior Forensic Latent Print Analyst of the U.S. Postal Inspection Service. The defendants presented three witnesses: Allan Bayle, a London-based consultant on fingerprint identification, with lengthy prior service as a fingerprint examiner at New Scotland Yard; Janine Arvizu, a laboratory quality auditor serving as Senior Technical Consultant at Consolidated Technical Services, Inc., a New Mexico firm; and Dr. Ralph Norman Haber, a psychometrician at Human Factors Consultants, a California firm.

A. The Testimony of the Government Witnesses

Stephen Meagher:

The first portion of Mr. Meagher's testimony was a run-through of the ACE-V process, visually illustrated by overhead projections of fingerprints whose distinctive patterns of "friction ridges" are frequently given further distinctive character by markings commonly termed "loops," "whorls," "arches," and "deltas."

[*Historical Note (not drawn from testimony*): "Galton points" take their name from Francis Galton, the multi-talented English scientist who was a cousin of Darwin's and a major figure in his own right. Starting in the late 1880s, Galton undertook to appropriate much of, and then to build upon, the pioneering fingerprint identification efforts of (1) another Englishman, William Herschel, serving in the Indian civil service, and (2) Henry Faulds, a Scottish physician serving as a medical missionary in Japan. Galton's efforts were brought into the mainstream of criminal investigation by Edward Henry, the Inspector General of Police in Bengal, who, in 1901, was called back to England as Assistant Commissioner (later, Commissioner) of Scotland Yard and promptly established the Yard's Fingerprint Branch. Galton and Henry have customarily been celebrated as the principal progenitors of fingerprint identification, with Herschel given an approving nod—while the foundational work of Faulds has, until very recently, been largely ignored. See generally Colin Beavan, *Fingerprints* (2001), "an elegantly written slim volume," Paul Shechtman, New York Law Journal, August 7, 2001, at 2 (book review); see also Nicholas Wright Gillham, *A Life of Sir Francis Galton* 231–249 (2001).[1] Fingerprinting was not, however, the most significant of Francis Galton's many lines of inquiry: The versatile, and indefatigably enterprising, Galton, did important work in fields as disparate as, inter alia, geography, biometrics and meteorology; but his most influential scientific contributions proved to be profoundly malign—an early student of genetics, Galton became the high priest of eugenics.]

   Although the observation of Galton points that are common to the latent print and the rolled print has traditionally been one of the mainstays of the "comparison" and "evaluation" stages of ACE-V, Mr. Meagher emphasized in his testimony that no minimum number of Galton points is required in order to achieve a reliable identification. In support of this, Mr. Meagher cited a 1973 pronouncement of the International Association for Identification, a similar pronouncement at an international conference held in Nurum, Israel, in 1995, and guidelines promulgated in 1997 by the Scientific Working Group on Friction Ridge Analysis Study and Technology. Mr. Meagher's testimony on this point is of some significance, because in my January 7 opinion, in concluding that the ACE-V process appeared to lack uniformly controlling standards, I noted that, on the basis of what I had gleaned from the *Mitchell* record, here and abroad there appeared to be a lack of uniformly controlling identification standards. What I said in the January 7 opinion was as follows:

> *Various witnesses at the* Mitchell *hearing testified that the ACE-V process is the method in general use among fingerprint examiners in the United States. However, the application of this method, in particular whether a minimum number of Galton*

---

1. In 1905 Faulds published *A Guide to Finger-Print Identification*. There shortly appeared, in the journal *Nature*, an anonymous review of Faulds's *Guide*. The review, written by Galton, announced that Faulds "overstates the value of his own work, belittles that of others . . ." Colin Beavan, at pages 189–190 of FINGER-PRINTS, after quoting from Galton's review, goes on to observe that:

> *Four years after writing this review, in 1909, Galton was knighted for his service to science. One year later, Faulds wrote repeatedly to the Home Secretary, Winston Churchill, asking for some similar recognition for his fingerprint contributions. The Home Secretary did not reply.*
>
> *Faulds made his last desperate plea through his Member of Parliament. On April 19, 1910, the Member stood up in the House of Commons, and asked Winston Churchill whether he had received correspondence from Faulds and what he intended to do about it. Churchill answered: "So far as the Home Office is concerned, I am informed that the adoption of the Finger Print System in 1904 was entirely due to the labours of Mr., now Sir, Francis Galton."*

points must be identified before a match can be declared, varies from jurisdiction to jurisdiction. Sergeant Ashbaugh testified that the United Kingdom employs a six-teen-point minimum, Australia mandates that twelve points be found in common, and Canada uses no minimum point standard. Test. Ashbaugh, Tr. July 7, 1999, at 144–45. In the United States, state jurisdictions set their own minimum point stan-dards, while the FBI has no minimum number that must be identified to declare an "absolutely him" match, Test. Meagher, Tr. July 8, 1999, at 105, but does rely on a twelve-point "quality assurance" standard, id. at 104. As described by the Havvard court, "there is no single quantifiable standard for rendering an identification opin-ion because of differences in both the quantity of characteristics shown in the latent print and the quality of the image." Havvard, 117 F. Supp. 2d at 853. While there may be good reason for not relying on a minimum point standard—or for requiring a minimum number, as some state and foreign jurisdictions do—it is evident that there is no one standard "controlling the technique's operation," Daubert, 509 U.S. at 594.

The bulk of Mr. Meagher's testimony was a description and assessment of the pro-ficiency tests administered annually to *certified* FBI fingerprint personnel (as I under-stand it, only certified examiners are presented by the government as fingerprint iden-tification witnesses in court)[2] in the years 1995–2001. Each person tested received a packet containing copies of a number of latent prints (whose source, although unknown to the test-taker, was known to the test-makers) and copies of a smaller number of known exemplars; the test-taker would then undertake to determine iden-tities, or non-identities, between the latent prints and the known exemplars. Between 55 and 71 persons were tested each year. The tests, while the same in structure from year to year, varied in content. The tests taken by almost all personnel were adminis-tered internally—*i.e.*, within the FBI Laboratory framework—by supervisory finger-

---

2. To become an FBI fingerprint examiner one must have a bachelor's degree—preferably as a science major—and then successfully complete a two-year in-house training program culminating in a three-day certifying examination. The rigorous qualification regime described by Mr. Meagher establishes the inapplica-bility to certified FBI fingerprint examiners of the recital in the January 7 opin-ion that "[t]here are no mandatory qualifications for individuals to become fin-gerprint examiners [footnote omitted], nor is there a uniform certification process." Mr. Meagher did not present testimony as to the standards—very likely quite varied—that govern qualification as a fingerprint examiner in state and local law enforcement agencies. Nor was there any occasion for him to give such testimony, since the question before this court involves the admissibility of fin-gerprint identification testimony by FBI fingerprint personnel. The January 7 opinion did, however, identify an apparent lack of uniform qualification stan-dards as a factor cutting against satisfaction of *Daubert's* concern for "the exis-tence and maintenance of standards controlling the technique's operation." 509 U.S. at 594.

print specialists who acted as test-makers. The test-makers (usually two each year, of whom Mr. Meagher was always one) were themselves tested annually, through a test similar in form to the internal test, which was created externally by the Collaborative Testing Service, a private entity which constructs tests for numerous American and foreign laboratories.

Mr. Meagher presented a tabulation of the proficiency test results for the seven years 1995–2001. According to that tabulation (Government Exhibit R-15), the aggregate test population was 447 (*not*, of course, 447 different people, since each certified FBI fingerprint examiner takes the proficiency test each year).

Sixteen of the 447 test takers were supervisory personnel who, having administered the internal test, took the external test. In the course of the seven years, one error was recorded on an external test: In 1995, the external test called for assessment of seven latent fingerprints and four known exemplar ten-print cards (*i.e.*, cards containing prints of all ten fingers); one person mistakenly identified a latent print as matching one of the known exemplars—a "false positive." All errors on the FBI fingerprint proficiency tests are inquired into; but a false positive—being mistakenly inculpatory—is thought by the FBI to call for particularly demanding scrutiny. The inquiry conducted with respect to the 1995 error on the external test led Mr. Meagher to conclude that the error was not one of faulty evaluation but of faulty recording of the evaluation—i.e., a clerical rather than a technical error.

The internal tests taken over the seven years numbered 431. These tests generated three errors, two in 1995 and one in 2000. Each of the three errors was a missed identification—i.e., a failure by the test taker to find a match between a latent print and a known exemplar which in fact existed; such an error is a "false negative" which, being mistakenly exculpatory, is regarded by the FBI as considerably less serious than a false positive.

In sum, the 447 proficiency tests administered in the seven years from 1995 through 2001 yielded four errors—a proficiency error rate of just under 1%.

Mr. Meagher was asked on direct examination whether, in the course of his career, he had learned, either directly or through conversations with colleagues, of any instances in which FBI fingerprint identification testimony presented in court had turned out to be false. The question was objected to—on the ground that an answer in the negative would not be probative that the identification testimony was in fact accurate—but I overruled the objection. Mr. Meagher did respond in the negative. At a later point in the hearing I recalled Mr. Meagher to the stand so that I could pursue a couple of issues about which he had given testimony. One of the questions I put to Mr. Meagher was whether he knew if, in any of the many criminal trials in which he had given testimony of a match (some sixty or more trials, it would appear), the defendant had been acquitted. Not surprisingly, Mr. Meagher responded that he couldn't really provide any information on that score since, after giving his testimony, he frequently had no occasion to learn of the outcome of the trial. I then asked Mr. Meagher whether he was aware of instances in which "identification testimony turned out to be mistaken" in instances of "criminal prosecutions in the United States not involving FBI fingerprint identification testimony." "[T]he answer to that," responded Mr. Meagher, "is I believe so, yes, and to cite an exact case, I can't do that for you, but when those kinds of things occur, they certainly do make the rounds within the community, and the practitioners are very aware of it, and the answer to that is yes. Yes there have been erroneous identifications testified to in court here in the United States by those other than the FBI. I certainly don't want to imply that there's many, but I am aware of a few." Mr. Meagher then recalled a case "right here in Philadelphia in which ultimately the prints did come to the FBI for confirmation verification or for us to render our own independent decision." On further questioning by counsel it appeared that the instance of mistaken fingerprint identification recalled by Mr. Meagher was the prosecution of Ricardo Jackson in the Court of Common Pleas in Delaware County, not in Philadelphia.

Kenneth O. Smith:

Mr. Smith's testimony addressed the preparation and content of the external fingerprint identification proficiency tests distributed to and graded by CTS for numerous forensic laboratories, both domestic and foreign, including the FBI Laboratory. Mr. Smith has been an adviser to CTS on these matters for several years and thus is very familiar with the CTS tests. CTS does not supervise the manner in which the tests are taken at the various laboratories, so one could not tell from the test results the conditions under which a test would have been taken in any particular laboratory (whether, for example, the test would have been taken collaboratively or individually by those tested). Mr. Smith was of the view that the difficulty of the CTS tests corresponds reasonably closely to the difficulty presented to fingerprint examiners by their day-to-day work.

B. The Testimony of the Defense Witnesses

Allan Bayle:

Mr. Bayle is "a fingerprint examiner and a forensic scene examiner." He served at New Scotland Yard for twenty-five years until June of last year when he moved to the private sector as a consultant. Mr. Bayle is a Fellow of the (UK) Fingerprint Society and, like Mr. Meagher, a member of the International Association for Identification. He has testified in English courts as a fingerprint expert "[h]undreds of times." Mr. Bayle had reviewed copies of the internal FBI proficiency tests before taking the stand. He found the latent prints utilized in those tests to be, on the whole, markedly unrepresentative of the latent prints that would be lifted at a crime scene. In general, Mr. Bayle found the test latent prints to be far clearer than the prints an examiner would routinely deal with. The prints were too clear—they were, according to Mr. Bayle, lacking in the "background noise" and "distortion" one would expect in latent prints lifted at a crime scene.[3] Further, Mr. Bayle testified, the test materials were deficient in that there were too few latent prints that were not identifiable; according to Mr. Bayle, at a typical crime scene only about ten per cent of the lifted latent prints will turn out to be matched. In Mr. Bayle's view the paucity of non-identifiable latent prints:

> *makes the test too easy. It's not testing their ability. It doesn't test their expertise. I mean I've set these tests to trainees and advanced technicians. And if I gave my experts these tests, they'd fall about laughing.*

On cross-examination, Mr. Bayle was shown Government Exhibit R-13—a latent print the government expects to introduce at the upcoming trial. (Mr. Bayle had seen Government Exhibit R-14, a blow-up of R-13, the day before). " . . . [I]sn't it correct,"

---

3. **Q:** Sir, could you explain background noise and distortion to the Court?

   A: Background noise is what we call the susbtrate. And it's like if you leave your mark [fingerprint] on a grain surface, the grain surface will show in the background, and that's interference. And that's what you'll get at most scenes of crime when you obtain them and actually lift the marks from that particular substrate.

   Q: Let me put it to you this way, if I put my marks or my fingerprints on the table, correct?

   A: Right.

   Q: The background noise would be the table, correct?

   A: The grain of the table, yes.

   Q: And the distortion would be the pressure that I've applied to my fingers—the tips of my fingers, correct?

   A: That's right.

   Q: And that's the distortion, is that right?

   A: That's part of the distortion, yes.

   Q: Okay. So is the background noise or distortion that's represented in those latent prints that you're taking a look at, is that representative of what you would find at a crime scene?

   A: No.

   Q: All right. Now, sir, at a crime scene, would you expect to see background noise and distortions?

   A: Yes, I do.

   Q: Now, sir, are the latent prints in the materials that you're looking at, are they difficult to match?

   A: No.

government counsel asked, "that what you're looking at right there is much easier than the latents that are in the test?" "Yes."

On cross-examination Mr. Bayle acknowledged his commitment to ACE-V:

Q: ... [I]n your field and what you teach is the methodology that has been spoken about in this Court and in *Mitchell*, as you know, ACE-V?

A: That's correct.

Q: Okay, and that is a methodology that you believe in. Correct?

A: It is.

Q: You believe it's reliable. Correct?

A: It is.

Q: And you use it day in and day out in your work assignments. Correct?

A: That's correct.

After calling Mr. Meagher back to the witness stand, I also recalled Mr. Bayle. I asked whether it was not the case that "there have been some instances . . . in the U.K. experience, even in recent years, of mistaken identifications presented in court?" In reply, Mr. Bayle described the current case of Scottish Police Officer Shirley McKie who was charged with perjury for giving testimony that a fingerprint lifted from a door frame at a murder scene was not hers. Four fingerprint experts testified that the print was Officer McKie's, but two American fingerprint experts—Pat Wertheim and David Grieve—gave contrary testimony and Officer McKie was acquitted. Also, according to Mr. Bayle, there was another misidentification in the same underlying case. The matter is not yet fully resolved: an inquiry is under way to try to find out what went wrong, and Mr. Bayle is lending his expertise to that inquiry. On further cross-examination of Mr. Bayle, government counsel noted that Messrs. Wertheim and Grieve had been witnesses in the *Daubert* phase of the *Mitchell* case.

Janine Arvizu and Ralph Norman Haber:
Ms. Arvizu's expertise is in the area of laboratory quality assessment. Dr. Haber is a psychometrician. Neither one professed any familiarity with fingerprint identification. But both appeared to be quite knowledgeable about the principles of effective skills testing. They were highly critical of the FBI proficiency tests. The test materials and uninformative attendant literature, taken together with the ambiguity as to the conditions governing the taking of the tests (e.g., may the test takers consult with one another? to what extent is taking the test perceived to be competitive with, or subordinated to, the performance of concurrent work assignments?), gave few clues as to what the test makers intended to measure. For both Ms. Arvizu and Dr. Haber, the stratospheric test success rate was hardly reassuring; to the contrary, it raised "red flags."

As to ACE-V itself, Dr. Haber offered the thought that "verification" was a misnomer for the final stage: a procedure in which a second fingerprint examiner knows the result arrived at by a previous examiner, and is asked to go over the same ground, would be better described as "ratification."

The Stipulation

Shortly before the close of testimony, government counsel presented, by stipulation, a correction of certain figures recited in the January 7 opinion. In that opinion I stated that:

> *Mr. Meagher had conducted a survey in which he sent Byron Mitchell's ten-print card and alleged latent fingerprints to state agencies. The ten-print card was to be compared with the state fingerprint records: the result—that only Pennsylvania, the state in which Mitchell had been incarcerated, reported a 'hit'—was significant confirmation of the uniqueness of fingerprints. The other aspect of the Meagher survey—a request that state agencies determine whether the latent prints matched the known Mitchell prints—offered scant support for the accuracy of fingerprint identification. Nine of the thirty-four responding agencies did not make an identification in the first instance. . . . While the survey results fall far short of establishing a "scientific" rate of error, they are (modestly) suggestive of a discernible level of practitioner error.*

The stipulation establishes that my statement that "[n]ine of the thirty-four responding agencies did not make an identification in the first instance" was erroneous in two respects: *First*, there were *thirty-nine* responding agencies, not *thirty-four*, each of the thirty-nine responding agencies having been sent *Mitchell's* ten-print card and two latent prints. Second (and more important), the recital that "[n]ine of the . . . responding agencies did not make an identification" was materially misleading: thirty of the thirty-nine responding agencies correctly identified—i.e., achieved a proper match with respect to—both latent prints; of the remaining nine, four in fact did correctly identify one of the two latents, but failed to identify the other; only five of the responding agencies did not identify either of the two latent prints.

The corrected figures call for some amendment of my conclusory observation, in the sentences quoted above from the January 7 opinion, that "the survey results . . . are (modestly) suggestive of a discernible level of practitioner error." If one were undertaking to calculate the "level of practitioner error," the figures reflected in the stipulation signify a larger denominator and a smaller numerator than my January 7 statement implied. Furthermore, as bearing on the issues before this court, it is important to note that whatever practitioner errors Mr. Meagher's survey may have been the catalyst of, those errors would have been those of examiners working for state agencies, not errors of FBI fingerprint examiners.

III

(1) Is ACE-V a "Scientific" Technique?

The opinion of January 7, which was based on the *Mitchell* record, undertook to respond to the parties' competing arguments as to whether ACE-V meets *Daubert*'s requirements. Characterizing ACE-V as "scientific" in the Rule 702 and *Daubert* sense, the government argued that the *Mitchell* record established that ACE-V met all four of the *Daubert* guidelines: (1) that "the theory or technique" is one that "can be (and has been) tested"; (2) that "the theory or technique has been subjected to peer review and publication"; (3) "in the case of a particular scientific technique, the court ordinarily should consider the known or potential rate of error . . . and the existence and maintenance of standards controlling the technique's operation"; and (4) "general acceptance" in the "'scientific community.'" 509 U.S. at 593–594. The defendants, reading the *Mitchell* record and *Daubert* differently, argued otherwise. In the January 7 opinion I accepted the battleground as the parties had defined it, and on that basis I concluded that: (1) and (2), ACE-V was not supported by "testing" or by "peer review" in the "scientific" sense contemplated by *Daubert*; (3) the rate of error was "in limbo" and consensus on controlling standards was lacking; and (4) while there was "general acceptance" of ACE-V in the fingerprint identification community, that community was not a "'scientific community'" in *Daubert*'s use of the term. But in reaching these conclusions I voiced some skepticism about the vocabulary that informed counsel's and my various analyses. "[T]he caveat must be added," I wrote, "that, in the court's view, the domain of knowledge occupied by fingerprint examiners should be described, in Rule 702 terms, by the word 'technical,' rather than by the word 'scientific,' the word the government deploys."

What is science? Science has to do with propositions that can be "tested or verified by observation or experiment."[4] ACE-V—the system of fingerprint identification that links Stephen Meagher of the United States, Allan Bayle of England, David Ashbaugh of Canada, and their counterparts in other countries—is not, in my judgment, itself a science. But its claim on the attention of courts derives from the fact that it is rooted in science—in the two propositions of which this court, in its January 7

---

4. Freeman J. Dyson, *Science & Religion: No Ends in Sight*, XLIX, THE NEW YORK REVIEW OF BOOKS (March 28, 2002) p. 4. Professor Dyson notes that "[t]he way a scientific argument goes is typically as follows: We have a number of theories to explain what we have observed. Most of the theories are probably wrong or irrelevant. Then somebody does a new experiment or a new calculation that proves that Theory A is wrong. As a result, Theory B now has a better chance of being right."

opinion, relying primarily on the testimony of Dr. William Babler,[5] took judicial notice: namely, that fingerprints are unique and are permanent. Principal credit for the initial observations and experiments supporting these propositions belongs to the four remarkable investigators and public officials whom I referred to in the historical note in section II of this opinion—Francis Galton, Edward Henry, William Herschel and, most particularly, Henry Faulds.[6]

---

5. With respect to uniqueness, some reliance was also placed on the corroborative testimony of Donald Ziesig.

6. The observations and experiments of Henry Faulds, while serving as a medical missionary in Japan, are admirably described by Colin Beavan, at pages 69–73 of his recent work, FINGERPRINTS, to which I have previously referred:

> *One day, while turning over ancient pottery fragments in his hands, Faulds noticed minute patterns of parallel lines impressed in the clay. He examined them closely, trying to discern their source. Some months earlier, Faulds had lectured his medical students on each of the five senses. During preparation for the lecture on touch, he had noticed the swirling ridges on his own fingertips. In a flash, he realized that the 2,000-year-old impressions he now examined in clay came from the ridges on the fingers of ancient potters.*
>
> *Did modern potters leave such marks, too? Faulds scoured the contemporary markets of Tokyo, closely examining the surfaces of current-day pottery. The marks were everywhere. On China tea sets in one market stall he noticed how "one peculiar pattern of lineations would reappear with great persistency, as if the same artist had left her sign-mark on her work." Suddenly it occurred to him that a piece of pottery could be matched to a particular potter by the ridge markings left in the clay. He had begun to suspect that finger-ridge patterns were unique to each individual, the basis for their use in identification. At first, Faulds paid little attention to this detail.*
>
> *At that time, Faulds did not fancy himself as a detective wanting to identify criminals, but as an anthropologist wishing to throw light on the origins of humanity. Since the 1860s, anthropologists had sought to classify populations according to their physical attributes. Among them, Paul Broca, who founded the Anthropological Society of Paris in 1859, had used measurements of the bony portions of the head and face to distinguish one group from another. By careful analysis, Broca showed, for example, that northern Europeans were distinctively more long-headed than central Europeans. Faulds hoped populations might be similarly classified by finger-ridge patterns. He thought the patterns might differ by race, era, and geography, much like Broca's facial characteristics.*
>
> *The Scottish doctor studied the fingerprints of his friends, his family, his grocers, even the workmen who came to his house. At first, Faulds examined their finger ridges directly, making sketches for his records. Next, he began recording their fingertips in wax. Finally, he hit on the technique of inking the fingertips and recording their impressions on paper. Twenty years earlier, William Herschel, unknown to Faulds, had begun collecting the prints of the thumb and first two fingers of his acquaintances. Now, Faulds began a similar practice,*

except for one crucial difference—he insisted on inking and printing all ten of his subjects' fingers, a move that would one day make fingerprint sets easier to differentiate in large criminal registers.

Faulds's collection of prints swelled to the thousands, but they all came from European and Japanese fingers. He needed a greater variety to determine whether finger-ridge patterns differed from race to race and area to area as he had postulated. In an effort to expand his data, he wrote more than a hundred letters to scientists around the world, asking their assistance in collecting fingerprints and including copies of specially created ten-digit fingerprint forms. Faulds received almost no response. "Some thought I was an advocate of palmistry . . . most took no notice whatever." Faulds's fingerprint studies had come to a dead end.

Coincidentally, during this period, the supply of medical alcohol at Faulds's hospital, kept in a bottle in a locked cabinet, ran inexplicably low. It had to be restocked again and again before Faulds finally realized that the bottle was emptying itself into some thirsty person's gullet. When he found a makeshift cocktail glass in the form of a laboratory measuring beaker, he examined its surface and discovered a nearly complete set of sweaty finger marks. Faulds searched his collection of fingerprint cards for a match, and found one. It belonged to one of his medical students—culprit discovered.

At first, Faulds did not recognize the new use for fingerprints he had unwittingly stumbled upon. Then, a month later, someone attempted to burgle the hospital by climbing up a wall and through a window. Local police accused a favorite member of Faulds's staff, but the ridge patterns in a sooty handprint found on the wall, Faulds found, did not match those of the accused. He showed his evidence to the police and exonerated the staff member.

This time Faulds saw the light. He remembered the crowds he had seen outside the Old Bailey, waiting for news of the trial of the Claimant. A filed set of the shipwrecked Roger Tichborne's fingerprints, Faulds realized, would have destroyed the Claimant's case in a moment. [Tichborne, the "Claimant" in a celebrated nineteenth century case was an imposter who claimed to be the long-lost heir of an aristocratic family]. Similarly, a fingerprint register of habitual criminals would foil their attempts to use false names and get lighter sentences. Faulds's conception was similar, in a way, to that of William Herschel, who, unknown to Faulds had one year earlier introduced fingerprints' official use in Hooghly, India. Herschel, however, used fingerprints only as a form of signature to authenticate documents. Faulds's idea had much farther-reaching ramifications. He realized fingerprints could solve the problem of identification that so troubled the British legal system.

Faulds was loath at first to publish his idea. He was plagued by a "most depressing sense of moral responsibility and danger. What if someone were wrongly identified and made to suffer innocently through a defective method? It seemed to me that a great deal had to be done before publicly proposing the adoption of such a scheme." Faulds first set out to prove conclusively that fingerprints were unique to each individual and, second, that they stayed the same throughout a person's life.

In one experiment, Faulds and his medical students shaved off their finger ridges with razors until no pattern could be traced. The ridges grew back, with-

(2) ACE-V as a "Technical" Discipline: *Daubert* Through the Prism of *Kumho Tire*
In adjusting the focus of inquiry from ACE-V's status as a "scientific" discipline to its status as a "technical" discipline, one modifies the angle of doctrinal vision. As noted in the January 7 opinion, the Court in *Kumho Tire* concluded that—contrary to the ruling of the Eleventh Circuit under review—*Daubert*'s pronouncements with respect to "scientific" expert testimony are also applicable to "technical" expert testimony. The *Kumho Tire* Court "also conclude[d] that a trial court may consider one or more of the more specific factors that *Daubert* mentioned when doing so will help determine that testimony's reliability. But, as the Court stated in *Daubert*, the test of reliability is 'flexible,' and *Daubert*'s list of specific factors neither necessarily nor exclusively applies to all experts or in every case. Rather, the law grants a district court the same broad latitude when it decides *how* to determine reliability as it enjoys in respect to its ultimate reliability determination." 526 U.S. at 141–142 (emphasis in original). Later in its opinion, the *Kumho Tire* Court, in explaining its rejection of the Eleventh Circuit's limitation of *Daubert* as applicable only to "scientific" evidence, stated: "We do not believe that Rule 702 creates a schematism that segregates expertise by type while mapping certain kinds of questions to certain kinds of experts. Life and the legal cases it generates are too complex to warrant so definitive a match." *Id.* at 151. The Court went on:

> To say this is not to deny the importance of *Daubert*'s gatekeeping requirement. The objective of that requirement is to ensure the reliability and relevancy of expert testimony. It is to make certain that an expert, whether basing testimony on professional studies or personal experience, employs in the courtroom the same level of intellectual rigor that characterizes the practice of an expert in the relevant field. Nor do we

---

out exception, in exactly the same patterns. They repeated the experiment, removing the ridges by any number of methods—by "pumice-stone, sand paper, emery dust, various acids, caustics and even spanish fly"—and each time the results were the same.

　　Next, Faulds studied infants to see if growth affected their fingertip patterns the way it dramatically changed the rest of their bodies. It didn't. Over a period of two years, he also examined the hands of large numbers of Japanese children and some thirty-five European children between the ages of five and ten. In no case did the ridge patterns vary. When an epidemic of scarlet fever swept through Japan, causing severe peeling of skin, Faulds again studied the fingerprints and found no before-and-after change.

　　"Enough had been observed," Faulds decided, "to enable me confidently, as a practical biologist, to assert the invariableness, for practical identification purposes, of the patterns formed by the lineations of human finger-tips." Fingerprints were permanent. Meanwhile, the many thousands of fingerprint sets collected and mutually compared by Faulds satisfied him that each person's fingerprint set was truly unique. He was finally ready to go public.

deny that, as stated in Daubert, *the particular questions that it mentioned will often be appropriate for use in determining the reliability of challenged expert testimony. Rather, we conclude that the trial judge must have considerable leeway in deciding in a particular case how to go about determining whether particular expert testimony is reliable. That is to say, a trial court should consider the specific factors identified in* Daubert *where they are reasonable measures of the reliability of expert testimony.*

Id. *at 152.*

The *Kumho Tire* Court's injunction that the gatekeeping requirement is designed to insure "that an expert . . . employs in the courtroom the same level of intellectual rigor that characterizes the practice of an expert in the relevant field" serves as a reminder that fingerprint identification is not a discipline that is confined to courtroom use. It is a discipline relied on in other settings—e.g., in identifying the dead in mass disasters. Properly to determine whether an FBI fingerprint examiner operates at a proper level of intellectual rigor when she comes to court as an expert witness, it becomes necessary, on this motion for reconsideration of my January 7 ruling, to reexamine the grounds on which I found that ACE-V did not satisfy three of the *Daubert* factors and only marginally met the fourth ("general acceptance" by the fingerprint community, which I deemed not a "scientific community"). In this reexamination there are two points to be addressed. One is the extent to which the several *Daubert* factors "are reasonable measures of the reliability of expert testimony." The other is whether the recent enlargement of the record—the three days of hearings on the motion for reconsideration—alters in some significant way the pertinent facts drawn from the *Mitchell* record.

(a) "peer review" and "general acceptance":

First I consider the "peer review" and "general acceptance" factors. The fact that fingerprint specialists are not "scientists," and hence that the forensic journals in which their writings on fingerprint identification appear are not "scientific" journals in *Daubert*'s peer review sense, does not seem to me to militate against the utility of the identification procedures employed by fingerprint specialists, whether on the witness stand or at the disaster site. By the same token, I conclude that the fingerprint community's "general acceptance" of ACE-V should not be discounted because fingerprint specialists—like accountants, vocational experts, accident-reconstruction experts, appraisers of land or of art, experts in tire failure analysis,[7] or others—have "techni-

---

7. Dennis Carlson, Jr., the proposed expert witness in *Kumho Tire*, was "an expert in tire failure analysis." 526 U.S. at 142.

"*[N]o one denies that an expert might draw a conclusion from a set of observations based on extensive and specialized experience. Nor does anyone deny*

cal, or other specialized knowledge"(Rule 702), rather than "scientific . . . knowledge" (id.), and hence are not members of what *Daubert* termed a "scientific community."

(b) "testing":

Next I consider the "testing" factor. The key to the admissibility of expert testimony under *Daubert* and *Kumho Tire* is reliability, and this, of course, derives directly from the text of Rule 702, which contemplates that "(1) the testimony is based upon sufficient facts or data, (2) the testimony is the product of reliable principles and methods, and (3) the witness has applied the principles and methods reliably to the facts of the case." Bearing this in mind, one would welcome "testing" in the *Daubert* sense as a criterion of reliability. Disagreeing with contentions that the "verification" phase of ACE-V constitutes *Daubert* "testing," or, in the alternative, that a century of litigation has been a form of "adversarial" testing that meets *Daubert*'s criteria, I concluded in the January 7 opinion that *Daubert*'s testing factor was not met, and I have found no reason to depart from that conclusion.

(c) "rate of error" and "standards controlling the technique's operation":

The last *Daubert* question to be addressed is whether *Daubert*'s third factor—"the known or potential rate of error . . . and the existence and maintenance of standards controlling the technique's operation"—offers support for fingerprint identification testimony. In the January 7 opinion, on the basis of the *Mitchell* record, I answered this question in the negative: I found no persuasive information with respect to rate of error. And with respect to "the existence and maintenance of [controlling] standards" I found

(1) "whether a minimum number of Galton points must be identified before a match can be declared, varies from jurisdiction to jurisdiction. Sergeant Ashbaugh testified that the United Kingdom employs a sixteen-point minimum, Australia mandates that twelve points be found in common, and Canada uses no minimum point standard. . . . In the United States, state jurisdictions set their own minimum point standards, while the FBI has no minimum number that must be identified to declare an 'absolutely him' match";

(2) there appeared to be no uniformly accepted qualifying standards for fingerprint examiners; and (3) the identification judgments made by fingerprint examiners at

---

that, as a general matter, tire abuse may often be identified by qualified experts through visual or tactile inspection of the tire. . . . As we said before . . . the question before the trial court was specific, not general. The trial court had to decide whether this particular expert had sufficient specialized knowledge to assist the jurors 'in deciding the particular issues in the case.'" Id. at 156. The district court declined to let Mr. Carlson testify. According to the Supreme Court, the district court "ultimately based its decision upon Carson's failure to satisfy either Daubert's factors or any other set of reasonable reliability criteria. In light of the record as developed by the parties, that conclusion was within the District Court's lawful discretion." Id. at 158.

ACE-V's "evaluation" stage—i.e., in determining whether there is a "match"—are "subjective."

What new light—if any—is shed upon rate of error, or upon controlling standards, by the recent three days of hearings?

(i) "rate of error":

The factual case presented by the government was chiefly devoted to demonstrating, through the testimony of Mr. Meagher, that certified FBI fingerprint examiners have scored spectacularly well on the in-house annual proficiency tests conducted by Mr. Meagher and his fellow supervisors from 1995 to date. (The testimony of Mr. Smith with respect to the CTS tests prepared for certain personnel (such as Mr. Meagher and his fellow FBI supervisors) at numerous forensic laboratories, while of some interest, added little to the government's case.) The evident theory of the government's demonstration was that, in the absence of actual data on rate of error, proficiency test scores of those who would be expert witnesses should be taken as a surrogate form of proof: if certified examiners rarely make a mistake on ACE-V proficiency tests, it stands to reason (so the theory would have it) that they rarely make a mistake when presenting ACE-V testimony in court.[8] To rebut the government's proof, the defense witnesses undertook to demonstrate that the proficiency tests were inadequate. Ms. Arvizu and Dr. Haber, knowing nothing about fingerprints but a good deal about skills-testing, gave pertinent testimony. But the full weight of the defense case rested with Mr. Bayle, a fingerprint specialist as knowledgeable and experienced as Mr. Meagher. In Mr. Bayle's view, the internal proficiency tests presented little challenge, principally because (a) the latent prints in the tests were, by and large, of substantially greater clarity than one would normally harvest from a crime scene, and (b) the latent prints in the tests included far fewer instances of non-identifiability than an examiner would routinely meet up with. "If I gave my experts these tests," said Mr. Bayle, "they'd fall about laughing." The government did get Mr. Bayle to acknowledge that one of the latent prints that is to figure in the upcoming trial is of very high clarity—a clarity exceeding that of most of the test latent prints. But that single example did not, in my view, blunt the larger point made by Mr. Bayle. On the record made before me, the FBI examiners got very high proficiency grades, but the tests they took did not.

---

8. The testimony with respect to FBI proficiency tests may also be taken as countering certain defense evidence, adduced on the Mitchell record (Def. Exhibits 2 and 3), referred to in footnote 24 of the January 7 opinion—evidence which seemed to show poor-to-mediocre results on proficiency tests taken in 1995 and 1998, and with respect to which the footnote opined that "these proficiency examination results may be taken as somewhat suggestive of practitioner error." But since it appears that those who took the proficiency tests referred to in the footnote were not FBI fingerprint examiners, any suggested relation between those test results and possible practitioner error would have no bearing on the fingerprint identification capabilities of FBI examiners.

The defense witnesses succeeded in raising real questions about the adequacy of the proficiency tests taken annually by certified FBI fingerprint examiners. It may be that further inquiry by qualified forensic specialists and persons versed in skills-testing will answer those questions in the FBI's favor. But on the present record I conclude that the proficiency tests are less demanding than they should be. To the extent that this is the case, it would appear that the tests can be of little assistance in providing the test makers with a discriminating measure of the relative competence of the test takers. But the defense witnesses offered not a syllable to suggest that certified FBI fingerprint examiners as a group, or any individual examiners among them, have not achieved at least an acceptable level of competence. The record shows that over the years there have been at least a few instances in which fingerprint examiners, here and abroad, have made identifications that have turned out to be erroneous. But Mr. Meagher knew of no erroneous identifications attributable to FBI examiners. Defense counsel contended that such non-knowledge does not constitute proof that there have been no FBI examiner errors. That is true, but nothing in the record suggests that the obverse is true. It has been open to defense counsel to present examples of erroneous identifications attributable to FBI examiners, and no such examples have been forthcoming. I conclude, therefore, on the basis of the limited information in the record as expanded, that there is no evidence that the error rate of certified FBI fingerprint examiners is unacceptably high.

(ii) "standards controlling the technique's operation":
The January 7 opinion found that three aspects of ACE-V manifested an absence of generally accepted controlling standards: (a) there appeared to be no agreed qualification standards for fingerprint examiners; (b) jurisdictions varied widely with respect to the minimum number of Galton points required for finding a "match"; (c) the ultimate "evaluation" judgment was termed "subjective." On reviewing these issues on the basis of the expanded record I reach the following conclusions:

(a) Whatever may be the case for other law enforcement agencies, the standards prescribed for qualification as an FBI fingerprint examiner are clear: To be hired by the FBI as a fingerprint trainee, one must be a college graduate, preferably with some training in one of the physical sciences; to become a certified fingerprint examiner, the trainee must complete the FBI's two-year in-house training program which winds up with a three-day certifying examination. The uniformity and rigor of these FBI requirements provide substantial assurance that, with respect to certified FBI fingerprint examiners, properly controlling qualification standards are in place and are in force.

(b) As previously noted, the *Mitchell* record pointed to wide disagreements, from jurisdiction to jurisdiction, with respect to the minimum number of Galton points required to permit an examiner to find a "match": sixteen points in the United Kingdom, twelve in Australia; no minimum number in Canada or in FBI fingerprint identification testimony in the United States. The absence of a Galton minimum under FBI auspices, as against maintenance of a high Galton threshold in the United Kingdom, the jurisdiction whose police first systematized fingerprint identification for law enforcement purposes, could be perceived as troublesome—i.e., connoting a lack of rigor in FBI standards. However, it appears that the July 7, 1999 *Mitchell* testimony with respect to the United Kingdom did not accurately reflect the then state of United Kingdom law and is now entirely out of date.

The *Mitchell* testimony failed to take account of a leading case decided some two months earlier—*Regina v. Buckley*, 143 SJ LB 159 (April 30, 1999), in which the Court of Appeal (Criminal Division) stated that "[i]f there are fewer than eight similar ridge characteristics, it is highly unlikely that a judge will exercise his discretion to admit such evidence and, save in wholly exceptional circumstances, the prosecution should not seek to adduce such evidence," whereas "[i]f there are eight or more similar ridge characteristics, a judge may or may not exercise his or her discretion in favour of admitting the evidence." The Court of Appeal then proceeded to list elements that should inform the trial judge's exercise of discretion:

How the discretion is exercised will depend on all the circumstances of the case, including in particular:

(i) *the experience and expertise of the witness;*

(ii) *the number of similar ridge characteristics;*

(iii) *whether there are dissimilar characteristics;*

(iv) *the size of the print relied on, in that the same number of similar ridge characteristics may be more compelling in a fragment of print than in an entire print; and*

(v) *the quality and clarity of the print on the item relied on, which may involve, for example, consideration of possible injury to the person who left the print, as well as factors such as smearing or contamination.*

In every case where fingerprint evidence is admitted, it will generally be necessary, as in relation to all expert evidence, for the judge to warn the jury that it is evidence opinion only, that the expert's opinion is not conclusive and that it is for the jury to determine whether guilt is proved in the light of all the evidence.

Id. Notably, the Buckley opinion prefaced its holding by succinctly narrating the history of English fingerprint identification jurisprudence—with special reference to changing standards with respect to minimum numbers of "similar ridge characteristics" (what we know as "Galton points). Excerpts from that history follow:

It has long been known that fingerprint patterns vary from person to person and that such patterns are unique and unchanging throughout life. As early as 1906, in R v Castleton 3 Cr App R 74, a conviction was upheld which depended solely on identification by fingerprints. At that time there were no set criteria or standards. But, gradually, a numerical standard evolved and it became accepted that once 12 similar ridge characteristics could be identified, a match was proved beyond all doubt.

In 1924, the standard was altered by New Scotland Yard, but not by all other police forces, so as to require 16 similar ridge characteristics. That alteration was made because, in 1912, a paper had been published in France by a man called Alphonse Bertillon. It was on the basis of his paper that the 16 similar ridge characteristics standard was adopted. However, in recent times, the originals of the prints used by Bertillon have been examined and revealed conclusively to be forgeries. It is therefore apparent that the 16 point standard was adopted on a false basis

* * * *

During the passage of time, there have, of course, in this area, as in the realms of much other expert evidence, been developments in knowledge and expertise. Of course, in practice, many marks left at the scene of a crime are not by any means perfect; they may be only partial prints; they may be smudged or smeared or contaminated. However, a consensus developed between experts that considerably fewer than 16 ridge characteristics would establish a match beyond any doubt. Some experts suggested that eight would provide a complete safeguard. Others maintained that there should be no numerical standard at all. We are told, and accept, that other countries admit identifications of 12, 10, or eight similar ridge characteristics and, in some other countries, the numerical system has been abandoned altogether.

* * * *

. . . . In 1988, the Home Office and ACPO (The Association of Chief Police Officers) commissioned a study by Drs Evett and Williams into fingerprint standards. They recommended that there was no scientific, logical or statistical basis for the retention of any numerical standard, let alone one that required as many as 16 points of similarity.

In consequence, ACPO set up a series of committees to consider regularising the position and to ensure that, if fingerprint identifications based on less than 16 points were to be relied upon, there would be clear procedures and protocols in place to establish a Nationwide system for training of experts to an appropriate level of competence, establishment of management procedures for the supervision, recording and monitoring of their work and the introduction of an independent and external audit to ensure the quality of the work done. In 1994 an ACPO report produced under the chairmanship of the Deputy Chief Constable of Thames Valley Police recommended changing to a non numerical system and the Chief Constable's Council endorsed that recommendation in 1996. Further discussions followed between the heads of all the Fingerprint Bureau in this country and ACPO. In consequence, a Fingerprint Evidence Project Board was established with a view to studying exhaustively the systems needed before moving nationally to a non numerical system. The first report of that body was presented on 25 March 1998 and recommended that the national standard be changed entirely to a non numerical system: a target date of April 2000 was hoped for, by which the necessary protocols and procedures would be in place. If and when that occurs, it may be that fingerprint experts will be able to give their opinions unfettered by any arbitrary numerical thresholds. The courts will then be able to draw such conclusions as they think fit from the evidence of fingerprint experts.

It is to be noted that none of this excellent work by the police and by fingerprint experts can be regarded as either usurping the function of a trial judge in determining admissibility or changing the law as to the admissibility of evidence.

As the *Buckley* opinion pointed out, the Fingerprint Evidence Project Board recommended in 1998 that by April of 2000 "the national standard be changed entirely to a non numerical system." April of 2000 turned out to be too ambitious a target date. But the projected change—based upon the consensus referred to in Buckley that there is no scientific basis for insisting on any given minimum of "similar ridge characteristics"—was accomplished as of June 11, 2001. The new regime was described in some detail in the House of Lords on February 25, 2002, in answers given by Lord Rooker on behalf of Her Majesty's Government to questions that had previously been 'put down,' in conformity with Parliamentary practice, by Lord Lester of Herne Hill:[9]

Lord Lester of Herne Hill *asked Her Majesty's Government:*
What standards are prescribed for fingerprint identification to be used in evidence in criminal trials. [H.L. 2699]

Lord Rooker: *The current standard prescribed for fingerprint identification is the non-numerical system which was introduced from 11 June 2001. This was after extensive consultation with the Lord Chancellor, the Attorney-General and other criminal justice system stakeholders.*

Although there is no set numerical standard to be satisfied before experts make a decision that a mark or impression left at a crime scene and a fingerprint were made by the same person, there are objective criteria which must be satisfied and must be

---

9. Lord Lester of Herne Hill (Anthony Lester QC), a leading barrister and also a leading public law scholar (see, e.g., LORD LESTER OF HERNE HILL QC & DAVID PANNICK QC, HUMAN RIGHTS LAW AND PRACTICE (1999)), has been a good friend of the undersigned for some thirty years, and so he seemed the logical person to ask about the current state of English fingerprint jurisprudence; as a result of that query I learned about Buckley and about the going into force on June 11, 2001 of the new fingerprint identification regime. What I certainly did not anticipate was that Lord Lester would undertake to enlarge his (and, by extension, my, and, by further extension, counsels') knowledge base by formally addressing questions to Her Majesty's Government. This is a method of legal research to which I could cheerfully become accustomed. And it was gratifying to be able to present to counsel and place on the record, in a Philadelphia courtroom on February 26, 2002, the research results provided by Lord Rooker to Lord Lester in the House of Lords on February 25, 2002.

capable of demonstration, eg in a court, before any such decision is made. There are also prescribed verification procedures which must be adhered to at all times before that decision is communicated to an investigating police officer and eventually to the courts.

Lord Lester of Herne Hill *asked Her Majesty's Government:*
What qualifications are prescribed for individuals to become fingerprint examiners for the purpose of giving evidence of identity in criminal trials. [H.L. 2700]

Lord Rooker: *All fingerprint experts commence their training with a foundation course of four weeks. They then need to complete five modules which should normally be completed within 12 to 18 months and are followed by a short assessment. Twelve months later, after a consolidation of skills and work experience on the job, they attend a two-week advanced course in which the emphasis is on court presentation and preparation of evidence. Even after the advanced course has been passed successfully, which is usually not less than three years after entering the training programme, the person will be permitted to attend court to give expert testimony only with the approval of their head of fingerprint bureau and chief constable.*

Lord Lester of Herne Hill *asked Her Majesty's government:*
Whether they consider that the determination that a fingerprint examiner makes when comparing a latent fingerprint with a known fingerprint for the purpose of establishing identity in criminal proceedings is a subjective determination in that no objective standard has been scientifically tested and no subjective process has been objectively tested; and, if not, what is the objective standard that is applied. [H.L. 2701]

Lord Rooker: *In determining whether or not a latent mark or impression left at a crime scene and a fingerprint have been made by the same person, a fingerprint examiner must apply set criteria in carrying out their comparison. The criteria are objective and can be tested and verified by other experts. It is the method which is of universal application by practitioners on behalf of either prosecution or defense, and has been in use from the first application of fingerprint/mark identification. Once the first fingerprint examiner has reached a conclusion that the mark or impression at the crime scene and a fingerprint have been made by the same person, that decision is subject to verification by two other fingerprint experts before the investigating officer is informed of the result. Any identification evidence presented in court will have been subject to these procedures.*

Instructing solicitors or barristers representing defendants can and regularly do ask that finger identification evidence be subjected to scrutiny by nominated fingerprint experts from outside the Police Service. Details of those experts can be obtained from registers maintained by the Law Society, the Expert Witness Institute or through the services of private companies who undertake independent forensic examinations. This is an external examination of Police Service practice and procedures which has been on going for many years.

The answers of Lord Rooker to the questions put by Lord Lester establish that there is no longer any significant lack of harmony between the FBI's fingerprint identification standards and those that prevail in English courtrooms. Further, the *Buckley* description of how, over the course of years, a consensus was arrived at in the United Kingdom that there was no scientific rationale for insisting on some minimum number of "similar ridge characteristics," offers weighty corroboration of the FBI's position as articulated by Mr. Meagher from the witness stand. In sum, I conclude that the minimum-Galton-point issue discussed in the January 7 opinion is now moot. Though a number of other countries may still observe Galton point minima, the fact that England has, after many years of close study, moved to the position which prevails in Canada and which the FBI has long subscribed to, leads me to conclude that there is sufficient uniformity within the principal common law jurisdictions to satisfy *Daubert*.

(iii) In the January 7 opinion, the aspect of the *Daubert* inquiry into "the existence and maintenance of standards controlling the technique's operation," 509 U.S. at 594, that was of greatest concern was the acknowledged subjectivity of the fingerprint examiner's stated opinion that a latent print and a known exemplar are both attributable to the same person. Government witnesses Meagher and Ashbaugh both described the "match" opinion as "subjective," and defense witness Dr. David Stoney agreed. I concluded that "[w]ith such a high degree of subjectivity, it is difficult to see how fingerprint identification—the matching of a latent print to a known print—is controlled by any clearly describable set of standards to which most examiners prescribe." On further reflection, I disagree with myself. I think my assessment stopped with the word "subjective" when I should have gone on to focus on the process the word describes. There are, to be sure, situations in which the subjectiveness of an opinion properly gives rise to reservations about the opinion's reliability.[10] But there are many situations in which an expert's manifestly subjective opinion (an opinion based, as Sergeant Ashbaugh said of the opinions of fingerprint examiners, on "one's personal knowledge, ability and experience") is regarded as admissible evidence in an American courtroom: a forensic engineer's testimony that a bottom-fire nailer's defective design caused an unintended "double-fire," resulting in injury to the plaintiff,

---

10. *Kumho Tire* may be regarded as one such situation. The Supreme Court, in the course of discussing several factors which might very properly have entered into the district court's decision (a decision the Supreme Court deemed "reasonable," 526 U.S. at 153) not to admit the testimony of plaintiff's expert in tire failure analysis, observed that the district court's "concerns might have been augmented by Carlson's repeated reliance on the 'subjective[ness]' of his mode of analysis in response to questions seeking specific information regarding how he could differentiate between a tire that actually had been overdeflected and a tire that merely looked as though it had been." 526 U.S. at 155.

Lauzon v. Senco Products, 270 F.3d 681 (8th cir. 2001); an electrical engineer's testimony that fire in a clothes drier was caused by a thermostat malfunction, *Maryland Casualty Co. v. Therm-O-Disc*, 137 F.3d 780 (4th Cir., 1998); a marketing researcher's testimony as to consumer interpretations of advertising claims, the testimony being based on a market survey of consumers. *Southard Sod Farms v. Stover Seed Co.*, 108 F.3d 1134 (9th Cir., 1997)."[11] In each instance the expert is operating within a vocational framework that may have numerous objective components, but the expert's ultimate opining is likely to depend in some measure on experiential factors that transcend precise measurement and quantification. As compared with the degree of subjectiveness inherent in one or more of the foregoing examples of expert opinion testimony, the subjective ingredients of opinion testimony presented by a competent fingerprint examiner appear to be of substantially more restricted compass. The defined characteristics of such testimony are illumined by the following exchange in the House of Lords on March 11, 2002:

> **Lord Lester of Herne Hill** asked Her Majesty's Government:
> *Further to the Written Answers by Lord Rooker on 25 February (WA 172-73), what are the objective criteria and prescribed verification procedures for fingerprint identification used in evidence in criminal trials. [HL3041]*
>
> **Lord Rooker:** *To determine whether or not a crime scene mark and a fingerprint impression have been made by the same person, the fingerprint examiner must carry out a process of analysis, comparison and evaluation by determining whether in each impression friction ridge features are of a compatible type; they are in the same relative positions to each other in the ridge structure; they are in the same sequence; there is sufficient quantitative and qualitative detail in each in agreement; and there are any areas of apparent or real discrepancy. The examiner must address all these issues before declaring that both mark and impression have been made by the same person.*
> *The next stage is verification. The examiner's conclusion must be verified independently by two other officers who must both be fingerprint experts. Any*

---

11. As to expert testimony about handwriting, note the limitations imposed by the district court in *United States v. Hines*, 55 F. Supp. 2d 62 (D. Mass. 1999), quoted from in the January 7 opinion; but cf. *United States v. Velasquez*, 64 F. 3d 844 (3d Cir. 1995). The handwriting case which was the mother of all handwriting cases was the *Howland Will Case (Robinson v. Mandell*, 20 F. Cas. 1027 (Cir. Ct. D. Mass. 1868)), in which Hetty Howland Robinson (later, Hetty Howland Robinson Green) sought a determination that she was the rightful heir of her aunt, Sylvia Ann Howland, under a will two copies of whose "second page" were signed with the aunt's name—by signatures asserted by the estate's executor to be forgeries. The fascinating tale of the trial was compellingly told by Louis Menand in *She Had To Have It*, THE NEW YORKER, April 23 & 30, 2001, p. 62, and retold by Menand in a chapter of THE METAPHYSICAL CLUB (2001).

mark/impression identification notified to investigating officers and presented in court will have, and must have, been subject to the above procedures.

In sum, contrary to the view expressed in my January 7 opinion, I am now persuaded that the standards which control the opining of a competent fingerprint examiner are sufficiently widely agreed upon to satisfy *Daubert's* requirements.

(3) Completing the *Daubert/Kumho Tire* Assessment

Having re-reviewed the applicability of the *Daubert* factors through the prism of *Kumho Tire*, I conclude that the one *Daubert* factor which is both pertinent and unsatisfied is the first factor—"testing." *Kumho Tire*, as I have noted above, instructs district courts to "consider the specific factors identified in *Daubert* where they are reasonable measures of the reliability of expert testimony." 526 U.S. at 152. Scientific tests of ACE-V—*i.e.*, tests in the *Daubert* sense—would clearly aid in measuring ACE-V's reliability. But, as of today, no such tests are in hand. The question, then, is whether, in the absence of such tests, a court should conclude that the ACE-V fingerprint identification system, as practiced by certified FBI fingerprint examiners, has too great a likelihood of producing erroneous results to be admissible as evidence in a courtroom setting. There are respected authorities who, it appears, would render such a verdict. In a recent OpEd piece in *The New York Times*, Peter Neufeld and Barry Scheck, who direct Cardozo Law School's Innocence Project, have this to say:

> *No one doubts that fingerprints can, and do, serve as a highly discriminating identifier, and digital photographic enhancement and computer databases now promise to make fingerprint identification more useful than ever before. But to what degree incomplete and imperfect fingerprints can be reliably used to identify individuals requires more scientific examination. . . . Forensic science has rarely been subjected to the kind of scrutiny and independent verification applied to other fields of applied and medical science. Instead, analysts testifying in courts about fingerprint analysis, bite marks, handwriting comparisons and the like have often argued that in their field the courtroom itself provided the test. . . . As the National Institutes of Health finance basic scientific research, the National Institute of Justice should put money into verification and validation before a technique of identification is admitted into court.*[12]

As explained in Part II of this opinion, I have found, on the record before me, that there is no evidence that certified FBI fingerprint examiners present erroneous identification testimony, and, as a corollary, that there is no evidence that the rate of error of certified FBI fingerprint examiners is unacceptably high. With those findings in mind, I am not persuaded that courts should defer admission of testimony with

---

12. *Will Fingerprinting Stand Up in Court?*, N.Y. TIMES, March 9, 2002, § A, p. 15, col. 1. The stated point of departure for the OpEd piece was the January 7 opinion in this case.

respect to fingerprinting—which Professors Neufeld and Scheck term "[t]he bedrock forensic identifier of the 20th century"—until academic investigators financed by the National Institute of Justice have made substantial headway on a "verification and validation" research agenda. For the National Institute of Justice, or other institutions both public and private, to sponsor such research would be all to the good. But to postpone present in-court utilization of this "bedrock forensic identifier" pending such research would be to make the best the enemy of the good.

IV

English and American trial courts have accepted fingerprint identification testimony for almost a century. The first English appellate endorsement of fingerprint identification testimony was the 1906 opinion in *Rex v. Castleton*, 3 Cr. App. R. 74. In 1906 and 1908, Sergeant Joseph Faurot, a New York City detective who had in 1904 been posted to Scotland Yard to learn about fingerprinting, used his new training to break open two celebrated cases: in each instance fingerprint identification led the suspect to confess[13]—important early indices of the reliability of fingerprint identification techniques when responsibly practiced. The first American court of last resort to consider the admissibility of such evidence was the Illinois Supreme Court: in *People v.*

---

13. Sergeant Faurot's two cases are described by Colin Beavan in FINGER-PRINTS:

> *Towards midnight on April 16, 1906, Detective Sergeant Joseph Faurot of the New York City Police was on patrol by the luxurious Waldorf–Astoria hotel, when he decided to make a quick tour of the Waldorf's corridors to see if the wealthy guests had attracted any thieves. By sheer luck, on the third floor, Faurot came across a British man sneaking out of someone else's suite in stockinged feet. Faurot arrested the Brit, who identified himself as James Jones and insisted that he was a gentleman of the highest social standing.*
>
> *At police headquarters, protesting that there was a perfectly innocent explanation for his behavior, Jones demanded his release. Faurot's colleagues advised him to accept Jones's explanation and let him go, or risk the disciplinary consequences of the British Consul's potential involvement. But Faurot, on a hunch, charged Jones as a hotel thief, put him in a cell, and sent his fingerprints to Scotland Yard, requesting a check for identification and possible criminal records. If Jones was the gentleman he said he was, Faurot would be in a lot of trouble. Until then, the Brit would have to dine on bread and water while Faurot waited for his reply.*
>
> *Before being transferred to sidewalk duty, Faurot had worked in the criminal records office at police headquarters, unsuccessfully trying to establish a workable identification system based on anthropometry. In 1904, when word of the Yard's fingerprint success reached New York, Police Commissioner William McAdoo shipped Faurot to London to study the new*

Jennings, 96 N.E. 1077 (1911), the court concluded that such evidence was admissible and affirmed appellant's murder conviction. The identification testimony in *Jennings* came from William M. Evans and Michael P. Evans of the Chicago Police Department's Bureau of Identification; Inspector Edward Foster of the Dominion Police in Ottawa, who "had studied the subject at Scotland Yard"; and Mary E. Holland, who "began investigation of finger print impressions in 1904, studied at Scotland Yard in 1908, passed an examination on the subject, and started the first bureau of identification in this country for the United States government at Washington." *Id.* at 1082. The court ruled:

> *From the evidence in this record we are disposed to hold that the classification of finger print impressions and their method of identification is a science requiring study. While some of the reasons which guide an expert to his conclusions are such as may be weighed by any intelligent person with good eyesight from such exhibits as we have here in the record, after being pointed out to him by one versed in the study of finger prints, the evidence in question does not come within the common experience of all men of common education in the ordinary walks of life, and therefore the court and jury were properly aided by witnesses of peculiar and special experience on this subject.*

Id. at 1083.

---

science. Faurot came home a zealous fingerprint convert, but he was not allowed by McAdoo's successor to set up a system. Nevertheless, Faurot's experience at London's Fingerprint Branch led him to send "Jones's" fingerprints to the Yard.

Fourteen days later, the Yard sent word that the prints matched those of Daniel Nolan, a known hotel thief with twelve convictions to his credit, who was wanted for stealing £800 from the house of a famous writer. The Yard's letter included two photographs of Nolan, the spitting image of the prisoner. Faurot had his man and, confronted with the evidence, Nolan admitted his true identity, and was sentenced to seven years in prison. Faurot's fingerprint identification, New York City's first, made a big splash across the front page of the New York Evening Post. "Police Learn Lesson from India," the headline proclaimed.

Faurot's second, more important fingerprint victory came in 1908, after the bloody body of Nellie Quinn was found in a rooming house on East 118th Street. Under Quinn's bed, Faurot found a bottle covered with fingerprints that did not belong to the girl. He suspected he might find a match among one of Quinn's "man friends," each of whom Faurot tracked down and fingerprinted, until he came across George Cramer, a plumber. Cramer's prints matched those on the bottle. Confronted with the fingerprint evidence, Cramer confessed that he had killed the girl in a drunken rage.

Pp. 190–191.

The *Jennings* opinion and Sergent Faurot's cases illustrate the extent to which American fingerprint identification programs depended, in their infancy, on lessons learned from Scotland Yard.[14]

In due course—as much of the testimony of Stephen Meagher, David Ashbaugh and Allan Bayle, and also the pronouncements of the Court of Appeal in *Buckley* and of Lord Rooker in the House of Lords, suggest—the techniques of North American fingerprint identification specialists appear to have reached a level of sophistication paralleling that of their English counterparts.

The opinion of the Court of Appeals in *Buckley* adumbrated the fingerprint identification regime which Her Majesty's Government has now put into force—an ACE-

---

14. The primacy of English endeavors is implicit in the succinct four paragraphs in which the fabled Eleventh Edition of the Encyclopedia Britannica, in 1913, gave fingerprint identification its blessing:

> The use of finger-prints as a system of identification (q.v.) is of very ancient origin, and was known from the earliest days in the East when the impression of his thumb was the monarch's sign-manual. A relic of this practice is still preserved in the formal confirmation of a legal document by "delivering" it as one's "act and deed." The permanent character of the finger-print was first put forward scientifically in 1823 by J.E. Purkinje, an eminent professor of physiology, who read a paper before the university of Breslau, adducing nine standard types of impressions and advocating a system of classification which attracted no great attention. Bewick, the English draughtsman, struck with the delicate qualities of the lineation, made engravings of the impression of two of his fingertips and used them as signatures for his work. Sir Francis Galton, who laboured to introduce finger-prints, points out that they were proposed for the identification of Chinese immigrants when registering their arrival in the United States. In India, Sir William Herschel desired to use finger-prints in the courts of the Hugli district to prevent false personation and fix the identity upon the executants of documents. The Bengal police under the wise administration of Sir E. R. Henry, afterwards chief commissioner of the London metropolitan police, usefully adopted finger-prints for the detection of crime, an example followed in many public departments in India. A transfer of property is attested by the thumb-mark, so are documents when registered, and advances made to opium-growers or to labourers on account of wages, or to contracts signed under the emigration law, or medical certificates to vouch for the persons examined, all tending to check the frauds and impostures constantly attempted.
>
> The prints depend upon a peculiarity seen in the human hand and to some extent in the human foot. The skin is traversed in all directions by creases and ridges, which are ineradicable and show no change from childhood to extreme old age. The persistence of the markings of the finger-tips has been proved beyond all question, and this universally accepted quality has been the basis of the present system of identification. The impressions, when examined, show that the ridges appear in certain fixed patterns, from

V regime which, stripped of any required minimum number of Galton points, corresponds almost exactly with the ACE-V procedures followed by the FBI.[15] It is to be expected that English trial judges, in accordance with *Buckley*, (1) will require a showing (or an agreement of the parties) that (a) a fingerprint examiner called as an expert witness is properly credentialed and (b) any prints presented in evidence will, at least arguably, possess the characteristics referred to by Lord Rooker as predicates for determining the existence, or the non-existence, of a match; and (2) will, subject to such a showing (or agreement of the parties), permit the examiner to give testimony before the fact-finder. The ACE-V regime that is sufficiently reliable for an English court is, I conclude, a regime whose reliability should, subject to a similar measure of trial court

---

which an alphabet of signs or a system of notation has been arrived at for convenience of record. As the result of much experiment a fourfold scheme of classification has been evolved, and the various types employed are styled "arches," "loops," "whorls" and "composites." There are seven subclasses, and all are perfectly distinguishable by an expert, who can describe each by its particular symbol in the code arranged, so that the whole "print" can be read as a distinct and separate expression. Very few, and the simplest, appliances are required for taking the print—a sheet of white paper, a tin slab, and some printer's ink. Scars or malformations do not interfere with the result.

The unchanging character of the finger-prints has repeatedly helped in the detection of crime. We may quote the case of the thief who broke into a residence and among other things helped himself to a glass of wine, leaving two finger-prints upon the tumbler which were subsequently found to be identical with those of a notorious criminal who was arrested, pleaded guilty and was convicted. Another burglar effected entrance by removing a pane of glass from a basement window, but, unhappily for him, left his imprints, which were referred to the registry and found to agree exactly with those of a convict at large; his address was known, and when visited some of the stolen property was found in his possession. In India a murderer was identified by the brown mark of a blood-stained thumb he had left when rummaging amongst the papers of the deceased. This man was convicted of theft but not of the murder.

The keystone to the whole system is the central office where the register or index of all criminals is kept for ready reference. The operators need no special gifts or lengthy training; method and accuracy suffice, and abundant checks exist to obviate incorrect classification and reduce the liability to error.

10 ENCYC. BRIT. 376 (1913).

15. One seeming difference between the two systems, which should be noted but may not be of great moment, is that the ACE-V procedure described by Lord Rooker calls for verification by two examiners, while the FBI's ACE-V procedure apparently does not, at least as a formal matter, require more than one verification in ordinary circumstances.

oversight, be regarded by the federal courts of the United States as satisfying the requirements of Rule 702 as the Supreme Court has explicated that rule in *Daubert* and *Kumho Tire*.

Conclusion

Motions for reconsideration are not favorites of the law. It is an important feature of a judge's job to arrive at a decision and then move on to the next issue to be decided, whether in the pending case or the case next to be addressed on the judge's docket. This judicial convention has special force for trial judges, for if a trial judge's ruling is mistaken it can, and if need arises will, be corrected on appeal. But there are occasions when a motion for reconsideration has its uses. This is such an occasion.

By agreeing to reconsider my prior ruling, I had the opportunity to acquire information not previously presented, or that I had not fully digested, on the record made in another courtroom more than two years ago. Through the efforts of government counsel, Stephen Meagher, heretofore a name in a transcript, became a real person, and through his live testimony I was able to get a substantially more rounded picture of the procedure—the FBI's ACE-V process of fingerprint identification—whose degree of reliability for expert evidentiary purposes it is my responsibility to determine. And, through the efforts of defense counsel, I had the opportunity to learn from Allan Bayle, a senior English fingerprint specialist, that one aspect of the FBI's system—the annual proficiency testing of FBI fingerprint examiners—may have shortcomings. But I also learned from Allan Bayle's testimony two more important truths: namely, that the ACE-V process employed by New Scotland Yard is essentially indistinguishable from the FBI's ACE-V process, and that this formidably knowledgeable and experienced veteran of the Yard—the legendary and actual source of the systematic and comprehensive utilization of fingerprint identification as an instrument of law enforcement—believes in ACE-V without reservation. Reopening the record also led me to educate myself about the legal framework with respect to the receipt in evidence of expert fingerprint identification testimony that has just been put into effect in England by Her Majesty's Government. That new legal framework—which departs very significantly from the regime I had read about in the *Mitchell* record—turns out to be substantially the same as the legal framework that our government, in the case at bar, has contended is appropriate for FBI fingerprint identification evidence.

Based on the foregoing considerations, I have concluded that arrangements which, subject to careful trial court oversight, are felt to be sufficiently reliable in England, ought likewise to be found sufficiently reliable in the federal courts of the United States, subject to similar measures of trial court oversight. In short, I have changed my mind. "Wisdom too often never comes, and so"—as Justice Frankfurter admonished himself and every judge—"one ought not to reject it merely because it comes late." *Henslee v. Union Planters Bank*, 335 U.S. 595, 600 (1949) (Frankfurter, J., dissenting); cf., *Wolf v. Colorado*, 338 U.S. 25, 47 (1949) (Rutledge, J., dissenting).

Accordingly, in an order filed today accompanying this opinion, this court GRANTS the government's motion for reconsideration of the January 7 order; VACATES the January 7 order; DENIES the defendants' Motion to Preclude the United States from Introducing Latent Fingerprint Evidence; and GRANTS the government's Motion in Limine to Admit Latent Prints.

At the upcoming trial, the presentation of expert fingerprint testimony by the government, and the presentation of countering expert fingerprint testimony by any of the defendants (see *United States v. Velasquez*, 64 F.3d 844, 848–852 (3d Cir. 1995)), will be subject to the court's oversight prior to presentation of such testimony before the jury, with a view to insuring that any proposed expert witness possesses the appropriate expert qualifications and that fingerprints offered in evidence will be of a quality arguably susceptible of responsible analysis, comparison and evaluation.

IN THE UNITED STATES DISTRICT COURT
FOR THE EASTERN DISTRICT OF PENNSYLVANIA
UNITED STATES OF AMERICA
v.
CARLOS IVAN LLERA PLAZA,
WILFREDO MARTINEZ ACOSTA,
and
VICTOR RODRIGUEZ
Cr. No. 98-362-10, 11, 12:

ORDER

For the reasons stated in the accompanying opinion dated today, this court GRANTS the government's motion for reconsideration of the January 7 order; VACATES the January 7 order; DENIES the defendants' Motion to Preclude the United States from Introducing Latent Fingerprint Evidence; and GRANTS the government's Motion in Limine to Admit Latent Prints.

Date: March 13, 2002 _____

Pollak, J.

APPENDIX

Federal Rules

This appendix contains those federal rules of evidence and procedure that contain provisions of special relevance to technical expert witnesses.

Federal Rules of Procedure

Rule 16. Pretrial Conferences; Scheduling; Management

Pretrial Conferences; Objectives.

In any action, the court may in its discretion direct the attorneys for the parties and any unrepresented parties to appear before it for a conference or conferences before trial for such purposes as

(1) expediting the disposition of the action;
(2) establishing early and continuing control so that the case will not be protracted because of lack of management;
(3) discouraging wasteful pretrial activities;
(4) improving the quality of the trial through more thorough preparation, and;
(5) facilitating the settlement of the case.

(b) Scheduling and Planning.

Except in categories of actions exempted by district court rule as inappropriate, the district judge, or a magistrate judge when authorized by district court rule, shall, after receiving the report from the parties under Rule 26(f) or after consulting with the attorneys for the parties and any unrepresented parties by a scheduling conference, telephone, mail, or other suitable means, enter a scheduling order that limits the time

(1) to join other parties and to amend the pleadings;

(2) to file motions; and

(3) to complete discovery.

The scheduling order may also include

(4) modifications of the times for disclosures under Rules 26(a) and 26(e)(1) and of the extent of discovery to be permitted;

(5) the date or dates for conferences before trial, a final pretrial conference, and trial; and

(6) any other matters appropriate in the circumstances of the case.

The order shall issue as soon as practicable but in any event within 90 days after the appearance of a defendant and within 120 days after the complaint has been served on a defendant. A schedule shall not be modified except upon a showing of good cause and by leave of the district judge or, when authorized by local rule, by a magistrate judge.

(c) Subjects for Consideration at Pretrial Conferences.

At any conference under this rule consideration may be given, and the court may take appropriate action, with respect to

(1) the formulation and simplification of the issues, including the elimination of frivolous claims or defenses;

(2) the necessity or desirability of amendments to the pleadings;

(3) the possibility of obtaining admissions of fact and of documents which will avoid unnecessary proof, stipulations regarding the authenticity of documents, and advance rulings from the court on the admissibility of evidence;

(4) the avoidance of unnecessary proof and of cumulative evidence, and limitations or restrictions on the use of testimony under Rule 702 of the Federal Rules of Evidence;

(5) the appropriateness and timing of summary adjudication under Rule 56 ;

(6) the control and scheduling of discovery, including orders affecting disclosures and discovery pursuant to Rule 26 and Rules 27 through 37 ;

(7) the identification of witnesses and documents, the need and schedule for fil-

ing and exchanging pretrial briefs, and the date or dates for further conferences and for trial;

(8) the advisability of referring matters to a magistrate judge or master;

(9) settlement and the use of special procedures to assist in resolving the dispute when authorized by statute or local rule;

(10) the form and substance of the pretrial order;

(11) the disposition of pending motions;

(12) the need for adopting special procedures for managing potentially difficult or protracted actions that may involve complex issues, multiple parties, difficult legal questions, or unusual proof problems;

(13) an order for a separate trial pursuant to Rule 42(b) with respect to a claim, counterclaim, cross-claim, or third-party claim, or with respect to any particular issue in the case;

(14) an order directing a party or parties to present evidence early in the trial with respect to a manageable issue that could, on the evidence, be the basis for a judgment as a matter of law under Rule 50(a) or a judgment on partial findings under Rule 52(c) ;

(15) an order establishing a reasonable limit on the time allowed for presenting evidence; and

(16) such other matters as may facilitate the just, speedy, and inexpensive disposition of the action.

At least one of the attorneys for each party participating in any conference before trial shall have authority to enter into stipulations and to make admissions regarding all matters that the participants may reasonably anticipate may be discussed. If appropriate, the court may require that a party or its representatives be present or reasonably available by telephone in order to consider possible settlement of the dispute.

(d) Final Pretrial Conference.
Any final pretrial conference shall be held as close to the time of trial as reasonable under the circumstances. The participants at any such conference shall formulate a plan for trial, including a program for facilitating the admission of evidence. The conference shall be attended by at least one of the attorneys who will conduct the trial for each of the parties and by any unrepresented parties.

(e) Pretrial Orders.
After any conference held pursuant to this rule, an order shall be entered reciting the action taken. This order shall control the subsequent course of the action unless modified by a subsequent order. The order following a final pretrial conference shall be modified only to prevent manifest injustice.

(f) Sanctions.

If a party or party's attorney fails to obey a scheduling or pretrial order, or if no appearance is made on behalf of a party at a scheduling or pretrial conference, or if a party or party's attorney is substantially unprepared to participate in the conference, or if a party or party's attorney fails to participate in good faith, the judge, upon motion or the judge's own initiative, may make such orders with regard thereto as are just, and among others any of the orders provided in Rule 37(b)(2) (B), (C), (D). In lieu of or in addition to any other sanction, the judge shall require the party or the attorney representing the party or both to pay the reasonable expenses incurred because of any noncompliance with this rule, including attorney's fees, unless the judge finds that the noncompliance was substantially justified or that other circumstances make an award of expenses unjust.

Rule 26. General Provisions Governing Discovery; Duty of Disclosure

Required Disclosures; Methods to Discover Additional Matter
  Initial Disclosures.

Except in categories of proceedings specified in Rule 26(a)(1)(E), or to the extent otherwise stipulated or directed by order, a party must, without awaiting a discovery request, provide to other parties:

(A) the name and, if known, the address and telephone number of each individual likely to have discoverable information that the disclosing party may use to support its claims or defenses, unless solely for impeachment, identifying the subjects of the information;

(B) a copy of, or a description by category and location of, all documents, data compilations, and tangible things that are in the possession, custody, or control of the party and that the disclosing party may use to support its claims or defenses, unless solely for impeachment;

(C) a computation of any category of damages claimed by the disclosing party, making available for inspection and copying as under Rule 34 the documents or other evidentiary material, not privileged or protected from disclosure, on which such computation is based, including materials bearing on the nature and extent of injuries suffered; and

(D) for inspection and copying as under Rule 34 any insurance agreement under which any person carrying on an insurance business may be liable to satisfy part or all of a judgment which may be entered in the action or to indemnify or reimburse for payments made to satisfy the judgment.

(E) The following categories of proceedings are exempt from initial disclosure under Rule 26(a)(1) :

  (i) an action for review on an administrative records

(ii)   a petition for habeas corpus or other proceeding to challenge a criminal conviction or sentence;

(iii) an action brought without counsel by a person in custody of the United States, a state, or a state subdivision;

(iv) an action to enforce or quash an administrative summons or subpoena;

(v)   an action by the United States to recover benefit payments;

(vi) an action by the United States to collect on a student loan guaranteed by the United States;

(vii) a proceeding ancillary to proceedings in other courts; and

(viii) an action to enforce an arbitration award.

These disclosures must be made at or within 14 days after the Rule 26(f) conference unless a different time is set by stipulation or court order, or unless a party objects during the conference that initial disclosures are not appropriate in the circumstances of the action and states the objection in the Rule 26(f) discovery plan. In ruling on the objection, the court must determine what disclosures—if any—are to be made, and set the time for disclosure. Any party first served or otherwise joined after the Rule 26(f) conference must make these disclosures within 30 days after being served or joined unless a different time is set by stipulation or court order. A party must make its initial disclosures based on the information then reasonably available to it and is not excused from making its disclosures because it has not fully completed its investigation of the case or because it challenges the sufficiency of another party's disclosures or because another party has not made its disclosures.

(2) Disclosure of Expert Testimony.

(A) In addition to the disclosures required by paragraph (1), a party shall disclose to other parties the identity of any person who may be used at trial to present evidence under Rules 702, 703, or 705 of the Federal Rules of Evidence.

(B) Except as otherwise stipulated or directed by the court, this disclosure shall, with respect to a witness who is retained or specially employed to provide expert testimony in the case or whose duties as an employee of the party regularly involve giving expert testimony, be accompanied by a written report prepared and signed by the witness. The report shall contain a complete statement of all opinions to be expressed and the basis and reasons therefor; the data or other information considered by the witness in forming the opinions; any exhibits to be used as a summary of or support for the opinions; the qualifications of the witness, including a list of all publications authored by the witness within the preceding ten years; the compensation to be paid for the study and testimony; and a listing of any other cases in which the witness has testified as an expert at trial or by deposition within the preceding four years.

(C) These disclosures shall be made at the times and in the sequence directed by the court. In the absence of other directions from the court or stipulation by the parties, the disclosures shall be made at least 90 days before the trial date or the date the case is to be ready for trial or, if the evidence is intended solely to contradict or rebut evidence on the same subject matter identified by another party under paragraph (2)(B), within 30 days after the disclosure made by the other party. The parties shall supplement these disclosures when required under subdivision (e)(1).

(3) Pretrial Disclosures.

In addition to the disclosures required by Rule 26(a)(1) and (2), a party must provide to other parties and promptly file with the court the following information regarding the evidence that it may present at trial other than solely for impeachment:

(A) the name and, if not previously provided, the address and telephone number of each witness, separately identifying those whom the party expects to present and those whom the party may call if the need arises;

(B) the designation of those witnesses whose testimony is expected to be presented by means of a deposition and, if not taken stenographically, a transcript of the pertinent portions of the deposition testimony; and

(C) an appropriate identification of each document or other exhibit, including summaries of other evidence, separately identifying those which the party expects to offer and those which the party may offer if the need arises.

Unless otherwise directed by the court, these disclosures must be made at least 30 days before trial. Within 14 days thereafter, unless a different time is specified by the court, a party may serve and promptly file a list disclosing (i) any objections to the use under Rule 32(a) of a deposition designated by another party under Rule 26(a)(3)(B), and (ii) any objection, together with the grounds therefor, that may be made to the admissibility of materials identified under Rule 26(a)(3)(C). Objections not so disclosed, other than objections under Rules 402 and 403 of the Federal Rules of Evidence, are waived unless excused by the court for good cause.

(4) Form of Disclosures; Filing.

Unless the court orders otherwise, all disclosures under Rules 26(a)(1) through (3) must be made in writing, signed, and served.

(5) Methods to Discover Additional Matter.

Parties may obtain discovery by one or more of the following methods: depositions upon oral examination or written questions; written interrogatories; production of documents or things or permission to enter upon land or other property under Rule

34 or 45(a)(1) (C), for inspection and other purposes; physical and mental examinations; and requests for admission.

(b) Discovery Scope and Limits.

Unless otherwise limited by order of the court in accordance with these rules, the scope of discovery is as follows:

(1) In General.

Parties may obtain discovery regarding any matter, not privileged, that is relevant to the claim or defense of any party, including the existence, description, nature, custody, condition, and location of any books, documents, or other tangible things and the identity and location of persons having knowledge of any discoverable matter. For good cause, the court may order discovery of any matter relevant to the subject matter involved in the action. Relevant information need not be admissible at the trial if the discovery appears reasonably calculated to lead to the discovery of admissible evidence. All discovery is subject to the limitations imposed by Rule 26(b)(2)(i), (ii), and (iii).

(2) Limitations.

By order, the court may alter the limits in these rules on the number of depositions and interrogatories or the length of depositions under Rule 30. By order or local rule, the court may also limit the number of requests under Rule 36. The frequency or extent of use of the discovery methods otherwise permitted under these rules and by any local rule shall be limited by the court if it determines that: (i) the discovery sought is unreasonably cumulative or duplicative, or is obtainable from some other source that is more convenient, less burdensome, or less expensive; (ii) the party seeking discovery has had ample opportunity by discovery in the action to obtain the information sought; or (iii) the burden or expense of the proposed discovery outweighs its likely benefit, taking into account the needs of the case, the amount in controversy, the parties' resources, the importance of the issues at stake in the litigation, and the importance of the proposed discovery in resolving the issues. The court may act upon its own initiative after reasonable notice or pursuant to a motion under Rule 26(c).

(3) Trial Preparation: Materials.

Subject to the provisions of subdivision (b)(4) of this rule, a party may obtain discovery of documents and tangible things otherwise discoverable under subdivision (b)(1) of this rule and prepared in anticipation of litigation or for trial by or for another party or by or for that other party's representative (including the other party's attorney, consultant, surety, indemnitor, insurer, or agent) only upon a showing that the party seeking discovery has substantial need of the materials in the preparation of the party's case and that the party is unable without undue hardship to obtain the substantial equivalent of the materials by other means. In ordering discovery of such materials when the required showing has been made, the court shall protect against disclosure of the mental impressions, conclusions, opinions, or legal theories of an attorney or other representative of a party concerning the litigation.

A party may obtain without the required showing a statement concerning the action or its subject matter previously made by that party. Upon request, a person not a party may obtain without the required showing a statement concerning the action or its subject matter previously made by that person. If the request is refused, the person may move for a court order. The provisions of Rule 37(a)(4) apply to the award of expenses incurred in relation to the motion. For purposes of this paragraph, a statement previously made is (A) a written statement signed or otherwise adopted or approved by the person making it, or (B) a stenographic, mechanical, electrical, or other recording, or a transcription thereof, which is a substantially verbatim recital of an oral statement by the person making it and contemporaneously recorded.

Federal Rules of Evidence

Rule 102. Purpose and Construction

These rules shall be construed to secure fairness in administration, elimination of unjustifiable expense and delay, and promotion of growth and development of the law of evidence to the end that the truth may be ascertained and proceedings justly determined.

Rule 104. Preliminary Questions

(a) Questions of admissibility generally.

Preliminary questions concerning the qualification of a person to be a witness, the existence of a privilege, or the admissibility of evidence shall be determined by the court, subject to the provisions of subdivision (b). In making its determination it is not bound by the rules of evidence except those with respect to privileges.

(b) Relevancy conditioned on fact.

When the relevancy of evidence depends upon the fulfillment of a condition of fact, the court shall admit it upon, or subject to, the introduction of evidence sufficient to support a finding of the fulfillment of the condition.

(c) Hearing of jury.

Hearings on the admissibility of confessions shall in all cases be conducted out of the hearing of the jury. Hearings on other preliminary matters shall be so conducted when the interests of justice require, or when an accused is a witness and so requests.

(d) Testimony by accused.

The accused does not, by testifying upon a preliminary matter, become subject to cross-examination as to other issues in the case.

(e) Weight and credibility.

This rule does not limit the right of a party to introduce before the jury evidence relevant to weight or credibility.

Rule 401. Definition of "Relevant Evidence"

"Relevant evidence" means evidence having any tendency to make the existence of any fact that is of consequence to the determination of the action more probable or less probable than it would be without the evidence.

Rule 402. Relevant Evidence Generally Admissible; Irrelevant Evidence Inadmissible

All relevant evidence is admissible, except as otherwise provided by the Constitution of the United States, by Act of Congress, by these rules, or by other rules prescribed by the Supreme Court pursuant to statutory authority. Evidence which is not relevant is not admissible.

Rule 403. Exclusion of Relevant Evidence on Grounds of Prejudice, Confusion, or Waste of Time

Although relevant, evidence may be excluded if its probative value is substantially outweighed by the danger of unfair prejudice, confusion of the issues, or misleading the jury, or by considerations of undue delay, waste of time, or needless presentation of cumulative evidence.

Rule 701. Opinion Testimony by Lay Witnesses

If the witness is not testifying as an expert, the witness testimony in the form of opinions or inferences is limited to those opinions or inferences which are (a) rationally based on the perception of the witness, and (b) helpful to a clear understanding of the witness' testimony or the determination of a fact in issue, and (c) not based on scientific, technical, or other specialized knowledge within the scope of Rule 702.

Rule 702. Testimony by Experts

If scientific, technical, or other specialized knowledge will assist the trier of fact to understand the evidence or to determine a fact in issue, a witness qualified as an expert by knowledge, skill, experience, training, or education, may testify thereto in the form of an opinion or otherwise, if (1) the testimony is based upon sufficient facts or data, (2) the testimony is the product of reliable principles and methods, and (3) the witness has applied the principles and methods reliably to the facts of the case.

Rule 703. Bases of Opinion Testimony by Experts

The facts or data in the particular case upon which an expert bases an opinion or inference may be those perceived by or made known to the expert at or before the hearing. If of a type reasonably relied upon by experts in the particular field in forming opinions or inferences upon the subject, the facts or data need not be admissible in evidence in order for the opinion or inference to be admitted. Facts or data that are otherwise inadmissible shall not be disclosed to the jury by the proponent of the opinion or inference unless the court determines that their probative value in assisting the jury to evaluate the expert's opinion substantially outweighs their prejudicial effect.

Rule 704. Opinion on Ultimate Issue

(a) Except as provided in subdivision (b), testimony in the form of an opinion or inference otherwise admissible is not objectionable because it embraces an ultimate issue to be decided by the trier of fact.

(b) No expert witness testifying with respect to the mental state or condition of a defendant in a criminal case may state an opinion or inference as to whether the defendant did or did not have the mental state or condition constituting an element of the crime charged or of a defense thereto. Such ultimate issues are matters for the trier of fact alone.

Rule 705. Disclosure of Facts or Data Underlying Expert Opinion

The expert may testify in terms of opinion or inference and give reasons therefor without first testifying to the underlying facts or data, unless the court requires otherwise. The expert may in any event be required to disclose the underlying facts or data on cross-examination.

Rule 706. Court-Appointed Experts

(a) Appointment.

The court may on its own motion or on the motion of any party enter an order to show cause why expert witnesses should not be appointed, and may request the parties to submit nominations. The court may appoint any expert witnesses agreed upon by the parties, and may appoint expert witnesses of its own selection. An expert witness shall not be appointed by the court unless the witness consents to act. A witness so appointed shall be informed of the witness' duties by the court in writing, a copy of which shall be filed with the clerk, or at a conference in which the parties shall have opportunity to participate. A witness so appointed shall advise the parties of the witness' findings, if any; the witness' deposition may be taken by any party; and the witness may be called to testify by the court or any party. The witness shall be subject to cross-examination by each party, including a party calling the witness.

(b) Compensation.

Expert witnesses so appointed are entitled to reasonable compensation in whatever sum the court may allow. The compensation thus fixed is payable from funds which may be provided by law in criminal cases and civil actions and proceedings involving just compensation under the fifth amendment. In other civil actions and proceedings the compensation shall be paid by the parties in such proportion and at such time as the court directs, and thereafter charged in like manner as other costs.

(c) Disclosure of appointment.

In the exercise of its discretion, the court may authorize disclosure to the jury of the fact that the court appointed the expert witness.

(d) Parties' experts of own selection.

Nothing in this rule limits the parties in calling expert witnesses of their own selection.

Rule 803. Subsection 18: (Exceptions to Hearsay)

(18) Learned treatises. To the extent called to the attention of an expert witness upon cross-examination or relied upon by the expert witness in direct examination, statements contained in published treatises, periodicals, or pamphlets on a subject of history, medicine, or other science or art, established as a reliable authority by the testimony or admission of the witness or by other expert testimony or by judicial notice. If admitted, the statements may be read into evidence but may not be received as exhibits.

Rule 901. Requirement of Authentication or Identification

(a) General provision.

The requirement of authentication or identification as a condition precedent to admissibility is satisfied by evidence sufficient to support a finding that the matter in question is what its proponent claims.

(b) Illustrations.

By way of illustration only, and not by way of limitation, the following are examples of authentication or identification conforming with the requirements of this rule:

(1) Testimony of witness with knowledge. Testimony that a matter is what it is claimed to be.

(2) Nonexpert opinion on handwriting. Nonexpert opinion as to the genuineness of handwriting, based upon familiarity not acquired for purposes of the litigation.

(3) Comparison by trier or expert witness. Comparison by the trier of fact or by expert witnesses with specimens which have been authenticated.

(4) Distinctive characteristics and the like. Appearance, contents, substance, internal patterns, or other distinctive characteristics, taken in conjunction with circumstances.

(5) Voice identification. Identification of a voice, whether heard firsthand or through mechanical or electronic transmission or recording, by opinion based upon hearing the voice at any time under circumstances connecting it with the alleged speaker.

(6) Telephone conversations. Telephone conversations, by evidence that a call was made to the number assigned at the time by the telephone company to a particular person or business, if (A) in the case of a person, circumstances, including self-identification, show the person answering to be the one called, or (B) in the case of a business, the call was made to a place of business and the conversation related to business reasonably transacted over the telephone.

(7) Public records or reports. Evidence that a writing authorized by law to be recorded or filed and in fact recorded or filed in a public office, or a purported public record, report, statement, or data compilation, in any form, is from the public office where items of this nature are kept.

(8) Ancient documents or data compilation. Evidence that a document or data compilation, in any form,

(A) is in such condition as to create no suspicion concerning its authenticity,
(B) was in a place where it, if authentic, would likely be, and
(C) has been in existence 20 years or more at the time it is offered.

(9) Process or system. Evidence describing a process or system used to produce a result and showing that the process or system produces an accurate result.

(10) Methods provided by statute or rule. Any method of authentication or identification provided by Act of Congress or by other rules prescribed by the Supreme Court pursuant to statutory authority.

Index

inform IT

Register
Your Book

at www.awprofessional.com/register

You may be eligible to receive:

- Advance notice of forthcoming editions of the book
- Related book recommendations
- Chapter excerpts and supplements of forthcoming titles
- Information about special contests and promotions throughout the year
- Notices and reminders about author appearances, tradeshows, and online chats with special guests

Contact us

If you are interested in writing a book or reviewing manuscripts prior to publication, please write to us at:

Editorial Department
Addison-Wesley Professional
75 Arlington Street, Suite 300
Boston, MA 02116 USA
Email: AWPro@aw.com

Visit us on the Web: http://www.awprofessional.com